SOLUTIONS MANUAL

INTRODUCTION TO MANAGEMENT ACCOUNTING

Thirteenth Edition

Charles T. Horngren
Stanford University

Gary L. Sundem
University of Washington

William O. Stratton
Pepperdine University

Upper Saddle River, New Jersey 07458

VP/Editorial Director: Jeff Shelstad
Acquisitions Editor: Wendy Craven
Assistant Editor: Sam Goffinet
Manager, Print Production: Christy Mahon
Production Editor & Buyer: Carol O'Rourke
Printer/Binder: Courier, Bookmart Press

Pearson Prentice Hall[TM] is a trademark of Pearson Education, Inc.

10 9 8 7 6 5 4 3 2 1
ISBN 0-13-144085-3

CONTENTS

Solutions by Chapter

GENERAL COMMENTS

Please read the textbook preface before examining this material. The scope and depth of a particular assignment schedule largely depend on the instructor's personal evaluation of the relative importance of various topics. In turn, his or her evaluation will be influenced by students' backgrounds and other courses in the curriculum. For example, many instructors requested a more straightforward coverage of activity-based costing in Chapter 4, primarily because most of their students were not accounting majors and needed only fundamental concepts. At the same time, others prefer a more demanding coverage such as for courses with accounting majors or graduate-level accounting courses. We have significantly revised the ABC coverage to address these needs, providing a three-tiered coverage (see pages xviii –xx for a detailed description including suggested text reading and problems to assign) that meets the needs of several course objectives. Because this book may be used in a wide variety of courses, several sample assignment schedules have been prepared. We recommend using these as a starting point for building a tailored schedule.

This edition contains both straightforward assignment material, homework that can be solved simply by referring to the presentations in the chapters, and more challenging problems, which require more thoughtful analysis.

This book's approach divorces product costing for financial reporting purposes from planning and control. For example, Chapters 1 through 11 assume that no changes take place in the level of beginning and ending inventories. This sharpens the analysis of planning and control, enhances clarity, and eases the learning process. The problems of product costing are then considered in Chapters 12 through 14. This whole approach may be unconventional, but classroom experience and experimentation have convinced us of its superiority over the traditional approach, which interweaves product costing, planning, and control. If students raise thorny questions regarding inventory valuation when Chapters 1 through 11 are being covered, we usually ask them to postpone their queries until Chapters 12 through 14 are discussed. If desired, Chapters 12 through 14 may be studied at any time after Chapter 4.

For comments on how to choose among the various problems in each chapter, see the section entitled "Comments on Choices of Problems in Each Chapter." Other teaching aids for use with this textbook are an Instructor's Manual (which includes chapter overviews, chapter outlines organized by objectives, teaching tips, a chapter quiz, transparency masters, suggested readings and a video guide that carefully integrates the videos into classroom lectures), Solutions Transparencies (which includes acetates for all the end-of-chapter assignments), a Test Item File (including multiple choice, true/false, comprehensive problems, short-answer problems, and critical thinking questions), the TestGen (a computerized testing package), On Location Video Library (which includes segments on companies such as Three Dog Bakery, Nantucket Nectars, Oracle, McDonalds, and many more), and PowerPoint slides. An Instructor's

Resource CD-ROM, complete with all instructor support materials, is available upon adoption.

Available for students is a Student Guide that provides overviews, study tips and chapter reviews formatted for easy note-taking, and self-tests including a variety of test questions to prepare for examinations. Spreadsheet Templates are also available for selected exercises and problems are identified in the text by a CD icon.

SAMPLE ASSIGNMENT SCHEDULES

Summary of Potential Assignments

Suggested alternative schedules are summarized here in terms of the relative percentage of time to be devoted to various chapters. Detailed assignment schedules are shown after this summary. These schedules all assume a straightforward coverage of ABC is desired. For a more in-depth coverage see Table A on pages xix –xx.

Alternative 1*				Alternative 2**			
Sequence A		Sequence B		Sequence A		Sequence B	
Chapter	Percentage of Time	Chapter	Percentage of Time	Chapter	Percentage of Time	Chapter	Percentage of Time
1	2%	1	2%	1	2%	1	2%
2	5	2	5	15	7	15	6
3	6	3	6	16	7	16	4
4	8	4	8	17	8	2	5
5 & 6	12	13	6	2	6	3	6
8	10	5 & 6	12	3	5	4	7
9	8	11	8	4	8	12	5
10	6	8	10	5 & 6	10	13	5
11	10	15	9	8	7	14	6
12	6	9	8	9	6	5 & 6	10
13	6	10	7	10	5	7	4
14	7	12	5	11	10	8	9
				12	5	9	6
						10	4
						11	7
Review or Exams	14	Review or Exams	14	Review or Exams	14	Review or Exams	14
Total	100%	Total	100%	Total	100%	Total	100%

*For students who have taken one term of elementary financial accounting immediately prior to this course.

** For students who have not taken elementary financial accounting recently. Students with no background in elementary financial accounting will have to spend more time on Chapters 15 and 16 than is suggested in the above tables.

Use of Fundamental Assignment Material

Some instructors may prefer to assign all the problems in either the A series or the B series of problems under "Fundamental Assignment Material". Each series includes a set of problems that covers the most important topics in the chapter. In addition to the A or B series, selected problems from "Additional Assignment Material" can be assigned as time allows. However, for those who wish to select particular problems in each chapter, some suggestions follow.

Alternative 1, Sequence A

Designed for one semester of 15 weeks with three 50-minute meetings per week. Note that longer semesters permit either more intensive or extensive coverage, depending on instructor preferences.

No. of Class Meeting	Chapter in Text	Problem Assignments	
		Normal: Based on Approximately Two Hours of Homework per session	Selected Additional Problems if Time Permits
1	Introduction.	See the section that follows shortly, "COMMENTS ON CHOICE OF PROBLEMS IN EACH CHAPTER."	
2	Ch. 1 - Perspective	A1, A3, 30	49
3	Ch. 2 - Excluding appendices	A1 (or 43 or 45) and A2 (or B1) and 30 (or 31)	42, 47
4	Appendices to Ch. 2	58 (or 59), 60 (or 61)	Any of 35-38, 65 or 66
5	Ch. 3	A1 & A3 (or B1 & B3)	47
6	Review Ch. 3	A2 or B2	57
7	Review Ch. 3	42, 51	53, 54 (appendix)
8	Ch. 4 (See discussion on p. xviii and Table A)	A1 (or B1), A2 (or B2)	1-9, 36, 41
9	Review Ch. 4	A4 (or B4), 13, 19, 20	44, 45
10	Review Ch. 4 (Consider jump to Ch. 12)	46, 47	38, 40
11	Ch. 5	A1, A2, 45 (or 47 or 48)	54
12	Review Ch. 5	B1	38 or 41
13	Review Ch. 5	58 (or B3)	50 or 51, 59, 60, 61
14	Ch. 6	A3 (or B3 or 59)	63
15	Review Ch. 6	A1 (or 60), any of 49, 50, 53, or 54	57
16	Review Ch. 6	56, 64	65, any of 29, 30, 50, or 51
	(Consider jump to Ch. 11)		
17	Ch. 7	Start A1 or B1	30, 32, 33, 35
18	Review Ch. 7	Finish A1 or B1	37 (or 46 for a multi-stage ABC problem)
19	Ch. 8	A1 (or B1 or 36 or 37)	Any of 24-27
20	Review Ch. 8	A3 or B2, 43	Any of 29-31, 33
21	Review Ch. 8	44, 45	41, 47
22	Review Ch. 8	A2, B3, 39	32, 48
23	Review Ch. 8 (Consider jump to Ch. 15)	50, 53	40

No. of Class Meeting	Chapter in Text	Problem Assignments: Normal: Based on Approximately Two Hours of Homework per session	Selected Additional Problems if Time Permits
24	Review for Exam		
25	*Test on Ch. 1 thru Ch. 8		
26	Ch. 9	A1 or B1, A2 or B2	50
27	Review Ch. 9	A3, B3, 46, 49	48, 52
28	Ch. 10	A1 or B1, B2	27, 37, 38, 39, 40
29	Review Ch. 10	A2, A3, A4 or B4,	44, 47, 50
30	Ch. 11	A1 or B1, 44 or 45	Any of 29-35
31	Review Ch. 11	38 or 39, 60	64
32	Review Ch. 11	49, 52	53, 69
33	Review Ch. 11	A3 (or B3), A4 (or B4)	A5 or B5 and any of 40-43
34	Review Ch. 11	46 or 47, 65	53, 66, 67
35	Ch. 12	A1 (or B2), B1 (or A3)	32 (or 33 or 34), 37
36	Review Ch. 12	A3 or B3	A2, 45
37	Review Ch. 12	A4 (or B4)	25 or 27 or 28, 34 or 35, 36
38	Ch. 13	A1 or B1	38 or 39
39	Review Ch. 13	A2 or B2, 28 or 29	Any of 41-46
40	Review Ch. 13	A3 or A4, B3 or B4	42, 43, 45, 64
41	Ch. 14	A1 or B1, 23, 25	Any of 24-27, 39 or 42
42	Review Ch. 14	A2 or B2, A3 or B3	29-32, 43
43	Review Ch. 14	A4 or B4	48
44	Final review		
45	Final examination		

*Some instructors devote time to discuss tests in subsequent sessions. We have found it more fruitful to hand out photocopied solutions and have students do their checking not on class time. An alternative is to have students correct their tests and turn in the corrected tests to be graded as a homework assignment (for credit). See the later section, "PRESENTATION OF SOLUTIONS IN CLASS."

Alternative 1, Sequence B

This is the same as the above, except that many instructors may prefer to interweave product costing and corresponding material on planning and control. Assignments 35-40 may be used immediately after meeting 10. Furthermore, assignments 30 through 34 may be used immediately after 16, and assignments 41 through 43 may be used immediately after 23.

Alternative 2, Sequence A

No. of Class Meeting	Chapter in Text	Problem Assignments	
		Normal: Based on Approximately Two Hours of Homework per session	Selected Additional Problems if Time Permits
1	Introduction		
2	Ch. 1 – Perspective	A1, A3, 30	49
3	Ch. 15 - Basic Concepts	A1 or B1, 25, 28, 38, or 39	24, 29
4	Review Ch. 15	A2 or B2 or 31	A3 or B3
5	Ch. 16	A1 or 42, A2 or 49, A3 or 50, A4 or 51	B1, B2, B3
6	Review Ch. 16	59, 60	41, 65, 67
7	Appendix 16A	56 or 68, 69	55, 58, 71
8	Ch. 17, Part One	A1 or B1, B3	
9	Review Ch. 17, Part One	A2 or B2, 35	A3, A4
10	Ch. 17, Part Two	A5, B5, 47	48
11	Appendix 17	37 or 38	50, 51
12-44	Same as alternative 1, Sequence A, from session 3 thru 37, omitting sessions 17 and 18.		
45	Final examination		

Students with no background in accounting will need to spend more time on Chapters 15, 16, and 17 than is suggested in the tables above. Some instructors may wish to omit parts of Chapters 16 and 17.

Alternative 2, Sequence B

This is basically the same as Alternative 2, Sequence A, except that those instructors who wish to cover the chapters on planning and control earlier in the course may prefer to delay sessions 7 through 11 until the end of the course. Moreover, the sessions for Chapters 10 and 17 may be deleted, whereas Chapters 7, 13, and 14 may be included.

Other Possibilities

Some instructors prefer to concentrate on a few chapters in greater depth and to delete other chapters. An example is expanding the coverage of activity-based costing to include cost-system design and use, and multistage ABC. When we use this approach, we delete Chapters 12 through 17 and occasionally Chapters 7 and 11. Other instructors prefer to cover all the chapters. To do so effectively, an instructor must obviously concentrate on the Normal Problem Assignments above and condense the number of sessions per chapter.

LINKING OF 12TH EDITION PROBLEMS TO THOSE IN THE 13TH EDITION

Users of the 12th Edition of *Introduction to Management Accounting* may have favorite problems that they want to continue to use. To help select a problem in the 13th Edition that is similar, the following table links the problems in the two editions. The first column for each chapter lists the problem numbers from the 12th Edition, and the second column shows the corresponding problem in the 13th Edition.

Chapter	Problems 12th Ed.	Problems 13th Ed.	Chapter	Problems 12th Ed.	Problems 13th Ed.	Chapter	Problems 12th Ed.	Problems 13th Ed.
1	A1	A1	2	25	25	2	61	64
	A2	A2	(cont.)	26	26	(cont.)	62	65
	A3	--		27	27		63	66
	B1	B1		28	28		64	68
	B2	B2		29	29		65	69
	B3	B3		30	30			
	27	27		31	31	3	A1	A1
	28	28		32	32		A2	A2
	29	29		33	33		A3	A3
	30	31		34	34		B1	B1
	31	30		35	35		B2	B2
	32	32		36	36		B3	B3
	33	--		37	37		25	25
	34	34		38	38		26	26
	35	35		39	39		27	27
	36	36		40	41		28	28
	37	37		41	42		29	29
	38	38		42	43		30	30
	39	39		43	44		31	31
	40	40		44	45		32	35
	41	41		45	46		33	36
	42	42		46	47		34	37
	43	43		47	49		35	38
	44	46		48	50		36	39
	45	44		49	51		37	40
	46	48		50	52		38	41
	47	45		51	53		39	42
	48	49		52	54		40	43
	49	51		53	55		41	44
	50	52		54	56		42	45
				55	58		43	46
2	A1	A1		56	59		44	47
	A2	A2		57	60		45	48
	B1	B1		58	61		46	49
	B2	B2		59	62		47	50
	24	24		60	63		48	51

Chapter	Problems 12th Ed.	Problems 13th Ed.
3 (cont.)	49	52
	50	53
	51	54
	52	55
	53	56
	54	57
	55	58
	56	60
	57	61

Chapter	Problems 12th Ed.	Problems 13th Ed.
4	A1	48
	A2	A3
	A3	A4
	B1	49
	B2	--
	B3	B4
	31	36
	32	37
	33	38
	34	41
	35	43
	36	46
	37	47
	38	--
	39	--
	40	52
	41	--
	42	53
	43	B3
	44	58
	45	54
	46	55
	47	56
	48	57
	49	61
	50	62
	51	63
	52	65
	53	66

Chapter	Problems 12th Ed.	Problems 13th Ed.
5	A1	A1
	A2	A2
	A3	A3
	B1	B1
	B2	B2
	B3	B3

Chapter	Problems 12th Ed.	Problems 13th Ed.
5 (cont.)	24	25
	25	26
	26	27
	27	28
	28	29
	29	30
	30	31
	31	32
	32	33
	33	34
	34	35
	35	36
	36	37
	37	38
	38	39
	39	40
	40	41
	41	42
	42	43
	43	44
	44	45
	45	46
	46	47
	47	48
	48	49
	49	50
	50	51
	51	52
	52	53
	53	54
	54	55
	55	56
	56	57
	57	58
	58	59
	59	61
	60	62
	61	64
	62	65

Chapter	Problems 12th Ed.	Problems 13th Ed.
6	A1	A1
	A2	A2
	A3	A3
	A4	A4
	B1	B1
	B2	B2

Chapter	Problems 12th Ed.	Problems 13th Ed.
6 (cont.)	B3	B3
	B4	B4
	B5	B5
	23	24
	24	25
	25	27
	26	28
	27	29
	28	30
	29	32
	30	33
	31	36
	32	37
	33	38
	34	39
	35	40
	36	41
	37	42
	38	43
	39	44
	40	45
	41	46
	42	47
	43	48
	44	49
	45	50
	46	51
	47	52
	48	53
	49	54
	50	55
	51	56
	52	57
	53	58
	54	59
	55	60
	56	61
	57	62
	58	63
	59	64
	60	65
	61	66
	62	68
	63	69

Chapter	Problems 12th Ed.	Problems 13th Ed.
7	A1	A1
	B1	B1
	21	22
	22	23
	23	24
	24	25
	25	26
	26	27
	27	28
	28	29
	29	30
	30	31
	31	32
	32	33
	33	34
	34	35
	35	36
	36	37
	37	38
	38	39
	39	40
	40	41
	41	42
	42	43
	43	44
	44	45
	45	48
	46	49
8	A1	A1
	A2	A2
	A3	A3
	B1	B1
	B2	B2
	B3	B3
	20	20
	21	21
	22	22
	23	23
	24	24
	25	25
	26	26
	27	27
	28	28
	29	29
	30	30
	31	31

Chapter	Problems 12th Ed.	Problems 13th Ed.
8 (cont.)	32	32
	33	33
	34	34
	35	35
	36	36
	37	37
	38	38
	39	39
	40	41
	41	42
	42	43
	43	44
	44	45
	45	46
	46	47
	47	48
	48	49
	49	50
	50	51
	51	40
	52	53
	53	54
	54	56
	55	57
9	A1	A1
	A2	A2
	A3	A3
	B1	B1
	B2	B2
	B3	46
	28	28
	29	29
	30	30
	31	31
	32	32
	33	33
	34	34
	35	35
	36	36
	37	37
	38	39
	39	40
	40	41
	41	42
	42	43
	43	44

Chapter	Problems 12th Ed.	Problems 13th Ed.
9 (cont.)	44	45
	45	48
	46	49
	47	50
	48	--
	49	--
	50	47
	51	52
	52	53
	53	54
10	A1	A4
	A2	A2
	A3	A3
	A4	A1
	B1	B3
	B2	B4
	B3	B1
	20	20
	21	21
	22	23
	23	31
	24	32
	25	33
	26	24
	27	25
	28	26
	29	27
	30	28
	31	29
	32	43
	33	44
	34	45
	35	46
	36	47
	37	48
	38	50
	39	34
	40	35
	41	37
	42	36
	43	38
	44	40
	45	39
	46	41
	47	42
	48	51

Chapter	Problems 12th Ed.	Problems 13th Ed.
10 (cont.)	49	53
	50	52
	51	54
	52	55

Chapter	Problems 12th Ed.	Problems 13th Ed.
11	A1	A1
	A2	A2
	A3	A3
	A4	A4
	A5	A5
	B1	B1
	B2	B2
	B3	B3
	B4	B4
	B5	B5
	23	25
	24	26
	25	27
	26	29
	27	30
	28	31
	29	32
	30	33
	31	34
	32	35
	33	36
	34	38
	35	39
	36	40
	37	41
	38	42
	39	43
	40	46
	41	47
	42	44
	43	45
	44	48
	45	49
	46	50
	47	51
	48	52
	49	53
	50	54
	51	55
	52	56
	53	62

Chapter	Problems 12th Ed.	Problems 13th Ed.
11 (cont.)	54	63
	55	57
	56	58
	57	60
	58	61
	59	64
	60	65
	61	66
	62	67
	63	69
	64	70

Chapter	Problems 12th Ed.	Problems 13th Ed.
12	A1	A3
	A2	A1
	A3	41
	A4	A4
	B1	B1
	B2	B2
	B3	B3
	B4	B4
	19	19
	20	20
	21	21
	22	22
	23	23
	24	24
	25	25
	26	26
	27	27
	28	28
	29	29
	30	30
	31	31
	32	32
	33	33
	34	37
	35	38
	36	39
	37	40
	38	42
	39	43
	40	44
	41	45
	42	46
	43	47

Chapter	Problems 12th Ed.	Problems 13th Ed.
12 (cont.)	44	49
	45	50

Chapter	Problems 12th Ed.	Problems 13th Ed.
13	A1	14-A1
	A2	13-A1
	A3	13-A2
	B1	14-B1
	B2	13-B1
	B3	13-B2
	18	14-15
	19	14-16
	20	13-29
	21	14-17
	22	14-20
	23	14-21
	24	14-22
	25	14-23
	26	14-24
	27	14-25
	28	14-26
	29	14-27
	30	--
	31	14-28
	32	--
	33	13-38
	34	--
	35	--
	36	13-39
	37	14-39
	38	14-40
	39	14-41
	40	--
	41	--
	42	14-42
	43	13-47
	44	13-48
	45	--
	46	13-49
	47	13-64
	48	13-65
	49	13-70
	50	--

Chapter	Problems 12th Ed.	Problems 13th Ed.
14	A1	14-A2
	A2	14-A3
	A3	14-A4

Chapter	Problems 12th Ed.	Problems 13th Ed.
14 (cont.)	B1	14-B2
	B2	14-B3
	B3	14-B4
	16	14-18
	17	--
	18	14-19
	19	14-31
	20	14-32
	21	14-33
	22	14-34
	23	14-35
	24	--
	25	--
	26	--
	27	14-36
	28	--
	29	--
	30	14-37
	31	14-38
	32	14-43
	33	14-44
	34	14-45
	35	14-46
	36	14-47
	37	--
	38	--
	39	14-48
	40	--
	41	--
	42	14-50
	43	14-51

Chapter	Problems 12th Ed.	Problems 13th Ed.
15	A1	13-A3
	A2	13-A4
	B1	13-B3
	B2	13-B4
	20	13-31
	21	13-32
	22	13-33
	23	13-34
	24	13-40
	25	13-41
	26	13-42
	27	13-43
	28	13-44
	29	13-45

Chapter	Problems 12th Ed.	Problems 13th Ed.
15 (cont.)	30	13-46
	31	13-50
	32	13-51
	33	13-52
	34	13-53
	35	13-54
	36	13-55
	37	13-56
	38	13-57
	39	13-58
	40	--
	41	13-59
	42	13-60
	43	13-61
	44	--
	45	13-62
	46	13-63
	47	13-66
	48	13-67
	49	13-68
	50	--
	51	--

Chapter	Problems 12th Ed.	Problems 13th Ed.
16	A1	15-A1
	A2	15-A2
	A3	15-A3
	B1	15-B1
	B2	15-B2
	B3	15-B3
	17	15-19
	18	15-20
	19	15-21
	20	15-23
	21	15-24
	22	15-25
	23	15-26
	24	15-27
	25	15-28
	26	15-29
	27	15-30
	28	15-31
	29	15-32
	30	15-33
	31	15-34
	32	15-35
	33	15-36

Chapter	Problems 12th Ed.	Problems 13th Ed.
16 (cont.)	34	15-37
	35	15-38
	36	15-39
	37	15-40
	38	15-42
	39	15-43

Chapter	Problems 12th Ed.	Problems 13th Ed.
17	A1	16-A1
	A2	16-A2
	A3	16-A3
	A4	16-A4
	B1	16-B1
	B2	16-B2
	B3	16-B3
	33	16-36
	34	16-37
	35	16-38
	36	16-39
	37	16-41
	38	16-42
	39	16-43
	40	16-44
	41	16-45
	42	16-46
	43	16-47
	44	16-48
	45	16-49
	46	16-50
	47	16-51
	48	16-52
	49	16-53
	50	--
	51	16-59
	52	16-60
	53	16-61
	54	16-62
	55	16-63
	56	16-64
	57	16-65
	58	16-66
	59	16-67
	60	--
	61	16-72
	62	16-73

Chapter	Problems 12th Ed.	Problems 13th Ed.	Chapter	Problems 12th Ed.	Problems 13th Ed.
18	A1	17-A1	19	A1	16-56
	A2	17-A2		A2	17-38
	A3	17-A3		B1	16-68
	A4	17-A4		B2	16-69
	A5	17-A5		B3	17-50
	B1	17-B1		21	16-40
	B2	17-B2		22	--
	B3	17-B3		23	17-28
	B4	17-B4		24	16-54
	B5	17-B5		25	--
	22	17-25		26	--
	23	17-26		27	16-57
	24	17-27		28	16-58
	25	17-29		29	--
	26	17-30		30	--
	27	17-31		31	--
	28	17-32		32	16-55
	29	17-33		33	--
	30	17-34		34	17-37
	31	17-35		35	--
	32	17-36		36	--
	33	17-39		37	16-70
	34	17-40		38	16-71
	35	17-41		39	--
	36	17-42		40	--
	37	17-43		41	17-51
	38	17-44		42	--
	39	17-45		43	--
	40	17-46			
	41	17-47			
	42	17-48			
	43	17-49			
	44	17-52			
	45	17-53			

COMMENTS ON CHOICES OF PROBLEMS IN EACH CHAPTER

Throughout the book, the "fundamental assignment material" contains two sets of problems, an "A" series (such as 1-A1 and 1-A2) and a "B" series (such as 1-B1 and 1-B2). To cover the basics of any chapter, you can assign either the "A" or the "B" series. To reinforce the basics or to explore issues in more depth, you can use items in the "additional assignment material". We especially encourage use of some of the cases. These are generally not overly long cases, but they allow discussion of material that is not straightforward. They are a good basis for class discussions.

The cognitive exercises in each chapter are short and designed to cover issues across the various value chain functions and disciplines other than accounting. These exercises present an opportunity to explore the role of accounting in support of other disciplines such as marketing, production, and general management.

The Excel application exercise in each chapter gives step-by-step instructions on how to use a spreadsheet to solve one of the chapter's problems. Use of a few of these exercises throughout the quarter will help students who do not already have spreadsheet expertise.

The collaborative learning exercise is designed for assignment to a group or for a class exercise. They will help students learn from one another.

The Internet exercise at the end of assignment material gives students an opportunity to relate the concepts presented in the text to actual company experiences. These exercises require the use of company Web sites. The information and format of these Web sites change frequently so the instructor should review each exercise prior to assigning it.

We especially encourage coverage of some of the ethics questions. There is at least one in each chapter. These provide a great basis for class discussion.

Chapter 1: Managerial Accounting and the Business Organization

The distinctions between scorekeeping, attention directing, and problem solving are frequently subject to argument. We do not find such disputes fruitful, so we cut them short. Despite their fuzziness, these distinctions help the student to recognize that accounting is a rich discipline that is not confined solely to data accumulation.

Problems 1-39 and 1-40 stress the cost-benefit approach to the design of systems. Problem 1-42 covers the value chain. Problems 1-A3, 1-35, 1-36, 1-45, 1-46, 1-47, and 1-49 cover ethics.

Chapter 2: Introduction to Cost Behavior and Cost-Volume Relationships

Problems 2-A1 and 2-A2 (or 2-B1 and 2-B2) cover the basic techniques, but any of 2-39 through 2-56 may be viewed as likely substitutes. There are plenty of good choices. Many instructors may prefer not to assign the appendices. Other problems in later chapters, such as 5-40 and 5-41 may be logically assigned in conjunction with Chapter 2. You may desire to examine Chapters 2 through 6 as a package before choosing particular assignments for each chapter.

Chapter 3: Measurement of Cost Behavior

Chapter 3 problems are designed with several purposes: (1) to measure fixed and variable cost behavior, (2) to stress the role of activity-based cost drivers, and (3) to predict costs with appropriate cost drivers. Problem 3-31 is a good, visual approach to cost behavior, and 3-39, 3-42, and 3-47 are different approaches to modeling cost behavior. Many of the problems involve non-output-volume-related cost drivers; these include 3-49, 3-52, 3-53, 3-54, 3-57, and 3-58. Problems 3-35, 3-37, 3-44, 3-45, 3-48, and 3-56 use cost behavior to predict costs. Several problems require least squares regression analysis: 3-52, 3-53, and perhaps 3-58. Two problems require understanding regression output but do not require the analysis itself: 3-42 and 3-51.

Chapter 4: Cost Management Systems and Activity-Based Costing

This chapter has been revised significantly from the previous edition. The focus of the revision is on presenting ABC material in three stages (see Table A): fundamental concepts, design and use, and advanced concepts. Many instructors teach courses that are designed to give only an overview of the fundamental concepts of management accounting. What is needed for these courses is a straightforward coverage of ABC and ABM. For such courses, we strongly recommend the Fundamental Concepts coverage shown in Table A. We have class tested this structure and find that students grasp the main concepts of ABC and ABM within 2 or 3 50-minute lectures.

For instructors wishing to extend ABC to cover the design and use of concepts, an additional 1-2 lectures are required. Table A gives guidance for such course coverage. Note that we cut back on the normal coverage of chapters 5 and 6 when this structure is used. Finally, for those who want a demanding and thorough coverage of ABC and ABM, Appendix 4 presents multi-stage process-based cost systems. This material is demanding and is designed for courses where students need to master ABC concepts.

Many instructors prefer to insert Chapters 12, 13, and 14 immediately after Chapter 4. This can be accomplished without breaking continuity. We prefer not to cover Chapter 14, the process-costing chapter, in an introductory course. There are too many other important and stimulating topics that deserve attention. Therefore, give serious consideration to omitting Chapter 14 completely, or perhaps you may wish to assign only its first part.

Table A

INTRODUCTION TO MANAGEMENT ACCOUNTING, 13 ED.
CHAPTER 4 COVERAGE RECOMMENDATIONS

	Fundamental Concepts	Design and Use of ABC Systems	Advanced (multistage) ABC
Text Pages	130 – 148 (19 pages)	148-161 (14 pages)	162-169 (8 pages)
Learning Objectives	1. Describe the purposes of cost management systems. 2. Explain the relationship between cost, cost objective, cost accumulation, and cost assignment. 3. Distinguish between direct, indirect, and unallocated costs. 4. Explain how the financial statements of manufacturers and merchandisers differ because of the types of goods they sell. 5. Understand the main differences between traditional and activity-based costing (ABC) systems and why ABC systems provide value to managers.	6. Design a cost accounting system that includes activity-based costing. 7. Use activity-based cost information to make strategic and operational control decisions.	8. Understand why multistage ABC systems give more value than two-stage ABC systems for strategic planning and operational control.
Topics	▪ Cost management systems ▪ Cost accounting systems ▪ Cost terms used when making strategic and operational control decisions ▪ Cost terms used for external reporting ▪ Traditional and ABC cost accounting systems ▪ Activity-based management	▪ Detailed illustration of two-stage ABC design and use ▪ Process maps ▪ Strategic and operational cost control decisions using ABM	▪ Key attributes of multistage ABC systems ▪ Illustration of multi-stage ABC ▪ Application of multi-stage with solution
Special Learning Aids	▪ Detailed illustration of cost allocation with several very similar exercises to reinforce understanding of fundamentals ▪ Business First example of ABC ▪ Making managerial decision boxes to emphasize key concepts ▪ Summary Problem for Your Review with detailed solution.	▪ Special graphics to aid learning ▪ Business First example of ABC ▪ Making managerial decision boxes to emphasize key concepts ▪ Summary Problem for Your Review with detailed solution.	▪ Special graphics to aid learning ▪ Detailed illustration of multistage ABC ▪ Business First example of ABC ▪ Making managerial decision boxes to emphasize key concepts ▪ Summary Problem for Your Review with detailed solution.

| Suggested Assignment Material | Use either the A or B series of Fundamental Assignment Problems. These problems are similar to the detailed illustrations in the text, enabling students to apply and learn the fundamental concepts using the text examples as a guide. Problems 4-A2 and 4-B2 continue the illustration presented in the text.

Additional assignment material:
Questions 1-9, 13, 19, 20

Exercises 36, 41, 44-45 extend the chapter illustration, 46-47 are favorites – financial services, customer costing, benchmarking | Questions 21-32

Exercises 37-40, 48 and 49

Problem 53

Excel Application Exercise 4-65

Cases 60 and 61 | Questions 34 and 35

Exercises 50 and 51

Problems 58 and 59

Case 62 – an extension of the financial services exercises 46 and 47. |
| Lecture Time Required | 2-3 50-minute lectures | 1-2 50-minute lectures | 1 50-minute lecture |

Chapter 5: Relevant Information and Decision Making: Marketing Decisions

Chapters 5 and 6 can help students learn much about how accounting data bear on decision making. Careful selection of assignment material in these two chapters is critical. Depending on the time available, our preferences in Chapter 5 follow: 5-A1, 5-A2, and 5-B1. Others that deserve special mention are 5-41, 5-46 through 5-48, and 5-61 and 5-62. The answer to 5-38 is obvious to most students, but it drives home a lesson to many students who are harder to convince. Problem 5-60 is a new problem that combines target costing and activity-based management.

Chapter 6: Relevant Information and Decision Making: Production Decisions

Problem 6-A3 is a special favorite that we always follow up (see 6-60). Problem 6-58 is a practical example of 6-60. Problems 6-B3 and 6-B4 are shortened versions of 6-A3 and 6-60. Problems 6-49, 6-51, 6-53, and 6-54 are short items that warrant consideration. Cases 6-64 and 6-65 provide more opportunity for discussion.

Many instructors prefer to insert Chapter 11 immediately after Chapter 6.

Chapter 7: The Master Budget

The exercises, 7-28 through 7-34, cover relatively simple elements of the master budget. The fundamental assignment problems, 7-A1 and 7-B1, are complete master budgets. Because these are time consuming, it may be best to build up to these with assignments that cover parts of the master budget if time permits. A new Case 7-46 links topics of activity-based budgeting and multi-stage ABC systems covered in chapter 4. If computer literacy is part of the course objectives, problems 7-41 and 7-42 should be assigned. Also consider a group assignment to create a spreadsheet that reproduces the master budget in the summary review problem at the end of the chapter, with a ground-rule that only formulas, no numbers, can appear in any of the master budget cells.

Chapter 8: Flexible Budgets and Variance Analysis

If time is short or if you do not wish to emphasize calculation of detailed price and usage variances, you may wish to assign only the first half of the chapter. Exercises 8-24 through 8-28 and problems 8-34 through 8-42 focus on flexible budgets without detailed variances. Most of these problems refer to textbook Exhibit 8-5, which provides a helpful template for solving this sort of problem. In addition, Case 8-53 introduces an activity approach to flexible budgeting that is worth considering given the current interest in activity analysis.

Problems that require detailed variance calculations refer to textbook Exhibits 8-7 or 8-9, which are concrete examples and useful templates for variance analysis. These references aid students by giving them a framework for organizing data and developing problem solutions.

Chapter 9: Management Control Systems and Responsibility Accounting

Chapter 9 problems focus on setting goals and objectives, developing incentives, and measuring performance toward objectives. Goals and objectives are covered in 9-32, 9-36, 9-42,and 9-50. Incentives are covered in 9-34 and 9-44. Performance measurement is in 9-37, 9-43, 9-48, and 9-49. Case 9-50 combines strategic pricing issues, cost behavior, and productivity; it is not a long case, but it is thought provoking. Problems 9-35, 9-45 and 9-48 cover the balanced scorecard, and the relationship between strategy and key success factors.

Chapter 10: Management Control in Decentralized Organizations

Many instructors will want to delay assigning Chapter 10 until the end of the course. Chapter 10 is easily divisible into two separate parts, one on performance measurement including economic value added and residual income measures and one on transfer pricing. In any event, the material can be covered on either of two levels: a brisk survey, which would concentrate on 10-A1 and 10-A2 (or 10-B1 and 10-B3), and problem 10-37 (comparison of EVA and residual income measures), or a deeper study, which would necessitate more than one class session.

There are several "nuts and bolts" problems: 10-A2, 10-A4, 10-B1, 10-B3, 10-24 through 10-27, and 10-31 through 10-33. Problems 10-26 and 10-40 deal with residual income. Problems 10-27, 10-37, 10-38, and 10-39 cover economic value added. Problem 10-47 provides perspective on transfer pricing, and 10-50 covers multinational transfer prices. Problem 10-34 introduces agency theory.

Case 10-52 (a special favorite) shows how the issues in Chapters 9 and 10 are closely related. We especially like 10-52 because it underscores the goal congruence and management effort aspects of designing management control systems. Too often, much material in this chapter is dismissed as being too "soft" or too qualitative for an accounting course. We disagree. We regard this chapter as the conceptual core of the course. It stresses the central questions that the designer of a control system must face, even though few pat answers are provided. Knowing what central questions to ask is an extremely important lesson for accountants and managers.

Chapter 11: Capital Budgeting

Many instructors want to introduce income taxes at the outset of capital budgeting. However, income tax considerations are not needed to grasp the essential ideas. The problem of determining what is relevant is far more imposing that any difficulties in using discounted cash flow tables. In addition to the fundamental assignment material, our favorite problems include 11-60, 11-49, 11-51, and 11-52. Problem 11-52 is of special interest because it has negative operating cash flows under both alternatives but a positive incremental operating cash flow. Cases 11-64, 11-65, and 11-66 address investment decisions in the new manufacturing environment. Problem 11-53 might be assigned in conjunction with Problem 11-62.

The "nuts and bolts" problems are 11-A1, 11-38, and 11-45 (or 11-B1, 11-39, and 11-44), 11-29 through 11-32, and 11-34.

Taxes complicate capital budgeting but do not change the basic concepts. Problems 11-A3 and 11-A4 (or 11-B3 and 11-B4) provide the most efficient way to drive the major points home regarding income taxes and discounted cash flow, but 11-A5 (or 11-B5) should also be used if there is time. Problems 11-40 and 11-41 provide informative basic exercises.

The appendix on inflation is covered in 11-46, 11-47, 11-62, and 11-63.

Chapter 12: Cost Allocation

Chapter 12 contains some technical details on cost allocation, and instructors who wish to avoid such detail can skip this chapter entirely. Others may want to insert this chapter and Chapter 13 immediately after Chapter 4.

Problem 12-A2 is comprehensive, covering the general framework for allocation, service department allocation, ABC, and process maps. Problems 12-A3 and 12-B1 contain the important basic ideas of cost allocation. Problems 12-A1, 12-B2, 12-25, and 12-40 compare direct and step-down methods of cost allocation. Activity-based costing is the focus of problems 12-B3, 12-25, 12-41, 12-42, and 12-43. Problems 12-34 through 12-36 illustrate and apply the chapter discussion for service-department cost allocation, process maps, ABC, and customer profitability. Choice of cost pools and allocation bases is covered in case 12-41, and case 12-42 presents multiple allocation bases. Joint product costs are the focus of problems 12-A4, 12-B4, 12-27, 12-28, and 12-44.

Chapter 13: Accounting for Overhead Costs

This chapter may be assigned without assigning Chapters 12. However, Chapter 8 should precede Chapter 13.

Assign this material carefully so that the student does some simple work first. Problems 13-A3 (or 13-B3), 13-A4 (or 13-B4 or 13-50), and 13-40 provide a basic introduction. Problems 13-41, 13-42, and 13-53 concentrate on essentials of absorption and direct costing. Cases 13-67 and 13-68 pursue the topic more deeply. The essentials of production volume variances are covered in 13-55. A recapitulation of all variances, as discussed in the first appendix, is presented in 13-45, 13-46, 13-62, and 13-63. Problem 13-59 covers the disposition of variances.

Please note the overall tone of this set of problems. The emphasis is on an overall perspective, not on detailed intricacies of variance analysis. In particular, consider the lessons that can be learned from 13-51 and 13-68.

Chapter 14: Job-Costing and Process-Costing Systems

This chapter is organized into two distinct parts – job-costing systems and process-costing systems.

Job-costing systems. Job-costing systems may be assigned without assigning process-costing systems (a subject we prefer to omit). Job costing may be studied at two levels or more. The first level would be confined to 14-A1 or 14-B1, which cover the basic points. At this first level, 14-20 to 14-24, 14-28, and 14-39 might also be considered.

There are many short straightforward exercises and problems. Consider 14-25, and 14-41. Nonmanufacturing situations are presented in 14-23 and 14-42.

Process-costing systems. The second part of the chapter on process-costing systems also may be studied as three independent sections. For example, many instructors may confine their coverage to process costing basics and do not cover the effects of beginning inventories and backflush costing. The second section considers the effects of beginning inventories. Others will skip this second section but cover the last section, which introduces backflush costing. The assignment material is divided accordingly. Problems 14-A2, 14-B2, 14-31 through 14-35, and 14-45 through 14-47 cover the basics of process costing. Problems 14-A3, 14-B3, 14-36 through 14-38 cover the weighted-average method. Finally, problems 14-A4, 14-B4, and 14-48 cover backflush costing.

Special Note on Chapters 15-17

Much of the assignment material in Chapters 15-17 is similar to that in this textbook's companion volume, *Introduction to Financial Accounting*. Students who have thoroughly studied that book will have little need to study Chapters 15-17 here, except as a review or to fill in gaps. For example, if there is time, many topics in the final two chapters of this book will deserve more careful study than may have been feasible in an earlier course. Consider intercompany investments, consolidations, and accounting for changing prices.

Chapter 15: Basic Accounting: Concepts, Techniques, and Conventions

This material can be used in a variety of ways, depending on the objectives of the course and the backgrounds of the students. For example, if we are teaching a class of managers some "financial accounting for non-financial executives," we usually assign either 15-A2 and 15-A3 (or 15-B2 and 15-B3). If we have more time, we also assign 15-A1 (or 15-B1), 15-24, and 15-25. For regular classes, we also like to assign 15-28 or 15-29.

The assignment material for Appendix 15B permits a study of the mechanics of bookkeeping and provides a deeper study of the general concepts of the chapter. If there is little time, it is unnecessary to cover the appendix on ledger accounts. *Subsequent chapters are not dependent on knowledge of T accounts.*

In sum, there is an ample supply of material that can be used for a quick survey or for a deep probing of basic accounting concepts and procedures. The amount of time devoted to the chapter will obviously depend on the instructor's purposes.

Chapter 16: Understanding Corporate Annual Reports: Basic Financial Statements

Although this chapter was not formally divided into major parts, instructors can pick and choose if they prefer. For instance, some instructors may wish to assign only the early part of the chapter and the statement of cash flows. Consider the following pertinent assignment material that covers the highlights: 16-A1 (or 16-B1), 16-41, 16-42, 16-59 through 16-63.

The statement of cash flows is covered in the fundamental assignment material (16-A2 through 16-A4, 16-B2 and 16-B3) and also by 16-43 through 16-53 and 16-64 through 16-67

Appendix 16A is covered in 16-54 through 16-58 and 16-68 through 16-71. Problems 16-56 and 16-68 are good basic problems that have solutions similar to first Exhibit 16-18 in the chapter.

Chapter 17: More on Understanding Corporate Annual Reports

Many instructors may not have time to cover the entire Fundamental Assignment Material. If so, Problem 17-B2 and 17-B3 may be the most serious candidates for homework assignments. Problem 17-35 provides a general overview of consolidated financial statements.

We always take a few minutes in class to stress the highlights of the consolidated balance sheet and income statement in the two big exhibits in the chapter.

To cover financial ratios, consider 17-A5, 17-B5, 17-36, and 17-48. We cover financial ratios only if the finance course does not.

Problems 17-37, 17-38, 17-50, and 17-51 cover Appendix 17. Problems 17-37 and 17-38 have solutions similar to Exhibit 17-8 of the text. When inflation is covered, there is a danger of getting too enmeshed in the *details* of how the four major methods differ. Some time should be devoted to the *measuring* of the differences, especially the strengths and weaknesses of the historical cost/constant dollar method in comparison with the other methods.

PRESENTATION OF SOLUTIONS IN CLASS

Instructors have a variety of views regarding the use of classroom time for homework solutions. Most instructors put solutions on a chalkboard or use overhead projectors. In turn, many students frantically copy the materials in their notes. Our practice is to reproduce the printed homework solutions for distribution either before, during, or after the discussion of a particular solution. The members of the class are glad to pay a modest fee to the school to cover the reproduction costs. In this way, students can spend more of their classroom time in thinking rather than writing. Furthermore, they have a complete set of notes.

Some instructors object to this procedure because it provides students with a "file" that can be passed along to subsequent classes. Students in subsequent classes will then use the "file" to avoid conscientious preparation of homework. There will always be some students who hurt themselves by not doing homework in an appropriate way. Why should the vast majority of students be penalized by withholding the printed solutions? The benefits of using printed solutions clearly outweigh the costs; we no longer fret about the few students who beat the system (and themselves).

Similarly, we distribute printed solutions to tests and examinations along with a summary of overall class performance. We do not devote class time to discussing these solutions. The students deserve feedback, but they have sufficient motivation to scrutinize the printed solutions and check their errors on an individual basis. In this way more class time is available for new material.

If students have complaints about grades, we usually ask them to cool off for 24 hours and then submit a written analysis of how they were unjustly treated. We then take these complaints in batches, regrade the papers, and return the papers. If the student then wants to have a person-to-person discussion of the matter, he or she is welcome to see us. This procedure may seem too impersonal, but we recommend it to those teachers (like us) who have been through some painful debates that have been inefficient and frustrating for both student and teacher.

Incidentally, key numbers from the solutions to each problem, which begin on p. xxix of this solutions manual, are available in quantities without charge from Accounting Editor, Prentice-Hall, Inc., Upper Saddle River, New Jersey 07458. Some instructors may wish to distribute these to the class at the start of the course.

CONDUCTING THE COURSE

From time to time we have received inquiries regarding how we teach a course in management accounting. The following "Notes on Classroom Procedures" explains our philosophy, and it can be handed out to students at the start of a course:

The following describes my general teaching style. I am placing this description in writing to avoid any misunderstanding; in the past, a few students have been misled about why I operate classes in a particular way.

In my view, the most effective and efficient use of classroom time aims at reinforcing or clarifying what the student has tried to learn on an individual basis (or sometimes a group basis) before entering the classroom. Therefore, optimal learning is achieved by (a) wholehearted preparation via studying the assigned readings and solving the assigned problems or cases; (b) discussion of the material by the students and teacher in class; and (c) the instructor's underscoring of the most important points via comments or short lectures (lecturettes). I rarely give lectures per se. My lectures are in the text or the readings.

Obviously, problems or cases are not ends in themselves; instead they are the means of focusing on central issues, concepts, or knowledge.

Given the foregoing, the success of this course depends on adequate preparation for classes by both students and teacher. It also requires participation during class--always participation of the mind and occasional participation of the mouth. Throughout the term, a variety of helpful questions arise from a variety of students. As in all situations throughout life, some individuals naturally speak more often than others. (We all realize that there is no necessary consistency between lots of talk and lots of comprehension of the subject matter.)

I use a call list for two major reasons: (a) to get acquainted with all the students in class so that I can at least link faces with names; and (b) to provide motivation and ensure widespread participation.

From time to time, you may come to class unprepared for a variety of reasons. In such instances, if you want to preclude the possibility of being called on, simply put your name on a slip of paper on the front desk before the session begins. In this way, everybody wins; I don't enjoy calling on students who are unprepared.

Unless otherwise specified, no assignments need to be handed in. However, as you know, the best preparation entails writing solutions and answers. Your contribution to the class via your solutions, comments, and questions is an essential part of the course. If you are absent from a particular class, you should hand in your solutions at the subsequent class. This requirement encourages an active rather than a passive role in the course.

Some of you may have unusually severe anxiety about being called on in class. If so, please see me after class during the first week of the quarter to discuss alternate arrangements. My use of a call list is not intended to be a terror tactic.

KEY AMOUNTS FROM SUGGESTED SOLUTIONS TO SELECTED PROBLEMS
For Students' Use in Checking Their Own Solutions

Introduction to Management Accounting, 13th Ed.
Horngren, Sundem, and Stratton

Chapter 1

1-A2	Tot. var., $178U	1-29	1, 7, 8 Production Decisions
1-B2	Actual, $14,340	1-30	3, 6, 7 Financial
1-B3	1. T		

Chapter 2

2-A1	1. 30,000; $30,000	2-47	1. $1,100
2-A2	1. $40,000	2-48	1. $71 million
2-B1	2. $32,000	2-49	3. $(660)
2-B2	1. $1,220	2-50	2. $144,000
2-28	3. Sales, $960,000	2-51	1. 40,000
2-29	1. Net inc., $70,000	2-52	1. 124
2-32	1. $60,000,000	2-53	3. 77.2%
2-33	2. 85,000 rooms	2-54	1. 38.9%
2-34	1. $23	2-55	1. 42,000
2-35	1. 267	2-56	1. $2.6 billion
2-36	2. 41,571	2-58	1. $140,000
2-37	2. 66,000	2-59	2. Net inc., $2,250,000
2-38	$1,800,000	2-60	2. 52.5%
2-40	2. P&G $4,800,000	2-61	1. a
2-41	1. $468	2-62	1. 15,000
2-42	1. £3,310,000	2-63	3. a. $542,000
2-43	2. 2,500	2-64	1. Old, $20,000; New, $60,000
2-44	1. 32.5 days	2-65	1. B-E: L, 170; D, 85
2-45	2. 10,000	2-66	1. 283,125
2-46	Operating profit, $1,677 million		

Chapter 3

3-A1	1. b; 3. a; 5. c; 7. c; 9. b;11. b	3-41	Var., £20/ton
3-A2	1. Sign A, $180 and $120	3-44	2. $3,000 fixed cost/week
3-A3	1. Var., $5.00	3-45	1. Var., $10,400U
3-B2	Act. anal., Z15, $64	3-48	Projected income $4,000
3-B3	FC, $50,000,000/month	3-49	1. Act. anal., Blooms, $4,140
3-32	2. B	3-50	2. $4,280.50
3-35	1. $3,000/month	3-52	3. $287.68
3-36	Disc., $86,000	3-54	2. a. # of boards, $149,133
3-37	B-E, 50,000 orders	3-55	2. $12,650
3-38	2. Var., $2.22/unit	3-57	2. 2003, $174.32/employee

Chapter 4

4-A1	Small Std. $35,600	4-46	Process other trans., $163,000
4-A2	1. Company GP 13.73%	4-47	1. Retail, $102.23
	2. Cell-Phone Casings GP 6.58%	4-52	2. X-1, $105,100
		4-53	Gross margin, ($4.175)
4-A4	1. $4.171	4-55	d. Breakeven $125,000
4-B1	Hand Tool parts $88	4-56	c. $2,000
4-B2	1. Company GP 17.4%	4-57	2. $4,000
	2. Cell-Phone casings GP 17.81%	4-59	1. Residential, $3.5259
		4-62	3. Retail, $141.89
4-B4	1. SA2, $16,000		

Chapter 5

5-A1	2. Inc. in op. income 46.1%	5-41	1. 66.7%
5-A2	1. Plain: $16, 24%	5-42	3. $201,600
5-A3	2. 50%	5-43	$3,160,000
5-B1	4. $150,000 decline	5-47	1. With, £103,000
5-B2	1. XY-7, 4/5 hour	5-49	1. 516,923
5-31	Difference, $50	5-51	1. Op. inc. @300,000, $220,000
5-32	1. $300 increase	5-52	1. 2nd option by $80
5-33	3. a. 30	5-53	1. Increase € 1,200
5-34	1. 300	5-54	1. $5
5-35	1. c. $24.80	5-58	2. $2.40
5-37	1. SFR 1,200 decrease	5-59	1. $31.05
5-40	1. $10	5-61	1. $1,550,000

Chapter 6

6-A1	3. $64,000	6-47	Sales, ZAR900,000
6-A2	1. $42,000	6-48	3. $90,000
6-A3	1. $22,000	6-49	2. 55.56%
6-A4	2. $337,000	6-50	2. 50%
6-B1	1. Difference, €2.5/unit	6-51	1. Difference, $100,000
6-B2	1. $300	6-52	1. $312,000
6-B3	Difference, $7,500	6-53	1. With, $4,604,840
6-B5	2. $1,050,000	6-54	1. With, $9.07
6-33	1. Difference, $10,000	6-55	1. €43,350
6-37	1. c	6-56	1. $192,000
6-38	1. $250	6-57	3. 30,000 units
6-39	1. Difference, $2,000	6-59	1. Difference, $3,000
6-40	2. $14.50	6-61	3. a. 468/show
6-41	$20,760	6-62	2. $550,000
6-43	2. $20,160	6-63	2. $250
6-44	2. $170,000	6-64	2. $10.00
6-45	c. ¥15,000,000	6-65	2. 50,000 units
6-46	k. $170,000,000	6-66	2. a. €111,000,000

Chapter 7

7-A1	1. Net inc., $59,820; cash bal., 8/31, $25,940	7-33	July purchases, $260,000
		7-34	1. $23,000
7-B1	1. Net inc., $16,367; cash bal., 3/31, $32,992	7-35	Cash, 6/30, $27,000
		7-36	Cash, 4/30, $129,000
7-26	2. Sales	7-37	Cash, 10/31, $13,115
7-27	$720,000	7-38	2. $594,000
7-28	1. $1,632,000	7-43	2. Inc., $772,000
7-29	3. $120,000	7-44	3. $1,756,000
7-30	July collections, $428,000	7-45	2. Total, $11,092,900
7-31	March collections, ¥225,600,000	7-46	Div. gross profit $947,600
7-32	$398,350		

Chapter 8

8-A1	2. $980,000 + $.80X	8-36	1. Act. op. inc., $104,400
8-A2	Activity-level var., $7,500U	8-38	1. Sales-act. var., RMB570,000
8-A3	2. Mat. usage, $750U	8-39	2. $9,900U
8-B1	2. Flex.-bud. var., $29,500U	8-40	1. Usage, $1,125U
8-B2	1. Lab. price var., $30,000F	8-41	Tot actual, $13,732
8-B3	2. 117,000 hours	8-43	Lab. usage var., $4,000U
8-24	$350,000	8-44	1. e. 6,500SFR U
8-25	@40,000, $11,500	8-45	2. Lab. price var., $855F
8-26	Dir. mat., $8/unit	8-46	1. Mat. pr. var., $5,400F
8-28	Flex.-bud. var., $7,500U	8-47	1. a. Usage, $600U
8-29	Mat. price var., B118,500F	8-48	Tot. cost, $140.80
8-30	1. $14.58	8-49	Dir. mat., $54.90
8-31	Lab. usage var., $10,200U	8-50	1. a. $9,200U
8-32	1. 13,010 hours	8-52	2. $(28,680)1. Flex.-bud. var., $10,000U
8-33	Mat. usage var., $7,500F	8-53	
8-34	Sales-act. var., $900,000U	8-54	2. Flex.-bud. var., $10,200F
8-35	Tot. flex.-bud. var., $32U		

Chapter 9

9-A2	Littleton seg. cont. $145,000	9-44	1. 640,000
9-A3	1. 2004, Intertel, $126,864	9-48	2. BTL only, 123
9-B2	Div. 2 seg. cont. ($360,000)	9-49	1. 20X3, 32.7 pounds/hr.
9-34	1. C, March, ¥413,500	9-52	1. B-E, $755,495
9-38	1. Dwtn. cont., $105,000		

Chapter 10

10-A1	3. B. $66,000	10-30	1. 20%
10-A2	1. $30,000 disadvantage	10-31	1. a. Overall, $1.30
10-A3	$26,000 advantage	10-32	2. $9 if excess capacity
10-A4	1. a. $4.50	10-33	1. £400
10-B1	1. b. ROI, 33%	10-35	2. Beta, ROI, 3%
10-B2	2002, $2,548 million	10-36	1. a. Pub./Info., 17.3%
10-B3	$3.35 per gallon	10-37	EVA, $(8,006,000)
10-B4	1. c. 5.88%	10-38	2002, $309,000,000
10-24	2. 4.6%	10-39	1. $2,502,194,000
10-25	A. 21%	10-40	1. Shoes, ROA, repl. cost, 18%
10-26	3. Y, $26,000	10-41	1. a. Plant, 10%
10-27	1. 2002, $(8,006,000)	10-48	$22 to $38
10-28	1. b. Fleet, 27%	10-50	1. $27.50 saved
10-29	1. J, ROI, 28%	10-51	1. $25,500 increase

Chapter 11

11-A2	$23,240	11-45	2. $5,240
11-A3	1. $(16,318)	11-46	1. $12,229
11-A4	1. $(89,690)	11-47	2. $75,838
11-A5	@ $65,000, Cash up $60,500	11-48	2. Difference, $(14,994)
11-B1	1. a. $10,668.00	11-49	Difference, $10,240
11-B2	$80,634	11-50	NPV, $12,679
11-B3	1. $(1,761)	11-51	Difference, £11,000
11-B4	2. $3,095	11-52	1. $21,000
11-B5	1. Cash inflow, $13,000	11-53	2. 45.2 trips
11-29	1. b. $21,216	11-54	2. $8,856
11-30	1. $381,300,000	11-55	2. $3,060
11-31	2. a. $501,920	11-56	$6,343
11-32	1. $427,838	11-57	NPV, $89,007
11-33	$811,200	11-58	6. ¥59,729,000
11-34	NPV, 20 yrs., $2,225	11-59	3. $35,878
11-35	$5,972	11-60	1. $6,637
11-36	1. $12,232	11-61	1. $11,550
11-37	2. 12%	11-62	1. NPV, $11,696
11-38	2. $9,069	11-63	2. $782
11-39	1. $4,862	11-64	1. NPV, Skr 487,040
11-40	Net inc., $48,000	11-65	2. $5,161,025
11-41	$530,000	11-66	NPV, $477,965
11-42	2. 2005, $2,240	11-67	Alt. C, NPV, $215,117
11-43	a. $67,570	11-69	Exp. NPV, ($558,070)
11-44	2. $11,114		

Chapter 12

12-A1	2. Tot., machining, $1,872,864	12-32	1. $.20
12-A2	4. Display type A, $16.27	12-33	4. To North, $562,500
12-A3	1. Northeast, $6 million	12-34	Whole company, $688,740
12-A4	2. B, $6,720,000	12-36	Customer type 1, $379,500
12-B1	1. Business, $72,000	12-37	1. Children's, $6,300
12-B2	3. a. $12.56	12-38	3. M1, $183.32
12-B3	1. Giant, $176.50	12-39	3. M1, $182.92
12-B4	2. Oat bran, $225,000	12-40	3. $6.875
12-23	2. $3,000	12-41	1. Model 1, ¥12,020
12-24	2. Sunnyville, $66,667	12-43	1. $1,488
12.25	2. Res., $401,250	12-44	2. To A, op. prof., $112
12-26	2. Assembly, $868,096	12-45	4. c. Prod. A, $270
12-27	2. B, $150,000	12-46	1. Board L, £199.35
12-28	2. B, $240,000	12-47	1. $216,750
12-29	3. $1,265,000		

Chapter 13

13-A1	3. $482.50	13-49	Last 6 months, $22,000 under
13-A2	1. Underapplied, $8,000	13-50	Under absorption, $6 increase
13-A3	1. $10,000	13-51	1. 20X5 variable cost net income, $100
13-A4	Gross margin, $2,160		
13-B1	2. Lower by $10,000	13-52	1. 20X5 variable cost net income, $100
13-B2	2. $20.00		
13-B3	2. $2,000	13-53	1. Absorption op. inc., $122,000
13-B4	Absorption op. inc., $447,000	13-54	1. Absorption op. inc., $228,400
13-35	Applied OH, $264,000	13-55	5. Fixed OH prod.-vol. var., $2,400F
13-36	80,000 direct labor hours		
13-37	2. b. $350,000	13-56	4. $75,000,000
13-38	Case 2, underapplied, $9	13-57	2. Flex. bud. var., $27,000U
13-39	No proration, $24,000 lower	13-58	1. Base c, 20X5, $13
13-40	Var. cost net income 20X6, $20	13-60	e. $1,146,500
13-42	1. $15,000	13-61	1.b. $45
13-43	¥1,260,000 unfavorable	13-62	Efficiency var., $3,600U
13-44	1.c. $11,000	13-63	Prod.-vol. var., €1,200U
13-45	Efficiency variance, 400U	13-64	Tot. mfg. cost, $95.03
13-46	Flexible-budget variance fixed, 1,500F	13-65	2.b. K156 total cost, SFr13,100
		13-66	3.a. $522,000
13-47	3. First Valley, $39,375	13-67	1.b. €1,545,000

Chapter 14

14-A1	2. WIP, $65,000	14-28	Case C, $7 per machine hour
14-A2	2. WIP, $11,000	14-31	WIP, $1,091,200
14-A3	2. WIP, $305,000	14-32	WIP, $38,220
14-B1	2. WIP, £32,000	14-35	Case B, 7,300
14-B2	2. WIP, $690,000	14-36	Conversion, 93,000
14-B3	WIP, $3,960	14-40	COGS, $871,000
14-20	2., 11	14-41	4., $53,500
14-22	2., 14	14-42	2., $31,25
14-25	1. Cost of houses sold, Oct., $605,000	14-45	3. $1,815,000
		14-46	WIP, 140,000
14-26	WIP, $5,000,000	14-47	WIP, £113,000
14-27	Finished goods, $32,000,000		

Chapter 15

15-A1	A, $30,000; H, $40,000
15-A2	2. Net inc., $4,000
15-A3	$45,000
15-B1	A, $1,228.4 million
15-B2	2. Net earn., $55 million
15-B3	$455,000,000
15-23	1. F
15-28	3. B189,000
15-29	2. X, $3,000; Y, $6,000
15-30	2. Net inc., $7,900
15-31	1. Cr.
15-32	1. T
15-36	1. Accrual op. inc., $63,300
15-38	a. $594,200,000
15-39	1. a. Net inc., $1,236 million
15-40	Net earn., $4,352 million

Chapter 16

16-A1	Ret. earn., $202,000
16-A2	Cash from op. act., $354,000
16-A4	1. Net inc., $120,000
16-B1	Inc. Tax. Payable, $1,157 mill.
16-B3	$1,590 million
16-41	Tot. assets, € 2,540
16-42	L.-T. inv., ¥15,000 million
16-43	$642,000
16-44	$358,000
16-45	$45,000
16-46	Cash from op. act., NK241,000
16-49	Cash from op. act., $217,000
16-51	Net inc., $15 million
16-52	Cash from op. act., $70 million
16-53	1. Cash from op. act., $31 mill.
16-54	1. a. $5,650
16-55	12/31/20X1, $70,000
16-56	LIFO, GM, $120,000
16-57	1. b. EPS, $.05
16-58	1. LIFO, GM, $280,000
16-59	2. $10 million
16-61	1. $197,817,000
16-63	Gain, $5,538,000
16-64	a. Operating
16-66	Cash fr. op. act., $2,349.5 mill.
16-68	2. a. Lower, $92
16-69	LIFO, taxes $48 lower
16-70	1. Op. Inc., $3.5 billion
16-71	2003 op inc., $1,921 million

Chapter 17

17-A2	2. Consol. net inc., $95 million
17-A3	2. Consol. net inc., $93 million
17-A5	1. a. $48 million
17-B2	2. Consol. net. inc., $600 mill.
17-B3	1. 22,110,000
17-B4	1. 2.225 times
17-B5	1. 1.24
17-29	$47 million; $50 million
17-30	2. Consol. net inc., $260,000
17-33	1. $124 million
17-34	1. Tot. assets, $490 million
17-35	Consol. net inc., $108 million
17-36	1. b. 20X2, 6.3%
17-37	1. Hold. gain, CC/ND, $60,000
17-38	CC/CD, inc. fr. cont. ops., $600
17-41	2. $3,088 million
17-43	1. ¥28,159,000,000
17-44	1. $1,736 million
17-45	2. $4.8 billion
17-46	2. $963.5 million
17-47	1. 5.695%
17-48	2. a. 1.1
17-50	1. c. HC/CD, $1,801.3 million

CHAPTER 1
COVERAGE OF LEARNING OBJECTIVES

LEARNING OBJECTIVE	FUNDA-MENTAL ASSIGN-MENT MATERIAL	CRITICAL THINKING EXERCISES AND EXERCISES	PROBLEMS	CASES, EXCEL, COLLAB., & INTERNET EXERCISES
LO1: Describe the major users and uses of accounting information.	A1, B1	31	37, 38, 40	52
LO2: Explain why ethics is important to management accountants.	A3	35, 36	45, 46, 47	49, 52
LO3: Describe the cost-benefit and behavioral issues involved in designing an accounting system.			39, 41	
LO4: Explain the role of budgets and performance reports in planning and control.	A2, B2	30	43	50
LO5: Discuss the role accountants play in the company's value chain functions.	A1, B1	28, 29, 32, 33, 34	37, 40, 42	
LO6: Contrast the functions of controllers and treasurers.	B3	27, 34	37, 43, 44	48
LO7: Explain why accounting is important in a variety of career paths.		28, 29		52
LO8: Identify current trends in management accounting.				51
LO9: Appreciate the import-ance of ethical conduct to professional accountants.	A3	35, 36	45, 46, 47	49, 52

CHAPTER 1
Managerial Accounting and the Business Organization

1-A1 (10-15 min.)

Because the accountant's duties are often not sharply defined, some of these answers could be challenged:

1. Attention directing and problem solving. Budgeting involves making decisions about planned activities – hence, aiding problem solving. Budgets also direct attention to areas of opportunity or concern – hence, directing attention. Reporting against the budget also has a scorekeeping dimension.
2. Problem solving. Helps a manager assess the impact of a decision.
3. Scorekeeping. Reports on the results of an operation. Could also be attention direction if scrap is an area that might require management decisions.
4. Attention directing. Focuses attention on areas that need attention.
5. Attention directing. Helps managers learn about the information contained in a performance report.
6. Scorekeeping. The statement merely reports what has happened.
7. Problem solving. The cost comparison is apparently useful because the manager wishes to decide between two alternatives. Thus, it aids problem solving.
8. Attention directing. Variances point out areas where results differ from expectations. Interpreting them directs attention to possible causes of the differences.
9. Problem solving. Aids a decision about where the parts should be made.
10. Scorekeeping. Determining a depreciation schedule is simply an exercise in preparing financial statements to report the results of activities.

1-A2 (15-20 min.)

1.

	Budgeted Amounts	Actual Amounts	Deviations or Variances
Room rental	$ 140	$ 140	$ 0
Food	800	1,008	208U
Entertainment	600	600	0
Decorations	220	190	30F
Total	$1,760	$1,938	$178U

2. Because of the management by exception rule, room rental and entertainment require no explanation. The actual expenditure for food exceeded the budget by $208. Of this $208, $150 is explained by attendance of 15 persons more than budgeted (at a budget of $10 per person) and $58 is explained by expenditures above $10 per person.

Actual expenditures for decorations were $30 less than the budget. If all desired decorations were purchased, the decorations committee should be commended for their savings.

1-A3 (10 min.)

All of the situations raise possibilities for violation of the integrity standard. In addition, the manager in each situation must address an additional ethical standard:

1. The General Mills manager must respect the confidentiality standard. He or she should not disclose any information about the new cereal.
2. Roberto must address his level of competence for the assignment. If his supervisor knows his level of expertise and wants an analysis from a "layperson" point of view, he should do it. However, if the supervisor expects an expert analysis, Roberto must admit his lack of competence.
3. The objectivity standard should cause Helen to decline to omit the information from her budget. It is relevant information, and its omission may mislead readers of the budget.

1-B1 (15-20 min.)

Because the accountant's duties are often not sharply defined, some of these answers could be challenged:

1. Scorekeeping. Records events.
2. Scorekeeping. Simply recording of what has happened.
3. Problem solving. Helps a manager decide between alternatives.
4. Attention directing. Directs attention to the use of overtime labor.
5. Problem solving. Provides information to managers for deciding between alternatives.
6. Attention directing. Directs attention to why nursing costs increased.
7. Attention directing. Directs attention to areas where actual results differed from the budget.
8. Problem solving. Helps the vice-president to decide which course of action is best.
9. Scorekeeping. Records costs in the department to which they belong.
10. Scorekeeping. Records actual overtime costs.
11. Attention directing. Directs attention to stores with either high or low ratios of advertising expenses to sales.
12. Attention directing. Directs attention to causes of returns of the drug.
13. Attention directing or problem solving, depending on the use of the schedule. If it is to identify areas of high fuel usage it is attention directing. If it is to plan for purchases of fuel, it is problem solving.
14. Problem solving. Provides information for deciding between two alternative courses of action.
15. Scorekeeping. Records items needed for financial statements.

1-B2 (10-15 min.)

1 & 2.

	Budget	Actual	Variance
Sales	$75,000	$74,860	$ 140U
Costs:			
Fireworks	$35,000	$39,500	$4,500U
Labor	15,000	13,000	2,000F
Other	8,000	8,020	20U
Profit	$17,000	$14,340	$2,660U

3. The cost of fireworks was $4,500 ÷ $35,000 = 13% over budget. Did fireworks suppliers raise their prices? Did competition cause retail prices to be lower than expected? There should be some explanation for the extra cost of fireworks. Also, the labor cost was $2,000 ÷ $15,000 =13% below budget. It would be useful to discover why this cost was saved. Both sales and other costs were very close to budget.

1-B3 (10 - 15 min.)

1. Treasurer. Analysts affect the company's ability to raise capital, which is the responsibility of the treasurer.
2. Controller. Advising managers aids operating decisions.
3. Controller. Advice on cost analysis aids managers' operating decisions.
4. Controller. Divisional financial statements report on operations. Financial statements are generally produced by the controller's department.
5. Treasurer. Financing the business is the responsibility of the treasurer.
6. Controller. Tax returns are part of the accounting process overseen by the controller.
7. Treasurer. Insurance, as with other risk management activities, is usually the responsibility of the treasurer.
8. Treasurer. Allowing credit is a financial decision.

1-1 Decision makers within and outside an organization use accounting information for three broad purposes:

1. Internal reporting to managers for planning and controlling operations.
2. Internal reporting to managers for special decision-making and long-range planning.
3. External reporting to stockholders, government, and other interested parties.

1-2 The emphasis of financial accounting has traditionally been on the historical data presented in the external reports. Management accounting emphasizes planning and control purposes.

1-3 The branch of accounting described in the quotation is management accounting.

1-4 Scorekeeping is the recording of data for a later evaluation of performance. Attention directing is the reporting and interpretation of information for the purpose of focusing on inefficiencies of operation or opportunities for improvement. Problem solving presents a concise analysis of alternative courses of action.

1-5 GAAP applies to publicly issued annual financial reports. Internal accounting reports are not restricted by GAAP.

1-6 Yes, but it covers more than that. The Foreign Corrupt Practices Act applies to all publicly-held companies and covers the quality of internal accounting control as well as bribes and other matters.

1-7 Users cannot easily observe the quality of accounting information. Thus, they rely on the integrity of accountants to be sure the information is accurate. Information that is unreliable is worthless, so if accountants do not have a reputation for integrity, the information they produce will not have value.

1-8   Three examples of service organizations are banks, insurance companies, and public accounting firms. Such organizations tend to be labor intensive, have outputs that are difficult to define and measure, and have both inputs and outputs that are difficult or impossible to store.

1-9   Two considerations are cost-benefit balance and behavioral effects. Cost-benefit balance refers to how well an accounting system helps achieve management's goals in relation to the cost of the system. The behavioral consideration specifies that an accounting system should be judged by how it will affect the behavior (that is, decisions) of managers.

1-10   Yes. The act of recording events has become as much a part of operating activities as the act of selling or buying. For example, cash receipts and disbursements must be traced, and receivables and payables must be recorded, or else gross confusion would ensue.

1-11   A budget is a prediction and guide; a performance report is a tabulation of actual results compared with the budget; and a variance reconciles the differences between budget and actual.

1-12   No. Management by exception means that management spends more effort on those areas that seem to be out of control and less on areas that are functioning as planned. This method is an efficient way for managers to decide where to put their time and effort.

1-13   No. There is no perfect system of automatic control, nor does accounting control anything. Accounting is a tool used by *managers* in their control of operations.

1-14   Information that is relevant for decisions about a product depends on the product's life-cycle stage. Therefore, to prepare and interpret information, accountants should be aware of the current stage of a product's life cycle.

1-15   The six functions are: (1) research and development – generation and experimentation with new ideas; (2) product and service process design – detailed design and engineering of products; (3) production – use of resources to produce a product or service; (4) marketing - informing customers of the value and features of products or services; (5) distribution – delivering products or services to customers; and (6) customer service – support provided to customers.

1-16   No. Not all of the functions are of equal importance to the success of a company. Measurement and reporting should focus on those functions that enable a company to gain and maintain a competitive edge.

1-17   Line managers are directly responsible for the production and sale of goods or services. Staff managers have an advisory function – they support line managers.

1-18   Management accountants are the information specialists, even in non-hierarchical companies. However, in such companies they are more directly involved with managers and are often parts of cross-functional teams.

1- 19   A treasurer is concerned mainly with the company's financial matters, the controller with operating matters. In large organizations, there are sufficient activities associated with both financial and operating matters to justify two separate positions. In a small organization the same person might be both treasurer and controller.

1-20   The four parts of the CMA examination are: (1) economics, finance, and management, (2) financial accounting and reporting, (3) management reporting, analysis, and behavioral issues, and (4) decision analysis and information systems.

1-21   This is not true. About one-third of CEOs come from finance or accounting backgrounds. Accounting is excellent preparation for top management positions because accountants are often exposed to many parts of the company early in their careers.

1-22 Changes in technology are affecting how accountants operate. They must be able to account for e-commerce transactions efficiently and safely, they often must integrate their accounting systems into ERP systems, and an increasing number are beginning to use XBRL to communicate information electronically.

1-23 The essence of the just-in-time philosophy is the elimination of waste, accomplished by reducing the time products spend in the production process and trying to eliminate the time spent in processes that do not add value to the product.

1-24 Moving tools and products that are in process from one location to another in a plant is an activity that does not add value to the product. So changing the plant layout to eliminate wasted movement and time improves production efficiency.

1-25 The four major responsibilities are: (1) *competence* - develop knowledge; know and obey laws, regulations, and technical standards; and perform appropriate analyses, (2) *confidentiality* - refrain from disclosing or using confidential information, (3) *integrity* - avoid conflicts of interest, refuse gifts that might influence actions, recognize limitations, and avoid activities that might discredit the profession, and (4) *objectivity* - communicate information fairly, objectively, and completely, within confidentiality constraints.

1-26 Standards do not always provide the needed guidance. Sometimes an action borders on being unethical, but it is not clearly an ethical violation. Other times two ethical standards conflict. In situations such as these, accountants must make ethical judgments.

1-27 (5-10 min.)

Typical activities associated with the treasurer function include:

- Provision of capital
- Investor relations
- Short-term financing
- Banking and custody
- Credits and collections
- Investments
- Risk management

Typical activities associated with the controller function include:

- Planning for control
- Reporting and interpreting
- Evaluating and consulting
- Tax administration
- Government reporting
- Protection of assets
- Economic appraisal

1-28 (5-10 min.)

Activities 2, 4, 5, and 6 are primarily associated with marketing decisions.

The management accountant would assist in these decisions as follows:

Boeing Company's pricing decision requires cost data relevant to the new method of distributing spare parts. Amazon.com will need to know the costs of the advertising program as well as the additional costs of other value chain functions resulting from increased sales. TexMex Foods will need to know the incremental revenues and incremental costs associated with the special order. Target Stores needs to know the impact on both revenues and costs of closing one of its stores.

<u>1-29</u>   (5-10 min.)

Activities 1, 7, and 8 are primarily associated with production decisions.

The management accountant would assist in these decisions as follows.

Porsche Motor Company needs an analysis of the costs associated with purchasing the part compared to the costs of making the part. Dell will need to know the costs of the training program and the savings associated with increased efficiencies in the setup and changeover activities. General Motors needs to know the costs and salvage values of the replacement equipment, the proceeds of the sale of the old equipment, and the operating savings associated with the use of the new equipment.

<u>1-30</u>   (5 min.)

1. Management	4. Management	7. Financial
2. Management	5. Management	
3. Financial	6. Financial	

1. Performance Report

	Budget	Actual	Variance	Explanation
Revenues	$220,000	$228,000	$8,000 F	Additional sales from new products*
Advertising cost	15,000	16,500	(1,500) U	New advertising Campaign
Net			$6,500 F	

* From the New Products Report, seven new products were added. This exceeded the plan to add six.

2. Factors that may not have been considered include:
   a. The costs of new products may have exceeded their price.
   b. Customer satisfaction with new products may not have been part of the new products report.
   c. Competitors' reactions to the Starbucks store's actions may not have been anticipated.
   d. External uncontrollable factors such as increases in operating costs, adverse weather, changes in the overall economy, new competitors entering the market, or key employee turnover may have decreased efficiency.

1-32   (5 min.)

1. Line, support
2. Staff, support
3. Staff, marketing
4. Line, marketing
5. Staff, support
6. Line, production

<u>1-33</u>   (30 min.)

Microsoft is a company that most students will know and have some understanding of what functions its managers perform. Nevertheless, this may not be an easy exercise for those who have little knowledge of how companies operate.

Research & development – Because software companies must continually come out with new products and upgrades to their current products this is a critical function for Microsoft. More than one-fourth of Microsoft's operating expenses are devoted to R&D.

Design of products, services, or processes – For Microsoft the design and R&D process probably overlap considerably. Product design is critical; process design is probably not. One essential part of design is beta testing – that is, field testing of new software. This quality-control step is essential to prevent customer dissatisfaction with new products.

Production – Microsoft produces disks and CD-ROMs and the manuals and packaging to go with them. However, they are increasingly delivering software over the Internet, which takes an initial process design and then few resources. It is not likely a major focus for Microsoft.

Marketing – Microsoft spends more on sales and marketing than on any other operating expense. Increasing competition in software sales makes marketing essential to the company's future. This function includes advertising and direct marketing activities, but it also includes activities of the company's sales force.

Distribution – This function is becoming simpler for Microsoft as it delivers more and more software over the Internet. Although the company must stay abreast of competitors in delivery methods, this is not likely to create a major competitive advantage or disadvantage for Microsoft.

Customer service – Customer service is important, but Microsoft tries to minimize its costs in this area by product design – making things work right without needing deep computer expertise. Still, poor customer service can severely impact a company, so Microsoft must attend to it.

Support functions – Most of the time these are not a major focus. There is one exception recently for Microsoft. Legal support has been front and center. The very future of the company was based on court judgments for which good legal support was essential.

<u>1-34</u> (15-20 min.)

The management accountant's major purpose is to provide information that helps *line managers* in making decisions regarding the planning and controlling of operations. The accountant supplies information for scorekeeping, attention directing, and problem solving. In turn, managers use this and other information for routine and non-routine decisions and for evaluating subordinates and the performance of sub-parts of the organization. Management accountants must walk a delicate line between (1) making sure that managers are properly using the pertinent information and (2) making sure that the managers, not the accountants, are doing the actual managing.

<u>1-35</u> (5 min.)

Other costs of a poor ethical environment include legal costs and costs due to high employee turnover. Other benefits of a good ethical environment include low employee turnover, low loss from internal theft, and improved customer satisfaction resulting from better quality and service (that result from a more productive work environment).

<u>1-36</u> (5 min.)

There are numerous examples.

"You understand how important it is to record this sale before year end, don't you?"

"Doing it this way is common for all companies in our business, so don't worry!"

"Trust me, the inventory is at the warehouse."

<u>1-37</u>   (15-20 min.)

This problem can form the basis of an introductory discussion of the entire field of management accounting.

1.   The focus of management accounting is on helping internal users to make better decisions, whereas the focus of financial accounting is on helping external users to make better decisions. Management accounting helps in making a host of decisions, including pricing, product choices, investments in equipment, making or buying goods and services, and manager rewards.

2.   Generally accepted accounting standards or principles affect both internal and external accounting. However, change in internal accounting is not inhibited by generally accepted principles. For example, if an organization wants to account for assets on the basis of replacement costs for internal purposes, no outside agency can prohibit such accounting. Of course, this means that organizations may have to keep more than one set of records. There is nothing immoral or unethical about having multiple sets of books, but they are
      expensive. Accounting data are commodities, just like butter or eggs. Innovations in internal accounting systems must meet the same cost-benefit tests that other commodities endure. That is, their perceived increases in benefits must exceed their perceived increases in costs. Ultimately, benefits are measured by whether better decisions are forthcoming in the form of increased net profits or cost savings.

3.   Budgets, the formal expressions of management plans, are a major feature of management accounting, whereas they are not as prominent in financial accounting. Budgets are major devices for compelling and disciplining management planning.

4.   An important use of management accounting information is the evaluation of performance, which often takes the form of comparison

of actual results against budgets, providing incentives and feedback to improve future decisions.

5. Accounting systems have an enormous influence on the behavior of individuals affected by them. Management accounting is more concerned with the likely behavioral effects of various accounting alternatives that may be adopted than is financial accounting.

1-38 (10 min.)

The main point of this question is that cost information is crucial for decisions regarding which products and services should be emphasized or de-emphasized. The incentives to measure costs precisely are far greater when flat fees are being received instead of reimbursements of costs.

Note, too, that nonprofit organizations and profit-seeking organizations have similar desires regarding management accounting. Accountability is now in fashion for many purposes, including justification of prices, cost control, and response to criticisms by investors (whether they be donors, taxpayers, or others).

When somebody's money is at stake, accounting systems get much love and attention. In a survey of 550 hospitals, hospital financial executives said that improved cost accounting systems "are crucial to responding to changes in hospital payment mechanisms and that better cost information is essential for more profitable and efficient operations." Hospitals will increasingly identify costs by product (type of case), not just by departments.

<u>1-39</u> (10 min.)

Paperwork and systems often seem to become ends in themselves. However, the rationale that should underlie systems design is the cost-benefit philosophy or approach that is implied in the quotation. The aim is to get the managers and their subordinates collectively to make better decisions under one system versus another system – for a given level of costs.

Marks & Spencer should look at each of the management accounting reports it produces with an eye toward how it helps managers make better decisions. Does it provide needed scorekeeping? Does it direct attention to aspects of operations that might need altering? Does it provide information for specific management decisions? These types of questions will help identify the benefit of the information in the report.

Then the company must consider the cost – not just the cost of collecting the data and preparing the reports, but the cost of educating managers to use the information and the cost of the time to read, digest, and act on the information. Too much information may be costly because it makes it time-consuming (and thus costly) to sift through the reams of information to find the few items that are important. And one cost may be the loss of important information because the total volume of information makes it too difficult to ferret out the important items.

1-40 (10 min.) Financial information is important in all companies. But how managers get and use financial information can differ depending on the culture and philosophies of the company.

Top executives of a company often represent a functional area that is critical to the comparative economic advantage of the company. If technology is crucial, engineers generally hold important executive positions. If marketing differentiates the company from others, marketing executives usually dominate. But regardless of the source of a company's competitive advantage, its success will eventually be measured in economic terms. They must attend to financial aspects to thrive and often even to survive.

Management accountants must work with the dominant managers in any organization. The modern trend toward use of cross-functional teams places management accountants at the center of the action regardless of what type of managers and executives dominate. Most companies realize that there is a financial dimension to almost every major decision, so they want the financial experts, management accountants, involved in the decisions. But to be accepted as an important part of these teams, the management accountants must know how to help managers in various functional areas. In General Mills, if accountants can't talk the language of marketing, they will not have great influence. In ArvinMeritor, if they do not understand the information needs of engineers they will not provide value.

<u>1-41</u> (10-15 min.)

1. Boeing's competitive environment and manufacturing processes changed greatly during the 1990s. An accounting system that served them well in their old environment would not necessarily be optimal in the 2000s. Boeing's management probably thought that changes in the accounting system were necessary to produce the kind of information necessary to remain competitive.

2. A cost-benefit criterion was probably used. Boeing's management may not have quantified the costs and the benefits, but they certainly assessed whether the new system would help decisions enough to warrant the cost of the system.

   Many of the benefits of a better accounting system are hard to measure. They affect many strategic decisions of an organization. Without accurate product costs, management will find it difficult to assess the consequences of their decisions. An accurate accounting system will help to price airplanes and other products competitively.

3. More accurate product costs will usually result in better management decisions. But if the cost of the accounting system that produces the more accurate costs is too high, it may be best to forego the increased accuracy. The benefit of better decisions must exceed the added cost of the system for a change to be desirable.

<u>1-42</u> (10 min.)

1.   There are many possible activities for each function of Nike's value chain. Some possibilities are:

Research and development – Determining changes in customers' tastes and preferences for shoes and sportswear to come up with new products (maybe the next "Air Jordans").

Product and service process design – Design a shoe to meet the increasing demands of competitive athletes.

Production – Determine where to produce products and negotiate contracts with the companies producing them.

Marketing – Signing prominent athletes to endorse Nike's products.

Distribution – Select the best locations for warehouses for distribution to retail outlets.

Customer service – Formulate return policies for products that customers perceive to be defective.

2.   Accounting information that aids managers' decisions includes:

Research and development – Trends in sales for various products, to determine which are becoming more and less popular.

Product and service process design – Production costs of various shoe designs.

Production – Measure total costs, including both purchase cost and transportation costs, for production in various parts of the world.

Marketing – The added profits generated by the added sales due to product endorsements.

Distribution – Storage and shipping costs for different alternative warehouse locations.

Customer service – The net cost of returned merchandise, to be compared with the benefits of better customer relations.

<u>1-43</u> (10-15 min.)   This problem can lead to a long or short discussion. Pointing out the problems can be done reasonably quickly. Formulating solutions can generate much discussion.

1. The appropriate accounting information presented correctly should be helpful to managers. It is clear that Belton does not regard the accounting performance reports as helpful. Some key problems are:

- Belton refers to "their" budget, meaning that the budget belongs to the controller's department, not him and his department. Managers should help formulate the budget and should accept it as a reasonable target.
- The controller's office shows up only when costs are over budget. Controllers should not be "policemen." They should be business advisors who provide continual assistance not occasional reprimand.
- Belton clearly does not understand the performance reports. An important role for the controller is education of managers in how to use accounting information.
- Belton believes the performance report has nothing to do with what happens on the shop floor. He may be right. Accounting reports often arrive too late and are not specific enough to be useful to front-line managers. If so, the reports should be changed or the results used differently.
- Paperwork takes time away from productive activity. This is especially a problem when the numbers have little value to those putting in the time.
- Budgeting is not taken seriously, so the numbers reported by Belton and his subordinates are not reliable.
- Things have gotten so bad that Belton had an attitude problem toward the controller's office. Palencia is meeting him for the first time, and he is already disrespectful of her.

2.   Palencia has major problems. Her first task is to get the cooperation of Belton, his subordinates, and those like them in other departments. This will probably involve changing the accounting reports received by the line managers, and it will certainly involve changes in how these reports are presented and used. If the reports are not useful, she needs to find out why. Then she can change the reports so that the managers find them helpful. If they have useful information, she needs to show managers how they can use the information to make better decisions.

Foremost, Palencia has to change the attitudes of the line managers toward the controller's department. This will take time, and it will require some specific instances where the controller or her staff provides information that the managers perceive as useful. To do this, she may need to change the accounting system to produce better information, and she needs to teach her controller's department staff how to present information in a nonthreatening way.

There is no one solution to Palencia's problems. Different managers would handle it in different ways. If students have had experience, there will be many suggestions about how to proceed. For students with little experience, it may be sufficient to point out the variety of possible approaches.

1-44 (10-15 min.)

Accountants become the information experts in many companies. In a company such as Marmon, with its many varied subsidiaries, the accounting system provides a link between the various operating companies. The accountants provide information about the operations of an individual unit, and they also show how the units fit together as parts of the Marmon Group.

Management accountants should work together with managers to determine what information the managers would find useful. Then the accountants should help devise systems to produce that information, provided that its value is greater than its cost. As such, management accountants are information consultants to managers. Decisions are still the domain of managers, but the accountants provide advice to help managers make better decisions.

Once, accountants were considered "corporate cops," staff members who reported on the failings of managers. They were primarily scorekeepers, but when the score showed something awry, they became informants - carriers of bad news to corporate headquarters. Managers resented them. But today, good management accountants are allies of managers. They provide information that helps managers make better decisions, which makes the managers look good. Everyone is better off when management accountants focus on providing the information that aids management decisions.

To be effective internal consultants, accountants must have a background in accounting and information systems. In addition, they must have knowledge of all the functions of business and all the areas of the value chain.

1.   Brigham's decisions violate standards of competence and integrity. Competence is violated because the most competent persons apparently are not being hired, jeopardizing the competence of the accounting department. Further, Brigham may be violating equal opportunity employment laws and regulations.

Integrity requires an accountant to avoid conflicts of interest, but hiring the sons of personal friends certainly appears to be a conflict of interest. Such hiring was possibly for the personal gain of Brigham at the expense of the company. Further, this practice subverts the company's equal employment opportunity policy.

2.   Myers's first step normally would be to discuss this situation with his boss. However, because the alleged unethical behavior is by his boss and Myers has already confronted him about it and been rebuffed, the next step seems warranted. This would involve going to Brigham's superior. (Alternately, some organizations have an individual, possibly called an ombudsperson, to whom Myers could report such concerns. Apparently McMillan Shipping Company does not have such a person.) If the matter could not be resolved at that level, he should continue up the line until reaching Paluska, the president. If equal employment opportunity is genuinely a company priority, Paluska should be very concerned about Brigham's actions.

What if the situation is not resolved to Myers's satisfaction after following the steps in the preceding paragraph? The final step is to go directly to the Board of Directors. If that is unsatisfactory, there may be no recourse but to resign, sending an explanatory memo to an appropriate high-level official of the company.

Should Myers go to the press so that they will put on pressure to change the hiring practices? Such a step is generally not appropriate. It would put Myers in the position of violating the ethical standard of confidentiality. The only person external to the firm with whom it is appropriate to discuss this issue is a confidential objective advisor.

<u>1-46</u>   (15-20 min.)

1.   Because of the standard of confidentiality, the information in the geologist's report should not be revealed.

2.   The standard of integrity would require one to reject the invitation.

3.   This is a difficult ethical problem, one that deserves discussion. Two ethical standards apparently conflict. Confidentiality would lead to nondisclosure, provided there was no legal requirement to do so. But objectivity would indicate that the information about the additional losses should be used in making the earnings prediction. The authors think that objectivity should take precedence here, but others might disagree.

4.   The standard of competence, and to some extent the standard of integrity, would lead one to research the tax law before deciding whether to deduct the item.

<u>1-47</u> (15-25 min.)

There are various possible answers. These are just some of the items that might be mentioned. The only area were the magazine is explicit in how it ranks companies is service to stockholders.

1) Stockholders - The magazine uses 3-year average returns to shareholders. Top companies were IBM and Motorola.

2) Community - Considers philanthropy, any foundation the company has, community service projects, educational outreach, scholarships, employee volunteerism, and so forth. Top companies were St. Paul Companies and General Mills.

3) Minorities and women – This includes both internal performance, such as percent of minority and women among employees, managers, and board members, any EEOC complaints, diversity programs in place, lawsuits, and accommodations for the disabled, and external performance, such as serving disadvantaged, low-income, minority, and other generally under-served populations. Top companies were Fannie Mae and IBM.

4) Employees – Considers wages relative to the industry, benefits paid, family-friendly policies, parental leave, team management, employee empowerment, and so forth. Top companies were Motorola and Herman Miller.

5) Environment – Considers positive programs in place such as pollution reduction, recycling, and energy-saving measures; as well as negative measures such as level of pollutants, EPA citations, fines, lawsuits, and other measures. Top companies were Herman Miller and IBM.

6) Non-U.S. stakeholders – Includes a wide variety of items such as providing good working conditions to foreign workers (e.g. avoiding sweatshops), supporting small-scale suppliers, and supporting world health initiatives. Top companies were Procter & Gamble and Avon.

7) Customers - Includes quality management programs, quality awards won, customer satisfaction measures, lawsuits, and so forth. Top companies were Motorola, IBM, Hewlett-Packard, and Fannie Mae.

<u>1-48</u>   (10-15 min.)

1.   Line authority is held by those managers directly responsible for the production and sales of goods or services. Staff authority is held by persons who have an indirect responsibility for the production and sale of goods and services. Staff members provide expertise, advice and support for line positions; line managers are directly responsible for achieving the basic objectives of the organization.

Conflicts between line and staff can arise for many reasons, ranging from the types of people that are generally attracted to each type of position to their responsibilities in the organization. Among the reasons are:

- Staff personnel tend to be younger, better educated, more professionally established.
- Line managers see staff managers as threats to their authority.
- Line managers are uncomfortable when they must rely on the knowledge and expertise of staff.
- Line managers often think staff managers overstep their authority and have a narrow view of the world.
- Staff managers often think line managers ignore their advice and resist their ideas.

2.   Chen has a staff position, providing advice to the controller. His main conflicts will probably arise with the chief accountant and the managers under him. He reports to the chief accountant's superior, but he prepares reports that affect the operations in the chief accountant's area of responsibility.

Paperman is in a staff position because accounting is not directly involved with sales or delivery of leasing services. He provides counsel and advice to all the line managers and most of the staff managers in the company. Conflicts may arise if he tries to exert

27

authority instead of just giving advice or if the other managers ignore his advice.

Hodge is in a line position because she is an integral part of the company's main line of business, leasing equipment. Her main conflicts are likely to arise in areas such as requisitioning of equipment
and billing of customers where she must rely on other departments over which she has no authority.

Burgstahler is in a staff position and offers advice to most other managers in the company. Conflicts might arise if managers perceive her advertising of positions or screening of candidates as not fulfilling their needs, or if she tries to exert her preferences instead of the hiring department's preferences into the advertising and screening activities. Conflicts can also arise in the performance evaluation functions, where she may be enforcing an unpopular policy.

1-49   (20-30 min.)

1.   In accordance with textbook Exhibit 1-7, "Standards of Ethical Conduct for Practitioners of Management Accounting and Financial Management," management accountants should not condone the commission of acts by their organization that violate the standards of ethical conduct. The specific standards that apply are:

   - competence. Management accountants have a responsibility to perform their professional duties in accordance with relevant laws and regulations.

   - confidentiality. Management accountants must refrain from disclosing confidential information unless legally obligated to do so. Rebecca Long may have a legal responsibility to take some action.

   - integrity. Management accountants have a responsibility to
     - refrain from either actively or passively subverting the attainment of the organization's legitimate and ethical objectives.
     - communicate favorable as well as unfavorable information and professional judgments or opinions.
     - refrain from engaging in or supporting any activity that would discredit the profession.

   - objectivity. Management accountants have a responsibility to communicate information fairly and objectively. They also should disclose all relevant information that could reasonably be expected to influence a user's understanding of reports, comments, and recommendations.

2. In accordance with Exhibit 1-7, the first alternative being considered by Rebecca Long, seeking the advice of her boss, is appropriate. To resolve an ethical conflict, the first step recommended is to discuss the problem with the immediate superior, unless it appears that this individual is involved in the conflict. In this case, it does not appear that Long's boss is involved.

Releasing the information to the local newspaper would be an inappropriate course of action. Communication of confidential information to anyone outside of the company is inappropriate unless there is a legal obligation to do so, in which case Long should contact the proper authorities.

Contacting a member of the board of directors would be an inappropriate action at this time. In accordance with Exhibit 1-7, Long should report the conflict to successively higher levels within the organization and turn to the board of directors only if the problem is not resolved at lower levels.

3. Assuming there is no established company policy in place to resolve the conflict, Long should report the problem to successively higher levels of management until it is satisfactorily resolved. There is no requirement for Long to inform her immediate supervisor of this action, because he is involved in the conflict. Long could also clarify the situation by confidential discussion with an objective advisor to obtain an understanding of possible courses of action. If the conflict is not resolved after exhausting all courses of internal review, Long may have no other recourse than to resign from the organization and submit an informative memorandum to an appropriate representative of the organization.

1-50 (20-30 min.) For the solution, see the Prentice Hall Web site, www.prenhall.com/

<u>1-51</u> (90 min. or more)

The purpose of this exercise is to learn about the practice of management accounting. Students often have the mistaken impression that accountants sit in the back room and prepare reports. These articles illustrate the varied skills and abilities that are necessary to be a successful management accountant.

The exercise also focuses on critical reading – identifying the most important points made in an article. It also shows how different students will focus on different aspects of each article. What one student considers important, others might think unimportant. Prioritizing the lessons will bring out differences in opinion, and create a need to form consensus from possibly conflicting views.

Finally, students should come away with a better understanding of why they are studying management accounting, whether they plan to be an accountant or simply a user of accounting information and services.

<u>1-52</u>   (30-45 min.)

NOTE TO INSTRUCTOR. This solution is based on the web site as it was in early 2004. Be sure to examine the current web site before assigning this problem, as the information there may have changed.

1. Management accounting and financial management.

2. The mission of the IMA is to
    a. Provide to members personal and professional development opportunities in management accounting, financial management, and information management through education, association with business professionals, and certification in management accounting and financial management.
    b. Ensure that the IMA is globally recognized by the financial community as a respected institution influencing the concepts and ethical practices of accounting, finance, and information management.

3. The IMA offers education through the use of online courses, journals, educational videos, study programs in workbook, disk and CD formats, corporate in-house programs, regional assistance programs and national conferences and seminars.

4. The IMA has a detailed code of ethics. It specifies accountants' obligations to the public, their profession, their organization, and to themselves. It also addressing how to solve ethical dilemmas. It make it clear that for accountants to fulfill their function in an organization, they must both be ethical and be perceived as being ethical.

5. The answer will depend upon the state where the student resides. The link provides the name of the chapters in the state, and a link to the president of each chapter, and chapter information.

CHAPTER 2
COVERAGE OF LEARNING OBJECTIVES

LEARNING OBJECTIVE	FUNDA-MENTAL ASSIGN-MENT MATERIAL	CRITICAL THINKING EXERCISES AND EXERCISES	PROBLEMS	CASES, EXCEL, COLLAB., & INTERNET EXERCISES
LO1: Explain how cost drivers affect cost behavior.		24,25, 27	39, 41	62
LO2: Show how changes in cost-driver activity levels affect variable and fixed costs.	A1, A2, B1, B2	24,25, 28, 29	39, 42, 43, 45, 49, 50, 51, 52, 53, 57	62, 63, 64, 67
LO3: Calculate break-even sales volume in total dollars and total units.	A1, A2, B1, B2	32,33,35	40, 42, 43, 44, 45, 47, 49, 50, 51, 53, 54, 56	62, 64, 67
LO4: Create a cost-volume-profit graph and understand the assumptions behind it.		30, 31	39	
LO5: Calculate sales volume in total dollars and total units to reach a target profit.	A1, A2, B1, B2	30, 31, 34, 35	40, 42, 43, 44, 45, 47, 49, 50, 51, 53	63, 64
LO6: Differentiate between contribution margin and gross margin.			45, 54	
LO7: Explain the effects of sales mix on profits (Appendix 2A).		36	58, 59	65
LO8: Compute cost-volume-profit relationships on an after-tax basis (Appendix 2B).	A1, B1	37, 38	60, 61	66

CHAPTER 2
Introduction to Cost Behavior and Cost-Volume Relationships

2-A1   (20-25 min.)

1.   Let N = number of units
       Sales = Fixed expenses + Variable expenses + Net income
    $1.00 N = $6,000 + $.80 N + 0
      $.20 N = $6,000
          N = 30,000 units

       Let S = sales in dollars
          S = $6,000 + .80 S + 0
      .20 S = $6,000
          S = $30,000

Alternatively, the 30,000 units may be multiplied by the $1.00 to obtain $30,000.

In formula form:

In units

$$\frac{\text{Fixed costs + Net income}}{\text{Contribution margin per unit}} = \frac{(\$6,000 + 0)}{\$.20} = 30,000$$

In dollars

$$\frac{\text{Fixed costs + Net income}}{\text{Contribution margin percent}} = \frac{(\$6,000 + 0)}{.20} = \$30,000$$

2. The quick way: (40,000 - 30,000) x $.20 = $2,000

Compare income statements:

	Break-even Point	Increment	Total
Volume in units	30,000	10,000	40,000
Sales	$30,000	$10,000	$40,000
Deduct expenses:			
Variable	24,000	8,000	32,000
Fixed	6,000	—	6,000
Total expenses	$30,000	$8,000	$38,000
Effect on net income	$ 0	$ 2,000	$ 2,000

3. Total fixed expenses would be $6,000 + $1,552 = $7,552

$$\frac{\$7,552}{\$.20/unit} = 37,760 \text{ units}; \quad \frac{\$7,552}{.20} = \$37,760 \text{ sales}$$

or 37,760 x $1.00 = $37,760 sales

4. New contribution margin is $.18 per unit; $6,000 ÷ $.18 = 33,333 units

33,333 units x $1.00 = $33,333 in sales

5. The quick way: (40,000 - 30,000) x $.16 = $1,600. On a graph, the slope of the total cost line would have a kink upward, beginning at the break-even point.

<u>2-A2</u>   (20-30 min.)

The following format is only one of many ways to present a solution. This situation is really a demonstration of "sensitivity analysis," whereby a basic solution is tested to see how much it is affected by changes in critical factors. Much discussion can ensue, particularly about the final three changes.

The basic contribution margin per revenue mile is $1.50 - $1.30 = $.20

		(1) Revenue Miles Sold	(2) Contribution Margin Per Revenue Mile	(3) (1)x(2) Total Contribution Margin	(4) Fixed Expenses	(5) (3)-(4) Net Income
1.		800,000	$.20	$160,000	$120,000	$ 40,000
2.	(a)	800,000	.35	280,000	120,000	160,000
	(b)	880,000	.20	176,000	120,000	56,000
	(c)	800,000	.07	56,000	120,000	(64,000)
	(d)	800,000	.20	160,000	132,000	28,000
	(e)	840,000	.17	142,800	120,000	22,800
	(f)	720,000	.25	180,000	120,000	60,000
	(g)	840,000	.20	168,000	132,000	36,000

2-B1 (15-20 min.)

1. $\dfrac{\$5,000}{(\$20-\$16)} = \dfrac{\$5,000}{\$4} = 1{,}250 \text{ units}$

2. Contribution margin ratio: $\dfrac{(\$40{,}000-\$30{,}000)}{(\$40{,}000)} = 25\%$

   $\$8{,}000 \div 25\% = \$32{,}000$

3. $\dfrac{(\$33{,}000+\$7{,}000)}{(\$30-\$14)} = \dfrac{\$40{,}000}{\$16} = 2{,}500 \text{ units}$

4. $(\$50{,}000 - \$20{,}000)(110\%) = \$33{,}000$ contribution margin;
   $\$33{,}000 - \$20{,}000 = \$13{,}000$

5. New contribution margin: $\$40 - (\$30 - 20\%$ of $\$30)$
   $= \$40 - (\$30 - \$6) = \$16$;

   New fixed expenses: $\$80{,}000 \times 110\% = \$88{,}000$;

   $\dfrac{(\$88{,}000+\$20{,}000)}{\$16} = \dfrac{\$108{,}000}{\$16} = 6{,}750 \text{ units}$

<u>2-B2</u>   (15-25 min.)

1.   176 x ($30 - $10) - $2,300 = $3,520 - $2,300 = $1,220

2.   a. 198 x ($30 - $10) - $2,300 = $3,960 - $2,300 = $1,660
            or (22 x $20) + $1,220 = $440 + $1,220 = $1,660

        b. 176 x ($30 - $12) - $2,300 = $3,168 - $2,300 = $868
            or $1,220 - ($2 x 176) = $868

        c. $1,220 - $220 = $1,000

        d. [(9.5 x 22) x ($30 - $10)] - ($2,300 + $300) = $4,180 - $2,600 = $1,580

        e. [(7 x 22) x ($33 - $10)] - $2,300 = $3,542 - $2,300 = $1,242

<u>2-1</u>   This is a good characterization of cost behavior. Identifying cost drivers will identify activities that affect costs, and the relationship between a cost driver and costs specifies how the cost driver influences costs.

<u>2-2</u>   Two rules of thumb to use are:
        a. Total fixed costs remain unchanged regardless of changes in cost-driver activity level.
        b. The per-unit variable cost remains unchanged regardless of changes in cost-driver activity level.

<u>2-3</u>   Samples of variable costs are the costs of merchandise, materials, parts, supplies, sales commissions, and many types of labor. Examples of fixed costs are real estate taxes, real estate insurance, many executive salaries, and space rentals.

<u>2-4</u>   Fixed costs, by definition, do not vary in total as volume changes. However, if fixed costs are allocated or spread over volume on a per-unit-of-volume basis, they decline *per unit* as volume increases.

2-5   Yes. Fixed costs per unit change as the volume of activity changes. Therefore, for fixed cost per unit to be meaningful, you must identify an appropriate volume level. In contrast, total fixed costs are independent of volume level.

2-6   No. Cost behavior is much more complex than a simple dichotomy into fixed or variable. For example, some costs are not linear, and some have more than one cost driver. Division of costs into fixed and variable categories is a useful simplification, but it is not a complete description of cost behavior in most situations.

2-7   No. The relevant range pertains to both variable and fixed costs. Outside a relevant range, some variable costs, such as fuel consumed, may behave differently per unit of activity volume.

2-8   The major simplifying assumption is that we can classify costs as either variable or fixed with respect to a single measure of the volume of output activity.

2-9   The same cost may be regarded as variable in one decision situation and fixed in a second decision situation. For example, fuel costs are fixed with respect to the addition of one more passenger on a bus because the added passenger has almost no effect on total fuel costs. In contrast, total fuel costs are variable in relation to the decision of whether to add one more mile to a city bus route.

2-10   No. Contribution margin is the excess of sales over all *variable* costs, not *fixed* costs. It may be expressed as a total, as a ratio, as a percentage, or per unit.

2-11   A "break-even analysis" does not describe the real value of a CVP analysis, which shows profit at any volume of activity within the relevant range. The break-even point is often only incidental in studies of cost-volume relationships.

2-12   No. break-even points can vary greatly within an industry. For example, Rolls Royce has a much lower break-even volume than does Honda (or Ford, Toyota, and other high-volume auto producers).

2-13   No. The CVP technique you choose is a matter of personal preference or convenience. The equation technique is the most general, but it may not be the easiest to apply. All three techniques yield the same results.

2-14   Three ways of lowering a break-even point, holding other factors constant, are: decrease total fixed costs, increase selling prices, and decrease unit variable costs.

2-15   No. In addition to being quicker, incremental analysis is simpler. This is important because it keeps the analysis from being cluttered by irrelevant and potentially confusing data.

2-16   Yes. Computer spreadsheets readily display various combinations of changes in selling prices, unit variable costs, fixed costs, and target profits.

2-17   Operating leverage is a firm's ratio of fixed to variable costs. A highly leveraged company has relatively high fixed costs and low variable costs. Such a firm is risky because small changes in volume lead to large changes in net income.

2-18   No. In retailing, the contribution margin is likely to be smaller than the gross margin. For instance, sales commissions are deducted in computing the contribution margin but not the gross margin.

2-19   No. CVP relationships pertain to both profit-seeking and nonprofit organizations. In particular, managers of nonprofit organizations must deal with tradeoffs between variable and fixed costs. To many government department managers, lump-sum budget appropriations are regarded as the available revenues.

2-20   Contribution margin could be lower because the proportion of sales of the product bearing the higher unit contribution margin declines.

2-21

$$\text{Target income before income taxes} = \frac{\text{Target after-tax net income}}{1 - \text{tax rate}}$$

2-22

$$\text{Change in net income} = \text{Change in volume in units} \times \text{Contribution margin per unit} \times (1 - \text{tax rate})$$

2-23   No. The individual is confused. Definitions of variable and fixed cost behavior are based on *total* cost behavior, not *unit* cost behavior.

2-24   The key to determining cost behavior is to ask, "If there is a change in the level of the cost driver, will the total cost of the resource change immediately?" If the answer is yes, the resource cost is variable. If the answer is no, the resource cost is fixed. Using this question as a guide, the cost of advertisements is normally variable as a function of the number of advertisements. Note that because the number of advertisements may not vary with the level of sales, advertising cost may be fixed with respect to the cost driver "level of sales." Salaries of marketing personnel are a fixed cost. Travel costs and entertainment costs can be either variable or fixed depending on the policy of management. The key question is whether it is necessary to incur additional travel and entertainment costs to generate added sales.

2-25   The key to determining cost behavior is to ask, "If there is a change in the level of the cost driver, will the total cost of the resource change immediately?" If the answer is yes, the resource cost is variable. If the answer is no, the resource cost is fixed. Using this question as a guide, the cost of labor can be fixed or variable as a function of the number of hours worked. Regular wages may be fixed if there is a commitment to the laborers that they will be paid for normal hours regardless of the workload. However, overtime and temporary labor wages are variable. The depreciation on plant and machinery is not a function of the number of machine hours used and so this cost is fixed.

Suggested value chain functions are listed below.

New Products	New Technology	New Positioning Strategies	New Pricing
▫ Marketing ▫ R & D ▫ Design	▫ R & D ▫ Design	▫ Marketing ▫ Support	▫ Marketing

2-27 (5 –10 min.)

Situation	Best Cost Driver	Justification
1.	Number of Setups	Because each setup takes the same amount of time, the best cost driver is number of setups. Data is both plausible, reliable, and easy to maintain.
2.	Setup Time	Longer setup times result in more consumption of mechanics' time. Simply using number of setups as in situation 1 will not capture the diversity associated with this activity.
3.	Cubic Feet	Assuming that all products are stored in the warehouse for about the same time (that is inventory turnover is about the same for all products), and that products are stacked, the volume occupied by products is the best cost driver.
4.	Cubic Feet Weeks	If some types of product are stored for more time than others, the volume occupied must be multiplied by a time dimension. For example, if product A occupies 100 cubic feet for an average of 2 weeks and product B occupies only 40 cubic feet but for an average of 10 weeks, product B should receive twice as much allocation of warehouse occupancy costs.

2-28   (5-10 min.)

1.   Contribution margin = $900,000 - $500,000   = $400,000
      Net income   = $400,000 - $330,000   = $ 70,000

2.   Variable expenses = $800,000 - $350,000   = $450,000
      Fixed expenses   = $350,000 - $ 80,000   = $270,000

3.   Sales   = $600,000 + $360,000   = $960,000
      Net income   = $360,000 - $250,000   = $110,000

<u>2-29</u>   (10-20 min.)

1.   d = c(a - b)
   $720,000 = 120,000($25 - b)
             b = $19
             f = d - e
                = $720,000 - $650,000 = $70,000

2.   d = c(a - b)
      = 100,000($10 - $6) = $400,000
   f = d - e
      = $400,000 - $320,000 = $80,000

3.   c = d ÷ (a - b)
      = $100,000 ÷ $5 = 20,000 units
   e = d - f
      = $100,000 - $15,000 = $85,000

4.   d = c(a - b)
      = 60,000($30 - $20)
      = $600,000
   e = d - f
      = $600,000 - $12,000 = $588,000

5.   d = c(a - b)
   $160,000 = 80,000(a - $9)
             a = $11
             f = d - e
                = $160,000 - $110,000 = $50,000

2-30 (10 min.)

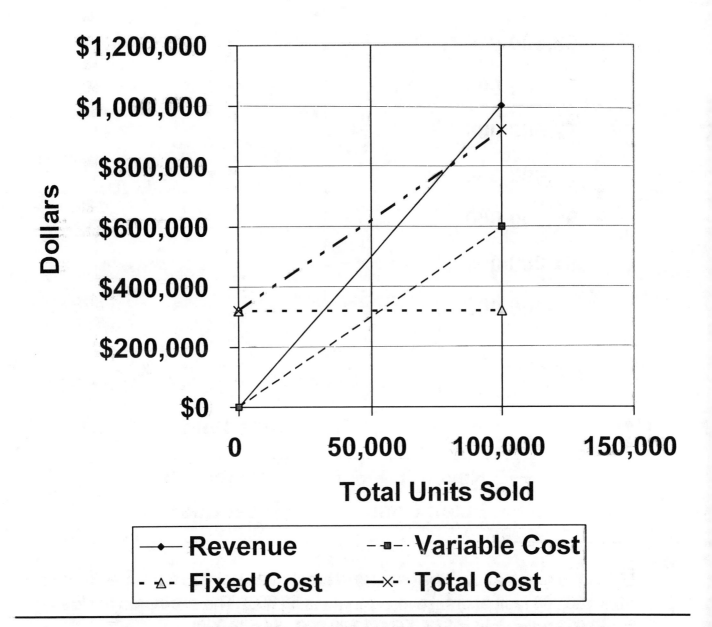

Using the graph above, the *estimated* breakeven point in total units sold is about 80,000. The *estimated* net income for 100,000 units sold is $80,000 ($1,000,000 - $920,000).

45

2-31 (10 min.)

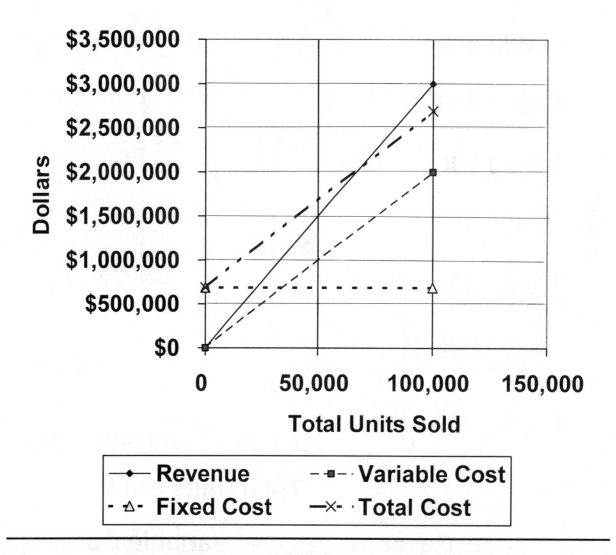

Using the graph above, the *estimated* breakeven point in total units sold is about 60,000 (actual breakeven volume is 58,800). The *estimated* net loss for 50,000 units sold is $88,000 ($1,500,000 - $1,588,000).

2-32 (10 min.)

1.
$$\text{Let TR} = \text{total revenue}$$
$$\text{TR} - .30(\text{TR}) - \$42,000,000 = 0$$
$$.70(\text{TR}) = \$42,000,000$$
$$\text{TR} = \$60,000,000$$

2. Daily revenue per patient = $60,000,000 ÷ 50,000 = $1,200. This may appear high, but it includes the room charge plus additional charges for drugs, x-rays, and so forth.

2-33 (15 min.)

1.

	100% Full	50% Full
Room revenue @ $50	$7,300,000 [a]	$3,650,000 [b]
Variable costs @ $10	1,460,000	730,000
Contribution margin	5,840,000	2,920,000
Fixed costs	3,400,000	3,400,000
Net income (loss)	$2,440,000	$ (480,000)

a) 400 x 365 = 146,000 rooms per year
146,000 x $50 = $7,300,000

b) 50% of $7,300,000 = $3,650,000

2.
$$\text{Let N} = \text{number of rooms}$$
$$\$50N - \$10N - \$3,400,000 = 0$$
$$N = \$3,400,000 ÷ \$40 = 85,000 \text{ rooms}$$
$$\text{Percentage occupancy} = 85,000 ÷ 146,000 = 58.2\%$$

2-34 (15 min.)

1. $23. To compute this, let X be the variable cost that generates $1 million in profits:

$$(\$48 - X) \times 800{,}000 - \$19{,}000{,}000 = \$1{,}000{,}000$$
$$(\$48 - X) = (\$1{,}000{,}000 + \$19{,}000{,}000) \div 800{,}000$$
$$\$48 - X = \$200 \div 8 = \$25$$
$$X = \$48 - \$25 = \$23$$

2. Loss of $600,000:

$$(\$48 - \$25) \times 800{,}000 - \$19{,}000{,}000$$
$$= (\$23 \times 800{,}000) - \$19{,}000{,}000$$
$$= \$18{,}400{,}000 - \$19{,}000{,}000$$
$$= (\$600{,}000)$$

2-35 (15-20 min.)

1.   Let N = number of occupied rooms per month
   $62N - $12N - $400,000 = $0
                        N = $400,000 ÷ $50
                        N = 8,000 per month or 267 per day

2.

   $62N - $12N - $400,000 = $100,000
                        N = $500,000 ÷ $50
                        N = 10,000 per month

3.   Let P = room rate per day
      Other contribution margin = $60,000 + $30,000 + $30,000 + $20,000
                                = $140,000

[.80(400)x30xP] + $140,000 - [.80(400)x30x$12] - $400,000 = $100,000
            9,600P + $140,000 - $115,200 - $400,000 = $100,000
                                        9,600P = $475,200
                                             P = $49.50

The latter answer indicates how hotels frequently may be inclined to reduce room rates if they can generate contribution margins from other hotel activities. The most prominent example is gambling conducted by hotels in Las Vegas and Atlantic City.

<u>2-36</u>   (15-20 min.)

1.   Let R = pints of raspberries and 2R = pints of strawberries
      sales - variable expenses - fixed expenses = zero net income
      $\$1.10(2R) + \$1.45(R) - \$.75(2R) - \$.95(R) - \$15,600 = 0$
      $\$2.20R + \$1.45R - \$1.50R - \$.95R - \$15,600 = 0$
      $\$1.2R - \$15,600 = 0$
      R = 13,000 pints of raspberries
      2R = 26,000 pints of strawberries

2.   Let S = pints of strawberries
      $(\$1.10 - \$.75) \times S - \$15,600 = 0$
      $.35S - \$15,600 = 0$
      S = 44,571 pints of strawberries

3.   Let R = pints of raspberries
      $(\$1.45 - \$.95) \times R - \$15,600 = 0$
      $\$.50R - \$15,600 = 0$
      R = 31,200 pints of raspberries

<u>2-37</u>   (10 min.)

1. $\$.50N - \$.40N - \$6,000 = \dfrac{\$288}{1 - .2}$

      $\$.10N = \$6,000 + \dfrac{\$288}{.8}$

      $\$.10N = \$6,000 + \$360$
      $N = \$6,360 \div \$.10 = 63,600 \text{ units}$

2. $\$.50N - \$.40N - \$6,000 = \dfrac{\$480}{1 - .2}$

      $\$.10N = \$6,000 + \dfrac{\$480}{.8}$

      $\$.10N = \$6,000 + \$600$
      $N = \$6,600 \div \$.10 = 66,000 \text{ units}$

2-38 (15 min.)

Several variations of the following general approach are possible:

$$\text{Sales - Variable expenses - Fixed expenses} = \frac{\text{Target after-tax net income}}{1 - \text{tax rate}}$$

$$S - .7S - \$470,000 = \frac{\$42,000}{(1 - .4)}$$

$$.3S = \$470,000 + \$70,000$$

$$S = \$540,000 \div .3 = \$1,800,000$$

Check:		
	Sales	$1,800,000
	Variable expenses (70%)	1,260,000
	Contribution margin	540,000
	Fixed expenses	470,000
	Income before taxes	$ 70,000
	Income taxes @ 40%	28,000
	Net income	$ 42,000

<u>2-39</u>   (10-15 min.)

The answer is $1,100,000.

Refined analysis:

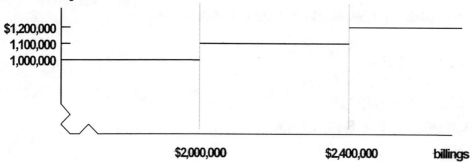

Practical analysis:

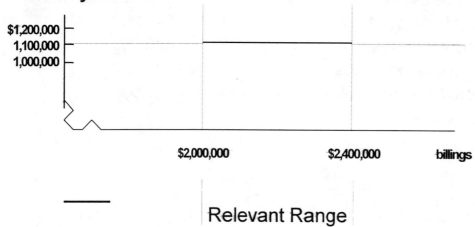

—   Relevant Range

2-40 (15-20 min.)

1. Microsoft: ($28,365 - $5,191) ÷ $28,365 = .82 or 82%

   Procter & Gamble: ($40,238 - $20,989) ÷ $40,238) = .48 or 48%

There is very little variable cost for each unit of software sold by Microsoft, while the variable cost of the soap, cosmetics, foods, and other products of Procter & Gamble is substantial.

2. Microsoft: $10,000,000 x .82 = $8,200,000

   Procter & Gamble: $10,000,000 x .48 = $4,800,000

3. By assuming that changes in sales volume do not move the volume outside the relevant range, we know that the total contribution margin generated by any added sales will be added to the operating income. Thus, we can simply multiply the contribution margin percentage by the changes in sales to get the change in operating income.

The main assumptions we make when we assume that the sales volume remains in the relevant range are that total fixed costs do not change and unit variable cost remain unchanged. This generally means that such predictions will apply only to small changes in volume – changes that do not cause either the addition or reduction of capacity.

2-41 (15-20 min.)

		Film	Refreshments	Total
1.	Revenue from admissions	$2,250	$270 [b]	$2,520
	Variable costs	1,125 [a]	162 [c]	1,287
	Contribution margin	$1,125	$108	$1,233
	Fixed costs:			
	Auditorium rental $330			
	Labor 435			765
	Operating income			$ 468

[a] .50 x $2,250 = $1,125

[b] .12 x $2,250 = $270

[c] .60 x $ 270 = $162

Some labor might be exclusively devoted to refreshments. Labor might be allocated, but such a discussion is not the major point of this chapter.

		Film	Refreshments	Total
2.	Revenue from admissions	$1,400.00	$168.00[b]	$1,568.00
	Variable costs	750.00[a]	100.80[c]	850.80
	Contribution margin	$650.00	$ 67.20	$ 717.20
	Fixed costs:			
	Auditorium rental $330			
	Labor 435			765.00
	Operating income (loss)			$ (47.80)

[a]   Guarantee is $750

[b]   .12 x $1,400 = $168

[c]   .60 x $168 = $100.80

3.   The offer would shift the risk completely to the movie producer, whereas ordinarily the theater owner bears a great deal of the risk. The owner is assured of a specified income; the producer then reaps the reward or bears the cost of the actual attendance level.

2-42 (15 min.)

1. Let X = amount of additional fixed costs for advertising

    $(1,100,000 \times £13) + £300,000 - .30(1,100,000 \times £13) - (£7,000,000 + X) = 0$

    $£14,300,000 + £300,000 - £4,290,000 - £7,000,000 - X = 0$

    $X = £14,600,000 - £11,290,000$

    $X = £3,310,000$

2. Let Y = number of seats sold

    $£13Y + £300,000 - .30(£13)Y - £9,000,000 = £500,000$

    $£9.10Y = £9,200,000$

    $Y = 1,010,989 \text{ seats}$

<u>2-43</u>   (20-30 min.)

Many shortcuts are available, but this solution uses the equation technique.

1. Let N = meals sold
    Sales - Variable expenses - Fixed expenses = Profit before taxes
    $19N - $10.60N - $21,000 = $8,400
       N = $29,400 ÷ $8.40
       N = 3,500 meals

2. $19N - $10.60N - $21,000 = $0
       N = $21,000 ÷ $8.40
       N = 2,500 meals

3. $23N - $12.50N - $29,925 = $8,400
       N = $38,325 ÷ $10.50
       N = 3,650 meals

4. Profit = $23(3,150) - $12.50(3,150) - $29,925
    Profit = $3,150

5. Profit = $23(3,450) -$12.50(3,450) - ($29,925 + $2,000)
    Profit = $36,225 - $31,925
    Profit = $4,300, an increase of $1,150.

    A shortcut, incremental approach follows:

Increase in contribution margin, 300 x $10.50 =	$3,150
Increase in fixed costs	<u>2,000</u>
Increase in profit	<u>$1,150</u>

<u>2-44</u> (10-15 min.)

1. The break even point is $65 fixed cost ÷ $2 per day = 32.5 days
2. The break even point is about $7 fixed cost ÷ [$2 – (.40x$2)] = 5.8 days
3. Let N = 50 days rented.

   Under the traditional system the total income is

   Revenue – variable cost – fixed cost   = $2xN - $0xN - $65
       = $100 - $65
       = $35

   Under the new system the income is

   Revenue – variable cost – fixed cost   = $2xN – (.4x$2xN) - $7
       = $100 - $40 - $7
       = $ 53

4. Under the traditional system there would be a loss of $53.

   $2x6 - $65 = ($53)

   Under the new system there would be an income of 20 ¢.

   $2x6 – (.4x$2x6) - $7 = $.20

5. Blockbuster reduces its risk substantially under the new system because it reduces its fixed cost.

<u>2-45</u>   (25-30 min.)

This problem raises more issues than are apparent at first glance. For instance, unless Hun-Tong is very wealthy and generous, he probably would not regard the five barbers as fixed costs over the entire possible range of volume. In short, if business declines precipitously, barbers would be discharged or laid off. Note how the later requirements demonstrate the effects of various mixes of variable and fixed costs on risks.

1.   Selling price-Unit variable costs = Contribution margin
        $13   - $1   = $12

2.   Fixed expenses (annual)
            Barbers' salaries (5 x $9.90 x 40 x 50) $ 99,000
            Rent and other fixed expenses (12 x $1,750)   21,000
                                                                $120,000

$$\text{B.E. Point} = \frac{\text{Total fixed expenses}}{\text{Contribution margin}} = \frac{\$120,000}{\$12} = 10,000 \text{ haircuts}$$

3.   Two valid approaches:

    (a)   Revenue (20,000 x $13) $260,000
            Variable expenses (20,000 x $1)   20,000
            Fixed expenses   120,000
            Operating income $120,000

    (b)   Haircuts in excess of break-even point:
                20,000 - 10,000 = 10,000 haircuts
            10,000 haircuts @ $12 = $120,000

4.   Even though fixed costs decline, the break-even point rises:
        Contribution margin per haircut = $13 - $1 - $6 = $6
        Fixed costs = (5 x $4 x 40 x 50)
            + (12 x $1,750) = $61,000

$$\text{Break-even point} = \frac{\$61,000}{\$6} = 10,167 \text{ haircuts}$$

5. Contribution margin = $13.00 - $1.00 - $7.00 = $5.00
    Fixed costs = $21,000 given

$$\text{Break-even point} = \frac{\$21,000}{\$5} = 4,200 \text{ haircuts}$$

6.
Revenue (20,000 x $13.00)	$260,000
Variable expenses @ $8.00	160,000
Contribution margin	$100,000
Fixed expenses	21,000
Operating income	$ 79,000

Thus, if volume is 20,000 haircuts, the new arrangement would increase the barbers' compensation from $99,000 to $140,000 and decrease operating income from $120,000 to $79,000. Note the risk-sharing here of the sales commission plan. Generally, the lower the fixed costs, the lower the risks, but the lower the rewards. If the volume declines markedly, Hun-Tong would still have an operating income as long as the total volume exceeds 4,200 haircuts. However, if volume soars to 20,000, Hun-Tong's operating income would be less than that of the hourly wage plan.

7. Let X = rate of commission

$$\$120,000 = 20,000(\$13) - \$20,000(\$1) - 20,000(\$13)X - \$21,000$$
$$= \$260,000 - \$20,000 - \$260,000X - \$21,000$$
$$\$260,000X = \$99,000$$
$$X = \frac{\$99,000}{\$260,000} = 38.1\%,$$

or 38.1% x $13 = $4.95 per haircut

Proof:
Contribution margin: $13.00 - $1.00 - $4.95 = $7.05
Operating income: (20,000 x $7.05) - $21,000 = $120,000

2-46 (10-15 min.) Amounts are in millions (rounded).

Net sales (1.10 x $27,630)	$30,393
Variable costs:	
Cost of goods sold (1.10 x $23,537)	25,891
Contribution margin	4,502
Fixed costs:	
Selling, administrative, and general expenses $2,423	
Interest expense 402	
Total fixed costs	2,825
Operating income	$ 1,677

The percentage increase in operating income would be ($1,677 ÷ $1,268) - 1 = .32 or 32%, compared with a 10% increase in sales. The contribution margin would increase by 10% or .10 x ($27,630 - $23,537) = $409 million. Because fixed costs would not change (assuming the new volume is within the relevant range), operating income would also increase by $409 million, from $1,268 million to $1,677 million. If all costs had been variable, costs would have increased by an additional .10 x $2,825 = $282 million, making operating income $1,677 - $282 = $1,395 million, a 10% increase over the 2002 operating income of $1,268 million. Because of the existence of fixed costs, the percentage increase in operating income will exceed the percentage increase in sales.

<u>2-47</u>   (15-25 min.)

1.   Average revenue per person $\underline{\$4.00 + 3(\$1.50) = \$8.50}$
      Total revenue, 200 @ $8.50 = $1,700
      Rent   600
      Total available for prizes
        and operating income $\underline{\$1,100}$

The church could award $1,100 and break even.

2.
Number of persons		100	200	300
Total revenue @ $8.50		$ 850	$1,700	$2,550
Fixed costs				
Rent	$600			
Prizes	1,100	1,700	1,700	1,700
Operating income (loss)		$ (850)	$ 0	$ 850

Note how "leverage" works. Being highly leveraged means having relatively high fixed costs. In this case, there are no variable costs. Therefore, the revenue is the same as the contribution margin. As volume departs from the break-even point, operating income is affected at a significant rate of $8.50 per person.

3.
Number of persons		100	200	300
Revenue		$ 850	$1,700	$2,550
Variable costs		200	400	600
Contribution margin		$ 650	$1,300	$1,950
Fixed costs: Rent	$200			
Prizes	1,100	1,300	1,300	1,300
Operating income		$ (650)	$ 0	$ 650

Note how the risk is lower because of less leverage. Fixed costs are less, and some of the risk has been shifted to the hotel. Note too that lower risk brings lower rewards and lower punishments. The income and losses are $650 instead of the $850 shown in part (2).

<u>2-48</u> (10-20 min.)

1. To compute eBay's operating income, we need to know its fixed and variable costs. We are given that its fixed costs are $37 million. We can calculate its variable costs in the first quarter of 2001 as follows:

Operating expenses - Fixed costs   = Variable costs
    $123 million   - $37 million   = $86 million

Since sales increased by 59% in 2002, variable costs should also have increased by 59%:

2002 variable costs = 1.59 x $86 million = $137 million

Therefore, we calculate 2002 operating income as follows:

operating income = revenues − variable cost − fixed cost
            =$245 million - $137 million - $37 million = $71 million

This is a 129% increase in operating income:

($71 million ÷ $31 million) − 1 = 129%

2. When sales increased 59%, operating income increased by 129%. This is an example of leverage. The variable cost percentage is $86 ÷ $154 = 56%. Thus, the contribution margin percentage is 100% - 56% = 44%. Every dollar of sales generates $.44 of operating income. The sales increase of $245 million - $154 million = $91 million generated $91 million x 44% = $40 million of operating income, while the original $154 million of sales had generated only $31 million of operating income. This is because the same $37 million of fixed cost applied at both level of sales. The total contribution margin from the $154 million of sales, $154 million x .44 = $68 million, had to first cover the $37 million of fixed costs, leaving only $31 million of operating income. The additional $91 million of sales caused no additional fixed costs, so its total contribution margin all becomes operating income.

2-49   (15-25 min.)

1.   Let N = number of hamburgers per month

$1.20N = $.70N + $1,560

  $.50N = $1,560

       N = 3,120 per month, or 3,120 ÷ 30 = 104 per day

2.   Multiply the answers in (1) by $1.20

    3,120 x $1.20 = $3,744 per month
      104 x $1.20 = $124.80 per day

3.   Hamburgers per month = (3,600 ÷ 2) = 1,800

Revenue per month, 1,800 x $1.20	$2,160
Variable expenses, 1,800 x $.70	1,260
Contribution margin, 1,800 x $.50	$ 900
Fixed expenses	1,560
Operating income (loss)	$ (660)

4.   Contribution margin on extra beers:

        Per day, 60 x $.60 = $36
      Per month, 30 x $36 = $1,080

Income would increase by $1,080, which more than offsets the $660 loss on the hamburger operation, making the net increase in operating income $1,080 - $660 = $420.

5.

Operating loss on hamburgers	$(660)
Desired contribution margin on extra beers	660
Overall effect on operating income	$ 0

Desired number of extra beers to provide overall effect on operating income of zero:

Per month = $660 ÷ .60 = 1,100 beers
Per day   = 1,100 ÷ 30 = 36.7 beers

Or, desired contribution margin per day is $660 ÷ 30 = $22
Daily number of beers = $22 ÷ $.60 = 36.7

Therefore, if Mac believed that the extra beers sold amounted to almost 37 daily instead of 60, the hamburger operation would have provided an overall effect on operating income of zero.

2-50 (40 min.)

1. Let N = the number of people to be admitted for the season

Revenue:

Rights for concession	$60,000
Admissions	$1.00N
Percentage of bets	10% of $25N = $2.50N

Total revenue = $60,000 + $3.50N

Expense:

Fixed costs:

Wages of cashiers	$ 150,000
Commissioner's salary	20,000
Maintenance	20,000
Utilities	40,000
Other expense	100,000
Purses	810,000
Total fixed costs	$1,140,000

Variable costs:
Parking is $4.80 per car or $.80 per person
(6 persons attend for each car, so $4.80 ÷ 6 = $.80)

Total expense = $1,140,000 + $.80N

(a) Break-even point:
$60,000 + $3.50N - $1,140,000 - $.80N = 0
$$\$2.70N = \$1,080,000$$
$$N = 400,000 \text{ people}$$

(b) Desired operating profit $270,000:
$60,000 + $3.50N - $1,140,000 - $.80N = $270,000
$$\$2.70N = \$1,350,000$$
$$N = 500,000 \text{ people}$$

2.
Previous level of attendance	600,000 people
20% increase in attendance	720,000 people
Total bets: 720,000 x $25	$18,000,000

Revenue:

Concession	$ 60,000
Admission	None
Percentage of bets (10% x $18,000,000)	1,800,000
Total revenue	$1,860,000

Expense:

Fixed	$1,140,000	
Variable ($.80 x 720,000)	576,000	$1,716,000
Operating profit		$ 144,000

3. The purses are doubled:

Previous fixed expense	$1,140,000
Additional purse money	810,000
New fixed expense	$1,950,000

Variable expense, $.80 per person
Revenue, $60,000+ $3.50N

$$\$60,000 + \$3.50N - \$1,950,000 - \$.80N = 0$$
$$\$2.70N = \$1,890,000$$
$$N = 700,000 \text{ people}$$

2-51 (30-40 min.)

1. Fixed costs:

Depreciation ($13,500 - $6,000) ÷ 3 =	$2,500
Insurance	700
Total fixed costs	$3,200

Variable costs:

Gas, $1.70 ÷ 17 miles	$.10
Oil, $30.00 ÷ 3,000 miles	.01
Maintenance, $240 ÷ 6,000 miles	.04
Variable cost per mile	$.15

Let N = Number of miles to break-even
Revenue - Variable costs - Fixed costs = 0
$.23N - $.15N - $3,200 = 0
N = $3,200 ÷ $.08 = 40,000 miles

2. An "equitable" mileage rate might be based on the actual number of business-related miles expected. The days not on the road are:

	Days
Weekends, 52 x 2	104
Vacation	10
Holidays	6
Home office	15
Not on the road	135
On the road, 365 - 135 =	230
Miles, 230 x 120 =	27,600

Let X = Reimbursement per mile to break even
27,600X = $3,200 + 27,600($.15)
27,600X - $3,200 - $4,140 = 0
X = $7,340 ÷ 27,600 = $.266

Therefore, a rate of $.27 seems more equitable than $.23.

2-52 (15-20 min.) Note in requirements 2 and 3 how the percentage declines exceed the 15% budget reduction.

1.   Let N = number of persons
     Revenue - variable expenses - fixed expenses = 0
     $900,000 - $5,000N - $280,000 = 0
                              5,000N = $900,000 - $280,000
                                   N = $620,000 ÷ $5,000
                                   N = 124 persons

2.   Revenue is now .85($900,000)   = $765,000
     $765,000 - $5,000N - $280,000 = 0
                              $5,000N = $765,000 - $280,000
                                    N = $485,000 ÷ $5,000
                                    N = 97 persons

     Percentage drop: (124 - 97) ÷ 124 = 21.8%

3.   Let y = supplement per person
     $765,000 - 124y - $280,000 = 0
                              124y = $765,000 - $280,000
                                 y = $485,000 ÷ 124
                                 y = $3,911

     Percentage drop: ($5,000 - $3,911) ÷ $5,000 = 21.8%

     Regarding requirements 2 and 3, note that the cut in service can be measured by a formula:

     $$\% \text{ cut in service} = \frac{\% \text{ budget change}}{\% \text{ variable cost}}$$

     The variable-cost ratio is $620,000 ÷ $900,000 = 68.9%

     $$\% \text{ cut in service} = \frac{15\%}{68.9\%} = 21.8\%$$

<u>2-53</u> (20 - 30 min.)

1. 2002 revenue = 80,122 million x .741 x $.132 = $7,837 million

    2001 revenue = 84,485 million x .724 x $.138 = $8,441 million

2. a) $3,000 million ÷ ($.138 - $.08) = 51,724 million revenue passenger miles

        51,724 ÷ 84,485 = 61.2 % load factor

    b) $3,000 million ÷ (.132 - $.08) = 57,692 million revenue passenger miles

        57,692 ÷ 80,122 = 72.0% load factor

3. $3,400 million ÷ ($.135 - $.08) = 61,818 million revenue passenger miles

    61,818 ÷ 80,122 = 77.2% load factor

2-54 (15-20 min.) Answers are in millions.

1.
Sales		$13,234
Variable costs:		
Variable costs of goods sold	$6,870	
Variable other operating expenses	1,219	8,089
Contribution margin		$ 5,145

Contribution margin percentage = $5,145 ÷ $13,234 = 38.9%

The contribution margin is sales less all variable costs, while gross margin is sales less cost of goods sold. The variable costs will include part of the costs of goods sold and also part of the other operating costs. Note that contribution margin can be either larger than or smaller than the gross margin. If most of the cost of goods sold and a good portion of the other operating costs are variable, then variable costs may exceed the cost of goods sold, and the contribution margin will be smaller than the gross margin. However, if a large portion of both the cost of goods sold and the other expenses are fixed, cost of goods sold may exceed the variable cost, resulting in the contribution margin exceeding the gross margin.

2. Predicted sales increase = $13,234 x .10 = $1,323
Additional contribution margin = $1,323 x .389 = $515
Fixed costs do not change
Predicted 2002 operating income = $345 + $515 = $860
Percentage increase in operating income = $515 ÷ $345 = 149%

3. Assumptions include:
   - Expenses can be classified into variable and fixed categories that completely describe their behavior within the relevant range.
   - Costs and revenues are linear within the relevant range.
   - 2002 volume is within the relevant range.
   - Efficiency and productivity are unchanged.
   - Sales mix is unchanged.
   - Changes in inventory levels are insignificant.

2-55 (20-30 min.)

Variable costs per box are ($.14 + $.22 + $.09), ($.14 + $.14 + $.09), and ($.14 + $.05 + $.09), or $.45, $.37, and $.28, respectively.

1. Let N = volume level in boxes that would earn same profit

$$\$7,840 + \$.45N = \$11,200 + \$.37N$$
$$\$.08N = \$3,360$$
$$N = 42,000 \text{ boxes}$$

2. As volume increases, the more expensive models would generate more profits. Compare the deluxe and jumbo models:

Let N = volume level in boxes that would earn same profit

$$\$20,200 + \$.28N = \$11,200 + .37N$$
$$\$.09N = \$9,000$$
$$N = 100,000 \text{ boxes}$$

Therefore, the decision rule is as shown below.

Anticipated Annual Sales Between	Use Model
0 - 42,000	Standard
42,000 - 100,000	Deluxe
100,000 and above	Jumbo

The decision rule places volume well within the capacity of each model.

3. No, management cannot use theater capacity or average boxes sold because the number of seats per theater does not indicate the number of patrons attending nor the popcorn-buying habits in different geographic locations. Each theater may have a different "boxes sold per seat" average with significant variations. The decision rule does not take into account variations in demand that could affect model choice.

2-56 (25 min.)

1. Break-even = $800 million ÷ ($65 million - $45 million)
    = $800 million ÷ $20 million = 40 airplanes

    Sales = $65 million x 40 = $2.6 billion

2. There are two efficient ways to compute the profit:
    a) (42 - 40) x $20 million = $40 million
    b) (42 x $20 million) - $800 million = $40 million

3. Operating profit = [42 x ($65 million - $43 million)] - $884 million
    = (42 x $22 million) - $884 million = $40 million

    Break-even = $884 million ÷ ($65 million - $43 million)
    = $884 million ÷ $22 million = 40.2 airplanes

    Although the change in cost structure does not change the operating profit at the projected level of sales, the break-even point increases from 40 to 40.2 airplanes. The additional fixed costs add to the risk of not breaking even. However, it also adds to the potential rewards if sales exceed the projected level of 42 airplanes.

4. Break-even = $800 million ÷ [$65 million - (1.1 x $45 million)]
    = $800 million ÷ $15.5 million
    = 51.6 airplanes

    Notice the substantial increase in the break-even point with a 10% increase in variable costs. Boeing might want an escalation clause in its contracts so that the price charged for airplanes increases with cost increases. They might want to enter into long-term contracts with suppliers to limit the possibilities for cost increases. Finally, they might want to undertake changes in their production process to limit cost increases.

2-57 (10-15 min.)

1. Kellogg has the higher fixed cost, while Post has the higher variable cost. Thus, the contribution margin for Kellogg will be higher. Kellogg will have more risk. Its profits increase faster as sales increase, but its profits decrease faster (or losses increase faster) as sales decrease.

2. Post provides more inventive to its sales force to increase sales. For each $1 of increased sales, Post pays more of that increase to the sales force, while Kellogg retains more of the increase for the company's profit.

3. A possible negative of the increased inventive for the Post sales force to increase sales is a motivation to increase those short-term sales at any cost. That is, the Post sales force might be motivated to sell customers product they don't need or to record sales that are not yet final. Many companies have found that too much emphasis on sales volumes can cause managers to take unethical actions to increase their sales levels. A main reason given for the failure of audit firm Arthur Andersen is an excessive emphasis on revenue generation that caused too little concern with quality and integrity.

2-58 (20-25 min.)

1. Net income (loss) = 250,000($2) + 125,000($3) - $735,000
    = $500,000 + $375,000 - $735,000
    = $140,000

2. Let B = number of units of beef enchiladas to break even (B)
    2B = number of units of chicken tacos to break even (C)

    Total contribution margin - fixed expenses = zero net income

    $3B + $2(2B) - $735,000 = 0
    $7B = $735,000
    B = 105,000
    2B = 210,000 = C

    The break-even point is 105,000 units of beef enchiladas plus
    210,000 units of chicken tacos, a grand total of 315,000 units.

3. If tacos, break-even would be $735,000 ÷ $2 = 367,500 units.
    If enchiladas, break-even would be $735,000 ÷ $3 = 245,000 units.

    Note that as the mixes change from 1 enchilada to 2 tacos, to 0 tacos
    to 1 enchilada, and to 1 taco to 0 enchiladas, the break-even point
    changes from 315,000 to 245,000 to 367,500.

4. Net income (loss) = 236,250($2) + 78,750($3) - $735,000
    = $472,500 + $236,250 - $735,000
    = $(26,250)

Let B = number of units of beef enchiladas to break even (V)
   3B = number of units of chicken tacos to break even (C)

Total contribution margin - fixed expenses = zero net income

$3B + $2(3B) - $735,000 = 0
$9B = $735,000
B = 81,667
3B = 245,000 = C

The major lesson of this problem is that changes in sales mix change break-even points and net incomes. The break-even point is 81,667 units of enchiladas plus 245,000 units of tacos, a total of 326,667 units. Thus, the unfavorable change in mix results in a net loss of $26,250 at the old total break-even level of 315,000 units. In short, the break-even level is higher because the sales mix is less profitable when tacos represent a higher proportion of sales. In this example, the budgeted and actual total sales in number of units were identical, but the proportion of product having the higher contribution margin declined.

2-59 (20-25 min.)

1. Let S = number of self-pay patients (S)
    4S = number of other patients (G)

$1,000S + $800(4S) - $600S - $600(4S) - $54,000,000 = 0
$1,000S + $3,200S - $600S - $2,400S = $54,000,000
$1,200S = $54,000,000
S = 45,000
4S = 180,000 = G

The break-even point is 45,000 self-pay patient days plus 45,000 x 4 = 180,000 other patient days, a grand total of 225,000 patient days.

2. Contribution margins:
    S = $1,000 - $600 = $400 per patient day
    G = $800 - $600 = $200 per patient day

    Patient days:
    S = .25 x 225,000 = 56,250
    G = .75 x 225,000 = 168,750

    Net income = 56,250 ($400) + 168,750($200) - $54,000,000
              = $22,500,000 + $33,750,000 - $54,000,000 = $2,250,000

    Let S = number of self-pay patients (S)
    3S = number of other patients (G)

$1,000S + $800(3S) - $600S - $600(3S) - $54,000,000 = 0
$1,000S + $2,400S - $600S - $1,800S = $54,000,000
$1,000S = $54,000,000
S = 54,000
3S = 162,000 = G

The break-even point is now lower (216,000 patient days instead of 225,000 patient days). The more profitable mix produces a net income of $2,250,000 at the 225,000 patient-day level.

2-60   (15-25 min.)

1.   Let N = number of rooms

$$\$105N - \$25N - \$9,200,000 = \frac{\$720,000}{(1-.4)}$$

$$\$80N - \$9,200,000 = \$1,200,000$$
$$\$80N = \$10,400,000$$
$$N = 130,000 \text{ rooms}$$

$$\$80N - \$9,200,000 = \frac{\$360,000}{(1-.4)}$$

$$\$80N - \$9,200,000 = \$600,000$$
$$\$80N = \$9,800,000$$
$$N = 122,500 \text{ rooms}$$

2. $\$105N - \$25N - \$9,200,000 = 0$

$$\$80N = \$9,200,000$$
$$N = 115,000 \text{ rooms}$$

Number of rooms at 100% capacity = 600 x 365 = 219,000
Percentage occupancy to break even = 115,000 ÷ 219,000 = 52.5%

3. Using the shortcut approach described in the chapter appendix:

$$\text{Change in net income} = \text{Change in volume in units} \times \text{Contribution margin in units} \times (1 - \text{tax rate})$$

= 15,000 x $80 x (1 - .40)

= 15,000 x $48

= $720,000, a large increase because of a high contribution margin per dollar of revenue.

Note that a 10% increase in rooms sold increased net income by $720,000 ÷ $1,680,000 or 43%.

Rooms sold	150,000	165,000
Contribution margin @ $80	$12,000,000	$13,200,000
Fixed expenses	9,200,000	9,200,000
Income before taxes	2,800,000	4,000,000
Income taxes @ 40%	1,120,000	1,600,000
Net income	$ 1,680,000	$ 2,400,000
Increase in net income		$720,000
Percentage increase		43%

2-61 (15-25 min.)

Current contribution margin = $16 - $10 - $2 = $4.
New variable costs per disk will be 130% of $10 + $2 = $13 + $2 = $15.

1.   a.   Break-even point $= \dfrac{\$600,000}{\$16 - (\$10 + \$2)} = 150,000$ CDs

2.   d.   Contribution margin: $16 - ($10 + $2) = $4
       Increased after-tax income: 10% x 200,000 x $4 x 60% = $48,000;
       or using formula at end of appendix:

$$\begin{array}{c}\text{Change in} \\ \text{net income}\end{array} = \begin{array}{c}\text{Change in volume} \\ \text{in units}\end{array} \times \begin{array}{c}\text{Contribution margin} \\ \text{in units}\end{array} \times (1\text{-tax rate})$$

$$= 20,000 \times \$4 \times (1 - .40)$$
$$= \$48,000$$

3.   a.   Let N = target sales in units

$$\begin{array}{c}\text{Target} \\ \text{sales}\end{array} - \begin{array}{c}\text{variable} \\ \text{expenses}\end{array} - \begin{array}{c}\text{fixed} \\ \text{expenses}\end{array} = \dfrac{\text{target after-tax net income}}{1 - \text{tax rate}}$$

$$\$16N - \$15N - \$600,000 = \dfrac{\$120,000}{(1 - .4)}$$

$$\$16N - \$15N - \$600,000 = \$200,000$$
$$N = 800,000 \text{ units}$$
$$\$16N = \$12,800,000$$

4.   b.   Let P = new selling price

Current contribution ratio is $4 ÷ $16 = .25
New contribution ratio is (P - $15) ÷ P = .25

$$.25P = P - \$15$$
$$.75P = \$15$$
$$P = \$15 \div .75$$
$$P = \$20$$

<u>2-62</u>   (25-35 min.)

1. $\dfrac{\$12,150,000}{\$810} = 15,000$ patient-days

2.   Variable costs = $\dfrac{\$3,300,000}{15,000} = \$220$ per patient-day

Contribution margin = $810 - $220 = $590 per patient-day

To recoup the specified fixed expenses:
    $5,900,000 ÷ $590 = 10,000 patient-days

3.   The fixed cost levels differ as the relevant range changes:

Patient-Days	Non-Nursing Fixed Expenses	Nursing Fixed Expenses	Total Fixed Expenses
10,000-12,000	$5,900,000	$1,350,000(a)	$7,250,000
12,001-16,000	5,900,000	1,575,000(b)	7,475,000

(a) $45,000 x 30 = $1,350,000
(b) $45,000 x 35 = $1,575,000

To break even on a lower level of fixed costs:
    $7,250,000 ÷ $590 = 12,288 patient-days

This answer exceeds the lower-level maximum; therefore, this answer is infeasible. The department must operate at a $7,475,000 level of fixed costs to break even: $7,475,000 ÷ $590 = 12,669 patient-days.

4.   The nursing costs would have been variable instead of fixed. The contribution margin per patient-day would have been $810 - $220 - $200 = $390. The break-even point would be higher: $5,900,000 ÷ 390 = 15,128 patient-days.

Some instructors might want to point out that hospitals have been under severe pressures to reduce costs. More than ever, nursing costs are controlled as variable rather than fixed costs. For example, more part-time help is used, and nurses may be used for full shifts but only as volume requires.

2-63 (10-15 min.)

1. Total variable cost = $10 x 75,000 = $750,000
   Total fixed cost = $1,000,000 - $12,000 - $750,000 = $238,000

2. Price = $1,000,000 ÷ 75,000 = $13.33
   Price = $1,700,000 ÷ 92,000 = $18.48

3. (a) Operating income = $1,700,000 - ($10 x 92,000) - $238,000
                         = $1,700,000 - $1,158,000
                         = $542,000

   (b) Operating income = $1,870,000 – ($10 x 101,200) - $238,000
                         = $1,870,000 - $1,250,000
                         = $620,000

   (c) Operating income = $1,530,000 – ($10 x 82,800) - $238,000
                         = $1,530,000 - $1,066,000
                         = $464,000

4. There are two reasons for the increased operating income: increased sales price and increased volume. The original sales price was $1,000,000 ÷ 75,000 = $13.33, creating a unit contribution margin of $13.33 - $10.00 = $3.33. The following year's sales price is predicted to be $1,700,000 ÷ 92,000 = $18.48, creating a unit contribution margin of $8.48. Even with no increase in sales volume, the extra contribution margin would increase operating income by ($8.48 - $3.33) x 75,000 = $386,250. Further, each of the 17,000 additional units would have a unit contribution margin $8.48, creating additional operating income of $8.48 x 17,000 = $144,160. The total extra operating income next year would be $386,250 + $144,160 = $530,410, which is within a rounding error of the $530,000 by which predicted the second year's income exceeds the first ($542,000 - $12,000 = $530,000).

2-64   (15-20 min.)

1.   Old: (Contribution margin x 600,000) - $580,000 = Budgeted profit
              [($3.10 - $2.10) x 600,000] - $580,000 = $20,000

      New: (Contribution margin x 600,000) - $1,140,000 = Budgeted profit
              [($3.10 - 1.10) x 600,000] - $1,140,000 = $60,000

2.   Old: $580,000 ÷ $1.00 = 580,000 units
      New: $1,140,000 ÷ $2.00 = 570,000 units

3.   A fall in volume will be more devastating under the new system
      because the high fixed costs will not be affected by the fall in
      volume:

      Old: ($1.00 x 500,000) - $580,000 = -$80,000 (a $80,000 loss)
      New: ($2.00 x 500,000) - $1,140,000 = -$140,000 (a $140,000 loss)

      The 100,000 unit fall in volume caused a $20,000 - (- $80,000) =
      $100,000 decrease in profits in the old environment and a $60,000 -
      (- $140,000) = $200,000 decrease in the new environment.

4.   Increases in volume create larger increases in profit in the new
      environment:

      Old: ($1.00 x 700,000) - $580,000 = $120,000
      New: ($2.00 x 700,000) - $1,140,000 = $260,000

      The 100,000 unit increase in volume caused a $120,000 - $20,000 =
      $100,000 increase in profit under the old environment and a $260,000
      - $60,000 = $200,000 increase under the new environment.

5.   Changes in volume affect profits in the new environment (a high
      fixed cost, low variable cost environment) more than they affect
      profits in the old environment. Therefore, profits in the old
      environment are more stable and less risky. The higher risk new
      environment promises greater rewards when conditions are
      favorable, but also leads to greater losses when conditions are
      unfavorable, a more risky situation.

2-65 (25-30 min.) This case is based on real data that has been simplified so that the numbers are easier to handle.

1.   Daily break-even volume is 85 dinners and 170 lunches:

First compute contribution margins on lunches and dinners:
Variable cost percentage= ($1,246,500 + $222,380) ÷ $2,098,400
                                    = 70%
Contribution margin percentage= 1 - variable cost percentage
                                    = 1 - 70% = 30%

Lunch contribution margin = .30 x $20 = $6
Dinner contribution margin = .30 x $40 = $12

Annual fixed cost is $170,940 + $451,500 = $622,440

Let X = number of dinners and 2X = number of lunches

12(X) + 6(2X) - $622,440 = 0
24(X) = 622,440
X = 25,935 dinners annually to break even
2X = 51,870 lunches annually to break even

On a daily basis:
Dinners to break even = 25,935 ÷ 305 = 85 dinners daily
Lunches to break even = 85 x 2 = 170 lunches daily or 51,870 ÷ 305 = 170 lunches daily.

To determine the actual volume, let Y be a combination of 1 dinner and 2 lunches. The price of Y is $40 + (2 x $20) = $80, and total volume in units of Y is $2,098,400 ÷ $80 = 26,230 and daily volume is 26,230 ÷ 305 = 86. Therefore, 86 dinners and 2 x 86 = 172 lunches were served on an average day. This is 1 dinner and 2 lunches above the break-even volume.

2. The extra annual contribution margin from the 3 dinners and 6 lunches is:

$$3 \times \$40 \times .30 \times 305 = \$10,980$$
$$+ \ 6 \times \$20 \times .30 \times 305 = \underline{\ \ 10,980}$$
Total $\qquad\qquad\qquad$ $\underline{\$21,960}$

The added contribution margin is greater than the $15,000 advertising expenditure. Therefore, the advertising expenditure would be warranted. It would increase operating income by $21,960 - $15,000 = $6,960.

3. Let Y again be a combination of 1 dinner and 2 lunches, priced at $80. Variable costs are .70 x $80 = $56, of which $56 x .25 = $14 is food cost. Cutting food costs by 20% reduces variable costs by .20 x $14 = $2.80, making the variable cost of Y $56 - $2.80 = $53.20 and the contribution margin $80 - $53.20 = $26.80. (This could also be determined by adding the $2.80 saving in food cost directly to the old contribution margin of $24.) The required annual volume in Y needed to keep operating income at $7,080 is:

$$\$26.80 \ (Y) - \$622,440 = \$7,080$$
$$\$26.80 \ (Y) = \$629,520$$
$$Y = 23,490$$
Therefore, daily volume = 23,490 ÷ 305 = 77 (rounded)

If volume drops no more than 86 - 77 = 9 dinners and 172 - 154 = 18 lunches, using the less costly food is more profitable. However, there are many subjective factors to be considered. Volume may not fall in the short run, but the decline in quality may eventually affect repeat business and cause a long-run decline. Much may depend on the skill of the chef. If the quality difference is not readily noticeable, so that volume falls less than, say, 10%, saving money on the purchases of food may be desirable.

2-66 (25-30 min.)

1. Break-even in pounds $=$ $\dfrac{\text{Annual fixed costs}}{\text{Contribution margin per pound}}$

    $= \dfrac{\$566,250}{(5.00 - \$3.00)} = 283,125$ pounds

2. Contribution margin ratio $= \$2.00 \div \$5.00 = 40\%$

    Old variable cost $= \$3.00$

    Only the cost of salmon is affected:
    New variable cost $= \$3.00 + .15\,(\$2.50) = \$3.375$

    $$\text{Let } S = \text{Selling price}$$
    $$\text{Selling price} - \text{Variable costs} = \text{Contribution margin}$$
    $$S - \$3.375 = .40S$$
    $$.60S = \$3.375$$
    $$S = \$5.625$$

    Check: $(\$5.625 - \$3.375) \div \$5.625 = 40\%$

3. Current income before taxes:
    $= 390,000 \times (\$5.00 - \$3.00) - \$566,250$
    $= \$780,000 - \$566,250 = \$213,750$

    Current income after taxes:
    $= \$213,750 \times .60 = \$128,250$

The problem can be solved by using units and then converting to dollar sales.

Let N = sales in pounds

$$\text{Sales - Variable expenses - Fixed expenses} = \frac{\text{Net income}}{1 - \text{tax rate}}$$

$$\$5.00N - [(\$3.00 + .15(\$2.50)]N - \$566,250 = \frac{\$128,250}{(1 - .4)}$$

$$\$5.00N - \$3.375N - \$566,250 = \$213,750$$

$$\$1.625N = \$780,000$$

$$N = 480,000 \text{ pounds}$$

$$\$5.00N = \$2,400,000 \text{ sales}$$

An alternative way to get the solution is:

$$\text{New contribution margin ratio} = \frac{\$5.00 - \$3.375}{\$5.00} = .325$$

New variable-cost ratio = 1.000 - .325 = .675

Let S = Sales

$$S = .675S + \$566,250 + \frac{(\$128,250)}{1 - .4}$$

$$.325S = \$780,000$$

$$S = \$2,400,000$$

4. Strategies might include:
    (a) Increase selling price by the $.375 cost increase.
    (b) Decrease other variable costs by $.375 per pound.
    (c) Decrease fixed costs by $.375 x 390,000 = $146,250.
    (d) Increase unit sales by 480,000 - 390,000 = 90,000 pounds.
    (e) Some combination of the above.

2-67 (30-40 min.) For the solution, see the Prentice Hall Web site, www.prenhall.com/

<u>2-68</u>   (30 min. or more)

The purpose of this problem is to develop an intuitive feel for the costs involved in a simple production process and to assess whether various costs are fixed or variable. Then students must assess the market to determine a price so that they can compute a break-even point.

Completing this problem can be done quickly or it can take much time. It might even be done in class, with students suggesting the various costs and predicting their levels. A complete analysis might involve finding the actual prices of the resources needed to make the product or service. This could lead to time-consuming research. Whatever approach is taken, students are led to see the real-world application of what they are learning.

<u>2-69</u>   (30-40 min.)

NOTE TO INSTRUCTOR. This solution is based on the web site as it was in early 2004. Be sure to examine the current web site before assigning this problem, as the information there may have changed.

1. Southwest Airlines serves 60 cities. Answers to several of the questions will depend on the student's choices of location and dates. Fares available include refundable anytime, restricted fares, advanced purchase fares, fun fares, and promotional fares. Different fares are offered because of the different costs incurred by SWA to serve customers who have different flying needs. Another factor causing different fares is the need to match products offered by competing airlines. Restrictions such as the requirement to make reservations at least 7 days in advance of travel are necessary to give SWA planning information in advance. Limiting the number of these reduced-price fares on each flight is necessary in order to keep open seats for customers who must travel on short notice.

2. The restricted fares, advance purchase fares, fun fares, and promotional fares are not available. Customers who need to travel with short notice are willing to pay more. Many business travelers fly with very short notice.

3. On a particular flight, price paid for a seat (assuming the same class seat) is not a cost driver. The various costs incurred by SWA will not change as a function of the price paid for a seat on a particular trip.

4. Operating revenues and operating expenses are reported for the current and prior year along with the percentage change. The operating revenues decreased from $5.555 billion in 2001 to $5.522 billion in 2002, a decrease of .6%. Operating expenses increased from $4.924 billion in 2001 to $5.104 billion in 2002, an increase of 3.7%. Thus, profits will fall significantly – as shown by the 33.9% drop in operating income.

5. To determine whether a particular cost or expense is fixed or variable, we must identify the cost driver with which costs might vary, the time period involved, and the relevant range. In this case, we are told that the cost driver is ASM. Assume that the period is one year, and the relevant range is the number of ASMs that can be available without adding to or subtracting from the current fleet of airplanes. Thus, adding ASMs means flying the existing airplanes for more hours.

Costs that would probably vary with ASMs are salaries, wages, and benefits, employee retirement plans, fuel and oil, maintenance materials and repairs, agency commissions, and landing fees and other rentals. Aircraft rentals and depreciation would probably be fixed costs. Some of these costs might be more directly caused by other cost drivers. For example, revenue passenger miles (RPM), that is number of passengers times the miles each flies, might drive agency commissions and possibly some salaries (for example, flight attendants whose number depends on how many passengers are on a particular flight).

CHAPTER 3
COVERAGE OF LEARNING OBJECTIVES

LEARNING OBJECTIVE	FUNDA-MENTAL ASSIGN-MENT MATERIAL	CRITICAL THINKING EXERCISES AND EXERCISES	PROBLEMS	CASES, EXCEL, COLLAB., & INTERNET EXERCISES
LO1: Explain step- and mixed-cost behavior.	A1,B1	26, 30, 31, 32	43,44,48,55	60, 61
LO2: Explain management influences on cost behavior.		27, 37	43	56, 59
LO3: Measure and mathematically express cost functions and use them to predict costs.	27	28, 33, 34, 35, 38 39, 40, 41 42	43, 45, 50 52, 54, 55	59, 61
LO4: Describe the importance of activity analysis for measuring cost functions.	A2,B2		46,49	57
LO5: Measure cost behavior using the engineering analysis, account analysis, high-low, visual-fit, and least-squares regression methods.	A3,B3	29, 33, 34, 38, 39 40, 41, 42	47, 50, 51 52, 53, 55	58, 61

CHAPTER 3
Measurement of Cost Behavior

<u>3-A1</u>   (20-25 min.)

Some of these answers are controversial, and reasonable cases can be built for alternative classifications. Class discussion of these answers should lead to worthwhile disagreements about anticipated cost behavior with regard to alternative cost drivers.

1.   (b) Discretionary fixed cost.
2.   (a) Purely variable cost with respect to revenue.
3.   (a) Purely variable cost with respect to miles flown.
4.   (d) Mixed cost with respect to miles driven.
5.   (c) Committed fixed cost.
6.   (b) Discretionary fixed cost.
7.   (c) Committed fixed cost.
8.   (a) Purely variable cost with respect to cases of Coca-Cola.
9.   (b) Discretionary fixed cost.
10.   (e) Step cost.
11.   (b) Discretionary fixed cost.

3-A2 (25-30 min.)

1. Support costs based on 60% of the cost of materials:

	Sign A	Sign B
Direct materials cost	$300	$150
Support cost (60% of materials cost)	$180	$ 90

Support costs based on $40 per power tool operation:

	Sign A	Sign B
Power tool operations	3	6
Support cost	$120	$240

2. If the activity analysis is reliable, by using the current method, Evergreen Signs is predicting too much cost for signs that use few power tool operations and is predicting too little cost for signs that use many power tool operations. As a result she could be losing jobs that require few power tool operations because her bids are too high -- she could afford to bid less on these jobs. Conversely, she could be getting too many jobs that require many power tool operations, because her bids are too low – given what her "true" costs will be, she cannot afford these jobs at those prices. Either way, her sign business could be more profitable if she better understood and used activity analysis. Evergreen Signs would be advised to adopt the activity analysis recommendation, but also to closely monitor costs to see if the activity analysis predictions of support costs are accurate.

3-A3 (25-30 min.)

1.   High-Low Method:

	Support Cost	Machine Hours
High month = September	$13,500	1,750
Low month = May	9,000	850
Difference	$ 4,500	900

$$\text{Variable cost per machine hour} = \frac{\text{Change in cost}}{\text{Change in cost driver}}$$

$$= \frac{\$4,500}{900} = \$5.00$$

Fixed support cost per month = Total support cost - Variable support cost

At the high point:
= $13,500 - $5.00 x 1,750
= $13,500 - $8,750
= $ 4,750

or at the low point:
= $ 9,000 - $5.00 x 850
= $ 9,000 - $4,250
= $ 4,750

2. The regression analysis results are somewhat different from the results of the high-low method. As a result, estimates of total support cost may differ considerably depending on the expected machine hour usage. For example, consider the following support cost estimates at three levels of machine hour usage (all within the relevant range):

		Machine Hour Usage		
		950 Hours	1,200 Hours	1,450 Hours
High-Low:				
Fixed		$4,750	$ 4,750	$ 4,750
Variable:	$5.00 x 950	4,750		
	$5.00 x 1,200		6,000	
	$5.00 x 1,450			7,250
Total		$9,500	$10,750	$12,000
Regression:				
Fixed		$2,728	$ 2,728	$ 2,728
Variable:	$6.77 x 950	6,432		
	$6.77 x 1,200		8,124	
	$6.77 x 1,450			9,817
Total		$9,160	$ 10,852	$12,545

Because the high-low approach has a lower variable cost estimate, the regression-based predictions exceed the high-low-based predictions by more at higher levels of machine usage. The high-low method used only two data points, so the results may not be reliable. Fernandez would be advised to use the regression results, which are based on all relevant data.

<u>3-B1</u> (20-25 min.)   The following classifications are open to debate. With appropriate assumptions, other answers could be equally supportable. For example, in #6, the health insurance would be a committed fixed cost if the number of employees will not change. This problem provides an opportunity to discuss various aspects of cost behavior. Students should make an assumption regarding the time period involved. For example, if the time period is short, say one month, more costs tend to be fixed. Over longer periods, more costs are variable.   They also must assume something about the nature of the cost. For example, consider #8. Repairs and maintenance are often thought of as a single cost. However, repairs are more likely to vary with the amount of usage, making them variable, while maintenance is often on a fixed schedule regardless of activity, making them fixed.

Another important point to make is the cost/benefit criteria applied to determining "true" cost behavior. A manager may accept a cost driver that is plausible but may have less reliability than an alternative due to the cost associated with maintaining data for the more reliable cost driver.

<u>Cost</u>	<u>Cost Behavior</u>	<u>Likely Cost Driver(s)</u>
1. Training cost	Discretionary fixed	Growth, cross-training*
2. Depreciation	Committed fixed	Capacity, service level*
3. Consulting	Discretionary fixed	Improvement policy*
4. Nursing supervisors	Step	Number of nurses, patients*
5. X-ray operating cost	Mixed	Capacity, number of patients
6. Insurance	Step	Number of employees*
7. Cancer research	Discretionary fixed	Research policy*
8. Repairs	Variable	Number of patients

*Not a required answer.

<u>3-B2</u>   (25-30 min.)

	Board Z15	Board Q52
Mark-up method:		
Material cost	$30	$55
Support costs (100%)	$30	$55
Activity analysis method:		
Manual Operations	16	7
Support costs (@$4)	$64	$28

The support costs are different because different cost behavior is assumed by the two methods. If the activity analyses are reliable, then boards with few manual operations are overcosted with the markup method, and boards with many manual operations are undercosted with the markup method.

<u>3-B3</u> (25-30 min.)

$$\text{Variable cost per machine hour} = \frac{\text{Change in Repair Cost}}{\text{Change in Machine Hours}}$$

$$= \frac{P260,000,000 - P190,000,000}{12,000 - 8,000}$$

$$= P17,500 \text{ per machine hour}$$

Fixed cost per month = total cost - variable cost
$$= P260,000,000 - P17,500 \times 12,000$$
$$= P260,000,000 - P210,000,000$$
$$= P\ 50,000,000 \text{ per month}$$

or
$$= P190,000,000 - P17,500 \times 8,000$$
$$= P190,000,000 - P140,000,000$$
$$= P\ 50,000,000 \text{ per month}$$

3-1   A cost driver is any output measure that is believed to cause costs to fluctuate in a predictable manner. For example, direct labor costs are probably driven by direct labor hours; materials costs are probably driven by levels of product output; and support costs may be driven by a variety of drivers, such as output levels, product complexity, number of different products and/or parts, and so on.

3-2   Linear cost behavior assumes that costs behave as a straight line. This line is anchored by an intercept, or fixed cost estimate, and total costs increase proportionately as cost driver activity increases. The slope of the line is the estimate of variable cost per unit of cost driver activity.

3-3   Whether to categorize a step cost either as a fixed cost or as a variable cost depends on the "size" of the steps (height and width) and on the desired accuracy of the description of step cost behavior. If the steps are wide, covering a wide range of cost driver activity, then within each range the cost may be regarded as fixed. If the steps are narrow and not too high, with small changes in cost, then the cost may be regarded as variable over a wide range of activity level, with little error. If the steps are narrow and high, covering big changes in cost, then the cost probably should not be regarded as variable, since small changes in activity level can result in large changes in cost.

3-4   Mixed costs are costs that contain both fixed and variable elements. A mixed cost has a fixed portion that is usually a cost per time period. This is the minimum mixed cost per period. A mixed cost also has a variable portion that is a cost per unit of cost driver activity. The variable portion of a mixed cost increases proportionately with increases in the cost driver.

3-5   In order to achieve the goals set for the organization, management makes critical choices – choices that guide the future activities of the organization. These choices include decisions about locations, products, services, organization structure, and so on. Choices about product or service attributes (mix, quality, features, performance, etc.), capacity (committed and discretionary fixed costs), technology (capital/labor considerations, alternative technologies), and incentives (standard-based performance evaluation) can greatly affect cost behavior.

3-6   Some fixed costs are called capacity costs because the levels of these fixed costs are determined by management's strategic decisions about the organization's expected levels of activities, or capacity.

3-7   Committed fixed costs are costs that are often driven by the planned scale of operations. These costs typically cannot be changed easily or quickly without drastically changing the operations of the organization. Typical committed fixed costs include lease or mortgage payments, property taxes, and long-term management compensation. Discretionary fixed costs are costs that may be necessary to achieve certain operational goals, but there are no contractual obligations to continue these payments. Typical discretionary fixed costs include advertising, research and development, and employee training programs. The distinction between committed and discretionary fixed costs is that discretionary fixed costs are flexible and could be increased or eliminated entirely on short notice if necessary, but committed fixed costs usually must be incurred for some time – greater effort is needed to change or eliminate them.

3-8   Committed fixed costs are the most difficult to change because long-term commitments generally have been made. These long-term commitments may involve legal contracts that would be costly to renegotiate or dissolve. Committed fixed costs also are difficult to change, because doing so may mean greatly changing the way the organization conducts its activities. Changing these committed fixed costs may also mean changing organization structure, location, employment levels, and products or services.

3-9 The primary determinants of both committed and discretionary fixed costs are elements of the organization's strategy relating to capacity, product attributes, and technology. These elements will determine long-term cost commitments (committed costs) and flexible spending responses to changes in the environment (discretionary costs).

3-10 Both planning for and controlling discretionary costs are important. It is hard to say that one is more important than the other, but certainly effective use of discretionary costs requires prior planning. One would not know, however, if these costs had been effective in meeting goals unless the organization has a reliable and timely control system – a means of checking accomplishments against goals.

3-11 High technology production systems often mean higher fixed costs and lower variable costs.

3-12 Incentives to control costs are means of making cost control in the best interests of the people responsible for making cost expenditures. A simple example will illustrate the use of incentives to control costs. Assume that you are an executive who travels for business, purchases professional literature, and keeps current with personal computer technology. Under one incentive system, you simply bill the organization for all your travel and professional expenses. Under another system, you are given an annual budget for travel and professional needs. Which system do you think would cause you to be more careful how you spend money for travel and professional needs? Most likely, the latter system would be more effective in controlling costs. Usually these incentives are economic, but other non-financial incentives may also be effective.

3-13 Use of cost functions, or algebraic representations of cost behavior, allows cost analysts or management to build models of the organization's cost behavior. These models can be used to aid planning and control activities. One common use of cost functions is in financial planning models, which are algebraic models of the cost and revenue behavior of the firm – extended C-V-P models similar to those discussed in Chapter 2.

3-14 A "plausible" cost function is one that is intuitively sound. A cost function is plausible if a knowledgeable analyst can make sound economic justifications why a particular cost driver could cause the cost in question. A "reliable" cost function is one that accurately and consistently describes actual cost behavior, past and future. Both plausibility and reliability are essential to useful cost functions. It is difficult to say that one is more important than the other, but one would not have much confidence in the future use of a cost function that is not plausible, even if past reliability (e.g., based on statistical measures) has been high. Likewise, one would not be confident using a cost function that is highly plausible, but that has not been shown to be reliable. The cost analyst should strive for plausible and reliable cost functions.

3-15 Activity analysis identifies underlying causes of cost behavior (appropriate cost drivers) and measures the relationships of costs to their cost drivers. A variety of methods may be used to measure cost functions, including engineering analysis and account analysis.

3-16 Engineering analysis is a method of identifying and measuring cost and cost driver relationships that does not require the use of historical data. Engineering analysis proceeds by the use of interviews, experimentation, and observation of current cost generating activities. Engineering analysis will be more reliable if the organization has had past experience with the activities.

Account analysis is a method of identifying and measuring costs and cost driver relationships that depend explicitly on historical cost data. An analyst selects a single cost driver and classifies each cost account as fixed or variable with respect to that cost driver. Account analysis will be reliable if the analyst is skilled and if the data are relevant to future uses of the derived cost function.

3-17 There are four general methods covered in this text to measure mixed costs using historical data: (1) cost account analysis, (2) high-low, (3) visual fit, and (4) regression.

- Account analysis looks to the organization's cost accounts and classifies each cost as either fixed, variable, or mixed with regard to an appropriate cost driver.
- High-low analysis algebraically measures mixed cost behavior by constructing a straight line between the cost at the highest activity level and that at the lowest activity level.
- Visual-fit analysis seeks to place a straight line among data points on a plot of each cost and its appropriate cost driver.
- Regression analysis fits a straight line to cost and activity data according to statistical criteria.

3-18 Engineering analysis and account analysis often are combined. One of the problems of account analysis is that historical data may contain past inefficiencies. Therefore, account analysis measures what costs were, not necessarily what they should be. Differences in future costs may be desired and/or anticipated, and account analysis alone usually will not account for these differences. Engineering analysis may be combined with account analysis to revise account-based measures for desired improvements in efficiency and/or planned changes in inputs or processes.

3-19 The strengths of the high-low method are also its weaknesses – the method is simple to apply since it does not require extensive data or statistical sophistication. This simplicity also means that the method may not be reliable because it may not use all the relevant data that are available, and choice of the two points to measure the linear cost relationship is subjective. The method itself also does not give any measures of reliability.

The visual-fit method is an improvement over the high-low method because it uses all the available (relevant) data. However, this method, too, may not be reliable since it relies on the analyst's judgment on where to place the line.

3-20 The cost-driver level should be used to determine the two data points to be used to determine the cost function.

3-21 Regression analysis is usually preferred to the high-low method (and the visual-fit method) because regression analysis uses all the relevant data and because easy-to-use computer software does the analysis and provides useful measures of cost function reliability. The major disadvantage of regression analysis is that it requires statistical sophistication to use properly. Because the software is easy to use, many users of regression analysis may not be able to critically evaluate the output and may be misled to believe that they have developed a reliable cost function when they have not.

3-22 This is a deceptive statement, because it is true on the face of it, but regression also has many pitfalls for the unwary. Yes, regression software provides useful output that can be used to evaluate the reliability of the measured cost function. If one understands the assumptions of least-squares regression, this output can be used to critically evaluate the measured function. However, the regression software cannot evaluate the relevance or accuracy of the data that are used. Even though regression analysis is statistically objective, irrelevant or inaccurate data used as input will lead to unreliable cost functions, regardless of the strength of the statistical indicators of reliability.

3-23 Plotting data helps to identify outliers, that is, observations that are unusual and may indicate a situation that is not representative of the environment for which cost predictions are being made. It can also show nonlinear cost behavior that can lead to transformations of the data before applying linear regression methods.

3-24 R^2 is a goodness-of-fit test. It tells us the percentage of variation in cost that is associated with changes in the cost driver.

<u>3-25</u> Control of costs does require measurement of cost behavior, either what costs have been or what costs should be. Problems of work rules and the like may make *changing* cost behavior difficult. There are tradeoffs, of course, and the instructor should expect that students could get into an impassioned debate over where the balance lies – union job protection versus improved efficiency. This debate gets to one of the major roles of accounting in organizations, and it is important that students realize that accounting does matter greatly to individuals, and, ultimately, to society.

<u>3-26</u> The fixed salary portion of the compensation is a fixed cost. It is independent of how much is sold. In contrast, the 5% commission is a variable cost. It varies directly with the amount of sales. Because the compensation is part fixed cost and part variable cost, it is considered a mixed cost.

<u>3-27</u> Both depreciation and research and development costs are fixed costs because they are independent of the volume of operations. Depreciation is generally a committed fixed cost. Managers have little discretion over the amount of the cost. In contrast, research and development costs are discretionary fixed costs because their size is often the result of management's judgment.

<u>3-28</u> Decision makers should know a product's cost function if their decisions affect the amount of product produced. To know the cost impact of their decisions, decision makers apply the cost function to each possible volume of production. This is important in many decisions, such as pricing decisions, promotion and advertising decisions, sales staff deployment decisions, and many more decisions that affect the volume of product that the company produces.

3-29 Regression analysis is a scientific method of fitting a cost-function line to observed costs. It is not subjective; that is, each cost analyst would come up with the same regression line, but different analysis might have different cost functions when using a visual fit method. In addition, regression analysis provides measures of how well the cost-function line fits the data, so that managers know how much reliance they can put in cost predictions that use the cost function.

3-30 (5 min.) Only (b) is a step cost.

(a) This is a fixed cost. The same cost applies to all volumes in the relevant range.
(b) This is a true step cost. Each time 15 students are added, the cost increases by the amount of one teacher's salary.
(c) This is a variable cost that may be different per unit at different levels of volume. It is not a step cost. Why? Because each unit of product requires a particular amount of steel, regardless of the form in which the steel is purchased.

3-31 (5 min.) The $5,000 is a fixed cost and the $45 per unit is a variable cost. By definition, adding a fixed cost and a variable cost together produces a mixed cost.

3-32 (10-15 min.)

1. Machining labor: G, number of units completed or labor hours
2. Raw material: B, units produced
3. Annual wage: C or E (depending on work levels), labor hours
4. Water bill: H, gallons used
5. Quantity discounts: A, amount purchased
6. Depreciation: E, capacity
7. Sheet steel: D, number of implements
8. Salaries: F, number of solicitors
9. Natural gas bill: C, energy usage

<u>3-33</u> (15 min.)

The analysis is faulty because of the following errors.

1. The scales used for both axes are incorrect. The space between equal intervals in number of orders and order-department costs should be the same.
2. The visual-fit line is too high. It appears that the line has been purposely drawn to pass through the (100,450) data point and the $200 point on the y-axis to simplify the analysis. A visual-fit line most often will not pass through any one data point. Choosing one point (any point) or a data point and the Y-intercept makes this similar to the high-low method, ignoring much of the information contained in the rest of the data.
3. The variable cost units are incorrect. The units should be expressed in thousands of dollars. Even if the derived total cost function was accurate, the resulting cost prediction is incorrect. The formula should be expressed as

Total cost (thousands of dollars) = 200 + $2.50 x Number of orders processed

Or

Total cost = $200,000 + $2,500 x Number of orders processed

This would result in a predicted total cost for 90 orders of

Total cost (thousands of dollars) = $200 + $2.50 x 90 = $425

Or

Total cost = $200,000 + $2,500 x 90 = $425,000.

Correct Analysis

The following chart has correctly constructed scales. The visual fit line shown indicates that fixed costs are $200,000 and variable cost is $2.25 per thousand orders – a lower slope than that shown in the text.

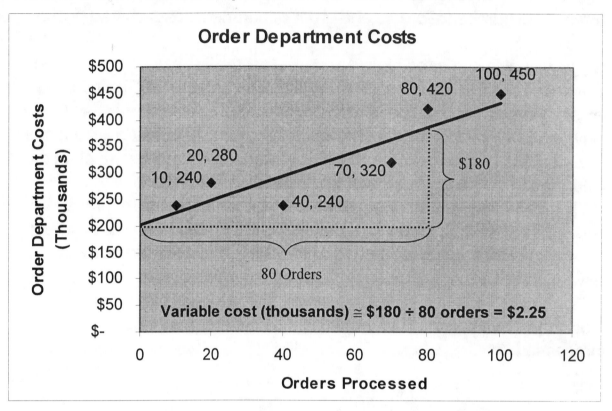

The total cost function is

Total cost (thousands of dollars) = $200 + $2.25 x Number of orders

Or

Total cost = $200,000 + $2,250 x Number of orders

The predicted total cost for 90 orders is

Total cost = $200,000 + $2,250 x 90 = $200,000 + $202,500 = $402,500.

<u>3-34</u> (15-20 min.)

Amounts are in millions.

1.

	2001	2002
Sales revenues	$57	$116
Less: Operating income (loss)	(19)	18
Operating expenses	$76	$ 98

2. Change in operating expenses ÷ Change in revenues = Variable cost percentage

($98 - $76) ÷ ($116 - $57) = $22 ÷ $59 = .37 or 37%

Fixed cost = Total cost – Variable cost
           = $76 - .37 x $57
           = $55
   or
           = $98 - .37 x $116
           = $55

Cost function = $55 + .37 x Sales revenue

3. Because fixed costs to not change, the entire additional total contribution margin is added to operating income. The $57 million sales revenue in 2001 generated a total contribution margin of $57 x (1 - .37) = $36, which was $19 short of covering the $55 of fixed cost. But the additional $59 million of sales revenue in 2002 generated a total contribution margin of $59 x (1 - .37) = $37 that could go directly to operating income because there was no increase in fixed costs. It wiped out the $19 operating loss and left $18 of operating income.

<u>3-35</u> (10-15 min.)

1. Fuel costs: $.20 x 15,000 miles per month = $3,000 per month.
2. Equipment rental: $6,000 x 7 x 3 = $126,000 for seven pieces of equipment for three months
3. Ambulance and EMT cost: $1,100 x (2,400/250) = $1,100 x 10 = $11,000 (must round up from 9.6 to 10)
4. Purchasing: $7,500 + $4 x 4,000 = $23,500 for the month.

<u>3-36</u> (10-15 min.) There may be some disagreement about these classifications, but reasons for alternative classifications should be explored.

Cost	Discretionary	Committed
Advertising	$20,000	
Depreciation		$ 47,000
Company health insurance*		15,000
Management salaries*		85,000
Payment of long-term debt		50,000
Property tax		32,000
Grounds maintenance	9,000	
Office remodeling	21,000	
Research and development	36,000	
Totals	$86,000	$229,000

* The behavior of costs such as these may depend on the company's philosophy. If the company is irrevocably committed to providing health insurance and to maintaining current management, they are committed. However, there may be situations where these become discretionary.

<u>3-37</u> (15-20 min.)

This problem extends the chapter analysis to preview short-run decision making and capital budgeting. This problem ignores taxes, investment cost, and the time value of money, which are covered in Chapter 11.

	Alternative 1	Alternative 2
Variable cost per order	$8.00	$4.00
Expected number of orders	70,000	70,000
Annual variable costs	$560,000	$280,000
Annual fixed cost	200,000	400,000
Annual total costs	$760,000	$680,000

Therefore, Alternative 2 is less costly than Alternative 1 by $80,000.

Let X = the break-even number of orders, the level at which expected costs are equal.

$$\text{Costs for Alternative 1} = \text{Costs for Alternative 2}$$
$$\$200,000 + \$8X = \$400,000 + \$4X$$
$$\$4X = \$200,000$$
$$X = 50,000 \text{ orders}$$

At 50,000 orders, the alternatives are equivalent. If order levels are expected to be below 50,000 orders, then Alternative 1 would have lower costs because fixed costs are lower. If orders are expected to be greater than 50,000, then Alternative 2 would have lower costs because variable costs are lower.

<u>3-38</u>   (20-25 min.) (A master of the scatter-diagrams with least-square regression lines and high-low lines appears in Exhibit 3-38 on the following page.)

This exercise enables a comparison of the high-low and visual-fit methods of decomposing mixed-costs into fixed and variable parts. Students find it interesting to compare their best guesses to the least-squares regression results. They find it interesting that a fairly complete and accurate analysis is possible based on a scatter-diagram and a little common sense. We normally have the class determine a "class best guess" before showing the transparency of the regression results.

The exercise also introduces students to the concept of a hierarchy of activity levels, although this topic is not covered in the text. The literature contains discussions of four general levels of activities. Recognizing each of these levels can be an aid in choosing appropriate cost drivers. These levels and example cost drivers are:

a.   Unit-level activities – performed each time a unit is produced (units of product, machine hours, labor hours).
b.   Batch-level activities – performed each time a batch of goods is processed or handled (number of orders processed, number of setups, number of material moves).
c.   Product-level activities – performed as needed to support the production of each different type of product (number of tests, number of parts, number of engineering change notices, hours of design time, number of inspections).
d.   Facility-level activities – sustain a facility's general manufacturing process (square footage, number of employees, hours of training).

In this exercise, a batch-level activity is involved – setups.

Exhibit 3-38 – Maintenance Costs (Thousands)

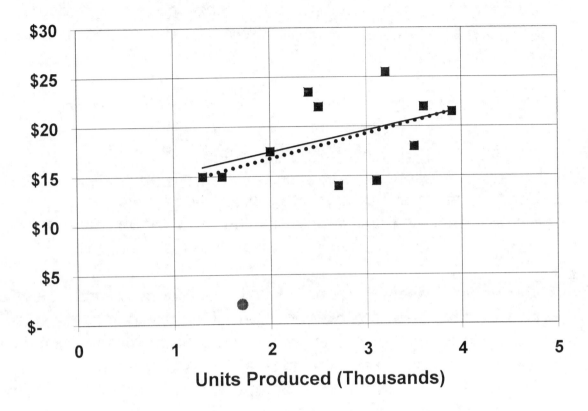

Units Produced (Thousands)

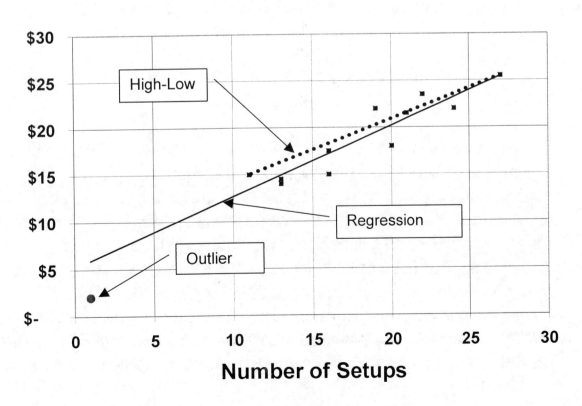

High-Low

Regression

Outlier

Number of Setups

1. Student answers will vary somewhat. Least-squares regression lines are given as a standard for comparison. Based on regression, the cost functions are:

    Maintenance costs = $13,108 + $2.17 x Units produced (000s)

    Maintenance costs = $5,162 + $751 x Number of setups

    The April observation should be ignored since it does not represent a typical month – it is an example of an outlier. Other examples would be strikes, abnormal downtime, or scheduled plant closings.

2. The high-low method uses only the highest and lowest activity levels. Note that using a scatter diagram, the high-low method can be used without knowing the exact figures. Fixed cost can be easily estimated using a straight edge and should be about $11,500 based on Units Produced and $7,500 based on Setups. Variable costs are estimated using the following computations:

    Variable maintenance costs = ($21,000 - $15,000)/(3,900 - 1,200)
                                         = $2.22 per unit

    Variable maintenance costs = ($25,500 - $15,000)/(27 - 11)
                                         = $656 per setup

3. Both cost drivers appear, on the surface, to be plausible. However, if maintenance activity is primarily associated with a "batch-level" activity such as setups, the setup driver is preferred. Of the three costs associated with maintenance activity, supplies and energy are probably variable, so salaries are the primary fixed costs. The monthly salary of two mechanics is $4,167 [(2 x $25,000)/12]. The cost function based on setups estimates fixed costs of about $5,200 (visual-fit method). This is much more plausible than the $15,200 estimate based on units of production. Students may inquire as to the use of "setup time" as an alternative to number of setups. Setup time

is an acceptable alternative that is often used when setup times differ among different products. Another consideration is data availability. Setup times by product may not be easily obtained or maintained.

Just looking at the two graphs, a linear cost function seems to fit the second graph much better than the first. Reliability of cost drivers is measured by the coefficient of determination, R-Squared. In the regressions used in requirement 1, only 21% of the past year's variability in maintenance costs can be explained by changes in the volume of units produced, whereas 85% of past fluctuations in costs can be explained by the number of setups performed. This confirms the visual observation.

3-39 (15-20 min.) The total cost for the month is $1,570 + (5 x $1,600) = $9,570, based on the following cost function information:

Cost	Fixed per month	Variable per computer
Phone	$ 50	
Utilities	65	
Advertising	75	
Insurance	80	
Materials		$1,500
Labor	1,300	100
Totals	$1,570 per month	$1,600 per computer

Algebraically, $y = \$1,570 + \$1,600x$,
          where y = total cost per month
              x = number of computers

<u>3-40</u> (5 min.)

All of the functions except (e) and (f) are linear cost functions. Both (c) and (d) are mixed costs. Note that (e) is not linear because X_1 and X_2 are multiplied, and (f) is not linear because it contains X_1^2.

<u>3-41</u> (5-10 min.)

$$\text{Variable cost per ton} = (£1,150,000 - £950,000) \div (45,000 - 35,000)$$
$$= \frac{£200,000}{10,000} = £20/\text{ton}$$

$$\text{Fixed cost} = £1,150,000 - (45,000 \times £20) = £250,000$$

$$\text{or} = £950,000 - (35,000 \times £20) = £250,000$$

$$\text{Cost function} = £250,000 + £20 \times \text{Number of tons}$$

<u>3-42</u> (10-15 min.)

The regression analysis results show that more was spent on building maintenance in months of low production volume than in months of high volume. The assistant controller erred in not thinking about the economic logic of this result. The result does not imply that intensive use of the building decreases maintenance costs. When production volume is low, workers do maintenance rather than work on production. When volume is high, little maintenance is done because workers are busy on production. This is a case where the regression analysis does not correctly separate costs into fixed and variable components. Considering the economic plausibility of a negative variable maintenance cost should make this readily apparent. A more correct analysis would probably show that maintenance costs are not related to direct labor, or, if there is a relationship, more labor should cause more maintenance because it implies more intensive use of the production facilities.

114

<u>3-43</u>   (50-60 min.) (Masters of the line graph and pie charts appear on the next two pages.)

1.   The line graph shows the plot of the total cost for each of the two options at various levels of capacity utilization. The outsource/ overtime option has a steeper slope due to the larger proportion of variable costs, especially beyond the 100% level of production when overtime premiums and outsourcing are required (note the kink in the line). At production (sales) levels below 100% of capacity, total costs are lower with the outsource/overtime option. At production levels above 100%, the build option becomes the low-cost option.

2.   Controlling risk usually means reducing the financial exposure of a company when business conditions turn unfavorable. Companies attempt to control this risk through various means – diversifying their product lines and markets and reducing fixed (committed) costs or converting fixed costs into variable costs. In this case, the outsource/overtime option avoids converting variable production costs into committed fixed (capacity) costs in order to retain cost control and hence reduce financial exposure.

As can be readily seen from the graph or the table, the benefit of the outsource/overtime option is the decreased financial exposure when production is low. Total costs of the outsource/overtime option at the 60% level of production are $8 million less than those of the build option. The cost of the outsource/overtime option is the lost profit when demand is high – total costs are $12 million higher at the 120% level. In essence, by choosing the outsource/overtime option, Ford is willing to forego $12 million of profit in the near term in order to reduce its financial exposure to an $8 million loss in the future. Why? Perhaps Ford's assessment of the probability of continued high demand is less than the probability of a future downturn, or perhaps Ford's key decision makers prefer to avoid risk.

BUILD VERSUS OUTSOURCE/OVERTIME OPTIONS

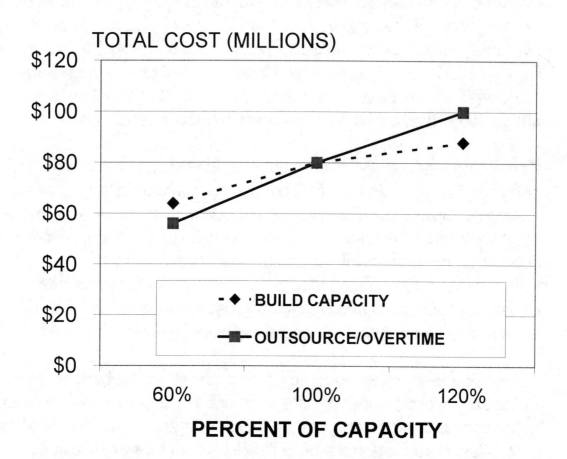

TOTAL COST (MILLIONS)

COST BEHAVIOR OF CAPACITY COSTS
(Millions)

Build Option @ 120% of Capacity

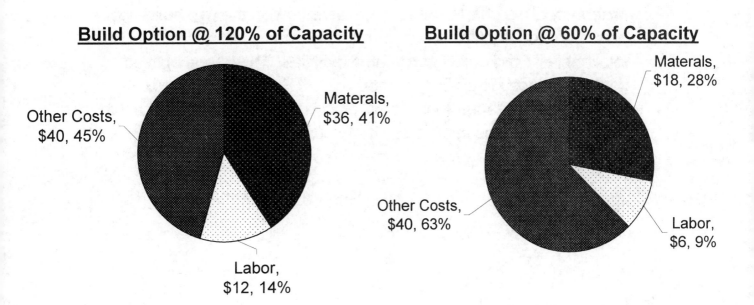

Other Costs, $40, 45%

Materals, $36, 41%

Labor, $12, 14%

Build Option @ 60% of Capacity

Materals, $18, 28%

Other Costs, $40, 63%

Labor, $6, 9%

Outsource/Overtime Option @ 120% of Capacity

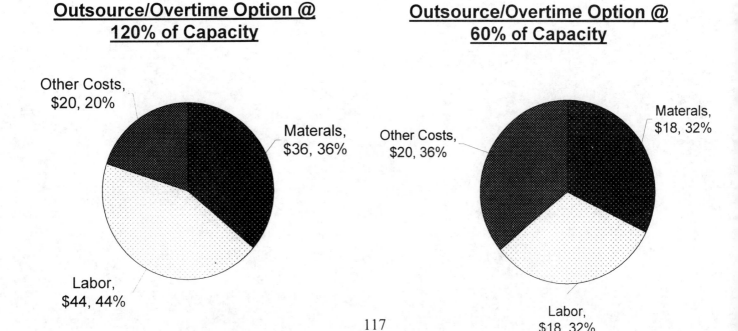

Other Costs, $20, 20%

Materals, $36, 36%

Labor, $44, 44%

Outsource/Overtime Option @ 60% of Capacity

Other Costs, $20, 36%

Materals, $18, 32%

Labor, $18, 32%

3.   Students' answers to this question will vary depending on their attitudes toward risk. This part of the problem helps students realize the value of different forms of analysis. We use pie charts to demonstrate one form of analysis – tables can also be used. The pie charts bring out the importance of fixed costs more readily than the line graph. The four pie charts can be used to point out the value of proportional pie charts. First, focus attention on the two build-option pies. Point out that fixed-cost percentages range from 45% to 63% of total costs if Ford builds automated facilities. This range of fixed costs is reduced to 20-36% of total costs if Ford continues to use overtime and outsourcing. However, comparing the size of the two 120% pies, it can be easily seen that Ford will sacrifice profits by not building if volume approaches the 120% level.

3-44 (30-35 min.)

1. The graph of weekly planned cost of jail guards versus number of prisoners shows that this cost is a step cost beyond 16 prisoners.

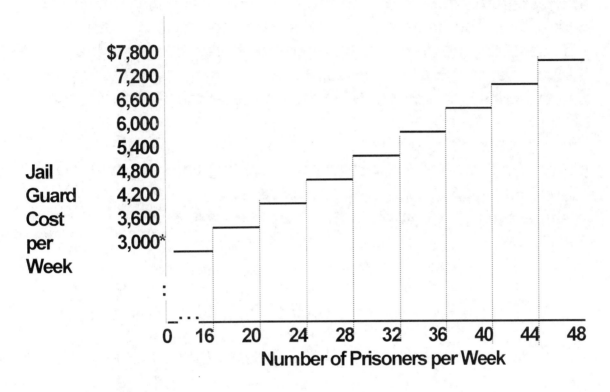

*($36,000/48) x 4

2. In January up to 16 prisoners are expected; therefore, $3,000 should be planned for jail guard costs. This represents the minimum staffing level, and would represent a fixed cost.

3.

Week	Actual Prisoners	Minimum Guard Cost
1	25	$ 4,800
2	38	6,600
3	26	4,800
4	43	7,200
Total		$23,400
Actual		$19,800
Variance		$ 3,600 under budget

119

This report indicates that Algona Beach spent less than planned for jail guards during July. It might appear that the county was extremely efficient because it spent less than planned. However, another interpretation of this report is that the jail was understaffed during the critical "busy" summer season. This could mean that prisoners were not adequately monitored and safeguarded during this time. The $3,600 savings might be small compared to damages awarded by the court to a prisoner who was harmed during the time of understaffing.

4.   The $3,000 fixed amount is the total weekly salary paid to the permanent guard staff. Each four prisoners (or portion thereof) above 16 requires an additional guard at a cost of $600 per week. On average, each additional prisoner costs $600 ÷ 4 or $150.

5.

Week	Actual Prisoners	Minimum Guard Cost	
1	25	$ 3,000+$150(25-16) =$	4,350
2	38	3,000+$150(38-16) =	6,300
3	26	3,000+$150(26-16) =	4,500
4	43	3,000+$150(43-16) =	7,050
Total			$22,200
Actual			$19,800
Variance			$ 2,400 under

Even though the variance of this report is much less than the previous one, this report is not necessarily more accurate. The average cost function predicted actual costs more closely, but if the cost behavior described in 3 above represents *committed* step costs due to state or federal regulations, then the amounts calculated in 3 are costs that the county should have incurred. On the other hand, the administrator of the county jail may try to hire guards according to the simplification of the minimum staffing cost behavior presented in 4, and expect that on average the jail will not be understaffed.

<u>3-45</u>   (25-30 min.)

1.

	Actual Costs	Planned Costs	Variance
Salaries	$66,400	8,000 x $7 = $56,000	$10,400 Unfavorable

2. If the cost measurements are reliable, then the audit office is overstaffed by approximately three auditors. Each auditor should be able to process 4 weeks x 5 days per week x 8 hours per day x 3 returns per hour or 480 returns during the 4-week period. The 8,000 returns should have been processed by 8,000 ÷ 480 or less than 17 auditors, three less than were employed. Alternatively, the $10,400 variance represents $10,400 ÷ ($830 x 4 weeks) or approximately 3 excess auditors.

3. The variance may be due to inefficiency of the auditors, improperly trained or inexperienced auditors, inaccuracy of the cost measures, a batch of unusually complex returns, or a combination of all these factors. The role of the cost variance is to identify where something is different than planned. The variance itself usually does not identify the *cause* of the variance, only that management attention may be required.

4. Besides number of returns, alternative cost drivers might include number of individual forms included in filed returns, number of pages of returns processed, and amount of taxes shown on returns filed.

<u>3-46</u> (10-15 min.)   One possible cost driver is shown, with cost behavior with respect to the cost driver in parentheses. Other cost drivers are also possible.

   a. Airplane fuel – Flight miles (variable)
   b. Flight attendants' salaries – Passenger miles (variable)
   c. Baggage handlers' salaries – Number of flights (variable)
   d. In-flight meals – Number of passengers (variable)
   e. Pilots' salaries – Hours of flight time (variable)
   f. Airplane depreciation – Flight miles (fixed)
   g. Advertising – This is a discretionary fixed cost for which identifying a cost driver is difficult.

<u>3-47</u>   (25-30 min.)

The first temptation may be to measure the cost behavior with the high-low method, using the cost and activity levels from 20X4 and 20X6 since they are the lowest and highest cost and activity levels given. However, Dr. Hyde has indicated that drug test procedures are both more numerous and more complex than they were in the past. Accordingly, if more and more expensive equipment has been acquired and more complex testing is commonplace to meet this new demand, then the past data may not be a relevant base for cost-behavior measurement. A simple graph of cost and activity illustrates the possible problems:

Cost of Test Procedures

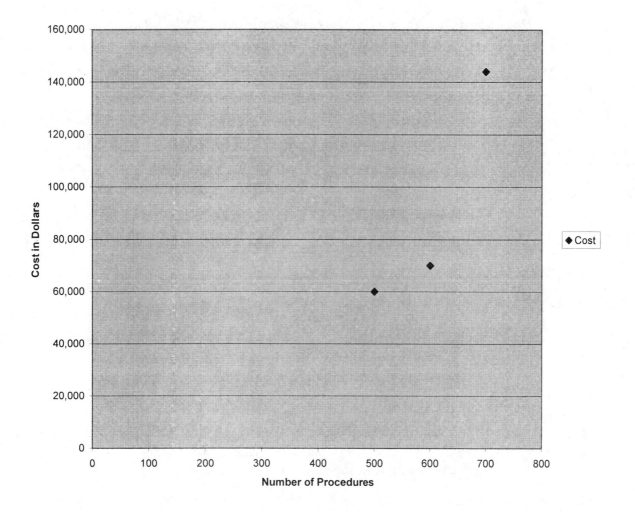

A line drawn through the points for the first two years will have a much different slope and intercept than that implied by the most recent year's experience. It is likely that cost behavior has changed significantly, and this cost behavior may not be revealed by the data currently available. New cost behavior probably has a higher intercept (greater fixed costs per month) and a steeper slope (greater variable cost per procedure) than in the past. More current data are required. Since the data given are monthly averages, the raw monthly data are probably available. One recommendation would be to disregard data from the first two years and to use monthly data from the third year to measure current cost behavior. It could well be that this analysis will indicate a need for the price increase demanded by Dr. Hyde.

3-48 (30-35 min.)

The data should be used to first determine variable expenses as a function (percentage) of tuition revenue. Then fixed expenses can be calculated. Since only two data points are available, the high-low method is the appropriate approach.

$$\text{Variable expenses} = \frac{\text{Change in expenses}}{\text{Change in revenues}} = \frac{\$730,000 - \$710,000}{\$770,000 - \$720,000}$$

$$= \frac{\$20,000}{\$50,000} = \underline{.4 \text{ or } 40\% \text{ of tuition revenue}}$$

Fixed expenses = Total expenses - Variable expenses
= $730,000 - .4 x $770,000
= $730,000 - $308,000
= $422,000 per year

or = $710,000 - .4 x $720,000
= $710,000 - $288,000
= $422,000 per year

Income for 20X4 may be predicted as follows:

LAKEVIEW SCHOOL
Projected Income
For the Year Ending August 31, 20X4

Tuition revenue		$710,000
Less: Variable expenses (.4 x $710,000)	$284,000	
Fixed expenses	422,000	706,000
Net Income		$ 4,000

Or, Net Income = Tuition revenue - variable expenses - fixed expenses
$$= \$710,000 - .4 \times \$710,000 - \$422,000$$
$$= .6 \times \$710,000 - \$422,000 = \underline{\$4,000}$$

Break-even tuition revenue may be found by setting Net Income = 0 and solving for the unknown tuition revenue, TR, as below:

$$0 = TR - .4TR - \$422,000$$
$$0 = .6TR - \$422,000$$
$$\$422,000 = .6TR$$
$$TR = \$703,333 \text{ at break-even}$$

<u>3-49</u> (20-25 min.)

1. Support cost measurement:

	Customer	
	<u>West Acres Plants</u>	<u>Beautiful Blooms</u>
Fixed charge method:		
Basic cost of FertiMix	$12,000	$12,000
Support cost @ 50%	<u>$ 6,000</u>	<u>$ 6,000</u>
Activity Analysis method:		
Lines of customized code	490	180
Estimated cost per line of		
customized code	<u>x $23</u>	<u>x $23</u>
Activity support cost	<u>$11,270</u>	<u>$ 4,140</u>

2. The activity analysis approach indicates that products requiring large amounts of customizing incur much more support cost than those that require relatively little customizing. The old approach leads to distorted costs that might lead to poor planning and control and either lost sales or unprofitable sales.

The benefits of adopting the activity analysis approach are (1) more accurate measures of support costs, (2) more competitive cost-based prices, (3) better planning of support costs, and (4) better control of support costs. The disadvantages are that the activity analysis will be more costly to implement and monitor (and may not be necessary for pricing if Des Moines Software's industry is not a competitive one).

3-50 (10-15 min.)

1. Variable cost/unit = ($1,131 - $655) ÷ (136 - 72) = $476 ÷ 64 = $7.4375
   Fixed cost = $1,131 - (136 x 7.4375) = $1,131 - $1,011.50 = $119.50
   Predicted cost for 510 units = ($119.50 x 4) + (510 x $7.4375) = $4,271.13

   Notice that the data are quarterly observations. Thus, the annual fixed cost is 4 times the computed (quarterly) fixed cost.

2. Predicted cost for 510 units = ($337 x 4) + (510 x $5.75) = $4,280.50

3. The regression analysis gives better cost estimates because it uses all the data to form a cost function. The two points used by the high-low method may not be representative of the general relation between costs and volume.

3-51 (35-40 min.)

If supplies cost is at least partly fixed with regard to production volume, then treating supplies cost as if it were purely variable (e.g., using the average supplies cost per unit of production as the variable cost rate) will result in predicting too little supplies cost at low levels of production and too much at high levels of production. See the graph below:

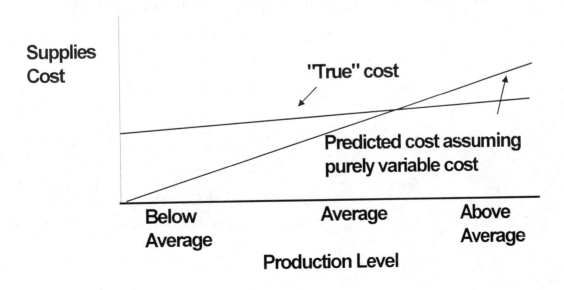

1. The preferred cost function uses "square feet of material used" as the cost driver for supplies cost. Although many other statistical criteria could be (should be) used to make this determination, this choice is based on the relative R-squared values. The R-squared measures the amount (percentage) of fluctuation (variation) in historical supplies cost that is associated with either number of tents or with square feet of material used. The cost function using square feet of material used has a much higher R-squared value and, therefore, is more closely associated with historical variations in supplies cost.

    The interpretation of the preferred cost function is that, based on past data, supplies cost has a fixed component, $1,900 per month, and a variable component, $0.072 per square foot of material used in a month. The total supplies cost function can be written as:

    Total supplies cost = $1, 900 per month + $0.072 x Square feet of material used

2. Approximately 68.6% of the variation in historical supplies cost is associated with variations in square feet of materials. The other 31.4% of variation in supplies cost (100% - 68.6%) depends on other factors, not included in the cost function. Square feet of materials used does not explain this 31.4% of the variation in supplies cost.

1.   The accompanying graphs can be used to discuss requirements 1-4.

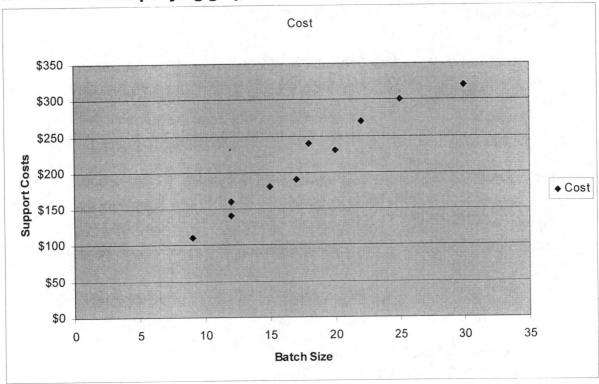

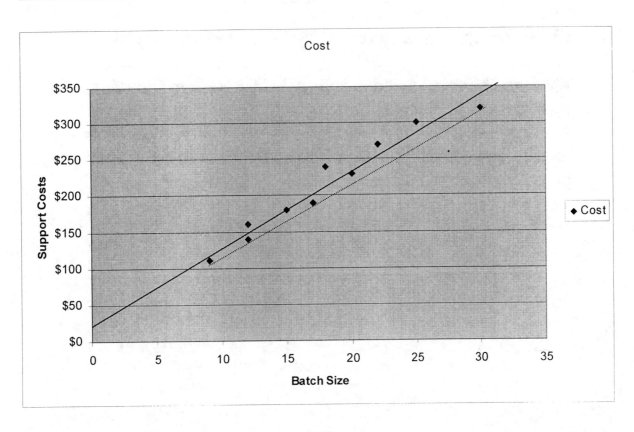

2. Regression Output:

Constant   24.42553

R Squared   0.955692

X Coefficient   10.53191

3. Support costs   = fixed cost + variable cost

                = \$24.43 + \$10.53 x 25

                = \$287.68

4.

	Support cost	Batch size
High Level	\$320	30
Low Level	110	9
Difference	\$210	21

$$\text{Variable cost} = \frac{\text{Change in cost}}{\text{Change in activity}} = \frac{210}{21} = \underline{\$10 \text{ per unit in batch}}$$

Fixed Cost = total cost - variable cost

           = \$320 - \$10x30   = $\underline{\$20 \text{ per batch}}$

Support costs of a batch of size 25 = \$20 + \$10 x 25 = \$270

Although the cost functions and cost estimates are fairly close, the manager would probably be better off using the regression result. The regression results appear to be very reliable and plausible. Since regression uses all the data and no data appear to be unusual (per the graph), there is little reason not to use the regression.

1.   The graphs are as follows:

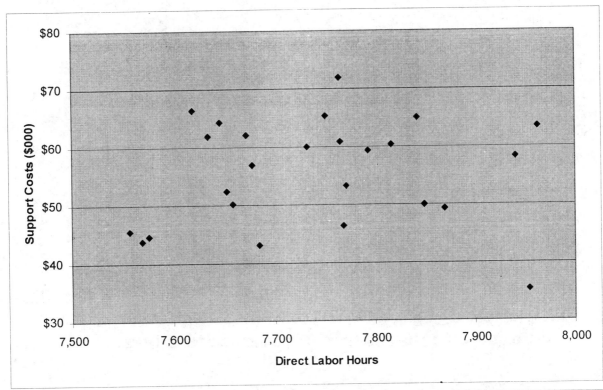

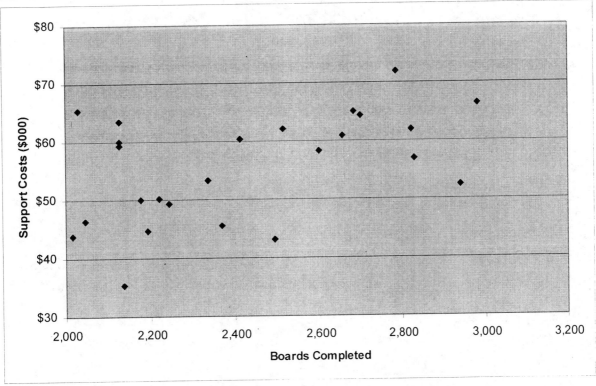

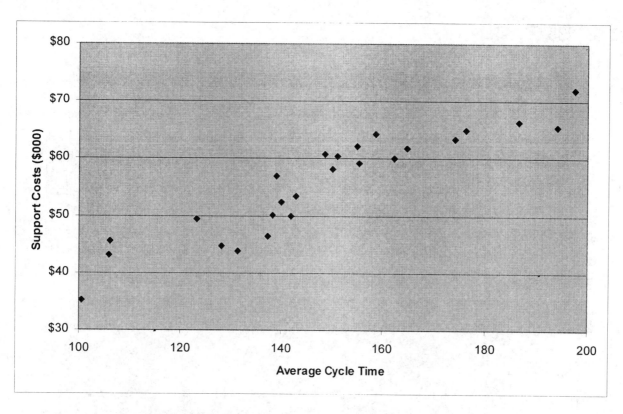

2. This output is generated by a spreadsheet. Regressions of circuit board support costs using the following as cost drivers:

Regression Output: Direct Labor Hours
Constant   9,466.871
R Squared   0.0059439
X Coefficient(s)   5.960404

Regression Output: Number of Boards Completed
Constant   21,810.742
R Squared   0.2219548
X Coefficient(s)   13.9454396

Regression Output: Cycle Time
Constant   6,572.774
R Squared   0.8540626
X Coefficient(s)   330.4828626

3.   The most plausible and reliable regression function, identifying the best single cost driver for American Micro Devices' circuit board support costs, appears to be the one that uses cycle time as the cost driver. (A multiple regression using both cycle time and number of boards is even better.) All of the functions are plausible – they indicate increasing support cost as the cost driver increases. The bases for choosing among the functions are the relative R-squareds of each function. Using cycle time as the cost driver generates the highest R-squared value of all the models using a single cost driver.

4.   The economic meaning of the function using cycle time as the cost driver is that circuit board support costs have a fixed component of $6,573 per week and a variable component of $330.48 per hour of average cycle time. Reducing cycle time by an average of one hour should reduce support costs by about $330.

<u>3-54</u>   (30-35 min.)

This problem anticipates the use of cost functions for pricing purposes. Alternatively, the instructor may wish to use this problem in conjunction with Chapter 5.

1.   One would expect that the third cost function, using average cycle time as the cost driver, would be the most reliable for explaining and predicting support costs. Although all the functions are plausible, average cycle time as a cost driver generates the highest R-squared, which means that it best explains past support costs. If the process remains unchanged, then this function should be reliable for predicting future support costs.

2.   The first part of this solution uses the cost function developed in problem 3-53. The second part uses the cost function given in the problem.

(a)   Cost function from 3-53:

Cost using Direct Labor Cost as the cost driver:
Fixed cost:	$9,467/wk x 3 weeks =	$ 28,401
Variable cost	$5.96 x 20,000 hours =	119,200
Total		$147,601

Cost using Number of Boards as the cost driver:
Fixed cost:	$21,811/wk x 3 weeks =	$ 65,433
Variable cost	$13.95 x 6,000 boards =	83,700
Total		$149,133

Cost using Average Cycle Time as the cost driver:
Fixed cost:	$6,573/wk x 3 weeks =	$ 19,719
Variable cost:	$330.48 x 180 hours x 3 weeks =	178,459
Total		$198,178

(b) Cost function from the problem:

Cost using Direct Labor Cost as the cost driver:

Fixed cost:	$9,000/wk x 3 weeks =	$ 27,000
Variable cost	$6 x 20,000 hours =	120,000
Total		$147,000

Cost using Number of Boards as the cost driver:

Fixed cost:	$20,000/wk x 3 weeks =	$ 60,000
Variable cost	$14 x 6,000 boards =	84,000
Total		$144,000

Cost using Average Cycle Time as the cost driver:

Fixed cost:	$5,000/wk x 3 weeks =	$ 15,000
Variable cost:	$350 x 180 hours x 3 weeks =	189,000
Total		$204,000

3. For this three-week period and the particular boards manufactured, the cycle time cost function yields materially different cost predictions. We know from the regression analyses that the direct labor function and, to a lesser degree, the number of boards function are not reliable functions. Unless there was something unusual about the production activity of those three weeks, American Micro Devices should use the cost estimates from the cycle time regression.

4. In a highly competitive environment, the market influences prices more than does cost. Therefore, setting prices by marking up costs, even if costs are accurate, is not a sufficient pricing policy. At a minimum, American Micro Devices should examine its prices compared to those of its competition in addition to comparing them to its costs.

3-55 (25-30 min.) This is not a difficult problem, but it forces students to think through cost and revenue behavior in a situation that differs from those illustrated in the text.

1. Fixed cost = $75,000 + $93,500 = $168,500
   Variable cost per student month = ($81,000 + $40,500) ÷ 2,700
                                   = $45 per student month

2. Revenues and fixed costs would not change.
   Variable costs would decrease by $45 for each of the students to whom lessons are not provided: (1,250-1,080) x $45 = $7,650
   Therefore, profits would increase by $7,650:
      2004-05 profit = $5,000 + $7,650 = $12, 650

3. To make a $5,000 profit, the contribution margin from the students served must equal the fixed cost plus the profit: $168,500 + $5,000 = $173,500.
   The contribution margin per student month is $100 - $45 = $55.
   Therefore, $173,500 ÷ $55 = 3,155 student months are needed.
   However, this is outside the relevant range for fixed costs. An additional facilities charge of $8,000 will be incurred, making the new required contribution margin $173,500 + $8,000 = $181,500.
   Students needed are: $181,500 ÷ $55 = 3,300 student months, or 3,300 ÷ 9 = 367 students.

(30-35 min.)

1. This is only a first pass; obviously Dr. White would be able to specify more precisely which are committed or discretionary costs.

Program Area	Committed	Discretionary
Administration:		
Salaries		
Administrator	$ 60,000	
Assistant		$35,000
Two secretaries	21,000	21,000
Supplies	35,000	
Advertising and Promotion		9,000
Professional meetings, dues, and		
literature		14,000
Purchased Services		
Accounting and billing	15,000	
Custodial and maintenance	13,000	
Security	12,000	
Consulting		10,000
Community mental health services		
Salaries (two social workers)	46,000	
Transportation *	5,000	5,000
Out patient mental health treatment		
Salaries		
Psychiatrist	86,000	
Two social workers	70,000	
Totals	$363,000	$94,000

* We assume that half of the transportation cost is discretionary.

2.   If all discretionary costs were eliminated, perhaps at least $94,000 could be saved. However, some of these "discretionary" cuts may seriously affect the ability of the health center to deliver its services. There does not seem to be much "fat" in this budget to begin with, and eliminating such items as transportation for social workers would mean that the community would have to come to the clinic rather than vice-versa. Cutting down on professional development opportunities of the staff could mean losing quality staff or reducing their quality over time. Dropping advertising and promotion may be the least painful since the center is apparently at capacity now. However, this could mean that individuals who really need the services will not find out about them. Eliminating the consulting may mean that the center cannot refer individuals with unique problems to specialists. Reducing levels of maintenance and custodial care may mean that more costly problems will develop in the future. Finally, eliminating the administrative assistant and one secretary will mean a greater burden for Dr. White and the remaining secretarial staff. Cutting these "discretionary" expenses may be necessary, but they will be painful.

3.   Dr. White should prepare for the worst but begin now to build her case for even higher resources given the past budget cuts and increasing demand for services at the center. Documentation of community needs, benefits provided by the center, and needs not being met is necessary. A good-faith effort to first eliminate any possible waste may convince budgetary authorities that no further budget cuts are necessary and even that some budget enhancement is desirable.

<u>3-57</u>   (45-50 min.)

This problem extends the use of activity analysis for control and transfer-pricing purposes. The instructor may wish to use this problem as a preview of later applications or in conjunction with Chapter 10.

1.   The number of employees may be an indicator of service department costs in general. If all users of service departments have roughly the same per capita usage of services, then using number of employees may be a simple and reasonably accurate and equitable means of charging for these costs. However, more specialized services may have more specific cost drivers that are not distributed according to number of employees, as is apparently the case of SS department costs at Southeast Pulp and Paper. Whether activity analysis is justified to identify and measure this cost behavior more accurately depends, of course, on the costs and benefits of the effort. This case is similar to the experience of Weyerhaeuser. Weyerhaeuser felt the effort was worthwhile, and while we do not have post-audit type information on the continued viability of activity analysis of service costs at Weyerhaeuser, we will assume that the benefits continue.

2.   2003 SS Cost per Employee $= \dfrac{\text{2003 SS Costs}}{\text{Number of Employees}}$

$= \dfrac{\$300,000}{1,721} = \$174.32$

2003 SS Cost per Report $= \dfrac{\text{2003 SS Costs}}{\text{Number of Reports}}$

$= \dfrac{\$300,000}{1,232} = \$243.51$

$$\text{2004 SS Cost per Employee} = \frac{\text{2004 SS Costs}}{\text{Number of Employees}}$$

$$= \frac{\$385,000}{1,295} = \$297.30$$

$$\text{2004 SS Cost per Report} = \frac{\text{2004 SS Costs}}{\text{Number of Reports}}$$

$$= \frac{\$385,000}{1,556} = \$247.43$$

	Total	Forest Mgmt	Lumber Products	Paper Products
2003 Number of Employees	1,721	762	457	502
2003 SS Costs Charged to Divisions via Employees ($174.32 x 762, etc.)		$132,832	$ 79,664	$ 87,509
2003 Number of Reports	1,232	410	445	377
2003 SS Costs Charged to Divisions via Reports ($243.51 x 410, etc.)		$99,839	$108,362	$91,803
2004 Number of Employees	1,295	751	413	131
2004 SS Costs Charged to Divisions via Employees ($297.30 x 751, etc.)		$223,272	$122,785	$38,946
2004 Number of Reports	1,556	412	432	712
2004 SS Costs Charged to Divisions via Reports ($247.43 x 412, etc.)		$101,941	$106,890	$176,170

It is clear that the other divisions have what they see are legitimate complaints. Each of the other divisions, Forest Management and Lumber Products, has reduced the number of employees, but not as drastically as the Paper Products division. The result has been that more of the SS department costs have been shifted to Forest Management and Lumber Products, even as Paper Products has increased its demands for SS services. It would appear that Paper Products is not paying its fair share of SS costs.

3. Charging for SS department costs on the basis of number of employees creates an incentive to reduce the number of employees or to add employees only if the added benefits exceed the wage/salary cost plus SS (and other service) department costs. Charging for SS costs based on the number of reports creates the incentive to demand additional reports only if their value to the division exceeds the cost charged. This latter form of charge, based on the department's cost driver(s), probably will permit planning and control of service department costs more effectively than using generic charges.

4. It appears that activity analysis should be extended to all of Southeast's service departments. Using number of employees as the basis for charging for service costs probably distorts incentives for divisions to control costs.

<u>3-58</u> (35-50 min.)

1.	See the accompanying graphs. One can discern two different cost behaviors that appear to mirror changes in the cost time series. Matching the cost table and the graph shows that both the intercept and the slope of the cost function have changed after week 13. After week 13, fixed costs have increased at the same time that variable costs per order have decreased. In fact, logistics costs seems to be an almost purely fixed cost after week 13.

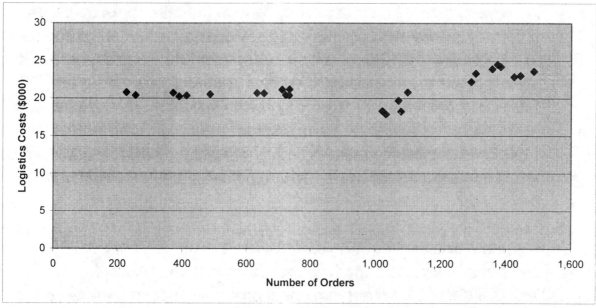

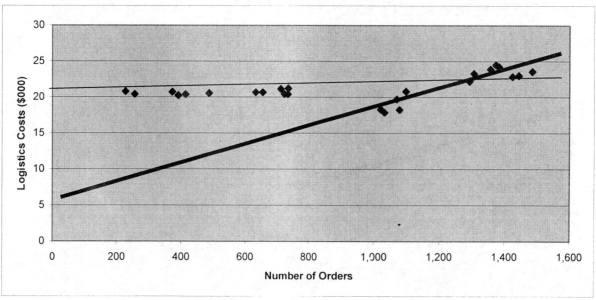

2. The first 13 weeks of data appear to be irrelevant to current cost behavior. Any measures of cost behavior that are to be used for current and future use should be based on the most recent data (weeks 14-25) only.

3. See the accompanying graph. The data do support Hudson's expectations: Fixed costs have increased, and variable costs have decreased. Regression analyses (though on limited numbers of observations) confirm this.

    Regression Output: Weeks 1-13
    Constant   5,497.172
    R Squared   0.8401874
    X Coefficient(s)   12.9031643

    Regression Output: Weeks 14-25
    Constant   20,337.16
    R Squared   0.1282178
    X Coefficient(s)   0.5556408

    However, average total logistics costs do not appear to have decreased. On logistics cost behavior alone, the switch does not seem to be justified. However, the new ordering system may be more flexible and may contribute to cost and quality savings in other departments. A full analysis of the benefits of the new ordering system should try to capture those benefits as well. If the ordering activity should increase greatly, the new system may be able to operate at lower total cost than the old system, but this level of activity would be well outside the relevant range of experience.

    In the last 12 weeks, the average number of orders is 528 per month. Under the old system, these would have cost $5,497 + (528 x $12.90) = $12,308. Under the current system the cost is $20,337 + (528 x $.56) = $20,633.

<u>3-59</u>   (20-30 min.) For the solution, see the Prentice Hall Web site, www.prenhall.com/

<u>3-60</u>   (10-30 min.)

The purpose of this exercise is to develop an understanding of different types of costs and their behavior. Assigning the problem ahead of time allows students to prepare lists of each type of cost, forcing them to think about types of cost and their behavior. However, the game could be played without advance preparation, especially if many students have some business experience.

<u>3-61</u> (40-60 min.)

NOTE TO INSTRUCTOR. This solution is based on the web site as it was in early 2004. Be sure to examine the current web site before assigning this problem, as the information there may have changed.

1.   For the 2002 annual report, the ten-year summary statistics section starts on page 14. The information found on the summary report includes operating revenues separated according to those earned from passenger, freight, and other sources, operating expenses, operating income, other income/expenses, tax expense and net income. The information also provides data on income per share, basic and diluted, dividends per share, total assets, long-term debt, and stockholders' equity. The report also includes two subsections, consolidated financial ratios and consolidated operating statistics.

2.   The information about revenues is divided into categories – passenger, freight, and other. The information about operating expenses is listed as one lump sum. It does not differentiate between costs associated with the differing types of revenues that are earned. This is likely due to the fact that the majority of the costs are incurred for providing passenger services and the freight costs are insubstantial in comparison. The firm also is not likely to want to

provide too much detail that the competitors for freight could use against SWA.

3. RPM is revenue passenger miles and ASM is available seat miles. The available seat miles is larger. The RPM is found by taking the number of passengers on each plane and multiplying it by the number of miles that the plane flies for that trip. This is done for all trips taken during the year. The ASM is determined by taking the number of seats on the plane and multiplying it by the miles that the plane flies for a trip. If all seats on the plane are filled with paying customers for all flights during the year, then the RPM and the ASM could be the same. The ASM is essentially a measure of capacity and RPM is a measure of how much of that capacity was used during the year. The actual RPMs and ASMs in miles are given for the year. The passenger revenue yield per RPM and operating revenue yield per ASM are provided, as is the operating expense per ASM.

4. and 5.

Using the high-low method, variable operating costs are:

	Op. Exp.	RPM
2002	$5,104,433	45,391,903
1999	3,954,011	36,479,322
Difference	$1,150,422	8,912,581

$$\text{Variable operating cost per RPM} = \frac{\text{Change in cost}}{\text{Change in cost driver}}$$

$$= \frac{\$1,150,422}{8,912,581} = \$0.1291$$

Fixed op. cost per year = Total operating cost - Variable operating cost

Using 2002: $5,104,433 – ($0.1291 x 45,391,903)

145

$$= \$5{,}104{,}433 - \$5{,}860{,}095$$
$$= -\$755{,}662$$

$$\text{Total operating cost per RPM} = \frac{2002 \text{ Operating Cost}}{2002 \text{ RPM}}$$

$$= \frac{\$5{,}104{,}433}{45{,}391{,}903} = \$0.1125$$

The total operating cost is <u>lower</u> than the variable operating cost, and the fixed cost is negative (impossible). This is not what would generally be expected. Airlines usually have large fixed costs and small variable costs.

6. As just explained, airlines usually have large fixed costs. In this case the high-low method is not accurate. The increase in costs between 1999 and 2002 may have included much investment in airplanes. If this investment in airplanes was driven by the demand for more RPMs, then it is part of long-run variable costs but not necessarily part of short-run variable costs. That is, it does not cost $0.1291 per passenger mile to add a passenger to a flight that is already scheduled. However, if attracting more passengers requires additional flights, and therefore additional airplanes, additional RPMs do generate $0.1291 of cost per RPM. The relationship between short- and long-run cost behavior may look like the graph on the next page.

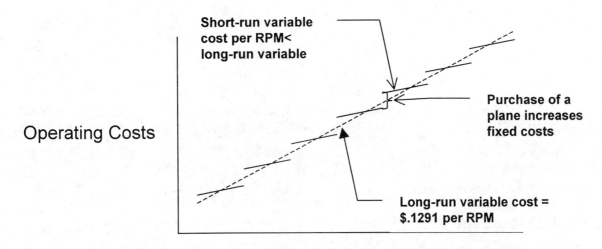

CHAPTER 4
COVERAGE OF LEARNING OBJECTIVES

LEARNING OBJECTIVE	FUNDA-MENTAL ASSIGN-MENT MATERIAL	CRITICAL THINKING EXERCISES AND EXERCISES	PROBLEMS	CASES, EXCEL, COLLAB. & INTERNET EXERCISES
LO1: Describe the purposes of cost management systems.		38	54	
LO2: Explain the relationship between cost, cost objective, cost accumulation, and cost assignment.		50,51	52	60,62,63
LO3: Distinguish between direct, indirect, and unallocated costs.	A1,B1	41,44,48,49	52,53	60
LO4: Explain how the financial statements of merchandisers and manufacturers differ because of the types of goods they sell.	B3			65,66
LO5: Understand the main differences between traditional and activity-based costing systems and why ABC systems provide value to managers.	A2,B2,B4		53,54	60,64,65,66
LO6: Design a cost accounting system that includes activity-based costing.	A3	40,46	54,58	60,61,62,63
LO7: Use activity-based cost information to make strategic and operational control decisions.	A2,A4	39,47	53,54,58	60,62,63,65
L08: Understand why multistage ABC systems give more value than two-stage systems for strategic planning and operational control (Appendix 4).		48,49,50,51	59	62,63

STATEMENT OF OPERATING INCOME
EXTERNAL REPORTING PURPOSE

Sales	$152,000
Cost of goods sold:	
Direct material	40,000
Indirect manufacturing	41,000
	81,000
Gross profit	71,000
Selling and administrative expenses:	
Commissions	15,000
Distribution to warehouses	10,400
Total selling and admin. expenses	25,400
Contribution to corporate expenses and profit	45,600
Unallocated expenses:	
Administrative salaries	8,000
Other administrative expenses	4,000
Total unallocated expenses	12,000
Operating income before tax	$ 33,600

OPERATING INCOME BY PRODUCT LINE
INTERNAL STRATEGIC DECISION MAKING PURPOSE

	Custom Detailed	Large Std.	Small Std.	Cost Type, Assignment Method
Sales	$32,000	$40,000	$80,000	
Direct material	5,000	15,000	20,000	Direct, Direct Trace
Indirect manufacturing	28,000[1]	5,000	8,000	Indirect, Allocation – Mach. Hours
	33,000	20,000	28,000	
Gross profit	(1,000)	20,000	52,000	
Commissions	1,500	3,500	10,000	Direct, Direct Trace
Distribution to warehouses	1,000[2]	3,000	6,400	Indirect, Allocation - Weight
	2,500	6,500	16,400	
Contribution to corporate expenses and profit	$(3,500)	$13,500	$35,600	

[1] Total machine hours is 1,400 + 250 + 400 = 2,050. Indirect manufacturing cost per machine hour is then $41,000 ÷ 2,050 = $20. The allocation to custom detailed is $20 x 1,400 machine hours = $28,000.

[2] Total weight shipped is 25,000 kg + 75,000 kg + 160,000 kg = 260,000 kg. Indirect distribution costs per kilogram is then $10,400 ÷ 260,000 kg = $0.04. The allocation to custom detailed is $0.04 x 25,000 kg = $1,000.

4-A2 (50-60 min.)

1. A summary of results follows.

	Pen Casings	Cell-Phone Casings	Company
Base Gross Profit Percentage	1.25%	38.75%	8.07%
Plan Gross Profit Percentage	6.25%	36.17%	13.73%
Support of Product Manager?	Moderate	None	
Support of President?	Moderate		

Exhibit A on the following page can be used to explain the impact of the controller's idea using the process map of the traditional costing system and the related financial reports. The controller's idea will result in an increase of 5% in the gross profit of the pen-casings line but a decrease of about 2.6% in the cell-phone line. The product manager of pen casings would probably give moderate support to the idea but the cell-phone casings manager would most likely not support the idea.

Although the company-level gross profit margin improves, the president's support may not be strong. Why? Top management is normally hesitant to support actions that do not have the unanimous support among product-line managers unless there is solid evidence of material improvement in profitability. While the overall gross margin percentage improves, the bottom line still is in red ink!

Perhaps the most important factor bearing on the president's support is lack of confidence in the accuracy of the cost and hence gross margin figures. Based on her own informal analysis, the president asked, "Why does an initiative that is solely focused on the cell-phone casing product line have little impact on this product's profitability while improving the profitability of the pen-casing line? Further, if overall company profitability increases, shouldn't this be reflected in improved profitability in the cell-phone casing line?"

Finally, the focus of improvement efforts should be directly on the pen-casing product line. This initiative deals mostly with the cell-phone line.

Exhibit A

Panel A Traditional Cost System

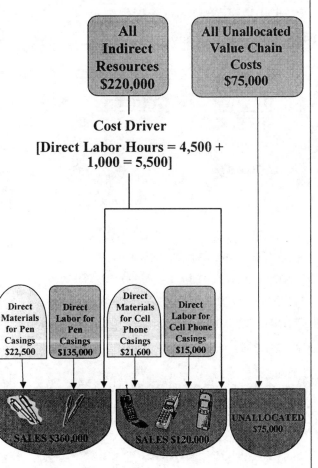

| All Indirect Resources $220,000 | | All Unallocated Value Chain Costs $75,000 |

Cost Driver

[Direct Labor Hours = 4,500 + 1,000 = 5,500]

| Direct Materials for Pen Casings $22,500 | Direct Labor for Pen Casings $135,000 | Direct Materials for Cell Phone Casings $21,600 | Direct Labor for Cell Phone Casings $15,000 |

SALES $360,000   SALES $120,000   UNALLOCATED $75,000

Panel B Pro-Forma Financial Reports

	STATEMENT OF OPERATING INCOME [EXTERNAL REPORTING PURPOSE]	Pen Casings	Cell Phone Casings
Sales	**$480,000**	$360,000	$120,000[1]
Cost of Goods Sold:			
Direct Material	**44,100**	22,500	21,600[2]
Direct Labor	**150,000**	135,000	15,000
Indirect Manufacturing	**220,000**	180,000[3]	40,000[4]
Cost of Goods Sold	**414,100**	337,500	76,600
Gross Profit	65,900	$ 22,500	$43,400
Corporate Expenses (Unallocated):	**75,000**		
Operating Loss	**($ 9,100)**		
Gross Profit Margin	**13.73%**[5]	6.25%	36.17%

CONTRIBUTION TO CORPORATE EXPENSES AND OPERATING INCOME [INTERNAL STRATEGIC DECISION MAKING AND OPERATIONAL-CONTROL PURPOSES]

1. $80,000 x .75 x 2
2. $12,000 x 2 x .90
3. $220,000 x [4,500/(4,500 + 1,000)]
4. $220,000 x [1,000/(4,500 + 1,000)]
5. $65,900/$480,000

What can be done to improve profitability of the pen casings? Can prices be raised without losing too much volume? Can operational improvements be made to lower the indirect manufacturing costs? The controller's idea is worthy of some support but it does not address the profitability issue head on.

2. Exhibit B on the following page is a process map that can be used to explain the impact of the controller's idea. Exhibit C that follows the end of the solution provides a detailed evaluation of the controller's idea.

	Pen Casings	Cell-Phone Casings	Company
Base Gross Profit Percentage	16.22%	(28.63%)	8.07%
Plan Gross Profit Percentage	16.11%	6.58%	13.73%
Support of Product Manager?	Neutral	Strong	
Support of President?	Strong		

The controller's idea will result in a slight decrease in the gross profit of the pen-casings line but a dramatic turnaround in the profitability of the cell-phone line. The product manager of pen casings would probably be neutral or even negative about the idea because the idea does not focus on operational improvements that directly affect the pen-casings line. The cell-phone casings manager would give strong support to the idea – this may save his/her job!

The president might note that the numbers agree with her informal analysis – generating confidence in the integrity of the cost accounting system. For reasons previously stated, the president would strongly support this idea while encouraging all managers involved to keep up the good work, reminding them that if all these predictions are realized, the company still is operating at a loss.

Exhibit B
Process Map of ABC System

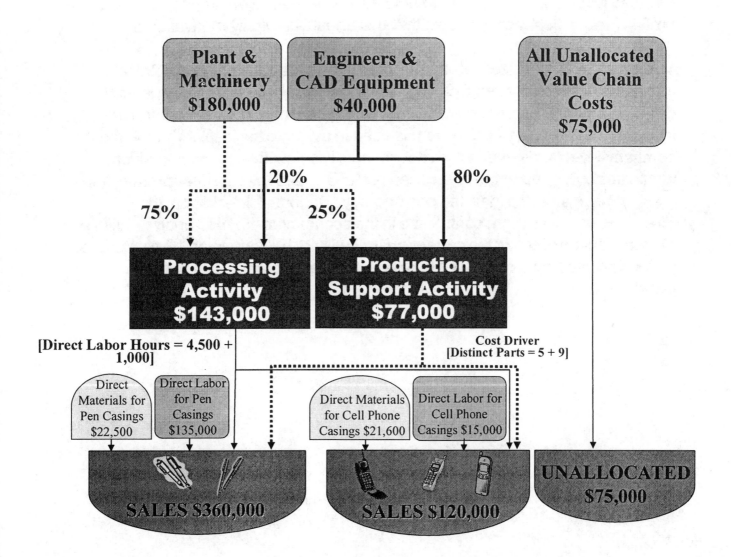

Plant & Machinery $180,000

Engineers & CAD Equipment $40,000

All Unallocated Value Chain Costs $75,000

20%   80%

75%   25%

Processing Activity $143,000

Production Support Activity $77,000

[Direct Labor Hours = 4,500 + 1,000]

Cost Driver
[Distinct Parts = 5 + 9]

Direct Materials for Pen Casings $22,500

Direct Labor for Pen Casings $135,000

Direct Materials for Cell Phone Casings $21,600

Direct Labor for Cell Phone Casings $15,000

UNALLOCATED $75,000

SALES $360,000

SALES $120,000

3. As vice president, you probably are pleased with the new ABC system. The cost drivers that are used to allocate activity costs appear to be plausible and reliable and thus probably represent a sound cause-effect model of operations. This will improve both the accuracy of product costing and operating managers' control over costs. Operating managers will be pleased with the ABC system because it helps them understand how their day-to-day work impacts costs and profits. From a behavioral perspective, this should be highly motivational.

This problem emphasizes the importance of the cost-accounting system to managers. Different systems can result in significantly different management decisions. In this case, the product-line managers' support for the controller's idea changes when an ABC system is used to evaluate the idea. Although the company-level gross margins do not change, it is possible that the president would strongly support the idea based on ABC data. Why? Neither product-line manager is against the idea and one strongly supports it. In addition, the president may have more confidence in the accuracy of the ABC analysis. While the substantial losses of the current quarter will not be completely eliminated, the serious profitability problem of the cell-phone casing product line has been reversed.

Exhibit C

PRO-FORMA FINANCIAL REPORTS FOR SIMPLE PLASTICS COMPANY
ACTIVITY-BASED COST ALLOCATION SYSTEM

	PANEL A STATEMENT OF OPERATING INCOME [EXTERNAL REPORTING PURPOSE]	PANEL B CONTRIBUTION TO CORPORATE COSTS AND PROFIT [INTERNAL STRATEGIC DECISION MAKING AND OPERATIONAL-CONTROL PURPOSES]	
		Pen Casings	Cell Phone Casings
Sales	$480,000	$360,000	$120,000
Cost of Goods Sold:			
Direct Material	44,100	22,500	21,600
Direct Labor	150,000	135,000	15,000
Processing Activity	143,000	117,000[1]	26,000[2]
Production Support Activity	77,000	27,500[3]	49,500[4]
Cost of Goods Sold	414,100	302,000	112,100
Gross Profit	65,900	$58,000	$7,900
Corporate Expenses (Unallocated):	75,000		
Operating Loss	($ 9,100)		
Gross Profit Margin	13.73%	16.11%	6.58%

1. $143,000 x [4,500 labor hours/(4,500 labor hours + 1,000 labor hours)]
2. $143,000 x [1,000 labor hours/(4,500 labor hours + 1,000 labor hours)]
3. $77,000 x [5 distinct parts/(5 distinct parts + 9 distinct parts)]
4. $77,000 x [9 distinct parts/(5 distinct parts + 9 distinct parts)]

This problem emphasizes the importance of the cost-accounting system to managers. Different systems can result in significantly different management decisions. In this case, the product-line managers' support for the controller's idea changes when an ABC system is used to evaluate the idea. Although the company-level gross margins do not change, it is possible that the president would strongly support the idea based on ABC data. Why? Neither product-line manager is against the idea and one strongly supports it. In addition, the president may have more confidence in the accuracy of the ABC analysis. While the substantial losses of the current quarter will not be completely eliminated, the serious profitability problem of the cell-phone casing product line has been reversed.

4-A3 (10-15 min.)

There can be many justifiable answers for each item other than the listed cost driver and behavior. The purpose of this exercise is to generate an active discussion regarding those chosen by Best Bank's managers. One point that should be emphasized is that many times managers choose cost drivers that are not the most plausible or reliable because of lack of data availability. Cost drivers are also used as a basis to allocate activity and resource costs and so the availability of data is often an important consideration.

	Activity or Resource	Cost Driver	Cost Behavior
a	R	Number of loan inquiries	V
b*	R	Number of square feet	F
c**	R	Number of person hours	F
d***	A	Number of investments	
e	A	Number of applications	
f	R	Number of person hours	V
g	R	Number of minutes	V
h	R	Number of person hours	F
i	A	Number of loans	
j	R	Number of computer transactions	V
k	A	Number of schedules	
l	R	Number of person hours	F

See the footnotes on the next page.

* An argument can be made that maintenance of the building is an activity. If this was the case, resources such as supplies and labor would be resources consumed, and several resource cost drivers would be needed. In addition, a separate resource and associated cost driver would be needed for insurance costs. However, the company had a contract for maintenance (fixed price), so this was a fixed-cost resource that was added to other occupancy costs such as insurance. The cost driver chosen for all these occupancy costs was square feet occupied by the various departments.

** Normally, the cost driver used for any labor resource is person hours. It is assumed that the staff person hours used are regular hours rather than overtime or temporary labor hours. Thus, the cost is fixed with respect to changes in hours used. As the hours used increases (decreases) the utilization of the resources increases (decreases) and eventually, management will need to make a decision whether to expand capacity (or whether to cut back on labor). This is an example of a step cost that is fixed over wide ranges of cost-driver level.

*** Students may try to determine the cost behavior of activities even though the problem requirements do not ask for it. Point out that activities almost always have mixed cost behavior because they consume various resources. Some of these are fixed-cost and others variable-cost resources. For example, the activity "research to evaluate a loan application" consumes such fixed-cost resources as manager labor time and computers (assumed owned by the bank). This activity also consumes variable-cost resources such as telecommunications time and external computing services.

4-A4 (30-35 min.)

1.

Cost/Activity: Cost Drivers	Cost per Driver Unit	Cost Driver Consumption, Part T151A*	Total Cost, Part T151A
Quality: Pieces scrapped	$ 80	1,000	$ 80,000
Production scheduling: Setups	500	12	6,000
Setup: Setups	1,200	12	14,400
Shipping: Containers shipped	5	500	2,500
Shipping admin.: Shipments	50	100	5,000
Production: Machine hours	150	500	75,000
Total indirect cost			$182,900
Direct materials			150,000
Total Cost of Part T151A			$332,900
Number of units produced			100,000
Cost per unit			$3.329
Selling price			7.500
Gross margin			$4.171
Gross margin percentage			55.6%

* .01 x 100,000; .00012 x 100,000; .00012 x 100,000; .005 x 100,000; .001 x 100,000; .005 x 100,000

2.   Assuming that the results of the activity analysis are accurate, Product T151A is much more profitable than RMP's existing costing system estimates. The existing system is overcosting product T151A by $6.00 – $3.329 = $2.671 or 80%! Chrysler's proposal can be accepted as long as the reduction in price is not significant. RMP should be aware, however, that the existing costing system is also *undercosting* some products, since all indirect costs are allocated. The activity-based costing system should be used to cost all product lines in order to identify RMP's "winners" as well as "losers."

Benefits of activity-based cost implementation include:

- More accurate costing of activities, products, customers, and other cost objects
- A solid foundation for activity-based management – using ABC information as a management tool for budgeting, planning, and control purposes
- An effective communication tool, since successful ABC implementation should involve all functional areas of the company

Costs of implementing ABC include:

- The cost of a pilot study includes salaries of managers who are dedicated to the study.
- Consultants are often necessary.
- Data collection is extensive since operational and financial data are often not available as required to support the new ABC system.
- It may be necessary to maintain an ABC system separate from the accounting system used for external reporting.

4-B1 (20-30 min.)

STATEMENT OF OPERATING INCOME
Thousands of Dollars

OPERATING INCOME BY PRODUCT LINE

		Tractor Imple-ments	Lawn Mower Parts	Hand Tool Parts	Cost Type, Assignment Method
Sales	$1,010	$350	$400	$260	
Cost of goods sold:					
Direct material	400	175	125	100	Direct, Direct Trace
Indirect manufacturing	94	68[1]	14	12	Indirect – Mach.Hrs
	494	243	139	112	
Gross profit	516	107	261	148	
Selling and administrative expenses:					
Commissions	55	25	20	10	Direct, Direct Trace
Distribution to warehouses	150	20[2]	80	50	Indirect - Weight
Total selling and administrative expenses	205	45	100	60	
Contribution to corporate expenses and profit	311	$ 62	$161	$ 88	
Unallocated expenses:					
Corporate salaries	7				
Other general expenses	5				
Total unallocated expenses	12				
Operating income before tax	$ 299				

[1] Total machine hours is 8,500 + 1,750 + 1,500 = 11,750. Indirect manufacturing cost per machine hour is then $94,000 ÷ 11,750 = $8. The allocation to tractor implements is $8 x 8,500 machine hours = $68,000.

[2] Total weight shipped is 100,000 kg + 400,000 kg + 250,000 kg = 750,000 kg. Indirect distribution costs per kilogram is then $150,000 ÷ 750,000 kg = $0.2. The allocation to tractor implements is $0.2 x 100,000 kg = $20,000.

<u>4-B2</u> (50-60 min.)

1. A summary of the analyses follows.

	Pen Casings	Cell-Phone Casings	Company
Base Gross Profit Percentage	1.25%	38.75%	8.07%
Plan Gross Profit Percentage	10.80%	37.20%	17.40%
Support of Product Manager?	Strong	None	
Support of President?			Moderate

Exhibit A on the following page can be used to explain the impact of the controller's idea using the process map of the traditional costing system and the related financial reports. The controller's idea will result in an increase of 9.55% in the gross profit of the pen-casings line but a decrease of 1.55% in the cell-phone line. The product manager of pen casings would probably give strong support to the idea but the cell-phone casings manager would most likely not support the idea.

Although the company-level gross profit margin improves, the president's support may not be strong. Why? There is not a strong consensus among product-line managers. Top management is normally hesitant to support actions that do not have the unanimous support among product-line managers unless there is solid evidence of material improvement in profitability. While the current loss would be reversed, the return on sales is still nominal at $3,500 \div \$480,000 = .73\%$.

Perhaps the most important factor bearing on the president's support is lack of confidence in the accuracy of the cost and hence gross margin figures. She probably will inquire whether the shift in the consumption percentages by the two activities is captured by the traditional costing system. Does the change in allocation rates from 90:10 to 82:18 based on direct labor hour changes accurately capture the impact of the operational changes? An informal analysis of the controller's idea might look like the following table.

Exhibit A

1. $80,000 x .75 x 2

Panel A   Traditional Cost System

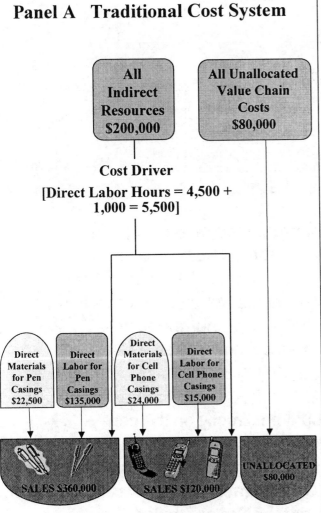

All Indirect Resources $200,000

All Unallocated Value Chain Costs $80,000

Cost Driver

[Direct Labor Hours = 4,500 + 1,000 = 5,500]

Direct Materials for Pen Casings $22,500

Direct Labor for Pen Casings $135,000

Direct Materials for Cell Phone Casings $24,000

Direct Labor for Cell Phone Casings $15,000

SALES $360,000

SALES $120,000

UNALLOCATED $80,000

Panel B   Pro-Forma Financial Reports

	STATEMENT OF OPERATING INCOME [EXTERNAL REPORTING PURPOSE]	CONTRIBUTION TO CORPORATE EXPENSES AND OPERATING INCOME [INTERNAL STRATEGIC DECISION MAKING AND OPERATIONAL-CONTROL PURPOSES]	
		Pen Casings	Cell Phone Casings
Sales	$480,000	$360,000	$120,000[1]
Cost of Goods Sold:			
Direct Material	46,500	22,500	24,000[2]
Direct Labor	150,000	135,000	15,000
Indirect Manufacturing	200,000	163,636[3]	36,364[4]
Cost of Goods Sold	396,500	321,136	75,364
Gross Profit	83,500	$ 38,864	$44,636
Corporate Expenses (Unallocated):	80,000		
Operating Income	$ 3,500		
Gross Profit Margin	17.40%[5]	10.80%	37.20%

2. $12,000 x 2
3. $200,000 x [4,500/(4,500 + 1,000)]
4. $200,000 x [1,000/(4,500 + 1,000)]
5. $83,500 ÷ $480,000

Operational Change	Likely Impact on the Consumption of Resources that Support:	
	Pen Casings	Cell-Phone Casings
Less purchasing work to supply parts for cell-phone casings		↓
Less engineering design work on cell phone casings		↓
Less equipment used to support cell-phone production		↓
Increase in cell-phone production		↑

Based on the informal analysis, the President probably would expect the profitability of cell-phone casings to improve and the profitability of pen casings to be unaffected. This disagrees with the numerical analysis. Given the propensity of managers to embrace numerical results, less weight will likely be given this analysis compared to the "objective" numbers. As a result, she may question the validity of the numerical analysis as well as the value of the traditional costing system!

Finally, the focus of improvement efforts should be directly on the pen-casing product line. This initiative deals mostly with the cell-phone line. What can be done to improve profitability of the pen casings? Can prices be raised without losing too much volume? Can operational improvements be made to lower the indirect manufacturing costs? The controller's idea is worthy of some support but it does not address the profitability issue head on.

2. Exhibit B on the following page is a process map that can be used to explain the impact of the controller's idea. Exhibit C at the end of the solution provides a detailed evaluation of the controller's idea.

	Pen Casings	Cell-Phone Casings	Company
Base Gross Profit Percentage	16.22%	(28.63%)	8.07%
Plan Gross Profit Percentage	17.26%	17.81%	17.40%
Support of Product Manager?	Neutral	Strong	
Support of President?			Strong

The controller's idea will result in a slight increase in the gross profit of the pen-casings line but a dramatic turnaround in the profitability of the cell-phone line. The product manager of pen casings would probably be neutral or slightly positive about the idea because the idea does not focus on operational improvements that directly affect the pen-casings line. The cell-phone casings manager would give strong support to the idea – this may save his/her job! The president would strongly support this idea while encouraging all managers involved to keep up the good work. Also, note that the numbers agree with the informal analysis – generating confidence in the integrity of the cost accounting system.

Exhibit B
Process Map for ABC System

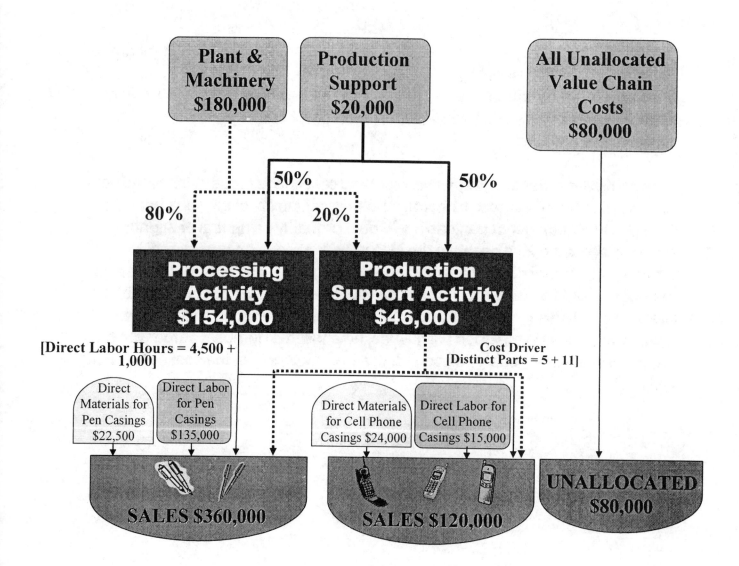

3. As vice president, you probably are pleased with the new ABC system. The cost drivers that are used to allocate activity costs appear to be plausible and reliable and thus probably represent a sound cause-effect model of operations. This will improve both the accuracy of product costing and operating managers' control over costs. Operating managers will be pleased with the ABC system because it helps them understand how their day-to-day work impacts costs and profits. From a behavioral perspective, this should be highly motivational.

This problem emphasizes the importance of the cost-accounting system to managers. Different systems can result in significantly different management decisions. In this case, the product-line managers' support for the controller's idea changes when an ABC system is used to evaluate the idea. Although the company-level gross margins do not change, it is possible that the president would strongly support the idea based on ABC data. Why? Neither product-line manager is against the idea and one strongly supports it. In addition, the president may have more confidence in the accuracy of the ABC analysis. The substantial losses of the current quarter have been completely eliminated and the serious profitability problem of the cell-phone casing product line has been reversed.

Exhibit C

PRO-FORMA FINANCIAL REPORTS FOR SIMPLE PLASTICS COMPANY
ACTIVITY-BASED COST ALLOCATION SYSTEM

PANEL A
STATEMENT OF OPERATING INCOME
[EXTERNAL REPORTING PURPOSE]

Sales	$480,000
Cost of Goods Sold:	
Direct Material	46,500
Direct Labor	150,000
Processing Activity	154,000
Production Support Activity	46,000
Cost of Goods Sold	396,500
Gross Profit	83,500
Corporate Expenses (Unallocated):	80,000
Operating Income	$ 3,500
Gross Profit Margin	17.40%

PANEL B
CONTRIBUTION TO CORPORATE COSTS AND PROFIT
[INTERNAL STRATEGIC DECISION MAKING AND OPERATIONAL-CONTROL PURPOSES]

	Pen Casings	Cell Phone Casings
Sales	$360,000	$120,000
Direct Material	22,500	24,000
Direct Labor	135,000	15,000
Processing Activity	126,000[1]	28,000[2]
Production Support Activity	14,375[3]	31,625[4]
Cost of Goods Sold	297,875	98,625
Gross Profit	$62,125	$21,375
Gross Profit Margin	17.26%	17.81%

1. $154,000 x [4,500 labor hours/(4,500 labor hours + 1,000 labor hours)]
2. $154,000 x [1,000 labor hours/(4,500 labor hours + 1,000 labor hours)]
3. $46,000 x [5 distinct parts/(5 distinct parts + 11 distinct parts)]
4. $46,000 x [11 distinct parts/(5 distinct parts + 11 distinct parts)]

4-B3 (25-30 min.)

1. Merchandise Inventories, 1,000 tents @ $97 .... $97,000

2. Direct materials inventory .... $ 50,000
    Work-in-process inventory   0
    Finished goods inventory   97,000
    Total inventories $147,000

3.

OUTDOOR EQUIPMENT COMPANY
Statement of Operating Income
For the Year Ended December 31, 20X4

Sales (9,000 units at $180)		$1,620,000
Cost of goods sold:		
Beginning inventory	$ 0	
Purchases	970,000	
Cost of goods available for sale	$970,000	
Less ending inventory	97,000	
Cost of goods sold (an expense)		873,000
Gross margin or gross profit		$ 747,000
Less other expenses: selling & administrative costs		180,000
Operating income (also income before taxes in this example)		$ 567,000

4.

MOUNTAIN SUPPLIES, INC.
Statement of Operating Income
For the Year Ended December 31, 20X4

Sales (9,000 units at $180)			$1,620,000
Cost of goods manufactured and sold:			
Beginning finished goods inventory		$ 0	
Cost of goods manufactured:			
Beginning WIP inventory	$ 0		
Direct materials used	530,000		
Direct labor	290,000		
Factory overhead	150,000		
Mfg costs during the year	$970,000		
Less ending work-in-process inventory	0	970,000	
Cost of goods available for sale		$970,000	
Less ending finished goods inventory		97,000	
Cost of goods sold (an expense)			873,000
Gross margin or gross profit			$ 747,000
Less other expenses: selling and administrative costs			180,000
Operating income (also income before taxes in this example)			$ 567,000

5. The balance sheet for the merchandiser (OEC) has just one line for inventories, the ending inventory of the items purchased for resale. The balance sheet for the manufacturer (MSI) has three items: direct materials inventory, work-in-process inventory, and finished goods inventory.

The income statements are similar except for the computation of cost of goods available for sale. The merchandiser (OEC) simply shows purchases for the year plus beginning inventory. In contrast, the manufacturer (MSI) shows beginning work-in-process inventory plus the three categories of cost that comprise manufacturing cost (direct materials, direct labor, and factory (or manufacturing) overhead) and then deducts the ending work-in-process inventory. The manufacturer then adds the beginning finished goods inventory to this cost of goods manufactured to get the cost of goods available for sale.

6. The purpose is providing aggregate measures of inventory value and cost of goods manufactured for external reporting to investors, creditors, and other external stakeholders.

4-B4 (20-30 min.)

1. The first step is to determine the cost per cost-driver unit for each activity:

Activity Center [Cost Driver]	Monthly Manufacturing Overhead	Cost-Driver Activity	Cost per Driver Unit
Material Handling [Direct materials cost]	$ 8,000	$200,000	$ 0.04
Engineering [Engineering change notices]	20,000	20	1,000.00
Power [Kilowatt hours]	16,000	400,000	0.04
Total Manufacturing Overhead	$44,000		

Next, the costs of each activity can be allocated to each of the three products:

PHYSICAL FLOW / ALLOCATED COST

Cost	SA2		SA5		SA9	
Material Handling	$.04 x 25,000	= $ 1,000	$.04 x 50,000	= $ 2,000	$.04 x 125,000	= $ 5,000
Engineering	$1,000 x 13	= 13,000	$1,000 x 5	= 5,000	$1,000 x 2	= 2,000
Power	$.04 x 50,000	= 2,000	$.04 x 200,000	= 8,000	$.04 x 150,000	= 6,000
Total		$16,000		$15,000		$13,000

2. Overhead rate based on direct labor costs:

$$\text{Rate} = \frac{\text{Total manufacturing overhead}}{\text{Total direct labor cost}} = \frac{\$44,000}{\$8,000} = \$5.50/\text{DL}\$$$

Overhead allocated to each product is:
SA2: $5.50 x 4,000 = $22,000
SA5: $5.50 x 1,000 =   5,500
SA9: $5.50 x 3,000 = 16,500
Total $44,000

Notice that much less manufacturing overhead cost is allocated to SA5 using direct labor as a cost driver. Why? Because SA5 uses only a small amount of labor but large amounts of other resources, especially power.

3. The product costs in requirement 1 are more accurate if the cost drivers are good indicators of the causes of the costs – they are both plausible and reliable. For example, kilowatt hours is certainly a better measure of the cost of power costs than is direct labor hours. Therefore, the allocation of power costs in requirement 1 is certainly better than in requirement 2. Materials handling and engineering are likewise more plausible. A manager would be much more confident in the manufacturing overhead allocated to products in requirement 1. Remember, however, that there are incremental costs of data collection associated with the more accurate ABC system. The benefit/cost criteria must be applied in deciding which costing system is "best."

4-1   A cost management system is a collection of tools and techniques that identifies how management's decisions affect costs. The three purposes of a CMS are to provide

1. cost information for operational control,
2. cost information for strategic decisions, and
3. aggregate measures of inventory value and cost of goods manufactured (or purchased) for external reporting to investors, creditors, and other external stakeholders.

4-2   The production manager needs operational control information. Setting the product mix is a strategic decision. The aggregate cost of inventory that appears on the balance sheet is information that is needed by external investors, creditors, and other stakeholders.

4-3   The major purpose of a detailed cost-accounting system is to measure costs for decision making and financial reporting. Cost accounting systems become more detailed as management seeks more accurate data for decision making.

4-4   The two major processes performed by a cost accounting system are cost accumulation and cost assignment.

4-5   Managers make important decisions on a daily basis. These decisions are based in large part on financial data that is provided by the cost accounting system. So it is critically important that the cost accounting system provide accurate and reliable financial information.

4-6   Cost objectives or cost objects include departments, products, territories, miles driven, bricks laid, patients seen, and potholes repaired.

4-7   No. Departments are objects of costing because they represent a logical grouping of activities for which a separate determination of costs is desired.

4-8   Direct costs can be identified specifically and exclusively with a given cost objective (that is, directly traced) in an economically feasible way. Indirect costs cannot be so identified. However, a plausible and reliable cost driver can be identified to be used to allocate resource costs to consuming resources, activities, or cost objects. When direct trace is not economically feasible nor can a plausible and reliable cost driver be found, costs should remain unallocated.

4-9   Yes, the same cost (for example, the department supervisor's salary) can be direct with respect to a department but indirect with respect to the variety of products flowing through a department (e.g., tables, chairs, and cabinets).

4-10   Yes. Economic feasibility means being "cost effective." That is, managers do not want cost accounting to be more expensive than its expected benefits.

4-11   Some costs can be physically linked with a department (or a product), but not in an economically feasible way. An example is the use of departmental meters for measuring power usage. Such devices would measure power costs as direct costs of a department. Otherwise, factory power costs usually are regarded by managers as indirect costs of individual departments. Managers often decide whether the resulting increased accuracy provided by individual power meters is worth their additional cost; thus, the test of economic feasibility will decide whether a particular cost is regarded as direct or indirect.

4-12   *For financial statement purposes*, the typical accounting system does not allocate costs associated with value-chain functions other than production to the physical units produced. However, for guiding decisions regarding product-pricing and product-mix decisions, many companies allocate all costs, including R&D, design, marketing, distribution, and customer service costs. However, the allocations of these costs may not be embedded in the system that generates financial statements.

4-13   Yes. The two criteria that should be met before any measure is used as a cost driver to allocate costs are economic plausibility and reliability. A measure should be plausible – make common sense. If managers cannot easily understand the logical relationship between a cost driver and the costs of an activity or resource, the resulting allocations will be perceived as arbitrary.

4-14   Production maintenance costs are normally indirect. Sales commissions normally can be directly traced to specific products. The costs associated with process design are normally unallocated because it is too difficult to identify plausible and reliable cost drivers.

4-15   Generally not. They are direct as far as the physical product is concerned, but in accounting for their cost it would usually be impractical to keep records of the amount of glue or tacks used in each unit of product. A more feasible method would be to consider these as supplies (indirect material).

4-16   Depreciation related to manufacturing activities is a product cost, not a period cost. Hence, it will become an expense as a part of manufacturing cost of goods sold. Thus, depreciation is not always an immediate expense.

4-17   "Expenses" denote all costs deducted from (matched against) revenues in a given period. "Costs" is a much broader term; for example, "cost" is used to describe an asset (the cost of inventory) and an expense (the cost of goods sold).

4-18   Unexpired costs are not confined to inventory costs. Other examples are plant, equipment, and miscellaneous deferred or prepaid costs such as insurance premiums.

4-19   Direct labor costs are incurred at the same time the direct labor is used in production. It is not purchased and stored for future use. Therefore, there is no direct labor inventory account.

<u>4-20</u>   Manufacturing is the transformation of materials into other goods through the use of labor and factory facilities. In contrast, merchandising companies (retailers or wholesalers) sell goods without changing their basic forms.

<u>4-21</u>   Normally, activities consume various resources including fixed-cost and variable-cost resources. As a result, the cost behavior of most activities is mixed. We often say that "activities consume resources and resources cost money."

<u>4-22</u>   The four steps are:

Step 1.   Determine cost objectives, key activities, resources, and related cost drivers.
Step 2.   Determine the relationships among cost objectives, activities, and resources.
Step 3.   Collect relevant data concerning costs and physical flow of cost-driver units among resources and activities.
Step 4.   Calculate and interpret the new activity-based cost information.

<u>4-23</u>   Percentages used as output measures for resources in a two-stage ABC system are not cost drivers as much as they are cost allocators. These percentages reflect management's estimates or measures of the amount of a resource that is consumed by an activity. The sum of percentages from any resource to consuming activities is 100%.

<u>4-24</u>   The accuracy of any cost system depends on the complexity of the operating system, the amount of indirect costs, and the reliability of the cost drivers used to allocate indirect costs. A simple operating system coupled with a well-designed traditional costing system with relatively little indirect costs and reliable cost drivers can be just as accurate in providing product or customer costs as a sophisticated ABC system. Such business environments rarely exist. Further, traditional costing systems do little to aid the operational control purpose of cost-management because they do not accumulate or report operational information about key business activities.

4-25   Six factors that explain why more and more organizations are adopting activity-based costing systems are:

1.   Fierce competitive pressure has resulted in shrinking margins, making accurate cost determinations essential. While companies may know that their overall margin is shrinking, they often do not have faith in the accuracy of the margins for *individual* products or services. Some are winners and some are losers – but which ones?

2.   Business complexity has increased, resulting in greater diversity in the types of products and services as well as customer classes. This means that the consumption of a company's shared resources also varies substantially across products and customers.

3.   New production techniques have increased the indirect proportion of total costs – that is, indirect costs are far more important in today's world-class manufacturing environment. In many industries direct labor is being replaced by automated equipment. It is not unusual for indirect cost to be more than 50% of total cost.

4.   The rapid pace of technology change has shortened product life cycles. This means that companies do not have time to make price or cost adjustments once costing errors are discovered.

5.   The costs associated with bad decisions that result from inaccurate cost determinations are substantial (bids lost due to overcosted products, hidden losses from undercosted products, failure to detect activities that are not cost effective, etc.).

6.   Computer technology has reduced the costs of developing and operating cost systems that track many activities.

4-26   One of the most significant non-value-added activities in any business is moving inventory, materials, and parts from one point to another during the production process. The time it takes for material-handling labor to move material can be reduced by changing the layout of machines. For example, one company changed its layout so several machines that were used to produce about 50% of its products were placed next to one another. This layout change reduced the distance and time required to move partially completed products from one machine to another. The cost savings were significant.

4-27 Activity-based management is using activity-based cost information to improve the operations of an organization. Managers use ABC information for decision making, planning, and controlling purposes. Cost information is vital for each of these purposes. The accuracy level of the cost information is a critical factor in determining the effectiveness of decision making, planning, and controlling.

4-28 Managers seek to eliminate, or at least reduce as much as possible, non-value-added activities. Separating these from value-added activities helps focus attention on the costs to be examined for potential reductions.

4-29 Benchmarking is the continuous process of comparing products, services, and activities against the best industry standards.

4-30 No two businesses are operated in the same manner, and often their competitive environments are significantly different. As a result, comparing either financial or operational measures to benchmarks under the assumption that "all things are equal" should be done with caution. Another important difference between businesses is the degree of accuracy of their cost accounting system. A financial measure such as "cost to serve a commercial customer" in a bank that allocates almost all of its operating costs should not be compared to a benchmark measure from another bank that allocates only a small portion of its operating costs.

4-31 A cost driver is an output measure for a resource or activity. In an ABC system, the costs of indirect resources that are consumed when activities are performed are allocated to these activities using appropriate output measures. Thus, these cost drivers are referred to as resource cost drivers.

After the costs of all resources consumed by an activity are accumulated into an activity cost pool, this cost must be allocated to products (or services or even other activities). This is done using the most appropriate (plausible and reliable) output measure. In practice, these measures are often referred to as cost drivers but they are more appropriately called activity cost drivers.

4-32 The simplest answer is to recommend a traditional costing system for the Youngstown plant and an ABC costing system for the Salem plant. Why? Because one of the primary purposes of any costing system is to provide as accurate cost information as possible subject to the benefit-cost criterion. There is always a tradeoff between the accuracy of a system and the costs to implement and maintain it. Generally, as the operations of a company become more complex, the diversity of demands upon resources increases across products (services). In order to accurately track resource costs in such a diverse operating environment, many cost pools are needed for the various activities – that is, an ABC system. Because the Youngstown plant operations are not complex, a simple (traditional) costing system probably provides sufficiently accurate cost information. Due to the complexity and diversity of the Salem plant operations, an ABC costing system should be considered.

4-33 In two-stage ABC systems, there are only two levels of allocation between resources used and the final cost objective. The first stage often consists of percentages representing the amount of effort used to perform the activities that consume the resources.

In multistage ABC systems, there is no limit on the number of allocations between resources and the final cost objective. In addition, multistage ABC systems have a distinctive operational flavor. There are many consumption rates that reflect the input/output relationships between activities and resources as well as between cost objects and activities.

4-34   These rates represent input/output relationships. Process improvements usually affect the input level required for a unit of output. For example, suppose the time required to perform a setup is currently 10 mechanic hours (say two persons working for 5 hours). By relocating tools needed to do the setup and providing more training, the time is reduced to 6 hours. This process improvement would be reflected in a lower resource consumption rate (from 10 to 6 labor hours per setup). As another example, on Exhibit 4-19, consider the resource consumption rate $r_2 = 25$ computer transactions per account verified. The total computer cost to verify 20,000 commercial accounts is (20,000 x 25 x $0.027) = $13,500. Suppose the number of transactions can be reduced to only 10 by using a new verification software feature. Suppose further that this new feature would raise the cost per transaction to $0.04. Now the total computer cost to verify the 20,000 commercial accounts is (20,000 x 10 x $0.04) = $8,000. This process improvement would result in a net savings of $5,500.

4-35   Resource consumption rates are almost always non-financial measures. The cost per driver unit is the total cost of an activity or resource divided by the total output flow of cost driver units.

4-36   When ever a resource is constraining the capacity to meet demand, a company can take the following actions:

- a. Reduce demand for the resource. In this case, this means either saying "no" to the increased business or deferring business (this may not be feasible).
- b. Increase capacity. The company can hire additional staff, outsource part of its order processing function, or permit overtime.
- c. Institute process improvements that reduce the consumption of the capacity-constraining resource. The company can investigate ways to reduce the resource consumption rates.

4-37 Managers use many tools and techniques to manage the organization. One of the fundamental tools used is the cost-accounting system. If the costs generated by the cost-accounting system are activity-based, then the resulting managerial applications are called activity-based management.

4-38 Cost planning and control (the strategic and operational purposes of a cost management system) requires information about processes, activities, and resources regardless of how many or few products are made. Cost reduction programs are most effective when managers understand the interrelationships between activities and resources. Thus, an ABC system often contributes significantly to an effective planning and control environment.

4-39 Benchmarking financial measures should be done with care. Many factors outside the influence of responsible managers can reduce the comparability of performance measures. For example, labor costs can vary substantially across regions. If the local labor rates in Youngstown are low compared to rates at the location of the department used in the text illustration, Youngstown may have the lowest cost per driver unit for those activities that are labor intensive such as processing deposits and withdrawals. Another factor is the scope of the ABC system. The Youngstown area customer care center may have chosen not to allocate many indirect costs that were allocated in the customer care center illustrated in the text. This would lower the costs accumulated in activity-cost pools and the resulting cost per driver unit.

4-40   The vast majority of businesses make hundreds or thousands of different products or services. It would be impossible to build a process map that depicts hundreds of different pens. So groups or families of products that have similar prices, volumes, activity-consumption rates, and resource consumption rates are formed. Then the average prices and rates are used to develop the process map and interrelationships. For example, the four pens and three cell phones may have prices and volumes as follows:

Pen type A:	100,000 @ $0.8500	= $ 85,000
Pen type B:	150,000 @ $0.7600	= $ 114,000
Pen type C:	120,000 @ $0.8200	= $ 98,400
Pen type D:	80,000 @ $0.7825	= $ 62,600
Cell phone type X:	3,000 @ $8.1000	= $ 24,300
Cell phone type Y:	3,000 @ $7.8000	= $ 23,400
Cell phone type Z:	4,000 @ $8.0750	= $ 32,300
	460,000	$ 440,000

The designer of the ABC system has three choices for cost objectives:

Choice 1: Use seven cost objects. This will give accurate individual prices and volumes but is the most costly to maintain.

Choice 2: Use one cost objective based on the overall average for all seven products. The average price is $440,000 ÷ 460,000 = $0.9565. This is the least costly system but the price used does not reflect any of the individual products. Thus, accuracy is very low which can lead to poor decision making.

Choice 3: Use two cost objectives (as was done in the chapter illustration). The pens product family has an average price of $360,000 ÷ 450,000 = $0.80. The cell phone product family has an average price of $80,000 ÷ 10,000 = $8.00. The average prices of both these product families is reasonably close to the individual prices, reflecting the homogeneity of the prices.

Clearly, there is a trade-off between the added cost of individual product costing and the benefits of more accurate individual product cost information. In most cases, a wise choice of homogeneous prices and production requirements yields adequate accuracy levels at a reasonable cost.

4-41 (10 min.)

This exercise emphasizes how a given cost item may be seen from different viewpoints. Classroom use of such exercises will get students *thinking* instead of *memorizing*. Surely, classroom discussion at this early stage of the course will not settle the student's mind on many issues. Exceptions can be cited for nearly every answer. The class will rarely be able to discuss more than half the items. This should not disturb the instructor. To accomplish the purpose of these problems, every item need not be discussed in prolonged detail.

	Manufacturing Costs	
	Direct (D) or Indirect (I)	Variable (V) or Fixed (F)
1.	I	F
2.	I	V
3.	I	V
4.	I	V
5.	I	F
6.	I	F
7.	I	V
8.	D	V
9.	D	V
10.	I	V

1. The cost of components used in products is almost always directly traceable and is a variable cost.

2. As volume changes over a wide range, the amount of supplies consumed for maintenance will also change so this cost is variable. However, there usually would not be an economically feasible way to trace these costs to individual products, so these costs would be indirect and allocated (normally the cost driver would be machine hours).

3. Training costs for mechanics would not vary as a function of volume of production assuming that no new products would be made and that no new mechanics would be hired. Training costs are indirect assuming that the training cannot be associated with only one product.

4. The wages of machine operators who work on only one product can be easily traced to the product. Probably these wages would not vary over wide ranges of volume and thus would be a fixed cost. We should note that if volume increases rapidly in a short time frame, it is often necessary to work overtime. In this case, the overtime portion of operator wages would be a variable cost.

4-43   (20 min.)

1.	c, f	7.	c, e	13.	a, f
2.	a, f	8.	c, e	14.	e, partly d, partly c
3.	a, e	9.	c, e	15.	b**, f
4.	c, f	10.	d, e	16.	c, e
5.	g*	11.	c, f	17.	c, f
6.	c, f	12.	c, g	18.	a, e

*Non-recurring items such as this are not classified as either variable or fixed.

**Could possibly be (c) if immaterial.

This problem emphasizes how a given cost item may be seen from different viewpoints. Classroom use of such problems causes students to *think* instead of *memorize*. Surely, classroom discussion at this early stage of the course will not settle the student's mind on many issues. Exceptions can be cited for nearly every answer. The class will rarely be able to discuss more than half the items. This should not disturb the instructor. To accomplish the purpose of these problems, every item need not be discussed in prolonged detail.

4-44   (10 min.)

Using Exhibit 4-6 and the chapter discussion of the Simple Plastics production and cost accounting system, the classification of these costs and resources is:

1.   D
2.   U
3.   I
4.   I
5.   D
6.   I
7.   I (a case can be made for this cost to be unallocated)
8.   U

<u>4-45</u> (20-25 min.)

The first step is determining the revised activity-cost pool amounts (stage 1).

Processing Activity Cost   = .90 x $180,000 + .30 x $40,000
                           = $162,000 + $12,000
                           = $174,000

Production Support Cost   = .10 x $180,000 + .70 x $40,000
                           = $18,000 + $28,000
                           = $46,000

Using the format from page 146, panel B,

	Contribution to Corporate Costs and Profit	
	Pen Casings	Cell Phone Casings
Sales	$360,000	$ 80,000
Cost of goods sold:		
Direct material	22,500	12,000
Direct labor	135,000	15,000
Processing	156,600	17,400
Production support	9,200	36,800
Cost of goods sold	323,300	81,200
Gross margin	$ 36,700	$ (1,200)

4-46 (15-20 min.)

Activity	Resource	Cost	Consumption Rate	Allocated Cost	Total Traceable Cost
Process New Accounts	Tellers	$350,000	10%	$35,000	
	Retail Sales Managers	$210,000	10%	$21,000	$56,000
Process Deposits and Withdrawals	Tellers	$350,000	60%	$210,000	
	Retail Sales Managers	$210,000	20%	$42,000	
	Managing Officer	$100,000	10%	$10,000	$262,000
Process Other Transactions	Tellers	$350,000	20%	$70,000	
	Retail Sales Managers	$210,000	30%	$63,000	
	Managing Officer	$100,000	30%	$30,000	$163,000

4-47 (20-25 min.)

1.

Activity	Total Cost	Annual Flow of Driver Units	Cost Per Driver Unit
Process new accounts	$ 56,000	540	$103.70370
Process deposits and withdrawals	262,000	163,000	1.60736
Process other transactions	163,000	49,000	3.32653

	Cost Per Driver Unit	Retail Customers		Commercial Customers	
		Driver Units	Cost	Driver Units	Cost
Process new accounts	$103.70370	500	$51,852	40	$4,148
Process deposits and withdrawals	1.60736	75,000	120,552	88,000	141,448
Process other transactions	3.32653	25,000	83,163	24,000	79,837
Total cost			$255,567		$225,433
Number of accounts			2,500		400
Cost per account			$102.23		$563.58

2. Benchmarking is not appropriate when different costing systems are used. If the benchmarks represent costs that result from branches that allocated significantly different resources or defined different activities, the results should not be compared.

3. The comparison below indicates that the Colorado City branch has much room for improvement especially in processing deposits and withdrawals. This assumes that the benchmarks used are appropriate.

	Open New Accounts	Process Dep. And With.	Process Other Trans.	Retail Cost Per Account	Commercial Cost Per Account
Benchmark	$81.67	$0.75	$3.050	$88.00	$508.00
Colorado City	$103.70	$1.61	$3.33	$102.23	$563.58

Answers can vary depending on the assumptions. For example, some companies would consider the order processing activity part of the distribution function in the value chain and would include this activity in the new ABC system. Others would consider this a support activity and leave it unallocated. Similarly, production scheduling can be considered part of the production function and thus be allocated under both traditional and ABC systems. Also, note that the cost drivers for the resource costs are not the same as those for the activity. For example, the cost driver for the activity order processing of customer orders might be number of orders, whereas the cost driver for the salaries of order processing staff is staff labor hours used.

Activity	Related Cost	Traditional	Multistage ABC
Setting up for a production run	Mechanic wages	Indirect (direct labor hours)	Indirect (mechanic labor time)
Purchasing materials and parts to be used in products	Materials and parts cost	Direct trace	Direct trace
Shipping sold products to customers (distributors)	Fuel used on company's fleet of trucks	Unallocated (period cost)	Indirect (miles)
Market research study	Salaries of market research staff	Unallocated (period cost)	Unallocated (R & D function not allocated)
Production scheduling	Salaries of production scheduling managers	Indirect (direct labor hours)	Indirect (hours of prod. scheduling managers)

Activity	Related Cost	Traditional	Multistage ABC
Purchasing materials and parts to be used in products	Salary of purchasing agents	Indirect (direct labor hours)	Indirect (material cost)
Order processing of customer orders	Salaries of order processing staff	Unallocated	Indirect (assuming this is part of the distribution function) (number of hours)
Preparing cost analyses	Salary of the cost accountant	Unallocated (administrative cost)	Unallocated
Designing a new product	Salaries of design engineers who are fully dedicated to this new product	Unallocated (R&D cost, which is a period cost)	Direct trace
Managing overall operations of the company	Salary of the executive	Unallocated (administrative cost)	Unallocated

4-49 (20-30 min.)

1. Answers can vary depending on the student's assumptions. For example, some company's would consider the order processing activity part of the distribution function in the value chain and thus would include this activity in the new ABC system. Others would consider this a support activity and thus leave it unallocated. Similarly, production scheduling can be considered part of the production function and thus be allocated under both traditional and ABC systems. Also, note that the cost drivers for the resource costs are not the same as those for the activity. For example, the cost driver for the activity "moving partially completed products from processing to assembly area" might be "number of moves," whereas the cost driver for the forklift salaries is labor hours used.

Activity	Related Cost	Traditional	Multistage ABC
Supervising production	Salaries	Indirect (direct labor hours)	Indirect (supervising hours)
Designing a prototype for a new product	Depreciation of computers	Unallocated	Indirect (number of parts)
Setting up for a production run	Depreciation of processing machinery	Indirect (direct labor hours)	Indirect (setup time or number of setups)
Purchasing materials and parts to be used in products	Materials and parts cost	Direct trace	Direct trace
Shipping sold products to customers (distributors)	Fuel used on company's fleet of trucks	Unallocated	Indirect (miles)
Market research study	Salaries of market research staff	Unallocated	Unallocated (R & D function not allocated)

Moving partially completed products from processing to assembly area	Salaries of forklift operators	Indirect (direct labor hours)	Indirect (number of forklift labor hours)
Purchasing materials and parts to be used in products	Travel costs to interview vendors	Unallocated (support activity)	Unallocated (support activity)
Customer inquiry	Telecommunications costs	Unallocated	Indirect (number of minutes)
Preparing cost analyses	Salary of cost accountant	Unallocated (support)	Unallocated (support)
Designing a new product	Salaries of design engineers fully dedicated to new product	Unallocated (design function not allocated)	Direct trace
President delivering a speech to a trade conference	Travel and entertainment costs	Unallocated (support)	Unallocated (support)

<u>4-50</u>   (15-20 min.)   The billing labor resource cost includes the wages of the billing labor team, an allocation of supervisor resource costs, and an allocation of occupancy resource costs. The bill-verifying labor resource cost includes the wages of the verifying labor team and an allocation of occupancy resource costs.

There are two cost-allocation paths from the billing labor team resource to the commercial accounts cost objective:

1. Billing labor → Bill verifying labor source → Bill verification activity → Commercial accounts
2. Billing labor → Billing activity → Commercial accounts

There is one cost-allocation path from the bill-verifying labor resource to commercial accounts cost objective.

Bill-verifying labor → Bill verifying labor source → Bill verification activity → Commercial accounts

<u>4-51</u>   (15-20 min.)   There are seven cost-allocation paths from the managing officer resource to the commercial accounts cost objective. The number of allocation stages for each of these paths is greater than two.

While it is not a requirement of the exercise, an interpretation of each path is given. Reviewing a few of these helps make the exercise more interesting.

Abbreviations:

MO = Managing officer
RSM = Retail sales managers
T = Tellers
ONA = Open new accounts
PDW = Process deposits and withdrawals
POT = Process other transactions
PLA = Process loan applications
BI = Background investigation

COM = Commercial accounts

Cost-Allocation Path	Interpretation
MO → RSM → T → ONA →COM	Managing officer supervises the retail sales managers. The retail sales managers supervise tellers who process new accounts for commercial customers.
MO → RSM → T → PDW → COM	Managing officer supervises the retail sales managers. The retail sales managers supervise tellers who process deposits and withdrawals for commercial customers.
MO → RSM → T → POT → COM	Managing officer supervises the retail sales managers. The retail sales managers supervise tellers who process other transactions for commercial customers.
MO → RSM → T → PLA → COM	Managing officer supervises the retail sales managers. The retail sales managers supervise tellers who process loan applications of commercial customers.
MO → RSM → POT → COM	Managing officer supervises the retail sales managers who process other transactions of commercial customers.
MO → RSM → BI → PLA → COM	Managing officer supervises the retail sales managers who perform background investigations as part of the loan application processing for commercial customers.
MO → BI → PLA → COM	Managing officer reviews the background investigation report as part of the loan application process for commercial customers.

<u>4-52</u> (20-30 min.)

This problem provides an overview of cost accumulation and allocation without getting bogged down in the intricacies of bookkeeping. Some instructors may prefer to assign the problem in conjunction with Chapter 13. In particular, note that the complication of under- and over-applied overhead is avoided in Chapter 4. For a fuller discussion, see Chapter 13.

1.   Amounts are in dollars.

	Machining	Finishing	Total
Direct material	91,000*	39,000	130,000
Direct labor	25,000**	50,000	75,000
Manufacturing overhead	38,000	42,000	80,000
Total	154,000	131,000	285,000

* 70% x $130,000
** 33.333% x $75,000

2.   Amounts are in dollars.

	X-1		
	Direct Material	Direct Labor	Mfg. Overhead
Machining	36,400*	7,500*	11,400*
Finishing	13,000**	20,000**	16,800**
Totals	49,400	27,500	28,200

* 40% x $91,000; 30% x $25,000; 30% x $38,000
** 1/3 x $39,000; 40% x $50,000; 40% x $42,000

	Y-1		
	Direct Material	Direct Labor	Mfg. Overhead
Machining	27,300*	7,500*	11,400*
Finishing	13,000**	20,000**	16,800**
Totals	40,300	27,500	28,200

* 30% x $91,000; 30% x $25,000; 30% x $38,000
** 1/3 x $39,000; 40% x $50,000; $40% x $42,000

	Z-1		
	Direct Material	Direct Labor	Mfg. Overhead
Machining	27,300*	10,000*	15,200*
Finishing	13,000**	10,000**	8,400**
Totals	40,300	20,000	23,600

* 30% x $91,000; 40% x $25,000; 40% x $38,000

** 1/3 x $39,000; 20% x $50,000; 20% x $42,000

Total Costs:

X-1 (49,400 + 27,500 + 28,200) =	$105,100
Y-1 (40,300 + 27,500 + 28,200) =	96,000
Z-1 (40,300 + 20,000 + 23,600) =	83,900
Accounted for	$285,000

4-53   (30-35 min.)

1.

Cost/Activity Center: Cost Drivers	Annual Traceable Cost	Annual Cost Driver Activity	Cost per Driver Unit	Cost Driver Consumption, Part H707	Total Cost, Part H707
Quality: Pieces scrapped	$ 800,000	10,000	$ 80	120	$ 9,600
Production scheduling: Setups	50,000	500	100	4	400
Setup: Setups	600,000	500	1,200	4	4,800
Shipping: Containers shipped	300,000	60,000	5	10	50
Shipping admin.: Shipments	50,000	1,000	50	5	250
Production: Machine hours	1,500,000	10,000	150	15	2,250
Total indirect cost	$3,300,000				$17,350
Direct materials					5,000
Direct labor					1,000
Total Cost of Part H707					$23,350
Cost per unit ($23,350 ÷ 2,000)					$11.675
Selling price					7.500
Gross margin					$ (4.175)
Gross margin percentage					(55.7%)

2.   Assuming that the results of the activity analysis are accurate, product H707 is much more costly than RMP's existing costing system esti-mates. The existing system is under-costing product H707 by $11.675 - $5.00 = $6.675 per unit or $6.675 ÷ $11.675 = 57%! General Motors' proposal should be rejected unless GM is willing to increase the price or RMP can significantly reduce its costs. RMP should be aware, however, that the existing costing system is also *overcosting* some products since all indirect costs are allocated (for example, see problem 4-A3). The activity-based costing system should be used to cost all product lines in order to identify RMP's "winners" as well as "losers."

Benefits of activity-based implementation include:
- More accurate costing of activities, products, customers, and other cost objects
- A solid foundation for activity-based management – using ABC information as a management tool for budgeting, planning, and control purposes

- An effective communication tool since successful ABC implementation should involve all functional areas of the company

Costs of implementing activity-based costing include:
- The cost of a pilot study includes salaries of managers who are dedicated to the study.
- Consultants are often necessary.
- Data collection is extensive since operational and financial data are often not available as required to support the new ABC system.
- It may be necessary to maintain an ABC system separate from the accounting system used for external reporting.

4-54   (60 min. or more)

The purpose of this exercise is to force students to look beyond the textbook. The library has many examples of applications of management accounting that show that topics presented in textbooks are of interest in the "real world".

The expectation in this exercise should not be for a detailed understanding of how a company applied activity-based costing. At this point in the course students should get a general impression of how textbook topics are being applied. Look for some expression of understanding the article, making sure that students are expressing the information in their own words. A brief, intuitive explanation is much better than a detailed description taken nearly verbatim from the article.

4-55   (20-30 min.)

This problem reviews Chapters 2 through 4. It attempts to nail down some terms that often give students trouble. Sharp distinctions should be made among gross profit, contribution margin, manufacturing cost of goods sold and variable manufacturing cost of goods sold. This and the succeeding problem were used originally as exam questions.

a, c, e. Answers (a), (c), and (e) can be computed without knowing either the contribution margin or the break-even point. Probably the easiest way to compute the answers is to prepare an income statement, filling in the known items, and then solving for the unknowns. The following are in thousands of dollars:

Sales		$100
Cost of goods manufactured and sold (i.e., manufacturing cost of goods sold):		
Direct material	$35	
Direct labor	25	
Variable manufacturing overhead	5**	
Fixed manufacturing overhead	15	
Total manufacturing cost of goods sold		80*
Gross profit		20
Selling and administrative expenses:		
Variable	15 ***	
Fixed	10	25
Net loss		$ (5)

*Answer (e) is simply 100 - 20 = 80.
**Answer (c) is 80 - (35 + 25 + 15) = 5.
***Total selling and administrative expenses = 5 + 20 = 25.
Then answer (a) is 25 - 10 = 15.

b.

Sales	$100
Direct materials	(35)
Direct labor	(25)
Variable manufacturing overhead	(5)
Variable selling and administrative	(15)
Contribution margin	$ 20

d. $$\text{Break-even} = \frac{\text{Fixed Mfg. overhead} + \text{Fixed Sell. \& adm.}}{\text{Contribution margin \%}}$$

$$= \frac{\$25,000}{.20} = \$125,000$$

4-56 (30-40 min.)

Probably the easiest way to compute the answers is to prepare an income statement, filling in the known items, and then solving for the unknowns.

a. The answer is $18,000, computed as follows, in thousands of dollars:

Sales		$100
Cost of goods sold:		
Direct material	$24	
Direct labor	28	
Variable manufacturing overhead	5	
Fixed manufacturing overhead	18[b]	
Total cost of goods sold		75[a]
Gross profit		$ 25

[a] $100 - 25 = 75$.
[b] $75 - (24 + 28 + 5) = 18$.

b. The answer is $13,000, computed using the following data in thousands of dollars:

Sales		$100
Variable costs:		
Direct material	$24	
Direct labor	28	
Variable manufacturing overhead	5	
Variable selling and administrative		
expenses	13[b]	
Total variable costs		70[a]
Contribution margin		$30

[a] $100 - 30 = 70$.
[b] $70 - (24 + 28 + 5) = 13$. Note that this can be computed without having to know the gross profit, the break-even point, or the fixed manufacturing overhead computed in part (a).

c.   The answer is $2,000, computed as follows:

Break-even point   = Total fixed costs ÷ Contribution margin percentage

∴ Total fixed costs = Break-even point x Contribution margin percentage
                    = $66,667 x .30
                    = $20,000

Now, Total fixed costs   = Fixed manufacturing overhead + Fixed selling and
                                                       administrative expense

$20,000 = $18,000 + X
      X = $2,000

Therefore, the answer is $2,000. Alternatively, full credit can be given
for an answer equal to $2,000 minus the answer in part (a), if that
happened to be wrong.

An alternate approach to part (c) is:

Let F = Total fixed expenses
Break-even point sales = Variable expenses + Fixed expenses
      $66,667 = .70($66,667) + F
            F = $66,667 - $46,667
              = $20,000

Then the fixed expenses can be analyzed as before.

4-57 (30-35 min.)

Putting fixed and variable costs into an income statement format and computing the missing items provides a framework for this solution.

		In Dollars
Sales		100,000
Variable expenses:		
Direct materials used	21,000	
Direct labor	16,000	
Variable manufacturing overhead	13,000	
Variable selling and administrative expenses	X	
Total variable expenses (100,000 - 40,000)		60,000
Contribution margin		40,000
Fixed expenses:		
Fixed manufacturing overhead	14,000	
Fixed selling and administrative expenses	Y	
Total fixed expenses (40,000 - 22,000)		18,000
Operating income		22,000

1. Since total variable expenses are $60,000, variable selling and administrative expenses must be $10,000:

$$X = 60,000 - (21,000 + 16,000 + 13,000)$$
$$= 10,000$$

2. Since total fixed expenses are $18,000, fixed selling and administrative expenses must be $4,000:

$$Y = 18,000 - 14,000$$
$$= 4,000$$

3. Cost of goods sold is the total production (or manufacturing) cost of the 1,000 sabres:

$$21,000 + 16,000 + 13,000 + 14,000 = 64,000.$$

4. a. ($4,000 + $14,000) ÷ ($40,000 ÷ 1,000) = $18,000 ÷ $40 = 450 units
    b. Let U = units
        $40U - $18,000 = $12,000
                    U = 750 units
    c. Let P = selling price
        Variable costs per unit = $60,000 ÷ 1,000 = $60
        Contribution margin per unit = P - $60
            900(P - $60) - $18,000 = $18,000
          900P - $54,000 - $18,000 = $18,000
                          900P = $90,000
                             P = $100

4-58 (25-30 min.)

a. Resource-consumption rates:

Computer: 32,960 ÷ 412 = 80 lines per document

Telecommunications: 1,236 ÷ 412 = 3 minutes per document

b. The total cost of the order processing department is

$28.1364 per document x 412 documents = $11,592.20

Let ICS = the total cost of the invoicing and collection staff. Then,

ICS = $11,592.20 – ($988.80 + $6,800.00 + $803.40)
     = $3,000.00

c. 412 documents x 0.5 order desk staff hours per document = 206 hours

d. The cost of the three activities is calculated as follows:

Order changes   = 15 change documents x $28.1364 per document
                   = $422.05

Returns processing = 153 return documents x $28.1364 per document
= $4,304.87

Order processing   = 244 order documents x $28.1364 per document
= $6,865.28

e. In November, 19 + 190 + 300 = 509 documents must be processed. Capacities of the invoice and collection and order desk staffs under the new collective bargaining agreement are 120 and 240 hours, respectively. The actual consumption of invoice collection staff time and order desk staff time is:

Invoice Collection Staff
509 documents x 0.25 invoice and collection staff hours per document
= 127.25 hours

Order Desk Staff

509 documents x 0.5 order desk staff hours per document
= 254.5 hours

The company will not be able to meet its order processing needs in November.

f. Whenever a resource is constraining the capacity to meet demand, a company can take the following actions:

1. Reduce demand for the resource. In this case this means either saying "no" to the increased business or deferring business (this may not be feasible).
2. Increase capacity. The company can hire additional staff, outsource part of its order processing function, or permit overtime.
3. Institute process improvements that reduce the consumption of the capacity-constraining resource. The company can investigate ways to reduce the resource consumption rates.

4-59 (50-60 min.)

1.

ACTIVITY	COST PER DRIVER UNIT	RESIDENTIAL ACCOUNTS DRIVER UNITS	COST	COMMERCIAL ACCOUNTS DRIVER UNITS	COST
Account inquiry	$13.806232	20,000	$276,125	5,000	$ 69,031
Billing	0.063516	1,440,000	91,463	1,000,000	63,516
Verification	4.664558			20,000	93,291
Other	0.038555	1,440,000	55,519	1,000,000	38,555
Total cost			$423,107		$264,393
No. of accounts			120,000		20,000
Cost per account			$ 3.5259		$13.21965

2. The service bureau's proposal is to provide billing and inquiry services for AT&T's customers for $4.30 per residential account and $8.00 per commercial account. From a strictly financial perspective, outsourcing commercial accounts would decrease AT&T's costs.

3. A table and bar chart are given on the next page. Both the two-stage and multistage ABC systems provide increased costing accuracy compared to the traditional costing system. Because the multistage system normally involves more detail as well as more involvement by operating managers, it provides the most accurate cost estimates of activities and final cost objectives.

For planning and control purposes, the multistage ABC system is superior. Why? Because it focuses on operational relationships. Many two-stage ABC systems do not model cost behavior. This is a major drawback because planning almost always involves changes in cost object levels. As the level of demand changes, so do variable costs. Thus, assuming all costs are fixed in two-stage systems effectively prohibits their use for planning purposes. Operational control frequently involves process improvement efforts. Such improvements can be easily modeled in multistage systems. Because two-stage systems have limited operational data, their usefulness for control purposes is also limited.

BILLING DEPARTMENT

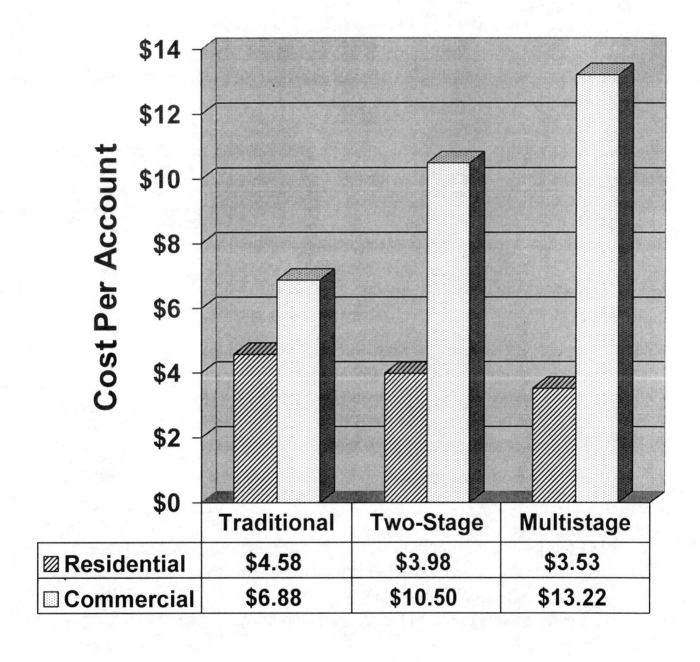

	Traditional	Two-Stage	Multistage
Residential	$4.58	$3.98	$3.53
Commercial	$6.88	$10.50	$13.22

207

4-60 (50-60 min.) Numbers except per unit amounts are in thousands.

This case focuses on activity-based costing in a service organization. It contains both straightforward numerical requirements and more conceptual, discussion-oriented issues. It contrasts a traditional cost accounting system with an ABC system.

1.

a) The indirect cost allocation rate is $2,850 / 5,700 = $.50 per check processed.

b)

	Retail Line	Business Line	Total
# checks processed	1,140	4,560	5,700
Cost / check processed	x$.50	x$.50	x$.50
Total cost	$ 570	$2,280	$2,850

c) Retail line = $570/$2,850 = 20%
   Business line = $2,280/$2,850 = 80%

d) Retail = $570/150 = $3.80
   Business = $2,280/50 = $45.60

e)

	Retail	Business
Revenue per account	$10.00	$40.00
Cost per account	3.80	45.60
Profit (loss) per account	$ 6.20	$(5.60)

f) The original cost system suggests that retail customers are profitable, but business customers are not. This suggests emphasizing retail customers. The bank would also try to make business customers more profitable, perhaps by increasing fees for services, reducing interest paid on business accounts, or requiring businesses to hold higher account balances.

2. Broken machines simply stop running. In contrast, "broken" or outdated cost systems continue producing potentially misleading costs. Consequently, managers need to recognize clues that the cost system needs refinement. Signs that Belltown's original cost system is broken include:

- Profits are declining even though the bank is serving more customers
- The CEO does not understand the results
- The customer mix is changing to more small retail customers and fewer large business customers, and these two different types of customers are likely to make different use of the bank's resources
- The cost system is an old (1988) single-allocation-base system
- The cost system has not changed since the new customer service call center was added
- The manager (Rose Martinez) does not trust the accounting system's numbers

3. Belltown has three activities, each with the following expected costs:
    Check payments: $440 + $700 = $1,140
    Teller withdrawals and deposits: $1,200
    Customer service call center: $450 + $60 = $510

The cost drivers and the estimated total quantity of each cost driver are:

Activity	Cost Driver	Units of Cost Driver
Check payments	Checks processed	5,700
Teller withdrawals and deposits	Teller transactions	400
Customer service call center	Customer calls to center	100

a. The indirect cost allocation rate for each activity is:
    Check payments:
        ($440 + $700)/5,700 = $.20 per check processed
    Teller withdrawals and deposits:
        $1,200/400 = $3 per teller transaction
    Customer call center:
        ($450 + $60)/100 = $5.10 per customer call

b. The quantity of cost driver activity in each customer line is (in thousands):

	Retail Line	Business Line	Total
Checks processed	1,140	4,560	5,700
Teller transactions	320	80	400
Customer calls to call center	95	5	100

Belltown must allocate costs from each cost pool to each customer line:

Activity	Total Indirect Cost Assigned To Retail Customer Line	Total Indirect Cost Assigned To Business Customer Line
Check payments:		
$.20 x (1,140; 4,560)	$ 228.00	$ 912.00
Teller withdrawals and deposits:		
$3 x (320; 80)	960.00	240.00
Customer call center:		
$5.10 x (95; 5)	484.50	25.50
Total indirect costs	$1,672.50	$1,177.50

You might note that this solution assumes that all calls to the call center are equally costly, as are all teller transactions. That is, business customers do not tend to take more or less time per call or per teller transaction than do retail customers.

c. The proportions of each activity's resources used by each customer line are:

	Retail	Business	Total
Check payments	1,140 (20%)	4,560 (80%)	5,700 (100%)
Teller withdrawals and deposits	320 (80%)	80 (20%)	400 (100%)
Customer call center	95 (95%)	5 (5%)	100 (100%)

d. The ABC indirect costs per retail and business customer are:
   Retail: $1,672.50/150 = $11.15
   Business: $1,177.5/50 = $23.55

e. The original cost system allocates all indirect costs based on the number of checks processed. Because retail customers write 20% of the checks, the original system allocated 20% of the indirect costs to retail customers and 80% of the indirect costs were allocated to business customers.

The ABC analysis shows that retail customers used much more than 20% of the other two activities: teller withdrawals and deposits and customer service call center. Retail customers made 80% of the teller transactions and 95% of the calls to the customer service center. Thus, the new ABC system allocates to retail customers 80% of the teller transaction costs and 95% of the customer service call center costs. Thus, the end result is that ABC allocates 59% (rather than 20%) of the indirect costs to retail customers and 41% (rather than 80%) of the indirect costs to business customers.

f. Using the new ABC data, the average profit per account for retail and business customers is:

	Retail	Business
Revenue per account	$10.00	$40.00
ABC cost per account	11.15	23.55
ABC profit (loss) per account	$(1.15)	$16.45
Original profit (loss) per account	$6.20	$(5.60)

The ABC system suggests that business customers are profitable, but retail customers are not – exactly opposite the conclusion based on the original cost data. This example illustrates how ABC can significantly affect management's strategy. The ABC data suggest that managers should emphasize business customers. The incentive system should provide more reward (e.g. larger bonuses) for adding business customers than for adding retail customers. In addition, the bank should try to make retail customers more profitable, perhaps by increasing fees for services, reducing interest paid on retail accounts, or requiring retail customers to maintain higher account balances.

4. a) The ABC data suggest that the plan to simply increase the number of checking account customers was not wise. Assuming it is easier to attract a given number of retail customers than business customers, it is not surprising that the incentive plan resulted in an influx of retail customers. Unfortunately, the ABC data suggest that the retail customers are not profitable. Given the existing revenue and cost structure, Belltown National Bank may want to provide a bonus based on attracting and retaining new business customers only. The bank should not encourage more retail customers until it changes the revenue structure (for example, by increasing the required minimum balance for retail checking accounts) or the cost structure (for example, by cutting back service at the customer service call center).

b) Two main benefits of ABC are:
   1) More accurate cost information
      a. Can help Belltown better price its services.
      b. Can help Belltown assess the profitability of different customers and/or different services. Such analyses can affect services offered and marketing strategy.
   2) Cost control
      a. Reduce consumption of costly cost drivers. For example, Belltown may want to encourage on-line banking to reduce the number of teller transactions.
      b. Reduce the indirect cost per unit of the cost driver. For example, train the customer service representatives to handle more calls per hour. This can reduce the cost per call if the bank can handle the call load with fewer customer service representatives.

c) The relative advantage of ABC, that is, when its benefits exceed its cost, is greatest:

1) When a company sells its products in a highly competitive industry. Then, accurate cost information is essential for setting competitive prices that still allow the company to earn a profit. Competitors will capitalize on a company's mis-pricing. In addition, ABC can pinpoint opportunities for cost savings, which increase the company' profit or are passed on to customers in lower sales prices.

2) When a company has high indirect costs. If indirect costs are low, it doesn't matter much how they are allocated.

3) When different customers/products/services use different amounts of the company's various resources.

4) When the company has sufficient information technology and accounting expertise to implement the system and to record cost driver data.

Belltown National Bank is in a highly competitive environment. Most of its costs are indirect. The retail and business customer lines use different amounts of the 3 resources, check processing, teller transactions, and customer service center calls. Given the magnitude of the data processing requirements, banks typically have advanced information technology and accounting expertise. All these factors suggest that the benefits of ABC are likely to outweigh the costs.

d) Non-accounting managers need to understand ABC because:

1) Non-accounting managers often serve on ABC teams. As in the case, ABC teams typically include managers familiar with operations – in addition to the accountants. ABC is not just an accounting exercise, and even managers who are not in the financial function may be involved in developing or updating an ABC system.

2) Managers need to understand ABC data to use it in decisions such as pricing, product and customer profitability analysis, cost control, etc.

<u>4-61</u> (30 min.)

1. and 2. The following are the most likely activities and resources that student will identify. There may be disagreements on the cost behavior – those listed below are probably most likely, but different behavior can be supported under different assumptions. Likewise, students might suggest other, equally reasonable, cost drivers, depending on their assumptions.

Activities	Cost Behavior	Cost Drivers
Setups		No. of setups
Molding process		Machine hours
Resources		
Maintenance mechanics	Fixed	Mechanic hours
Supervisors	Fixed	No. of people
Molding machine operators	Fixed	Operator hours
Machine supplies	Variable	Machine hours
Energy	Variable	Kilowatt hours
Building	Fixed	Square footage
Molding machines	Fixed	Machine hours

4-62 (2-3 hours)

1.

Loan applications per retail customer	0.1
Loan applications per commercial customer	0.25
Teller labor hours per new account	1.5
Teller labor hours to process a deposit or withdrawal	0.05
Teller labor hours to process other transactions	0.15
Teller labor hours to process a loan application	0.4
Computer transactions to process a loan application	38
Retail sales manager time (hours) to perform a background investigation	1.75
Managing officer time (hours) to perform a background investigation	0.5
Computer transactions to perform a background investigation	45
Telecommunication time (minutes) to perform a background investigation	35
Managing officer labor hours spent supervising retail sales managers	0.15
Cost of computer services per transaction	0.05

2.

ACTIVITY	TRACEABLE COST	ANNUAL NUMBER OF DRIVER UNITS	COST PER DRIVER UNIT
Process new accounts	$22,824	540	$42.27
Process deposits and withdrawals	$260,896	163,000	$1.60
Process other transactions	$332,908	49,000	$6.79
Process loan applications	$61,371	350	$175.35

3.

	COST PER DRIVER UNIT	RETAIL CUSTOMERS		COMMERCIAL CUSTOMERS	
		NUMBER OF DRIVER UNITS	COST	NUMBER OF DRIVER UNITS	COST
Process new accounts	$42.27	500	$21,135	40	$1,691
Process deposits and withdrawals	$1.60	75,000	$120,000	88,000	$140,800
Process other transactions	$6.79	25,000	$169,750	24,000	$162,960
Process loan applications	$175.35	250	$43,838	100	$17,535
Total cost			$354,723		$322,986
Number of accounts			2,500		400
Cost per account			$141.89		$807.47

4. Exhibits 4-62A and 4-62B at the end of the solution show the operational and financial measures of the Colorado City branch as a percent of the benchmarks for the branches in the Better Bank system that deployed MSABC systems. Each operational and financial measure is greater than the benchmark, indicating that process improvements are needed throughout operations at the Colorado City branch.

From the Exhibit 4-62A, processing loan applications and the background investigation should be carefully investigated to determine why their productivity measures are significantly greater than the benchmark.

From Exhibit 4-62B, special attention should be given to the processing of deposits and withdrawals, and processing loan applications. Since the total cost of processing deposits and withdrawals is very large ($260,800), priority should be given to process improvements in this activity.

5. The labor analysis is shown in Exhibit 4-62C at the end of the solution.

Total estimated cost savings from process improvement program:

RESOURCE	SAVINGS
Teller labor	$75,000
Supervision of tellers	0
Computers	14,980
Telecommunications	919
Total Cost Savings	$90,899

Exhibit 4-62A
Billing Department Operating Measures as a Percent of Benchmark

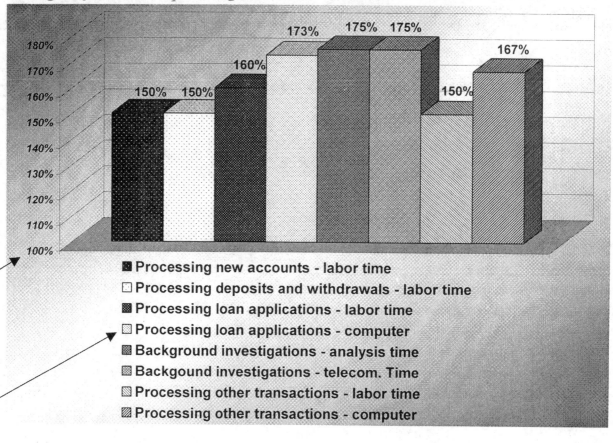

38 transactions ÷ 22 transactions = 1.7273 or 173% of the benchmark

The benchmark for each productivity measure is set to 100%. Divide each Colorado city measure by the benchmark amount.

Exhibit 4-62B
Billing Department Financial Measures as a Percent of Benchmark

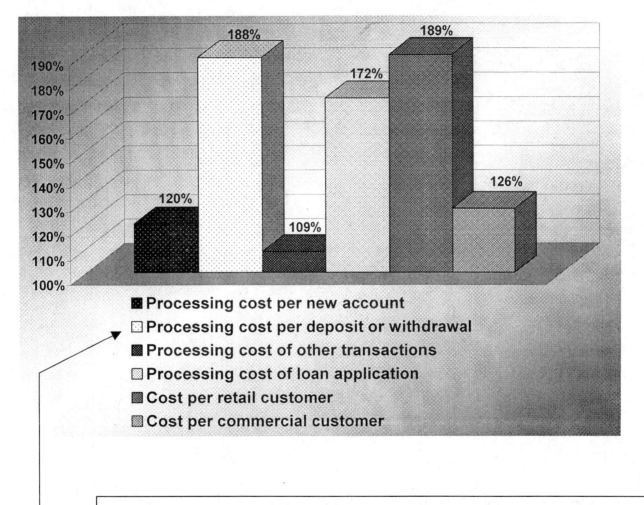

$$1.601 \div 0.85 = 1.88 \text{ or } 188\% \text{ of the benchmark}$$

Exhibit 4-62C
Teller Labor Analysis

	OPEN NEW ACCOUNTS	PROCESS DEPOSITS AND WITHDRAWALS	PROCESS OTHER TRANSACTIONS	PROCESS LOAN APPLICATIONS	TOTAL
Current resource consumption (hours): Current rate x Current driver units	1.5 x 540 = 810.0	.050000 x 163,000 = 8,150.0	.15 x 49,000 = 7,350.0	.40 x 350 = 140.0	
Benchmark resource consumption (hours): Benchmark rate x Current driver units	1.0 x 540 = 540.0	.033333 x 163,000 = 5,432.8	.10 x 49,000 = 4,900.0	.25 x 350 = 87.5	
Teller labor time savings (hours)	270.0	2,717.2	2,450.0	52.5	5,489.7
Teller labor cost savings					$75,000*

* Labor cost per person = $350,000 ÷ 14 = $25,000.
  Total labor cost savings = full-time equivalent positions saved x $25,000
  Full-time positions saved = 5,489.7 ÷ 1,500 = 3.7 positions
Total labor cost savings = 3 x $25,000 = $75,000.

4-63 (60 min. or more)

1. Before implementing the process modeling approach to ABC, AT&T allocated some billing costs on the basis of *number of invoices produced.*

2. The business billing center was selected for the pilot study at AT&T. The overall goals of the pilot study from the managers' perspective included gaining an understanding of the center's operations and identifying value-adding activities.

3. Cost objects were the product and service types. Activities included printing, sorting, dispatching, validating data, correcting errors, and monitoring the billing process. Resources included labor pools, computers, facilities, and paper. Cost drivers included square feet, pages printed, printer hours, and labor hours.

4. The "billing" activity (cost driver is "pages printed") consumes billing labor time (cost driver is "labor hours") at some rate. If it takes 1 labor hour for every 400 pages printed, the rate, or consumption characteristic is, $1 \div 400 = 0.0025$ labor hours per page.

5. AT&T considered the flowchart "critical" because it "revealed how the organization conducted business. Managers were able to see how cost flows are a function of operations (activities) and how they (activities) consume costly resources." Recall that this was one of the overall goals for the pilot study.

6. From Exhibit 4-18, there were 20,000 inquiries (driver units) for the inquiry activity and each inquiry costs $13.806232 for a total of $276,124.64. A similar calculation would be made for the billing and other activities. The sum of these three activity costs is the total cost to support residential customers.

7. Using data from Exhibit 4-18, the percent of billing department costs associated with inquiry investigation (both account inquiry and correspondence) is $345,155.81 ÷ $687,500 = 50.2%.

8. Account inquiry associates were given access to additional operating systems allowing end-to-end responsibility for inquiry investigation. Training was also given to associates in the use of these systems. The elimination of referrals to other working groups resulted in reductions in investigation time, improved service, and cost reductions. This is a good example of ABM – how ABC is used to improve operations.

4-64 (50-60 min.) For the solution, see the Prentice Hall Web site, www.prenhall.com/

4-65 (60 min. or more)

Answers will vary based on the industry and particular company chosen.

<u>4-66</u>   (25 – 30 min.)

NOTE TO INSTRUCTOR. This solution is based on the web site as it was in early 2004. Be sure to examine the current web site before assigning this problem, as the information there may have changed.

1. The site suggests that you should "Surprise them with a Bear-Gram gift!" The current offering changes as the holidays and seasons change, so the focus item will vary.

2. A Bear-Gram is a unique idea that is the creative alternative to flowers and guaranteed to last forever. The Bear-Gram is a hand-crafted Teddy Bear that is guaranteed for life. The Classic Teddy Bears are made in Vermont, and no two are alike. Customers have a choice of over 100 different outfits and accessories to personalize their Teddy Bear for every interest or special occasion. The Bear-Gram includes a delicious candy treat and a personalized message inside a gift card. It includes a fun, colorful gift box that has a game inside and an air hole to ensure your Teddy Bear gets lots of air on its journey.

3. Each Vermont Teddy Bear is individually made. No two bears are alike. Teddy bears can be made in four different colors, vanilla, buttercream, honey, and dark chocolate. There are also accessories to go with the bear. Any of the accessories may be ordered to be shipped with the bear.

4. A classic Vermont Teddy Bear is born online. Activities include designing new teddy bears, fur cutting, sewing, dressing, order processing, and shipping. The fur cutting activity requires labor, equipment (hydraulic press), power, and occupancy. Labor, equipment, and occupancy are probably fixed-cost resources. Power is a variable-cost resource. A cost driver for fur cutting might be either labor hours or machine hours. A cost driver for the order processing activity could be either number of orders or line items ordered.

5. Any company that has complexity in one or more function of its value chain is a good candidate for ABC. In addition, any company can benefit

from the increased understanding of its business that results from implementing an ABC system. As the Vermont Teddy Bear Factory grows from a small to a medium-sized firm, it will undoubtedly realize increased complexity across its value chain. Having a good cost management system in place, including an ABC system, will be of significant value.

6. The balance sheet shows one account labeled "Inventory." In footnote number 2 we find that the inventory account has three separate accounts – raw material, work-in-process, and finished goods. For the 2003 year the inventories were: raw materials – $483,547, work-in-process – $459,565, and finished goods – $3,835,327. All three inventories increased from the previous year.

7. Based only on the financial statements as presented, one cannot tell if the firm is a manufacturer or a merchandiser. The income statement shows that the firm had sales and cost of goods sold. We need to look in the footnotes for details such as the inventory accounts.

CHAPTER 5
COVERAGE OF LEARNING OBJECTIVES

LEARNING OBJECTIVE	FUNDA-MENTAL ASSIGN-MENT MATERIAL	CRITICAL THINKING EXERCISES AND EXERCISES	PROBLEMS	CASES, EXCEL, COLLAB. & INTERNET EXERCISES
LO1: Discriminate between relevant and irrelevant information for making decisions.	A1,B1	29,31	53	
LO2: Apply the decision process to make business decisions.		30,31	53	
LO3: Decide to accept or reject a special order using the contribution margin technique.	A1,B1	32	46,47,52,53,54	62
LO4: Choose whether to add or delete a product line using relevant information.	B3	37	52,56	
LO5: Compute a measure of product profitability when product is constrained by a scarce resource.	A2,B2	36	50,53,58	63
LO6: Identify the factors that influence pricing decisions in practice.		26,27,39,40	45,48,49,54	64
LO7: Compute a target sales price by various approaches, and compare the advantages and disadvantages of these approaches.	A3	27,40,41,42	47,48,53	
LO8: Use target costing to decide whether to add a new product.	A4,B4	28,43,44	59,60,61	

CHAPTER 5
Relevant Information and Decision Making: Marketing Decisions

5-A1 (25-30 min.)

1. A contribution format, which is similar to Exhibit 5-3, clarifies the analysis.

	Without Special Order	Effect of Special Order		With Special Order
Units	2,000,000	150,000		2,150,000
		Total	Per Unit	
Sales	$10,000,000	$660,000	$4.40[1]	$10,660,000
Less variable expenses:				
Manufacturing	$ 3,600,000	$300,000	$2.00[2]	$ 3,900,000
Selling & administrative	800,000	37,500	.25[3]	837,500
Total variable expenses	$ 4,400,000	$337,500	$2.25	$ 4,737,500
Contribution margin	$ 5,600,000	$322,500	$2.15	$ 5,922,500
Less fixed expenses:				
Manufacturing	$ 2,900,000	0	0.00	$ 2,900,000
Selling & administrative	2,000,000	0	0.00	2,000,000
Total fixed expenses	$ 4,900,000	0	0.00	$ 4,900,000
Operating income	$ 700,000	$322,500	$2.15	$ 1,022,500

[1] $660,000 ÷ 150,000 = $4.40

[2] Regular unit cost = $3,600,000 ÷ 2,000,000 = $1.80

Logo   .20

Variable manufacturing costs $2.00

[3] Regular unit cost = $800,000 ÷ 2,000,000 = $ .40

Less sales commissions not paid (3% of $5)   (.15)

Regular unit cost, excluding sales commission $ .25

2. Operating income from selling 7.5% more units would increase by $322,500 ÷ $700,000 = 46.1%. Note also that the average selling price on regular business was $5.00. The full cost, including selling and administrative expenses, was $4.65. The $4.65, plus the 20¢ per logo, less savings in commissions of 15¢ came to $4.70. The president apparently wanted $4.70 + .08($4.70) = $4.70 + .376 = $5.076 per pen.

Most students will probably criticize the president for being too stubborn. The cost to the company was the forgoing of $322,500 of income in order to protect the company's image and general market position. Whether $322,500 was a wise investment in the future is a judgment that managers are paid for rendering.

5-A2 (10 min.)

1. Contribution margins:
    Plain = $66 - $50 = $16
    Professional = $100 - $70 = $30

    Contribution margin ratios:
    Plain = $16 ÷ $66 = 24%
    Professional = $30 ÷ $100 = 30%

2.

		Plain	Professional
a.	Units per hour	2	1
b.	Contribution margin per unit	$16	$30
	Contribution margin per hour	$32	$30
	Total contribution for 20,000 hours	$640,000	$600,000

3. For a given capacity, the criterion for maximizing profits is to obtain the greatest possible contribution to profit for each unit of the limiting or scarce factor. Moreover, fixed costs are irrelevant unless their total is affected by the choice of products.

<u>5-A3</u>   (15-20 min.)

The purpose of this problem is to underscore the idea that any of a number of general formulas might be used that, properly employed, would achieve the *same* target selling prices. Desired sales = $7,500,000 + $1,500,000 = $9,000,000.

The target markup percentage would be:

1.   100% of direct materials and direct labor costs of $4,500,000.

   Computation is: $\dfrac{\$9,000,000 - \$4,500,000}{\$4,500,000} = 100\%$

2.   50% of the full cost of jobs of $6,000,000.

   Computation is: $\dfrac{\$9,000,000 - \$6,000,000}{\$6,000,000} = 50\%$

3. $\dfrac{\$9,000,000 - (\$3,500,000 + \$1,000,000 + \$900,000)}{\$5,400,000} = 66.67\%$

4. $\dfrac{\$9,000,000 - \$7,500,000}{\$7,500,000} = 20\%$

5.

$$\frac{\$9,000,000 - (\$3,500,000 + \$1,000,000 + \$900,000 + \$300,000)}{\$5,700,000}$$

$$= \frac{\$3,300,000}{\$5,700,000} = 57.9\%$$

If the contractor is unable to maintain these profit percentages consistently, the desired operating income of $1,500,000 cannot be obtained.

<u>5-A4</u> (15-20 minutes)

1. Revenue ($360 x 70,000) $25,200,000
    Total cost over product life   16,600,000
    Estimated contribution to profit $ 8,600,000
    Desired (target) contribution to profit
        40% x $25,200,000 $10,080,000
    Deficiency in profit $ 1,480,000

The product should not be released to production.

2. Previous total estimated cost $16,600,000
    Cost savings from suppliers
        .20 x .70 x $8,000,000   1,120,000
    Revised total estimated cost $15,480,000
    Revised total contribution to profit:
        $25,200,000 - $15,480,000 $ 9,720,000
    Desired (target) contribution to profit $10,080,000
    Deficiency in profit $ 360,000

The product should not be released to production.

3. Previous revised total estimated cost from
        requirement 2. $15,480,000
    Process improvement savings:
        .25 x .30 x $8,000,000 $600,000
    Less cost of new technology   220,000   380,000
    Revised total estimated cost   15,100,000
    Revised total contribution to profit:
        $25,200,000 - $15,100,000 $10,100,000
    Desired (target) contribution to profit $10,080,000
    Excess contribution to profit $ 20,000

The product should be released to production.

5-B1 (30-40 min.)

1.

DANUBE COMPANY
Income Statement
For the Year Ended December 31, 20X0

		Total	Per Unit
Sales		$40,000,000	$20.00
Less variable expenses:			
Manufacturing	$19,000,000		
Selling & administrative	9,000,000	28,000,000	14.00
Contribution margin		$12,000,000	$ 6.00
Less fixed expenses:			
Manufacturing	$ 5,000,000		
Selling & administrative	6,000,000	11,000,000	5.50
Operating income		$ 1,000,000	$ 0.50

2. Additional details are either in the statement of the problem or in the solution to requirement 1:

	Total	Per Unit
Full manufacturing cost	$24,000,000	$12.00
Variable cost:		
Manufacturing	$19,000,000	$ 9.50
Selling and administrative	9,000,000	4.50
Total variable cost	$28,000,000	$14.00
Full cost = fully allocated cost*		
Full manufacturing cost	$24,000,000	$12.00
Selling and administrative expenses	15,000,000	7.50
Full cost	$39,000,000	$19.50
Gross margin ($40,000,000 - $24,000,000)	$16,000,000	$ 8.00
Contrib. margin ($40,000,000 - $28,000,000)	$12,000,000	$ 6.00

* Students should be alerted to the loose use of these words. Their meaning may not be exactly the same from company to company. Thus, "fully allocated cost" in some companies may be used to refer to manufacturing costs only.

3. Ricardo's analysis is incorrect. He was on the right track, but he did not distinguish sufficiently between variable and fixed costs. For example, when multiplying the additional quantity ordered by the $12 full manufacturing cost, he failed to recognize that $2.50 of the $12 full manufacturing cost was a "unitized" fixed cost allocation. The first fallacy is in regarding the total fixed cost as though it fluctuated like a variable cost. *A unit fixed cost can be misleading if it is used as a basis for predicting how total costs will behave.*

A second false assumption is that no selling and administrative expenses will be affected except commissions. Shipping expenses and advertising allowances will be affected also – unless arrangements with Costco on these items differ from the regular arrangements.

The following summary, which is similar to Exhibit 5-3, is a correct analysis. The middle columns are all that are really necessary.

	Without Special Order 2,000,000	Effect of Special Order 100,000		With Special Order 2,100,000
Units				
		Total	Per Unit	
Sales	$40,000,000	$1,700,000	$17.00	$41,700,000
Less variable expenses:				
Manufacturing	$19,000,000	$ 950,000	$ 9.50	$19,950,000
Selling and administrative	9,000,000	330,000	3.30*	9,330,000
Total variable expenses	$28,000,000	$1,280,000	$12.80	$29,280,000
Contribution margin	$12,000,000	$ 420,000	$ 4.20	$12,420,000
Less fixed expenses:				
Manufacturing	$ 5,000,000	0	0.00	$ 5,000,000
Selling and administrative	6,000,000	20,000	0.20	6,020,000
Total fixed expenses	$11,000,000	20,000	0.20	$11,020,000
Operating income	$ 1,000,000	$ 400,000	$ 4.00	$ 1,400,000

* Regular variable selling and administrative expenses,

$9,000,000 ÷ 2,000,000 =	$ 4.50
Less: Average sales commission at 6% of $20 =	(1.20)
Regular variable sell. and admin. expenses, less commission	$ 3.30
Fixed selling and administrative expenses, special	
commission, $20,000 ÷ 100,000	.20

231

Some students may wish to enter the $20,000 as an extra variable cost, making the unit variable selling and administrative cost $3.50 and thus adding no fixed cost. The final result would be the same; in any event, the cost is relevant because it would not exist without the special order.

Some instructors may wish to point out that a 5% increase in volume would cause a 40% increase in operating income, which seems like a high investment by Danube to maintain a rigid pricing policy.

4.   Ricardo is incorrect. Operating income would have declined from $1,000,000 to $850,000, a decline of $150,000. Ricardo's faulty analysis follows:

Old fixed manufacturing cost per unit,	
$5,000,000 ÷ 2,000,000 =	$2.50
New fixed manufacturing cost per unit,	
$5,000,000 ÷ 2,500,000 =	2.00
"Savings"	$ .50
Loss on variable manufacturing costs per unit,	
$9.20 - $9.50	(.30)
Net savings per unit in manufacturing costs	$ .20

The analytical pitfalls of unit-cost analysis can be avoided by using the contribution approach and concentrating on the totals:

	Without Special Order	Effect of Special Order	With Special Order
Sales	$40,000,000	$4,600,000[a]	$44,600,000
Variable manufacturing costs	$19,000,000	$4,750,000[b]	$23,750,000
Other variable costs	9,000,000	0	9,000,000
Total variable costs	$28,000,000	$4,750,000	$32,750,000
Contribution margin	$12,000,000	$ (150,000)[c]	$11,850,000

[a] 500,000 x $9.20 selling price of special order

[b] 500,000 x $9.50 variable manufacturing cost per unit of special order

[c] 500,000 x $.30 negative contribution margin per unit of special order

No matter how fixed manufacturing costs are unitized, or spread over the units produced, their total of $5,000,000 remains unchanged by the special order.

5-B2 (15 min.)

1. If fixed manufacturing cost is applied to product at $1.00 per machine hour, it takes $.80 ÷ $1.00, or 4/5 of an hour to produce one unit of XY-7. Similarly, it takes $.20 ÷ $1.00 or 1/5 of an hour to produce BD-4.

2. If there are 100,000 hours of capacity:

   XY-7: 100,000 hours ÷ 4/5 = 125,000 units.
   BD-4: 100,000 hours ÷ 1/5 = 500,000 units.

   Total contribution margins show that BD-4 should be produced, generating an increase of $250,000 in the contribution margin.

	Per Unit	Units	Total
XY-7	$6.00 - ($3.00 + $2.00) = $1.00	125,000	$125,000
BD-4	$4.00 - ($1.50 + $2.00) = $ .50	500,000	$250,000

<u>5-B3</u> (15-20 min.)

All amounts are in thousands of British pounds.

The major lesson is that a product that shows an operating loss based on fully allocated costs may nevertheless be worth keeping. Why? Because it may produce a sufficiently high contribution to profit so that the firm would be better off with it than any other alternative.

The emphasis should be on totals:

	Existing Operations	Replace Magic Department With	
		General Merchandise	Electronic Products
Sales	6,000	-600 + 300 = 5,700	-600 + 200 = 5,600
Variable expenses	4,090	-390 + 210^a = 3,910	-390 + 100^b = 3,800
Contribution margin	1,910	-210 + 90 = 1,790	-210 + 100 = 1,800
Fixed expenses	1,110	-100 + 0 = 1,010	-100 + 25 = 1,035
Operating income	800	-110 + 90 = 780	-110 + 75 = 765

^{a}(100% - 30%) x 300
^{b}(100% - 50%) x 200

The facts as stated indicate that the magic department should not be closed. First, the total operating income would drop. Second, fewer customers would come to the store, so sales in other departments may be affected adversely.

<u>5-B4</u>   (10-15 min.)

1.   Cost-plus pricing is adding a specified markup to cost to cover those components of the value chain not included in the cost plus a desired profit. In this case the markup is 35% of production cost.

Price charged for piston pin = 1.35 x $50.00 = $67.50. If the estimated selling price is only $46 and this price cannot be influenced by Caterpillar, a manager would be unlikely to favor releasing this product for production.

2.   Target costing assumes the market price cannot be influenced by companies except by changing the value of the product to consumers. The price charged would then be the $46 estimated by market research.

The highest acceptable manufactured cost or target cost, TC, is

	Dollars
Target Price	$ 46.00
Target Cost	TC
Target Gross Margin	$.35TC

$$46 - TC = .35TC$$
$$1.35TC = 46$$
$$TC = 46 \div 1.35 = \$34.07$$

3.   The required cost reduction over the product's life is

Existing manufacturing cost	$50.00
Target manufacturing cost	34.07
Required cost reduction	$15.93

Steps that Caterpillar managers can take to meet the required cost reduction include value engineering during the design phase, Kaizen costing during the production phase, and activity-based management throughout the product's life.

5-1   Precision is a measure of the accuracy of certain data. It is a quantifiable term. Relevance is an indication of the pertinence of certain facts for the problem at hand. Ideally, data should be both precise and relevant.

5-2   Decisions may have both quantitative and qualitative aspects corresponding to the nature of the facts being considered before deciding. Quantitative implications of alternative choices can be expressed in monetary or numerical terms, such as variable costs, initial investment, etc. Other relevant features may not be quantifiable, such as the quality of life in a choice between locating in Chicago or New York. The advantage of quantitative information is that it is more objective and often easier to compare alternatives than with qualitative judgments.

5-3   The accountant's role in decision-making is primarily that of a technical expert on relevant information analysis, especially relevant costs. The accountant is usually an information provider, not the decision maker.

5-4   No. Only future costs that are different under different alternatives are relevant to a decision.

5-5   Past data are unchangeable regardless of present or future action and thus would not differ under different alternatives.

5-6   Past costs may be bases for formulating predictions. However, past costs are not inputs to the decision model itself because past costs cannot be changed by the decision.

5-7   The commonalty of approach is the focus on the differences between expected outcomes of different available alternatives.

5-8   The lesson here is important. No matter how fixed costs are spread for *unit* product costing purposes, the *total* fixed costs will be unchanged (even though fixed costs *per unit* may change).

5-9 Yes. The costs that make a difference when a product or department is being deleted are the avoidable costs.

5-10 No. Avoidable costs are all costs (both variable and fixed) that will not continue if an ongoing operation is changed or deleted.

5-11 Four examples of scarce factors are: (a) labor hours, (b) money (investment capital), (c) supervisory hours, and (d) computer hours.

5-12 Customers are one of the factors influencing pricing decisions because they can buy or do without the product, they can make the product themselves, or they can usually purchase a similar product from another supplier.

5-13 Target cost per unit is the average total unit cost over the product's life cycle that will yield the desired profit margin.

5-14 Value engineering is a cost-reduction technique, used primarily during the design function in the value chain, that uses information about all value chain functions to satisfy customer needs while reducing costs.

5-15 Kaizen costing is the Japanese term for continuous improvement during manufacturing.

5-16 In target costing, managers start with a market price. Then they try to design a product with costs low enough to be profitable at that price. Thus, prices essentially determine costs.

5-17 Customer demands and requirements are important in the product development process. Many companies seek customer input on the design of product features. Companies purchase many of the materials used in products. They have to work with suppliers to get the lowest cost for these materials.

5-18   Not necessarily. There are other important factors that management must consider before discontinuing a product. The product may be necessary to round out a product line. The product may be the company's attempt to break into a new market area or new product class.

5-19   The variable costs of a job can be misused as a guide to pricing. However, the adjusted markup percentages based on variable costs can have the same price result as those based on total costs, plus they have the advantage of indicating the minimum price at which any sale may be considered profitable even in the short run.

5-20   Three examples of pricing decisions are (1) pricing new products, (2) pricing products sold under private labels, and (3) responding to new prices of a competitor's products.

5-21   Three popular markup formulas are (1) as a percentage of variable manufacturing costs, (2) as a percentage of total variable costs, and (3) as a percentage of full costs.

5-22   Two long-run effects that inhibit price cutting are (a) the effects on longer-run price structures and (b) the effects on longer-run relations with customers.

5-23   Full costs are more popular than variable costs for pricing because price stability is encouraged and in the long run all costs must be recovered to stay in business.

5-24   Executives usually use full costs for setting "normal" prices and the contribution approach for special, non-recurring orders.

5-25   No. There is a confusion between total fixed costs and unit fixed costs. Increasing sales volume will decrease unit fixed costs, but not total fixed costs. This assumes that the volume increase results in operating levels that are still within the relevant range.

5-26 Marginal cost is the additional cost resulting from producing and selling one additional unit. It changes as production volume changes, often decreasing up to a point and then increasing. Variable cost is the accountant's approximation to marginal cost. It remains constant over the relevant range of volume. Because the difference between these two costs often is not material (within the relevant range), in such cases we can use the variable-cost estimate of marginal cost for decision-making purposes.

5-27 Pricing decisions must be made within legal constraints. These laws help protect companies from predatory and discriminatory pricing. Predatory pricing involves setting prices so low that they drive competitors out of the market. Discriminatory pricing is charging different prices to different customers for the same product or service.

5-28 Managers are directly involved in the research and development and the design functions. During the initial product research phase, managers often are involved in surveys, focus groups (with major airlines), and other market research activities to explore the potential for a new product. During process and product design, managers help with such tasks as negotiations with suppliers and cost analyses. Production managers provide input regarding cost reduction ideas. Marketing managers provide input regarding customer needs (a super large plane with > 500 seats versus more medium-sized planes that can serve more markets). Distribution managers provide input regarding the costs of various channels of distribution. Finally, managers involved with customer relations provide input regarding the likely cost-to-serve profile for expected customers for a new product.

5-29 (5 min.)

All the data given are historical costs. Most students will identify the $6 and $7 prices as relevant. They will also declare that the $2 price of popcorn is irrelevant. Press them to see that the relevant admission prices are expected *future* costs that will differ between the alternatives. The past prices are being used as a basis for *predicting* the future prices.

Similarly, the *past* prices of popcorn were not different. Hence, they are regarded as irrelevant under the assumption that the *future* prices will not differ.

5-30 (20 min.) Some students may forget to apply the 10% wage rate increase to both alternatives.

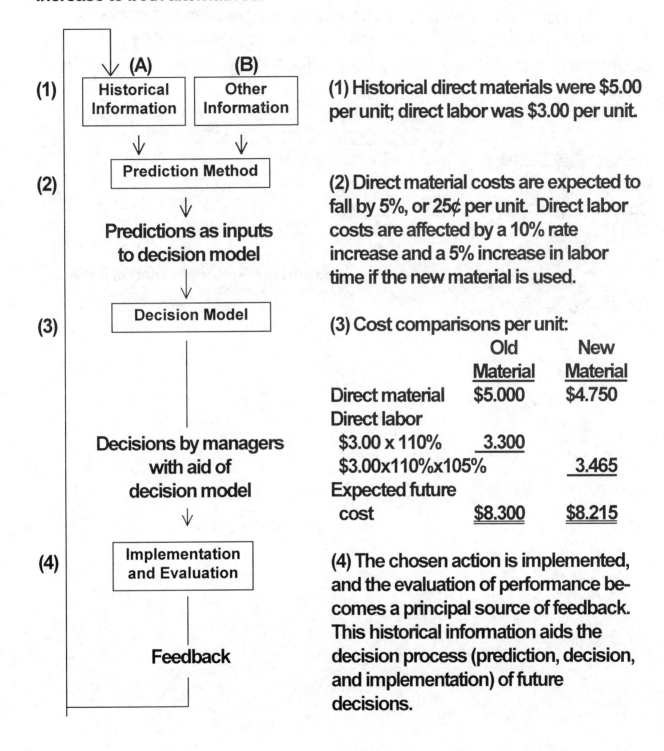

(1) Historical Information (A)   Other Information (B)

(1) Historical direct materials were $5.00 per unit; direct labor was $3.00 per unit.

Prediction Method

(2) Predictions as inputs to decision model

(2) Direct material costs are expected to fall by 5%, or 25¢ per unit. Direct labor costs are affected by a 10% rate increase and a 5% increase in labor time if the new material is used.

(3) Decision Model

Decisions by managers with aid of decision model

(3) Cost comparisons per unit:

	Old Material	New Material
Direct material	$5.000	$4.750
Direct labor		
$3.00 x 110%	3.300	
$3.00x110%x105%		3.465
Expected future cost	$8.300	$8.215

(4) Implementation and Evaluation

Feedback

(4) The chosen action is implemented, and the evaluation of performance becomes a principal source of feedback. This historical information aids the decision process (prediction, decision, and implementation) of future decisions.

<u>5-31</u> (10 min.)

Relevant costs are the future costs that differ between alternatives. Among the irrelevant costs are the cost of tickets to the symphony, automobile costs, and baby-sitting cost for the first four hours. The relevant costs are:

	Symphony	Game	Difference
Tickets, 2 @ $20 each	$0	$40	$40
Parking	0	6	6
Baby-sitting, 1 extra hour @ $4	0	4	4
Total	$0	$50	$50

The baseball game is $50 more costly to the Petrocelis than is the symphony.

5-32 (10-15 min.)

1. Operating income would increase by $300 if the order is accepted.

	Without Special Order	Effect of Special Order	With Special Order
Units	2,000	100	2,100
Sales	$36,000	$1,500	$37,500
Purchase cost	20,000	1,000	21,000
Variable printing cost	4,000	200	4,200
Total variable cost	24,000	1,200	25,200
Contribution margin	12,000	300	12,300
Fixed cost	8,000	0	8,000
Operating income	$ 4,000	$ 300	$ 4,300

2. If maximizing operating income in the short run were the only goal, the order should be accepted. However, if qualitative considerations favoring rejection are worth more than the $300 increase in operating income, the manager would reject the offer. For example, accepting the offer from F. C. Kitsap may generate similar offers from other clubs who now willingly pay the $18 normal price. Lost profits on such business might more than offset the $300 gain on this sale. On the other hand, this might be a way of gaining F. C. Kitsap as a regular customer who will then buy other items that generate a profit well in excess of the $300.

5-33 (20 min.)

1.

Total Variable Costs

Volume in Number of Lunches

$6

Total Fixed Costs

$120

Volume in Number of Lunches

Total Costs

Variable

Fixed

Volume in Number of Lunches

2. There are correct ways and incorrect ways to analyze the data. A correct way follows:

$$
\begin{aligned}
\text{Total cost} &= \text{Total FC} + \text{Total VC} \\
&= \$120 \text{ per year} + \$6 \text{ per lunch} \\
\text{Let X} &= \text{The number of lunches} \\
\text{Then, Unit cost} &= (\$120 \div X) + \$6 \\
\text{If 1 lunch, Unit cost} &= (\$120 \div 1) + \$6 = \$126.00 \text{ per lunch} \\
\text{If 12 lunches, Unit cost} &= (\$120 \div 12) + \$6 = \$16.00 \text{ per lunch} \\
\text{If 200 lunches, Unit cost} &= (\$120 \div 200) + \$6 = \$6.60 \text{ per lunch}
\end{aligned}
$$

244

3.   (a) The CPA can compare either total annual costs or unit costs. Let X = the total number of lunches in question.

	Total Costs		Unit Costs	
	Elsewhere	At Club	Elsewhere	At Club
In general	$ 10X	$120+$ 6X	$10.00	($120÷X)+$6
For 1 lunch.........................	$ 10	$120+$ 6 = $126	$10.00	$126.00
For 12 lunches..................	$ 120	$120+$ 72 = $192	$10.00	$ 16.00
For 200 lunches	$2,000	$120+$1,200 =$1,320	$10.00	$ 6.60

Let X = Number of lunches
$10X = $120 + $6X
X = 30 lunches is point of indifference.

(b) Elsewhere, 250 x $10 $2,500
    At Club, $120 + 250($6)   1,620
    Savings $ 880

The preceding parts concentrated on how total costs behave in relation to chosen volume levels. *Generally, the decision maker should take a straightforward, analytical approach by thinking in terms of total costs rather than unit costs.* By keeping an eye on the total picture, the manager is less likely to fall into some analytical traps that come from misinterpreting *unit* costs. In addition, of course, the qualitative aspects should not be ignored. For example, there may be an intangible benefit of dining with actual and potential clients at the luncheon club.

5-34 (15 min.)

1. Except for the advertising costs, the fixed costs are irrelevant in this situation.

    The contribution margin per student is:

    $14,000 - $7,900 = $6,100

    Break-even point for the campaign is:

    $1,830,000 ÷ $6,100 = 300 students.

    2. 350 x $6,100 = $2,135,000

    3. 100 x $6,100 = $610,000

5-35 (10 min.)

1.

		Cost per Unit of Product		
	Variable manufacturing cost	$ 9.00	$ 9.00	$ 9.00
	Variable selling and admin. cost	4.00		4.00
(a)	Total variable cost	$13.00		
	Fixed manufacturing cost		6.00*	6.00
(b)	Full manufacturing cost		$15.00**	
	Fixed selling and administrative cost			5.80*
(c)	Full cost			$24.80

   * Fixed manufacturing cost, $3,000,000 ÷ 500,000 = $6.00

     Fixed selling and admin. cost, $2,900,000 ÷ 500,000 = $5.80

 ** This amount must be used by U.S. companies for inventory valuation in reports to shareholders.

2. Full cost is often called fully allocated cost.

<u>5-36</u>   (20 min.)

1.   These warehouse stores attempt to maximize profits by cutting prices
and increasing turnover. Since profit is the product of contribution
margin and total sales, it can be affected by changing either. Total
profit can be increased if the added turnover brought about by a
lowering of price brings in more contribution margin than was lost by
the price cut. They also try to minimize fixed costs by limiting their
investment in buildings and equipment.

Characteristics: (a) choose product lines and sizes that move quickly
and avoid stocking slow-moving items and sizes; (b) stock lower
cost, lower quality items; (c) rely heavily on self service; and (d)
attempt to cut costs by providing fewer services, and (e) build low-
cost buildings in a place where property costs are not too high.

2.   Such a criterion by itself gives no indication what total contribution
margin (TCM) can be expected. Sales turnover or sales volume must
be used also. The rate of return on assets is determined by

TCM = Unit contribution margin x Total sales

If sales turnover can be assumed to be fairly constant among items,
then such a figure as a 20% average target gross profit might be
meaningful.

<u>5-37</u> (10-15 min.)

1. The key is to focus on lost revenues and avoidable costs:

Revenues, 600 hours @ SFR12 per hour		SFR7,200
Avoidable costs*:		
Teacher salaries	SFR5,200	
Supplies	800	6,000
Decrease in operating income		SFR1,200

*In addition to the avoidable costs shown, there might be some savings in sanitary engineering (less cleaning necessary) and depreciation (less wear and tear on equipment). Unless these savings are more than the SFR1,200 decrease in operating income, the school will be worse off financially without the after-school care program.

2. Among the qualitative factors to consider are that the after-school care program might attract students to the regular program, it provides additional compensation to teachers, and there is a social need for such programs.

5-38 (20 min.)

This solution may be obvious to most students. However, the use of this problem in executive programs and regular classes has shown that some students need this exercise before they become convinced that the "unitization" of fixed costs can be misleading. Moreover, in decision-making in general, the use of *total* rather than *unit* cost is nearly always less confusing.

This special order increases revenue by $390,000 and variable costs by $420,000. Total fixed costs are unchanged at $300,000. This $300,000 is unaffected regardless of how they are allocated to units of product. Therefore, net income will be affected only by the changes in revenue and variable costs.

Summary of regular operations:

	Per Unit	Total
Revenue	$2.00	$600,000
Variable costs	1.40	420,000
Contribution margin	$ .60	$180,000
Fixed costs	1.00	300,000
Net income	$ -.40	$-120,000

The new business would alter the picture as follows, assuming fixed costs are "spread" on a 50/50 basis:

	Regular	Special	Total
Revenue	$600,000	$ 390,000	$ 990,000
Variable costs	420,000	420,000	840,000
Contribution margin	$180,000	$ -30,000	$ 150,000
Fixed costs	150,000	150,000	300,000
Net income	$ 30,000	$-180,000	$-150,000

No matter how the fixed costs are spread, the total fixed costs will be $300,000 and the total net loss will be $150,000. This is true despite the fact that fixed costs *per unit* have fallen from $1.00 to $.50. The moral is: beware of unit fixed costs.

Some instructors may want to emphasize how the unitization of fixed costs differs. That is, the unit cost depends on the production volume chosen as the denominator.

$$\text{Fixed costs per unit} = \frac{\text{Total fixed costs}}{\text{Production volume}} = \frac{\$300,000}{300,000 \text{units}} = \$1$$

$$\text{or} \quad \frac{\$300,000}{600,000 \text{units}} = \$.50$$

The *total* fixed cost is unaffected by what volume is chosen as the denominator for computing the cost per unit.

Using the graphs like those in the chapter:

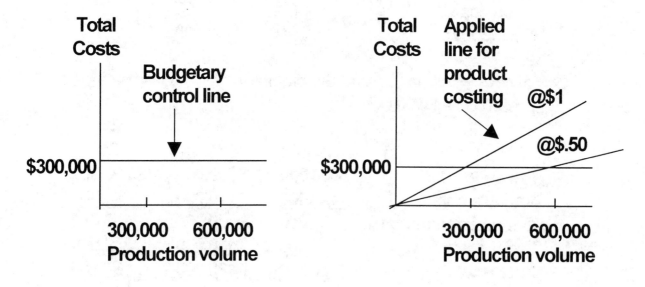

250

<u>5-39</u>   (10-15 min.)

Pricing policies always seem to spark much student interest. This "break-even" philosophy is similar to the "base or bulk volume" philosophy favored by many executives. That is, the "normal" pricing applies to the bulk or base of the business, but price-cutting can be applied to incremental business.

In the case of the auto business, this normal-incremental pricing is applied by many dealers in the manner described in the problem. Many observers think such pricing is nonsense, unless it is a response to changes in demand and in competitor pricing.

Why do some observers think that such pricing is nonsense? Because prices should be influenced by customer demand and competition, not by where sales happen to be on a break-even graph. Ordinarily, a pricing strategy should aim to maximize the contribution margin, all other things being equal. Some critics maintain that it is foolhardy to cut a price to the same potential customer just because he or she appears on, say, May 27 rather than on May 23.

As prospective customers, most rational people would shop for a car during the final two or three days of the month.

5-40 (15 min.)

1. Assuming that total fixed costs are the same at production levels of 6,000 and 10,000 units, the analysis can focus on contribution margins:

    CM@ $12: 6,000 units x ($12-$6) = $36,000
    CM@ $10: 10,000 units x ($10 - $6) = $40,000

    Profits will be $40,000 - $36,000 = $4,000 higher at the $10 price.

2. Subjective factors include image in the marketplace (higher price may give image of quality), market penetration (satisfied customers may become repeat customers), and effects on the sales force.

5-41 (10 min.)

1. ($60,000 - $36,000) ÷ $36,000 = 66.7%

2. ($60,000 - $50,000) ÷ $50,000 = 20%

3. ($60,000 - $30,000) ÷ $30,000 = 100%

5-42   (10-15 min.)

1.   (150% x $30,000) + ($75 x 2,000 hours) = $45,000 + $150,000 = $195,000

2 & 3.

Materials and supplies, at cost	$ 30,000
Hourly pay for consultants	70,000
Fringe benefits for consultants	24,000
Total variable cost	$124,000
Avoidable fixed costs	9,000
Minimum bid	$133,000
Unavoidable fixed costs	35,000
Total cost	168,000
Desired mark-up, 20% x $168,000	33,600
Bid to achieve desired profit	$201,600

5-43   (10 min.)

Unit Target Cost   = Target Price - Target Profit

$$= \quad \$65 \quad\quad - \quad .20 \times \$65$$

$$= \quad \$52$$

Total Target Cost ($52 x 80,000)	$ 4,160,000
Less cost to design and develop	1,000,000
Total target cost to manufacture, sell, distribute and service the toothbrush	$ 3,160,000
Unit target cost to manufacture, sell, distribute and service the toothbrush ($3,160,000 ÷ 80,000)	$39.50

Note that the unit amounts are averages over the entire product life cycle. Thus, $65 is the expected average selling price and $39.50 is the average cost to manufacture, sell, distribute, and service the toothbrush product. The initial selling price may be substantially higher than $65 and the initial costs may also be higher than $39.50. Continuous improvements across the value chain (kaizen costing) will bring down the costs just as competitive market forces will very likely bring down the price.

5-44 (15 – 20 min.)

1. Unit Target Cost = Target Price - Target Profit

$$= \quad \$230 \quad - \quad .2 \times \$230$$

$$= \quad \$184$$

Existing Unit Cost = Total Cost over Product Life ÷ Total Demand

$$= \quad \$10,200,000 \quad ÷ \quad 50,000$$

$$= \quad \$204$$

The new product should not be released to production.

2. Total Cost Savings = .4 x $5,000,000 - $1,000,000 = $1,000,000

On a per unit basis, this savings is $1,000,000 ÷ 50,000 = $20

The new expected average unit cost will be reduced to $204 - $20 = $184 which is the target cost. So the new product should be released to production.

5-45 (10 min.)

This problem raises issues for which there are no right answers. Determining the types of product promotion activities that are ethically and legally appropriate is not an easy question, and the role of price discrimination is especially difficult.

For a company to legally charge different prices to different customers, it usually must show a cost difference in serving the customers. But many companies promote their products by charging a zero price (i.e., giving free samples for a limited amount of the product). Is this case any different than a breakfast cereal company sending free samples through the mail? If so, how? Further, establishing physicians' confidence in the medication has a potential long-run benefit; does this justify giving the drug free to physicians? In addition, physicians need to know how to administer the drug and how to look for possible side effects, so are the free samples justified as an educational investment? Or are the free drug samples essentially bribes to convince physicians to prescribe the new drug?

What about the difference in price between hospital and retail pharmacies? GLPI may think that if a hospital pharmacy starts a patient on the new drug, he or she will stay on it even if further purchases are from a retail pharmacy. Does this justify a price differential? Or it may be that distribution costs are less to hospital pharmacies than to retail pharmacies. Is this difference enough to justify a $15 difference in price?

Students are likely to disagree on the appropriateness of the policies, and some may feel passionately about their opinion. At some time the discussion should be turned to the effect of cost on the pricing policies. For example, a lead-in question may be whether the eventual price of $50 is fair for a product whose production cost is only $12. Then it can proceed to considering whether a cost differential can justify the $15 difference between the prices to hospital and retail pharmacies. Finally, the issue of price and incentives to physicians can be addressed. This last issue may be the first one students want to focus on, and it may be the one with the most ethical content, but it should not be the sole issue discussed.

5-46 (10-15 min.)

	Contribution Approach	Fully Allocated Cost Approach
1. Sales	$39,000	$39,000
Fully allocated operating expenses		45,000
Variable operating expenses (80% x $45,000)	36,000	
Apparent change in operating income	$ 3,000	$ (6,000)

2. A decision not to accept the order means that short-run income would be $3,000 lower. In effect, Transnational invests $3,000 to maximize long-run benefits. Goldmark can find the contribution approach helpful because he can weigh decisions of this sort by asking whether the probability of long-run benefits (not encouraging price-cutting by competitors, not encouraging customers to expect lower prices) is worth a quantifiable present investment equal to the contribution margin ($3,000 in this case).

Students should be alerted to the fact that, by itself, the contribution approach does *not* say "go forth and cut prices." All it does is quantify a manager's options more sharply.

<u>5-47</u>   (20-25 min.)

1.   Net income would be increased by £3,000 if the order were taken:

	Without the Order	Effect of the Order	With the Order
Sales	£1,100,000	£19,800	£1,119,800
Direct material	£ 280,000	£ 5,600	£ 285,600
Direct labor	320,000	6,400	326,400
Variable overhead	240,000*	4,800	244,800
Fixed overhead	160,000	0	160,000
Total costs	£1,000,000	£16,800	£1,016,800
Operating income	£ 100,000	£ 3,000	£ 103,000

*   Variable overhead is total overhead - fixed overhead, or £400,000 - £160,000 = £240,000. Variable overhead rate = £240,000 ÷ £320,000 = 75% of direct labor.

2.   A contribution approach to pricing might appear as follows:

Selling price		£19,800
Direct materials	£5,600	
Direct labor	6,400	
Variable overhead at 75% of direct labor	4,800	
Total variable cost		16,800
Contribution margin		£ 3,000

The contribution approach essentially attempts to provide a measure of the decrease in immediate net income that would result from rejecting an order. This is the contribution margin forgone. Traditional approaches to pricing do not supply such a number. In part (1), the £3,000 tells Smythe that she is *investing* £3,000 now to uphold her pricing policies. She can then assess whether preserving such policies and the long-run pricing structure is worth an investment of such magnitude. She also may assess whether accepting marginal business will cause this customer to seek such concessions regularly. Alternatively, Smythe may want to make such concessions occasionally to attract new customers.

A possible contribution margin formula may be illustrated as follows:

Direct material	£ 5,600
Direct labor	6,400
Variable overhead at 75% of direct labor	4,800
Total variable cost	£16,800
Markup at 30.95%* of £16,800	5,200
Target selling price	£22,000

*Normal markup percentage = (£22,000 - £16,800) ÷ £16,800 = 30.952%

Note that the markup of 30.952% is much higher than the 10% used previously because the markup must provide for the recovery of fixed overhead as well as the making of net income. The key to the contribution approach is its intelligent use with full recognition that total variable cost is *not* total cost.

An alternative way to compute the target selling price would provide for a two-step markup:

Total variable cost	£16,800
Fixed costs, 19.048%* of £16,800	3,200
Total costs	£20,000
Markup, 11.905%** of £16,800	2,000
Target selling price	£22,000

 * 160 ÷ (280 + 320 + 240) = 19.048%
** 100 ÷ 840 = 11.905%

5-48 (15-20 min.)

1.

	Year to Date	Final Course Enrollment		Grand Totals
		30	10 More	
Tuition revenues	$2,000,000	$6,000	$1,000	$2,007,000
Costs of courses	800,000	4,000	600	804,600
Contribution margin	1,200,000	2,000	400	1,202,400
General administrative expenses	400,000	0	0	400,000
Operating income	$ 800,000	$2,000	$ 400	$ 802,400

2. The same general considerations influence pricing decisions in profit-seeking and nonprofit organizations. The exception is price-setting by many government-owned entities, which often is heavily affected by legislative bodies. The familiar three Cs – customers, costs, and competition – do influence price setting.

Executive education is highly competitive; the rates for top-flight teachers are relatively high; and customers often do without or conduct their own in-house training. The offering of discounts is often risky. It may alienate full-paying customers, may lead to widespread price-cutting, and may encourage the particular customers to bargain hard regarding course after course.

The setting of tuition in private universities is similar to setting prices in private industry. *Customers* may go to the *competition* – to other private or public universities. *Costs* must be recovered if the institution is to survive. Of course, tuition is only one part of a university's revenue. Private institutions are especially dependent on endowment income and on donations from friends and alumni.

<u>5-49</u>   (15 min.)

1.   Contribution margin from direct sales = $15 - $2 = $13
     Contribution margin from sales to distributor = $50 - $2 = $48

     Total contribution from sales to distributors
          = (14,000 x 10) x $48 = $6,720,000

          Tape sales @ $15 to get CM of $6,720,000 = $6,720,000 ÷ $13 = 516,923. So more than 516,923 tapes would have to be sold directly to customers.

2.   The cost of producing and promoting the movie is irrelevant to this decision.

3.   Total contribution from direct sales = 30 million x ($15.50 - $2) = $405 million.

     Sales at CM of $48 to get contribution of $405 million:
          $405,000,000 ÷ $48 = 8,437,500 tapes
          Sales per store = 8,437,500 ÷ 14,000 = 603 tapes

     It is unlikely that Disney would have been able to sell 603 tapes per video store. The decision to sell directly to consumers appears to have been wise.

<u>5-50</u>   (20 min.)   This is a classic problem of the application of the contribution approach.

	Basic	Marginal	Total
Number of flights per month	3,000	120	3,120
Available seats	300,000	12,000	312,000
Seats filled	156,000	2,400	158,400
Percent filled	52%	20%	51%
Revenue	$31,200,000	$240,000	$31,440,000
Variable expenses	21,840,000	120,000	21,960,000
Contribution margin	$ 9,360,000	$120,000	$ 9,480,000

Continental's approach was described by Chris F. Whelan, vice president in charge of economic planning, who made the scheduling decisions. He used a marginal (variable cost) approach, which was described as follows:

Whelan considers that the bulk of his scheduled flights have to return at least their fully allocated costs. Overhead, depreciation, and insurance are very real expenses and must be covered. The out-of-pocket approach comes into play, says Whelan, only after the line's basic schedule has been set.

"Then you go a step farther," he says, and see if adding more flights will contribute to the corporate net. Similarly, if he's thinking of dropping a flight with a disappointing record, he puts it under the marginal microscope: "If your revenues are going to be more than your out-of-pocket costs, you should keep the flight on."

By "out-of-pocket costs" Whelan means just that: The actual dollars that Continental has to pay out to run a flight. He gets the figure not by applying hypothetical equations but by circulating a proposed schedule to every operating department concerned and finding out just what extra expenses it will entail. If a ground crew already on duty can service the plane, the flight isn't charged a penny of their salary expense. There may even be some costs eliminated in running the flight; they won't need employees to roll the plane to a hanger, for instance, if it flies on to another stop.

Most of these extra flights, of course, are run at off-beat hours, mainly late at night. At times, though, Continental discovers that the hours aren't so unpopular after all. A pair of night coach flights on the Houston-San Antonio-El Paso-Phoenix-Los Angeles leg, added on a marginal basis, have turned out to be so successful that they are now more than covering fully allocated costs.

Alternative. Whelan uses an alternative cost analysis closely allied with the marginal concept in drawing up schedules. For instance, on his 11:11 p.m. flight from Colorado Springs to Denver and a 5:20 a.m. flight the other way, Continental uses Viscounts that, though they carry some cargo, often go without a single passenger. But the net cost of these flights is less than would be the rent for overnight hangar space for the Viscount at Colorado Springs.

And there's more than one absolute-loss flight scheduled solely to bring passengers to a connecting Continental long-haul flight; even when the loss on the feeder service is considered a cost on the long-haul service, the line makes a net profit on the trip.

Continental's data handling system produces weekly reports on each flight, with revenues measured against both out-of-pocket and fully allocated costs. Whelan uses these to give each flight a careful analysis at least once a quarter. But those added on a marginal basis get the fine-tooth-comb treatment monthly.

The business on these flights tends to be useful as a leading indicator, Whelan finds, since the off-peak traffic is more than normally sensitive to economic trends and will fall off sooner than that on the popular-hour flights. When he sees the night coach flights turning in consistently poor showings, it's a clue to lower his projections for the rest of the schedule.

5-51 (15-20 min.)

1. Total variable costs are $.90 + $.20 = $1.10 per boomerang.
    Total fixed costs are $300,000 + $50,000 = $350,000

Volume in units	200,000	250,000	300,000
Sales @ $3.00	$600,000	$750,000	$900,000
Total variable costs @ $1.10	220,000	275,000	330,000
Contribution margin	380,000	475,000	570,000
Fixed costs	350,000	350,000	350,000
Operating income	$ 30,000	$125,000	$220,000
Operating income as a percentage of sales	5.0%	16.7%	24.4%

2. Note the significant difference in predictions. For example, the correct analysis indicates $30,000 operating income at a 200,000 volume level; the incorrect analysis indicates $100,000 operating income. The manager's tabulation is incorrect because it assumes that all costs are variable. The presence of a larger proportion of fixed costs causes much wider swings in operating income when volume deviates from the volume used to develop the full costs per boomerang.

5-52 (15-20 min.)

1. Extra revenue from option 1: ($30 - $15) x 30 passengers = $450
    Extra costs for option 1: ($2.20 - $.20) x 65 mi + $400 = $530
    Therefore, the second option (adding a car to an existing train) is
    more profitable by $530 - $450 = $80.

    Costs that are the same for both alternatives are irrelevant. These
    include the cost of the tour guide, cost of moving the car or car and
    engine to the main track, and depreciation.

2. This depends on the total additional revenues and costs for option 2:

Revenues: $15 x 30		$450.00
Costs: Fuel - 65 mi x $.20/mi	$ 13.00	
Tour guide	150.00	
Moving car	40.00	
Total additional cost		203.00
Extra profit		$247.00

    This option is definitely profitable, generating extra profit of $450 -
    $203 = $247. The cost of the tour guide and the cost of moving the car
    to the main track are relevant for this decision because they would be
    incurred only if the agreement with the tour agent is accepted. The
    depreciation remains irrelevant as long as excess cars are available.

5-53 (15-20 min.)

1. Net income will be increased by 300 x (€40 - €26 - €10) = €1,200.

2. The variable manufacturing costs per unit: €26.

3. €180,000, €60,000, €30,000, €10; i.e., all numbers are irrelevant except €26.

4. Selling price: €180,000 ÷ 2,000 units = €90

Total sales: 2,400 x 2 x €90 =		€432,000
Less expenses:		
Fixed: €60,000 + €30,000 + €100,000* =	€190,000	
Variable: 2,400 x 2 x (€26 + €10) =	172,800	362,800
Net income		€ 69,200

*Depreciation: €500,000 ÷ 5 = €100,000.

5-54 (15-25 min.)

1. Budgeted fixed manufacturing overhead per unit:
    $$\$10,000,000 \div 2,000,000 = \$5$$

2. Relevant items:

Additional sales	$1,200,000
Additional manufacturing costs, 100,000 x $10	$1,000,000
Additional selling and administrative expenses	10,000
Total relevant costs	$1,010,000
Additional operating income	$ 190,000

    Fixed manufacturing costs are irrelevant because their total will be the same regardless of the special order being accepted or rejected.

3. Students may raise many points, including:

    a. Whether the president is willing to "invest" $190,000 in forgone operating income now to preserve a marketing policy or to prevent a general weakening of prices among competitors.

    b. Whether accepting the order now may lead to more profitable orders from the same customer subsequently.

4. Budgeted fixed manufacturing overhead rate would be $10,000,000 ÷ 1,000,000 = $10. However, the *additional* operating income in requirement 2 would be unaffected by how fixed costs are "unitized." (Of course, the original budgeted operating income would have been different, but that is irrelevant in requirement 2.)

<u>5-55</u> (20-30 min.)   When this problem was used in an exam, it was well done by students who used contribution margin analysis in total dollars. A number of students attempted to force a decision by means of analysis of unit costs or by break-even analysis, failing to consider the effect of sales volume on profits. A number of good solutions were marred by failure to draw specific conclusions.

Output and pricing:

Volume	Price	CM per Unit	Total Contribution Margin
50,000	$25	9	$450,000
60,000	24	8	480,000
70,000	23	7	490,000
80,000	22	6	480,000

The contribution margin per unit decreases as volume increases.

Output of 70,000 at selling price of $23 yields the largest contribution margin. However, this is in excess of capacity.

Maximum at present capacity: 60,000 units output at $24
= Contribution margin of $480,000

To increase capacity:

Investment	$200,000
Useful life	10 years
Cost per year ($200,000 ÷ 10)	$ 20,000

By increasing capacity to 70,000 units, which maximizes the total contribution margin, the company gains an additional $10,000 in contribution margin but incurs an additional fixed cost of $20,000.

Conclusions: Do not invest in new capacity. Sell at $24.
              Produce 60,000, the maximum capacity now available.

<u>5-56</u>   (15-20 min.)

1.

	Designer	Moderately Priced
Items that can be displayed in 8,000 square feet	300	400
Contribution margin per item	$120	$65
Contribution margin per turnover of inventory	$36,000	$26,000
Relative number of turnovers for a given time period	2	3
Total contribution margin for a given time period	$72,000	$78,000

Students should recognize that square feet of floor space is the limiting or scarce factor. Note that the contribution margin *percentage* and the contribution margin *per item* are greater for the designer items. Nevertheless, the moderately priced items will generate a larger contribution margin *in total*. Why? Because more moderately priced items are sold in any given period of time. The analysis above implies sales of 300 x 2 = 600 designer items versus 400 x 3 = 1,200 moderately priced items. The designer items should be dropped.

2.   The solution in requirement 1 assumes that moderately priced items can outsell designer items 3 to 2 and that the store will be 100% full of such items. Interdependencies between the items are ignored. If these factors do not hold, some combination of the two items may be preferable.

Additional considerations include the investment in inventories, the number of sales personnel, the skills and training of sales personnel, and the degree of substitutability between the types of items.

This problem could also be addressed on a unit basis. Suppose one designer item is displayed and sold in a given time period. How many moderately priced items could be sold in the same period? First, compute how many moderately priced items would be displayed:

Moderate priced items displayed   = 4/3 x designer items displayed
                                                  = 4/3 x 1 = 1 1/3

For each item displayed, 1 1/2 moderately priced items would be sold in the same time period that 1 designer item is sold. Why? Because turnover of designer items is 2/3 that of moderately priced items, which implies that turnover of moderately priced items is 1 1/2 times that of designer items. Therefore,

Moderate priced items sold   = 1 1/2 x 1 1/3 x designer items sold
                                       = 2 x designer items sold

Gulf Coast Fashions can use a given amount of space to sell either 1 designer item or 2 moderately priced items. Contribution margins are:

Designer items	Moderately priced items
1 x $120 = $120	2 x $65 = $130

The contribution is greater from selling 2 moderately priced items than from selling 1 designer item.

<u>5-57</u>   (15 min.)

The standard line should be produced. The major lesson here is that gross profit *per unit* of product is not necessarily indicative of the relative profitability of products. In this case the limiting factor (scarce resource) is production capacity. The most desirable product is the one that maximizes the contribution to profit for the given production capacity. In this case, the standard product will yield a $14 contribution per hour of machine time, while the premium product will yield $12:

	Per Unit	
	Standard	Premium
Selling price	$28	$38
Variable costs	14	20
Contribution margin per unit of product	$14	$18
Divide by machine time per unit of product	÷ 1	÷1.5*
Contribution margin per hour of machine time	$14	$12

Comparisons of gross profit percentages do not help in these instances, because they are not dependent on the scarce resource, machine time. (Of course, the rate of return on investment may be affected by different required amounts of assets, but that complication is not introduced here.)

* $9 ÷ $6 = 1.5 hours of machine time required per unit of premium product. This is the key to the solution because it means that, if the full productive capacity is allocated to one of the products, the company could produce fewer premium products than standard products. Many students are not comfortable with this idea until an example is explained.

Assume total fixed overhead of $360,000 and total machine hours of 60,000. The fixed overhead rate would be $6 per hour. (This is also $6 per standard unit.) But because $9 is charged per premium unit, the hours of machine time must be $9 ÷ $6 = 1.5 hours per unit. Therefore, only 40,000 units of the premium product could be produced: 60,000 ÷ 1.5 = 40,000. (Proof: at $9 fixed overhead each, total fixed overhead is $9 x 40,000 = $360,000.)

<u>5-58</u> (30-50 min.)

This might be assigned at the end of the next chapter as a review of two chapters. This problem is more challenging than nearly all of the others in this chapter. Accordingly, this solution is more elaborate than is really necessary to answer the question.

1. The total amount of fixed overhead is common to all alternatives. Therefore, it is irrelevant to this analysis. The scarce resource is hours of capacity. The objective is to maximize the contribution per hour:

	Subcomponents	Plug-in Assemblies	Difference
Revenue per unit	$2.20	$5.30	
Variable cost per unit	1.40	3.30	
Contribution per unit	$ .80	$2.00	$-1.20
Contribution per hour	$ 48.00*	$ 40.00**	$ 8.00
Hours available	x 600,000	x 600,000	
Total contribution	$28,800,000	$24,000,000	$4,800,000

  * $ .80 x 60 units per hour = $48.00
** $2.00 x 20 units per hour = $40.00

Plug-in assemblies should be dropped because it is diverting the limited resource from a more profitable use. Note that the sales manager is incorrect. These decisions should not be reached by "all-costs" allocations and consequent computations of net profits or losses on units of product. Each plug-in assembly is making $2.00 contribution to profit and to the recovery of fixed costs, but it takes three times as long to get a plug-in assembly.

2. The lowest price must yield a contribution of $28,800,000. The contribution per unit would be $28,800,000 divided by the number of units produced in one year, or:

$28,800,000 ÷ (600,000 hours x 20 unit per hour)
= $28,800,000 ÷ 12,000,000 units = $2.40 per unit

Because the contribution is currently $2.00 per unit at a selling price of $5.30, the minimum acceptable price must be $5.70 in order to provide a unit contribution of $2.40.

To double check, consider the following:

| | 100% of Capacity | |
	To Subcomponents	To Plug-in Assemblies
Sales in units	36,000,000	12,000,000
Sales at $2.20 and $5.70	$79,200,000	$68,400,000
Variable costs at $1.40 and $3.30	50,400,000	39,600,000
Contribution margin	$28,800,000	$28,800,000
Fixed costs*	21,600,000	21,600,000
Operating income	$ 7,200,000	$ 7,200,000

*36,000,000 x Unit fixed overhead rate of $.60, and 12,000,000 x Unit fixed overhead rate of ($1.20 + the $.60 transferred-in), respectively.

3. Note that this increase in variable cost per hour is common to both alternatives. That is, the variable processing cost would rise by $14.40 per hour:
Variable overhead = 40% of old fixed overhead
= .4 x $21,600,000 = $8,640,000
Variable overhead rate per hour = $8,640,000 ÷ 600,000 = $14.40

The contribution per hour is therefore reduced from $48 to $33.60 for subcomponents and from $40 to $25.60 for plug-in assemblies. Note that the crucial difference per hour is still $8.00. The critical question in relevant cost analysis is: what difference does it make?

Incidentally, many individuals often jump to the conclusion that relevant cost analysis is simple: variable costs are always relevant, and fixed costs are irrelevant. This is an example where the variable overhead cost is irrelevant. (For that matter, in this case, the labor cost, another variable cost, is also irrelevant.) Irrelevant costs can be included in the analysis. But, *if they are analyzed correctly*, they will not make any *difference* between alternatives. If analyzed incorrectly, they will provide misleading information.

In short, the answer here is the same as the answers to (1) and (2). The lowest acceptable price is still $5.70. To prove this, use the same format as in (2):

	100% of Capacity	
	To Subcom- ponents	To Plug-in Assemblies
Sales in units	36,000,000	12,000,000
Sales at $2.20 and $5.70	$79,200,000	$68,400,000
Variable costs* at $1.64 and $4.02	59,040,000	48,240,000
Contribution margin	$20,160,000	$20,160,000
Fixed costs**	12,960,000	12,960,000
Operating income	$ 7,200,000	$ 7,200,000

*$1.40 + ($14.40 ÷ 60 units) = $1.64, and
$3.30 + ($14.40 ÷ 20 units) = $4.02
**.6 x $21,600,000 = $12,960,000

Finally, note that the fixed costs could be ignored completely in all of the above requirements. If you want to include them, you may – but, if the fixed costs are analyzed correctly, they won't affect the decisions. In part (2), $21.6 million of fixed costs would be deducted no matter what product mix is chosen; in part (3), $12.96 million of fixed costs would be deducted under any alternative.

5-59 (10-15 min.)

1. | Manufacturing cost | $27.00 |
    | Gross margin, 15% x $27.00 | 4.05 |
    | Price | $31.05 |

    Memphis would not produce a motor because it would not be able to sell them at $31.05, assuming that market research is right about the market price of $25.00 Even with no profit margin, the cost of $27 exceeds the price of $25.

2. Using target costing, Memphis would begin with the market price of $25.00. From this, managers would compute the largest acceptable manufacturing cost:

    | Price | $25.00 |
    | Less gross margin | 3.26* |
    | Manufacturing cost | $21.74 |

    *Price = Cost + (.15 x Cost)
    $25.00 = 1.15 x Cost
    Cost = $25.00 ÷ 1.15 = $21.74
    Margin = $25.00 - $21.74 = $3.26

3. Memphis managers would have to determine if they could design the garage-door-opener motor and its production process in a way that manufacturing costs were below $21.74. Both the design specifications for the motor and the production process would need to be looked at. If there is no way to reduce production costs to $21.74 or below, the product should not be produced. However, target costing forces managers to examine ways to lower the production costs through product and process design. Instead of taking the design and process as givens and then examining the market to see if Memphis can sell the product for a high enough price, the company's managers will try to design a product and process that meets the constraints of the market.

5-60 (35-45 min.)

	Cost per driver unit	C-200472		C-200473		C-200474		C-200475	
		Number of units	Cost	Number of units	Cost	Number of units	Cost	Number of units	Cost
Direct material	$1.60/ pound	2,000	$ 3,200	1,000	$ 1,600	4,000	$ 6,400	600	$1,280
Setup/maintenance	$1,015/ setup	10	10,150	4	4,060	12	12,180	5	5,075
Processing	$370/ mach. hr.	20	7,400	12	4,440	32	11,840	12	4,440
Marketing	$860/order	30	25,800	10	8,600	50	43,000	16	13,760
Customer service	$162/sales call	55	8,910	35	5,670	20	3,240	28	4,536
Total existing cost			$55,460		$24,370		$76,660		$29,091
Total demand in units			2,000		1,400		4,000		600
Existing cost per unit			$ 27.73		$ 17.41		$ 19.17		$ 48.49
Target cost per unit			$ 23.40*		$ 16.80		$ 21.00		$ 30.00
Required cost reduction			$ 4.33		$ 0.61		$ 0		$ 18.49
RCR as a percent of market price			11.1%		2.2%		0%		37.0%
Decision			Redesign product and process using value engineering		Release to production and set kaizen cost improvement plan		Release to production		Abandon subject to approval

* Target cost = (1 – desired contribution percentage) x market price = (1 - .40) x $39 = $23.40.

5-61 (20 min.)

1. Contribution margin = $800 - ($475 + $25) = $300
   Total contribution = $300 x 44,000 mowers = $13,200,000
   Total fixed costs = 7 years x ($900,000 + $50,000) = $6,650,000
   Development costs = $5,000,000

   Life cycle profit = $13,200,000 - $6,650,000 - $5,000,000
   = $1,550,000

2. Desired profit = .10 x ($800 x 44,000) = $3,520,000

   The life cycle profit is $3,520,000 - $1,550,000 = $1,970,000 short of what is desired. Therefore, unless some changes can be made, Southeast will not enter the riding lawn mower market.

3. A target costing company does not quit when the first cost estimate comes in too high. Managers establish a target cost and try to adjust design, production and marketing processes to meet the target cost. In this case, the target cost is:

Revenue	$35,200,000
Desired profit	3,520,000
Target cost	$31,680,000

   Expected costs are:

Variable production costs	$20,900,000
Fixed production costs	6,300,000
Variable selling costs	1,100,000
Fixed selling costs	350,000
Development costs	5,000,000
Total costs	$33,650,000

If total costs can be reduced by at least $1,970,000, to $31,680,000 or less by changes in the product's design, the production process design, or production or selling methods, this will begin to be a profitable product.

<u>5-62</u>   (30 – 40 min.)

Fixed overhead allocation rate per machine hour
    = €2,160,000 ÷ 90,000 = €24
Variable overhead allocation rate = €40 - €24 = € 16

St. Tropez should not accept either order. The company does not have adequate plant capacity to manufacture the order of 20,000 jewelry cases from Lyon Inc. without subcontracting. The order from Avignon Co. does not yield St. Tropez a positive contribution margin.

The calculations showing that St. Tropez does not have the necessary plant capacity in the second quarter to produce the order for 20,000 jewelry cases are as follows:

Annual plant capacity	<u>90,000</u> machine hours
Monthly plant capacity	7,500 machine hours
Estimated monthly capacity use .8 x 7,500	<u>6,000</u> machine hours
Excess capacity per month	1,500 machine hours
Period involved, second quarter	<u>x 3</u> months
Total excess capacity available	<u>4,500</u> machine hours

Machine hours required to produce 20,000 jewelry cases
    = Number of cases x machine hours per case
    = 20,000 x .25 = 5,000 hours.

The Lyon Inc. order for 20,000 jewelry cases would require 5,000 machine hours, but only 4,500 machine hours are available in the second quarter.

Computations related to the order from Avignon Co. are as follows:

Price offered per case		€ 85.0
Variable production cost per case:		
Raw materials	€42.5	
Direct labor, .5 hours @ €60	30.0	
Overhead, .5 machine hours @ €16*	8.0	80.5
Contribution margin per case		€ 4.5
Number of cases		x 7,500
Total contribution margin		€33,750
Fixed costs related to the order:		
Setup costs	€15,000	
Special device	25,000	40,000
Loss from taking the order		€ (6,250)

*Fixed costs are not relevant in this case and should be omitted.

The Avignon Co. order should be rejected because it is unprofitable in the short run with the present price and cost structure.

5-63 (20 – 30 min.) For the solution, see the Prentice Hall Web site, www.prenhall.com/

<u>5-64</u>   (60 min. or more)

Pricing tends to be more of an "art" rather than a "science" in small firms. In large firms, students will find a wide variety of tools and techniques but will most likely get interesting answers to all the recommended questions.

Perhaps the most significant factor that influences the process for establishing a pricing policy is company size. For many small companies, the process is simple. For example, one restaurant prices using a formula of three times the cost of material used in each menu item. This markup is designed (hoped) to cover all the operating costs in the restaurant's value chain beyond direct material (food cost). Other important factors commonly mentioned include market conditions and the experience level of management.

Target costing is not often mentioned. Some form of cost plus pricing is most often used. When target costing is used and managers are asked to explain the target-costing process, it is often discovered that only some elements of a fully developed target costing process are used.

Students may discover that different pricing policies are used for different product or service families in the same firm. This is particularly true for large companies that compete in many different markets.

5-65   (50 – 60 min.)

NOTE TO INSTRUCTOR. This solution is based on the web site as it was in early 2004. Be sure to examine the current web site before assigning this problem, as the information there may have changed. As of January 2004, the Web address for Colgate-Palmolive was www.colgate.com.

1. In its 2002 Annual Report, the major component of Colgate's strategy is investing in innovative new products with growth potential. According to William Shanahan, President, "successful new products" drove market share gains and a worldwide unit volume increase of 4.5% in 2002. In 2002, 40% of sales came from products introduced in the past 5 years. The company supports this strategy by focusing on the R & D and marketing value chain functions. The company that places an emphasis on rapid product development needs relevant information regarding expected revenues and costs for proposed new products. The company will also need to have reliable estimates of the impact of its advertising and promotion on sales. If a company uses an ABC system as discussed in chapter 4, the impact of increased sales from new products will be estimated via increased activity levels as well as higher variable costs and capacity utilization. This information is very relevant in Colgate's planning process.

2. The importance of Colgate's code of conduct can be measured several ways. A search of the 2002 annual report indicates that "code of conduct" is mentioned 10 times. The following references give a good feel for codes priority at Colgate.

   From management's letter to shareholders:

   "Proud to uphold Colgate's reputation as a company with the highest ethical standards, Colgate people around the world adhere to a global Code of Conduct that guides us in managing with respect and living our values of Caring, Global Teamwork and Continuous improvement around the world. Our Code of

Conduct is a set of principles that guides our relationships with one another, our business partners, consumers, shareholders and the communities in which we live and work."

From pages 9 and 13 of the annual report:

Training also encompasses our values. For example, in less than one year, 2,500 supervisors, managers and executives throughout the Colgate world will have completed "Business Integrity: Colgate's Values at Work." This training experience ensures a thorough and consistent understanding of the Company's ethical business and professional standards and practices as expressed in Colgate's Code of Conduct.

3. As of February 2004, the latest new-product press release was on January 25, 2004. The product discussed in the news release is Colgat4 Kids Toothpaste and Toothbrush featuring Sponge Bob Squarepants and friends. This appears to be a variation of an existing product.

4. The company displays its major product groups and major market regions using a moving heading page. In January 2004, three laundry detergents were listed. The information provided is sketchy with little differentiation made between the different detergents. The site gives no guidance as to when to use a product. It basically provides a list and some advertising information on selected items. The site does not indicate which detergent is best for a particular stain. It does give information about how to pretreat a wide variety of stains. There is not enough information to select the best detergent for a problem. They say Fab should be used or any other detergent.

5. The company's financial strategy is to continuously improve gross margin percentage, reduce overhead (sales, general, and administrative expenses), and increase advertising. The income statement and other disclosures in the annual report provide sufficient data to evaluate the effectiveness of the company's strategy.

By emphasizing high-profit-margin products, and implementing numerous cost reduction programs, the gross margin percentage has improved steadily from 52.7% in 2000 to 54.6% in 2002 (from the comparative consolidated statements of income). Sales, general, and administrative expenses (a good surrogate for overhead) have declined from 32.8% of sales to 32.6% of sales during this same period, even with higher advertising costs.

Advertising costs are included in sales, general, and administrative expenses. The amount of advertising costs is not given in the footnotes or the financial statement. Management's letter, however, states that spending for effective marketing programs increased absolutely and as a percentage of sales. Management's Discussion and Analysis of Financial Condition and Results of Operations states that "total advertising support behind Colgate brands . . . increased 8% in 2002. Included in selling, general, and administrative expenses is media spending of $486.6, $509 and $550.0 [million] in 2002, 2001, and 2000, respectively.

The resulting substantial cash savings are the primary source supporting increased R & D and advertising for rapid new product development. When all components of Colgate's strategy are taken together, the company's overall profitability improved as measured by net profit margin (net income ÷ sales). Net profit margin has increased steadily from 11.8% in 2000 to 13.9% in 2002.

CHAPTER 6
COVERAGE OF LEARNING OBJECTIVES

LEARNING OBJECTIVE	FUNDA-MENTAL ASSIGN-MENT MATERIAL	CRITICAL THINKING EXERCISES AND EXERCISES	PROBLEMS	CASES, EXCEL, COLLAB. & INTERNET EXERCISES
LO1: Use opportunity cost to analyze the income effects of a given alternative.		24,29,30,31, 32,41,43	49,50,62	
LO2: Decide whether to make or to buy certain parts or products.	A1,B1	25,33,34,35,	51,52	64,65,68
LO3: Decide whether a joint product should be processed beyond the split-off point.	A2,B2	36,37,	55,63	67
LO4: Identify irrelevant information in disposal of obsolete inventory.		27,38,	56,58	
LO5: Decide whether to keep or replace equipment.	A3,B3,B4	39,41	57,59,60	
LO6: Explain how unit costs can be misleading.		26,40		
LO7: Discuss how performance measures can affect decision making.	B4	42	59,60	
LO8: Construct absorption and contribution format income statements and identify which is better for decision making.	A4,B5	28,44,45,46, 47,48		66

CHAPTER 6
Relevant Information and Decision Making: Production Decisions

6-A1   (20 min)

1.   The key to this question is what will happen to the fixed overhead costs if production of the boxes is discontinued. Assume that all $60,000 of fixed costs will continue. Then, Sunshine State will lose $36,000 by purchasing the boxes from Weyerhaeuser:

Payment to Weyerhaeuser, 80,000 x $2.40	$192,000
Costs saved, variable costs	156,000
Additional costs	$ 36,000

2.   Some subjective factors are:
   - Might Weyerhaeuser raise prices if Sunshine State closed down its box-making facility?
   - Will sub-contracting the box production affect the quality of the boxes?
   - Is a timely supply of boxes assured, even if the number needed changes?
   - Does Sunshine State sacrifice proprietary information when disclosing the box specifications to Weyerhaeuser?

3.   In this case the fixed costs are relevant. However, it is not the depreciation on the old equipment that is relevant. It is the cost of the new equipment. Annual cost savings by not producing the boxes now will be:

Variable costs	$156,000
Investment avoided (annualized)	100,000
Total saved	$256,000

The payment to Weyerhaeuser is $256,000-$192,000 = $64,000 less than the savings, so Sunshine State would be $64,000 better off subcontracting the production of the boxes.

6-A2 (15 min.) Table is in thousands of dollars.

1,2.

	(a) Sales Beyond Split-Off	(b) Sales at Split-Off	(a)-(b) Incremental Sales	(c) Separable Costs Beyond Split-Off	(a)-(b)-(c) Incremental Gain or (Loss)
A	230	54	176	190	(14)
B	330	28	302	300	2
C	175	54	121	100	21
Increase in overall operating income from further processing of A, B, and C					9

The incremental analysis indicates that Products B and C should be processed further, but Product A should be sold at split-off. The overall operating income would be $42,000, as follows:

Sales: $54,000 + $330,000 + $175,000		$559,000
Joint cost of goods sold	$117,000	
Separable cost of goods sold:		
$300,000 + $100,000	400,000	517,000
Operating income		$ 42,000

Compare this with the present operating income of $28,000. That is, $230,000 + $330,000 + $175,000 - ($190,000 + $300,000 + $100,000 + $117,000) = $28,000. The extra $14,000 of operating income comes from eliminating the $14,000 loss resulting from processing Product A beyond the split-off point.

<u>6-A3</u> (30-40 min.)

Problem 6-60 is an extension of this problem. The two problems make a good combination.

1. Operating inflows for each year, old machine:
      $910,000 - ($810,000 + $60,000) $40,000
      Operating inflows for each year, new machine:
      $910,000 - ($810,000 + $25,000*) $75,000

      * $60,000 - $35,000

Cash flow statements (in thousands of dollars):

	Keep			Buy		
			Three			Three
	Year	Years	Years	Year	Years	Years
	1	2 & 3	Together	1	2 & 3	Together
Receipts, inflows from operations	40	40	120	75	75	225
Disbursements:						
Purchase of "old" equipment	(87)*	–	(87)	(87)	–	(87)
Purchase of "new" equipment:						
Total costs less proceeds						
from disposal of "old"						
equipment ($99,000-$16,000)	–	–	–	(83)	–	(83)
Net cash inflow (outflow)	(47)	40	33	(95)	75	55

*Assumes that the outlay of $87,000 took place on January 2, 2004, or sometime during 2004. Some students will ignore this item, assuming correctly that it is irrelevant to the decision. However, note that a statement for the entire year was requested.

The difference for three years taken together is $22,000 ($55,000 - $33,000). Note particularly that the $87,000 book value can be omitted from the comparison. Merely cross out the entire line; although the column totals will be affected, the net difference will still be $22,000.

2. Income statements (in thousands of dollars):

	Keep		Buy		
		Three			Three
	Years	Years	Year	Years	Years
	1, 2 & 3	Together	1	2 & 3	Together
Sales	910	2,730	910	910	2,730
Expenses:					
Other expenses	810	2,430	810	810	2,430
Operating of machine	60	180	25	25	75
Depreciation	29	87*	33	33	99
Total expenses	899	2,697	868	868	2,604
Loss on disposal:					
Proceeds ("revenue")	–	–	(16)	–	(16)
Book value ("expense")	–	–	87	–	87*
Loss	–	–	71	–	71
Total charges	899	2,697	939	868	2,675
Net income	11	33	(29)	42	55

*As in part (1), the $87,000 book value can be omitted from the comparison without changing the $22,000 difference. This would mean dropping the depreciation item of $29,000 per year (a cumulative effect of $87,000) under the "keep" alternative, and dropping the book value item of $87,000 in the loss on disposal computation under the "buy" alternative.

Difference for three years together, $55,000 - $33,000 = $22,000.

Note the motivational factors here. A manager may be reluctant to replace simply because the large loss on disposal will severely harm the profit performance in Year 1.

3.   The net difference for the three years taken together would be unaffected because the item is a past cost. You can substitute any number for the original $87,000 figure without changing this answer.

For example, examine how the results would change in part (1) by inserting $1 million where the $87,000 now appears (in thousands of dollars):

		Keep: Three Years Together	Buy: Three Years Together	Difference
Receipts		120	225	105
Disbursements:				
Purchase of old equipment		(1,000)	(1,000)	0
Purchase of new equipment:				
Gross price	99			
Disposal proceeds of "old"	16	–	(83)	(83)
Net cash outflow		(880)	(858)	22

In sum, this may be a horrible situation. The manager really blundered. But keeping the old equipment will compound the blunder to the cumulative tune of $22,000 over the next three years.

4.   Diplomatically, Lee should try to convey the following. All of us tend to indulge in the erroneous idea that we can soothe the wounded pride of a bad purchase decision by using the item instead of replacing it. The fallacy is believing that a current or future action can influence the long-run impact of a past outlay. *All* past costs are down the drain. Nothing can change what has already happened.

The $87,000 has been spent. Subsequent accounting for the item is irrelevant. The schedules in parts (1) and (2) clearly show that we may *completely* ignore the $87,000 original outlay and still have a correct analysis. The important point is that the $87,000 is not an element of difference between alternatives and, therefore, may be safely ignored. The only relevant items are those expected future items that will *differ* between alternatives.

5.   The $87,000 purchase of the original equipment, the sales, and the other expenses are irrelevant because they are common to both alternatives. The relevant items are the following (in thousands of dollars):

	Three Years Together	
	Keep	Buy
Operating of machine (3 x $60; 3 x $25)	$180	$ 75
Incremental cost of new machine:		
Total cost		$99
Less proceeds of old machine		16
Incremental cost	–	83
Total relevant costs	$180	$158
Difference in favor of buying		$ 22

6-A4 (40-50 min.)

1.

COLUMBIA COMPANY
Contribution Income Statement
For the Year Ended December 31, 2004
(in thousands of dollars)

Sales		$1,800
Less variable expenses		
Direct material	$400	
Direct labor	330	
Variable manufacturing overhead (Schedule 1)	150	
Total variable manufacturing cost of goods sold	$880	
Variable selling expenses	60	
Variable administrative expenses	23	
Total variable expenses		963
Contribution margin		$ 837
Less fixed expenses:		
Fixed manufacturing overhead (Schedule 2)	$232	
Selling expenses	240	
Administrative expenses	121	
Total fixed expenses		593
Operating income		$ 244

COLUMBIA COMPANY
Absorption Income Statement
For the Year Ended December 31, 2004
(in thousands of dollars)

Sales		$1,800
Less manufacturing cost of goods sold:		
Direct material	$400	
Direct labor	330	
Manufacturing overhead (Schedules 1 and 2)	382	
Total manufacturing cost of goods sold		1,112
Gross margin		$ 688
Less:		
Selling expenses	$300	
Administrative expenses	144	444
Operating income		$ 244

COLUMBIA COMPANY
Schedules of Manufacturing Overhead
For the Year Ended December 31, 2004
(in thousands of dollars)

Schedule 1: Variable Costs		
Supplies	$ 20	
Utilities, variable portion	40	
Indirect labor, variable portion	90	$150
Schedule 2: Fixed Costs		
Utilities, fixed portion	$ 12	
Indirect labor, fixed portion	40	
Depreciation	110	
Property taxes	20	
Supervisory salaries	50	232
Total manufacturing overhead		$382

2. Change in revenue $200,000
   Change in total contribution margin:
      Contribution margin ratio in part 1 is $837 ÷ $1,800 = .465
      Ratio times increase in revenue is .465 x $200,000 $ 93,000
   Operating income before change   244,000
   New operating income $337,000

   This analysis is readily done by using data from the contribution
   income statement. In contrast, the data in the absorption income
   statement must be analyzed and split into variable and fixed
   categories before the effect on operating income can be estimated.

6-B1 (15-20 min.)

1.

	Make		Buy	
	Total	Per Unit	Total	Per Unit
Purchase cost			€10,000,000	€50
Direct material	€5,500,000	€27.5		
Direct labor	1,900,000	9.5		
Factory overhead, variable	1,100,000	5.5		
Factory overhead, fixed avoided	1,000,000	5.0		
Total relevant costs	€9,500,000	€47.5	€10,000,000	€50
Difference in favor of making	€ 500,000	€ 2.5		

The numerical difference in favor of making is €500,000 or €2.5 per unit. The relevant fixed costs are €1,000,000, not €2,500,000.

2.

	Make	Buy and Leave Capacity Idle	Buy and Rent
Rent revenue	–	–	€ 1,250,000
Obtaining of components	€(9,500,000)	€(10,000,000)	€(10,000,000)
Net relevant costs	€(9,500,000)	€(10,000,000)	€(8,750,000)

The final column indicates that buying the components and renting the vacated capacity will yield the best results in this case. The favorable difference is €9,500,000 - €8,750,000 = €750,000.

6-B2 (15 min.)

1.

Sales ($400 + $600 + $100)		$1,100
Costs:		
Raw materials	$700	
Processing	100	
Total		800
Profit		$300

2.

Sales ($860 + $850 + $175)		$1,885
Costs:		
Joint costs	$800	
Frozen dinner costs	470	
Salisbury steak costs	200	
Tanning costs	80	
Total costs		1,550
Profit		$ 335

Although it is more profitable to process all three products further than it is to sell them all at the split-off point, it is important to look at the economic benefit from further processing of each individual product.

3. Steaks to frozen dinners:

Additional revenue from processing further ($860 - $400)	$460
Additional cost for processing further	470
Increase (decrease) in profit from processing further	$ (10)

Hamburger to Salisbury steaks:

Additional revenue from processing further ($850 - $600)	$250
Additional cost for processing further	200
Increase (decrease) in profit from processing further	$ 50

Untanned hide to tanned hide:

    Additional revenue from processing further ($175 - $100) $75

    Additional cost for processing further   80

    Increase (decrease) in profit from processing further $ (5)

Only the hamburger should be processed further, because it is the only product whose additional revenue for processing further exceeds the additional cost. The resulting profit would be $350:

Sales ($400 + $850 + $100)		$1,350
Costs:		
Joint costs	$800	
Further processing of hamburger	200	
Total cost		1,000
Profit		$ 350

6-B3   (15-20 min.)

1.

| | Three Years Together | | |
	Keep	Replace	Difference
Cash operating costs	$42,000	$22,500	$19,500
Old equipment, book value:			
Periodic write-off as depreciation	15,000	-	
or lump-sum write-off	-	15,000*	
Disposal value		-3,000*	3,000
New equipment, acquisition cost		15,000**	- 15,000
Total costs	$57,000	$49,500	$ 7,500

*In a formal income statement, these two items would be combined as
"loss on disposal" of $15,000 - $3,000 = $12,000.
**In a formal income statement, written off as straight-line depreciation of
$15,000 ÷ 3 = $5,000 for each of three years.

2.

| | Three Years Together | | |
	Keep	Replace	Difference
Cash operating costs	$42,000	$22,500	$19,500
Disposal value of old equipment	-	-3,000	3,000
New equipment, acquisition cost	-	15,000	- 15,000
Total relevant costs	$42,000	$34,500	$ 7,500

This tabulation is clearer because it focuses on only those items that
affect the decision.

3. The prospective benefits of the replacement alternative:

3 x ($14,000 - $7,500) =	$19,500
Deduct initial net cash outlay required, $15,000 - $3,000 =	12,000
Difference in favor of replacement	$ 7,500

Of course, the new equipment is likely to be faster, thus saving operator
time. The latter is important, but it is not quantified in this problem.

<u>6-B4</u> (10 min.)

1. The replacement alternative would be chosen because the county would have $7,500 more cash accumulated in three years.

2. The keep alternative would be chosen because the higher overall costs of photocopying for the first year would be shown for the replacement alternative (under accrual accounting):

| | First Year | |
	Keep	Replace
Cash operating costs	$14,000	$ 7,500
Depreciation expense	5,000	5,000
Loss on disposal		12,000
Total costs	$19,000	$24,500

Thus, the performance evaluation model might motivate the manager to make a decision that would be undesirable in the long run.

1.   KINGLAND MANUFACTURING
                          Contribution Income Statement
                       For the Year Ended December 31, 2004
                           (In thousands of dollars)

Sales			$10,000
Less variable expenses:			
Direct material		$4,000	
Direct labor		2,000	
Variable indirect manufacturing costs (Schedule 1)		960	
Total variable manufacturing cost of goods sold			$6,960
Variable selling expenses:			
Sales commissions	$500		
Shipping expenses	300	800	
Variable clerical salaries		400	
Total variable expenses			8,160
Contribution margin			$ 1,840
Less fixed expenses:			
Manufacturing (Schedule 2)		$ 582	
Selling (advertising)		200	
Administrative-executive salaries		100	
Total fixed expenses			882
Operating income			$ 958

KINGLAND MANUFACTURING
Absorption Income Statement
For the Year Ended December 31, 2004
(In thousands of dollars)

Sales			$10,000
Less manufacturing cost of goods sold:			
Direct material		$4,000	
Direct labor		2,000	
Indirect manufacturing costs (Schedules 1 and 2)		1,542	7,542
Gross profit			$ 2,458
Selling expenses:			
Sales commissions	$500		
Advertising	200		
Shipping expenses	300	$1,000	
Administrative expenses:			
Executive salaries	$100		
Clerical salaries	400	500	1,500
Operating income			$ 958

KINGLAND MANUFACTURING
Schedules 1 and 2
Indirect Manufacturing Costs
For the Year Ended December 31, 2004
(In thousands of dollars)

Schedule 1: Variable Costs

Cutting bits	$ 60	
Abrasives for machining	100	
Indirect labor	800	$ 960

Schedule 2: Fixed Costs

Factory supervisors' salaries	$100	
Factory methods research	40	
Long-term rent, factory	100	
Fire insurance on equipment	2	
Property taxes on equipment	10	
Depreciation on equipment	300	
Factory superintendent's salary	30	582
Total indirect manufacturing costs		$1,542

2. Operating income would increase from $958,000 to $1,050,000, computed as follows:

Increase in revenue	$500,000
Increase in total contribution margin:	
Contribution margin ratio in contribution income statement is $1,840 ÷ $10,000 = .184.	
Ratio times revenue is .184 x $500,000	$ 92,000
Increase in fixed expenses	0
Operating income before increase	$958,000
New operating income	$1,050,000

The above analysis is readily calculated by using data from the contribution income statement. In contrast, the data in the absorption income statement must be analyzed and divided into variable and fixed categories before the effect on operating income can be estimated.

6-1   An opportunity cost does not entail a disbursement of cash at any future time, whereas an outlay cost does entail an additional disbursement sooner or later.

6-2   The $800 represents an opportunity cost. It is the amount forgone by rejecting an opportunity. It signifies that the value to the owner of keeping those strangers out of the summerhouse for that two-week period is at least $800.

6-3   Accountants do not ordinarily record opportunity costs in accounting records, because those records are traditionally concerned with real transactions rather than possible transactions. It is impossible to record data on all lost opportunities.

6-4   A differential cost is any difference in total cost or revenue between two alternatives. A differential cost is an incremental cost when one of the alternatives contains all the costs of the other plus some additional costs. The additional costs are the incremental costs – which are also differential.

6-5   No. Incremental cost has a broader meaning. It is the addition to total costs by the adoption of some course of action. Another term, marginal cost, is used by economists to indicate the addition to costs from the manufacture of *one* additional unit. Of course, marginal cost is indeed the incremental cost of one unit.

6-6   The decline in costs would be called differential or incremental savings.

6-7   Not necessarily. Qualitative factors can favor either making or buying. Often factors such as product quality and assurance of delivery schedules favor making. However, sometimes establishing long-term relationships with suppliers is an important qualitative factor favoring the purchase of components.

6-8   The choice in many cases is not really whether to make or buy. Instead, the choice is how best to use available capacity.

6-9   Joint products are two or more manufactured products that (1) have relatively significant sales values and (2) are not separately identifiable as individual products until their split-off point. Examples of joint products include chemicals, lumber, flour, and meat.

6-10   The split-off point is where the individual products produced in a joint process become separately identifiable. Costs before the split-off point are irrelevant for decisions about the individual products. They affect the decision about whether to undertake the entire production process, but they do not influence decisions about what to do with the individual products.

6-11   Yes. Techniques for assigning joint-product costs to individual products are useful only for product costing, not for deciding on further processing after the split-off point. The product must be considered separately at that point apart from its historical cost. The proper basis of the decision on further processing is a comparison of incremental revenue versus incremental expense between the alternatives of selling at the split-off point and processing further.

6-12   No. Once inventory has been purchased, the price paid is a sunk cost. It is true that selling at a price less than $5,000 would produce a reported loss. However, a sale at any price above $0 is economically beneficial provided that the only alternative is to scrap the inventory.

6-13   No. Sunk costs are irrelevant to the replacement decision.

6-14   No. Past costs are not relevant because they cannot be affected by a decision. Although past costs are often indispensable for formulating predictions, past costs themselves are not the predictions that are the inputs to decision models. Clear thinking is enhanced by these distinctions.

6-15   Only b and c are relevant.

a. Book value of old equipment is *irrelevant* to a replacement decision because it does not change under any alternative and cannot be realized.

b. Disposal value of old equipment is *relevant* to a replacement decision because it can either be realized (by replacement) or forgone (by continued use).

c. Cost of new equipment is *relevant* to a replacement decision because it can be incurred (by replacement) or avoided (by continued use).

6-16   Yes. Some expected future costs may be irrelevant because they will be the same under all feasible alternatives.

6-17   Yes. The statement is correct in terms of *total* variable costs.

6-18   Two reasons why unit costs should be analyzed with care in decision making are:

1. Most unit costs are stable only over a certain range of output, and care must be taken to see that allowances are made when alternatives are considered outside that range.

2. Some unit costs are an allocation of fixed costs; thus when a higher volume of output is being considered, unit cost will decrease proportionately, and vice versa.

Two other reasons are mentioned in the text:

1. Some unit costs are based on both relevant and irrelevant factors and should be broken down further before being considered.

2. Unit costs must be reduced to the same base (denominator) before comparing or combining them.

6-19   Sales personnel sometimes neglect to point out that the unit costs are based on outputs far in excess of the volume of their prospective customer.

6-20   An inconsistency between a decision model and a performance evaluation model occurs when a decision about whether to replace a piece of equipment is based on the cash flow effects over the life of the equipment but a manager's performance evaluation is based on the first year's reported income. The loss on disposal of the equipment is irrelevant for decision purposes, but it affects the first year income, hence the performance evaluation.

6-21   The wide use of income statements to evaluate performance may overly influence managers to maximize short-run performance that may hurt long-run performance. They may pass up profitable opportunities to replace equipment because of the large loss on disposal shown on the first year's income statement.

6-22   The contribution approach has several advantages over the absorption approach, including a better analysis of cost-volume-profit relationships, clearer presentation of all variable costs, and more relevant arrangement of data for such decisions as make-or-buy or product expansion.

6-23   The terms that describe an income statement that emphasizes the differences between variable or fixed costs are *contribution approach*, *variable costing*, or *direct costing*.

6-24   Yes, this statement is generally correct. Accountants record transactions. But opportunity cost is the cost of transactions that do not occur (or have not occurred yet). It is the cost of opportunities forgone. Managers usually have much better information about forgone opportunities than do accountants.

6-25   Deciding whether to outsource payroll functions requires estimates of the cost of designing, maintaining, and using a payroll system internally compared to the cost of a contract with an outside supplier. To operate an internal payroll system requires hiring personnel with the needed expertise in both legal/governmental issues affecting payroll and information processing to implement a system. Small companies often find it less costly to outsource payroll to a company that has broad expertise in these areas.

6-26 Whenever total costs are unitized by dividing by total units and the resulting unit costs are then used to predict new total costs based on a different level of production, errors are being made. If the new production level is higher, predicted total costs are overestimated. If the new production level is lower, predicted total costs are underestimated. Never unitize fixed costs if the resulting unit cost will be used for planning purposes! Consider the following simple example:

	Fixed Cost	Variable Cost	Total
Total	$100	$100	$200
Units	10	10	10
Unit Cost	$10	$10	$20

If a new planned number of units is 20, what will be the new, predicted total cost?

The _correct_ cost function and cost prediction is

Total Cost = $100 + $10 x Number of units
        = $100 + $10 x 20
        = $300

The correct cost function is based on the two amounts that are constant within the relevant range – the _total fixed cost_ and the _unit variable cost_.

The _incorrect unitized_ cost function and incorrect and overestimated prediction is

Total Cost = $20 x Number of units
        = $20 x 20
        = $400

It is easy to see that the error comes from treating fixed costs as if they were variable.

6-27 The amount paid for inventory is a sunk cost. Once a company has the inventory, it cannot change what it paid for it. Thus the only relevant issue is what can be done with the inventory. If there is a choice of selling the inventory for less than what the company paid for it or not selling it at all, it is certainly better to get something rather than nothing for it.

6-28 Managers generally find contribution margin income statements more useful, especially if they are concerned with short-term results. The contribution margin statement provides information on the immediate profit impact of increases or decreases in sales.

<u>6-29</u> (10-15 min.)

1.

	Independent Practice	Employee	Difference
Operating revenues	$320,000	$90,000	$230,000
Operating expenses	220,000	–	220,000
Income effects per year	$100,000	$90,000	$ 10,000

	Choose Independent Practice	
Revenues		$320,000
Expenses:		
Outlay costs	$220,000	
Opportunity cost of employee compensation	90,000	310,000
Income effects per year		$ 10,000

Each tabulation produces the key difference of $10,000. As a general rule, we favor using the first tabulation. It offers a straightforward presentation of inflows and outflows under sharply stated alternatives.

2.

	Choice as Employee	
Revenue		$ 90,000
Expenses:		
Outlay costs	$ 0	
Opportunity cost of accounting practice	100,000	100,000
Income effects per year		$ (10,000)

If the employee alternative is selected, the key difference in favor of becoming a sole practitioner is again $10,000. Bridgeman is sacrificing $10,000 to avoid the risks of an independent practice.

6-30 (10-15 min.)

	Alternatives Under Consideration		
	(1)	(2)	(1) - (2)
	Sell, Rent, and Invest in Bonds	Hold Present Home	Difference
Revenue	$12,000*	$ -	$12,000
Less: Outlay cost	10,000	6,000	4,000
Income effects per year	$ 2,000	$(6,000)	$ 8,000

*6% x $200,000

Advantage of selling home is $2,000 + $6,000 = $8,000. Obviously, if rent is higher, the advantage decreases.

The above analysis does not contain explicit opportunity costs. If opportunity costs were a part of the analysis, the following presentation applies (whereby the interest on investment in bonds is not listed as a separate alternative but is regarded as a forgone alternative):

	Alternative Chosen: Hold Present Home

Opportunity cost	$2,000
Outlay cost	6,000
Income effects per year	$8,000

As before, the advantage of selling the home and renting is $8,000. The opportunity cost of home ownership is $12,000 - $10,000 = $2,000.

6-31 (15-20 min.) Opportunity cost is the maximum available contribution to profit forgone by using limited resources for a particular purpose (page 252). In this case, the opportunity cost of the machine when analyzing the alternative to produce 12-oz. bottles of Juice Cocktails is the larger of the $90,000 contribution margin from additional sales of the 100% Juices or the $75,000 proceeds from the sale of the machine. The $160,000 historical cost of the machine is a past cost and thus irrelevant.

6-32 (15-20 min.) The first tabulation is probably easier to understand, but the choice of a tabulation is a matter of taste:

	(a) Expand Laboratory Testing	(b) Expand Eye Clinic	(c) Rent to Gift Shop
Revenues	$320,000	$500,000	$11,000
Expenses	290,000	480,000	0
Income effects per year	$ 30,000	$ 20,000	$11,000

Treating the gift shop as the forgone (rejected) alternative, the tabulation is:

	(a) Expand Laboratory Testing		(b) Expand Eye Clinic	
Revenue		$320,000		$500,000
Expenses:				
Outlay costs	$290,000		$480,000	
Opportunity cost, rent forgone	11,000	301,000	11,000	491,000
Income effects per year		$ 19,000		$ 9,000

The numbers favor laboratory testing, which will generate a contribution to hospital income that is $10,000 greater than the eye clinic's. The numbers have been analyzed correctly under both tabulations. Both answer the key query: What difference does it make? As a general rule, we prefer using the first tabulation. It is a straightforward presentation.

<u>6-33</u>   (15 min.)

1.   It is easiest to analyze total costs, not unit costs.

	Make	Purchase
Direct materials	$300,000	
Avoidable overhead costs:		
Indirect labor	30,000	
Supplies	20,000	
Allocated occupancy cost	0	
Purchase cost		$340,000
Total relevant costs	$350,000	$340,000

The difference in favor of purchasing is $350,000 - $340,000 = $10,000.

2.   Because the quantitative difference is small, qualitative factors may dominate the decision. Companies using a just-in-time system need assurance of both quality and timeliness of supplies of materials, parts, and components. A small, local company may not be reliable enough for Bose. In essence, Bose may be willing to "invest" $10,000, the quantitative advantage of purchasing, in order to have more control over the supply of the components.

The division manager may have made the right decision for the wrong reason. He incorrectly ignored avoidable fixed costs, leading to a mistaken belief that making the components was less costly by $.40 per unit or $40,000 in total. The $50,000 of avoidable fixed costs makes the purchase option less costly by $10,000. If the manager's decision is to make the component, it should be because forgoing profits of $10,000 has a long-run qualitative benefit of more than $10,000, not because the bid is greater than the variable cost.

6-34 (20-25 min.)

Nantucket Nectars should make the bottles.

	Make		Buy	
	Total	Per Bottle	Total	Per Bottle
Purchase cost			$250,000	$.250
Direct materials	$85,000	$.085		
Direct labor	30,000	.030		
Variable overhead	60,000	.060		
Avoidable fixed overhead	60,000	.060		
Total relevant costs	$235,000	$.235	$250,000	$.250
Difference in favor of making	$15,000	$.015		

6-35 (15-20 min.)

	Make	Buy and Leave Facilities Idle	Buy and Use Facilities for Other Activities	Buy and Rent Out Facilities
Contribution from other activities			$ 75	
Rent revenue				$ 55
Relevant cost of bottles	$(235)	$(250)	(250)	(250)
Net relevant costs	$(235)	$(250)	$(175)	$(195)

Nantucket Nectars should buy the bottles and use the facilities for other activities.

<u>6-36</u> (10 min.)

Product M should not have been processed further. The only valid approach is to concentrate on the separable costs and revenues *beyond* split-off:

	Sell at Split-off as M	Process Further as Super M	Difference
Revenues, 2,500,000 gallons @30¢ & 38¢	$750,000	$950,000	$200,000
Separable costs beyond split-off	–	225,000	225,000
Income effects for April	$750,000	$725,000	$ (25,000)

The joint costs do not differ between alternatives and are irrelevant to the question of whether to sell or process further. The next table (not required) confirms the results (in thousands):

	Alternative 1			Alternative 2			Differential
	L	M	Total	L	Super M	Total	Effects
Revenues	$1,000	$750	$1,750	$1,000	$950	$1,950	$200
Joint costs			$1,600			$1,600	—
Separable costs		—			225	225	225
Total costs			$1,600			$1,825	$225
Income effects			$ 150			$ 125	$ (25)

<u>6-37</u> (10 min.)

1. Answer (c): $8,000 ÷ 2,000 = $4.00

2. Answer (a): Product A is the only product that produces an incremental profit ($42,000 - $25,000) - $9,000 = $8,000.

313

<u>6-38</u>   (5-10 min.)

1.   The only relevant item is the $250 to be received for the calendars. No
     additional costs will be incurred. Therefore, profit will be $250 higher
     if the offer is accepted than if it is rejected.

2.   The amount paid for the calendars is irrelevant. Even if $1 million had
     been paid for the calendars, the added profit from selling them for
     $250 is $250. The $900 paid is a past cost, a sunk cost, that will not be
     affected by the decision.

<u>6-39</u>   (15-20 min.)

1.   The difference in total costs over the five years is $2,000 in favor of
     replacement, computed as follows:

	Five Years Together		
	Keep	Replace	Difference
Cash operating costs	$22,500	$10,000	$ 12,500
Old machine (book value):			
Depreciation	5,000	–	
or			–
Lump-sum write-off	–	5,000	
Disposal value	–	-2,000	2,000
New machine: Acquisition cost	–	12,500	-12,500
Total costs	$27,500	$25,500	$ 2,000

2.   The loss on disposal of the old machine combines the lump-sum
     write-off (an irrelevant item) with the disposal value (a relevant item),
     $5,000 - $2,000 = $3,000 loss on disposal. Because of the inclusion of
     an irrelevant item, this amount does not affect the computation in
     requirement 1. It is best to keep the lump-sum write-off and the
     disposal value separate, as is done in the table in requirement 1.

6-40 (10 min.)

1. Variable cost $ 90,000
    Fixed cost   110,000
    Total cost $200,000

    Cost per unit, $200,00 ÷ 10,000 $ 20.00

2. Variable cost $180,000
    Fixed cost   110,000
    Total cost $290,000

    Cost per unit, $290,000 ÷ 20,000 $ 14.50

3. The two unit costs are equally accurate (or, more appropriately, equally inaccurate). Unit costs that include unitized fixed costs are always suspect. A unit cost that includes fixed costs will be accurate at only one volume; using it at any other volume will be misleading.

6-41 (10 min.)

The original investment is the "cash equivalent" cost. "Excess" trade-in allowances, such as the $1,500 in this instance, are really reductions in the "list price." The $1,260 sales tax is added to the original cost. The problem is silent regarding how the sales tax is computed. The original investment is:

List price	$21,000
Less price allowance, $4,500 - $3,000	1,500
Cash equivalent cost before sales tax	$19,500
Sales tax	1,260
Cash equivalent cost	$20,760

The annual cash operating costs are irrelevant. Another way of computing the $20,760 is:

Cash payment ($21,000 - $4,500 + $1,260)	$17,760
Opportunity cost of truck traded in	3,000
Total cost	$20,760

(10 min.)

The $9 million is gone. It is irrelevant for decision purposes. The relevant comparison is whether to invest $5 million in the division or to invest it elsewhere:

	Sell Division	Hold Division
Investment required	$5 million	$5 million
Income generated	?	$500,000 yearly*

*This assumes that the division has truly "turned around" and will now make a net profit of $500,000 per year for the foreseeable future.

The $5 million is relevant because Lake Forest is forgoing the opportunity to invest it elsewhere for some return. If projects or divisions of comparable risk can be expected to generate more than $500,000 yearly, the division should be sold.

<u>6-43</u>   (10-15 min.)

The purpose of this problem is to sharpen the student's concept of "opportunity cost." Daily fees are $140 x 6 hours, or $840.

1.   The difference in annual income is $241,920 - $221,760 = $20,160:

	(a) Work	(b) Don't Work
Work, $840 x 6 days x 48 weeks	$241,920	
Don't work on every other Saturday:		
$840 x 5 days x 24 weeks		$100,800
$840 x 6 days x 24 weeks		120,960
Totals	$241,920	$221,760

2.   The calculation in (1) seems awkward and unnecessary. The opportunity cost is the maximum amount forgone by not working on every other Saturday, which is $840 x 1 day x 24 weeks, or $20,160. This is really the key number because it answers the crucial question, "What difference does it make?" Opportunity cost is defined as the maximum available contribution to profit forgone by using limited resources for a particular purpose.

3.   If she has already decided to take the day off, her opportunity cost is zero because in any case she would not see patients. Note that opportunity cost is a "situation-specific" concept. If one of the possible alternatives is not even allowed into the feasible set by the decision maker, its financial effects are irrelevant. On the other hand, if she decided to repair her car instead of keeping the appointments with patients on a *working* Saturday, her opportunity cost for the day would be $840; for half a day, $420.

<u>6-44</u>   (10 min.) This is a basic exercise. Answers are in thousands of dollars.

1.   210 + 150 + 170 = 530
2.   700 - 530 = 170
3.   170 - 150 = 20
4.   150 + 170 = 320

<u>6-45</u>   (10-15 min.) This is a basic exercise.

Sales		¥770
Variable expenses:		
Direct materials	¥290	
Direct labor	140	
Variable factory overhead	<u>60</u>	
(a) Variable manufacturing cost of goods sold	¥490	
Variable selling and admin. expenses	<u>100</u>	
Total variable expenses		<u>590</u>
(b) Contribution margin		¥180
Fixed expenses:		
Fixed factory overhead	¥120	
Fixed selling and administrative expenses	<u>45</u>	<u>165</u>
(c) Operating income		<u>¥ 15</u>

6-46 (15-20 min.)

This is a straightforward exercise in basic terms and relationships. To fill all the blanks, both absorption and contribution income statements must be prepared. Data are in millions of dollars. Required answers are in italics.

	Absorption Approach		Contribution Approach	
Sales		$920		$920
Direct materials used	$350		$350	
Direct labor	210		210	
Variable indirect manufacturing costs	100		100	
f. *Variable manufacturing cost of goods sold*			660	
Variable selling and administrative expenses			90	
Total variable expenses				750
k. *Contribution margin*				170
Fixed factory overhead	50		50	
g. *Manufacturing cost of goods sold*		710		
j. *Gross profit*		210		
Fixed selling and administrative expenses	80		80	130
Variable selling and administrative expenses	90	170		
Operating income		$ 40		$ 40

320

6-47   (10-20 min.) Answers are in thousands of rands.

$$\text{Prime costs} = \text{Direct material} + \text{Direct labor}$$
$$600 = 370 + DL$$
$$DL = 230$$

The body of a model income statement follows. The computations are explained for each item that was originally blank. Numbers given in the problem are in bold.

Sales, 780 + 120		ZAR900
Direct materials	ZAR370	
Direct labor, 600 - 370	230	
Factory overhead, 780 - (370 + 230)	180	
Manufacturing cost of goods sold		780
Gross margin		ZAR120
Selling and administrative expenses*		100
Operating income		ZAR 20

*120 - 20

6-48 (15-20 min.) The data are placed in the format of the income statement, and the unknowns are computed as shown:

Sales		$970
Variable expenses		
Direct materials	$210	
Direct labor	170	
Variable factory overhead	110	
Variable manufacturing cost of goods sold		490 [1]
Variable selling and administrative expenses		280 [2]
Total variable expenses (970 - 200)		770
Contribution margin		200
Fixed expenses		
Fixed factory overhead	90 [3]	
Fixed selling and administrative expenses	100	190
Operating income		$ 10

[1] 210 + 170 + 110 = 490
[2] 970 - 200 = 770; 770 - 490 = 280
[3] Total fixed expenses = 200 - 10 = 190
    Fixed factory overhead = 190 - 100 = 90

6-49 (15-25 min.)

1.

	With American Airlines Personnel	Without American Airlines Personnel
Contribution margin for October 20:		
$100 x 50	–	$5,000 – Var. Cost
$ 50 x 50	$2,500 – Var. Cost	–

Opportunity cost is a slippery term, so we are reluctant to be overly rigid about its definition during classroom sessions. The strict definition would be that the opportunity cost is $5,000 less the variable cost of maintaining the rooms–the maximum profit forgone by rejecting the best forsaken alternative. Nevertheless, some students will insist that the $5,000 - $2,500 = $2,500 difference between the alternatives is the opportunity cost.

On December 28, the opportunity cost would be 10 x $80 – Var. Cost = $800 – Variable cost.

2.   The simplest approach is:

$$\text{Let } X = \% \text{ of occupancy}$$
$$\text{Then } \$90X = \$50$$
$$X = \$50 \div \$90 = 55.56\%$$

A longer approach follows. To be indifferent, Marriott would have to generate the same rent as the American Airlines contract which is $50 x 50 rooms x 365 days = $912,500.

$$\text{Let } Y = \text{Number of rooms per day @ } \$90$$
$$\$90(Y)365 = \$912,500$$
$$\$32,850Y = \$912,500$$
$$Y = 27.778 \text{ rooms per day}$$

Percentage of occupancy of the 50 rooms = 27.778 ÷ 50
= .55556
= 55.56%

To check the answer:
$90 x .55556(50) x 365 = $912,507 (higher than $912,500 because of rounding up to .55556)

6-50 (10-15 min.)

1. Contribution margin from airlines: ($50 - $10)(50)(365) = $730,000
   General contribution margin: ($90 - $10)(50)(365)(.53) = $773,800
   Marriott should reject the contract.

   Compare the answers to 6-49 and 6-50. Note that the answer to requirement 2 of 6-49 (55.56%) implies that the answer to 6-50 should be to accept the contract. Why? Because general occupancy (53%) is expected to be less than the indifference point. However, when variable costs are considered, Marriott should reject the contract.

2.
$$\text{Let } X = \text{occupancy rate}$$
$$(\$90 - \$10)(50)(365)(X) = \$730,000$$
$$\$1,460,000X = \$730,000$$
$$X = .50 \text{ or } 50\% \text{ occupancy rate}$$

<u>6-51</u> (10-20 min.)

The point of requirement 2 is to emphasize that the essence of make or buy is how to best utilize facilities.

1.

	Make		Buy	
	Total	Per Unit	Total	Per Unit
Purchase cost			$1,050,000	$21
Direct material	$400,000	$ 8		
Direct labor	300,000	6		
Variable factory overhead	150,000	3		
Fixed factory overhead that can be avoided by not making	100,000	2		
Total relevant costs	$950,000	$19	$1,050,000	$21
Difference in favor of making	$100,000	$ 2		

2.

	Make	Buy and Leave Facilities Idle	Buy and Rent	Buy and Use Facilities for Oil Filters
Rent revenue	$ -	$ -	$ 65,000	$ -
Contribution from other products	-	-	-	200,000
Obtaining of parts	(950,000)	(1,050,000)	(1,050,000)	(1,050,000)
Net relevant costs	$(950,000)	$(1,050,000)	$ (985,000)	$ (850,000)

The analysis indicates that buying the parts and using the vacated facilities for the production of other products is the alternative that should yield the best results in this instance. The advantage over making the parts is $950,000 - $850,000, = $100,000.

6-52 (35-50 min.)

Note: Requirement 2 of this problem usually gives trouble to students; because Requirement 2 takes considerable class time for a clear explanation, you may prefer to assign Requirement 1 only.

1. There are several ways to approach this problem. The easiest is probably to concentrate on the difference in the total contribution margin. The total fixed costs of $780,000, before considering the increase in advertising, will be unaffected and may be ignored. Production and sales will decline by 10%, from 60,000 to 54,000 units:

	60,000 Units	54,000 Units	Difference
Sales at $90 and $98, respectively	$5,400,000	$5,292,000	
Variable costs at $70*	4,200,000	3,780,000	
Contribution margin	$1,200,000	$1,512,000	$312,000

*$35 + $12 + $8 + $15

Advertising may be increased by $312,000 without affecting the current operating income level of $420,000 (contribution margin of $1,200,000 minus fixed expenses of $780,000).

2. If the total fixed costs do not change, the company will need a total contribution margin of $1,200,000 from the two products together. How many units of the new product can be sold? The clue to the production capacity of the plant is in how fixed factory overhead was unitized: $300,000 ÷ $6 per unit = 50,000 units of expected sales.

New product budget @ 50,000 Units:

Sales at $40	$2,000,000
Variable costs at $30*	1,500,000
Contribution margin, new product	$ 500,000

*Direct material	$ 6
Direct labor	12
Variable factory overhead	8
Variable selling expense, 10% x $40	4
Total variable costs per unit	$30

Therefore, the needed contribution margin on the old product is $1,200,000 - $500,000, or $700,000.

Sales, 60,000 units at $90	$5,400,000
Contribution margin needed	700,000
Total variable costs that can be sustained	$4,700,000
Variable selling costs at $9*	540,000
Maximum that may be paid to the supplier	$4,160,000

*$15 less 40% = $9 or 60% ($15 x 60,000) = $540,000

Maximum unit purchase price, $4,160,000 ÷ 60,000 = $69.33.

If students do not accept the above analysis, the following proof may be helpful (in thousands):

	Old	Difference	New Product 1	New Product 2
Sales	$5,400	$2,000	$5,400	$2,000
Variable costs	4,200	2,000	4,700*	1,500
Contribution margin	$1,200	$ -	$ 700	$ 500
Fixed manufacturing costs	300	-	-	300
Fixed selling costs	480	-	380**	100**
Total fixed costs	$ 780	$ -	$ 380	$ 400
Operating income	$ 420	$ -	$ 320	$ 100

*An alternate approach to this whole solution is to use the above format and solve toward the unknown purchases figure. The $4,700,000 is the maximum allowable variable cost. Because $540,000 of the $4,700,000 represents selling expense, the remainder, $4,160,000 must be the maximum that may be paid to the supplier.

**This allocation uses the $2.00 unit cost figure for the new product and assigns the remaining fixed costs to the old product. Note, however, that how the total fixed selling costs are allocated is irrelevant because total fixed costs are unaffected by allocation methods or by how such costs are assigned to products.

6-53 (15-25 min.)

1.

	Alternative	
	Without Contract	With Contract
Contribution margin:		
(200 rooms x 365 days)($85 - $12)(.85)	$4,529,650	
(200 - 40)(365)($85-$12)(.95)		$4,050,040
(40)(365)($50 - $12)		554,800
Total contribution margin	$4,529,650	$4,604,840
Difference in favor of contract	$75,190	

2. Let X = contribution margin per room

$$(40)(365)(X) + \$4,050,040 = \$4,529,650$$
$$14,600X = \$479,610$$
$$X = \$32.85$$

Add back variable cost: $32.85 + $12.00 = $44.85

Note how this room rate is the "point of indifference." The manager has $50.00 - $44.85 = $5.15 of leeway to bargain on contract rates.

329

6-54 (10-20 min.)

The basic message here is that airlines can maintain the same revenue per mile even in the face of switching by some passengers to lower fares.

1.

	Without Discount	With Discount
Revenue, 75 @ $.12	$9.00	
Revenue		
72 @ $.12		$8.64
6 @ $.072		.43
Total per airplane mile	$9.00	$9.07

Note that a minor (4%) gain in passengers will be beneficial. Note, too, that airlines have negligible variable costs of adding a few passengers in otherwise empty seats.

Some instructors may want to use the language of "opportunity costs" here, but such language is not really necessary and may be confusing. For example, some observers would say that the three passengers who switch cause an opportunity cost of 3 x $.12 or $.36 that is more than offset by the added revenue of 6 x $.072 or $.43.

2. Let X = number of passengers who switch

Revenue with discount = Revenue without discount

$$50(.60)(\$.12) = X(\$.12)$$
$$50(\$.072) = \$.12(X)$$
$$\$3.60 = \$.12(X)$$
$$X = \$3.60 \div \$.12 = 30 \text{ passengers}$$

Check:	Without Discount	With Discount
Revenue, 75 @ $.12	$9.00	
Revenue:		
(75 - 30) @ $.12		$5.40
50 @ $.072		3.60
Total per airplane mile	$9.00	$9.00

Therefore, if more than 20 of the 50 discount passengers are "new," that is, they would not have flown without the discount, there is more revenue with the discount plan. The indifference point results in 95 passengers, 50 paying the discount fare and 45 paying full fare.

6-55 (25-40 min.)

1. Sets result in a 20% sales increase: 1,250 x 1.20 = 1,500 dresses.

	Percent of Total	Total Number of			Total
		Dresses	Capes	Handbags	
Complete sets	70%	1,050	1,050	1,050	
Dress and cape	6	90	90		
Dress and handbag	15	225		225	
Dress only	9	135			
Total units if accessories are introduced	100%	1,500	1,140	1,275	
Unit sales if accessories are not introduced		1,250	—	—	
Incremental sales		250	1,140	1,275	
Incremental contribution margin per unit		€ 650	€ 40	€ 20	
Total incremental contribution margin		€ 162,500	€45,600	€25,500	€ 233,600

Additional costs
  Additional cutting cost (1,500 x €36)   € 54,000
  Additional material cost (250 x €320)   80,000
  Cutting cost on additional dresses (250 x €100) 25,000
  Lost remnant sales (1,250 x €25)   31,250
                                                            190,250
Incremental profit   €   43,350

2. Nonquantitative factors that could influence management in its decision to manufacture matching capes and handbags include:
   - accuracy of forecasted increase in dress sales.
   - accuracy of forecasted product mix.
   - company image from dress manufacturer only to a more extensive supplier of women's apparel.
   - competition from other manufacturers of women's apparel.
   - whether there is adequate capacity (labor, facilities, storage, etc.).

6-56 (15-30 min.)

1.
Sales: 10,000 x 12 x $12			$1,440,000
Less expenses: Direct materials	$ 4.20		
Direct labor	.60		
Overhead	1.50		
Selling	4.10		
10,000 x 12 x $10.40			1,248,000
Operating income [or: (10,000 x 12) ($12 - $10.40)]			$ 192,000

2.
Sales	
10,000 x 12 x 120% x $11 = 144,000 x $11	$1,584,000
Less variable expenses:	
($4.20 + $.60 + $.70 + $3.00)(144,000)	1,224,000
Contribution margin	$ 360,000
Less fixed expenses: ($.80 + $1.10)(120,000)	228,000
Operating income	$ 132,000

(A common student error is to use 144,000 units at old fixed costs per unit.)

3.
Cost to obtain order: $6,000 ÷ 5,000	$1.20
Direct materials	4.20
Direct labor	.60
Variable overhead	.70
Variable selling expenses: 60% of $3.00	1.80
Minimum price for special order	$8.50

4. The variable selling expenses only $3.00

6-57 (15-20 min.)

1. The salesman's analysis is faulty because it includes depreciation on the old equipment, which is irrelevant. Moreover, both the total and unit costs are based on an annual volume of 40,000 units, which may not necessarily be accurate. A correct analysis would compare the old machine cost of ($6 variable cost x expected volume) with the new machine cost of ($4 variable cost x expected volume + $60,000 fixed cost).

2.

	New Machine	Old Machine
Units	20,000	20,000
Variable costs	$ 80,000	$120,000
Straight-line depreciation	60,000	-
Total cost	$140,000	$120,000
Unit cost	$7.00	$6.00

3.   Let X = Number of units

$$\$60,000 + \$4X = \$6X$$
$$X = 30,000 \text{ units}$$

<u>6-58</u>   (15 min.)

Marketing management misjudged the life of the old freight cars. This may raise questions about the accuracy of the estimated useful life of the new freight cars. However, the unexpired costs of the old freight cars are not relevant to this decision. The conceptual error being made by the operating manager is the failure to distinguish between two decisions: the original decision and the current decision. Instead, he is mixing the two so that neither is evaluated correctly.

The current decision should be influenced solely by expected future revenues and outlays, including the capital investment. The book value of the old equipment is *per se* irrelevant. The current decision should not carry the burden of past blunders.

The past decision should be audited. In this instance, hindsight reveals that marketing management was overly optimistic. The key question is whether unwarranted optimism is being used again to justify additional outlays.

Some instructors may wish to point out how decisions such as these might be affected by the long-term relationships with a big customer at this and other locations. Many decisions have such interdependencies.

<u>6-59</u> (15-30 min.)

1.   Cost Comparison–Replacement of Equipment
                              Relevant Items Only

	Three Years Together		
	Keep	Replace	Difference
Cash operating costs	$30,000	$18,000	$12,000
Disposal value of old equipment		-3,000	3,000
Acquisition cost–new equipment		12,000	-12,000
Total relevant costs	$30,000	$27,000	$ 3,000

The advantage of replacement is $3,000 for the three years together.

2.   Cost Comparison–Replacement of Equipment
                        Including Relevant and Irrelevant Items

	Three Years Together		
	Keep	Replace	Difference
Cash operating costs	$30,000	$18,000	$12,000
Old equipment (book value):			
Periodic write-off as depreciation	9,000		
or			—
Lump-sum write-off		9,000*	
Disposal value	—	-3,000*	3,000
New equipment, acquisition cost	—	12,000**	-12,000
Total costs	$39,000	$36,000	$ 3,000

*In a formal income statement, these two items would be combined
  as "loss on disposal" of $9,000 - $3,000 = $6,000.
** In a formal income statement, written off as straight-line depreciation
  of $12,000 ÷ 3 = $4,000 for each of the three years.

3.

	Keep	Replace
Cash operating costs	$10,000	$ 6,000
Depreciation expense	3,000	4,000
Loss on disposal ($9,000 - $3,000)	—	6,000
Total charges against revenue	$13,000	$16,000

Assuming the manager is evaluated on the basis of the division's profitability, the performance evaluation model for the first year indicates a difference *in favor of keeping*: $16,000 - $13,000 = $3,000. As indicated earlier in this solution, such a decision would result in $3,000 <u>less</u> income over the next three years together. However, some managers would adhere to the short-run view and not replace the equipment.

6-60 (10 min.)

This problem extends problem 6-A3. It should not be assigned without also assigning 6-A3.

1. The "replace" alternative would be chosen because it enhances cumulative wealth.

2. The division would show lower income for the first year under the "replace" alternative. The manager who wants to show better short-run performance will oppose replacement.

3. The answers to the first two parts probably would be unaffected. The point is that decision models and performance evaluation models may conflict in nonprofit organizations too. Moreover, the money in the budget appropriation may have been spent. In addition, there is a higher likelihood of unfavorable publicity and also a danger of cuts in subsequent budget appropriations.

<u>6-61</u> (20 min.)

The numbers in this case are a slight modification of those given in an article in the *New York Times*, November 21, 1994.

1.

	On Broadway	Off Broadway
Attendance	400	400
Revenue	$176,000	$128,000
Expenses	206,000*	82,000
Net profit (loss)	$ (30,000)	$ 46,000

*$82,000 + $124,000 = $206,000

2.

	On Broadway	Off Broadway
Attendance	750	375
Revenue	$330,000	$120,000
Expenses	206,000	82,000
Net profit	$124,000	$ 38,000

3. a. $206,000 ÷ $55 = 3,745 weekly attendance
        3,745 ÷ 8 = 468 per show attendance
    b. $82,000 ÷ $40 = 2,050 weekly attendance
        2,050 ÷ 8 = 256 per show attendance

4.

	On Broadway	Off Broadway
Attendance	600	400
Revenue	$264,000	$128,000
Expenses	206,000	82,000
Net profit	$ 58,000	$ 46,000

Total profit for a 26-week run:
    On Broadway: ($58,000 x 26) - $1,295,000 = $213,000
    Off Broadway: ($46,000 x 26) - $ 440,000 = $756,000

5. Total profit for a 100-week run:
        On Broadway: ($58,000 x 100) - $1,295,000 = $4,505,000
        Off Broadway: ($46,000 x 100) - $ 440,000 = $4,160,000

6. a. $1,295,000 ÷ $58,000 = 22.3 weeks

    b. $ 440,000 ÷ $46,000 =   9.6 weeks

7. Let X be the length of run in weeks at which on-Broadway profit
    equals off-Broadway profit:

    $58,000 X - $1,295,000 = $46,000 X - $440,000

    $12,000 X = $855,000

    X = 71.25 weeks

8. Mr. Simon's decision depends on both his predictions of attendance
    on Broadway versus off Broadway and his attitude toward risk. The
    on-Broadway production has more risk because of its bigger up-front
    investment. If the attendance figures in requirements 4 and 5 are
    accurate (400 off-Broadway and 600 on-Broadway), the off-Broadway
    alternative is better for any runs less than 71.25 weeks. Because this
    is a long run and many successful shows have runs shorter than 50
    weeks, it appears that the off-Broadway alternative might be best.
    However, if attendance on Broadway can exceed 600 per show,
    especially if it approaches the capacity of 1,000 per show, there is
    much more money to be made on Broadway.

    There is a trend for non-musical plays to be produced off Broadway
    because of the large investment required on Broadway. Many plays
    do not last beyond a few weeks, and even filling a theater to capacity
    would require more than a 5-week run just to recoup the initial
    investment. Weekly profit would be ($55 x 1,000 x 8) - $206,000 =
    $234,000, so it would take $1,295,000 ÷ $234,000 = 5.5 weeks to break
    even. There is less risk off Broadway, especially because it takes
    many fewer theatergoers to reach the break-even point. For example,
    at capacity operations it takes 5.5 x 8 x 1,000 = 44,000 attendees to
    break even on Broadway. Off Broadway it requires only a little more
    than half that number:

    ($40 x 500 x 8) - $82,000 = $78,000 weekly profit

    $440,000 ÷ $78,000 = 5.6 weeks to break even

    5.6 x 8 x 500 = 22,400 attendees to break even.

<u>6-62</u>   (15-20 min.)

1.   The opportunity cost of the land is 10% x $15,000,000 = $1,500,000.

2.   Costs saved by closure of tomato farm:

Variable production costs	$ 550,000
Shipping costs	200,000
Saved fixed costs	300,000
Opportunity cost of land	1,500,000
Total	$2,550,000

Cost of purchasing tomatoes:
   8,000,000 lbs. x $.25/lb. = $2,000,000

Net savings to Agribiz from closing the tomato farm and buying tomatoes on the market is $2,550,000 - $2,000,000 = $550,000.

3.   The main ethical issue involves the impact of the plant closure on employees and on the community.

<u>6-63</u>   (10–15 min.)

1.   Assuming that reprocessing creates beans of acceptable quality, Starbucks should reprocess the beans because it generates more profit than selling them as-is.

Sell as is:	$2.65 x 1,000 = $2,650	
Reprocess:	Revenue, $3.70 x 1,000	$3,700
	Reprocessing cost	(600)
	Shipping cost	(200)
	Total	$2,900

2.

Sell as is	$2,650
Reprocess	2,900
Advantage to reprocessing	$ 250

3.   The cost of buying and roasting the original beans is irrelevant.

6-64 (30-40 min.)

1. Minnetonka Corporation should *make* the bindings.

    Cost saved by purchasing bindings:

Material, 20% x $30	$ 6.00
Labor, 10% x $35	3.50
Overhead, 10% x $5*	.50
Total	$10.00
Cost to buy per pair	$10.50

    *Total overhead is $15 per pair
    Allocated overhead is $100,000 ÷ 10,000 = $10 per pair
    Therefore, variable overhead is $15 - $10 = $5 per pair.

2. Minnetonka Corporation would *not pay more than* $10 each because that is the cost to make the product internally.

3. At a volume of 12,500 pair, Minnetonka should *buy* the bindings. The cost of buying 12,500 pair is $131,250. The cost of making 12,500 pair is:

12,500 x $10	$125,000	
Added fixed costs	10,000	
Total	$135,000	
Buying the bindings will save		$ 3,750

    Making the bindings saves variable costs of $.50 per pair. If sales exceed $10,000 ÷ $.50/pair = 20,000 pair, it is cheaper to make the bindings.

4. Minnetonka Corporation needs 12,500 pair of bindings. The cost to buy 12,500 pair is $131,250. The cost to make 10,000 and buy 2,500 is:

Cost to make 10,000 pair	$100,000
Cost to buy 2,500 pair	26,250
Total	$126,250

Therefore, Minnetonka should choose this latter course of action, which saves $5,000.

5. There are many nonquantifiable factors that Minnetonka should consider in addition to the economic factors calculated above. Among such factors are:

a. The quality of the purchased bindings as compared to Minnetonka-produced bindings.
b. The reliability of delivery to meet production schedules.
c. The financial stability of the supplier.
d. Development of an alternate source of supply.
e. Alternate uses of binding manufacturing capacity.
f. The long-run character and size of the market.

6-65 (30-45 min.)

1. The $10,000 disposal value of the old equipment is irrelevant because it is the same for either choice. This solution assumes that the direct department fixed overhead is avoidable. You may want to explicitly discuss this assumption.

Cost Comparison for Make or Buy Decision

	At 60,000 Units Normal Volume	
	Make	Buy
Outside purchase cost at $1.00	-	$60,000
Direct material at $.30	$18,000	–
Direct labor and variable overhead at $.10	6,000	–
Depreciation ($188,000 - $20,000) ÷ 7	24,000	–
Direct departmental fixed overhead** at $.10 or $6,000 annually	6,000	–
Totals	$54,000*	$60,000

*On a unit basis, which is very dangerous to use unless proper provision is made for comparability of volume:

Direct material	$.30
Direct labor and variable overhead	.10
Depreciation, $24,000 ÷ 60,000	.40
Other fixed overhead**, $6,000 ÷ 60,000	.10
Total unit cost	$.90

Note particularly that the machine sales representative was citing a $.24 depreciation rate that was based on 100,000 unit volume. She should have used a 60,000 unit volume for the Rohr Company.

**Past records indicate that $.05 of the old unit cost was allocated fixed overhead that probably will be unaffected regardless of the decision. *This assumption could be challenged.* This total of $3,000 ($.05 x 60,000 units) could be included under *both* alternatives, causing the total costs to be $57,000 and $63,000, and the unit costs to be $.95 and $1.05, respectively. Note that such an inclusion would have no effect on the difference between alternatives.

Also, this analysis assumes that any idle facilities could not be put to alternative profitable use. The data indicate that manufacturing rather than purchasing is the better decision—before considering required investment.

2.

	At 50,000 Units		At 70,000 Units	
	Make	Buy	Make	Buy
Outside purchase at $1.00	-	$50,000	-	$70,000
Direct material at $.30	$15,000	–	$21,000	–
Direct labor and variable overhead at $.10	5,000	–	7,000	–
Depreciation	24,000	–	24,000	–
Other direct fixed overhead	6,000	–	6,000	–
Totals	$50,000	$50,000	$58,000	$70,000

At 70,000 units, the decision would not change. At 50,000 units, Rohr would be indifferent. The general approach to calculating the point of indifference is:

$$\text{Let } X = \text{Point of indifference in units}$$
$$\text{Total costs of making} = \text{Total costs of buying}$$
$$\$.30X + \$.10X + \$24,000 + \$6,000 = \$1.00\,X$$
$$\$30,000 = \$.60\,X$$
$$X = 50,000 \text{ units}$$

3.   Other factors would include: Dependability of estimates of volume needed, need for quality control, possible alternative uses of the facilities, relative merits of other outside suppliers, ability to renew production if price is unsatisfactory, and the minimum desired rate of return. Factors that are particularly applicable to the evaluation of the outside supplier include: short-run and long-run outlook for price changes, quality of goods, stability of employment, labor relations, and credit standing.

6-66   (25-35 min.)

1.

LAGRANDE CORPORATION
Contribution Income Statement
For 2004
(In millions of Euros)

Sales		€ 900
Less variable expenses:		
Manufacturing cost of goods sold	€ 400	
Selling and administrative expenses	140	540
Contribution margin		360
Less fixed expenses:		
Manufacturing costs	180	
Selling and administrative expenses	60	240
Operating income		€ 120

2. (a)

Sales: €900 x 90% x 130%	€ 1,053
Variable expenses: €540 x 130%	702
Contribution margin	351 *
Fixed expenses	240
Operating income	€ 111

*Alternative computation of contribution margin:	
Sales after a 10% reduction in prices:	
€ 900 x 90%	€ 810
Variable expenses	540
Contribution margin before volume change	270
Add 30% of € 270	81
Estimated new contribution margin	€ 351

(b) Contribution margin: €360 x 110%   € 396
     Fixed expenses: €240 + 30   270
     Operating income   € 126

(c) Sales   € 900
     Variable expenses:
        Manufacturing: €400 x 85%   €340
         Selling and administrative   140   480
     Contribution margin   420
     Fixed expenses: €240 + € 80   320
     Operating income   € 100

(d) Sales: €900 x 120% x 105%   € 1,134
     Variable expenses:
        Manufacturing: €400 x 120%   €480
        Selling and administrative:
          €140 x 120% x 125%   210   690
     Contribution margin   444 **
     Fixed expenses:
        Manufacturing   €180
        Selling and administrative: €60 x 2   120   300
     Operating income   € 144

     **Alternate computation of contribution margin:
        Sales after a 5% increase in prices:
          €900 x 105%   € 945
        Variable expenses:
          Manufacturing   €400
          Selling and admin. after a 25% increase
            in unit costs: €140 x 125%   175   575
        Contribution margin before volume change   370
         Add 20% of €370   74
        Estimated new contribution margin   € 444

(e)   These computations are good examples of "sensitivity analysis"–
        testing various inputs to a model to measure the effects on
        estimated outputs. This is a _planning_ procedure. An important
        point to make with students is that the contribution form of income
        statement is much more appropriate for these purposes than the
        absorption form.

        The analysis is readily calculated by using data from the
        contribution income statement. In contrast, the data in the
        absorption income statement must be analyzed and split into
        variable and fixed categories before the effect on operating income
        can be estimated.

3.   Alternatives (a) and (c) are clearly undesirable because they produce
        less operating income than the status quo. Either alternative (b) or
        alternative (d) would be better than the status quo. However, if both
        alternatives cannot be undertaken simultaneously, and if there is no
        subjective reason to favor alternative (b), alternative (d) seems best. It
        produces €144 – €126 = €18 (or 18 million Euros) more operating
        income than alternative (b). It would also be worth looking into the
        possibility of conducting the sales promotion campaign in alternative
        (b) together with the redesign of selling and administrative operations
        mentioned in alternative (d).

6-67   (25 - 30 min.)   For the solution, see the Prentice Hall Web site,
        www.prenhall.com/

<u>6-68</u>   (60 min. or more)

This exercise provides experience searching the literature of a particular subject as well as developing a better understanding of outsourcing decisions. Students will research the literature individually and then share their findings with their group.

Requirements 2 and 3 help develop critical thinking. The articles are not likely to answer these questions directly, but students will probably be able to infer answers from the information given.

The short report in requirement 4 will help develop an ability to select the most important points from the literature and report them in a way that is helpful to others.

<u>6-69</u>   (30-45 min.) NOTE TO INSTRUCTOR. This solution is based on the web site as it was in early 2004. Be sure to examine the current web site before assigning this problem, as the information there may have changed.

1.   The topics are "shop", "coffee club", "about GMCR", "learn about coffee", and "social and environmental initiatives." No, the information that would be provided for each link would be different. That is the reason that the different links are highlighted.

2.   To find out information concerning the financial statements, the place to look would be in the "about GMCR" section (then under investor services). In 2002 the firm had a profit of $5,970,000. The biggest cost the firm encountered was cost of sales (product costs). No, the firm did not pay any dividends. The firm has never paid any dividends and does not plan to start paying them in the foreseeable future. Instead, the profits are being reinvested in the firm. Thus, if I wanted an income producing stock, this would not be a logical investment choice.

3.   To learn more about coffee, you would click on the link "learn about coffee." The links that likely would provide information about coffee

differences, based solely on the titles given to such links, would be "Best coffee for you", "Learning about specialty coffee", "Coffee history", "Coffee glossary", and possibly "Frequently asked questions".

The solution to the information provided will depend on which link the student selects. If students pick "Best coffee for you", they will find links to help them identify the best coffee for them – looking at categories such as American, African, Indonesian, Light roasted, Dark roasted, Decaffeinated Coffees, Organic Decaf, Flavored Coffees, and Flavored Decaffeinated Coffees. Below each of these is a listing of blends and types that fall into each category. If students select "learning about specialty coffees", then they will find coffee facts that answer the questions where, how, what, when, who, and why. If students go for "the history of coffee", they will discover information concerning the history in a time-line format of coffee, coffee houses, migration of coffee across the world, and also products made to go into coffee. Students selecting the glossary will find an extensive listing of terms and definitions associated with coffee and coffee brewing. A look at the frequently asked question section shows that a couple of questions on the list do discuss the differences between types of coffee. None of the links present information about prices of coffee. This information would likely be a major factor of difference between differing types of coffee.

4. Green Mountain Coffee provides information regarding the environment, environmental actions the company has taken and awards it has won, the organizations, including those in the coffee community and those in the local community, that the company supports. The information, while interesting, would not help in determining how the product tasted, nor would it tell about the quality of the product. However, such information might be relevant to an investor who wants to invest only in socially conscious companies or one who believes that socially conscious companies will have an advantage if the government imposes costs (taxes) based on the company's impact on the environment.

CHAPTER 7
COVERAGE OF LEARNING OBJECTIVES

LEARNING OBJECTIVE	FUNDA-MENTAL ASSIGN-MENT MATERIAL	CRITICAL THINKING EXERCISES AND EXERCISES	PROBLEMS	CASES, EXCEL, COLLAB. & INTERNET EXERCISES
LO1: Explain the major features and advantages of a master budget.	A1,B1	22,24,26	39	
LO2: Follow the principal steps in preparing a master budget.	A1,B1	29	40	43,45
LO3: Prepare the operating budget and the supporting schedules.	A1,B1	28,29,30,31	40	43,45,46,48
LO4: Prepare the financial budget.	A1,B1	27,29,32,33,34,35	36,37,38	43,44,47,48
LO5: Explain the difficulties of sales forecasting.		23	42	49
LO6: Anticipate possible human relations problems caused by budgets.		25	40	
LO7: Use a spreadsheet to develop a budget (Appendix 7).			41,42	

CHAPTER 7
The Master Budget

7-A1 (60-90 min.)

1.
Exhibit I
COMPUTER SUPERSTORES, INC.
Mall of America Store
Budgeted Income Statement
For the Three Months Ending August 31, 2005

Sales		$1,500,000
Cost of goods sold (.60 x $1,500,000)		900,000
Gross profit		$ 600,000
Operating expenses:		
Salaries, wages, commissions	$300,000	
Other expenses	60,000	
Depreciation	7,500	
Rent, taxes and other fixed expenses	165,000	532,500
Income from operations.		$ 67,500
Interest expense*		6,180
Net income		$ 61,320

*From Exhibit II, $318,000 of principal is outstanding during June and July, and $318,000 - $212,000 = $106,000 is outstanding during August. The interest expense accrued is then

$318,000 x .10 x 2/12 + $106,000 x .10 x 1/12

= $5,300 + $883 = $6,183, rounded to $6,180.

Note that this accrual is independent of the cash interest actually paid ($3,530 and $1,530).

Exhibit II
COMPUTER SUPERSTORES, INC.
Mall of America Store
Budgeted Statement of Cash Receipts and Disbursements
For the Three Months Ending August 31, 2005

	June	July	August
Beginning cash balance	$29,000	$25,000	$25,470
Minimum cash balance desired	25,000	25,000	25,000
(a) Available cash balance	$ 4,000	$ 0	$ 470
Cash receipts & disbursements:			
Collections from customers			
(schedule b)	$ 376,000	$ 607,000	$454,000
Payments for merchandise			
(schedule d)	(420,000)	(240,000)	(240,000)
Fixtures	(55,000)	-	-
Salaries, wages, commissions,			
@ 20% x sales	(140,000)	(80,000)	(80,000)
Other variable expenses,			
@ 4% x sales	(28,000)	(16,000)	(16,000)
Fixed expenses	(55,000)	(55,000)	(55,000)
(b) Net cash receipts & disbursements	$(322,000)	$ 216,000	$63,000
Excess (deficiency) of cash before			
financing (a + b)	(318,000)	216,000	63,470
Financing:			
Borrowing, at beginning of period	$ 318,000	$ -	$ -
Repayment, at end of period	-	(212,000)	(61,000)
Interest, 10% per annum	-	(3,530)*	(1,530)**
(c) Total cash increase (decrease)			
from financing	$318,000	$(215,530)	$(62,530)
(d) Ending cash balance (beginning			
balance + b + c)	$ 25,000	$ 25,470	$ 25,940

*10% x $212,000 x 2/12 = $3,533, rounded to $3,530
**10% x $ 61,000 x 3/12 = $1,525, rounded to $1,530.

Exhibit III
COMPUTER SUPERSTORES, INC.
Mall of America Store
Budgeted Balance Sheet
August 31, 2005

Assets		Equities	
Cash (Exhibit II)	$ 25,940	Accounts payable	$180,000
Accounts receivable*	432,000	Notes payable	45,000**
Merchandise inventory	180,000	Accrued interest payable	1,120***
Total current assets	$637,940	Total current liabilities	$226,120
Net fixed assets:		Owners' equity:	
$168,000 less		$511,000 plus net	
depreciation of $7,500	160,500	income of $61,320	572,320
Total assets	$798,440	Total equities	$798,440

*July sales, 20% x 90% x $400,000 $ 72,000
 August sales, 100% x 90% x $400,000   360,000
 Accounts receivable (to Exhibit III) $432,000

** $318,000 - $212,000 - $61,000 = $45,000

*** Interest expense of $6,180 less the $3,530 + $1,530 = $5,060 paid

	June	July	August	Total
Schedule a: Sales Budget				
Credit sales	$630,000	$360,000	$360,000	$1,350,000
Cash sales	70,000	40,000	40,000	150,000
Total sales (to Exhibit I)	$700,000	$400,000	$400,000	$1,500,000

Schedule b: Cash Collections

	June	July	August
Cash sales	$ 70,000	$ 40,000	$ 40,000
On accounts receivable from:			
April sales	54,000	-	-
May sales	252,000	63,000	-
June sales	-	504,000	126,000
July sales	-	-	288,000
Total collections (to Exhibit II)	$376,000	$607,000	$454,000

Schedule c: Purchases Budget	May	June	July	August
Desired purchases:				
60% x next month's sales	$420,000	$240,000	$240,000	$180,000

Schedule d: Disbursements for Purchases

		June	July	August
Last month's purchases (to Exhibit II)		$420,000	$240,000	$240,000
Accounts payable, August 31, 2005 (to Exhibit III)				$180,000
Cost of goods sold (to Exhibit I)		$420,000	$240,000	$240,000

Schedule e: Operating Expense Budget
and
Schedule f: Payments for Operating Expenses

		June	July	August
Salaries, wages, commissions, other @24% of sales		$168,000	$ 96,000	$ 96,000

2.   This is an example of the classical short-term, self-liquidating loan. The need for such a loan often arises because of the seasonal nature of many businesses. In times of peak sales, the payroll and suppliers must be paid in cash that is not then available. The basic source of cash is proceeds from sales to customers. However, credit is extended to customers so that there is a lag between the sale and the collection of the cash. When the cash is collected, it in turn may be used to repay the loan. The amount of the loan and the timing of the repayment are heavily dependent on the credit terms that pertain to both the purchasing and selling functions of the business.

7-B1 (60-120 min.) $ refers to New Zealand dollars.

1. See Exhibits I, II, and III and supporting schedules a, b, c, d.

2. The cash budget and balance sheet clearly show the benefits of moving to just-in-time purchasing (though the transition would rarely be accomplished as easily as this example suggests). However, the company would be no better off if it left so much of its capital tied up in cash – it has merely substituted one asset for another. At a minimum, the excess cash should be in an interest bearing account – the interest earned or forgone is one of the costs of inventory.

	January	February	March
Schedule a: Sales Budget			
Total sales (100% on credit)	$62,000	$75,000	$38,000
Schedule b: Cash Collections			
60% of current month's sales	$37,200	$45,000	$22,800
30% of previous month's sales	7,500	18,600	22,500
10% of second previous month's sales	2,500	2,500	6,200
Total collections	$47,200	$66,100	$51,500

	December	January	February	March
Schedule c: Purchases Budget				
Desired ending inventory	$39,050	$ 6,000	$ 6,000	$ 6,000
Cost of goods sold	12,500	31,000	37,500	19,000
Total needed	$51,550	$37,000	$43,500	$25,000
Beginning inventory	16,000	39,050	8,050	6,000
Purchases	$35,550	$ -	$35,450	$19,000
Schedule d: Disbursements for Purchases				
100% of previous month's purchases		$35,550	$ -	$35,450
March 31 accounts payable				$19,000

Exhibit I
VICTORIA KITE
Budgeted Statement of Cash Receipts and Disbursements
For the Three Months Ending March 31, 2005

	January	February	March
Cash balance, beginning	$ 5,000	$ 5,100	$37,692
Minimum cash balance desired	5,000	5,000	5,000
(a) Available cash balance	0	100	32,692
Cash receipts and disbursements:			
Collections from customers			
(Schedule b)	47,200	66,100	51,500
Payments for merchandise			
(Schedule c)	(35,550)	-	(35,450)
Rent	(8,050)	(250)	(250)
Wages and salaries	(15,000)	(15,000)	(15,000)
Miscellaneous expenses	(2,500)	(2,500)	(2,500)
Dividends	(1,500)	-	
Purchase of fixtures	-	-	(3,000)
(b) Net cash receipts & disbursements	$ (15,400)	$ 48,350	$(4,700)
Excess (deficiency) of cash before			
financing (a + b)	$(15,400)	$ 48,450	$27,992
Financing:			
Borrowing, at beginning of period	$ 15,500	$ -	$ -
Repayment, at end of period	-	(15,500)	
Interest, 10% per annum	-	(258)	
(c) Total cash increase (decrease)			
from financing	$ 15,500	$(15,758)	$ -
(d) Cash balance, end (beginning			
balance + c + b)	$ 5,100	$ 37,692	$32,992

Exhibit II
VICTORIA KITE
Budgeted Income Statement
For the Three Months Ending March 31, 2005

Sales (Schedule a)		$175,000
Cost of goods sold (Schedule c)		87,500
Gross margin		$ 87,500
Operating expenses:		
Rent*	$17,250	
Wages and salaries	45,000	
Depreciation.	750	
Insurance	375	
Miscellaneous	7,500	70,875
Net income from operations		$ 16,625
Interest expense		258
Net income		$ 16,367

*(January-March sales less $10,000) x .10 plus 3 x $250

Exhibit III
VICTORIA KITE
Budgeted Balance Sheet
March 31, 2005

Assets

Current assets:

Cash (Exhibit I)	$32,992	
Accounts receivable*	22,700	
Merchandise inventory (Schedule c)	6,000	
Unexpired insurance	1,125	$62,817
Fixed assets, net: $12,500 + $3,000 - $750		14,750
Total assets		$77,567

Liabilities and Stockholders' Equity

Liabilities:

Accounts payable (Schedule d)	$19,000	
Rent payable.	16,500	
Dividends payable	1,500	$37,000
Stockholders' equity**		40,567
Total liabilities and stockholders' equity.		$77,567

*February sales (.10 x $75,000) plus March sales (.40 x $38,000) = $22,700

**Balance, December 31, 2004	$25,700
Add: Net income.	16,367
Total	$42,067
Less: Dividends declared.	1,500
Balance, March 31, 2005	$40,567

7-1   Budgeting is primarily attention directing because it helps managers to focus on operating or financial problems early enough for effective planning or action.

7-2   Strategic planning covers no specific time period, is quite general, and often is not built around financial statements. Long-range planning usually has a 5- or 10-year horizon and consists of financial statements without much detail. Budgeting usually has a horizon of one year or less, and consists of financial statements with much detail.

7-3   No. Capital relates to the investment in productive assets, and capital budgeting is a method of planning and controlling these investments.

7-4   Continuous budgets add a month in the future as the month just ended is dropped. The target for the next eleven months need not be changed. Therefore, each monthly budget, or target, is established twelve months ahead of time. Some companies revise the budgets for the next eleven months in addition to adding a month. However, most such companies compare results to the original budget (a fixed target) in addition to comparing them to the latest revised budget.

7-5   No. Continuous budgets cover a constant future planning period by dropping the current month and adding a future month to the budget as each month passes. Pro forma statements are defined as those which include not actual figures but estimated or forecasted figures. All budgets are thus pro forma statements.

7-6   Budgeted performance is better than past performance as a basis for judging current performance because the budget contains no hidden inefficiencies and can be founded on current rather than past economic conditions.

7-7   Budgets are especially important in environments that are rapidly changing. They force managers to look forward. Budgets allow systematic reactions to change. They force analysis of the factors that are bringing about the changes.

7-8 Budgeting is beneficial because it encourages careful planning, allows both continuous and periodic evaluation of current operations, and facilitates coordination between subunits.

7-9 No. When budgeting in done correctly, it is an important aid to managers. Managers need time to plan and coordinate their various activities. Budgeting forces them to take time from the day-to-day problems and focus on longer-term issues.

7-10 An operating budget is used as a guide for production and sales, while a financial budget is used to control the receipt and disbursement of funds.

7-11 The sales forecast is the starting point for budgeting because all other operating activities of the company are affected by the volume of sales.

7-12 Operating expenses are costs charged to the income statement in a particular period. Some operating expenses may be associated with the sales of the period, and others may be costs of being in business for the period. Disbursements for these operating expenses, that is, the cash payments for them, may come in a previous period (assets purchased in one period and depreciated over future periods) or a future period (wages accrued in a period but paid in the next period), as well as during the period.

7-13 A cash budget is an attempt to regulate the flow of cash in optimum fashion.

7-14 A sales forecast is simply a prediction of sales under a given set of conditions. A sales budget reflects a commitment to establish the conditions to generate the predicted level of sales.

7-15 The sales forecast is influenced by past patterns of sales, estimates made by the sales force, general economic conditions, competitors' actions, changes in prices, market research studies, and advertising and sales promotion plans.

7-16   Budgeting will be effective only if it is accepted by those managers who are responsible for controlling costs. Since their performance will be measured against the budget, they must be educated in the assumptions underlying the budget and convinced of its objectivity and relevance.

7-17   Both functional and activity-based master budgets begin with the forecasted demand for products or services. However, whereas functional budgets then determine the inventory, materials, labor, and overhead budgets, the activity-based budget focuses on determining the demand for key activities. This demand is measured by the cost-driver unit for each activity. Then the budgeted resource consumption rates are used to set the budgets for resources such as materials, labor, and overhead. The focus on activities and consumption rates in activity-based budgeting is what managers believe offers value from an operational control perspective.

7-18   Financial planning models are mathematical statements of the relationships in the organization among all the operating and financial activities and of other major internal and external factors that may affect the financial results of decisions.

7-19   No. Financial planning models can help simplify the process of budgeting. But planning models are only as good as the assumptions and inputs used to build them. Managers must understand the models to provide appropriate assumptions and inputs. If managers do not understand budgeting, using financial planning models can result in GIGO (garbage in, garbage out).

7-20 Setting up the master budget on a spreadsheet is time-consuming – the first time. However, if it is done properly, with maximum flexibility, then the ease of subsequent use probably will more than offset that initial cost. Ultimately, though, the master budget system must meet the cost-benefit test. Improved budgeting systems are only worthwhile if they offer net benefits. It is also a fact that all large, well-managed companies have computerized master budget systems. Preparing and revising the master budget of a large company just would not be feasible without the aid of a computer.

7-21 Spreadsheets can be used to make a mathematical model of an organization. It may take much effort to create the model, but once it is in place it can be used over and over again with minimal effort. Such a model is especially useful for sensitivity analysis, which is the asking of "what if" questions.

7-22 Budgets that are used primarily for limiting spending are subject to much "game playing." Accurate forecasts and estimates give way to strategies designed to justify increased budgets. Budgets should have a much larger role in the effective and efficient management of an organization. A budget should be a decision tool. It helps managers project the results of their decisions, thereby aiding them in making the right decisions. It also provides a base for adapting to change. The management uses of a budget require accurate forecasts and estimates, and anything that results in loss of budget accuracy will limit the usefulness of the budget as a decision tool.

7-23 Accurate sales forecasts are essential to budgeting. Sales personnel are often "closest to the action" and therefore in the best position to make accurate forecasts. They are in direct contact with customers, and often they are the first to notice trends. A central staff function, such as market research, can set parameters for forecasting and give some common ground rules. But usually it is important to get sales personnel heavily involved because they have information that no one else has.

7-24   Budgets are helpful to all segments of an organization. Segments with both revenues and expenses can show a budgeted profit. Other segments, those that have only expenses such as a research and development department, still have to plan their operations. It is important to predict the resources needed to meet the segment's objectives so that needed resources can be obtained. Budgeting may be used to express an agreement between the segment and top management about what activities the segment is to undertake. The planning that comes through a good budget process is important to all segments.

7-25   A key to employee acceptance of a budget is participation. Budgets created with the active participation of all affected employees are generally more effective than budgets imposed on subordinates. If a budget is to help direct future activities, employees must accept the budget. Acceptance means believing that the budget reflects a desired future path for the organization. If a manager has been a participant in determining the future path – that is, helped develop the budget – he or she is more likely to accept it as a desirable objective.

7-26   (5 min.)

1. a. Budgeted income statement
   b. Budgeted balance sheet
   c. Cash budget
   d. Capital budget

2. Sales budget (or operating budget)
3. Sales budget
4. Continuous (rolling)
5. Overall goals of the organization

7-27   (10-15 min.)

Adventure.Com needs $720,000 of venture capital. It needs the following amounts:

Initial capital investment	$300,000
First year cash outflow (12 x $30,000)	360,000
Second year cash outflow [12 x ($30,000 - $25,000)]	60,000
Total	$720,000

At the beginning of 2007, the cash receipts exceed the cash disbursements, so no additional cash is needed.

7-28 (10-15 min.)

1.   Cost + (.25 x Cost) = Sales
                    1.25 x Cost = $2,040,000
                          Cost = $1,632,000

2.   Best path to success is to sketch the Cost of Goods Sold section of an income statement. Start with the cost of goods sold and work upwards.

July Cost of Goods Sold Schedule

Beginning inventory (.30 x $2,170,000 ÷ 1.25)	$ 520,800
Add: Purchases	X
Cost of goods available for sale	$2,288,000
Less: Final inventory (.30 x $2,300,000 ÷ 1.25)	552,000
Cost of goods sold ($2,170,000 ÷ 1.25)	$1,736,000

X = $1,736,000 + $552,000 - $520,800 = $1,767,200

<u>7-29</u>   (25-30 min.)

1. July collections include:

May sales billed June 10, .18 x .5 x $750,000	$ 67,500
June sales billed June 20, .18 x .5 x $800,000	72,000
June sales billed July 10, .80 x .5 x $800,000 x .98	313,600
July sales billed July 20, .80 x .5 x $900,000 x .98	352,800
Total	$805,900

2. September collections from August sales:

August sales billed September 10, .80x.5x$900,000x.98	$352,800
August sales billed August 20, .18 x .5 x $900,000	81,000
Total	$433,800

3. .80 x .25 x $600,000 = $120,000

4.

Ending inventory, .80 x .25 x $900,000	$180,000
Merchandise needed for current month's sales,	
.80 x $800,000	640,000
Total needs	820,000
Beginning inventory, .80 x .25 x $800,000	160,000
Purchases	$660,000

5.

	July	August
Ending inventory, .80 x .25 x next month's sales	$180,000	$120,000
Merchandise needed for current month's sales,		
.80 x sales	720,000	720,000
Total needs	900,000	840,000
Beginning inventory, .80 x .25 x current month's sales	180,000	180,000
Purchases	$720,000	$660,000
Payments, 1/2 of current purchases, 1/2 of preceding		
month's purchases, .5 x $720,000 + .5 x $660,000		$690,000

7-30 (15 min.) This is straightforward. It follows the illustration in the chapter very closely. All amounts are in dollars.

	June	July	August
Sales budget			
Credit sales, 30%	120,000	132,000	150,000
Cash sales, 70%	280,000	308,000	350,000
Total sales, 100%	400,000	440,000	500,000
Cash collections budget			
Cash sales this month	280,000	308,000	350,000
100% of last month's credit sales	120,000	120,000	132,000
Total collections	400,000	428,000	482,000

7-31 (15-25 min.) This problem is slightly more complex than 7-30. All amounts are in thousands of Japanese yen.

	January	February	March
Sales budget			
Credit sales, 80%	144,000	168,000	192,000
Cash sales, 20%	36,000	42,000	48,000
Total sales	180,000	210,000	240,000
Cash collections budget			
Cash sales this month	36,000	42,000	48,000
50% of this month's credit sales	72,000	84,000	96,000
40% of last month's credit sales	62,400	57,600	67,200
10% of next-to-last month's credit sales	18,000	15,600	14,400
Total collections	188,400	199,200	225,600

7-32 (10-15 min.)

Collections from:

January sales:	$300,000 x 12%	$ 36,000
February sales:	$400,000 x 10% x 99%	39,600
	$400,000 x 25%	100,000
March sales:	$450,000 x 50% x 99%	222,750
Total cash collections		$398,350

7-33 (15-20 min.) This is straightforward. It follows the illustration in the chapter very closely. All amounts are in dollars. Some students need to be reminded that merchandise inventories are carried at cost, not at selling prices.

QUANTRILL FURNITURE MART
Purchases and Disbursements Budgets

	June	July	August
Purchases budget			
Ending inventory	220,000	270,000	240,000
Cost of goods sold, 60% of sales	264,000	210,000	240,000
Total needed	484,000	480,000	480,000
Beginning inventory	250,000	220,000	270,000
Purchases	234,000	260,000	210,000
Disbursements for purchases			
10% of this month's purchases	23,400	26,000	21,000
80% of last month's purchases	144,000*	187,200	208,000
10% of second-last month's purchases	25,000**	18,000	23,400
	192,400	231,200	252,400

*.80 x 180,000 = 144,000
**.10 x 250,000 = 25,000

7-34 (20-25 min.) This is straightforward. Except for requirement 1, it follows the illustration in the chapter very closely. All amounts are in euros.

1. $200,000 - [15,000 + .9(.6 \times 300,000)] = 200,000 - [15,000 + .9(180,000)]$
$$= 200,000 - 177,000$$
$$= 23,000$$

2.

BARCELONA S.A.
Purchases and Disbursements Budgets

	June	July	August
Purchases budget			
Ending inventory*	166,200	198,600	231,000
Cost of goods sold, 60% of sales	180,000	168,000	204,000
Total needed	346,200	366,600	435,000
Beginning inventory	200,000	166,200	198,600
Purchases	146,200	200,400	236,400
Disbursements for purchases			
80% of last month's purchases	120,000	116,960	160,320
20% of this month's purchases	29,240	40,080	47,280
Disbursements for purchases	149,240	157,040	207,600

*Inventory targets, end of month:

June: $15,000 + .9(0.6 \times 280,000) = 15,000 + .9(168,000) = 166,200$

July: $15,000 + .9(0.6 \times 340,000) = 15,000 + .9(204,000) = 198,600$

August: $15,000 + .9(0.6 \times 400,000) = 15,000 + .9(240,000) = 231,000$

368

7-35 (20 min.) This is a straightforward exercise.

RALEIGH COMPANY
Cash Budget
For the Month Ended June 30, 2004
(in thousands)

Cash, May 31, 2004		$ 15
Receipts:		
Collections from customers from:		
June sales (.80 x $290)	$232	
May sales (.5 x 24)*	12	
April sales	16	260
Cash available for needs		$275
Disbursements:		
On accounts payable of May 31	$145	
On June purchases, .25 x $192	48	
Wages	36	
Utilities	5	
Advertising	10	
Office expenses	4	248
Cash, June 30, 2004		$ 27

*$24,000 = 20% of May sales, 10% of which or half the remainder will be collected in June. All of April's remaining sales will be collected in June.

7-36   (20-25 min.) The collections from March sales are a bit tricky. Note that the *receivable* balance from March sales at March 31 is $450,000; therefore, four fifths (because 40/50 will be collected in April and 10/50 will be collected in May) will be received in April.

KIM NEWS AND GIFTS
Budgeted Statement of Cash Receipts and Disbursements
For the Month Ending April 30, 20X4

Cash balance, March 31, 20X4		$ 80,000
Add receipts, collections from customers:		
From April sales, 1/2 x $1,000,000	$500,000	
From March sales, 4/5 x $450,000	360,000	
From February sales	60,000	920,000
Total cash available before current financing		$1,000,000
Less disbursements:		
Merchandise purchases, $450,000 x 40%	$180,000	
Payment on accounts payable	460,000	
Payrolls	90,000	
Insurance premium	1,500	
Other expenses	45,000	
Repayment of loan and interest	94,500	871,000
Cash balance, April 30, 20X4		$ 129,000

7-37 (40-60 min.)

BOUQUET COMPANY
Statement of Estimated Cash Receipts and Disbursements
For the Month of October 2004

Cash balance, September 30, 2004		$ 4,800
Receipts, collections of receivables (Schedule 1)		29,340
Total cash available		$34,140
Less disbursements:		
Merchandise purchases (Schedule 2)	$17,000	
Variable expenses (Schedule 3)	3,125	
Fixed expenses (Schedule 3)	900	21,025
Cash balance, October 31, 2004		$13,115

Schedule 1, Collections of Accounts Receivable:

		Collected in October	
	Sales	Percent	Amount
From August sales	$12,000	6%	$ 720
From September sales	$36,000	30%	10,800
From October sales	$30,000	60% x 99%	17,820
Total October collections			$29,340

Schedule 2, Payments for Merchandise:

	September	October
Target ending inventory	$ 9,000*	$ 6,600*
Goods sold	21,600	18,000
Total needs	$30,600	$24,600
Beginning inventory	10,800*	9,000*
Purchases	$19,800	$15,600
Payments, 2/3 x $15,600 October purchases		$10,400
Accounts payable, end of September,		
1/3 x $19,800 purchases		6,600
Total payments in October		$17,000

* (12/20)(.5)(30,000) = $9,000; (12/20)(.5)(36,000) = $10,800;
(12/20)(.5)(22,000) = $6,600

Schedule 3, Selling and General Administrative Expenses:

Total selling and general administrative expenses	$61,500
Less fixed expenses	24,000
Total variable expenses for year (vary with sales)	$37,500

October variable expenses:
$37,500 x (October sales ÷ Year's sales) =
$37,500 x ($30,000 ÷ $360,000) $ 3,125

Total fixed expenses	$24,000
Less depreciation (no current cash outlay)	13,200
Total cash required for fixed expenses for year	$10,800

October cash required for fixed expenses:
$10,800 ÷ 12 $ 900

7-38 (30 - 40 min.)

1. The Ritz-Carleton's monthly cash budget is:

	January	February	March	April	May	June
Revenues	$2,137,500	$2,137,500	$1,912,500	$1,912,500	$1,575,000	$1,575,000
Collections:						
Previous Mo. Sales	$ 598,500	$ 598,500	$ 598,500	$ 535,500	$ 535,500	$ 441,000
This Mo. Sales	1,282,500	1,282,500	1,147,500	1,147,500	945,000	945,000
Next Mo. Sales	213,750	191,250	191,250	157,500	157,500	157,500
Total collections	2,094,750	2,072,250	1,937,250	1,840,500	1,638,000	1,543,500
Disbursements:						
Variable costs	256,500	256,500	229,500	229,500	189,000	189,000
Fixed salaries	400,000	400,000	400,000	400,000	400,000	400,000
Fixed operating costs	120,000	120,000	120,000	120,000	120,000	120,000
Interest payments						3,000,000
Total disbursements	776,500	776,500	749,500	749,500	709,000	3,709,000
Net cash inflow	$1,318,250	$1,295,750	$1,187,750	$1,091,000	$ 929,000	($2,165,500)

	July	August	September	October	November	December	Total
Revenues	$1,575,000	$1,575,000	$1,575,000	$1,575,000	$1,912,500	$2,137,500	$21,600,000
Collections:							
Previous Mo. Sales	$ 441,000	$ 441,000	$ 441,000	$ 441,000	$ 441,000	$ 535,500	$ 6,048,000
This Mo. Sales	945,000	945,000	945,000	945,000	1,147,500	1,282,500	12,960,000
Next Mo. Sales	157,500	157,500	157,500	191,250	213,750	213,750	2,160,000
Total collections	1,543,500	1,543,500	1,543,500	1,577,250	1,802,250	2,031,750	21,168,000
Disbursements:							
Variable costs	189,000	189,000	189,000	189,000	229,500	256,500	2,592,000
Fixed salaries	400,000	400,000	400,000	400,000	400,000	400,000	4,800,000
Fixed operating costs	120,000	120,000	120,000	120,000	120,000	120,000	1,440,000
Interest payments						3,000,000	6,000,000
Total disbursements	709,000	709,000	709,000	709,000	749,500	3,776,500	14,832,000
Net cash inflow	$ 834,500	$ 834,500	$ 834,500	$ 868,250	$1,052,750	($1,744,750)	$ 6,336,000

2. Increase in revenues: 6 mo. x .05 x 300 rooms x $250 x 30 days = $675,000

   Increase in costs: 6 mo. x .05 x 300 rooms x $30 x 30 days = $81,000

   Increase in profit = $675,000 - $81,000 = $594,000

374

<u>7-39</u> (15 min.)

1.   Possible cost-saving actions would probably focus on one or more of
      the activities of the Shipping and Receiving Department. Tulchin might
      start with the non-value added activities, handling and record-keeping.
      For example, if the number of moves could be cut by 40%, the entire
      $43,335 could be saved. Reorganizing the warehouse is one way to try
      to achieve such savings. The activity-based budget also shows that
      the highest-cost activity is shipping, so that might be the best place to
      look for cost savings from changing processes.

2.   Regardless of what methods are selected to achieve cost savings, the
      activity-based budget seems to be a better starting point. The
      traditional budget does not show directly how changes in activities
      might affect costs, whereas the activity-based budget does.

<u>7-40</u> (25-30 min.)

1.   An optimistic preliminary budget might be as follows, assuming level
      sales volume, a $.94 per pound price, and a 2% decrease in variable
      costs.

Sales, 1.6 million pounds @ $.94/pound	$1,504,000
Variable costs	(862,400)
Fixed costs, primarily depreciation	(450,000)
Pretax profit	$ 191,600

      This budget does not meet the $209,000 profit goal. Kosta has a
      dilemma of submitting a realistic budget that does not meet Dunlop's
      goal or preparing an unrealistic budget. To meet the profit target, she
      might assume that prices will not fall, sales levels will be maintained,
      and some fixed costs will be saved. Although the following budget is
      not one Kosta believes in, she might be forced to submit it (or
      something similar) to headquarters:

Sales, 1.6 million pounds @ $.95/pound $1,520,000
Variable costs, .98 x $880,000   (862,400)
Fixed costs, primarily depreciation   (448,600)*
Pretax profit $ 209,000
*$1,520,000 - $862,400 - $209,000

2.   Two major problems are the arbitrary setting of budget targets by top management and the draconian measures used when a budget is not met, even if the shortfall is small or reasonable explanations for the shortfall are given.

3.   Apparently the preliminary financial results are as follows:

Sales, 1.6 million pounds @ $.945/pound $1,512,000
Variable costs, .98 x $880,000   (862,400)
Fixed costs, primarily depreciation   (450,000)
Pretax profit $ 199,600

Extending the depreciable lives of fixed assets by 2 years could increase this profit to $214,600, well above the target. But doing so would be manipulating the accounting system to achieve desirable results. When the estimates of depreciable lives were first made, there may have been much uncertainty in the estimates. However, changing the accounting method to make the financial results look better is an ethical violation.

Managers should not be able to change accounting methods just to make their performance look better (or in this case, to save their job). Although changing the depreciation schedule is not ethical, it is easy to see how the budgeting process creates an incentive for such unethical behavior. If the budget and reporting process makes excellent performance appear deficient, there may be great temptation for managers to manipulate the system.

7-41 (50-90 min.) This spreadsheet is constructed so that only formulas are entered in the disbursements and operating income schedules. You can compare the total operating income figures at the bottom of each spreadsheet to assess the effects of each scenario. Amounts are in dollars.

1 and 2.

Table of Budget Data	June	July	August	
Sales forecasts	375,000	330,000	420,000	
Growth	0%	0%	0%	
	375,000	330,000	420,000	
Cost of goods sold percentage			70%	
Misc. expense percentage			6%	
Sales commissions			10%	
Employee salaries per month			22,000	
Rent per month			6,000	
Insurance expense per month			450	
Depreciation per month			2,850	
Disbursements for Operating Expenses (2a)				
Cost of goods sold	262,500	231,000	294,000	787,500
Commissions	37,500	33,000	42,000	112,500
Salaries	22,000	22,000	22,000	66,000
Miscellaneous	22,500	19,800	25,200	67,500
Rent	6,000	6,000	6,000	18,000
Total	350,500	311,800	389,200	1,051,500

377

Operating Income (2b)	June	July	August	Total
Sales	375,000	330,000	420,000	1,125,000
Cost of goods sold	262,500	231,000	294,000	787,500
Gross margin	112,500	99,000	126,000	337,500
Operating expenses				
Commissions	37,500	33,000	42,000	112,500
Salaries	22,000	22,000	22,000	66,000
Miscellaneous	22,500	19,800	25,200	67,500
Rent	6,000	6,000	6,000	18,000
Insurance	450	450	450	1,350
Depreciation	2,850	2,850	2,850	8,550
Total	91,300	84,100	98,500	273,900
Operating income	21,200	14,900	27,500	63,600

3a.

Table of Budget Data	June	July	August			Total
Sales forecasts	375,000	330,000	420,000			
Growth	5%	5%	5%			
	393,750	346,500	441,000			
Cost of goods sold percentage			70%			
Misc. expense percentage			6%			
Sales commissions			10%			
Employee salaries per month			22,000			
Rent per month			6,000			
Insurance expense per month			450			
Depreciation per month			2,850			
Disbursements for Operating Expenses						Total
Cost of goods sold	275,625	242,550	308,700			826,875
Commissions	39,375	34,650	44,100			118,125
Salaries	22,000	22,000	22,000			66,000
Miscellaneous	23,625	20,790	26,460			70,875
Rent	6,000	6,000	6,000			18,000
Total	366,625	325,990	407,260			1,099,875

Operating Income	June	July	August	Total
Sales	393,750	346,500	441,000	1,181,250
Cost of goods sold	275,625	242,550	308,700	826,875
Gross margin	118,125	103,950	132,300	354,375
Operating expenses				
Commissions	39,375	34,650	44,100	118,125
Salaries	22,000	22,000	22,000	66,000
Miscellaneous	23,625	20,790	26,460	70,875
Rent	6,000	6,000	6,000	18,000
Insurance	450	450	450	1,350
Depreciation	2,850	2,850	2,850	8,550
Total	94,300	86,740	101,860	282,900
Operating income	23,825	17,210	30,440	71,475

380

3b.

Table of Budget Data	June	July	August	Total
Sales forecasts	375,000	330,000	420,000	
Growth	-2%	-2%	-2%	
	367,500	323,400	411,600	
Cost of goods sold percentage			70%	
Misc. expense percentage			6%	
Sales commissions			0%	
Employee salaries per month			52,500	
Rent per month			6,000	
Insurance expense per month			450	
Depreciation per month			2,850	
Disbursements for Operating Expenses				
Cost of goods sold	257,250	226,380	288,120	771,750
Commissions	0	0	0	0
Salaries	52,500	52,500	52,500	157,500
Miscellaneous	22,050	19,404	24,696	66,150
Rent	6,000	6,000	6,000	18,000
Total	337,800	304,284	371,316	1,013,400

Operating Income	June	July	August	Total
Sales	367,500	323,400	411,600	1,102,500
Cost of goods sold	257,250	226,380	288,120	771,750
Gross margin	110,250	97,020	123,480	330,750
Operating expenses				
Commissions	0	0	0	0
Salaries	52,500	52,500	52,500	157,500
Miscellaneous	22,050	19,404	24,696	66,150
Rent	6,000	6,000	6,000	18,000
Insurance	450	450	450	1,350
Depreciation	2,850	2,850	2,850	8,550
Total	83,850	81,204	86,496	251,550
Operating income	26,400	15,816	36,984	79,200

7-42 (50-90 min.) These spreadsheets contain data from the problem in the top of the spreadsheet space. Computations of operating expenses are accomplished with formulas that reference the table. Comparing the summary calculations of operating expenses (labeled TOTAL OPERATING EXPENSE) allows the user to assess the effects of alternate scenarios.

1. Table of Budget Data

Cost behavior				
Cost	Fixed	Variable	Quantity / display	
17" Displays		$100	5	
15" Displays		$40	5	
Indirect	$40,000	$16/component		
Packaging	$8,000	$4 / display		
Shipping	$8,000	$2 / display		
TOTAL OPERATING EXPENSE	$19,206,000			

Sales forecasts

Month	17" Displays	15" Displays
Sales mix	1	1.25
Sales growth	1	1
1 October	3,200	4,000
2 November	2,400	3,000
3 December	5,600	7,000
4 January	3,200	4,000
5 February	3,200	4,000
6 March	2,400	3,000
7 April	2,400	3,000
8 May	2,800	3,500

Operating expenses

Month	Components	Indirect	Packaging	Shipping	Total
1 October	$2,400,000	$616,000	$36,800	$22,400	$3,075,200
2 November	1,800,000	472,000	29,600	18,800	2,320,400
3 December	4,200,000	1,048,000	58,400	33,200	5,339,600
4 January	2,400,000	616,000	36,800	22,400	3,075,200
5 February	2,400,000	616,000	36,800	22,400	3,075,200
6 March	1,800,000	472,000	29,600	18,800	2,320,400
Totals	$15,000,000	$3,840,000	$228,000	$138,000	$19,206,000

2. Table of Budget Data

Cost behavior			
Cost	Fixed	Variable	Quantity / display
17" Displays		$100	5
15" Displays		$40	5
Indirect	$40,000	$16 / component	
Packaging	$8,000	$4 / display	
Shipping	$8,000	$2 / display	
TOTAL OPERATING EXPENSE	$16,639,680		
Sales forecasts		17" Displays	15" Displays
Sales mix		1	1.25
Month	Sales growth	0.9	0.9
1 November	2,400	2,160	2,700
2 December	5,600	5,040	6,300
3 January	3,200	2,880	3,600
4 February	3,200	2,880	3,600
5 March	2,400	2,160	2,700
6 April	2,400	2,160	2,700
7 May	2,800	2,520	3,150

Operating expenses					
Month	Components	Indirect	Packaging	Shipping	Total
1 November	$1,620,000	$428,800	$27,440	$17,720	$2,093,960
2 December	3,780,000	947,200	53,360	30,680	4,811,240
3 January	2,160,000	558,400	33,920	20,960	2,773,280
4 February	2,160,000	558,400	33,920	20,960	2,773,280
5 March	1,620,000	428,800	27,440	17,720	2,093,960
6 April	1,620,000	428,800	27,440	17,720	2,093,960
Totals	$12,960,000	$3,350,400	$203,520	$125,760	$16,639,680

3. Table of Budget Data

Cost behavior			
Cost	Fixed	Variable	Quantity / display
17" Displays		$100	5
15" Displays		$40	5
Indirect	$40,000	$16 / component	
Packaging	$8,000	$4 / display	
Shipping	$8,000	$2 / display	
TOTAL OPERATING EXPENSE	$18,240,600		

Sales forecasts

	17" Displays	15" Displays
Sales mix	1	1.5
Sales growth	0.9	0.9

Month	17" Displays	15" Displays
1 December	5,600	7,560
2 January	3,200	4,320
3 February	3,200	4,320
4 March	2,400	3,240
5 April	2,400	3,240
6 May	2,800	3,780
7	0	0
8	0	0

Operating expenses

Month	Components	Indirect	Packaging	Shipping	Total
1 December	$4,032,000	$1,048,000	$58,400	$33,200	$5,171,600
2 January	2,304,000	616,000	36,800	22,400	2,979,200
3 February	2,304,000	616,000	36,800	22,400	2,979,200
4 March	1,728,000	472,000	29,600	18,800	2,248,400
5 April	1,728,000	472,000	29,600	18,800	2,248,400
6 May	2,016,000	544,000	33,200	20,600	2,613,800
Totals	$14,112,000	$3,768,000	$224,400	$136,200	$18,240,600

1.   On January 1, Columbia Civic Theater needs to borrow $2,057,000, on April 1 it needs an additional $510,000, on September 31 it can repay $2,014,000, but on October 1 it must again borrow $675,000. This can be seen from the following analysis (in thousands of dollars):

	Qtr. 1	Qtr. 2	Qtr. 3	Qtr. 4
Beginning cash balance	208	200	200	200
Minimum cash balance desired	200	200	200	200
Available cash balance	8	0	0	0
Cash receipts & disbursement:				
Collections from customers (1)	883	1,893	4,504	2,024
Payments for supplies (2)	(780)		(200)	
Other expenses (3)	(30)	(30)	(30)	(30)
Payments for payroll (4)	(2,046)	(2,100)	(2,100)	(2,100)
Major equipment (5)			(100)	(300)
Small equipment (6)	(60)	(60)	(60)	(60)
Mortgage principal (7)		(125)		(125)
Mortgage interest (8)		(88)		(84)
Interest on working capital (9)	(32)			
Net cash receipts & disbursements	(2,065)	(510)	2,014	(675)
Excess (deficiency) of cash				
before financing	(2,057)	(510)	2,014	(675)
Financing:				
Borrowing (at beginning of quarter)	2,057	510		675
Repayment (at end of quarter)			(2,014)	
Total cash increase (decrease)				
from financing	2,057	510	(2,014)	675
Ending cash balance	200	200	200	200

Explanations (see next page):

(1) Collections are revenues for the quarter less the increase (or plus the decrease) in accounts receivable.

(2) Payments for supplies in the first quarter are the accounts payable carried over from 2004 and in the third quarter (July) are the purchases in June. December's purchases will be paid for in 2006.

(3) Other expenses are $10,000 per month, paid as incurred.

(4) Payroll payments in the first quarter are those of December 2004 ($646,000) plus the $700,000 from each of January and February. Each other quarter they are three $700,000 payments.

(5) $100,000 of major equipment payments are made in September, October, November, and December.

(6) Small equipment payments are $20,000 each month.

(7) The mortgage payments semi-annually are $4,000,000 ÷ 32 = $125,000.

(8) $3,500,000 x .025 = $87,500, rounded to $88,000; $3,375,000 x .025 = $84,375, rounded to $84,000.

(9) The $32,000 payment is the interest that was payable at the end of 2004.

The result of 2005 operations will be an increase in the working capital loan from $1,588,000 (without the accrued interest) to $2,816,000, an increase of $1,228,000:

	Qtr. 1	Qtr. 2	Qtr. 3	Qtr. 4
Beginning loan	$1,588	$3,645	$4,155	$2,141
Additional borrowing	2,057	510	(2,014)	675
Ending loan	$3,645	$4,155	$2,141	$2,816

Quarterly interest expense @8% is:

Qtr. 1	Qtr. 2	Qtr. 3	Qtr. 4	Total
$72,900	$83,100	$83,100	$56,320	$295,420

2. Columbia Civic Theater's projected income statement and balance sheet for 2005 are (in thousands):

COLUMBIA CIVIC THEATER
Income Statement
For the Year Ended December 31, 2005

Revenues		$11,059
Expenses:		
Salary & wages	$8,400	
Supplies	800	
Depreciation	500	
Other	120	
Total expenses		9,820
Operating margin		1,239
Interest:		
Mortgage	172	
Loan	295	467
Net income		$ 772

COLUMBIA CIVIC THEATER
Balance Sheet
December 31, 2005

Assets		Liabilities & Equities	
Cash	$ 200	Loan payable	$ 2,816
Receivables	6,195	Accrued interest payable	295
Supplies inventory	600	Accounts payable	700
Total current assets	6,995	Payroll payable	700
Fixed assets	5,949	Current mortgage	250
Total assets	$12,944	Total current liabilities	4,761
		Mortgage payable	3,000
		Total liabilities	7,761
		Equities	5,183
		Total liabilities & equities	$12,944

3.   This requirement asks for a Statement of Cash Flows. Such a statement is not shown in Chapter 7, but it is covered in Chapter 16. Students who do not have a background in financial accounting might be directed to skip this requirement. Amounts are in thousands.

COLUMBIA CIVIC THEATER
Statement of Cash Flows
For the Year Ended December 31, 2005

Cash flows from operating activities:	
Cash receipts	$9,304 [11,059 – 1,755]
Cash disbursements:	
Supplies	(980) [780 + 200]
Payroll	(8,346) [2,046 + (3 x 2,100)]
Interest	(204) [32 + 88 + 84]
Other	(120)
Net cash provided (used) by operations	(346)
Cash flows from investing activities:	
Investment in plant and equipment	(640)
Net cash used for investing activities	(640)
Cash flows from financing activities:	
Principal payments on mortgage	(250)
Receipts from bank loan	1,228 [2,816 – 1,588]
Net cash provided by financing activities	978
Net increase (decrease) in cash	(8)
Beginning cash balance, 1/1/2005	208
Ending cash balance, 12/31/2005	$ 200

4.   Columbia Civic Theater has a net income of $772,000 but a shortfall in cash requiring borrowing of $1,228,000. This is not uncommon for a growing organization. However, it is borrowing on a short-term basis via a working capital loan, while the need seems to be a long-term need. The $640,000 of investment is clearly long-term, but the $346,000 needed for

operations also appears to be a long-term need unless receivables can be collected more quickly. Therefore, Columbia should consider additional long-term borrowing, possibly a second mortgage. The organization is in danger of defaulting on its loan because it cannot meet the condition that it be paid off at least once a year, so it needs a loan without such a stipulation.

7-44   (40-60 min.)

1.

ST. JOHN HOSPITAL
Budgeted Cash Receipts
For the Quarter Ending September 30, 2004
(in thousands)

	Calculation	July	August	September
May: 3rd-party billings	.9 x 6000 x .2	$1,080		
May: patient billings	.1 x 6000 x .4	240		
June: 3rd-party billings	.9 x 6000 x .2		$1,080	
June: patient billings	.1 x 6000 x .4		240	
June: 3rd-party billings	.9 x 6000 x .5	2,700		
June: patient billings	.1 x 6000 x .4	240		
July: 3rd-party billings	.9 x 5400 x .2			$ 972
July: patient billings	.1 x 5400 x .4			216
July: 3rd-party billings	.9 x 5400 x .5		2,430	
July: patient billings	.1 x 5400 x .4		216	
July: 3rd-party billings	.9 x 5400 x .2	972		
July: patient billings	.1 x 5400 x .1	54		
August: 3rd-party billings	.9 x 6000 x .5			2,700
August: patient billings	.1 x 6000 x .4			240
August: 3rd-party billings	.9 x 6000 x .2		1,080	
August: patient billings	.1 x 6000 x .1		60	
Sept: 3rd-party billings	.9 x 6600 x .2			1,188
Sept: patient billings	.1 x 6600 x .1			66
Total receipts from billings		$5,286	$5,106	$5,382
Endowment fund income		210	210	210
Total cash receipts		$5,496	$5,316	$5,592

2.

Budgeted Cash Disbursements
For the Quarter Ending September 30, 2004
(in thousands)

		July	August	September
Salaries:	$1,800 + (.2 x $5,400)	$2,880		
	$1,800 + (.2 x $6,000)		$3,000	
	$1,800 + (.2 x $6,600)			$3,120
Purchases, previous month		1,450	1,500	1,800
Interest				540
Total cash disbursements		$4,330	$4,500	$5,460

3.

Budgeted Cash Receipts and Disbursements
For the Third Quarter, 2004
(in thousands)

Beginning cash balance	$ 350
Budgeted cash receipts ($5,496 + $5,316 + $5,592)	16,404
Less budgeted cash disbursements ($4,330 + $4,500 + $5,460)	(14,290)
Budgeted cash balance, September 30, 2004	$ 2,464
Minimum cash balance (.1 x $2,200)	(220)
Cash available for capital expenditures	$ 2,244
Budgeted capital expenditures	(4,000)
Borrowing needed on October 1, 2004	$ (1,756)

7-45 (50-60 min.)

1.

WESTERN IDAHO STATE UNIVERSITY
Projected Enrollment, Credits, and Faculty
Academic Year 2004-05

	Undergraduate	Graduate	Total
Expected enrollment[a]	3,528	1,890	5,418
Average credit hours	25	20	-
Total credit hours[b]	88,200	37,800	126,000
Full-time-equivalent enrollment[c]	2,940	1,575	4,515
Credit hours per faculty member[d]	720	360	1,080
Total faculty needed[e]	122.5	105	227.5

[a]98% x 3,600 = 3,528; 105% x 1,800 = 1,890
[b]25 x 3,528 = 88,200; 20 x 1,890 = 37,800
[c]88,200 / 30 = 2,940; 37,800 / 24 = 1,575
[d]24 x 30 = 720; 18 x 20 = 360
[e]88,200 / 720 = 122.5; 37,800 / 360 = 105

2.

WESTERN IDAHO STATE UNIVERSITY
Faculty Salaries Budget
Academic Year 2004-05

	Faculty Needed	Average Salary	Total Faculty Salaries
Undergraduate	122.5	$48,760	$ 5,973,100
Graduate	105.0	48,760	5,119,800
Total	227.5		$11,092,900

3.

WESTERN IDAHO STATE UNIVERSITY
Tuition and Legislative Revenue Budget
Academic Year 2004-05

	Undergrad Division	Graduate Division	Total
Total credit hours	88,200	37,800	126,000
Less: Scholarship credit hours*	900	1,200	2,100
Tuition paying credit hours	87,300	36,600	123,900
Tuition per credit hour	x $70	x $70	x $70
Total tuition budget	$6,111,000	$2,562,000	$8,673,000
Full time equivalent students	2,940	1,575	4,515
Legislative apportionment per full-time equivalent student	x $780	x $780	x $780
Total legislative apportionment	$2,293,200	$1,228,500	$3,521,700

*30 x 30 = 900; 50 x 24 = 1,200

4.

WESTERN IDAHO STATE UNIVERSITY
Annual Budget Shortfall
Academic Year 2004-05

Budgeted operating expenditures:

Faculty salaries	$11,092,900
Operation and maintenance of facilities:	
Salaries and wages (1.06 x $240,000)	254,400
Other ($260,000 + $12,000)	272,000
General Administrative	525,000
Library:	
Acquisitions	155,000
Operations	200,000
Health Services	50,000
Intramural athletics	60,000
Intercollegiate athletics	245,000
Insurance and retirement	560,000
Interest	75,000
Total budgeted operating expenditures	$13,489,300
Budgeted revenues:	
Tuition	$ 8,673,000
Legislative apportionment	3,521,700
Endowment income	210,000
Auxiliary services	335,000
Intercollegiate athletics	300,000
Total budgeted operating revenues	$13,039,700
Deficit from operations	$ 449,600
Budgeted capital expenditures	575,000
Total cash needed from fund-raising*	$ 1,024,600

*13,489,300 + 575,000 - 13,039,700

1.

	Standard	Custom	Division
Sales (schedule a)	$1,300,000	$400,000	$1,700,000
Cost of goods sold :			
Direct material (schedule b)	300,000	60,000	360,000
Direct labor (schedule c)	120,000	30,000	150,000
Processing (schedule g):			
$38.60 x 3,500 MH	135,100		
$38.60 x 500 MH		19,300	154,400
Production support:			
$704 x 25 runs	17,600		
$704 x 100 runs		70,400	88,000
Cost of goods sold	572,700	179,700	752,400
Gross profit	$ 727,300	$220,300	$ 947,600

Schedule a: Sales budget

	Standard	Custom
Price per package	$ 26	$ 400
Demand	50,000	1,000
Sales	$1,300,000	$400,000

Schedule b: Direct material budget

	Standard	Custom
Cost per package	$ 6	$ 60
Demand	50,000	1,000
Direct material cost	$300,000	$60,000

Schedule c: Direct labor budget

	Standard	Custom
Demand in packages	50,000	1,000
Consumption rate	0.1 hours/pkg	1.4 hours/pkg
Budgeted labor hours	5,000	1,400
Capacity per laborer	1,500	1,500
Laborers required (round up)	4	1
Cost per laborer	$30,000	$30,000
Budgeted direct labor cost	$120,000	$30,000

Schedule d : Activity driver-level budget

	Standard	Custom	Tot. MH	Standard	Custom	Tot. Runs
Demand (pkgs)	50,000	1,000		50,000	1,000	
Consumption rate (activity level per package)	.07 MH	.5 MH		.0005 runs	.1 runs	
Activity level	3,500	500	4,000	25	100	125

Schedule e: Fixed-cost resource budget

	Processing Function	Production Support Function	Total
Activity-level budget (see Sch. d)	4,000	125	
Consumption rate	1 MH/MH	20 MH/Run	
Resource driver level	4,000 MH	2,500 MH	6,500 MH
Capacity			1,900 MH/Mch.
Required number of machines 6,500 ÷ 1,900 = 3.4			4
Budgeted cost ($40,625 x 4 machines)			$162,500

Schedule f: Variable-cost resource budget

	Processing Function	Production Support Function	Total
Activity-level budget (see Sch. d)	4,000 MH	125 Runs	
Consumption rate	.1 MwHr/MH	1.5 MwHr/Run	
Resource driver level	400 MwHr	187.5 MwHr	587.5 MwHr
Budgeted cost ($136 per MwHr)			$79,900

Schedule g: Function-cost budgets

	Processing Function	Production Support Function
Variable cost, from sch. f	$136/MwHr x 400 MwHr = $ 54,400	$136/MwHr x 187.5 MwHr = $25,500
Fixed cost, from sch. e	$162,500 x 4,000 MH/6,500 MH = 100,000	$162,500 x 2,500 MH/6,500 MH = 62,500
Total	$154,400	$88,000
Cost per driver unit	$154,400 ÷ 4,000 MH = $38.60	$88,000 ÷ 125 runs = $704

2.   There are many different charts that can be used to evaluate the 2005 budget. Exhibits 7-46A , 7-46B, and 7-46C on the following pages are examples. Each of these charts depict the relationship

Gross profit = Revenue – (Direct material + Direct labor + Processing cost + Production support cost).

So

Revenue = Gross profit + Direct material + Direct labor + Processing cost + Production support cost.

Exhibit 7-46A
Components of Revenue, By Product and Division

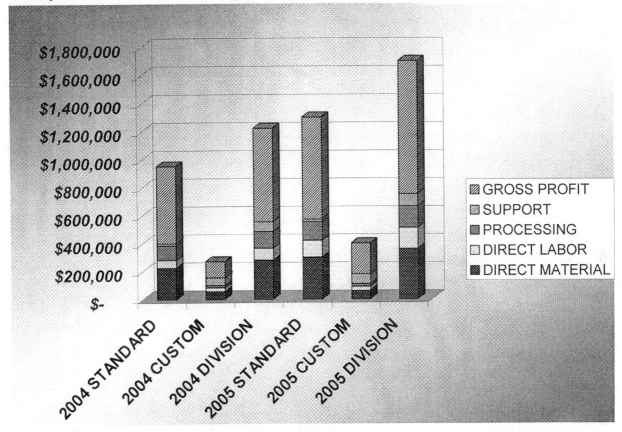

It is clear that the standard bracket product line accounts for most of the
profit in the division and this will continue in 2005.

Exhibit 7-46B
Common-Sized Financial Analysis

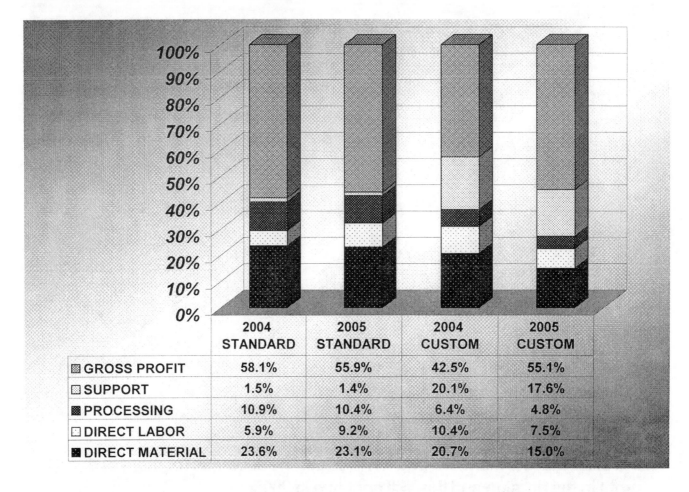

	2004 STANDARD	2005 STANDARD	2004 CUSTOM	2005 CUSTOM
▨ GROSS PROFIT	58.1%	55.9%	42.5%	55.1%
▨ SUPPORT	1.5%	1.4%	20.1%	17.6%
▨ PROCESSING	10.9%	10.4%	6.4%	4.8%
▨ DIRECT LABOR	5.9%	9.2%	10.4%	7.5%
▨ DIRECT MATERIAL	23.6%	23.1%	20.7%	15.0%

Gross profit percentage for standard brackets will decrease due to a substantial increase in direct labor costs. Gross profit percentage of custom solutions will increase significantly as a result of decreases in each of the components.

Exhibit 7-46C
Common-Sized Statements of Revenue Components
2004 Actual and 2005 Budget

2004 ACTUAL RESULTS

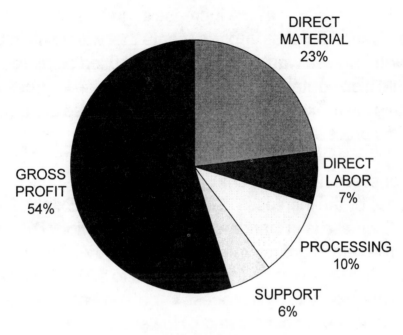

2005 BUDGET

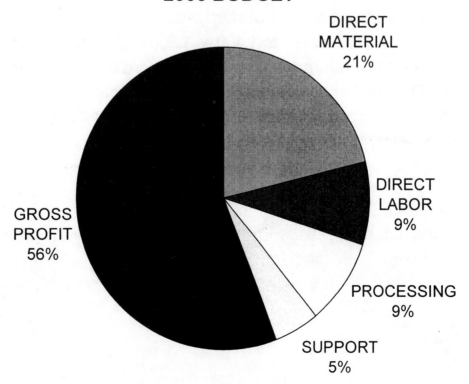

The pie charts in Exhibit 7-46C are an alternative means to evaluate the changes planned in the 2005 budget.

It is easy to see from the size of the pie charts that substantial revenue growth is planned. This $(1,700,000 - 1,222,000) \div 1,222,000 = 39.1\%$ increase in revenue will generate a $= 41.9\%$ increase in gross profit. The primary reason is the planned process improvements that will result in cost reductions. Normally, we would also expect that fixed costs remaining constant would also contribute to the greater increase in gross profit. However, in this case, fixed costs will increase because of hiring of direct labor and a new processing machine.

The planned cost savings in material, processing, and support are mitigated to a large degree by the increases in direct labor cost. Exhibit 7-46B shows that this labor increase is in standard bracket production. The result is a modest improvement in gross profit from 54% to 56%. Text Exhibit 7-17 shows that the increase in wages from $28,000 to $30,000 was offset for the custom solutions products by a process improvement in consumption rate from 1.6 to 1.4 labor hours per package. However, there is no such planned process improvement for the standard bracket products. From schedule c, the planned labor utilization for standard bracket production is $5,000 \div 6,000$ labor hours $= 83.3\%$ compared to $1,400 \div 1,500 = 93\%$ for custom solutions. It would only take a small improvement in standard bracket labor efficiency from 0.1 to .09 hours per package to result in a reduction of 1 laborer with resulting cost savings of $30,000 (50,000 pkg x .09 hours/pkg = 4,500 hours or 3 laborers, one less than before the improvement).

7-47   For the solution, see the Prentice Hall Web site, www.prenhall.com/

<u>7-48</u> (30-60 min.)

The purpose of this exercise is to prepare a budget for an organization (an individual student) that is familiar to all students and to see the effect of assumptions on the budget. Each student will have some ideas about both the revenue and expense budgets of a typical student, but these ideas will likely vary across students. They will experience the process of negotiation needed to get a budget that the group can agree on.

When the groups get together and compare budgets, it will be instructive to see how different groups make different assumptions that lead to different budgets. This should reinforce the importance of assumptions to the budget process and show how decisions made during the budget process affect the resulting budget.

<u>7-49</u> (30-45 min.) NOTE TO INSTRUCTOR. This solution is based on the web site as it was in early 2004. Be sure to examine the current web site before assigning this problem, as the information there may have changed.

1.   There are 12 brand lines under the corporation shell. They are Carnival Cruise Lines, Princess Cruises, Holland America Line, Seabourn Cruise Line, Windstar, P&O Cruises, Cunard Line, Ocean Village, Swan Hellenic, Costa, AIDA, and P&O Cruises Australia. Each brand has a slightly different focus. While several are cruise lines, each of the lines focuses on a different part of the world or offers a different class of cruise. Different names allow for the association or branding of a particular line with a particular type of cruise. For instance, the Windstar focuses on the exotic locations and the sailing ship experience while Carnival focuses on more of a festive atmosphere on board ship – that is, fun times. The corporation also operates 3 riverboats on the Danube River and several tour companies.

2.   Total revenues in fiscal 2003 were $6,718 million. The occupancy percentage was 103.4%. Notice that occupancy is greater than 100%. How can one explain this? For Carnival, it means that capacity is defined as two persons per room, so when more than two persons occupy a room capacity

utilization is greater than 100%. If they budget for only 100% capacity for the fiscal 2004 and assume no increase in capacity, using the 2003 annual report, the budgeted capacity for 2004 is 33,309,785 ÷ 1.034 = 32,214,492 cruise days. However, the company expects added capacity next year, so their budget should include revenues from the extra capacity also.

3.   According to management's estimate, capacity will increase 17.5% in 2004 and another 9.2% in 2005. Thus, budgeted cruise days at 100% occupancy for the next two years would be:

   2004: 1.175 x 32,214,492 = 37,852,028 cruise days

   2005: 1.092 x 37,852,028 = 41,334,414 cruise days

Of course, with added cruise days there would be added costs. If added cruise days were achieved by making better use of existing capacity, costs would probably not increase proportionately with the volume. Some fixed costs would not be likely to change. However, since the added volume requires adding capacity, costs would probably increase nearly proportionally to the increase in volume. A few fixed costs, for example corporate headquarters costs, might not increase much, but even costs that are fixed for a given level of capacity will increase if capacity needs to be increased.

4.   The prices for cruises of the same length to the same location are not all the same. They differ according to when the cruise dates are – high season or low season – and also according to the level of capacity utilization that the particular cruise has achieved. The firm's goal is to have the maximum capacity utilization possible for each cruise. If demand is high for a particular cruise, then the firm will be able to command a higher price and still fill the cabins. Since much of the cost of the cruise is likely to be fixed in nature, the firm will incur the cost even if they don't fill the cabins. Thus, a price that covers variable cost and contributes to fixed costs will be preferred to an empty cabin. Destinations or dates that are less popular are cheaper because once the company schedules the cruise, it is in its best interests to fill as many cabins as possible as long as the price is above the variable costs. Last-minute deals can be especially cheap if a particular cruise looks like it is likely to have excess capacity.

CHAPTER 8
COVERAGE OF LEARNING OBJECTIVES

LEARNING OBJECTIVE	FUNDA-MENTAL ASSIGN-MENT MATERIAL	CRITICAL THINKING EXERCISES AND EXERCISES	PROBLEMS	CASES, EXCEL, COLLAB., & INTERNET EXERCISES
LO1: Distinguish between flexible budgets and master (static) budgets.	A1			
LO2: Use flexible-budget formulas to construct a flexible budget based on the volume of sales.	A1,	24, 25, 26 27	43, 49, 50	52, 53, 55, 57, 58
LO3: Prepare an activity-based flexible budget.			43	54
LO4: Explain the performance evaluation relationship between master (static) budgets and flexible budgets.	B1	20, 21	34, 36, 37 38, 42, 51	54, 56, 57
LO5: Compute flexible-budget variances and sales-activity variances.	A1, A2, B1	20, 21, 27 28	34, 35, 36 37, 38, 39 42, 51	52, 53, 54, 55, 56, 57, 58
LO6: Compute and interpret price and usage variances for inputs based on cost-driver activity.	A3, B2	22, 29, 30 31, 32, 33	40, 41, 44, 45, 46, 47, 48, 51	55, 57, 58
LO7: Compute variable overhead spending and efficiency variances.	B3	23	40, 41, 44, 45 46, 47, 48, 51	

CHAPTER 8
Flexible Budgets and Variance Analysis

8-A1 (30-45 min.) Amounts are in thousands.

1.
<u>Flexible Budget Amounts</u>

Revenue	<u>$7,000</u>	<u>$8,000</u>	<u>$9,000</u>
Fuel	$ 140	$ 160	$ 180
Repairs and maintenance	70	80	90
Supplies and miscellaneous	700	800	900
Variable payroll	<u>4,690</u>	<u>5,360</u>	<u>6,030</u>
Total variable costs	<u>$5,600</u>	<u>$6,400</u>	<u>$7,200</u>
Supervision	$ 180	$ 180	$ 180
Rent	160	160	160
Depreciation	480	480	480
Other fixed costs	<u>160</u>	<u>160</u>	<u>160</u>
Total fixed costs	<u>$ 980</u>	<u>$ 980</u>	<u>$ 980</u>
Total costs	<u>$6,580</u>	<u>$7,380</u>	<u>$8,180</u>
Operating income	<u>$ 420</u>	<u>$ 620</u>	<u>$ 820</u>

2. $980,000 per quarter plus .80 of revenue.

3. Variances are defined as deviations of actual results from plans. The total variances in the problem can be subdivided to provide answers to two broad questions:

  (a) What portion is attributable to not attaining a predetermined level of volume or activity? This variance is called the *sales activity variance.*

  (b) What portion is attributable to nonvolume effects? This variance is often called the *flexible-budget variance*, which is composed of *price* and *efficiency* variances.

The existing performance report, which is based solely on a *static* budget, cannot answer these questions clearly. It answers (a) partially, because it compares the revenue achieved with the original targeted revenue. But the report fails to answer (b). A complete analysis follows:

Summary of Performance
(in thousands)

	(1) Actual Results at Actual Activity Level	(2) (1)-(3) Flexible Budget Variances	(3) Flexible Budget for Actual Sales Activity	(4) (3)-(5) Sales Activity Variances	(5) Master (Static) Budget
Net revenue	$7,600	$ -	$7,600	$400 U	$8,000
Total variable costs	6,223	143U	6,080	320 F	6,400
Contribution margin	$1,377	$143U	$1,520	$ 80U	$1,600
Fixed costs	981	1U	980	-	980
Operating income	$ 396	$144U	$ 540	$ 80U	$ 620

U = Unfavorable

Column (4) focuses on the effects of sales volume. It shows that a $400,000 drop in sales activity caused a $80,000 decrease in contribution margin and hence a $80,000 drop in operating income.

Column (2) generally focuses on efficiency. Without a flexible budget, operating inefficiencies cannot be isolated from the effects of changes in sales activity. Cost control performance may be reported in more detail, where the focus is on efficiency (in thousands):

	Actual Costs	Flexible Budget Allowance*	Budget Variance
Fuel	$ 157	$ 152	$ 5U
Repairs and maintenance	78	76	2U
Supplies and miscellaneous	788	760	28U
Variable payroll	5,200	5,092	108U
Supervision	183	180	3U
Rent	160	160	-
Depreciation	480	480	-
Other fixed costs	158	160	2F
Totals	$7,204	$7,060	$144U

U = Unfavorable
*For $7,600,000 revenue.

(20-30 min.)

	A	B	C
			Master Budget Based on Standard Inputs Allowed for Planned Outputs
		Flexible Budget Based on	
	Actual Overhead Costs Incurred	Actual Outputs x Expected Prices	Achieved x Expected Prices
Systems consulting, variable	$37,000	90 requests x $500 = $45,000	(75 requests x $500) = $37,500

Flexible-budget variance (A - B) $37,000 - $45,000 = $8,000 F	Activity-level variance (B - C) $45,000 - $37,500 = $7,500 U
Master budget variance (A - C) $37,000 -$37,500 = $500 F	

Systems consulting, fixed	$77,000 (given)		$65,000

Master budget variance (A - C)
$77,000 - $65,000 =
$12,000 U

1. Direct materials: 5 lb. x $10.00 = $ 50.00
    Direct labor: 5 hrs. x $25.00 =   125.00
    Total $175.00

2. The standard costs expected are based on actual output achieved,
    not scheduled or budgeted output.

	A	B	C
			Flexible Budget Based on
	Actual Cost Incurred:	Flexible Budget Based on	Expected Inputs for Actual Outputs
	Actual Inputs x	Actual Inputs x	Achieved x
	Actual Prices	Expected Prices	Expected Prices
In general:	$xxx	$xxx	$xxx

	Price variance	Usage variance
	(A - B)	(B - C)
	Flexible-budget variance (A - C)	

Direct Materials	2,700 lbs x $8.50 = $22,950	2,700 lbs x $10.00 = $27,000	525 units x 5 x $10.00 = $26,250

Price variance (A - B) = $22,950 - $27,000 = $4,050 F	Usage variance (B - C) $27,000 - $26,250 = $750 U
Flexible-budget variance (A - C) $22,950 - $26,250 = $3,300 F	

	A	B	C
Direct Labor	2,850 hr x $26.00 = $74,100	2,850 hr x $25.00 = $71,250	525 units x 5 hr x $25.00 = $65,625

Price variance (A - B) = $74,100 - $71,250 = $2,850 U	Usage variance (B - C) = $71,250 - $65,625 = $5,625 U
Flexible-budget variance (A - C) $74,100 - $65,625 = $8,475 U	

3. Among the possible explanations for the performance are:

(a) Were substandard materials used because they were cheaper, resulting in higher waste than usual? (Note the tradeoff resulted in a net favorable materials variance.)

(b) Net savings in material costs may be undesirable if they cause inefficient use of direct labor, too.

(c) Direct labor is expensive. A wage rate that is 4% above the standard rate can be significant in total amount.

8-B1 (15-20 min.)

1.
TAX PREPARATION SERVICES, INC.
Summary Performance Report

	Actual Results at Actual Activity Level	Flexible Budget Variances	Flexible Budget for Actual Activity Level	Sales Activity Variances	Master Budget
Physical units (clients)	3,000	-	3,000	500F	2,500
Sales	$1,080,000	$30,000F	$1,050,000	$175,000F	$875,000
Variable costs	800,000	50,000U	750,000	125,000U	625,000
Contribution margin	$ 280,000	$20,000U	$ 300,000	$ 50,000F	$250,000
Fixed costs	159,500	9,500U	150,000	-	150,000
Operating income	$ 120,500	$29,500U	$ 150,000	$ 50,000F	$100,000

2.
Master budget operating income		$100,000
Variances:		
Sales activity variances	$50,000F	
Flexible-budget variances	29,500U	20,500F
Actual operating income		$120,500

8-B2 (20-30 min.)

1.

	A	B	C
			Flexible Budget Based on Standard Inputs for Actual Outputs Achieved x
	Actual Cost Incurred: Actual Inputs x Actual Prices	Flexible Budget Based on Actual Inputs x Expected Prices	Expected Prices
Direct Materials	115,000 lb x $8 = $920,000	115,000 lb x $7 = $805,000	14,400 units x 10 x $7 = $1,008,000

Price variance (A - B) = $920,000 - $805,000 = $115,000 U	Usage variance (B - C) $805,000 - $1,008,000 = $203,000 F
Flexible-budget variance (A - C) = $920,000 - $1,008,000 = $88,000F	

	A	B	C
Direct Labor	30,000 hr x $12 = $360,000	30,000 hr x $13 = $390,000	14,400 units x 2 hr x $13 = $374,400

Price variance (A - B) = $360,000 - $390,000 = $30,000 F	Usage variance (B - C) $390,000 - $374,400 = $15,600 U
Flexible-budget variance (A - C) $360,000 - $374,400 = $14,400 F	

2. Tradeoffs may have been made in each category. More expensive materials may have been acquired with the hope of achieving less waste. Less expensive labor may have been used that caused more inefficiency. The overall effects were favorable, at least as measured by these variances. Management also should be concerned with effects of these tradeoffs on quality, on-time delivery, customer satisfaction, and so on.

8-B3 (20-30 min.) If the total overhead incurred is $203,200, of which $134,500 is fixed, then variable overhead was $203,200 - $135,500 = $67,700. The following analysis should be helpful. All given items are designated by an asterisk (*).

	A	B	C
			Flexible Budget Based on Standard Inputs
		Flexible Budget Based on Actual	Allowed for Actual
	Actual Overhead Costs Incurred	Inputs x Expected Prices	Outputs Achieved x Expected Prices
Billing department-variable overhead	$67,700	$67,700 + $2,500* = $70,200; 117,000 hr x 10* x $.06* = $70,200	$70,200 - $7,500 = $62,700 = 104,500 hr x 10* x $.06*

Spending variance $2,500* F	Efficiency variance $6,000 U - $1,500 F= $7,500 U
Flexible-budget variance (A - C) $5,000* U	

1. $7,500U. The efficiency variance is computed by subtracting the spending variance from the flexible-budget variance, $5,000 – (-$2,500). Note that this computation can be made independently of the next two requirements.

2. 117,000 hours. The actual hours can be computed by adding the price variance to the actual variable overhead and then dividing the result by $.60: ($67,700 + $2,500) ÷ $.60 = 117,000 hours. Alternatively, this answer could be obtained by taking the answer in part (3) and adding 12,500 hours because the unfavorable efficiency variance represents 12,500 hours of work ($7,500 ÷ $.60).

3. 104,500 hours. The standard hours allowed for output achieved can be computed in one of two ways:

(a)   Take the answer in part (2) and deduct 12,500 hours: 117,000 - 12,500 = 104,500 hours.

(b)   Deduct the efficiency variance from the $70,200 and then divide the result, $62,700, by $.60: ($70,200 - $7,500) ÷ $.60 = 104,500 hours.

8-1   Favorable variances arise when actual costs are less than budgeted costs (or actual revenue exceeds budgeted revenue). Unfavorable variances mean that actual costs are greater than budgeted costs (or actual revenue falls short of budgeted revenue).

8-2   Yes. Flexible budgets are flexible only with respect to variable costs. There is no point in scaling down the fixed cost budget in proportion to actual output when the actual fixed costs don't behave that way.

8-3   No. A flexible budget adjusts costs as the *level of activity* changes, not as prices change.

8-4   The use of flexible budgeting requires cost formulas or functions to predict what costs should be at different levels of cost driver activity. These flexible-budget cost formulas are possible only if cost behavior is understood.

8-5   A "flex" in a flexible budget generally refers to adjustments made because of changes in volume. Activities that have variable costs will therefore generate "flexes" in the budget, but those activities that drive only fixed costs will not have a "flex."

8-6   No. Performance can be either effective or efficient or both or neither. For example, the targeted sales level (effectiveness) may be achieved or not, independent of whether the actual level of operations used the appropriate amount of resources (efficiency).

417

8-7 A master budget variance is the difference between the originally planned (master budget) amount and the actual amount. A flexible-budget variance is the difference between the actual amount and the amount that is expected for the actual level of output achieved.

8-8 Favorable and unfavorable variances do not necessarily mean good and bad performance, respectively. They mean simply that actual results differed from the standards. Differences may arise from inaccurate standards, or they may be the result of factors that are beyond the control of management. Variances should be a signal to ask the question "why," but they do not automatically give the answer.

8-9 No. The primary function of a control system is *explanation*, not placing blame.

8-10 Sales activity variances are most often the responsibility of marketing managers. However, if factors such as quality of product and meeting of delivery schedules impact the volume of sales, production managers who affect quality and delivery may also affect the sales activity variance.

8-11 A perfection (or ideal) standard disregards all imperfections and human errors and thus is rarely attained. A currently attainable standard can be closely approached by keeping all inefficiencies down to a minimum level, and it can be occasionally surpassed by exceptional effort.

8-12 The first interpretation is that standards are set just tightly enough so that employees regard their fulfillment as highly probable if they exert normal effort and diligence. The second interpretation is that standards are set more tightly so that employees regard their fulfillment as possible though unlikely.

8-13 There is much room for measurement error when a standard is set. Consequently, random fluctuations around the standard can really be conceived of as defining the band of acceptable outcomes rather than as variances from a precise standard. The standard is often the midpoint of the band of acceptable outcomes.

8-14   Price variances should be computed even if prices are outside of company control because the use of a standard price will still be helpful for measuring production performance. By separating price effects from efficiency effects, the efficiency variances are not affected by price changes.

8-15   Some common causes of unfavorable usage or efficiency variances are improper handling, poor quality of material, poor workmanship, changes in methods, new workers, slow machines, breakdowns, and faulty designs.

8-16   Failure to meet price standards is often the responsibility of the purchasing officer, but responsibility may be shared with the production manager if he or she has frequent rush orders for materials. Of course, market conditions may be such that it is beyond the control of anyone in the company to attain the price standard.

8-17   The variable overhead efficiency variance does not measure the performance of the managers who are responsible for overhead. It is an overhead cost that a company occurs because it has not controlled its cost driver, not because it has not controlled its overhead.

8-18   Overhead control techniques are different from direct material cost control techniques because:

1.   Cost drivers are generally more complex and less obvious.
2.   Responsibility is split among various people.
3.   A large percentage of overhead costs may be fixed or joint in nature.

8-19   The variable overhead spending variance is not the result of only price changes, as is the labor price variance, but also includes such factors as inadequate attention to cost control and imperfect identification and measurement of cost drivers for cost estimates.

8-20   The impact of changes in sales volume on profit depends on the amount of variable versus fixed costs. If sales (revenues) drop 10%, the contribution margin drops by 10% also, but fixed costs will not change (assuming the new sales volume remains in the relevant range). With operating profit of $100 on sales of $1,000, total costs must have been $900. Suppose half of those costs were fixed. Then, the contribution margin would be $1,000 - $450 = $550. A 10% drop in sales would cost the company 10% x $550 = $55, not $10.

8-21   Changes in production volume will affect variable costs but not fixed costs, provided that the new production level remains within the relevant range. If production volume increases by 10%, costs will increase by less than 10% if there are any fixed costs. Suppose that half of the production costs for 100 units are fixed and half are variable. That means that per unit variable costs are ($1,000 x .5) / 100 = $5. Producing an extra 10 units should cause an extra cost of $50, giving a total cost of $1,050 for 110 units. The production manager should have a cost target of $1,050, not $1,100.

8-22   If a purchasing manager saves money by paying less per pound than planned, we want to make sure this savings did not come at the expense of quality. By examining the material usage variance, we can see whether more than planned of the cheaper material had to be used. Perhaps there was more scrap or waste because of using inferior materials. One might also examine the labor usage variance. Inferior materials may also be harder to handle, thus requiring additional labor time. Or, partially completed products might have to be scrapped when defects are found, wasting not only the materials put into the product but also the labor used up to the point it is scrapped.

8-23 Unfavorable variable-overhead efficiency variances arise when there is waste in the usage of the cost driver used to apply the variable overhead. To know who is responsible for the unfavorable variable-overhead efficiency variance we need first to know what cost driver is used for applying the variable overhead and second to determine who is responsible for controlling that cost driver. If Birmingham Company uses direct labor hours as the cost driver for applying variable overhead, then the plant manager is responsible for the variable-overhead efficiency variance. Why? Because he or she is responsible for controlling direct labor costs.

8-24 (10 min.)

Variable cost is $204,000/24,000 units = $8.50 per unit
Budgeted cost = $8.50(30,000) + $95,000 = $350,000

8-25 (10 min.)

Mileage	30,000	40,000	50,000
Fuel @ $.15	$ 4,500	$ 6,000	$7,500
Depreciation	5,500	5,500	5,500
Total	$10,000	$11,500	$13,000

8-26 (10 min.) Answers are in italics.

	Budget Formula per Unit	Various Levels of Output		
Units		6,000	7,000	8,000
Sales	$18	$108,000	$126,000	$144,000
Variable costs:				
Direct material	8	48,000	56,000	64,000
Hand labor	3	18,000	21,000	24,000
Fixed costs:				
Depreciation		16,000	16,000	16,000
Executive salaries		42,000	42,000	42,000

8-27 (10-15 min.)

The manager's delight is unjustified. A more informative analysis is obtained when a flexible budget is introduced:

	Actual Costs	Flexible-Budget Variance	Flexible Budget	Sales Activity Variance	Master Budget
Units of product	6,800	-	6,800	1,200U	8,000*
Direct materials	$ 99,000	$10,600U	$ 88,400	$15,600F	$104,000
Direct labor	37,600	3,600U	34,000	6,000F	40,000
Total	$136,600	$14,200U	$122,400	$21,600F	$144,000

*$104,000/$13 = 8,000 or $40,000/$5 = 8,000

Note that the manager should have expected lower costs when volume was 15% less than the master budget. But the manager was unable to bring the costs below the amounts in the flexible budget. Costs of $21,600 were saved by producing 1,200 fewer units than planned, but the manager spent $14,200 more than expected to produce the 6,800 units.

8-28 (10-15 min.)

	A	B	C
	Actual Results at Actual Activity Level	Flexible Budget for Actual Pounds of Activity	Master Budget
Materials support:	$170,000 (given)	650,000 lb x $.25 = $162,500	750,000 lb x $.25 = $187,500

Flexible-budget variance (A - B) $170,000 - $162,500 = $7,500 U	Materials-activity variance (B - C) $162,500 - $187,500 = $25,000 F
Master-budget variance (A - C) $170,000-$187,500 = $17,500 F	

8-29 (10-15 min.)

Cost Incurred: Actual Inputs x Actual Prices	Flexible Budget Based on Actual Inputs x Expected Prices	Flexible Budget Based on Standard Inputs Allowed for Actual Outputs Achieved x Expected Prices
7,900 sq. yd x B695 = B5,490,500	7,900 sq. yd. x B710 = B5,609,000	7,600 sq. yds. x B710 = B5,396,000

7,900 x (B695 - B710) = Price variance, B118,500F	(7,900 - 7,600) x B710 = Usage variance, B213,000U

<u>8-30</u> (15-20 min.)

1.   Price variance per hr. = Total price variance/ Actual hrs.
                                    = $1,015 ÷ 1,750
                                    = $.58, unfavorable

     Actual labor rate (price) = Standard price + Price variance
                                    = $14.00 + $.58
                                    = $14.58

2.   Flexible-budget labor variance = Price variance + Usage variance
                              $1,855 = $-1,015 + X
                                   X = $2,870, favorable

           Usage variance = Standard price x Difference in hours
                  $2,870 = $14.00 x Difference in hours

     Difference in hours = $2,870 ÷ $14.00
                          = 205

Because the variance is favorable, the standard hours allowed must be 1,750 + 205 = 1,955.

The analytical framework follows. All given items are designated by an asterisk (*).

Actual Hours x Actual Price	Actual Hours x Expected Price	Standard Hours x Expected Price
1,750 hrs.*	1,750 hrs.*	1,955 hrs.
x $14.58	x $14.00*	x $14.00*
= $25,515	= $24,500	= $27,370

1,750* x $.58	205 x $14.00*
= Price variance, $1,015U*	= Usage variance, $2,870F
Flexible-budget variance, $1,855F*	

<u>8-31</u>   (10 min.)

Material usage variance
    = Difference in pounds x Standard price
    = (16,500 - 18,000) x $3
    = $4,500, favorable

Labor usage variance
    = Difference in hours x Standard price
    = (46,700 actual hours - 45,000 standard hours) x $6
    = $10,200, unfavorable

<u>8-32</u>   (10-20 min.)

1.   Usage variance = (Actual hours - Standard hours) x Standard rate
             $14,140 = (Actual hours - 12,000) x $14.00
             $14,140 = $14.00 x (Actual hours) - $168,000
        Actual hours = $182,140 ÷ $14.00 = 13,010
                       or
        Excess hours, $14,140 ÷ $14.00   1,010
        Standard hours   <u>12,000</u>
        Total actual hours   <u>13,010</u>

2.   Price variance
        = Actual quantity purchased x (Actual price - Standard price / unit)
             $-288 = 1,800 x (Actual price - $4.50)
             $-288 = 1,800 x (Actual price) - $8,100
        Actual price = $7,812 ÷ 1,800 = $4.34
                    or
        Standard price $4.50
        Variance per unit, $288 ÷ 1,800   <u>.16F</u>
        Actual price   <u>$4.34</u>

<u>8-33</u> (10-15 min.)

Direct material:
  Price variance: $154,000 - $165,000 = $11,000F
  Usage variance: $165,000 - $172,500 = $7,500F
  Flexible-budget variance: $154,000 - $172,500 = $18,500F

Direct labor:
  Price variance: $79,200 - 74,000 = 5,200U
  Usage variance: $74,000 - $71,300 = $2,700U
  Flexible-budget variance: $79,200 - $71,300 = $7,900U

You may wish to call the students' attention to tradeoffs. For example, more efficient use of materials may be attained by more careful work that takes more time than allowed by the labor standard.

<u>8-34</u> (10-15 min.) (in thousands)

	(1)	(2)	(3)	(4)	(5)
		(1)-(3)		(3)-(5)	
	Actual Results at Actual Prices	Flexible-Budget Variances	Flexible Budget for Actual Sales Output Achieved	Sales Activity Variances	Master Budget
Revenue	$ 4,000	$ -	$4,000	$1,000U	$5,000
Variable costs	400	-	400	100F	500
Contribution margin	$ 3,600	$ -	$3,600	$ 900U	$4,500
Fixed costs	4,910	410U	4,500	-	4,500
Operating income	$(1,310)	$410U	$ (900)	$ 900U	$ -

U = Unfavorable

Note that this is an example of a "high fixed cost" or "highly leveraged" organization. This means a high sensitivity of operating income in relation to changes in revenue. Income plummeted in this case, but would have soared if the change in revenue had been $1,000,000 in the opposite direction.

8-35 (15-25 min.)

1.

	Actual Results	Flexible-Budget Variance	Flexible Budget	Sales Activity Variance	Master Budget
Attendees	90	-	90	15F	75
Revenue	$3,255	$105F	$3,150	$525F	$2,625
Chicken dinners	1,670	86U	1,584	264U	1,320
Beverages	466	74F	540	90U	450
Club rental	81	0	81	0	81
Music	875	125U	750	0	750
Profit	$ 163	$ 32U	$ 195	$171F	$ 24

2. If all costs had behaved as budgeted, the extra 15 attendees would have produced an extra $171 of profit ($525 more revenue and $264 + $90 = $354 more cost). The sales activity variance summarizes this effect of volume. Revenue was $105 over budget for the number of attendees. Maybe three tickets were sold to persons who did not attend. Costs ran $86 + $125 - $74 = $137 more than the budget for 90 attendees. Dinner cost was $86 over budget; this is not easily explained – did the caterer charge extra costs? Beverages were under budget by $74. The band seems to have played (or at least was paid for) an extra half hour.

8-36 (20-30 min.)

1.

	Actual Results at Actual Prices	Flexible-Budget Variances	Flexible Budget	Sales Activity Variances	Static (Master) Budget
Physical units	80,000	-	80,000	8,000F[a]	72,000
Sales	$806,400[c]	$ 6,400F	$800,000[b]	$80,000F	$720,000
Variable costs	492,000	12,000U	480,000	48,000U	432,000[g]
Contribution margin	314,400[d]	5,600U	320,000	32,000F	288,000
Fixed costs	210,000[e]	10,000U	200,000	-	200,000
Operating income	$104,400[f]	$15,600U	$120,000	$32,000F	$ 88,000

[a]80,000 - 72,000
[b]720,000/72,000 = $10 per unit; $10 x 80,000 = 800,000
[c]800,000 + 6,400
[d]806,400 - 492,000
[e]200,000 + 10,000
[f]314,400 - 210,000
[g]480,000/800,000 = .60; 720,000 x .60 = 432,000

2. Sales were 8,000 units higher than originally budgeted. This higher sales volume should have produced an operating income of $120,000 (up from $88,000 by $80,000(1 - .6) = $32,000). However, only $104,400 was achieved. Sales prices were higher by $6,400, but costs exceeded the flexible budget by $12,000 + $10,000 = $22,000:

Actual operating income		$104,400
Variances:		
Sales prices	6,400F	
Sales volume	32,000F	
Variable costs	12,000U	
Fixed costs	10,000U	16,400F
Master budgeted operating income		$ 88,000

428

8-37 (20-30 min.) There is a need to work from the knowns to the unknowns.

CORTEZ CREDIT SERVICES
Analysis of Income Statement
For the Year 20X1
(in thousands)

	(1)	(2) (1)-(3) Flexible-Budget Variances	(3) Flexible Budget	(4) (3)-(5) Sales Activity Variances	(5) Master Budget
Reports	700	-	700	100U	800
Sales @ $50	$35,000	$ -	$35,000	$5,000U	$40,000
Variable costs	11,400	900U	10,500	1,500F	12,000*
Contribution margin	$23,600	$ 900U	$24,500	$3,500U	$28,000
Fixed costs	21,800	800U	21,000	-	21,000
Operating income	$ 1,800	$1,700U	$ 3,500	$3,500U	$ 7,000

* Contribution margin = 70% x (800 x $50) = $28,000; $40,000 sales - $28,000 contribution margin = $12,000 variable costs; at master budget level of 800,000 reports, variable costs are $15 per report.

Note: The variance in fixed costs is properly a flexible-budget variance—not a sales activity variance. The variances in Column (4) are traceable *solely* to changes in volume: The effects of price and efficiency changes and any other types of spending changes are presented in Column (2).

The $7,000,000 budgeted income was not attained because (a) *volume* was down by 100,000 reports, causing a $3,500,000 shortfall in contribution margin. In addition, our *prices* paid for services (commissions) were higher, and the *efficiency* of our workers receiving wages was lower; together these totaled $900,000. Finally, we spent $800,000 in excess of our advertising budget.

8-38 (15-20 min.)

1. The sales activity variance is RMB570,000 favorable, and the flexible-budget variance is RMB 390,000 unfavorable. The following numbers are in millions of Chinese RMBs):

	Actual Results at Actual Activity Level	Flexible-Budget Variances	Flexible-Budget for Actual Sales Activity	Sales Activity Variances	Master Budget
Sales	9.20	—	9.20	1.90 F	7.30
Variable costs	6.83	.39 U	6.44	1.33 U	5.11
Contribution margin	2.37	.39 U	2.76	.57 F	2.19
Fixed costs	1.80	—	1.80	—	1.80
Operating income	.57	.39 U	.96	.57 F	.39

2. The RMB 180,000 favorable master-budget variance in 2005 resulted from the increase in volume. In fact, if there had been no cost overruns in 2005, profits would have increased by RMB 570,000. In 2006 sales volume falls to its 2005 budgeted level, and if the franchise maintains the actual cost structure of 2005, its profits would fall well below the level budgeted for 2005. If another RMB 390,000 unfavorable flexible-budget variance occurs in 2006, profit would be zero.

8-39 (20-25 min.)

1. Monetary amounts are in thousands of dollars

	Actual Results at Actual Prices	Flexible-Budget Variance	Flexible Budget	Sales Activity Variances	Master Budget
Millions of passenger miles	1,650	-	1,650	150F	1,500*
Revenue	303,600**	26,400U	330,000	30,000F	300,000
Variable expenses	200,000	14,500F	214,500***	19,500U	195,000
Contribution margin	103,600	11,900U	115,500	10,500F	105,000
Fixed expenses	83,000	3,000U	80,000	-	80,000
Operating income	20,600	14,900U	35,500	10,500F	25,000

*300,000 /$.20 = 1,500,000
**330,000 - .08(330,000) = 303,600
***(195,000 ÷ 300,000) x 330,000 = 214,500

		Actual Results at Actual Prices	Flexible-Budget Variance	Flexible Budget	Sales Activity Variances	Master Budget
2.	Jet fuel	108,900	9,900U*	99,000	9,000U	90,000

*Price variance of .10 x $99,000 = $9,900U

$9,900 of the $14,500 flexible budget variance for variable expenses, or 68%, was caused by the extra fuel cost.

<u>8-40</u>   (30-45 min.) The computations of variances are straightforward, although the context is different from that in the text. The explanation of variances is potentially complex and difficult.

1. Nursing price variance

> = Actual cost - (Actual hours x Standard rate)
> = $33,150 - (2,075 x $15)
> = $33,150 - $31,125 = $2,025U

Nursing usage variance

> = (Actual hours - Standard hours allowed) x Standard rate
> = [2,075 - (4,000 x .5)] x $15
> = 75 x $15 = $1,125U

2. Efficiency variance

> = (Actual hours - Std. hours allowed) x Variable overhead rate
> = (2,075 - 2,000) x $10 = $750U

Spending variance

> = Actual cost - Actual hours x Variable overhead rate
> = $20,340 - (2,075 x $10)
> = $20,340 - $20,750 = $410F

3. The nursing price and usage variances are unfavorable. This may be due to inefficient scheduling. More nurses are being used than are required, and a higher proportion than is normal are in the high wage rate categories.

But this might be exactly what is expected when volume increases. The nurses who perform the extra work that physicians usually handle are probably highly skilled, and, therefore, are paid more than average. Thus, the average pay rate for nurses increases. Further, as the hospital sees additional patients, nurses may bear nearly the entire added load. Why? Because physicians may already be at capacity. Therefore, although at a volume of 3,800 patients nurses average .5 hours per patient, they put in more than .5 hours with each additional patient because they pick up some physician tasks as well as their own normal tasks. Suppose a physician spends an average of .5 hours on each patient case. Since additional physician time may not be available, nurses might average a full hour for each additional patient, the .5 hour that they normally spend plus the .5 hour a physician usually spends.

It appears that Dr. Mortensen has controlled supplies and other variable costs quite well. Of the $1,340 unfavorable variance, $1,000 is due to the added volume. An additional $750 is due to the use of extra nursing hours; that is, the variable overhead efficiency variance arises solely due to the use of extra nursing hours. The spending for supplies and other variable overhead is $410 less than expected. This reflects both price and quantity effects for the supplies and other variable overhead.

8-41 (20-30 min.) This is an excellent basic problem in flexible budgeting.

1.
UNIVERSITY OF SCOTLAND MOTOR POOL
Monthly Budget Report
For March 20X1

	March Actual	Monthly Flexible Budget	Under (over)
Gasoline	£ 8,200	£ 7,700	£(500)
Oil, minor repairs, parts and supplies	1,290	1,400	110
Outside repairs	50	234	184
Insurance	416	416	-
Salaries and benefits	1,800	1,800	-
Depreciation	1,976	1,976	-
Totals	£13,732	£13,526	£ (206)
Number of automobiles	26	26	-
Actual kilometers	140,000	140,000	-
Cost per kilometer	£ .0981	£ .0966	£(.0015)

Supporting Calculations for Monthly Budget Amounts:
Gasoline: (140,000 km ÷ 8 km per liter) x £.44 per liter = £7,700
Oil, etc.: 140,000 km x £.01 per km = £1,400
Outside repairs: (£108 per auto x 26 autos) ÷ 12 months = £234
Insurance:
  Annual cost for one auto = £4,800 ÷ 25 autos = £192 per auto
  Annual cost for 26 autos = 26 x £192 = £4,992
  Monthly cost = £4,992 ÷ 12 = £416
Salaries and benefits:
  No change, monthly cost = £21,600 annual cost ÷ 12 months = £1,800
Depreciation:
  Annual depreciation per auto = £22,800 ÷ 25 autos = £912
  Annual depreciation for 26 autos = £912 x 26 = £23,712
  Monthly depreciation = £23,712 ÷ 12 = £1,976

2. Outside automobile repairs are a function of the use of the automobile over its lifetime. However, these repairs occur irregularly throughout the year and the life of the car. A monthly budget figure based upon a per mile charge becomes questionable. Therefore, the use of one-twelfth of the estimated annual outside repair costs adjusted for the number of cars in operation during a month would appear to be more reasonable. Further, repairs probably occur more frequently in low-volume months, so the favorable variance in this high-volume month is not surprising.

8-42   (50-70 min.)

The following notation applies to requirements 1-3.

TC = Total cost
F_I = Fixed costs of the Account Inquiry activity center
F_C = Fixed costs of the Correspondence activity center
F_B = Fixed costs of the Account Billing activity center
F_V = Fixed costs of the Bill Verification activity center
V_I = Variable cost per labor hour in the Account Inquiry activity center
V_C = Variable cost per letter in the Correspondence activity center
V_B = Variable cost per line in the Account Billing activity center
V_V = Variable cost per account in the Bill Verification activity center
HR = Account Inquiry labor hours
LR = Letters of correspondence issued
LN = Lines printed
AC = Commercial accounts verified

1.

Activity Center	Flexible-Budget Formula
Account Inquiry	$F_I + V_I \times HR = \$156,380 + \$24.22^{(1)} \times HR$
Correspondence	$F_C + V_C \times LR = \$25,584 + \$3.50^{(2)} \times LR$
Account Billing	$F_B + V_B \times LN = \$81,400 + \$0.063^{(3)} \times LN$
Bill Verification	$F_V + V_V \times AC = \$78,050 + \$0.54^{(4)} \times AC$

(1) $\$79,910 \div 3,300$ (3) $\$154,377 \div 2,440,000$

(2) $\$9,800 \div 2,800$ (4) $\$10,797 \div 20,000$

2.

Flexible Budget – Account Inquiry Activity Center

	Budget Formula:	Cost Driver: Number of Labor Hrs. (HR)		
		3,000	4,000	5,000
Variable Costs	$24.22/HR	$ 72,660	$ 96,880	$121,100
Fixed Costs	$156,380	156,380	156,380	156,380
Total Flexible Budget		$229,040	$253,260	$277,480

Flexible Budget – Correspondence Activity Center

	Budget Formula:	Cost Driver: Number of Letters (LR)		
		2,500	3,000	3,500
Variable Costs	$3.50/LR	$ 8,750	$10,500	$12,250
Fixed Costs	$25,584	25,584	25,584	25,584
Total Flexible Budget		$34,334	$36,084	$37,834

436

Flexible Budget – Account Billing Activity Center

	Budget Formula:	Cost Driver: Number of Lines (LN)		
		2,000,000	2,500,000	3,000,000
Variable Costs	$0.063/LN	$126,000	$157,500	$189,000
Fixed Costs	$81,400	81,400	81,400	81,400
Total Flexible Budget		$207,400	$238,900	$270,400

Flexible Budget – Bill Verification Activity Center

	Budget Formula:	Cost Driver: Number of Accounts (AC)		
		15,000	20,000	25,000
Variable Costs	$0.54/AC	$ 8,100	$10,800	$13,500
Fixed Costs	$78,050	78,050	78,050	78,050
Total Flexible Budget		$86,150	$88,850	$91,550

3. $TC = F_I + F_C + F_B + F_V + V_I \times HR + V_C \times LR + V_B \times LN + V_V \times AC$
$= 341,414 + 24.22 \times HR + 3.50 \times LR + .063 \times LN + .54 \times AC$

4.

Activity Center	Actual Costs	Flexible Budget	Flexible-Budget Variances
Account Inquiry	$235,400	$262,948[1]	$27,548F
Correspondence	38,020	36,959[2]	1,061U
Account Billing	285,000	264,100[3]	20,900U
Bill Verification	105,320	90,200[4]	15,120U
Total Costs	$663,740	$654,207	$9,533U

(1) $156,380 + (24.22 \times 4,400) = \$262,948$
(2) $25,584 + (3.50 \times 3,250) = \$36,959$
(3) $81,400 + (0.063 \times 2,900,000) = \$264,100$
(4) $78,050 + (0.54 \times 22,500) = \$90,200$

8-43 (25-30 min.)

	Cost Incurred: Actual Inputs x Actual Prices	Flexible Budget Based on Actual Inputs x Expected Prices	Flexible Budget Based on Standard Inputs Allowed for Actual Outputs Achieved x Expected Prices
Direct materials	3,300 lbs. x $.96 = $3,168	3,300 lbs. x $1.00 = $3,300	3,000 lbs. x $1.00 = $3,000

	3,300 x ($.96 - $1.00) = Price variance $132F	(3,300 - 3,000) x $1.00 = Usage variance $300U
	Flexible-budget variance, $168U	

	Cost Incurred: Actual Inputs x Actual Prices	Flexible Budget Based on Actual Inputs x Expected Prices	Flexible Budget Based on Standard Inputs Allowed for Actual Outputs Achieved x Expected Prices
Direct labor	5,500 hrs. x $7.60 = $41,800	5,500 hrs. x $8.00 = $44,000	5,000 hrs x $8.00 = $40,000

	5,500 x ($7.60 - $8.00) = Price variance $2,200F	(5,500-5,000) x $8.00 = Usage variance, $4,000U
	Flexible-budget variance, $1,800U	

	Cost Incurred: Actual Inputs x Actual Prices	Flexible Budget Based on Actual Inputs x Expected Prices	Flexible Budget Based on Standard Inputs Allowed for Actual Outputs Achieved x Expected Prices
Variable overhead	5,500 hrs x $.86 * = $4,730	5,500 hrs. x $.80 = $4,400	5,000 hrs. x $.80 = $4,000

	5,500 x ($.86 - $.80) = Spending variance, $330U	(5,500-5,000) x $.80 = Efficiency variance, $400U
	Flexible-budget variance, $730U	

U = Unfavorable, F = Favorable

* The average variable overhead price is unnecessary to comply with the requirements of the problem. It was computed by dividing $4,730 by 5,500 hours.

8-44 (30-35 min.) The format of the solution may seem awkward at first, but students find that it provides perspective on the analysis of variances. SFR = Swiss Franc.

1.

Cost Incurred: Actual Inputs x Actual Prices	Flexible Budget Based on Actual Inputs x Expected Prices	Flexible Budget Based on Standard Inputs Allowed for Actual Outputs Achieved x Expected Prices
4,300 lbs. X 15.5SFR =66,650SFR	4,300 lbs x 16SFR = 68,800SFR	4,000 lbs. x 16SFR = 64,000SFR

4,300 x .5SFR= Price variance, 2,150SFR F	300 x 16SFR = Usage variance, 4,800SFR U
Flexible-budget variance, 2,650 SFR U	

6,300 hrs. x 30.5SFR = 192,150SFR	6,300 hrs. x 30SFR = 189,000SFR	6,000 hrs. x 30SFR = 180,000SFR

6,300 x .5SFR = Price variance, 3,150SFR U	300 x 30SFR Usage variance, 9,000SFR U
Flexible-budget variance, 12,150SFR U	

69,500SFR	6,300 hrs. x 10SFR = 63,000SFR	6,000 hrs. x 10SFR = 60,000SFR

Spending variance, 69,500 - 63,000 = 6,500SFR U	300 x 10SFR = Efficiency variance, 3,000SFR U
Flexible-budget variance, 9,500SFR U	

2. The flexible-budget allowance for any *variable* cost is the *same as* (is equal to) the total standard quantity allowed for the good units produced times the standard price.

The budget allowance under standard costing for variable costs always depends on *output*, the units produced. Therefore, the budget for 4,000 units is, as shown above, 4,000 units x 1 1/2 hours x 30SFR = 180,000SFR. For 5,000 units, the budgetary allowance would be 5,000 units x 1 1/2 hours x 30SFR = 225,000SFR. Note again that a budget can be established *after the fact* – after the number of units produced is known.

8-45 (30-50 min.)

1.
Department Performance Report
Direct Labor and Variable Overhead

Actual hours		5,700
Standard hours allowed, 2/3 hour x 8,100 units		5,400
Excess hours		300

	Actual Costs Incurred	Budget Based on 5,400 Standard Direct Labor Hours Allowed for 8,100 Good Units Produced	Flexible Budget Variance to be Explained
Direct labor	$29,070	$28,350	$720F
Variable overhead:			
Lubricants @$.60	$ 2,910	$ 3,240	$330F
Other supplies @$.30	1,845	1,620	225U
Rework @$.60	3,690	3,240	450U
Other indirect labor @ $1.50	8,550	8,100	450U
Total variable overhead	$16,995	$16,200	$795U

2. Summary explanation:

	Incurred: Actual Hours x Actual Price	Flexible Budget: Actual Hours x Expected Price	Flexible Budget: Standard Hours Allowed x Expected Price
Direct labor	5,700 hrs. x $5.10 = $29,070	5,700 hrs. x $5.25 = $29,925	5,400 hrs. x $5.25 = $28,350

	5,700 x $.15 = Price variance, $855F	300 x $5.25 = Usage variance, $1,575U

Flexible-budget variance, $720U

	Incurred	Flexible Budget: Actual Hours x Expected Price	Flexible Budget: Standard Hours Allowed x Expected Price
Variable overhead	$17,100 less spending variance = $17,100 - $105F = $16,995	5,700 hrs. x $3.00 = $17,100	5,400 hrs. x $3.00 = $16,200

Spending var. = flexible-budget var. - usage var. = $795 U - $900 U = $105 F	Efficiency variance = $17,100 - $16,200 = $900 U

Flexible-budget variance, $795U

3.	The subdivision of the budget variance for variable overhead into *spending* and *efficiency* variances is similar to the split of the total direct labor variance into a *price* variance and a *usage* variance. However, the interpretation is quite different.

The efficiency variance for variable overhead measures the extra overhead costs (or savings) incurred solely because direct labor usage exceeded (or was less than) the standard direct labor hours allowed. When variable overhead is closely related to labor time, fluctuations in overhead costs should correspond with variations in labor time. Both the labor usage and overhead efficiency variances are measured by multiplying a standard price times the difference between actual hours and standard hours allowed.

The variable overhead *spending* variance is similar to the labor *price* variance, but its causal factors encompass more than price changes alone. Other causes include poor budget estimates for one or more individual overhead items, variation in attention and control regarding individual costs, and erratic behavior of specific overhead items that have been squeezed for convenience into a budget formula that assumes strictly variable behavior and relation to one volume base – labor hours. For example, material handling within the factory (getting material to the workbench) is more closely related to goods *started* during a period than to standard hours allowed for work done.

8-46 (30-40 min.)

1. Material price variance = ($5.50 - $5.30) x 27,000 = $5,400 F
    Material usage variance = $5.50 x (27,000 - (60 x 430)) = $6,600 U

    Labor rate variance = ($15.90 - $16.00) x 660 = $66 F
    Labor usage variance = $16.00 x (660 - (1.5 x 430)) = $240 U

    Overhead flexible-budget variance = $5,335 - (($5.76 x 430) + $2,808)
                                                   = $50.20U

2. The person in charge of purchasing saved $5,400 by purchasing direct materials for $.20 per pound below standard cost. However, more of the material was used, causing an unfavorable usage variance of $6,600. If the purchase of low-quality materials caused the excess usage, the net effect was an unfavorable variance of $1,200.

    There was a small savings of $66 because the average wage rate was $.10 per pound below standard. However, more than the standard amount of labor was used, costing $240. If the hiring lower quality (and therefore lower paid) workers caused the entire excess usage, the net effect is $174 unfavorable.

    The excess labor might also have been related to the excess use of materials. If some processing is complete before the defective materials are identified, some labor would also be wasted in the process. Thus, the $240 unfavorable labor usage variance might be caused by the purchase of low quality materials.

    The overhead variance is not large, but it too is unfavorable; more overhead costs were incurred than would be expected for the production of 430 kayaks.

3.   Suppose variable overhead varies with total labor hours. Then the overhead variance can be broken into a variable-overhead efficiency variance and an overhead spending variance (but the overhead spending variance cannot be broken into fixed and variable components without more information):

Var. OH/DLH = $5.76 ÷ 1.5 = $3.84

Var.-overhead efficiency variance = $3.84 x (660 - (1.5 x 430)) = $57.60 U
Overhead spending variance = $5,335 - (($3.84 x 660) + $2,808)= $7.40 F

The unfavorable variable overhead efficiency variance indicates that $57.60 of overhead costs were incurred because of the excess use of labor. Whatever caused the extra labor hours also caused this variance. Control of overhead itself was good, as shown by the favorable $7.40 overhead spending variance.

Note: None of the variances indicate <u>why</u> actual costs differed from standard costs. The variances point toward possible causes and lead managers to ask the right questions about possible causes. The explanations above are possible causes, but they cannot be known for sure until managers do further exploration.

8-47 (15-20 min.)

1. Direct Materials:
   Price variance = ($7.80 - $8.00) x 2,775 = $555F
   Usage variance = (2,775 - 2,700) x $8 = $600U
   Total direct materials variance = $21,645 - (900 x $24)
                                   = $21,645 - $21,600 = $45U

   Overhead:

	Actual Results at Actual Prices	Flexible Budget for Actual Output Achieved	Flexible-Budget Variances
Supplies	$ 2,132	$ 2,250	$118F
Power	1,612	1,572	40U
Rent and other building services	2,775	2,815	40F
Factory labor	1,618	1,500	118U
Depreciation	4,500	4,500	0
Total overhead	$12,637	$12,637	$ 0

2. MPM does not account separately for the price (rate) and quantity of labor. Therefore, labor price and usage variances cannot be computed. Many highly automated companies account for labor this way. Because labor is a small proportion of cost in some automated manufacturing processes, it is not worth the cost to monitor price and efficiency effects. MPM treats labor as a fixed overhead cost. Therefore, the company does not expect to adjust the amount of labor used as volume changes. Therefore, it compares the actual labor cost to a fixed monthly budget of $1,500.

8-48 (10-20 min.)

Raw material	(a) Initial mix	(b) Allowance for reduction	(c) Required quantity a ÷ b*	(d) Unit cost	Standard material cost (c x d)
Altium	24 kg	.8	30 kg	$2.20	$ 66.00
Bollium	19.2 ltr	.8	24 ltr	1.95	46.80
Credix	10 kg	1.0	10 kg	2.80	28.00

Standard material cost –
  20-liter container $140.80

* Instead of being divided by the 0.8, the first two items could be multiplied by 1.25 to obtain the same answer.

8-49 (25-35 min.) This problem is not straightforward. It is complicated by the need to include an allowance for defective units in the standard costs. Note that many accountants now object to standard costing because of the "acceptability" of allowing for defects in the standards.

Direct Materials

Pounds in final product	3.2
Allowance for normal scrap	.4
Total pounds per finished unit	3.6
Allowance for defective units	.9*
Total pounds per good unit	4.5
Standard price per pound	$12.20**
Standard direct material cost per good unit	$54.90

*Defective units = 20% x total units or 25% of good units;
  Material allowance for defectives = .25 x 3.6 lb. = .9 lb.
**$11.40 price of materials + $.80 shipping and handling

Direct Labor

Hours of actual machining per unit	4.00
Allowance for nonproductive time	1.00*
Total hours per finished unit	5.00
Allowance for defective units	1.25**
Total hours per good unit	6.25
Standard rate per hour	$ 28.00***
Standard direct labor cost per good unit	$175.00

*For every 4 hours worked there is 1 hour of nonproductive time.
**Defective units = 20% x total units or 25% of good units;
  Direct labor allowance for defectives = .25 x 5 hr = 1.25 hr.

***Basic rate	$20.00
Fringe benefits	6.00
Payroll taxes	2.00
Total labor rate	$28.00

8-50 (50-75 min.)

1.   a.   Sales-activity variance = Budgeted unit contribution margin x Difference between the master budget sales in units and the actual sales in units

$$= \$9.20 \times (9,000 - 8,000)$$
$$= \$9,200 \text{ unfavorable}$$

This variance is labeled as a sales-activity variance because it quantifies the impact on income of the deviation from an original sales target – while holding price and usage factors constant. Of course, the failure to reach target sales may be traceable to a number of causes beyond the control of the marketing force, including strikes, material shortages, and storms.

        b.   The budget formulas in Exhibit 8-2 are the basis for the following answers. The alert student will note that budgeted contribution margin and operating income are in the 8,000-unit column of Exhibit 8-2.

Budgeted contribution margin = $9.20 x 8,000 = $73,600
Budgeted operating income
    = $73,600 - $70,000 fixed costs = $ 3,600
Budgeted direct material = $10.00 x 8,000 = $80,000
Budgeted direct labor = $8.00 x 8,000 = $64,000

2.

	Cost Incurred Actual Inputs x Actual Prices	Flexible Budget Based on Actual Inputs x Expected Prices	Flexible Budget Based on Standard Inputs Allowed for Actual Output Achieved x Expected Prices
Direct Materials	42,000 lbs. x $1.86 = $78,120	42,000 lbs. x $2.00 = $84,000	(8,000 units x 5) x $2.00 = $80,000

42,000 x ($1.86-$2.00) = Price variance, $5,880F	(42,000 - 40,000) x $2.00 = Usage variance, $4,000U
Flexible-budget variance, $1,880F	

	Cost Incurred Actual Inputs x Actual Prices	Flexible Budget Based on Actual Inputs x Expected Prices	Flexible Budget Based on Standard Inputs Allowed for Actual Output Achieved x Expected Prices
Direct Labor	4,140 hrs. x $16.40 = $67,896	4,140 hrs. x $16.00 = $66,240	(8,000 units x .5 hrs. x $16.00) or (4,000 hrs. x $16) = $64,000

4,140 x ($16.40-$16.00) = Price variance, $1,656U	(4,140 - 4,000) x $16.00 = Usage variance, $2,240U
Flexible-budget variance, $3,896U	

3.   The purchasing manager for Dominion apparently purchased material for $.14 per pound less than the standard, saving the company $5,880. However, the company used more of the material, perhaps because poor quality of the materials caused excessive waste. The cost of the extra material was $4,000, leaving a net saving of $1,880. But this is not necessarily the end of the analysis. Both price and usage variances for labor were unfavorable. Possibly scrapping of the materials came after they had been partly processed, entailing a wasting of labor as well. If the quality of materials caused the entire extra usage of 140 hours of labor, $2,240 should be compared to the net saving of $1,880, making the material-purchase decision a poor economic decision. In addition, the labor price variance may be related, also. If the extra usage of labor caused the use of overtime and the overtime premium caused the increase in average labor rates, the $1,656 unfavorable price variance might also be caused by the materials. If all of these causation links apply, the total effect of purchasing the cheaper materials is:

Material price variance	$5,880 F
Material usage variance	4,000 U
Labor usage variance	2,240 U
Labor rate variance	1,656 U
Total variance	$2,016 U

8-51   (30 min.) The solution is given in the textbook after the problem itself.

8-52 (15-20 min.)

1. Variable costs, 2004: $114, 750 + $204,000 + $153,000 + 21% x ($204,000 + $153,000) + ($194,250 - $181,500) = $559,470.

Therefore, variable cost per visit are $559,470 ÷ 17,000 = $32.91.

Fixed costs are $181,500 + [$676,200 - .20 x (204,000 + $153,000)] = $786,300.

Cost Function: $32.91 per visit variable and $786,300 per year fixed.

2.

Revenues ($75 per visit; 18,000 visits)		$1,350,000
Variable costs:		
Supplies	$ 121,500	
Physician salaries	216,000	
Nurse salaries	162,000	
Overhead	79,380	
Administrative	13,500	
Total variable cost		592,380
Fixed costs:		
Overhead	604,800	
Administrative Expenses	181,500	
Total fixed costs		786,300
Net Loss		$ (28,680)

3.
Variance to explain: $28,680 - $15,500 = $13,180 F
Sales Volume variance = 400 visits x ($75 - $32.91) = $16,836 F
Flexible Budget Variance = $13,180 - $16,836 = $3,656 U

a) The extra 400 units generated $16,836 additional profit.
b) Costs were higher than expected for 18,400 visits by $3,656.

The total effect was a smaller loss than budgeted, caused entirely by the additional 400 visits. The benefit of the additional visits was offset partly by spending $3,656 more than budgeted for this level of volume.

8-53 (35-45 min.)

1. Printing department costs for the first month:

	A	B	C
		Flexible Budget Based on Standard Inputs Allowed for Actual Outputs Achieved x	
	Actual Cost Incurred: Actual Inputs x Actual Prices	**Expected Prices**	**Master Budget**
Printing	$50,000	40,000 pages x $1.00 = $40,000	35,000 pages x $1.00 = $35,000

Flexible-budget variance (A - B) = $50,000 - $40,000 = $10,000 U	Printing activity variance (B - C) = $40,000 - $35,000 = $5,000 U
Static budget variance (A - C) $50,000 - $35,000 = $15,000 U	

2. The static budget was inaccurate for the reasons given in the problem: all types of jobs requested more printing, and both government and central administration jobs used more four-color and graphics printing. Printing activity was higher, and the mix of types of jobs differed from what was expected. Likely explanations are that (1) the $1.00 charge per page is an average printing cost, but costs per page can differ greatly with relative complexity, (2) the printing department has not identified the appropriate cost drivers to enable it to charge for the costs the department incurs. All the users recognize that four-color, graphic printing is a bargain, and simple printing is too expensive. As a result, everyone wishes to use more of the low-price, high complexity printing.

3. a. The ABC analysis is an attempt to measure the costs of printing complexity. If the analysis is accurate, then four-color printing jobs will cost at least $1.35 per page ($.35 + $1.00) plus pre-press costs. Simple, black-and-white jobs will cost only $.35 per page. Costs charged for the various jobs will reflect their complexity and should result in more efficient use of printing services. Since the costs of different types of jobs will vary under this new system, it is critical that the ABC estimates are accurate. Chapter 3 discusses methods for measuring cost behavior.

   b. These cost estimates are themselves averages per type of cost because some portions of the printing department costs are fixed in the short run. There is some controversy over whether these fixed costs should be spread over normal or expected levels of cost driver activity. Not "unitizing" these costs preserves the distinction between fixed and variable cost behavior. Under this approach, fixed costs would be recovered by an annual or monthly charge based on expected usage. An objection is that this merely passes the fixed cost problem along to the line units who are selling products or services to external customers. An alternative approach is to unitize these costs over expected or normal cost driver activity and charge users as if all costs were variable. If cost driver activity expectations are accurate, there should not be significant static budget variances. Large errors in forecasting, however, will lead to large budgeting errors because total fixed costs charged will not equal total fixed costs incurred.

   c. Costs of commercial jobs:

	Old System	ABC System
27,500 pages	@$1/page = $27,500	@$.35/page =$9,625
27,500 use color	–	@ $1.00/color page = $27,500
Total cost	$27,500	$37,125

(40-50 min.)

Before proceeding to answer the questions asked, it is helpful to get a good understanding of the cost behavior. The costs of the outpatient clinic can be broken down into budgeted fixed and variable costs as follows:

	Fixed	Variable	
Cost	Total	Total	Per Unit
Physicians	$240,000		
Nurses and technicians		$180,000	$45
Supplies		60,000	15
Overhead	180,000	72,000	18
Total	$420,000	$312,000	$78

1.   Whether Bellevue Community Hospital would save money by closing its outpatient clinic depends on what fixed costs it might avoid if the clinic were closed. The budgeted contribution margin is $180 - $78 = $102 per patient, giving a total contribution from 4,000 patients of 4,000 x $102 = $408,000. If the hospital can avoid more than $408,000 of the $420,000 of fixed costs, it would be financially better off without the clinic. It is likely that the $240,000 of physician cost would be saved; the hospital would not need to employ any physicians for the clinic. It is hard to tell whether any of the $180,000 of fixed overhead would be saved, but it is unlikely that Bellevue would save more than $168,000, especially since $30,000 of the fixed overhead is an allocation of hospital-wide administrative costs that are unlikely to change much and $37,500 is depreciation on equipment. The only way that it seems likely to achieve a financial advantage by closing the clinic is if the closure frees up resources that are valuable to the hospital.

2.   The difference between the static budget loss of $12,000 and the actual loss of $22,200 can first be divided into a sales volume variance and a flexible-budget variance:

A	B	C
Actual	Flexible Budget	Master Budget
Profit (Loss)	Profit (Loss)	Profit (Loss)
$(22,200)	$102 x 3,800 -	$102 x 4,000 -
	$420,000 =	$420,000 =
	$(32,400)	$(12,000)

Flexible-budget variance (A - B) = $(22,200) - $(32,400) = $10,200 F	Sales activity variance (B - C) = $(32,400) - $(12,000) = $20,400 U
Static budget variance (A - C) $(22,200) - $(12,000) = $10,200 U	

Therefore, the main explanation of the additional loss is the decrease in volume. In fact, the loss of volume cost Bellevue $20,400, and cost savings of $10,200 reduces the overall shortfall to only $10,200.

The $10,200 flexible-budget variance can be further analyzed by cost category. First, consider the physician cost. Since physician costs are fixed, we can only compute a total physician cost variance: $240,000 - $233,000 = $7,000 F.

Nurse and technician costs are variable and have a standard rate of $30 per hour and an actual rate of $182,700 ÷ 5,800 = $31.50. A total of 5,800 hours was used; standard hours allowed for 3,800 patients is 1.5 hrs./patient x 3,800 patients = 5,700. Price (rate) and usage variances are as follows:
   Price (rate) variance = ($30 - $31.50) x 5,800 = $8,700 U
   Usage variance = (5,800 – 5,700) x $30 = $3,000 U

Supplies cost is variable, but we have no measure of amount used. Therefore, we can compute only a total supplies variance: $15 x 3,800 - $58,500 = 1,500 U.

From the information given, the overhead variance cannot be computed in any more detail than a total overhead variance: [($18 x 3,800) + $180,000] - $232,000 = $248,400 - $232,000 = $16,400 F

Therefore, the total flexible-budget variance can be explained as follows:

Physician variance	$ 7,000 F
Nurse & technician rate variance	8,700 U
Nurse & technician usage variance	3,000 U
Supplies variance	1,500 U
Overhead variance	16,400 F
Total flexible-budget variance	$10,200 F

One possible explanation for this pattern of variances is that nurses have been covering some time that physicians usually cover. The physician may not be spending full time in the clinic. Nurses and technicians are spending more time per patient than is budgeted, and that may be causing overtime premiums, which might explain the unfavorable rate variance. The large favorable overhead variance is more difficult to explain from the information given. It might be possible (though this is just speculation) that some expensive equipment was not fully utilized at the clinic and was moved to the hospital. This might explain why the volume was down (i.e., those who needed that equipment went to the hospital rather than the clinic) and why the fixed charges to the clinic were reduced.

8-55 (45 – 60 min.)

1.

Revenue (2,000x$200)	$400,000
Variable costs (2,000 x $139)	278,000
Contribution margin	$122,000
Fixed costs	56,000*
Operating income	$66,000

* Fixed costs = ($18 + $10) x 2,000 = $56,000.

2.

Master budget variance = $66,000 - $47,740 = $18,260 U

Sales volume variance = 200 x ($200 - $139) = $12,200 F
Flexible bud. var. = $392,260 – ($139x2,200 + $56,000) = $30,460 U
Master budget variance $18,260

Material variances:
    Housing variance = $44,000 – 2,200 x $20 $ 0
    PCB variances:
        PCB price variance = ($16 - $15) x 4,700 $ 4,700 U
        PCB usage variance = (4,700 – 4,400) x $15 4,500 U
        Total PCB variance = $75,200 – 2,200 x $30 $ 9,200 U
    Reading heads variances: $13,200 U
        RH price variance = ($11 - $10) x 9,200 $ 9,200 U
        RH usage variance = (9,200 – 8,800) x $10 4,000 U
        Total RH variance $13,200 U
Total material variances $22,400 U

Labor variances:

    Assembly variances:

        Assembly rate variance = ($8 - $8) x 3,900   0

        Assembly usage var. = ($4,400 – 3,900) x $8 $4,000 F

        Total assembly variances $4,000 F

    PCB variances:

        PCB rate variance = ($9.90 - $9) x 2,400 $2,160 U

        PCB usage variance = (2,400 – 2,200) x $9   1,800 U

        Total PCB variances $3,960 U

    Reading heads variances:

        RH rate variance = ($11 - $10) x 3,500 $3,500 U

        RH usage variance = ($3,500 – 3,300) x $10   2,000 U

    Total RH variances $5,500 U

Total labor variances $5,460 U

Overhead variances:

    Variable OH efficiency var. = (9,800 – 9,900) x $2 $ 200 F

    Variable OH spending var. = $18,800 – (9,800 x $2) 800 F

    Fixed OH spending variance = $37,600 - $36,000 1,600 U

Total overhead variances $ 600 U

Selling & administrative var. = $22,000 - $10 x 2,000 $2,000 U

Total flexible-budget variances $30,460 U

From these variances we learn that operations were not very efficient. The extra 200 units of sales increased income before taxes by $12,200, but this was more than offset by operating inefficiencies that cost Balmer $30,460, leaving the company short of budget by $30,460 - $12,200 = $18,260.

The material variances and the RH and PCB labor variances were all unfavorable and quite large, explaining much of the shortfall income. The bright spots were assembly labor and variable overhead, which had small favorable variances. But, all in all, the performance was significantly below expectations.

<u>8-56</u> (20-30 min.) For the solution, see the Prentice Hall Web site, www.prenhall.com/

<u>8-57</u> (60 min. or more)

The purpose of this exercise is to understand the difficulty of setting standard costs for even simple products or services. For many products or services, identifying the direct material and direct labor inputs may not be hard, but even identifying the overhead support can be a challenge. Students are likely to make various assumptions, which can lead to very different standard costs in all cost categories.

Requirements 2 and 3 also lead to consideration (albeit it implicitly) of many of the behavioral issues organizations may have in setting standards. Different managers have different objectives and different levels of knowledge. These must be combined into a single standard cost estimate.

If class time allows, it may be useful to have one or more groups present their standard costs to the class and describe how they were determined. The class may have suggestions that the group failed to consider – possibly some implicit assumptions that would not necessarily hold true.

<u>8-58</u> (30-50 min.)

NOTE TO INSTRUCTOR. This solution is based on the web site as it was in early 2004. Be sure to examine the current web site before assigning this problem, as the information there may have changed.

1.   Hershey's Web site seem primarily directed to customers. It is part of the company's advertising effort. In 2004, Hershey was showing Sugar Free Chocolate Candy, Kit Kat Bites, Hershey's Mini Kisses to Go, and King Size Reese's Peanut Butter Cups as new products. When you click on the product, you get an animated ad promoting the product.

2. Hershey produces products not only for the United States, but also exports to 90 countries worldwide. Because Hershey produces more than 100 different products, a flexible budget would be much more useful than a static budget. The reason is that determining the exact number of each item that would be needed in a given period would be impossible to predict. Consumers don't always buy the same items in the same quantities from year to year.

3. The master budget would show a 5% increase in net sales and variable costs but no increase in fixed costs. Based on actual 2002 results, the assumed 2003 master budget would project income before income taxes of $715,528:

	2002	2003
Net sales	$4,120,317	$4,326,333
Variable cost (cost of sales)	2,561,052	2,689,105
Contribution margin	1,559,265	1,637,228
Fixed costs	921,700	921,700
Income before income taxes	$ 637,565	$ 715,528

If sales increased 8%, one would expect income before income taxes to increase by 8% of the contribution margin, or 8% x $1,559,265 = $124,741. Actual income before income taxes increased by 10% x $637,565 = $63,757, to $637,565 + $63,757 = $701,322, or less than what would be expected. The master budget variance would be $715,528 – $701,322 = $14,206 U. Under these assumptions, and despite an 8% rather than 5% increase in sales, income fell short of the master budget by $14,206. The sales activity variance, the contribution margin on the added 3% of sales (an 8% rather than 5% increase), would be 3% x $1,559,265= $46,778 F. Thus, the flexible budget variance must have been $14,206 + $46,778 = $60,984 U. Either there were some inefficiencies or many of the costs assumed to be fixed were actually variable.

CHAPTER 9
COVERAGE OF LEARNING OBJECTIVES

LEARNING OBJECTIVE	FUNDA-MENTAL ASSIGN-MENT MATERIAL	CRITICAL THINKING EXERCISES AND EXERCISES	PROBLEMS	CASES, EXCEL, COLLAB., & INTERNET EXERCISES
LO1: Describe the relationship of management control systems to organizational goals.		28, 30, 36		50, 52, 53, 54
LO2: Use responsibility accounting to define an organizational subunit as a cost center, a profit center, or an investment center.	A1	28	43	
LO3: Develop performance measures and use them to monitor the achievements of an organization.		32, 35, 36	42, 44, 45	50
LO4: Explain the importance of evaluating performance and how it impacts motivation, goal congruence, and employee effort.	A1, B1	30, 33, 34, 37	42, 43, 48	50, 52, 53, 54
LO5: Prepare segment income statements for evaluating profit and investment centers using the contribution margin and controllable-cost concepts.	A2, B2	38	43	52, 54
LO6: Use a balanced scorecard to recognize both financial and nonfinancial measures of performance.	B3	35	45	
LO7: Measure performance against quality, cycle time, and productivity objectives.	A3, B1	31, 33, 39, 40, 41	46, 47, 48, 49	50, 51
LO8: Describe the difficulties of management control in service and nonprofit organizations.		29, 37		50, 53

CHAPTER 9
Management Control Systems and Responsibility Accounting

9-A1 (20 min.)

Admittedly, Midwest Electronics Company may have a legitimate claim against the supplier, but for the sake of discussion assume that the supplier has a smart attorney and would win the case.

The penalty of $30,000 should be charged to the purchasing department. Jean Trudeau may have done everything in her power to see that the special part was delivered on time, but she must realize that she is the one who is responsible for purchasing necessary material when it is needed. Trudeau may not have control over her suppliers and subsequent delivery, but it is her responsibility, and hers alone as far as Midwest Electronics is concerned, to have the purchased parts when they are needed. She is the one person in the organization who has the most influence over delivery. Everybody makes mistakes. The important point is to minimize the number of mistakes and also to understand fully that the extensive control reflected in responsibility accounting is the necessary balance to the great freedom of action that individual executives are given.

Other questions to discuss are: Did the sales department behave responsibly in accepting the order with penalty? Is it conceivable that a careful statistical study of delays by suppliers would permit the development of an "expected amount" of penalty to be incurred in a probabilistic sense, which then could be budgeted as part of the purchasing department's costs?

Discussions of this problem have again and again revealed a tendency among students (and among accountants and managers) to "fix the blame" – as if the variances arising from a responsibility accounting system should pinpoint misbehavior and provide answers. The point is that no accounting system or variances can provide answers ipso facto. However, variances can ask questions. In this case, in deciding where the penalty should be assigned, the student might inquire who should be asked in this situation – not who should be blamed.

<u>9-A2</u> (30-40 min.) See Exhibit 9-A2.

<u>9-A3</u> (15-20 min.)

1. Without adjusting for inflation, it appears that both companies had large increases in productivity in terms of revenues per employee.

	1998	**2004**
Intertel	$\dfrac{\$7,658,000,000}{75,900} = \$100,896;$	$\dfrac{\$9,667,000,000}{76,200} = \$126,864$
Telemark	$\dfrac{\$5,831,000,000}{56,600} = \$103,021;$	$\dfrac{6,764,000,000}{54,800} = \$123,431$

However, the 1998 productivity measures should be expressed in 2004 dollars for comparability:

	1998		**2004**
Intertel	$\dfrac{(1.2 \times \$7,658,000,000)}{75,900} = \$121,075$		126,864*
Telemark	$\dfrac{(1.2 \times \$5,831,000,000)}{56,600} = \$123,625$		123,431*

*Same as above for 2004.

2. Using the productivity measures that are correctly adjusted for inflation, we see that Telemark had very little change in productivity between 1998 and 2004. In contrast, Intertel increased its productivity by $126,864 - $121,075 = $5,789 per employee, an increase of $5,789 \div 121,075 = 4.8\%$. Although Telemark had a decrease in number of employees and Intertel had an increase, the larger sales increase for Intertel led to a higher productivity number. While Telemark had slightly higher productivity in 1998, Intertel has the higher productivity in 2004.

EXHIBIT 9-A2 Answers are in thousands of dollars.

	Company as a Whole	Breakdown into Two Divisions — Denver Division	Breakdown into Two Divisions — Colorado Springs Division	Breakdown of Denver Division — Not Allocated	Breakdown of Denver Division — Downtown	Breakdown of Denver Division — Littleton	Breakdown of Colorado Springs Division — Not Allocated	Breakdown of Colorado Springs Division — Downtown	Breakdown of Colorado Springs Division — Plaza	Breakdown of Colorado Springs Division — Airport
Net Sales	8,000	3,200	4,800		2,400	800		2,400	1,200	1,200
Variable costs:										
Cost of merchandise sold	5,000	2,000	3,000		1,500	500		1,500	750	750
Variable operating expenses	640	280	360		240	40		240	60	60
Total variable costs	5,640	2,280	3,360		1,740	540		1,740	810	810
Contribution margin	2,360	920	1,440		660	260		660	390	390
Less: Fixed costs controllable by segment managers	960	335	625	130	125	80	180	125	160	160
Contribution controllable by segment managers	1,400	585	815	(130)	535	180	(180)	535	230	230
Less: Fixed costs controllable by others	490	140	350	35	70	35	70	70	105	105
Contribution by segments	910	445	465	(165)	465	145	(250)	465	125	125
Less: Unallocated costs	110									
Income before income taxes	800									

464

9-B1 (15-20 min.)

1. It is not possible to determine the validity of Betty LaGrande's claim. It would be valid only if, on a proportional basis, the number of unidentified rejects caused by the other departments were greater than their proportionate number of identified rejects. Although the claims cannot be substantiated, a legitimate issue has been raised. The rejects charged to all the departments contain amounts not clearly attributable to the respective departments. This violates the concept that performance measures should not contain items outside the control of the manager. Further, a manager's effort to control the variation will be influenced by the result she can get from her actions. The fact that some of the variation could be caused by other departments will reduce the amount of the reported rejects within her control.

2. There are two solutions to this problem. First, remove the apportioned rejects from the reports and charge the managers with only the rejects identified with their department. Second, if the number of unidentified rejects is large and represents a large dollar value (which could be reduced if adequate information as to cause were available), then Hassan Company should consider inspection at the end of each department.

9-B2   (30-35 min.)

1.   See Exhibit 9-B2.

2.   The incremental costs of running such sightseeing tours can be identified with much more confidence than in many other instances. Net income will be improved by the excess of tour revenue over such costs; routine allocations of other operating costs and indirect costs do not seem relevant to the decision to run such tours. Those railroads that do not run such tours either:

   (a)   Do not expect incremental revenue to exceed incremental costs; or
   (b)   Even if profits could be enhanced, may not want to engage in any activity that will improve short-run profits because their long-run objective may be to reduce their passenger business as much as possible.

3.   If the entire $60,000 of separable discretionary fixed costs can be avoided by dropping No. 2, net income would decrease by the controllable contribution of $340,000. If not, net income would decrease by between $340,000 and $400,000. In addition, the loss of income would be reduced by any part of the separable committed costs that might be saved.

Exhibit 9-B2

GOLDEN SPIKE RAILROAD
Income Statement
For the Year Ended December 31, 20X3
(in thousands of dollars)

| | Railroad as a Whole | Breakdown into Two Divisions | | Possible Breakdown of Passenger Traffic Only | | | |
		Freight Traffic	Passenger Traffic	Not Allocable	Division No.1	No.2	No.3
Revenue	80,000	72,000	8,000	-	4,000	3,200	800
Variable costs	45,000	36,000	9,000	-	3,300	2,800	2,900
Contribution margin	35,000	36,000	(1,000)	-	700	400	(2,100)
Separable discretionary fixed costs	8,000	7,600	400	80	240	60	20
Contribution controllable by segment managers	27,000	28,400	(1,400)	(80)	460	340	(2,120)
Separable committed costs	25,000	20,000	5,000	1,000	3,000	700	300
Contribution by segments	2,000	8,400	(6,400)	(1,080)	(2,540)	(360)	(2,420)
Unallocated costs	800						
Income before income taxes	1,200						

467

9-B3 (25 min)

1. Students will come up with many possible measurements. Among the possibilities are:

Financial:
    a. Growth in profitability
       Number of new clients
       Revenues from new clients

Customer:
    a. Number of face-to-face meetings with clients
       Customer survey – satisfaction scores
    b. Number of cases completed on time
       Customer survey – how well needs were met

Internal:
    a. Number of team-based cases handled
       Number of staff generated entries to Intranet
    b. Internal conflicts and number successfully resolved
       Employee survey – ranking in internal communications
    c. Number of staff-generated solutions
       Ratio of partners to legal staff

Learning:
    a. Voluntary turnover
       Employee survey – satisfaction with environment
    b. Percentage of underrepresented minorities
       Diversity of undergraduate degrees
       Variety of skills and interests represented

2. The firm will want to balance the benefits from the balanced scorecard with the costs of using it. The firm might routinely collect customer satisfaction scores at the end of each case. It might collect employee satisfaction scores once or twice a year. The key will be to set up a system to 1) carefully define each measure, 2) collect the needed information, and 3) use the information to provide feedback on performance. For measures such as number of new clients or number of face-to-face meetings, collecting the information will be easy. For more subjective measures, such as customer or employee satisfaction, the firm must devise detailed measurement methods. These must be accepted as reasonable bases on which to assess performance. Finally, the firm must set up a system for weekly, monthly, quarterly, or annual reporting of the measures and evaluation of performance based on these reports.

3. The impact of a balanced scorecard will be greater if the firm bases individual performance evaluations and compensation on the scorecard results. This can have both benefits and drawbacks. Among the benefits are 1) aligns staff priorities with firm priorities, 2) focuses staff attention on reaching the firm's strategic goals, and 3) provides motivation to increase performance in areas that are important to the firm. Drawbacks include 1) imperfect measures may lead to dysfunctional behaviors and 2) focus on items measured in the balanced scorecard may lead to neglect of non-measured items. Whether to tie compensation to the balanced scorecard results is a matter of judgment – whether the benefits outweigh the drawbacks.

9-1   A management control system is a logical integration of techniques to gather and use information to make planning and control decisions, to motivate employee behavior, and to evaluate performance.

9-2   A management control system

- clearly communicates the organization's goals
- ensures that managers and employees understand the specific actions required to achieve goals
- communicates the results of actions across the organization, and
- ensures that managers can adjust to changes in the environment.

9-3   The major components of a management control system are:

- Setting goals, measures and targets
- Developing and executing the plan
- Monitoring actions and reporting results of actions
- Evaluating and rewarding performance

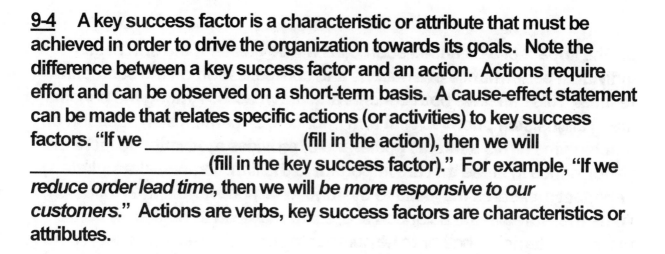

9-4   A key success factor is a characteristic or attribute that must be achieved in order to drive the organization towards its goals. Note the difference between a key success factor and an action. Actions require effort and can be observed on a short-term basis. A cause-effect statement can be made that relates specific actions (or activities) to key success factors. "If we _____ (fill in the action), then we will _____ (fill in the key success factor)." For example, "If we *reduce order lead time*, then we will *be more responsive to our customers*." Actions are verbs, key success factors are characteristics or attributes.

9-5   Goals without performance measures may not be completely useless, but performance measures greatly enhance the achievement of goals. They provide signals to managers about whether goals are being achieved.

9-6   Some typical corporate goals other than those which improve profit are (a) growth, (b) highest quality products, (c) market domination, (d) excellent social service, (e) highest prestige, and (f) improved productivity.

9-7   Key success factors are those aspects of performance that are essential to achieve if the organization is to be successful. Management examines an organization's strategic plan and major goals and decides what factors are most important to achieving its goals. These are the key success factors.

9-8   Examples of sacrificing long-range goals to short-run performance gain are:

a. Wasteful disposal of inventory to improve the turnover rate.
b. Wasting prime materials by adhering to restrictive goals for by-products.
c. Maintaining peak personnel efficiency by refusing to rotate assignments for long-range flexibility and individual improvement.
d. Postponing desirable maintenance and repairs.

<u>9-9</u>   Three types of responsibility centers are:
   • Cost center - responsibility for control of costs
   • Profit center - responsibility for both costs and revenues
   • Investment center - responsibility for both profit and investment.

<u>9-10</u>   Investment centers go a step farther than profit centers. Both measure profits, but an investment center also compares that profit to investment using measures such as return on investment, residual income or EVA.

<u>9-11</u>   Good performance measures will:
   • Relate to the organization's goals.
   • Balance long-term and short-term considerations.
   • Reflect key activities of the organization.
   • Be affected by managers' actions.
   • Be easily understood by managers.
   • Be used in evaluating and rewarding managers.
   • Be reasonably objective and easily measured.
   • Be used consistently.

<u>9-12</u>   Some nonfinancial measures of performance are percentage of products delivered on time, number of defective units produced, setup time for a batch of production, average time from order to delivery, and pounds of output per direct labor hour.

<u>9-13</u>   Performance evaluation provides feedback to managers about how well they are achieving their goals. Goal congruence and motivation are two aspects important to achieving an organization's goals through managers' actions and decisions. Goal congruence is achieved if managers seek the goals sought by top management – that is, managers aim in the direction that is best for the organization. Managerial effort is exertion toward a goal. A good performance evaluation system provides the managers with appropriate goals and the incentive to achieve the goals.

9-14 Managers are expected to explain the entire profit of a profit center. They have the best information to assess the causes of the profit. But they should be evaluated on controllable profit. The objective in evaluation is to measure the effect of the manager's actions on the profit, and changes in profit due to factors beyond a manager's control do not indicate anything about the impact of the manager's actions.

9-15 No. Variable costs vary in direct proportion to output, and fixed costs do not. However, a fixed cost may be controllable by some person or group, and it is almost always controllable in the long run. Variable costs may be uncontrollable for very short periods once a decision has been made to perform some activity.

9-16 No. By deducting separable discretionary costs from the contribution margin a better measure of short-run performance is obtained, which might be called the "short-run performance margin," or contribution controllable by segment managers.

9-17 Examples of segments are divisions, territories, branches, product lines, and stores.

9-18 Managers should be judged on how well they attain their currently attainable objectives, focusing on deducting controllable costs from revenues, whereas the subunit should be judged on its performance as an economic investment.

9-19 No. The contribution margin format does not ignore items that are not a part of the contribution margin. Rather, it separates costs by their behavior (variable and fixed) and by who can control the cost.

9-20 A balanced scorecard is a performance report that contains measures of all the key financial and nonfinancial variables that are important for a company to prosper. Many companies find this a useful tool to help managers focus on the multidimensional factors that make an organization successful.

9-21   Key performance indicators are measures that drive the organization to achieve its goals.

9-22   The four categories are:

(a) prevention – costs incurred to prevent the production of defective products or services,
(b) appraisal – costs incurred to identify defective products or services,
(c) internal failure – costs of defective products that are scrapped or reworked, and
(d) external failure – costs caused by delivery of defective products or services to customers.

9-23   Many companies are finding that it is less costly to prevent defects than it is to identify and correct defects.

9-24   Control of nonfinancial performance requires setting objectives, measuring results, and evaluation of results by comparing outcomes to expectations (or objectives). This is the same sequence indicated by control of financial performance.

9-25   Three measures of productivity are:

(a) $$\frac{\text{Standard direct labor hours allowed for good output achieved}}{\text{Actual direct labor hours of input}}$$

(b) $$\frac{\text{Sales revenue}}{\text{Direct labor cost}}$$

(c) $$\frac{\text{Sales revenue}}{\text{Number of employees}}$$

9-26   Comparing productivity measures over time is complicated by changes in the production process and by inflation. Changes in the production process that substitute one input for another and make productivity with respect to the replaced input appear to increase, but productivity with respect to the input that is increased will appear to decrease. Further, if either input or output (but not both) are measured in monetary terms, inflation can distort productivity measures across time.

9-27   Yes. There are several reasons that developing control systems in nonprofit organizations is more difficult than in profit-seeking organizations, including:

(a) There are often multiple goals, and often the goals are not explicit.
(b) The types of people in nonprofit organizations, frequently professionals, are often less receptive to the demands imposed by control systems.
(c) There is no single, measurable objective such as profit.
(d) The relationship of inputs to outputs is hard to specify.
(e) A large portion of the costs are discretionary fixed costs, which are the hardest to manage through a control system.

Nevertheless, control systems can be valuable to nonprofit organizations.

9-28   This question cannot be answered directly from the text. It requires students to think about an issue closely related to those in the text.

An article in *FE: The Magazine for Financial Executives* (Vol. 1, No. 8) addresses these questions. After studying several large firms that encourage innovation, the author concluded that such firms had not abandoned sound financial controls or even watered them down. "The companies surveyed had achieved superior financial results and had sound financial systems in place ...The CFO [Chief Financial Officer] in each firm knew the key financial factors needed for the company's success, and had a financial control system to carefully track that success" (p.36).

The article made two structure-oriented and five process-oriented suggestions to adapt a financial control system to foster innovation. Regarding structure:

1.   "The primary focus should be on setting up profit centers. A decentralized organization allows for expanding profit center accounting. Profit center accountability in turn permits more discretion and enhances innovation. Our study indicated that flexibility and entrepreneurial decision-making can be fostered by a well-structured profit center reporting system."

2.   "A second structural factor in a large, decentralized organization committed to innovation calls for divisional financial executives to have a direct, solid-line reporting to the divisional general manager. However, a solid-line reporting of divisional financial executives to a corporate senior financial executive virtually precludes an entrepreneurial spirit at the division level."

The process-related suggestions are these:

a. Planning – "The successful entrepreneurial firms...have a well-developed strategy...The strategy is well understood through all levels of management...Highly structured, precisely quantified planning is not done...Planning is directed toward allowing flexibility and changes dictated by the changing business environment."

b. Budgeting – "An annual budget, with interim breakouts, is well accepted as essential for any successful business. An entrepreneur is not greatly burdened by and accepts the need for stating in numbers his or her program for the coming 12 months."

c. Resource allocation – "Approval systems for capital expenditures frequently require extensive reporting to higher levels of management...The CFO should measure the needs for capital controls against the driving force of an innovation entrepreneur. Achieving a fair balance is not easy."

d. Reporting – "A profit center seeking to be independent and innovative can lose its thrust if it perceives that every action is being followed by corporate headquarters through the monthly financial reporting. The challenge is to provide a system that maintains financial strength while allowing the flexibility and independence that produce superior results through innovation and entrepreneurism."

e. Analyzing operating results – "One factor in this area stood out: the frequent reference to comparisons of actual results to budget, giving full weight to noncontrollable factors and to changed conditions."

9-29   A municipality is similar to many other organizations. When a municipality delegates decisions to middle-managers, top management should be informed about activities and motivate managers to act in the best interests of the municipality. A responsibility accounting system can be a great aid. Identifying responsibility centers is an important first step. Developing a system to report the financial results of each responsibility center enables top management to know the city's financial situation. Before developing the IFMS, New York City officials did not know exactly why the desperate financial situation had developed. IFMS allows them to anticipate financial demands. It also allows a check on managers who might tend to be fiscally irresponsible. The financial results of a responsibility center should affect performance evaluation. Of course, non-financial matters also affect evaluations. But New York City provides a good case study in the consequences of not identifying and measuring the financial responsibilities of managers and how adding such measures can lead to organizational success.

9-30   In an article in the Web magazine Optimize (April 2003) Bruce Guptill discussed customer-centric metrics. The four most popular metrics were 1) customer satisfaction, 2) customer loyalty, 3) decreased complaints, and 4) increased customer behavior. In addition, Volvo might consider results from research by third parties such as J. D. Power & Associates, market share data, and time from order to fulfillment. Students may come up with many more potential metrics.

9-31   Quality, cycle time, and productivity are related because improvements in cycle time and productivity are dependent upon high quality processes and inputs. High quality depends on good product (or service) and process designs, highly trained employees, and commitment to continuous improvement. These factors also lead to improvements in cycle time and productivity.

<u>9-32</u> (5 min.)

There are many possible answers for each company or organization. Examples are:

- Northwest Airlines: Percent on-time arrivals, capacity utilization
- Wal Mart: Number of standard stocking units (sku's); sales per square foot of space
- Hewlett-Packard: Number of new products, product development time
- New York Department of Motor Vehicles: cost of services, number of licenses issued per employee

<u>9-33</u> (20 min.)

Plant maintenance should be charged the standard rate of $14.00. The $6.00 hourly rate difference ($20.00 - $14.00) could be charged to Loss from Idle Capacity or some similar account, or from a control viewpoint, the $6.00 rate difference should be charged to the individual who is primarily responsible for deciding to retain the welders rather than to lay them off.

Charging plant maintenance the standard rate of $14.00 assumes that the welders are qualified to do the normal plant maintenance work. It is up to the plant maintenance supervisor to get $14.00 worth of work from the welders. The $6.00 hourly rate difference should certainly not be charged to plant maintenance since the regular help need be paid only $14.00.

Because the welders must be retained in order to maintain high quality workmanship, and perhaps the reputation and sales position of the company, a conceptual case could even be made for treating the $6.00 as an asset because the decision to keep high-priced personnel implies a future cost saving, possibly in hiring and training new employees, or a future revenue enhancement. This is rarely done in practice.

9-34 (35 min.)

1. Compensation:
   If quota is met: ¥50,000 + ¥68,000+.05 x (actual-quota)
   If quota is not met: ¥50,000

	Clerk		
	A	B	C
January	¥ 50,000	¥118,000	¥193,000
February	190,750	118,000	50,000
March	226,000	50,000	413,500
April	50,000	118,250	50,000

2. Notice the wide variation in month-to-month sales, which are under the control of the salesclerks, and the absurdity of the method of figuring sales quotas in relation to this salary bonus plan. The salesclerks would naturally be tempted to manipulate their sales to maximize their personal income.

Realizing the above mentioned points and the hopelessness of continually increasing sales by 3% a month, the salesclerks would try to just meet their quota or surpass it by a substantial amount.

With the relatively small-volume sales territory, salesclerk B would just try to meet his or her quota several months running and then have a low volume month to bring the quota down in preparation for another run of months of just meeting the quota.

Salesclerks A and C, with larger volume territories, are better off financially to surpass their sales quotas by substantial amounts and then have a slack month to bring down their quotas in preparation for a large bonus the following month.

Given sales quotas of 103% of the previous month's actual sales, the bonus of ¥68,000 plus 5% commission on sales over quota is extremely high and provides incentive for manipulation rather than overall sales effort.

The bonus system should be eliminated, and the base salary should be increased. If an incentive is to be provided, the quotas should reflect a normal month's sales and not be related directly to the previous month's sales. Most companies believe a bonus payment should be small in relation to basic compensation and should be related to actual sales effort rather than to clever manipulation. Moreover, any bonus plan should be tied to performance over a longer time span than one month. A yearly span would not tempt nearly as much manipulation.

9-35 (10 min.)

Students may classify some of these measures differently from that shown here. The point should be made that the important feature in a balance scorecard is to have all perspectives represented.

PERFORMANCE MEASURE	PERSPECTIVE
Return on sales	Financial
Retention of target customers	Customer
Net cash flow	Financial
Training hours	Learning and growth
Employee turnover rate	Learning and growth
Material handling cost per unit	Internal process, financial
Market share	Customer
Product development cycle time	Internal process
Revenue growth in segments	Financial
Occupational injuries and illness	Learning and growth
Days sales in inventory	Internal process, financial
Average cost per invoice	Internal process, financial

<u>9-36</u> (10-15 min.) Students will suggest many different goals and measures in each category. This solution lists one possibility for each of the five areas.

Customer Satisfaction -
Goal: Reduce customer waiting time
Measure: Average time from check-in until seeing a physician
Efficient use of lab tests -
Goal: Reduce unnecessary lab tests
Measure: Lab tests per patient (possibly by diagnosis)
Usage of physician time -
Goal: Decrease time physicians spend on administrative and clerical tasks
Measure: Patients seen per hour of physician time or, better, percentage of physician time spent with patients
Maintain state-of-the-art facilities -
Goal: Provide patients with access to latest technology
Measure: Amount of capital expenditures or, better, percent of equipment below standard
Overall financial performance -
Goal: ROI exceeding the 75th percentile in the industry
Measure: Return on investment

This is a good time to discuss the cost/benefit tradeoff with possible performance measures. Sometimes the best performance metric is just too costly to measure. For example, use of physician time is better measured by the percentage of their working time that is spent seeing patients than by number of patients per hour of physician time. But the better measure requires physicians to log the time they spend on various activities. This may be too costly, both in terms of the time it takes and the resistance from physicians, so a less desirable surrogate such as patients per hour, might be used.

<u>9-37</u>   (15-20 min.)

Increasing sales activity can be related to increased number of new accounts; thus many stock brokerages set objectives for its brokers to make a set number of "cold calls" to solicit investments from potential clients. However, a large number of small accounts probably do not have the same impact on sales as a few large accounts. The brokerage firm must be careful not to divert its employees' energies so much to finding new accounts that research, analysis, and existing accounts are neglected. Service firms have found that it is much more profitable to retain existing customers than to find new customers. Therefore, customer retention has become a major objective, and performance is measured on activities that are believed to aid in retaining profitable customers. These measures include how quickly phones are picked up, how quickly inquiries are answered, accessibility of data bases, and so on.

9-38 (15 - 20 min.)

1.

	Company	Downtown	Jamesville
Revenues	$1,700,000	$850,000	$850,000
Variable costs	1,105,000	510,000	595,000
Contribution margin	595,000	340,000	255,000
Fixed costs controllable by restaurant managers	175,000	125,000	50,000
Contribution controllable by restaurant managers	420,000	215,000	205,000
Fixed costs controllable by others	290,000	110,000	180,000
Contribution by restaurant	130,000	$105,000	$25,000
Unallocated costs	70,000		
Operating income	$ 60,000		

2. a. The new restaurant in Jamesville is not yet as profitable as the downtown restaurant. Apparently the advertising campaign necessary to build up the customer base in Jamesville weighs heavily on the profits of the Jamesville restaurant. However, both have a positive contribution after subtracting all costs that the company can specifically identify with a particular restaurant.

b. The two managers have almost equal levels of performance, with the Downtown manager having $10,000 more controllable contribution. The lower contribution margin in Jamesville is offset by its lower rent and other fixed costs that the manager controls. Although the two managers reach their level of profitability by different means (that is, by a different mix of costs), they seem to both be performing well.

<u>9-39</u>   (10-15 min.)

The figure on the next page can be used as both a solution to this exercise and point of further discussion by making a transparency or duplicating copies for students. It represents the current reality as espoused by "total-quality" guru Deming and attested to by most firms today. Note how the total cost of quality is higher for firms producing inferior quality products or services. Deming predicted this by pointing to the close relationship between quality and costs such as waste, rework, returns, lost sales, and inspection.

In the TQM approach *all* phases of the company's operations are incorporated in the quality program. For example, the quality of incoming materials and parts is higher. This reduces (or eliminates) the need for appraisal (and associated costs), while failures that result from poor quality are also reduced. Another example of a win-win scenario is training employees to reduce errors resulting in cost savings from reduced inspection (appraisal) and internal and external failures. If the cost savings from reduced appraisal activity exceeds the training costs (prevention), the prevention and appraisal cost curve will shift downward while the internal and external failure costs also are lower.

Figure for 9-39 – from p. 435 of 12th Edition

(10-15 min.)

1. One trend is the overall upward trend in defective units. The overall rate of defective units has about doubled in the 8 weeks, from about .75% the first week to 1.4% in the 8th week.

    A second trend is a weekly trend, with low defects on Monday and increasing each day of the week, with the most defects produced on Friday.

2. It is essential to arrest and reverse the overall trend toward more defective units. Even by the first week of this eight-week period, the defective rate was well above the target of .5%, and it grew each of the eight weeks. The control chart will not tell what actions are needed to reverse this trend, but it focuses attention on the problem and allows managers to explore potential solutions.

    The weekly pattern is also disturbing. There is no reason that defect rates must increase as the week goes on. Apparently employees come in refreshed on Monday and are quite attentive to quality. This attentiveness drops steadily until, by Friday, they don't seem to pay much attention to quality. Incentives for better quality late in the week might work, or the company may try changing the work patterns so that employees are not bored, tired, or whatever else besets them by Friday.

(20-30 min.)

Week	Units completed	Total cycle time	Average cycle time
1	564	14,108	25.0
2	544	14,592	26.8
3	553	15,152	27.4
4	571	16,598	29.1
5	547	17,104	31.3
6	552	16,673	30.2

The cycle time objective was met only in the first week. After that, however, cycle time generally has steadily increased. With knowledge of the acceptable control limit, an analyst probably could determine within the third or fourth week that cycle time is tending to be out of control. Corrective action could have been initiated before increased cycle times lead to higher costs and possible difficulty in meeting schedules.

A control chart approach shows the increasing cycle time graphically:

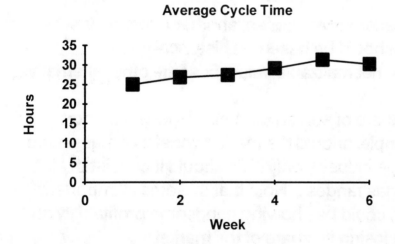

<u>9-42</u>   (20-35 min.)

The purpose of this problem is to get students to recognize that measurements affect behavior and that accounting measurements tend to place too much focus on short-run results. An exhaustive study of the eight goals is impossible and unwarranted at this stage of the course. The aim is to provide an overview, a perspective on where accounting often fits in management control.

1.   Students may add many alternative measurements in each of the following categories.

  a. Profitability. Total dollars of profit. Percentage of profit on sales. Rate of return on investment. Residual income. General Electric chose residual income, which is described in Chapter 10. The imputed interest rate should be established as closely as possible to the point at which discontinuance of the business would be considered. Using residual income, a manager maximizes an absolute amount (residual income) rather than a rate.

  Regardless of the alternative chosen, another question is whether the measurement should be based on historical costs, replacement costs, net realizable value, or some other alternative.

  b. Market position. Share of served markets. How is a market defined? For example, should the market consist of that served by the electric-range industry only? Or should it consist of all ranges, including gas ranges? Note that this area is important because a division could be showing handsome profitability and simultaneously be losing its share of the market.

c. Productivity. This measure attempts to gauge efficiency. Productivity focuses on physical and/or financial relationships between inputs and outputs. Through the years, there have been various attempts, both by General Electric and others, to measure productivity for a division (as opposed to an individual worker or small cost center, where the measurement difficulties are less imposing). G.E. has changed its approach through the years, and it still has not found a completely satisfactory measure. As a rule, all measures should be adjusted for changes in unit prices because price changes should not affect measures of productivity. G.E. believes that productivity must be tied to all the factors of production, not just labor alone. For example, the company has used the following measure:

$$\frac{\text{Sales Billed}}{\text{Employee Compensation} + \text{Facilities Charge} + \text{Direct Materals Costs} + \text{Business Services Costs}}$$

d. Product leadership. This still tends to be a qualitative evaluation, but at least it should be conducted routinely on a standard evaluation form. Among the questions asked are: How does each product compare with its competition and general company standards? Where is the research conducted? Who introduced the basic product (for example, did G.E. or Westinghouse introduce the electric toothbrush)? Trends are important.

e. Personnel development. The objective of this area is to assure the steady flow of promotable employees. An inventory of various executive positions is taken to see whether orderly succession in the hierarchy is likely. Among the various programs that are evaluated are: recruitment, training, review, and counseling.

f. Employee attitudes. Among these measurements are employee turnover, absenteeism, and results of attitude surveys.

g. Public responsibility. Measures are routine but less precise, as you might expect. Explicit surveys of executive participation in community affairs and public attitudes are used.

h. Balance between short-range and long-range goals. This balance is not measured separately. It is included in the eight-point list to reinforce the basic idea of the entire measurements project. Note that areas (2) through (7) essentially counteract the built-in tendency of the accounting profitability measurements to stress short-range results.

2. By its very reliance on the other goals, G.E. must believe that profitability cannot encompass all the other goals. Nevertheless, profitability is usually dominant and other goals play a secondary (though still important) role.

9-43 (30 min.)

1. McBride Cadillac/Hummer

	Parts and Service	Vehicles
Sales	$600,000	$2,400,000
Cost of sales		$1,920,000
Parts and service materials	$180,000	-
Parts and service labor	240,000	-
Sales commissions	-	48,000
Subtotal	$420,000	$1,968,000
Mark-up on "variable" material and labor*	$180,000	$ 432,000
Parts and service overhead	$ 60,000	-
Advertising	-	$ 120,000
Sales salaries	-	60,000
General dealership overhead	120,000	
Operating expenses	$180,000	$ 180,000
Net income	$ 0	$ 252,000

*Roughly equivalent to contribution margin.

2. The operating statement by departments would be the same as (1) through "mark-up on variable material and labor." At that point an effort should be made to allocate general overhead to the two departments insofar as such allocations can be accomplished without reliance on arbitrary assumptions. The remaining general overhead should not be allocated at all. Assume that $72,000 of the $120,000 general overhead can be allocated with confidence, and that $48,000 cannot. The bottom of the income statement could appear as follows:

	Parts and Service	Vehicles	Total
Markup on "variable" material and labor	$180,000	$432,000	$612,000
Parts and service overhead	$ 60,000	$ -	
Advertising	-	120,000	
Sales salaries	-	60,000	
Direct allocation of general overhead	12,000	60,000	
Total expenses directly charged To departments	$ 72,000	$240,000	312,000
Departmental contribution to net income	$108,000	$192,000	$300,000
General overhead not allocable			48,000
Net income of the dealership as a whole			$252,000

3. The first approach is artificial in the sense that only one function of the dealership is regarded as a source of net income. A more modern approach is to view a dealership as a department store with three or more *profit centers* (segments of a business that have revenue as well as expenses), such as new vehicles, used vehicles, and parts and service. Each is regarded as an independent venture. Each contributes its individual segment margin to the overall dealership overhead which cannot be directly or obviously assigned to a specific profit center.

9-44 (35-45 min.)

1. A = 800,000   X = .50
    F = 800,000   Y = .80
                       Z = 1.00

    Performance = (Y x F) + X(A - F)
                = (.80 x 800,000) + .50(800,000 - 800,000)
                = 640,000

2. A = 800,000
    F = 700,000

    Performance = (Y x F) + X(A - F)
                = (.80 x 700,000) + .50(800,000 - 700,000)
                = 560,000 + 50,000
                = 610,000

    A = 800,000
    F = 900,000

    Performance = (Y x F) - Z(F - A)
                = (.80 x 900,000) - 1.00 x (900,000 - 800,000)
                = 720,000 - 100,000
                = 620,000

Notice that when F < A, increasing F by one TV gains Y and loses X, a net gain of Y - X = .80 - .50 = .30. When Chavez predicts production 100,000 TVs below actual, it costs him a .30 x 100,000 = 30,000 point drop in the performance measure. Therefore, there is an incentive not to predict a volume below the expected actual volume. Likewise, when F > A, decreasing F by one TV gains Z and loses Y, a net gain of Z - Y = 1.00 - .80 = .20. The overly optimistic forecast causes a .20 x 100,000 = 20,000 point drop in the performance measure. There is an incentive not to predict a volume above the expected actual volume. The system motivates a forecast equal to the expected actual volume.

3.   When actual volume falls short of target, additional production increases the performance measure by $Z = 1.0$ per TV. It is worthwhile to achieve as much production as possible. When actual volume exceeds forecast, additional production increases the production measure by .50 per TV, still creating an incentive for continued production.

9-45 (15-20 min.) Students may suggest a variety of measures. There is not a right measure for each objective. Listed below are some possible measures:

1. Maintain strong financial health
   a. Daily cash balance
   b. Percentage increase in sales and income
   c. Return on investment or residual income (or EVA)
2. Provide excellent service to customers
   a. Customer satisfaction surveys
   b. Average time from receipt of order to shipping
   c. Percent of products returned by customers, or amount of allowances for quality defects.
   d. Number and dollar amount of exclusive supplier agreements.
3. Be among the industry leaders in product and process innovations
   a. Percent of sales from products less than 2 years old
   b. Dollars (or percent of sales) spent on process improvements
4. Develop and maintain efficient, state-of-the-art production processes
   a. Cost per unit
   b. Average delay from projected date of availability to actual delivery

9-46   (20-30 min.)

1.   (a)   Prevention cost – This includes costs incurred to prevent the production of defective products, such as programs to train personnel, simplified production processes, and improved production planning. These costs have increased between 2001 and 2003 both in absolute amount and as a percent of total quality cost. Apparently more attention is now being given to the prevention of defects.

   (b)   Appraisal cost – These costs are incurred to identify defective products. They include testing, inspection, and various other quality control procedures. Although these costs were a larger percentage of total quality costs in 2003 than 2001, their total amount has increased in almost direct proportion to the increase in product cost. Therefore, appraisal procedures have probably remained much the same as in 2001.

   (c)   Internal failure cost – These are the costs of items scrapped and the costs of rework to correct defects in products. These costs are up slightly as a percentage of total quality costs but down significantly in absolute amount. Despite higher product costs, much less is being spent on defective units. Most likely this means that the money spent on prevention has decreased the number of defective units being scrapped or reworked.

   (d)   External failure cost – These are costs caused by delivery of defective units, including warranty expenses and sales returns and allowances. There has been a dramatic decrease in this cost, probably because fewer defective units are being delivered to customers.

2.   The overall costs of quality are much lower in 2003 than in 2001. The decrease comes primarily in the two categories of internal and external failure costs. Red Lake is following a popular approach to modern quality control: preventing defects is less costly than identifying and correcting them. By increasing spending on prevention of defects, Red Lake has reduced overall quality costs.

In addition to the costs in the quality cost report, companies should be concerned with potential lost sales if customers receive a large proportion of defective units. Red Lake's decrease in external failure costs probably means that it is delivering fewer defective units, and therefore there will also be smaller opportunity costs due to lost sales.

9-47   (20 – 30 min.)

From a customer perspective, simply lowering the mean delivery time without any change in the variability does little to address customers' concerns about certainty of delivery dates. To see this, compute the standard deviation before six sigma and compare to the standard deviation after six sigma.

	Before Six Sigma	After Six Sigma
	30	22
	12	20
	11	5
	13	8
	26	19
	14	8
	16	7
	20	12
	24	18
	14	21
Standard Deviation	6.6	6.6
Mean	18	14

Although the mean delivery time has been reduced by 22.2%, the variability of delivery times has not changed. This means that a customer who plans on delivery on a particular date is no more certain that the delivery will take place within a specified range than before the Six Sigma improvement. This is an important factor for planning purposes.

9-48 (20-30 min.)

This problem is similar to the problem in the chapter, with a slight difference. The purchase of BTL and the pooling of its operating statistics may be misleading because of fundamental differences in operations. The approach to the problem is to back out United's normal growth from the 20X1 figures.

1. **United only**

	20X0	20X1
Customer lines	14,615,000	15,054,000
Employees	72,350	74,520
Lines per employee	202	202

Productivity in 20X1 remained at the same level as in 20X0.

2.

	United with BTL	BTL Only
Customer lines	19,994,000	19,994,000 - 15,054,000 = 4,940,000
Employees	114,590	114,590 - 74,520 = 40,070
Lines per employee	174	123

The low productivity of BTL reduces the productivity of the combined company.

3. The employees of the acquired company probably will not be able to immediately achieve the level of productivity achieved by United's other employees. A rapid change to increase their productivity could lead to labor unrest and political difficulties. A dramatic increase in productivity at BTL probably also will require considerable investment in improved technology and in education and training of employees.

9-49 (20-30 min.)

1.   The best productivity measure based on the physical measures given is: pounds of laundry processed ÷ direct-labor-hours worked. Comparing 20X1 and 20X3:

$$\underline{\text{20X1}} \qquad\qquad\qquad \underline{\text{20X3}}$$

$$\frac{1{,}360{,}000}{45{,}100} = 30.2 \text{ pounds/hour} \qquad \frac{1{,}525{,}000}{46{,}650} = 32.7 \text{ pounds/hour}$$

Productivity has increased by 32.7 - 30.2 = 2.5 pounds/hour, an increase of 2.5 ÷ 30.2 = 8.3%.

2.   The best productivity measure based on the financial measures given is: sales revenue ÷ direct labor cost. Comparing 20X1 and 20X3:

$$\underline{\text{20X1}} \qquad\qquad\qquad \underline{\text{20X3}}$$

$$\frac{\$720{,}000}{\$316{,}000} = 2.28 \qquad\qquad \frac{\$1{,}394{,}000}{\$498{,}000} = 2.80$$

By this measure, productivity has increased by .52 ÷ 2.28 = 22.8%. There are three explanations for this large increase: 1) increase in physical productivity, as shown in requirement 1; 2) increase in revenue per pound at a rate greater than inflation ($720,000 ÷ 1,360,000 = $.53 in 20X1 compared to $1,394,000 ÷ 1,525,000 = $.91 in 20X3, an increase of (.91 - .53) ÷ .53 = 72%); and 3) increase in wage rates per hour more than inflation ($316,000 ÷ 45,100 = $7.01 in 20X1 compared to $498,000 ÷ 46,650 = $10.68 in 20X3, an increase of ($10.68 - $7.01) ÷ $7.01 = 52%).

3.   This productivity measure mixes financial and physical measures. Therefore, it is essential to adjust for inflation. Expressing both 20X1 and 20X3 productivity measures in 20X3 dollars:

$$\underline{\text{20X1}}$$

$$\frac{(\$720,000 \times 1.4)}{45,100} = \$22.35/\text{hour}$$

$$\underline{\text{20X3}}$$

$$\frac{\$1,394,000}{46,650} = \$29.88/\text{hour}$$

This measure shows an increase in productivity of ($29.88 - $22.35) ÷ $22.35 = 33.7%. It incorporates the increase in physical productivity and the revenue increase at greater than the inflation rate, but it excludes the effect of wage rate changes that was included in the solution to requirement 2.

9-50 (30 min.)   There are numerous solutions to this case. Here is one possible solution. An alternative solution would be to try to increase the productivity of the employees.

1 & 2. Rico Estrada is faced with difficult tradeoffs. His subgoal of retaining a skilled and motivated work force is threatened by new, competitive pressures. As Estrada loses accounts, he is spreading his (discretionary fixed) labor costs over fewer accounts, and the average cost rises. If he tries to maintain his customary 25% markup, Estrada will become less competitive and probably will lose even more accounts. This has been termed the cost "death spiral," and if left unchecked could lead to bankruptcy. Estrada must find a solution or he eventually will not be able to cover his costs.

It is likely that Estrada can maintain quality service and customer satisfaction with a reduced work force. By November it appears that Estrada has $41 - (680 \div 20) = 7$ excess employees unless this is a temporary downturn in business. This excess employment is costing Estrada $7 \times \$3,000 = \$21,000$ per month (ignoring taxes and fringe benefits). If Estrada could save this amount, he could reduce the average cost per account as shown:

Number of accounts	680
Average monthly cost per account	$191
Total monthly cost (680 x $191)	$129,880
Less: salary savings	21,000
Revised monthly cost	$108,880

CDS's current price:

Average cost	$191.00
Markup @ 25%	47.75
CDS's price	$238.75

Competitor's price, 80% x $238.75 $191.00

Possible CDS Responses:

a. Maintain current markup of 25%:
    Target cost $191 ÷ 1.25 = $152.80
    Total cost   680 x $152.80 = $103,904
    Required cost reduction $108,880 - $103,904 = $4,976
    Required employee reduction @ $3,000 each   Approximately 2

b. Reduce markup to 15%:
    Target cost $191 ÷ 1.15 = $166.09
    Total cost   680 x $166.09 = $112,941
    Required cost reduction   None

To maintain the current 25% markup, Estrada would have to achieve a target cost of $152.80, but that would entail further cost savings of $4,976, or about two more employees. Estrada could avoid further layoffs by reducing his desired markup, but then the business may not be as attractive to him.

It is likely that the business will become even more competitive on the service dimensions, so a skilled, motivated work force will be critical to keeping current customers and regaining lost customers. Can Estrada reduce his work force and maintain the loyalty of the remaining employees? This will be difficult, but it may be necessary, and it may be at least partly accomplished through attrition and/or early retirements.

The equipment lease in August was probably in response to business growth, which now appears to be unnecessary. Can Estrada get out of the lease? If so, he may be able to cut costs further and/or retain some employees that otherwise would be laid off. Perhaps the best approach would be for Estrada to present the work force with the magnitude of the problem and enlist their aid in solving it. There are numerous stories in the business press about innovative solutions developed by employees who are able to achieve significant productivity increases. This could even lead to a purchase of the company by the employees.

<u>9-51</u>   (30-40 min.)

Answers will vary. In 2003 the following quotes appeared on the companies' Web sites:

3M – "3M employees continuously challenge the upper limits of product reliability and capability through process and product innovation and the application of proven quality principles. Underlying this effort is a strong corporate commitment to the Six Sigma strategy for achieving breakthrough performance in all areas of our business. Six Sigma is a disciplined methodology of continuous improvement, which requires thorough process and product understanding to reduce inherent variability or defects. It is clearly focused on customer-driven expectations and on data-driven decisions."

Motorola – "As founder of the Six Sigma quality initiative, Motorola continues their dedication towards continuous improvement for manufacturing process quality. To achieve these quality standards, Motorola required accurate and reliable ways to measure production activity. The result was the creation of the Manufacturing Pulse software suite of tools to collect real-time, critical data directly from the shop floor for continuous monitoring and maintenance of Six Sigma quality levels. Dedication to Six Sigma is the foundation for a long time commitment to best-in-class electronics manufacturing software tool development."

Dow Chemical – "Six Sigma will deliver $1.5 billion in EBIT [Earnings Before Interest and Taxes] cumulatively from the combined impact of revenue growth, cost reductions and asset utilization. Six Sigma is a methodology, a tool set and a mindset that accelerates the implementation of business strategies. At the close of 2001, Dow was more than half way toward its $1.5 billion cumulative financial goal set for year-end 2003."

General Electric – "In the beginning of our Six Sigma initiative (a statistical method for deriving near-perfect quality, equivalent to 3.4 defects per million operations), we needed to train more than 100,000 people in its science and methodology - improving efficiency and reducing variance in our internal operations. From there, our Operating System drove the initiative from just improving products to better designing them. Now Six Sigma is the way we work. We all speak a common language of CTQs (critical-to-quality), DPMOs (defects per million opportunities), FMEAs (failure mode effect analysis), and Needs Assessment Maps (to name just a few). Today our Six Sigma efforts are focused squarely on our customers, helping them improve their products and services in new and exciting ways."

There are many more quotes on the Web sites, and those shown here may have been replaced. Nevertheless, it is very likely that each Web site will contain many references to six sigma because it is a central tenet to the operations in each of the four companies.

9-52 (60-90 min.)

This problem provides a comprehensive review of many of the techniques and terms that were introduced in previous chapters. It might be used as a final examination. *You may wish to skip part (7).*

Some answers are based on the following detailed master budget:

	Product		
	A	B	Division
Sales, 50,000 at $10.00 and 70,000 at $6.00	$500,000	$420,000	$920,000
Variable manufacturing costs at $7.50 and $3.00	375,000	210,000	585,000
Contribution margin	$125,000	$210,000	$335,000
Fixed discretionary manufacturing costs	4,500	8,500	13,000
Contribution controllable by product managers	$120,500	$201,500	$322,000
Fixed committed manufacturing costs	40,500	76,500	117,000
Contribution by products*	$ 80,000	$125,000	$205,000
Unallocable fixed costs:			
Manufacturing (committed)			$ 25,000
Selling and administrative (discretionary)			72,000
Selling and administrative (committed)			48,000
Total unallocable fixed costs			$145,000
Operating income			$ 60,000

*This is the answer to part (2).

Note: Fixed manufacturing costs = $740,000 - $585,000 = $155,000, subdivided into components of $13,000 + $117,000 + $25,000 = $155,000.

Answers to requirements:

1. Contribution margin ratio: $335,000 \div $920,000 = .364$
   Break-even point: ($145,000 + $130,000) \div .364 = $755,495$
   Contribution margin per unit, A: $10.00 - $7.50 = 2.50
   Contribution margin per unit, B: $ 6.00 - $3.00 = 3.00

2. See the footnote to the analysis above.

3.

	Product		
	A	B	Total
Selling and administrative expenses:			
Discretionary, 53/117 and 64/117	$32,615	$39,385	$ 72,000
Committed, 50/120 and 70/120	20,000	28,000	48,000
Totals	$52,615	$67,385	$120,000

There is an arbitrary distinction between the allocation bases. The purpose of this part is to ask whether *budgeted* or *actual* numbers should be used as bases for allocating these costs. The chapter discusses this issue. Another point worth discussing is whether the *actual* costs or only the *budgeted* costs should be allocated. The answer often depends on the extent of controllability by the product managers (if any controllability exists). Of course if the product managers have zero influence over the level of costs, they should not be allocated.

4. This raises the issue of incentives and goal congruence. Product A has the higher selling price but the lower contribution margin ($10.00 and $2.50 for A versus $6.00 and $3.00 for B). The resulting incentives to push the higher-priced product will likely contribute less to the firm's overall profit performance (all other things equal).

5. Actual results were:

	Product A	B	Total
Sales, 53,000 units at $10.00 and 64,000 units at $6.00	$530,000	$384,000	$914,000
Variable manufacturing costs:			
Material	$134,500	$102,400	
Labor	156,350	50,000	
Overhead	108,650	50,000	
Total variable manufacturing costs	$399,500	$202,400	601,900
Contribution margin			$312,100
Fixed manufacturing costs* $147,300			
Fixed selling and administrative costs 116,000			263,300
Operating income			$ 48,800

*The $749,200 given in the problem minus $601,900, also given, equals $147,300.

The "controllable contribution" is the actual contribution margin less the fixed *discretionary* costs, which would be:

Actual contribution margin		$312,100
Total actual fixed costs	$263,300*	
Committed fixed costs, which are the same as those budgeted (because there are no variances),		
$117,000 + $25,000 + $48,000	190,000	73,300
Contribution controllable by segment managers		$238,800

*Selling & administrative expenses	$ 116,000
Fixed manufacturing costs,	
$749,200 - $601,900	147,300
Total actual fixed costs	$263,300

6. The analysis rests *solely* on master budgeted sales and costs versus actual sales and costs *at budgeted unit prices*:

	Actual Sales at Budgeted Prices	Budgeted Sales at Budgeted Prices	Sales Activity Variance
Product A:			
Sales	$530,000	$500,000	
Variable costs	397,500*	375,000	
Contribution margin	$132,500	$125,000	$ 7,500F
Product B:			
Sales	$384,000	$420,000	
Variable costs	192,000**	210,000	
Contribution margin	$192,000	$210,000	$18,000U
Contribution margin for both products	$324,500	$335,000	$10,500U

*53,000 units x $7.50
**64,000 units x $3.00

7.

	Cost Incurred: Actual Inputs x Actual Prices	Flexible Budget Based on Actual Inputs x Expected Prices	Flexible Budget Based on Standard Inputs Allowed for Actual Outputs Achieved x Expected Prices
Product A Direct materials	538,000 pieces x $.25 = $134,500	538,000 pieces x $.25 = $134,500	530,000 pieces x $.25 = $132,500

Price variance, 0 | Usage variance, $2,000U

Flexible-budget variance, $2,000U

Labor	53,000 hours x $2.95 = $156,350	53,000 hours x $3.00 = $159,000	53,000 hours x $3.00 = $159,000

Price variance, $2,650F | Usage variance, 0

Flexible-budget variance, $2,650F

Variable overhead	53,000 hours x $2.05 = $108,650	53,000 hours x $2.00 = $106,000	53,000 hours x $2.00 = $106,000

Spending variance, $2,650U | Efficiency variance, 0

Flexible-budget variance, $2,650U

Product B

Direct materials

320,000 lbs.	320,000 lbs.	320,000 lbs.
x $.32	x $.30	x $.30
= $102,400	= $96,000	= $96,000

Price variance, $6,400U	Usage variance, 0

Flexible-budget variance, $6,400U

Labor

20,000 hours	20,000 hours	19,200 hours
x $2.50	x $2.50	x $2.50
= $50,000	= $50,000	= $48,000

Price variance, 0	Usage variance, $2,000U

Flexible-budget variance, $2,000U

Variable overhead

20,000 hours	20,000 hours	19,200 hours
x $2.50	x $2.50	x $2.50
= $50,000	= $50,000	= $48,000

Spending variance, 0	Efficiency variance, $2,000U

Flexible-budget variance, $2,000U

Check:

	Product A	Product B	Total
Material	$2,000U	$ 6,400U	
Labor	2,650F	2,000U	
Variable overhead	2,650U	2,000U	
Totals	$2,000U	$10,400U	$12,400U

Total actual variable costs [item (6) in problem statement]		$601,900
Standard variable costs:		
Product A: 53,000 x $7.50	$397,500	
Product B: 64,000 x $3.00	192,000	589,500
Total variance		$ 12,400U

Summary of all variances:			
Budgeted operating income			$60,000
Variances:			
Sales activity variance		$10,500U	
Price and efficiency variances for variable costs		12,400U	
Budget variance for fixed costs:			
Actual*	$263,300		
Budgeted**	275,000	11,700F	
Total variances			11,200U
Actual operating income			$48,800

*See actual results in solution to requirement 5.
**$13,000 + $117,000 + $145,000.

9-53   (45 min.) For the solution, see the Prentice Hall Web site,
       www.prenhall.com/

9-54   (60 min. or more)

       The purpose of this exercise is to develop goals and objectives for a
familiar organization. By working in teams, students may see the possibly
conflicting objectives of various stakeholder groups. They will also see
how difficult it can be to develop measures for some seemingly obvious
goals. For example, quality of education is certainly a goal of a university
department. But how does one measure this quality? Standardized tests
are often suggested, but they may motivate "teaching to the test" rather
than generating overall quality. Eventual success in a career might be
used, but it is available only after a long delay.

       If the optional interview is obtained, it will be useful to see how the
faculty member's goals and objectives differ from those of the student
group. Does the faculty member have a different perspective? Would
legislators (for a state university) or a board of trustees (for a private college
or university) have an even different perspective? What about the staff of
the university? The interview might lead to a better understanding of how
difficult it is to set goals and objectives for an organization with many
diverse stakeholders.

9-55 (50 – 60 min.)

NOTE TO INSTRUCTOR. This solution is based on the web site as it was in early 2004. Be sure to examine the current web site before assigning this problem, as the information there may have changed.

1. According to the 2002 annual report, the success drivers are customer focus (putting the consumer at the heart of everything the company does), strategic choices (focus on core strengths, fast-growing, high-margin, asset-efficient businesses), operational excellence (focus on execution on all levels), financial discipline (focus on corporate governance, ethics, and internal controls), organization structure (consolidated categories and brands into Global Business Units), and brand building (branding gives consumers a choice of a reliable product amid a world of uncertainty).

2. P&G lists 22 different categories broken into 5 major subgroups: 1) personal and beauty, 2) health and wellness, 3) house and home, 4) baby and family, and 5) pet nutrition and care. The household cleaner category includes Bounty, Swifter, and Mr. Clean products. The firm wants to build established brands. The first step would be identifying the top brands in the household cleaner category. Bounty and Mr. Clean are well-established brand names with several specific products under each brand name. Swifter is less well known, thus may need additional investment in brand awareness.

Financial measures might include gross margin, contribution margin, product-line return on investment, residual income or economic value added for major business segments or the company as a whole. Nonfinancial measures might include market share, increase in market share for key brands, brand recognition, brand loyalty, and number of new markets.

3. The Web site lists 7 different skill areas that are needed for success at P&G. Each answer will be unique based on the student's own motivation and interpretation.

CHAPTER 10
COVERAGE OF LEARNING OBJECTIVES

LEARNING OBJECTIVE	FUNDA-MENTAL ASSIGN-MENT MATERIAL	CRITICAL THINKING EXERCISES AND EXERCISES	PROBLEMS	CASES, EXCEL, COLLAB., & INTERNET EXERCISES
LO1: Define decentralization and identify its expected benefits and costs.	A2, A4, B4	22, 23		55
LO2: Distinguish between responsibility centers and decentralization.			43	52
LO3: Explain how the linking of rewards to responsibility center results affects incentives and risk.		20	34, 40	
LO4: Compute ROI, residual value and economic value added (EVA) and contrast them as criteria for judging the performance of organizational segments.	A1, A4, B1, B2, B4	21, 24, 25, 26, 27, 29	35, 36, 37, 38, 39, 40	54
LO5: Compare the advantages and disadvantages of various bases for measuring the invested capital used by organizational segments.		21, 28, 30	41	
LO6: Define transfer prices and identify their purpose.	A2, A3, A4, B3, B4	23	43, 44, 45, 46, 51	52
LO7: State the general rule for transfer pricing and use it to assess transfer prices based on total costs, variable costs, and market prices.	A2, A3, A4, B1, B3, B4	31, 32	43, 44, 45, 46, 49, 51	52
LO8: Identify the factors affecting multinational transfer prices.		33	50	
LO9: Explain how controllability and management by objectives (MBO) aid the implementation of management control systems.				53

CHAPTER 10
Management Control in Decentralized Organizations

10-A1 (10-15 min.) Dollar amounts are in thousands.

	Division A	Division B	Division C
	A	**B**	**C**
Return on sales:			
$180 ÷ $3,600	5%		
$126 ÷ $1,800		7%	
$ 90 ÷ $9,000			1%
Capital turnover:			
$3,600 ÷ $1,000	3.6		
$1,800 ÷ $600		3	
$9,000 ÷ $900			10
Rate of return on invested capital:			
$180 ÷ $1,000 (or 3.6 x 5%)	18%		
$126 ÷ $600 (or 3 x 7%)		21%	
$ 90 ÷ $900 (or 10 x 1%)			10%

2. If ROI is used for judging relative performance, B is best for this period. Other factors deserving discussion include the risks faced by each division and the short-run versus long-run implications of current performance.

3.

	Division A	Division B	Division C
	A	**B**	**C**
Income	$180	$126	$90
Imputed interest	100	60	90
Residual income	$ 80	$ 66	$ 0

Division A has the highest residual income. Although its ROI is less than that of Division B, its investment base is sufficiently high and its ROI is sufficiently above the imputed interest rate to make Division A's residual income higher.

1. Assume that fixed costs are unaffected. The company as a whole will not benefit if Atlantic buys on outside:

Purchase costs from outsider, 2,000 units at $300	$600,000
Less: Savings in variable costs by reducing Southern's output, 2,000 at $285	570,000
Disadvantage to company as a whole	$ 30,000

2. Company will benefit if Atlantic buys on outside:

Purchase costs from outsider, 2,000 units at $300		$600,000
Less:		
Savings in variable costs as above	$570,000	
Savings related to other production operations	40,500	610,500
Advantage to company as a whole		$ 10,500

3. Company will benefit if Atlantic buys on outside:

Purchase costs from outsider, 2,000 units at $270	$540,000
Less: Savings in variable costs as above	570,000
Advantage to company as a whole	$ 30,000

4. As president, I probably would not want to become immersed in these disputes. If arbitration is necessary, it probably should be conducted by some other officer on the corporate staff. One possibility is to have the immediate line boss of the two managers make a decision.

   If decentralization is to be strictly adhered to, the arbitrator should probably do nothing under any of the conditions described. If no forced transfer were made, Atlantic would go outside, resulting in an optimal decision for the overall company in parts (2) and (3) but not in part (1).

Of course, in part (1) if the manager of Southern understood cost-volume-profit relationships, and if he wanted to maximize his short-run net income, he would probably accept a price of $300. This would bring a contribution to the divisional profit of 2,000 x ($300 - $285), or $30,000.

Suppose, however, that he refuses to meet the price of $300. This would mean that the company will be $30,000 poorer in the short run. Should top management interfere and force a transfer at $300? This would undercut the philosophy of decentralization. Many managers would not interfere because they would view the $30,000 as the price that has to be paid for mistakes made under decentralization. But how high must this price go before the temptation to interfere would be irresistible? $40,000? $50,000? How much? On the other hand, the Southern manager may realize that $30,000 is being sacrificed but may have decided that it is worth more than $30,000 to achieve some long-term subjective benefits.

In sum, the point of this question is that any super structure that interferes with lower-level decision-making weakens decentralization. Of course, such interference may occasionally be necessary to prevent horrendous blunders. But recurring interference and constraints simply transform a decentralized organization into a centralized organization.

10-A3 (10 min.)

The company as a whole would benefit because the $30,000 disadvantage from purchasing on the outside would be more than offset by the additional contribution margin on sales to other customers:

Southern's sales to other customers,	
2,000 units at $325	$650,000
Variable costs, at $297	594,000
Contribution margin	$ 56,000

The net advantage would be $56,000 minus $30,000, or $26,000.

10-A4 (30-35 min.)

1. a. 25% of $900,000= $225,000 target net income

   Let X = Unit sales price
   Dollar sales = Variable expenses + Fixed expenses + Operating income
   150,000X = 150,000($1) + $300,000 + $225,000
   X = $675,000 ÷ 150,000 = $4.50

   b. Expected asset turnover = $675,000 ÷ $900,000 = .75

   c. Return on sales
   = $225,000 ÷ $675,000 = 33 1/3%

2. a, b.

	Sales Volume		
	150,000 Units*	180,000 Units	120,000 Units
Sales, at $4.50	$675,000	$810,000	$540,000
Variable expense, at $1.00	$150,000	$180,000	$120,000
Fixed expenses	300,000	300,000	300,000
Total expenses	$450,000	$480,000	$420,000
Operating income	$225,000	$330,000	$120,000
Rate of return on $900,000 assets	25.0%	36.7%	13.3%

   *Column not required.

   A summary analysis of these three cases, in equation form, follows:

	Return on Sales	x	Turn-over	=	Rate of Return
Volume 150,000	33.33%	x	.75	=	25.0%
Volume 180,000	40.74%	x	.90	=	36.7%
Volume 120,000	22.22%	x	.60	=	13.3%

3. Average available assets would decrease by $150,000, from $900,000 to $750,000. Fixed overhead would be $300,000 - $22,500 = $277,500. Results would be:

	Sell 105,000 Units	Sell 150,000 Units	Difference 45,000 Units
Sales, 105,000 units at $4.50 and 45,000 at $2.25	$472,500	$573,750	$101,250
Variable expenses, at $1.00	$105,000	$150,000	$ 45,000
Fixed expenses	277,500	300,000	22,500
Total expenses	$382,500	$450,000	$ 67,500
Operating income	$ 90,000	$123,750	$ 33,750
Total assets needed	$750,000	$900,000	$150,000
Rate of return on assets	12.0%	13.8%	22.5%

Based on the information given, he should sell at the $2.25 price. Both divisions and the company as a whole will benefit from such a decision. Although the original overall target rate of return of 25% is unattainable, the division will nevertheless earn a better rate of return with the intracompany business than without it. The additional units will earn a 22.5% incremental rate of return, which exceeds the 12.0% rate earned on 105,000 units. As a result, the overall rate of return would increase from 12.0% to 13.8%, as shown in the schedule above.

Despite this economic analysis, the Toronto Division manager may still decide against transferring goods at such a low price. For example, she may feel entitled to a higher profit. This would mean that the company would undoubtedly be worse off if the incremental costs of the other division are $2.25. Should top management interfere and force a transfer of $2.25? Such intervention would weaken the decentralization structure. Obviously, authoritarian action sometimes may be needed to prevent costly mistakes. But recurring interference and constraints simply transform a decentralized organization into a centralized organization. Of course, if managers repeatedly make costly dysfunctional decisions, the costs of decentralization may exceed the benefits. Then a more centralized organizational design may be desirable.

10-B1 (30-45 min.)

1. The percentage return for each project is as follows:

Project	Percentage Return
1	24%
2	33%
3	13%
4	16%
5	21%
6	30%

a. Under assumption (a), projects 1, 2, 5, and 6 would be taken.

Total investment	$7,650,000
Total return	$2,005,500
Return on investment	26.2%
Residual income	$ 858,000*

*$2,005,500 - ($7,650,000 x .15)

The manager taking the above projects would be following the company rule.

b. Under assumption (b), the rational manager will take only project 2, since this gives a return on investment of $627,000 ÷ $1,900,000 = 33% (and a residual income of $627,000 - ($1,900,000 x .15) = $342,000). To take any further projects at lower returns would lower the overall return on capital invested. It should be noted that if this were not a new division with no capital at this time, the manager under this alternative would take only those projects which would not lower the expected rate of return on presently-invested capital.

c. Under assumption (c), the manager will take projects 1, 2, 4, 5 and 6.

Total investment $8,600,000
Total return $2,157,500
Return on capital invested   25.1%
Residual income $ 867,500*
*$2,157,500 - ($8,600,000 x .15)

2. To maximize the earnings of the company as a whole, the division manager should be instructed to maximize residual income. The essence of the concept of residual income is that it requires the manager to take all projects which promise a positive return to the company over and above the cost of the capital invested. This will maximize total *return* to the company for the capital it has available. To maximize ROI or to use a target rate above the cost of capital means that the company (assuming that it has the money to invest) is passing up profitable opportunities. Note that by taking project 4, the division manager lowered his ROI from assumption (a) but *raised* the residual income. Project 3 would lower residual income since its gross return on investment is less than the cost of the capital needed.

10-B2 (10 min.) Amounts are in millions.

1.	2001	2002
Adjusted before-tax operating profit	$5,352	$5,458
Less:		
Cash taxes	(1,496)	(1,508)
Capital charge (10% x $12,750		
and 9% x $15,574)	(1,275)	(1,402)
EVA	$2,581	$2,548

2. Although Coca Cola's profit increased in 2002, its EVA fell slightly. Therefore, Coca Cola created more value for its shareholders in 2001 than in 2002. However, given the state of the economy in 2002, this performance was not bad relative to that of many other companies. CFO Magazine publicizes Stern Stewart's ranking of organizations according to their EVA performance. In their July 2003 issue (cfo.com), Coca Cola had a 2002 EVA of $2,496 million. This result differs slightly from the above calculation because of other adjustments Stern Stewart makes.

10-B3 (20 min.)

The appropriate transfer price is $3.35 per gallon. In general, internal profit centers should conduct both buying and selling at bona fide market price quotations. As long as the market prices are met, the buying divisions must purchase from the internal divisions. In this way, both divisions and the corporation as a whole will maximize operating income:

	Ice Cream Machine	
	Including Sales to Denali Drive-In	Excluding Sales to Denali Drive-In
Sales*	$31,025	$26,000
Variable costs @ $2.10	16,800	13,650
Contribution margin	$14,225	$12,350
Fixed costs	6,800	6,320
Operating margin	$ 7,425	$ 6,030

*6,500 gallons @ $4 + 1,500 gallons @ $3.35; 6,500 gallons @ $4

Purchase should be kept inside because the overall company operating income will be higher by $7,425 - $6,030 = $1,395. In other words, Arctic Enterprises is better off by $1,395 with sales to the Denali Drive-In:

Purchases from outside	$5,025
Less: Savings in fixed costs	(480)
Savings in variable costs by reducing	
Arctic's output, 1,500 gallons @ $2.10	(3,150)
Net savings from inside purchases	$1,395

10-B4 (30-45 min.)

1. a. Contribution margin per unit = ¥7,000 - ¥4,800 = ¥2,200
        Total contribution = ¥2,200 x 3,400 units = ¥7,480,000
        Operating income = ¥7,480,000 - ¥6,080,000 = ¥1,400,000
        ROI = ¥1,400,000 ÷ ¥12,500,000 = 11.2%

    b. Revenue = ¥7,000 x 3,400 units = ¥23,800,000
        Capital turnover = ¥23,800,000 ÷ ¥12,500,000 = 1.90

    c. Return on sales
        = ¥1,400,000 ÷ ¥23,800,000 = 5.88%

2. a. Desired operating income
        = 20% x ¥12,500,000 = ¥2,500,000
        Let X = units to be sold to reach desired return
        ¥2,200 x X units = ¥6,080,000 + ¥2,500,000
        X = ¥8,580,000 ÷ ¥2,200 = 3,900 units

    b. Let Z = required decrease in total assets

Operating income	÷	total assets = .20
(¥1,400,000 + .1Z)	÷	(¥12,500,000 - Z) = .20
.3Z	=	¥1,100,000
Z	=	¥3,666,667
Operating income	=	¥1,400,000 + .1 (¥3,666,667) = ¥1,766,667
Total assets	=	¥12,500,000 - ¥3,666,667 = ¥8,833,333
ROI	=	¥1,766,667 ÷ ¥8,833,333 = 20%

3. Examine the operating income and rate of return on assets with and without the 1,400-unit transfer (amounts are thousands of Japanese Yen):

	Sell 2,400 units	Sell 3,800 units	Difference 1,400 units
Sales, 2,400 units @ ¥7,000 and 1,400 units @ ¥6,000	16,800	25,200	8,400
Variable costs, ¥4,800/unit	11,520	18,240	6,720
Fixed costs	4,900	6,080	1,180
Total costs	16,420	24,320	7,900
Operating income	380	880	500
Total assets needed	10,000	12,500	2,500
Rate of return on assets	3.8%	7.0%	20%

Based on the information given, the Kyoto division should sell 1,400 units to the European Marketing division at the ¥6,000 price. Both divisions and the company as a whole will benefit from such a decision. Although the original overall target rate of return of 20% is unattainable, the division will nevertheless earn a better rate of return with the intracompany business than without it. The additional units will earn a 20% incremental rate of return, which exceeds the 3.8% rate earned on 2,400 units. As a result, the overall rate of return will increase from 3.8% to 7.0%, as shown in the schedule above.

Despite this economic analysis, the manager may still decide against transferring goods at such a low price. For example, he may feel entitled to a higher profit. This would mean that the company would undoubtedly be worse off in the short run if the European Marketing division must pay the equivalent of ¥6,000 to purchase the games elsewhere. Should top management interfere and force a transfer at ¥6,000? Such intervention would weaken the decentralization structure. Obviously, top management intervention sometimes may be needed to prevent costly mistakes. But recurring interference and constraints simply transform a decentralized organization into a centralized organization. Of course, if managers repeatedly make costly dysfunctional decisions, the costs of decentralization may exceed the benefits. Then a more centralized organizational design may be desirable. Further, the Kyoto manager may acknowledge the ¥500,000 loss by not transferring but believe that some long-run objective is worth the ¥500,000 short-term sacrifice.

10-1 Benefits of decentralization include: 1) lower-level managers may make better decisions because they have better knowledge of local conditions; 2) managers develop their management skills so that there are more managers qualified to move up in the organization; and 3) managers have higher status and therefore are more highly motivated.

Costs of decentralization include: 1) managers may make decisions that are not in the best interest of the organization because they are not aware of or not interested in facts that don't pertain to their own segment; 2) managers may perform functions at the division level that would be less costly if centralized; and 3) the cost of information to coordinate and control activities may increase with decentralization.

10-2 One of the limitations in decentralization is lack of knowledge in segments of the organization. This is especially true in geographically decentralized operations. Accounting systems give a common language and structure for sharing information throughout an organization. Sophisticated communications systems make this information available without delay. Many companies have "data warehouses" that let managers anywhere in the organization have immediate access to whatever accounting information they want.

10-3 It is more difficult to hold managers of nonprofit organizations responsible for performance because inputs and outputs are generally more difficult to measure. Without reliable performance measures, granting managerial freedom is more risky.

10-4 No. Profit centers facilitate decentralization, but one can exist without the other. They are different concepts, as the chapter explains.

10-5 Decentralization is usually most successful in organizations where segments are relatively independent. If segments buy from or sell to one another, or if there are many common customers or suppliers, decentralization is less likely to be desirable.

10-6 The major advantage of the rate of return analysis of performance is its attention to the required asset investment in relation to operating income.

10-7 ROI is affected by a division's income and the amount of its investment. You can also think of ROI as a factor of return on sales and capital turnover.

10-8 Economic value added (EVA) is after-tax operating income minus the after-tax weighted-average cost of capital multiplied by the sum of long-term liabilities and stockholders' equity. Companies can improve EVA by

- Investing in products or projects that generate more after-tax operating income than the cost of the capital used,
- Divesting in products or projects that do not generate enough after-tax operating income to cover the cost of the capital used,
- Reducing the weighted-average cost of capital, and
- Increasing the after-tax operating income without using more invested capital

An alternative definition of the capital charge portion of the EVA equation is the product of the after-tax weighted-average cost of capital multiplied by the sum of working capital and non-current assets. The equivalency of these two definitions can be shown as follows:

Total assets = Total liabilities + Stockholders' equity

Current assets + Non-current assets = Current liabilities + Long-term debt + Stockholders' equity

Current assets - Current liabilities + Non-current assets = Long-term debt + Stockholder's equity

The right-hand side of the above equation represents the capital structure of an organization - that is, how capital is financed. The left-hand side represents the actual capital – working capital and non-current assets. Either definition can be used.

10-9   Division A's manager would reject the proposed project because it would reduce the division's ROI. Division B's manager would accept the proposed project because it would increase the division's ROI. Both managers would be motivated to accept the proposed project based on its impact on division residual income because the project's return is greater than the imputed cost of invested capital.

10-10 Four possible definitions of invested capital are:

1.   Total assets
2.   Total assets employed
3.   Total assets less current liabilities
4.   Stockholders' equity

10-11 Not necessarily. Using a historical cost accounting system *with budgets* is not backward looking. Budgets force managers to plan for the future, including predicting future prices.

10-12 The use of gross book value rather than net book value of assets to compute ROI may affect the speed with which managers replace assets. Gross book value leads to more rapid replacement. A manager who suggests using gross book value probably has assets that are relatively new compared to those in other divisions. When net book value is used, the manager's relatively new assets are valued considerably higher than older assets because they have little accumulated depreciation. When gross book value is used, accumulated depreciation is irrelevant and there is less difference between the values of older assets and newer assets.

10-13 Companies need transfer-pricing systems to accurately determine the efficiency of various divisions of a company's operation when using profit or investment centers. If inefficiency exists somewhere in a corporation that does not employ a transfer - pricing system, it is much harder to pin down the area or process that is most directly responsible. In addition, transfer pricing is an attention-directing device that highlights good performance and motivates personnel to maintain efficiency. Transfer pricing systems also preserve segment autonomy.

10-14 Using full costs can mask the real behavior of a cost. Any transfer price that includes a fixed cost element makes a fixed cost in the producing department look like a variable cost to the buying department. Using actual costs can pass on inefficiencies and make planning difficult for the buying department. The amount of the transfer is not known until actual costs are available, and factors beyond the control of the buying department can affect the transfer price.

10-15 If a producing division has idle capacity, a transfer price at or close to the variable cost will usually be optimal. Why? Because it costs the firm as a whole only the variable costs to produce the item to be transferred. If the buying division is willing to pay more than the variable cost for the item, the benefit from the transfer must exceed the cost. However, if there is not idle capacity, the selling (producing) division, and hence the firm as a whole, gives up the contribution it would obtain from selling to outside customers or using the resource for some other use. A higher transfer price would be optimal in order to assure that the value to the buying division is at least as great as the sacrifice made by the selling division to transfer the item internally.

10-16 Variable-cost transfer prices can also lead to dysfunctional decisions. For example, the chapter includes an illustration of a situation where the producing division has no excess capacity and variable-cost transfers may cause dysfunctional decisions.

10-17 Negotiated transfer prices are likely to lead to better transfer pricing decisions because those with the best knowledge are making the decisions. On the other hand, valuable time and effort can be lost in the negotiating process.

10-18 Multinational transfer prices are influenced by the relative income-tax rates in the countries in which the producing and purchasing divisions are located. They are also influenced by import duties and restrictions on flows of capital between countries.

10-19 In organizations using management by objectives (MBO), managers and their superiors jointly formulate and agree on the goals and plans for the forthcoming period. Managers are then evaluated against these agreed-upon goals and plans.

10-20 Agency theory specifies how to trade off incentive, risk, and the cost of measuring performance.

10-21 No. ROI and residual income create different motivations for managers. Goal congruence and managerial effort would usually be accomplished better by residual income.

10-22 Profit measures and other performance measures by themselves do not cause unethical behavior. However, the way managers use them may. Managers charged with meeting performance targets by whatever means possible might resort to unethical means. Thus, it is important that management control systems not only include the right performance measures, but they must also specify how management should use these measures in evaluating managers.

10-23 When top management second-guesses divisional managers frequently, many advantages of decentralization are lost. Segment autonomy disappears. Essentially, top management intervention implies that top managers know more about the local market conditions than do segment managers. If this is indeed the case, a decentralized operation may not be appropriate.

10-24 (10 min.) Dollar amounts are in thousands.

1. Turnover of capital = Sales ÷ Invested capital
    = $130,000 ÷ $50,000
    = 260%, or 2.6 times

2. Return on sales = $6,000 ÷ $130,000
    = 4.6%

3. Return on Investment = $6,000 ÷ $50,000 = 12%
    or ROI = 2.6 x 4.6% = 12%

10-25 (5 min.)

The basic equation: ROI = Income percentage of revenue x Capital turnover

A:	7%	x 3	=	21%
B:	24%	÷ 3%	=	8
C:	20%	÷ 4	=	5%

10-26 (15-20 min.)

1.   The filled-in blanks are underscored:

	Division		
	X	Y	Z
Invested capital, $182,000 ÷ .14	$1,000,000	$1,300,000	$1,250,000
Income, .05 x $2,000,000	$ 100,000	$ 182,000	$ 150,000
Revenue, $1,250,000 x 3	$2,000,000	$3,640,000	$3,750,000
Return on sales, $182,000 ÷ $3,640,000	5%	5%	4%*
Capital turnover, $2,000,000 ÷ $1,000,000; $3,640,000 ÷ $1,300,000	2	2.8	3
Rate of return on invested capital	10%**	14%	12%***

*$150,000 ÷ $3,750,000 = 4%
**5% x 2.0 = 10.0% or $100,000 ÷ $1,000,000 = 10%
***$150,000 ÷ $1,250,000 = 12% or   4% x 3 = 12%

2.   If the criterion for judging relative performance is ROI, Division Y is best for this period. Other factors deserving attention include the relative risks faced by each division and the short-run versus long-run implications of current performance.

3.

	Division		
	X	Y	Z
Income	$ 100,000	$182,000	$150,000
Capital charge	120,000	156,000	150,000
Residual income	($ 20,000)	$ 26,000	$ 0

10-27 (10 – 15 min.) Dollar amounts are in thousands.

1.

2002:	Adjusted operating profit after tax ($115,352 - $22,903)	$ 92,449
	Capital charge (.087 x $1,154,653)	100,455
	EVA	$ (8,006)
2001:	Adjusted operating profit after tax ($107,593 - $16,468)	$ 91,125
	Capital charge (.096 x $942,811)	90,510
	EVA	$ 615

2. Briggs and Stratton's overall performance declined substantially, with EVA decreasing from a positive $615,000 to a negative $8,006,000. This is despite an increase in the adjusted after-tax operating profit from $91,125,000 to $92,449,000. Because of the large increase in invested capital, the capital charge increased by nearly $10 million.

10-28 (20 min.)

1.

	Fleet	Speedy
Assets	$2,000,000	$2,000,000
Liabilities	800,000	0
Stockholders' equity	1,200,000	2,000,000
Income before interest	400,000	400,000
10% interest	80,000	0
Net income	$ 320,000	$ 400,000
Rate of return on:		
Assets	20%	20%
Stockholders equity	27%	20%

2.   When an asset base is used for measuring return, the investor sources for the assets are ignored and so is interest. Rate of return, as used here, means 20% gross rate of return (that is, before interest expense) on total assets. The use of long-term debt can have an impact on the return based on stockholders' equity. However, the 27% rate of return on stockholders' equity does not distinguish between the basic earnings rate on total assets and the various costs of obtaining and using the funds. In other words, top management has two major functions: operating and financing. Measures of operational performance (how assets are employed) should not be influenced by financing decisions (how funds for investing are obtained). Fleet Footwear in effect has paid 10% for the use of $800,000, which in turn has earned a gross return of 20%. This method of financing benefited the stockholders handsomely.

10-29 (20-30 min.) This problem presses the student more than those immediately preceding it. Dollar amounts are in thousands.

1.

	Division		
	J	K	L
Income: .20 x $3,000;			
.15 x $16,000	$ 210	$ 600	$ 2,400
Revenue: $210 ÷ .07;			
$600 ÷ .04;			
3 x $16,000	$3,000	$15,000	$48,000
Invested capital: $3,000 ÷ 4	$ 750	$ 3,000	$16,000
Income percentage of			
revenue, 15% ÷ 3	7%	4%	5%
Capital turnover, 20% ÷ 4%	4	5	3
Rate of return on invested capital,			
$210,000 ÷ $750,000	28%	20%	15%
Cost of invested capital	20%	12%	12%*
Residual income,			
$210 - (.20 x $750);			
$600 - (.12 x $3,000)	$ 60	$ 240	$ 480

*$2,400,000 - $480,000 = $1,920,000;
  $1,920,000 ÷ $16,000,000 = 12%

2.   This requirement can generate much discussion or little discussion, as the instructor desires. Using ROI as the criterion, J is the best performer. Using residual income as the criterion, L is the best performer. Note that this company uses different interest rates for different divisions, probably because of wide variations in risks. Note, too, that residual income, an absolute amount, is always easier to generate by large divisions.

10-30 (15 min.)

1 & 2.

Year	Income Before Depreciation	Depreciation	Operating Income	Net Book Value*	(2) Rate of Return	Gross Book Value	(1) Rate of Return
1	80,000	50,000	30,000	125,000	24%	150,000	20%
2	80,000	50,000	30,000	75,000	40%	150,000	20%
3	80,000	50,000	30,000	25,000	120%	150,000	20%

* ($150,000 + $100,000) ÷ 2; ($100,000 + $50,000) ÷ 2; etc.

3.   Carrasquel might prefer the net book value because it always gives a higher ROI. However, if all divisions used net book value, her decision might change. Relative to other divisions, she might pass up the highest rates of return, which could occur in the Ocala Division after she transfers out.

10-31 (10 min.)

1.

	(b) Process Further		(a) Sell to Outsiders at Transfer Point	
	Binding Division Performance	Overall Performance	Binding Division Performance	Overall Performance
Selling Price	$8.50	$8.50	$—	$6.30
Variable costs:				
Printing Division	$5.00			$5.00
Binding Division	2.80			—
Total variable costs	7.80	7.80	—	5.00
Contribution to net income	$ .70	$ .70	$—	$1.30

2. If the transfer price is based on variable cost, the manager of the Binding Division would want the product processed further. But this would hurt overall company performance. The essential question is whether the Binding Division should offer the final product in the market at all. The incremental revenue of $2.20 is less than the incremental cost of $2.80.

10-32 (10-15 min.)

1. If wheels were available for $13 each in the market, Omaha would not be willing to pay more than $13 to Lincoln. If wheels could not be purchased in the market, the maximum price would be $20, computed as follows:

Sales price	160
Variable costs (except for wheels)	120
Contribution available for wheels and to cover fixed costs and profit	$ 40

    The $40 must pay for two wheels, so the most that can be paid per wheel is $40÷2 = $20. The manager of the Omaha Division would likely not pay the entire amount of $20 per wheel, because that would leave no contribution to fixed costs plus profit. However, any price less that $20 would produce a positive contribution margin and therefore be better than not producing the bicycles.

2. Because there is excess capacity, any transfer price above the variable cost of $9 would result in a positive contribution margin. No price below $9 would be acceptable. If there were no excess capacity, the minimum transfer price would be the market price of $13. Why? Because the Lincoln division would have to forgo $13 of revenue from an external sale in order to transfer a wheel internally.

1. Glasgow is better off using a £400 transfer price. A £400 transfer price places an extra £400 - £200 = £200 of income in Japan instead of Sweden, while a £200 transfer price places an extra £200 of income in Sweden instead of Japan. In addition, the £400 transfer price adds to the import taxes paid to Sweden. The net effect is as follows:

Japanese income is £200 higher, .3 x £200 more taxes	£ (60)
Swedish income is £200 lower, .6 x £200 less taxes	120
Swedish import tax, .1 x £200 more taxes	(20)
Net reduction in taxes from £400 transfer price	£ 40

2. The total taxes saved by the £400 transfer price is £40 per unit.

10-34 (20-25 min.)

1. The two contracts illustrate the tradeoff between incentive and risk in employment contracts. The bonus contract provides more incentive to generate profits than does the straight salary. This should benefit U.K. International. On the other hand, it may cause the manager to focus too much on short-run profitability. Further, it imposes risk on the manager. A manager demands extra compensation to bear this risk. If the vice-president/personnel is correct, the expected cost to U.K. International of this risk is £9,000 (the amount by which the expected compensation with the bonus plan exceeds the straight salary). The choice should be based on whether the extra incentive under the bonus plan is likely to be worth at least £9,000 to U.K. International.

Another factor to consider is what type of manager will be attracted by each type of contract. Sometimes it is hard to determine a manager's qualifications at the time of hiring. The manager knows his or her abilities better than does the company. Highly qualified managers would seek contracts with a bonus. Why? They would be confident that they would do better than average and therefore receive compensation above what the firm expects an average manager to receive. The opposite is true for less qualified managers. Because U.K. International receives £9 of every £10 of extra profit generated, attracting a highly qualified manager is likely to be advantageous.

2. Managers are generally risk averse. This means that they prefer a contract with less risk to one with more risk if the expected compensation does not differ. It does not mean that managers avoid risks, only that they want to be compensated for such risk-seeking. If a risky contract has an expected compensation high enough, it will be preferred to a given risk-free contract. For U.K. International, a quality manager willing to accept a straight-salary contract at £40,000 might not accept a risky bonus contract with an expected compensation of £40,000. Extra compensation must be paid to offset the added risk.

The U.K. International Trading Company should recognize that besides normal operating risk, they have imposed an added risk in the bonus contract. Because the contract is in British currency, possible movement in exchange rates adds to the noncontrollable factors affecting the bonus, hence it increases the risk.

(25 min.)

1. The two separate components highlight certain features of profitability that are not revealed by the single calculation.
   a. The importance of turnover as a key to profits is stressed.
   b. The importance of sales volume is explicitly recognized.
   c. It reduces important elements to ratios instead of dollar figures. This often enhances comparability of different divisions, businesses, and time periods.
   d. The breakdown stresses the possibility of trading off turnover for margin so as to increase the average rate of return at a given level of output.

2.

	Company		
	Alpha	Beta	Gamma
Return on sales	15%	15%	1%
Turnover on capital	x 2	x 0.2	x 3
Return on investment	30%	3%	3%

Income and investment alone shed little light on comparative performance because of disparities in size between Alpha and the other two companies. Thus, it is impossible to say whether Beta's low rate of return in comparison with Alpha's is attributable to its larger capital or to its lower income. The fact that Beta and Gamma have identical income and capital suggests that the same conditions underlie the low rate of return, but this conclusion is erroneous.

Introducing sales to measure level of operations helps to disclose specific areas for more intensive investigation. Beta does as well as Alpha in terms of profit margin; both companies earn 15% on sales. But Beta has a much lower turnover of capital than does Alpha. Whereas a dollar of investment in Alpha supports two dollars in sales each period, a dollar investment in Beta supports only 20 cents in sales each period. This suggests that the analyst should look carefully at Beta's investment. Is the company keeping an inventory larger than necessary for its sales volume? Are receivables being collected promptly? Or did Alpha acquire its fixed assets at a price level which was much lower than that at which Beta purchased its plant?

On the other hand, Gamma's turnover is higher than Alpha's, but Gamma's margin on sales is much lower. Why? Are its operations inefficient, are its material costs too high, or does its location entail high transportation costs?

Analysis of return on capital raises questions such as the foregoing. When answers are obtained, basic reasons for differences between rates of return may be discovered. For example, in Beta's case, it is apparent that the emphasis will have to be on increasing turnover by reducing investment or increasing sales. Most likely, Beta cannot appreciably increase its rate of return simply by increasing its return on sales. In contrast, Gamma's management should concentrate on increasing the return on sales.

3.   Beta has a high profit margin and a low turnover. It is in an industry such as jewelry or other luxury goods. In contrast, Gamma has a low profit margin and a high turnover. It might be a grocery chain or a discount retail establishment.

<u>10-36</u> (15-20 min.)

1. (a) Entertainment $223.0 ÷ $1,272.2 = 17.5%
        Publishing/Information   122.4 ÷   705.5 = 17.3%
        Consumer/Commercial Finance   244.6 ÷ 1,235.0 = 19.8%

    (b) Entertainment $1,272.2 ÷ $1,120.1 = 1.14
        Publishing/Information   705.5 ÷ 1,308.7 =   .54
        Consumer/Commercial Finance 1,235.0 ÷   924.4 = 1.34

    (c) Entertainment $223.0 ÷ $1,120.1 = 19.9%
        Publishing/Information   122.4 ÷ 1,308.7 = 9.4%
        Consumer/Commercial Finance   244.6 ÷   924.4 = 26.5%

2. This requirement can lead to a lengthy discussion of what causes differences in the three measures computed in requirement 1. The obvious difference is the low return on investment in the Publishing/ Information segment. It is worth noting that this difference arises primarily because of the low capital turnover in the segment. The Publishing/Information segment is generating less than half as much sales revenue per dollar of invested capital as either of the other two segments.

10-37 (25 – 30 min.) Amounts in thousands.

	Residual Income	Economic Value Added
Income from operations	$ 118,358	$ 118,358
Net Adjustments for EVA		(3,006)
Provision for taxes	(27,390)	
Cash taxes		(22,903)
After-tax operating income	90,968	92,449
Average capital for EVA (adjusted)		1,154,653
Average total assets, (1,349,033 + 1,296,195) ÷ 2	1,322,614	
Average current liabilities, (266,023 + 242,182) ÷ 2	(254,103)	
Average capital for residual income	1,068,511	
Cost-of-capital percentage	8.7%	8.7%
Capital charge	92,960	100,455
Residual income or EVA	$ (1,992)	$ (8,006)

10-38 (10-15 min.) Amounts are in millions.

1. 2002 EVA = $9,893 - $8,825 - $349 - (9.5% x $4,320) = $309

    2001 EVA = $9,489 - $8,475 - $332 - (9.5% x $3,875) = $314

2. EVA decreased slightly from $314 million to $309 million. In a poor economy, this was reasonably good performance. Both years showed positive EVA and therefore positive value creation. These EVA numbers are less than the EVA of $487 million that Nike had in 1997, which (according to CEO Phillip H. Knight) was "the best year we have ever had, the best anyone has ever had in our business." However, they are better than Nike's EVA in 1999 and 2000.

10-39 (10-15 min.)

1. Weighted-average cost of capital:
    30% x 5% = 1.5
    70% x 11% = 7.7
                 9.2%

    EVA = $5,458,000,000 - $1,523,000,000 – (9.2% x $15,574,000,000)
          = $2,502,192,000

2. Coca-Cola's EVA of $2.5 billion is very high. This means that Coca-Cola generated $2.5 billion of value for its shareholders above the normal return expected on an investment. However, note that this is an accounting measure of value, and it is not necessarily equivalent to the market return on a share of Coca-Cola stock.

10-40 (20-30 min.) Dollar amounts are in thousands.

	Shoes	Clothing	Accessories
Historical Cost:			
Net assets	$15,000	$44,000	$27,000
Operating income	2,700	6,750	5,000
Capital charge	1,500	4,400	2,700
Residual income	1,200	2,350	2,300
Rate of return on net assets	18.0%	15.3%	18.5%
Replacement Cost:			
Net assets	$15,000	$55,000	$48,000
Operating income	2,700	6,150	3,900
Capital charge	1,500	5,500	4,800
Residual income	1,200	650	(900)
Rate of return on net assets	18.0%	11.2%	8.1%

Neither base is foolproof regarding the evaluation of an individual *manager's* performance. First, the short-run emphasis of such measures includes only a part of the activities that promote profitability in the long-run. Second, the environmental conditions facing a particular division plus unfavorable carryover of past mistakes may severely hamper *divisional* performance even though the *manager* is clearly superior by any test other than rate of return or residual income. That is, the "best" managers are often deliberately given the sickest divisions precisely because they have the most ability to improve a sad situation. *Improvement* or *fulfilling tailor-made budgeted targets* may be the best tests of *management* performance as distinguished from *divisional* performance.

2. The following rankings exist:

	Rate of Return		Residual Income	
	On Historical Cost	On Replacement Cost	On Historical Cost	On Replacement Cost
First	Accessories	Shoes	Clothing	Shoes
Second	Shoes	Clothing	Accessories	Clothing
Third	Clothing	Accessories	Shoes	Accessories

3. In this case, if historical cost is the base, the use of rate of return on net assets ranks Accessories first, whereas residual income ranks Clothing first. Used indiscriminately, each method has its drawbacks, regardless of whether historical cost or replacement cost is used as a base. Rate of return inhibits divisions with high rates from expansion, whereas residual income tends to favor large divisions that earn in excess of the cost of capital.

Replacement costs are more helpful than historical costs as indicators of the relative profitability of *divisions* because they are usually good approximations of the current economic sacrifice being made to conduct such operations. As for managers, their ability to meet *budgeted* goals, however measured, is paramount. Students, professors, and managers have disagreements regarding which asset base is preferable.

<u>10-41</u> (50-60 min.)

1.   See Exhibit 10-41 on the following page.

2.   Some major companies, including du Pont and Monsanto Chemical, have used gross assets as an investment base. One reason often cited for using undepreciated cost is that it partially compensates for the impact of the changing price level on historical cost. However, if a company desires to use replacement cost as a base, it should not try to tailor historical costs to the measurement problems of changing prices; the results of such hybrid attachments can be unreliable.

The reasoning in support of the gross assets base must be aligned with the purpose for its use: appraisal of company results as a whole (column 11 of the answer to requirement 1) or appraisal of a plant's or division's performance (column 6). A company's performance as a whole is the responsibility of top management. When profits are made, depreciation is recouped out of sales revenue. If dividends are paid in the amount of net income, cash may accumulate in the amount of the annual $100,000 depreciation (column 8). (No cash is kept in the business from earnings, but there is a conversion of fixed assets into cash as measured by depreciation.) To count original cost plus the cash accumulation as a part of the investment base (column 10) is duplication; it does not provide as useful a base as net assets. In contrast, a plant manager's or division manager's performance often is best analyzed by using gross assets as the investment base (column 6). The reinvestment of the cash accumulation in the amount of depreciation charges may be beyond the manager's control.

EXHIBIT 10-41

Rate of Return on Assets Using Original Cost of Fixed Assets vs. Using Net Book Value of Fixed Assets

| | Plant Performance | | | | | | | Company Performance | | | | | |
| | Fixed Assets | | | | | Rate of Return | | Total Cash | | Gross Assets | | Net Assets | |
Year	Gross Cost (1)	Accumulated Depreciation (2)	Net Value, End of Year (3)	Average Book Value for Year* (4)	Annual Net Income (5)	On Gross Cost (6)	On Average Book Value (7)	Accumulation** (8)	Average*** Cash for Year (9)	Base (10)	Rate of Return (11)	Base (12)	Rate of Return (13)
1	$400,000	$100,000	$300,000	$350,000	$40,000	10.0%	11.4%	$100,000	$ 50,000	$ 450,000	8.9%	$400,000	10.0%
2	400,000	200,000	200,000	250,000	40,000	10.0%	16.0%	200,000	150,000	550,000	7.3%	400,000	10.0%
3	400,000	300,000	100,000	150,000	40,000	10.0%	26.7%	300,000	250,000	650,000	6.2%	400,000	10.0%
4	400,000	400,000	0	50,000	40,000	10.0%	80.0%	400,000	350,000	750,000	5.3%	400,000	10.0%

* 1/2 (Beginning balance plus Ending balance), e.g., 1/2($300,000+$200,000) = $250,000 for year 2.

** Assume that sales and expenses except depreciation are on a cash basis, and that dividends equal net income. Thus cash in the amount of the depreciation charge will accumulate each year.

*** This situation is unrealistic in the sense that idle cash is being accumulated without being reinvested to earn a return.

Those who favor gross asset value as a base state that it facilitates comparisons among plants or divisions. If income moves downward as a plant ages, the decrease in earning power will be evident under a gross asset base, while the constantly decreasing net asset base will reflect a possibly deceiving higher rate of return in later years (column 7).

The proponents of using net book value as a base maintain that it is less confusing because (a) it is consistent with the total assets shown on the conventional balance sheet and (b) it is consistent with net income computations, which include deductions for depreciation. Using net book value prevents duplication of the same asset in the base and shows a constantly rising rate of return on plant performance. See column 7. Note that the inclusion of the cash accumulation and *gross fixed assets* duplicates the same item, so that the total fixed and current gross asset base rises from year to year.

The definition of income should be consistent with the definition of the capital base to which it is related. Thus, interest expense is ordinarily excluded in computing incomes that are related to asset bases, while interest expense is deducted in computing income that is related to stockholders' equity bases. Nonrecurring items are ordinarily excluded when current operating performance is to be appraised.

<u>10-42</u> (30-40 min.)

The issues in this problem are covered briefly in a section in the chapter. This problem was originally used on a final examination. In particular, note that the quotation is dealing with *how to evaluate performance*, as distinguished from decisions to buy, hold, or sell assets.

A basic question, then, is why we bother to evaluate performance. Fundamentally, it is to assist future decisions and to provide managers with incentives toward organizational goals. One set of numbers may be appropriate for evaluating the economic performance of a segment, whereas a different set may be appropriate for appraising an individual manager's performance. The last sentence in the problem clearly recognizes this distinction, but students tend to pay insufficient attention to it in their solutions. Of course, the major reason for the distinction is that events uncontrollable by the manager sometimes dominate the economic performance of an entity; simultaneously, the manager may be doing either a superhuman or an abysmal job with respect to the critical factors under his or her control.

The issues presented in the statement assume the following logical pattern:

1.   Economic values are the best for performance measurement.
2.   Replacement values will probably be less than economic value throughout an asset's life.
3.   Market (exit) value is inherently less than or equal to (usually the former) economic value for a given asset.
4.   Use of economic value is infeasible; hence, replacement value should be used.
5.   Replacement value will facilitate the evaluation of the division's performance more easily than the division manager's performance.

The statement correctly establishes economic value as the "ideal" measure of an asset's value. The statement fails to disclose the characteristics of economic value that make it "infeasible." Infeasibility probably refers to the difficulty of determining (a) cash flows in the future and (b) the appropriate discount rate to be applied to those flows in the present value process.

The statement presents a reasonable case in favor of replacement value over exit value.

Some remarks might be made about the fact that replacement costs of highly specialized assets may be more difficult to obtain than a direct approximation of their economic values via discounted cash flow techniques.

The biggest defect of the commentary is its failure to mention the cost and value of information tradeoffs in deciding whether some "current" value basis for evaluation of performance is superior to continuing to use historical cost.

10-43 (20-30 min.)

Where market prices are not available as a foundation for setting transfer prices, the prices bear an artificiality that severely limits the significance of rate-of-return or other performance measures. The whole idea of decentralization is the manager's independence; unless a manager can resort to buying and selling outside the company, his or her profit center is essentially in a centralized company. Nevertheless, profit centers may promote more goal congruence than cost centers.

The rule to be used is that goods and services should be transferred at a price equivalent to that prevailing in an outside market at the time of transfer. Where the internal division meets these selling prices, the buying division must purchase internally. Market prices establish the ceiling for transfer-pricing. In many instances, a lower price may easily be justified, particularly where high-volume purchases are made or where selling costs are less.

In the two cases cited, the transfer prices should be no higher than those that could be obtained consistently by buying the used cars, parts, or services from outside parties.

10-44 (30 min.)

1. Both the Pump Division and the company as a whole will benefit if the $28.00 price is met. If not, 75% of the pump volume will disappear, and gross margin will fall to $250,000 as follows:

Sales, 250,000 at $38		$9,500,000
Variable costs, at $25	$6,250,000	
Fixed costs	3,000,000	
Total costs		9,250,000
Gross margin		$ 250,000

If the $28 price is met, the Pump Division will show a gross margin of $2,500,000 as follows:

	To Automotive Division	To Outsiders	Total
Sales:			
750,000 at $28	$21,000,000		
250,000 at $38		$9,500,000	$30,500,000
Variable costs	$18,750,000	$6,250,000	25,000,000
Fixed costs	2,250,000	750,000	3,000,000
Total costs	$21,000,000	$7,000,000	$28,000,000
Gross margin	$ 0	$2,500,000	$ 2,500,000

The rejection of intracompany business will slash margins by $2,500,000 - $250,000 = $2,250,000. Alternatively, the acceptance of intracompany business will result in a contribution margin of $3.00 per pump ($28 less $25 variable costs) or $3.00 x 750,000 = $2,250,000 which otherwise will be forgone.

2. Yes, the division should reject intracompany sales and concentrate on outside sales since the gross margin would be $4,000,000, whereas the gross margin if automotive division business were accepted would be $3,500,000. The gross margin would increase by $500,000 as follows:

Sales, 1,000,000 at $36		$36,000,000
Variable costs, at $28	$28,000,000	
Fixed costs	5,000,000	
Total costs		33,000,000
Gross margin (new proposal)		$ 3,000,000
Gross margin (accepting intracompany business)		2,500,000
Difference		$ 500,000

10-45 (30 min.)

1. The U.S. Division should not supply the European Division with the sound system for the $6.90 per unit price. The U.S. Division is operating at capacity and would lose $4.10 ($11.00 - $6.90) for each part sold to the European Division. The management performance of the U.S. Division is measured by return on investment and dollar profits; selling to the European Division at $6.90 per unit would adversely affect those performance measures.

2. Japan Electronics would be $5.90 better off, in the short run, if the U.S. Division supplied the European Division the part for $6.90 and the Game Box was sold for $62.50. If the $10.00 per unit for fixed overhead and administration is an allocation of costs the European Division incurs regardless of the Game Box order, Japan Electronics would lose $4.10 in cash flow for each sound system sold to the European Division but gain at least $10.00 from each Game Box the European Division sells, a net gain of $10.00 - $4.10 = $5.90.

3. In the short run there is an advantage to Japan Electronics of transferring the sound system at the $6.90 price and thus selling the Game Box for at least $62.50. To make this happen, Japan Electronics could overrule the decision of the U.S. Division management. This action would be counter to the purposes of decentralized decision-making. If such action were necessary on a regular basis the decentralized decision-making inherent in the divisionalized organization would be a sham.

   Alternatively, the problem could be placed back with the European Division. Even if the European Division had to pay the market price of $11.00, the contract would increase its profit. The variable cost would be $28.10 + $11.00 + $17.50 = $56.60. As long as the European Division has excess capacity, its profit would increase by at least $5.90 (i.e., $62.50 - $56.60) per Game Box. Therefore, both the European division and Japan Electronics as a whole would be better off if the transfer were made at market price. It is up to the European Division managers to find a way to price the Game Box at $62.50 or more even when the sound system is transferred at $11.00.

10-46 (20-25 min.)

1. The Ashville Division manager would not buy the lumber for $70 and would not produce the chairs. The division would lose $5 on each chair produced at that price:

Revenue per chair		$94
Division cost per chair:		
Lumber	$70	
Manufacturing	23	
Selling	6	99
Division loss per chair		$ (5)

However, the company as a whole would benefit by $17 per chair if the chairs were produced and sold:

Revenue per chair		$94
Additional costs per chair:		
Lumber	$48	
Manufacturing	23	
Selling	6	77
Total contribution per chair		$17

Therefore, the policy to transfer at fully allocated costs motivates the manager to make a decision not in the best interests of the company as a whole.

2. When there is no idle capacity at the Georgolina Mill, transferring lumber to the Ashville Division causes the Mill to pass up sales to outside customers. Compare the total contribution from selling the lumber to the total contribution from using the lumber to build chairs and selling the chairs:

Sell Lumber

Revenue	$72
Total additional costs:	
Variable cost of lumber	$48
Total contribution margin	$24

Build and Sell Chair

Revenue		$94
Total additional costs:		
Variable cost of lumber	$48	
Manufacturing	23	
Selling	6	77
Total contribution margin		$17

The company is $7 better off with the contribution of $24 from selling lumber rather than $17 from selling the chair.

Another way to view this problem is that, if the lumber can be sold for $72, using it to build a chair adds $94 - $72 = $22 of additional revenue. The additional costs are $23 + $6 = $29. The company is $7 worse off if it spends $29 to gain $22 in revenue.

10-47 (25-30 min.)

1. Cost of QualType:

   ($.25 x 120 pages) + (100 copies per page x $.014 x 120 pages)
   = $30.00 + $168.00 = $198.00

   Thus, Jiffy Press, at a bid price of $180.25, is the least expensive. In addition, the reports would be ready sooner. If the San Jose office is not directed by top management to do otherwise, Maxima - San Jose would choose Jiffy Press. If QualType got the business that would occupy idle capacity, Maxima would have .60 x $198.00 = $118.80 contribution to fixed costs, which it would not have if QualType didn't get the business. Thus, giving the business to Jiffy Press is not an optimal economic decision from the entire corporation's point of view. If the decision maker at San Jose gives the business to QualType due to top management's encouragement, his decision would be optimal economically.

2. If QualType has idle capacity, the minimum transfer price is its variable costs, .40 x $198.00 = $79.20. If QualType can get other orders outside at $198.00, the minimum transfer price should be $198.00. The best outside bid, $180.25, generally provides an appropriate transfer price.

3. The optimal decision might be to go with Jiffy Press since one to two days may be saved in getting the reports to the client. Potential future earnings for consulting services would be greater than the contribution forgone. However, it is uncertain whether the delay would affect the client's decision to utilize Maxima's services in the future. The client's goodwill towards Maxima is also determined by other factors such as the competence of the individuals in Maxima, the quality of the report, the price of the report, and the time required for the report to be prepared up until the time of printing.

4. Top management has decreased the sense of autonomy of Maxima - San Jose in suggesting that QualType be utilized. This could affect morale and cause dysfunctional behavior, particularly since QualType's quality is poor.

10-48 (10 - 15 min.)

The minimum transfer price is $22. Any price below $22 would cause the Fabricating Division to lose profit. In fact, the minimum transfer price could be slightly above $22 if the Fabricating Division, despite its current situation with excess capacity, would limit its future flexibility by agreeing to the production and transfer.

The maximum price is $38, the price at which the Assembly Division could buy the subassembly on the market. It might be slightly less than $38 if the Assembly Division can save some transportation or handling costs by buying internally, or if it can be more confident in the quality when purchasing internally.

<u>10-49</u>   (15 min.)

This simple example provides a good opportunity to discuss the issue of moving profits from one division to another through transfer prices. The setting is different from any presented in the chapter.

Michelin certainly has an incentive to transfer tires at as low a price as possible. A €1 larger transfer price shifts €1 of profit from Michelin's parent-company account to its subsidiary's account. Michelin retains 100% of its parent-company profits, but it gets only 70% of the subsidiary's profits. Thus, for every €1 addition to the transfer price, Michelin Group loses €1 and gains only €.70, a net loss of €.30.

Of course, the minority shareholders of Stomil Olsztyn want as much profit as possible transferred to their company. Thus, they favor a high transfer price. Each extra €1 of transfer price gains them €.30 in profit. Suppose Stomil Olsztyn could sell the tires on the market and receive a contribution of €9 rather than the contribution of €5 they get from Michelin. Then, the minority shareholders would gain 30% x €4 = €1.20 per tire.

A key to a fair transfer price is Stomil Olsztyn's alternative opportunities. If the subsidiary could sell the same tire on the market for a net price (market price less discounts less costs incurred to sell on the market that the subsidiary does not incur on sales to Michelin) of more than €25, the transfer price is too low. Or, if it uses resources that could make alternative products that would have a contribution margin greater than €5, the price is too low. In such cases, Michelin is gaining at the expense of the minority shareholders of Stomil Olsztyn.

Arms-length negotiation between managers of Michelin and Stomil Olsztyn may lead to optimal transfer prices, provided that both seek to maximize their own unit's profits.

10-50 (15 min.)

1. The optimal transfer price is $650 per unit:

    (a) Tax savings with $650 transfer price:
    $[.60 \times (\$650-\$400)] - [.34 \times (\$650 - \$400)]$
    $= \$150 - \$85 = \$65$

    (b) Additional duty with $650 transfer price:
    $.15 \times (\$650-\$400) = \$37.50$

    (c) Advantage of $650 transfer price over $400 transfer price:
    $\$65 - \$37.50 = \$27.50$

2. The changes make the $400 transfer price optimal:

    (a) Additional taxes with $400 transfer price:
    $[.50 (\$650 - \$400)] - [.34 (\$650-\$400)]$
    $= \$125 - \$85 = \$40$

    (b) Duty savings with $400 transfer price:
    $.20 (\$650-\$400) = \$50$

    (c) Advantage of $400 transfer price over $650 transfer price:
    $\$50 - \$40 = \$10$

Multinational transfer pricing is heavily affected by the constraints of various countries' laws on taxes and tariffs. Moreover, the resulting transfer prices complicate the evaluation of the performance of the managers and the economic investments in a particular country.

<u>10-51</u> (15-20 min.)

1. 1,500 units x ($37 - $20) = $25,500 increase in operating income if units are purchased inside.

2. Variable manufacturing costs of $20 per unit.

3. Currently available outside purchase price of $37 per unit.

4. (a) Benefit of $25,500 from the Dayton Division's viewpoint, but disadvantage of 1,500 units x ($40 - $20) = $30,000 from the Cleveland Division viewpoint. Therefore, net decrease in Ohio Instruments Company operating income of $4,500.

    (b) Benefit of zero to the Dayton Division, but disadvantage of ($40 - $37) (1,500) = $4,500 to the Cleveland Division. Net decrease in Ohio Instruments Company operating income of $4,500.

5. (a) Cleveland Division's current ROI = $36,000 ÷ $300,000 = 12%. Proposed investment earns an ROI = $2,200 ÷ $20,000 = 11%. Therefore, the Cleveland Division's ROI will decrease if the proposal is accepted.

    (b) $2,200 - .09($20,000) = $400 increase in the Cleveland Division residual income, so the Cleveland Division would accept proposal.

10-52 (25-35 min.)

This is a favorite problem. In a short space, it gets to the heart of the problems of a control system: goal congruence and effort. In particular, it focuses on how the widespread accounting convention of writing off engineering costs as immediate expenses may inhibit wise investments. It is also a good problem on the motivational impact of cost allocations, so it might be assigned in conjunction with Chapter 12.

1. The strong points of the present plan include the tendency of the ECD manager to hire the optimal number of engineers and to use them efficiently. At first glance, the production managers will also tend to behave in similar fashion. In addition, the user receives no surprises because the total cost of each "contract" is known in advance.

    The weakest point of the present plan is not explicitly pinpointed in the case. (We usually do not raise this point until the proposed plan is discussed.) Why is top management considering a switch to a "no-charge" system? To encourage greater use of ECD services! Such services are evidently being under-used. A likely reason for small usage is that the "expense" borne in the first year may exceed the prospective savings for the first year. Therefore, even if the investment is justified on a longer-run basis, the production managers feel too much pressure for short-run performance to look beyond the current year. (Moreover, many managers are transferred or promoted nearly every year.)

    Under the proposed plan, the ECD manager may continue to hire engineers until their marginal cost exceeds the marginal savings. But a tenser atmosphere is likely. ECD services would be a "free good." When the selling price is zero, the production managers will increase their demand. The ECD manager (or some committee) will have to determine priorities. In contrast, the present plan uses a "market price" system of sorts. Priorities are determined by a negotiated contract at a predetermined price.

2.   Most students will favor the present system, although a minority may like the proposed system. Of course, other systems are possible. For example, an *internal* accounting system could capitalize the ECD costs and amortize them over the "useful life" of the expected cost savings. The latter system would then provide a method of performance evaluation (incentive) that would be consistent with the decision model (long-run net savings) apparently favored by top management.

Again, in the final analysis, the choice of a system will depend on top management's prediction of the impact of the particular method on the collective decisions of the affected managers. In this instance, incidentally, top management adopted the proposed plan.

A major lesson here is that internal accounting systems are neither inherently good nor inherently bad. The role of *timing* and the wishes of *top management* dramatically affect the choice of a system. Thus, a particular system may solve the problems of goal congruence and effort for a year or two or more. However, as time passes, the system invariably warrants correction or revamping.

For example, after a class discussion of this case in an executive program, a French executive said in effect:

> "This case is one that I've experienced. A few years ago, our top management adopted the no-charge system to spur heavier use of our central research and development department. Five years later we returned to a charge system, because our central staff had ballooned to an intolerable level."

In *both* instances, the choice of the system could have been correct.

Finally, the literature on agency theory emphasizes risk congruence. That is, incentives may be designed to encourage or discourage risk-taking. The existing system discourages risk-taking on the part of individual managers because they have less chance to have a diversified portfolio of projects. The proposed system shifts the risk to the ECD manager. Because this manager can attain a diversified portfolio, he may accept more risky projects. Top management may prefer the latter.

<u>10-53</u> (20-30 min.)

1. Management by Objectives (MBO) is a formal system for developing and making measurable the goals for each position in the organization for a given time period. Mutually agreed upon goals are set for each subordinate with his or her superior. Both agree on the objectives to be met and how they will be measured.

    Advantages most often claimed for the MBO system include:

    1. Increased subordinate motivation to accomplish goals.
    2. Channeling of subordinate efforts toward organizationally recognized goals rather than individual goals.
    3. Increased development of subordinate abilities through the systematic establishment of goals by subordinates.
    4. Improved performance appraisal accuracy over time because substantive measures are used rather than subjective supervisor evaluation.
    5. Increased communication between subordinate and superior.

    Disadvantages associated with MBO include:

    1. Likely emphasis on short-run rather than long-run consequences.
    2. Difficulty in dealing with non-quantifiable factors.
    3. Emphasis on organizational rather than personal goals, needs, and wants.
    4. The increased emphasis on counseling often requires too much time.
    5. Limited effectiveness in turbulent or less-structured environments.

2. The human value premises of MBO suggest that subordinates will attempt 100% achievement if they accept a clear and tangible set of objectives. Inherent in MBO is the premise that goal formation is a joint process, where individual subordinates are involved in setting goals for their activities and developing programs that lead to attainment of organizational goals. In addition, the MBO system allows for adjustments to be made in goals to account for errors that may have occurred during the formation of them. During the appraisal process of MBO, recognition should be given for partial achievement of goals as well as for reaching the various goals.

Roger Chavez does not incorporate the human value premises of MBO in his management style for the following reasons:

1. Goal setting at Fresno Company is not a joint process. Chavez assumes that only he can establish organizational and individual goals. Subordinates apparently are not consulted.
2. Chavez has assumed that no errors have been made in assigning objectives.
3. Apparently no analysis was conducted to determine the cause for any lack of achievement.
4. It is likely that Chavez failed to use periodic review sessions to help subordinates find ways to meet their goals.

<u>10-54</u> (25-30 min.) For the solution, see the Prentice Hall Web site, www.prenhall.com/

<u>10-55</u> (40 min. or more)

The purpose of this exercise is to recognize that return on investment, a summary performance measure, is composed of two parts that may differ greatly by company and by industry. It also requires students to find publicly available information about a company, possibly using the Internet to do so.

Requirement 1 is an individual exercise in information gathering and analysis. Requirement 2 brings in the group aspect. By comparing results across companies, students should be able to see that some businesses generate returns on their investment through large margins (e.g., computer software companies), while some have high capital turnover (e.g. grocery stores). Strategies to improve ROI can emphasize either increasing margins or turnover.

If class time permits, reports from the groups would be worthwhile. In as little as 10 minutes of class time, students can see the variety in margins and turnover. They can also be reminded that the ultimate objective is return of investment, so focus on either margins or turnover without at least maintaining the other is not productive.

<u>10-56</u> (40-50 min.)

NOTE TO INSTRUCTOR. This solution is based on the web site as it was in early 2004. Be sure to examine the current web site before assigning this problem, as the information there may have changed.

1. The main focus is on being able to make a reservation or locating a Marriott hotel in a particular city and state (or even country). The site is a promotional tool as well as the portal to information about Marriott. The highlighted promotion on the home page will change often; at this writing it was about earning a free weekend with Marriott Rewards.

2. The home page has links to each of Marriott's brands. Each appears to operate at least somewhat independently. They are good candidates for treatment as investment centers. Why? Each segment probably has some control over its investment decisions. If not investment centers, the segments are likely to be profit centers.

3. For 2002, the firm reported information on five segments, four of which are in the "lodging" subcategory. The lodging segments are full-service, select-service, extended-stay, and timeshare. The nonlodging segment is synthetic fuel. Information was reported on sales, profit, depreciation and amortization, assets, goodwill, and capital expenditures for each segment.

4. Using average balances for assets, the ROI calculations are:

Segment	2002	2001
Full-service	$397 ÷ $3,408.5 = 11.6%	$294 ÷ 3,423.5 = 8.6%
Select-service	$130 ÷ $851 = 15.3%	$145 ÷ $963 = 15.1%
Extended-stay	$(3) ÷ $320 = (0.9)%	$55 ÷ $382.5 = 14.4%
Timeshare	$183 ÷ $2,167 = 8.4%	$147 ÷ $1,871.5 = 7.9%
Synthetic fuel	$(134) ÷ $54 = (248)%	N/A (new in 2002)

5. Using average balances for assets, the ROI for the corporation was $573 ÷ $8,701.5 = 6.6% in 2002 and $641 ÷ $8,672 = 7.4% in 2001. In determining whether or not to use this return as a measure of how well a segment performed depends on several factors, for example: Does each of the segments have autonomy to operate independent of central management? Do segment managers have control over sales and investments? The answers to these questions help determine the appropriate type of responsibility center to use as well as the performance measures.

6. Marriott primarily provides lodging services. If one segment provides lodging to employees of another segment, transfer prices are necessary. This is unlikely to comprise a large percentage of the business of any of the segments. Nevertheless, the company may have a policy such as charging a low transfer price if a hotel has excess capacity but charging the rack rate if a particular hotel is full.

Marriott may also transfer services (cleaning, repairing, etc.) between different brands of hotels. Fore example, Marriott may have full-service hotels and extended-stay hotels in the same area that use services available from one another. They may also transfer furniture between hotels. The transfer prices for these exchanges would likely fall between variable cost and market values.

CHAPTER 11
COVERAGE OF LEARNING OBJECTIVES

LEARNING OBJECTIVE	FUNDA-MENTAL ASSIGN-MENT MATERIAL	CRITICAL THINKING EXERCISES AND EXERCISES	PROBLEMS	CASES, EXCEL, COLLAB., & INTERNET EXERCISES
LO1: Describe capital budgeting decisions and use the net present value (NPV) method to make such decisions.	A1, A2, B1 B2	26, 29, 30 31, 32, 33 34, 35, 36 37, 38, 39	48, 49, 50 51, 28, 53 59, 61	65, 66, 67 68
LO2: Evaluate projects using sensitivity analysis.	.	38, 39	64, 68	
LO3: Calculate the NPV difference between two projects using both the total project and differential approaches.			48, 49	
LO4: Identify relevant cash flows for NPV analyses.		25, 27	48, 49, 50 51, 52, 53 54, 57, 58	64, 65, 66 67
LO5: Compute the after-tax net present values of projects.	A3, A4, B1 B2	40, 41, 42 43	54, 55, 56 57, 61, 62	67
LO6: Explain the after-tax effect of cash of disposing of assets.	A5, B5	28	55, 56	67
LO7: Use the payback model and the accounting rate-of-return model and compare them with the NPV model.		38, 44, 45	58, 59	
LO8: Reconcile the conflict between using an NPV model for making a decision and using accounting income for evaluating the related performance.			60	
LO9: Compute the impact of inflation on a capital-budgeting project.		46, 47	62, 63	

CHAPTER 11
Capital Budgeting

11-A1 (15-25 min.) Answers are printed in the text at the end of the assignment material.

11-A2 (20-30 min.) This is a straightforward exercise.

1 & 2. The model indicates that the computers should be acquired because the net present value is positive.

	14% Discount Factor	Total PV @ 14%	Sketch of Cash Flows (in thousands) 0	1	2	3
Cash effects of operations, $150,000	2.3216	$348,240		150	150	150
Investment		(325,000)	(325)			
Net present value		$ 23,240				

<u>11-A3</u> (20-30 min.) This is a straightforward exercise.

1. The model indicates that the computers should not be acquired.

	12% Discount Factor	Total PV @ 12%	Sketch of Cash Flows (in thousands)			
			0	1	2	3
Cash effects of operations, $300,000(1-.40)	2.4018	$432,324		180	180	180
Cash effect of depreciation, savings of income taxes:						
$220,000 x .40 = $88,000	2.4018	211,358		88	88	88
Total after-tax effect on cash		643,682				
Investment		(660,000)	(660)			
Net present value		$ (16,318)				

2. The computers should be acquired. The net present value rises, and now it is positive:

    After-tax impact of disposal on cash: .60($90,000 - 0) = $54,000
      PV is $54,000 x .7118 = $38,437
    Net present value as above   (16,318)
    New net present value $22,119

3. This requirement demonstrates that the choice of a discount rate often is critical to a decision.

    Applying an 8% discount factor:
      $300,000(1 - .40) x 2.5771 = $463,878
      $220,000 x .40 x 2.5771 =   226,785
                                  $690,663
    Investment   (660,000)
    NPV is positive, so acquire $ 30,663

11-A4 (25-30 min.)

1. Cash effects of operations:

Before tax annual cash inflow	$ 360,000
Taxes @ 40%: 360,000 x .4	144,000
After-tax cash inflow	$ 216,000
Present value @ 16%: $216,000 x 4.8332	$1,043,971

Cash effects of depreciation*:

Year	Tax Savings**	PV factor	Present Value
1	.1429 x $1,500,000 x .4 = $ 85,740	.8621	$73,916
2	.2449 x 1,500,000 x .4 = 146,940	.7432	109,206
3	.1749 x 1,500,000 x .4 = 104,940	.6407	67,235
4	.1249 x 1,500,000 x .4 = 74,940	.5523	41,389
5	.0893 x 1,500,000 x .4 = 53,580	.4761	25,509
6	.0892 x 1,500,000 x .4 = 53,520	.4104	21,965
7	.0893 x 1,500,000 x .4 = 53,580	.3538	18,957
8	.0446 x 1,500,000 x .4 = 26,760	.3050	8,162
Total present value			$366,339

*Short-cut using Exhibit 11-7: .6106 x .40 x $1,500,000 = $366,360, which differs from the $366,339 computed above only because of a rounding error.

**Factors .1429, .2449, etc. are from Exhibit 11-6.

Summary:

Present value of cash effects of operations	$1,043,971
Present value of cash effects of depreciation	366,339
Total after-tax effect on cash	$1,410,310
Investment	(1,500,000)
Net present value is negative, so don't acquire	$ (89,690)

2.   The 7-year MACRS analysis will apply regardless of the economic life
      of the equipment. The only change from requirement 1 will be the
      added five years of cash effects from operations:

      PV of $216,000 per year for 5 years at 16%
        = 3.2743 x $216,000 = $707,249
      To account for the delay of 10 years before
        savings begin: $707,249 x .2267 $160,333*
      NPV as above   (89,690)
      NPV is positive, so acquire. $ 70,643

*Or, $216,000(5.5755 - 4.8332) = $216,000 x .7423 = $160,337, which differs
  from $160,333 only because of a rounding error.

11-A5 (5-10 min.)

      Many students forget to add the cash proceeds to the tax effect.
Answers are in dollars.

(a) Cash proceeds	65,000	30,000
Book value	50,000	50,000
Gain (loss)	15,000	(20,000)

Effect on income taxes at 30%:
      (b) Tax saving (inflow effect)   6,000
      (c) Tax paid (outflow effect) (4,500)

Total after-tax effect on cash
      (a) plus (b)   36,000
      (a) minus (c)   60,500

11-B1 (15-20 min.)

1. Using the right table is essential. Factors for this part are from Table 1:
   (a) PV = $12,000 x .8890 = $10,668.00
   (b) PV = $12,000 x .7513 = $9,015.60
   (c) PV = $12,000 x .6407 = $7,688.40

2. Use Table 2: (a) PV = $15,000 x 4.4518 = $66,777.00
   (b) PV = $15,000 x 3.7908 = $56,862.00
   (c) PV = $15,000 x 3.2743 = $49,114.50

3. Use Table 2: (a)   PV = annual withdrawal x F
   $400,000 = annual withdrawal x 7.7217
   Annual withdrawal = $400,000 ÷ 7.7217 = $51,802.06

   (b)   PV = annual withdrawal x F
   $400,000 = annual withdrawal x 6.1446
   Annual withdrawal = $400,000 ÷ 6.1446 = $65,097.81

4. Contract B has the higher present value:

Year	Present Value @14% From Table 1	Present Value of Contract A	Present Value of Contract B
1	.8772	$175,440	$394,740
2	.7695	230,850	269,325
3	.6750	270,000	202,500
4	.5921	296,050	118,420
Total		$972,340	$984,985

<u>11-B2</u> (20-30 min.) This is a straightforward exercise.

1 & 2. The model indicates that the equipment should be acquired because the net present value is positive.

	14% Discount Factor	Total PV @ 14%	Sketch of Cash Flows (in thousands) 0 1 2 3 4 5
Cash effects of operations, $140,000	3.4331	$ 480,634	140 140 140 140 140
Investment		(400,000)	(400)
Net present value		$ 80,634	

<u>11-B3</u> (20-30 min.) This is a straightforward exercise.

1. The model indicates that the equipment should not be acquired.

	14% Discount Factor	Total PV @ 14%	Sketch of Cash Flows (in thousands) 0 1 2 3 4 5
Cash effects of operations, $140,000(1-.40)	3.4331	$ 288,380	84 84 84 84 84
Cash effect of depreciation, savings of income taxes*:	3.4331	109,859	32 32 32 32 32
Total after-tax effect on cash		$ 398,239	
Investment		(400,000)	(400)
Net present value		$ (1,761)	

*Depreciation is $400,000 ÷ 5 = $80,000 per year;
annual tax savings is $80,000 x .40 = $32,000.

2. The equipment should be acquired. The net present value is positive.

After-tax impact of disposal on cash:
.60($25,000 - 0) = $15,000
PV is $15,000 x .5194 = $ 7,791
Net present value as above   (1,761)
New net present value $ 6,030

3. Applying 10% discount factors:
$140,000(1 - .40)(3.7908) = $ 318,427
$80,000(.40)(3.7908) =   121,306
                                                                  $ 439,733
Investment   (400,000)
NPV is positive, so acquire. $ 39,733

11-B4 (25-30 min.)

1. See Exhibit 11-B4 on the following page for requirement 1.

2. The major reason for this requirement is to underscore the fact that the present value of the depreciation tax savings is unchanged regardless of the length of the economic life of the asset.

PV of the $52,650 to be received in the 6th year,
$52,650 x .4104 factor = $21,608
NPV as above   (18,513)
NPV is positive, so acquire. $ 3,095

EXHIBIT 11-B4

1.

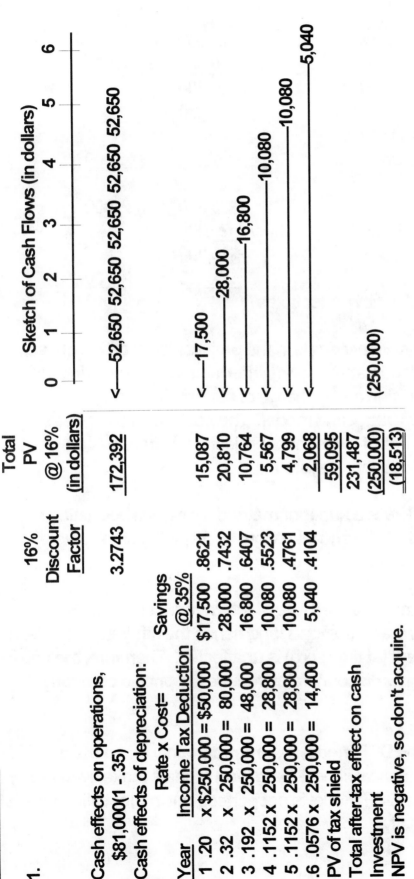

Sketch of Cash Flows (in dollars)

	0	1	2	3	4	5	6
		52,650	52,650	52,650	52,650	52,650	

	17,500
	28,000
	16,800
	10,080
	10,080
	5,040

(250,000)

		16%	Total PV @ 16% (in dollars)
		Discount Factor	
Cash effects on operations, $81,000(1 - .35)		3.2743	172,392

Cash effects of depreciation:

Year		Rate x Cost= Income Tax Deduction	Savings @ 35%			Total PV @ 16% (in dollars)
1	.20 x $250,000 =	$50,000	$17,500	.8621		15,087
2	.32 x 250,000 =	80,000	28,000	.7432		20,810
3	.192 x 250,000 =	48,000	16,800	.6407		10,764
4	.1152 x 250,000 =	28,800	10,080	.5523		5,567
5	.1152 x 250,000 =	28,800	10,080	.4761		4,799
6	.0576 x 250,000 =	14,400	5,040	.4104		2,068

PV of tax shield						59,095
Total after-tax effect on cash						231,487
Investment						(250,000)
						(18,513)

NPV is negative, so don't acquire.

Note: The cash effects of MACRS depreciation can be computed more easily using Exhibit 11-7. Present value of tax savings = Original cost x Tax rate x Factor from 11-7 = $250,000 x .35 x .6753 = $59,089. This differs slightly from the $59,095 calculated above because of rounding error.

<u>11-B5</u> (5-10 min.)

1.	Book value	$20,000	
	Sale price	10,000	$ 10,000
	Net loss	$10,000	
	Tax savings	x .30	3,000
	Net immediate cash inflow, including tax savings		$13,000

2.	Sales price	$35,000	$35,000
	Book value	20,000	
	Net gain	$15,000	
	Income tax	x .30	(4,500)
	Net immediate cash inflow, after taxes		$30,500

<u>11-1</u>   The accountant has a limited role in the project identification phase. In the selection phase, accountants provide information for predicting cash inflows and outflows and often are in charge of summarizing the information using a capital budgeting model. The postaudit phase uses information about the results of investment projects; this information usually comes from the accounting system.

<u>11-2</u>   Discounted cash flow is a superior method for capital budgeting because it measures profitability and takes into account the time value of money.

<u>11-3</u>   No. A higher minimum desired rate of return reduces the present value of future cash inflows and outflows, and hence the difference between them. The initial investment (at time zero) is unaffected. Therefore, the net present value is less. Higher discount rates reduce the price a company should be willing to pay.

<u>11-4</u>   No. It is true that the DCF model assumes certainty and perfect capital markets. But all practical capital budgeting models make even more limiting assumptions. The DCF model is not perfect, but in most situations it is the best practical alternative.

11-5 Yes, double counting does occur if depreciation expense is considered separately. The cost of an investment is represented by its cash outflow at year zero. An additional consideration of depreciation would be double counting. Note, however, that the tax savings from depreciation is considered separately.

11-6 No. The IRR and NPV models generally make the same decision. Suppose we compute the NPV of a project using the cost of capital as the discount rate. If its NPV is greater than zero, then its IRR is generally greater than the cost of capital.

11-7 The real options model recognizes the value in allowing investment in stages – that is, contingent investments. If the investment can be adjusted after gaining the information from the early stages, we can make better decisions about late-stage investments. Projects that allow this ability to make adjustments are often better than similar investments that require the entire investment up front.

11-8 Sensitivity analysis is especially appropriate for organizations that do not have accurate cash flow predictions. Sensitivity analysis can help a manager decide whether it is worth gathering information to improve cash flow predictions.

11-9 The differential approach should lead to the same choice between alternatives as the total approach because it merely disregards the factors that are constant for each alternative: those that make no difference.

11-10 The NPV model is appropriate for all types of investments. However, with some types of investments, such as those in advanced technology, NPV must be carefully applied. Many qualitative effects should be either quantified as best as possible and included in the model, or they should be considered as subjective factors in addition to the NPV analysis.

11-11 The marginal tax rate is the rate paid on *additional* amounts of pretax income. In contrast, the average tax rate is the total taxes paid divided by the total pretax income.

11-12 No. Two sets of books are appropriate. The objectives of tax reporting and shareholder reporting differ; therefore, the rules for reporting to each differ. If tax rules were used for financial reporting, users of the statements would not receive the information they judge to be most useful. Likewise, if tax authorities accepted financial reporting rules, certain social goals sought by the taxation system would not be met.

11-13 Tax avoidance is the achieving of a reduction in income tax payments through legal means; tax-evasion achieves the same end through illegal means. Tax avoidance is considered moral; tax evasion, immoral. Tax avoidance uses the rules of the system (tax laws) in an optimum way; tax evasion disregards the rules.

11-14 No. Companies have an obligation to shareholders to avoid taxes where it is legal to do so. Tax evasion is clearly unethical as well as illegal.

11-15 Accelerated rather than straight-line depreciation is to be preferred for tax purposes because it provides a bigger present value of tax savings by reducing taxable income more during the earlier years of an asset's life. Because of the time value of money, immediate tax savings are more valuable than tax savings in the future.

11-16 Yes. Two streams may be identified: (a) inflows from operations and (b) savings of income tax outflows (which are often regarded in capital budgeting as additions to inflows).

11-17 Because of the time value of money, the earlier a company takes tax deductions and thereby saves taxes, the larger the present value of the tax savings.

11-18 Yes. MACRS treats assets as if they were purchased at midyear, so they have depreciation effects for one tax year more than the number of years of their depreciable lives. For example, if a company purchases a three-year MACRS asset during 2004 and pays taxes on a calendar year basis, its depreciation begins July 1, 2004, and extends through June 30, 2007, affecting taxes in 4 years (2004 through 2007).

11-19 No. Depreciation is never a cash outlay. The depreciation amount is used to predict the income tax cash effect, but depreciation itself is not a cash effect.

11-20 It is useful to learn the "payback" and "accounting rate-of-return" methods of capital budgeting because they are widely used today. In addition, the payback method may give a rough indication of riskiness, and the accounting rate of return shows a project's effect on an accrual accounting income statement. The comparative advantage of discounted cash flow can also be seen by contrast. Surveys show that most companies use more than one method to evaluate capital budgeting projects, so it is likely that you will need to understand more than DCF models.

11-21 The basic flaw in the payback method is that it does not compare the total profitability of alternative projects. It simply measures the rate of recoupment of the initial investment.

11-22 If a company makes capital-budgeting decisions using DCF and performance evaluations using accrual accounting numbers, a conflict may arise. Often accrual accounting can show low profits in the early years of a project's life because of high depreciation, write-offs of old equipment that is being replaced, or slow growth in revenues as the company penetrates new markets. Such low accrual accounting profits might discourage managers from making investments that have a positive net present value.

11-23 The three components of the market or nominal interest rate are: 1) risk-free element, or pure rate of interest, 2) business-risk element, and 3) inflation element.

11-24 The correct analysis under inflation (a) uses a required rate that includes an element attributable to inflation and (b) explicitly adjusts the predicted operating cash flows for the effects of inflation.

11-25 It is difficult to predict the cash flows to be received from an investment in research and development (R&D) because there is so much uncertainty involved. The manager's assertion that this is impossible is not uncommon. However, even investments in R&D must, on average, return more than the cost of capital if they are to be desirable investments. Therefore, it is usually worth the effort to predict, as well as possible given the uncertainties, the possible outcomes of R&D activities and their effect on the company's cash flows. From that, a net present value can be computed.

11-26 The net present value of an investment project represents the increase (or decrease) in the value of the firm from investing in the project, provided the cash flows and cost of capital are estimated correctly. Thus, implementing a positive net present value project will increase the company's value, while implementing a negative net present value project will decrease it.

11-27 The direct cash flows are the easiest to predict. These would include the investment in the new machine (less any salvage value of the old machine), the savings in labor and other variable operating costs because of the decreased production time per unit, and the estimated salvage value of the new machine at the end of its economic life. Those more difficult to measure are revenue from increased sales because of higher quality or more timely delivery schedules, cost savings from reworking defective units because of the more accurate standards of the new machine, and decreased storage costs because the faster production process allows quicker adaptation to changes in demand and thus less need for large inventories.

<u>11-28</u> The first situation is reasonably clear. There is no legal or ethical reason not to take the depreciation allowed by the tax law. The second is much more problematic. Investing offshore is generally not illegal, although its ethics might be questionable. If the offshore investment is really a sham to avoid (or evade) taxes while the company still takes advantage of the business climate provided in the U. S. for most of its business, it is not contributing to society as much as it is taking from it. But even more questionable is the use of transfer prices to move profits into a tax haven. Again, there may be no technical illegality (although there are laws relating to transfer prices that might be violated), artificially transferring profits from the society in which the company really earns them to a tax haven where the company is located only for the tax purposes is certainly of dubious ethics.

<u>11-29</u> (10-15 min.)

1. The present value is $200,000 and the annual payments are an annuity, requiring use of Table 2:
    (a) $200,000 = annual payment x 11.2578
    annual payment = $200,000 ÷ 11.2578 = $17,765
    (b) $200,000 = annual payment x 9.4269
    annual payment = $200,000 ÷ 9.4269 = $21,216
    (c) $200,000 = annual payment x 8.0552
    annual payment = $200,000 ÷ 8.0552 =$24,829

2. (a) $200,000 = annual payment x 8.5595
    annual payment = $200,000 ÷ 8.5595 = $23,366
    (b) $200,000 = annual payment x 7.6061
    annual payment = $200,000 ÷ 7.6061 = $26,295
    (c) $200,000 = annual payment x 6.8109
    annual payment = $200,000 ÷ 6.8109 =$29,365

3. (a) Total payments = 30 x $21,216 = $636,480
    Total interest paid = $636,480 - $200,000 = $436,480
    (b) Total payments = 15 x $26,295 = $394,425
    Total interest paid = $394,425 - $200,000 = $194,425

<u>11-30</u> (10 min.)   The initial step on solving present value problems focuses on a basic question: Which table should I use? No computations should be made until you are convinced that you are using the correct table.

1.   Use Table 1, row 4, 12% column. Citibank will lend $381,300,000. The $600 million is a future amount. Its present value is:

PV = $600,000,000 x .6355 = $381,300,000

2.   Use Table 2, row 4, 12% column. Citibank will lend $455,595,000. The $150 million is a uniform periodic payment at the end of a series of years. Therefore, it is an annuity. Its present value is:

PV_A = $150,000,000 x 3.0373 = $455,595,000

In particular, note that Citibank is willing to lend more than in requirement 1 even though the interest rate is the same. Why? Because the bank will get its money back more quickly.

<u>11-31</u> (10-20 min.)

1.   a. PV = $800,000(.6355) = $508,400
        b. PV = $800,000(.5523) = $441,840

2.   The annual rates would be halved and the periods doubled.
        Present values decline:

        a. PV = $800,000(.6274) = $501,920
        b. PV = $800,000(.5403) = $432,240

3.   Present values rise because the money is repaid more quickly:

        a. PV = $200,000(3.0373) = $607,460
        b. PV = $200,000(2.7982) = $559,640

<u>11-32</u> (10-15 min.)

1. $150,000 = Future amount x .3506

        Future amount = $150,000 ÷ .3506
                       = $427,838

2. $150,000 = Future annual amount x 4.6389

        Future annual amount = $150,000 ÷ 4.6389
                             = $32,335

<u>11-33</u> (10 min.)

The deferral cost Duncan $811,200 in present value, computed as follows:

Present value of $4,000,000 in 2 years	$3,188,800
Present value of $4,000,000 today	4,000,000
Sacrifice in present value	$ 811,200

A more detailed analysis follows:

Year	Present Value @ 12% from Table 1	Present Value of Original Contract	Present Value of Revised Contract
20X5	1.0000	$12,000,000	$ 8,000,000
20X6	.8929	12,500,600	12,500,600
20X7	.7972	12,755,200	15,944,000
Total		$37,255,800	$36,444,600

Difference ($37,255,800 - $36,444,600) = $811,200

<u>11-34</u> (20-25 min.) This basic exercise develops comfort with the tables and the NPV method.

	8	18	20	28
Number of years				
Amount of annual cash inflow	$10,000	$13,749[b]	$ 9,000	$ 8,000
Required initial investment	$40,776[a]	$80,000	$65,000	$30,000
Minimum desired rate of return	14%	20%	12%[c]	25%
Net present value	$ 5,613	($13,835)	$2,225	$ 1,938[d]

[a] (4.6389 x $10,000) - $5,613 = $46,389 - $5,613 = $40,776

[b] (4.8122 x CF) - $80,000 = ($13,835); CF = ($80,000 - $13,835) ÷ 4.8122 = $13,749

[c] (F x $9,000) - $65,000 = 2,225; F = $67,225 ÷ $9,000 = 7.4694
On the 20 year row, the factor 7.4694 is a 12% rate

[d] PV Factor for 25% on 28-year row is 3.9923
$8,000 x 3.9923 = $31,938
NPV = $31,938 - $30,000 = $1,938

<u>11-35</u> (10 min.)

Buy. The net present value is positive.

Initial outlay *	$(25,000)
Present value of cash operating savings, from 12-year, 12% column of Table 2, 6.1944 x $5,000	30,972
Net present value	$ 5,972

* The trade-in allowance really consists of a $5,000 adjustment of the selling price and a bona fide $10,000 cash allowance for the old equipment. The relevant amount is the incremental cash outlay, $25,000. The book value is irrelevant.

<u>11-36</u> (10-15 min.)

1. The quickest solution is to "net" the flows for each year:

    1. $200,000 - $150,000 = $ 50,000 ⎤
    2. 250,000 - 200,000 =   50,000 ⎬ an annuity of 3 payments (a)
    3. 300,000 - 250,000 =   50,000 ⎦
    4. 400,000 - 300,000 =   100,000 ⎤ an annuity of 2 payments
    5. 450,000 - 350,000 =   100,000 ⎦ deferred three years (b)

(a) $50,000 x 2.3216	$116,080
(b) $100,000 x 1.6467 x .6750	111,152
Total	$227,232
Less initial investment	215,000
Net Present Value (NPV)	$ 12,232

    Various other approaches would reach the same answer, but they would involve more computations.

2. The NPV is positive because at a 12% rate, the present value of the net inflows will be higher than at 14%, so NPV will increase.

<u>11-37</u> (10-15 min.)

1.   NPV @ 10% = 10,000 x 3.7908 = $37,908 - $36,048 = $1,860
        NPV @ 12% = 10,000 x 3.6048 = $36,048 - $36,048 = $0
        NPV @ 14% = 10,000 x 3.4331 = $34,331 - $36,048 = $(1,717)

2.   The IRR is the interest rate at which NPV = $0; therefore, from
        requirement 1 we know that IRR = 12%.

3.   The NPV at the company's cost of capital, 10%, is positive, so the
        project should be accepted.

4.   The IRR (12%) is greater than the company's cost of capital (10%), so
the project should be accepted. Note that the IRR and NPV models give the
same decision.

<u>11-38</u> (30-45 min.)

This problem deals essentially with sensitivity analysis, which asks how the basic forecasted results will be affected by changes in the critical factors (useful life, cash flows) that influence rate of return.

1. $\$25,000 \div \$5,000 = 5$ years

2.   NPV= ($\$5,000$ x 6.8137) - $\$25,000$ = $\$9,069$

3.   a) NPV = ($\$5,000$ x 3.7908) - $\$25,000$ = ($\$6,046$)
       b) NPV = ($\$5,000$ x 8.5136) - $\$25,000$ = $\$17,568$

4.   NPV = ($\$3,500$ x 6.8137) - $\$25,000$ = ($\$1,152$)

5.   NPV = ($\$4,000$ x 5.3349) - $\$25,000$ = ($\$3,660$)

<u>11-39</u> (15-20 min.)

1.   NPV = ($\$15,000$ x 3.7908) - $\$52,000$ = $\$56,862$ - $\$52,000$ = $\$4,862$

2.   (a) NPV = ($\$15,000$ x 3.1699) - $\$52,000$ = $\$47,549$ - $\$52,000$ = $\$(4,451)$
       (b) NPV = ($\$15,000$ x 4.8684) - $\$52,000$ = $\$73,026$ - $\$52,000$ = $\$21,026$

3.   (a) NPV = ($\$12,000$ x 3.7908) - $\$52,000$ = $\$45,490$ - $\$52,000$ = $\$(6,510)$
       (b) NPV = ($\$18,000$ x 3.7908) - $\$52,000$ = $\$68,234$ - $\$52,000$ = $\$16,234$

4.   (a) NPV = ($\$18,000$ x 4.8684) - $\$52,000$ = $\$87,631$ - $\$52,000$ = $\$35,631$
       (b) NPV = ($\$12,000$ x 3.1699) - $\$52,000$ = $\$38,039$ - $\$52,000$ = $\$(13,961)$

5.   (Savings x 3.7908) - $\$52,000$ = 0
                          Savings = $\$52,000 \div 3.7908$
                          Savings = $\$13,717$

11-40 (5-10 min.) In thousands of dollars.

(S)	Sales	<u>530</u>
(E)	Expenses excluding depreciation	350
(D)	Depreciation	<u>100</u>
	Total expenses	<u>450</u>
	Income before income taxes	80
(T)	Income taxes at 40%	<u>32</u>
(I)	Net income	<u><u>48</u></u>

Cash effects of operations:

(S - E)	Cash inflow from operations, 530 - 350 =	180
	Income tax outflow at 40%	<u>72</u>
	After-tax inflow from operations	108

Effect of depreciation:

(D)	Depreciation, $100	
	Income tax savings at 40%	<u>40</u>
	Total after-tax effect on cash	<u><u>148</u></u>

Total after-tax effect on cash is
either S - E - T = 530 - 350 - 32 = 148 or I + D = 48 + 100 = 148

11-41 (5-10 min.)

Cash effects of operations:

Cash inflow from operations: $1,200,000 - $600,000	$600,000
Income tax outflow @ 35%	210,000
After-tax inflow from operations (excluding depreciation)	$390,000

Effects of depreciation:

Depreciation, $400,000	
Income tax savings @ 35%	140,000
Total after-tax effect on cash	$530,000

11-42 (10 min.)

The month and day on which an asset is acquired does not affect its tax depreciation. The half-year convention is applied to all assets.

	2004	2005
1. 3-year property: 33.33% and 44.45% of $30,000	$9,999	$13,335
2. 5-year property: 20% and 32% of $7,000	1,400	2,240
3. 5-year property: 20% and 32% of $5,000	1,000	1,600
4. 7-year property: 14.29% and 24.49% of $4,000	572	980

11-43 (10 min.)

This problem could be solved by specifying appropriate schedules of tax savings and computing the present values. However, the process would be extremely time-consuming. The steps outlined in the chapter make the computations quite simple.

(a)	$240,000 x .35 x .8044 =	$ 67,570
(b)	$560,000 x .40 x .7733 =	$173,219
(c)	$ 55,000 x .50 x .6106 =	$ 16,792
(d)	$910,000 x .35 x .7059 =	$224,829
(e)	$400,000 x .25 x .5492 =	$ 54,920

593

11-44 (10-15 min.)

Annual addition to profit = 40% x $25,000 = $10,000.

1. Payback period is $30,000 ÷ $10,000 = 3 years. It is not a good measure of profitability because it ignores returns beyond the payback period and it does not account for the time value of money.

2. NPV = $11,114. Accept the proposal because the NPV is positive.
   Computation: NPV = ($10,000 x 4.1114) - $30,000
   = $41,114 - $30,000 = $11,114

3. $$ARR = \frac{\text{increase in average cash flow - increase in depreciation}}{\text{initial investment}}$$

   =($10,000 - $5,000) ÷ $30,000 = 16.7%

11-45 (15 min.)

1. $12,000 ÷ $3,000 = 4 years

2. $3,000 x 5.7466 = $17,240. The company should buy because the net present value is a positive $17,240 - $12,000 = $5,240.

3. $$ARR = \frac{\$3,000 - (\$12,000 \div 8 \text{ years})}{\$12,000} = \frac{\$1,500}{\$12,000} = 12.5\%$$

<u>11-46</u> (30 min.)

1 & 2. See Exhibit 11-46 on the following page for requirements 1 and 2.

The footnotes for the exhibit follow:

[a] Be sure to use a nominal discount rate, which includes an element attributable to inflation, and adjust the predicted cash flows for inflationary effects. Each year is adjusted for anticipated inflation: $68,750 x 1.04, $68,750 x 1.04^2, $68,750 x 1.04^3, etc.

[b] The annual savings in income taxes will be unaffected by inflation. Why? Because the income-tax deduction must be based on original cost of the asset in year 0 dollars. Amounts are 45% of (.20 x $300,000), (.32 x $300,000), (.192 x $300,000), (.1152 x $300,000), (.1152 x $300,000), and (.0576 x $300,000).

[c] Shortcut using Exhibit 11-7: .6211 x .45 x $300,000 = $83,849, which differs from the $83,852 calculated above only because of rounding error.

[d] A common error is to adjust the discount rate as above but *not* adjust the predicted cash inflows.

3. The method of Requirement 1 is correct. The required rate of return includes an inflation element, and the cash inflows are adjusted for inflation. In Requirement 2 the required rate of return includes an inflation element, but the cash inflows are not adjusted for inflation. This understates the cash flows, so the net present value is understated. The incorrect method would lead to underinvestment, because desirable investments would be rejected.

EXHIBIT 11-46

Sketch of Relevant Cash Flows
(in dollars)

Timeline: 0   1   2   3   4   5   6

		At 20 Percent	
		P.V. Factor	Present Value
1. Correct Analysis			
Cash operating inflows:[a]			
Pretax inflow in year-0 dollars	$125,000		
Tax effect at 45%	56,250		
After-tax effect	$ 68,750		
	(71,500)	.8333	$ 59,581
	(74,360)	.6944	51,636
	(77,334)	.5787	44,753
	(80,428)	.4823	38,790
	(83,645)	.4019	33,617
Subtotal			$228,377
Cash effect of depreciation:[b]			
Savings in income taxes	(27,000)	.8333	22,499
	(43,200)	.6944	29,998
	(25,920)	.5787	15,000
	(15,552)	.4823	7,501
	(15,552)	.4019	6,250
	(7,776)	.3349	2,604
			83,852[c]
Investment in equipment	(300,000)	1.0000	(300,000)
Net present value			$ 12,229
2. Incorrect Analysis			
Cash operating inflows after taxes[d]	68,750 (yrs 1–5)	2.9906	$205,604
Tax effect of depreciation (same as above)			83,852
Investment in equipment	(300,000)	1.0000	(300,000)
Net present value			$ (10,544)

See footnotes on the previous page.

<u>11-47</u> (30-40 min.) Answers are in Mexican pesos.

1.   After-tax cash operating savings,
      .6 x 160,000 = 96,000
      PV of cash operating savings, 96,000 x 3.1272   300,211
      Income tax savings from depreciation
      .4 x (420,000 ÷ 5) = .4 x 84,000 = 33,600
      PV = 33,600 x 3.1272   105,074
      PV of total savings   405,285
      Required outlay at time zero   (420,000)
      Net present value   (14,715)

      Note how income taxes have a two-edged effect. They chop the
      present value of the cash operating savings by 40%, but the
      depreciation deduction provides income tax savings.

2.   See Exhibit 11-47 on the following page for requirement 2.

3.   The analysis in Requirement 2 is correct. The cash flows and the
      required rate of return incorporate the 10% rate of inflation. In
      Requirement 1, the 18% required rate of return includes an inflation
      element, but the predicted cash flows ignore inflationary effects.

EXHIBIT 11-47

All numbers are expressed in Mexican pesos.

2.

	18% PV Factor	Total Present Value
Cash operating savings:*	.8475	89,496
	.7182	83,426
	.6086	77,764
	.5158	72,498
	.4371	67,580
Total		390,764
Income tax savings from depreciation *not* changed by inflation, see 1	3.1272	105,074
Total		495,838
Required outlay at time zero	1.0000	(420,000)
Net present value		75,838

Sketch of Relevant Cash Flows
(in thousands)

0	1	2	3	4	5
	105,600	116,160	127,776	140,554	154,609
	33,600	33,600	33,600	33,600	33,600
(420,000)					

*Amounts are computed by multiplying (160 x .6) = 96,000 by 1.10, 1.10^2, 1.10^3, etc.

598

11-48 (30-35 min.)

1.   <u>Annual Operating Cash Flows</u>

	Ricoh	Kodak	Difference
Salaries	$49,920(a)	$41,600(b)	$ 8,320
Overtime	1,728(c)	–	1,728
Repairs and maintenance	1,800	1,050	750
Toner, supplies, etc.	3,600	3,300	300
Total annual cash outflows	$57,048	$45,950	$11,098

(a) ($ 8 x 40 hrs.) x 52 weeks x 3 employees = $320 x 52 x 3 = $49,920

(b) ($10 x 40 hrs.) x 52 weeks x 2 employees = $400 x 52 x 2 = $41,600

(c) ($12 x 4 hrs.) x 12 months x 3 machines = $ 48 x 12 x 3 = $ 1,728

<u>Initial Cash Flows</u>

	Ricoh	Kodak	Difference
Purchase of Kodak machines	$ –	$54,000	$54,000
Sale of Ricoh machines	–	-3,000	-3,000
Training and remodeling	–	4,000	4,000
Total	$ –	$55,000	$55,000

	PV of $1.00 Discounted at 12%	Present Value of Cash Flows 0	Annual Cash Flows 1	2	3	4	5
TOTAL PROJECT APPROACH:							
Kodak:							
Initial cash outflow	1.0000	$(55,000)					
Operating cash flows	3.6048	(165,641)	(45,950)	(45,950)	(45,950)	(45,950)	(45,950)
Total		$(220,641)					
Ricoh:							
Operating cash flows	3.6048	$(205,647)	(57,048)	(57,048)	(57,048)	(57,048)	(57,048)
Difference in favor of retaining Ricoh		$(14,994)					
INCREMENTAL APPROACH:							
Initial investment	1.0000	$(55,000)					
Annual operating cash savings	3.6048	40,006	11,098	11,098	11,098	11,098	11,098
Net present value of purchase		$(14,994)					

2. The Ricoh machines should not be replaced by the Kodak equipment.

Net savings = (Present value of expenditures to retain Ricoh machines) less (Present value of expenditures to convert to Kodak machines)

= $205,647 - $220,641 = $(14,994)

3. a. How flexible is the new machinery? Will it be useful only for the presently intended functions, or can it be easily adapted for other tasks that may arise over the next 5 years?
   b. What psychological effects will it have on various interested parties?

11-49 (40 min.)

Total project Analysis	At 10% for 7 Years		Sketch of Cash Flows (in thousands)							
	PV Factor	Present Value	0	1	2	3	4	5	6	7
Replace (A)										
Recurring cash maintenance cost	4.8684	$ (4,868)		(1.0)	(1.0)	(1.0)	(1.0)	(1.0)	(1.0)	(1.0)
Recurring cash operating cost savings*	4.8684	73,026		15.0	15.0	15.0	15.0	15.0	15.0	15.0
Disposal value of old machine	1.0000	5,000	5.0							
Initial investment	1.0000	(72,000)	(72.0)							
Overhaul, end of 4th yr.	0.6830	(4,781)					(7.0)			
Disposal value of new machine	0.5132	2,566								5.0
Present value of net cash outflows		$ (1,057)								
Keep (B)										
Recurring cash maintenance cost	4.8684	$ (5,842)		(1.2)	(1.2)	(1.2)	(1.2)	(1.2)	(1.2)	(1.2)
Overhaul at end of 6th yr. (Machine 5 yrs. old)	0.9091	(5,455)	(6.0)							
Present value of net cash outflows		$(11,297)								
Difference in favor of replacement		$ 10,240								

*Some students will challenge this item as not being a "real" saving,
because the laborer will merely be transferred to other work. However, this
solution assumes that the laborer will engage in some productive work
somewhere in the organization; therefore, the railroad will indeed be able to
avoid hiring other people for such productive work and will save the overall
organization $15,000, one-half of the laborer's annual compensation.

Differential Analysis	At 10% for 7 Years PV Factor	Present Value	Sketch of Cash Flows (in thousands) 0	1	2	3	4	5	6	7
Replace (A)										
Recurring cash maintenance savings	4.8684	$ 974		.2	.2	.2	.2	.2	.2	.2
Disposal value of old machine	1.0000	5,000	5.0							
Initial investment	1.0000	(72,000)	(72.0)							
Overhaul, end of 4th yr.	0.6830	(4,781)					(7.0)			
Disposal value of new machine	0.5132	2,566								5.0
Recurring cash operating savings	4.8684	73,026		15.0	15.0	15.0	15.0	15.0	15.0	15.0
Overhaul avoided at end of 6th year	0.9091	5,455		6.0						
Net present value of replacement		$ 10,240								

11-50 (30 min.)

The initial purchase cost of the golf course and the operating receipts and disbursements for the first season of ownership are irrelevant to the present decision. The relevant annual costs which Ms. Bogey should take into consideration are:

Electricity, (300 x 1 kw) x (130 x 5 hrs.) x $.08 per kw hr.	$15,600
Labor cost, 130 x $75	9,750
Light bulb cost	1,500
Repairs and maintenance of lighting system, .04 x $94,000	3,760
Property taxes, .017 x $94,000	1,598
Total additional operating expenses	$32,208

Annual revenue from night operations:

Years 1 and 2: 130 x $450	$58,500
Years 3, 4, and 5: 130 x $300	$39,000

One-time cash flows:

Present value of initial investment	$94,000
Salvage value, year 5	$35,000

Example of Cash Flow Analysis

	Revenue	Expenses		Net Flow	PV Factor	PV of Cash Flows
Year 1	$58,500	- $32,208	=	$26,292	.9091	$23,902
Year 2	58,500	- 32,208	=	26,292	.8264	21,728
Year 3	39,000	- 32,208	=	6,792	.7513	5,103
Year 4	39,000	- 32,208	=	6,792	.6830	4,639
Year 5	74,000	- 32,208	=	41,792	.6209	25,949
Present value of cash flows						$81,321

Since the present value of the annual cash flows is $12,679 less than the initial investment of $94,000, the proposed lighting system should not be installed. If significant increases in revenue were predictable, the plan might become attractive to Ms. Bogey.

11-51 (20-25 min.)

	PV Factor	Total Present Value	Sketch of Cash Flows (in thousands)					
			0	1	2	3	4	5
Old machine:								
Operating cash outflows	3.00	£(156,000)		(52)	(52)	(52)	(52)	(52)
Disposal value*	.40	1,600						4
Present value		£(154,400)						
New machine:								
Net cash outlay (£62,000– £15,000)	1.00	£ (47,000)	(47)					
Operating cash outflows	3.00	(120,000)		(40)	(40)	(40)	(40)	(40)
Disposal value*	.40	1,600						4
Present value		£(165,400)						
NPV in favor of old machine		£ 11,000						

*Could be excluded from both alternatives because they are the same amounts.

The old machine minimizes the present value of future costs by £11,000. Variations of the above analysis might exclude the £4,000 disposal values. The net quantitative difference between the alternatives should be the same no matter what approach is used, as long as such approach is used correctly.

<u>11-52</u> (30-35 min.) This is one of our favorite problems. The heart of the solution extends through the first paragraph of the response to requirement 2. The remainder is amplification.

	Analysis of Cash Flows		
	Present		Proposed	Difference
Revenue		$200,000	$15,000*	
Expenses:				
Miscellaneous	$100,000			
Salaries	110,000	210,000	13,000	
Net cash flow from operations		$ (10,000)	$ 2,000	$12,000
Required investment:				
Equipment		$ -	$19,000**	
Termination pay		-	32,000	
Total		$ -	$51,000	$51,000

*10% x $150,000 = $15,000 commission.
** An acceptable alternative would be to show $3,000 and $22,000, respectively. The incremental investment would still be $19,000.

1. Present value of $12,000 per year for
    10 years at 10% = $12,000 x 6.000 $72,000
    Required investment   51,000
    Net present value $21,000

The requirements of the problem focus on the incremental approach. The total project approach could view the problem as choosing the alternative that minimizes the net present value of the future costs:

Present:
  Operating cash outflows, $10,000 x 6.000 $(60,000)
Proposed:
  Operating cash inflows, $2,000 x 6.000 $ 12,000
  Termination pay   (32,000)
  Equipment   (19,000)
  Total $(39,000)
Difference in favor of proposed investment $ 21,000

2.   The minimum amount of annual revenue that BACR would have to receive to justify the investment would be that amount yielding an incremental net present value of zero. As the initial investment is constant, any change in the incremental net present value is due solely to a change in the amount of revenue. Therefore, the maximum drop in the incremental net present value of $21,000 equals the maximum drop in the present value of the revenue stream. This implies a maximum drop of $21,000 ÷ 6 = $3,500 in *annual* revenue and a minimum amount of annual revenue of $15,000 - $3,500 = $11,500.

Let X = Revenue at point of indifference, where net present value is zero

NPV = PV of (New annual cash flows - Old annual cash flows) − Required investment

$$0 = 6.000[(X - 13,000) - (-10,000)] - 51,000$$
$$0 = 6.000(X - 13,000 + 10,000) - 51,000$$
$$0 = 6.000(X - 3,000) - 51,000$$
$$0 = 6.000X - 18,000 - 51,000$$
$$6.000X = 69,000$$
$$X = 11,500$$

Part 2 demonstrates sensitivity analysis, where the manager may see the potential impact of the possible errors in the forecasts of revenue. Such analysis shows how much of a margin of safety is available. In this case, his "best guess" is revenue of $15,000 (part 1). Sensitivity analysis shows him that a decline of revenue would have to occur from $15,000 to $11,500 before the rate of return on the project would decline to the minimum acceptable level.

The following alternative approach to solving requirement 2 is longer, but it
    may be clearer for many students:

If 10% is the minimum acceptable rate of return, the minimum acceptable net
    present value must be zero, using the 10% rate:

NPV = PV of future cash flows - Initial investment
Let X = Annual cash inflow
Then 0 = 6.000(X) - $51,000
    X = $51,000 ÷ 6.000 = $8,500

Present value of $8,500 per year for 10 years at 10% = $8,500 x 6.000	$51,000
Required investment	51,000
Net present value	$ 0

Many students will stop at this point, giving an answer of $8,500. But
the requirement asks for the minimum amount of *revenue*, as
distinguished from the *difference in cash flows*. The following
analysis shows that revenue can fall to $11,500. Note also that there
can be negative cash flows under both alternatives; the alternative
with the least negative cash flow is preferable:

	Present	Proposed	Difference in Cash Flows
Revenue	$200,000	$11,500	
Expenses	210,000	13,000	
Net cash flow from operations	$ (10,000)	$ (1,500)	$8,500

11-53 (30-40 min.)

1.

End of Year	PV of $1.00 Discounted at 20%	Present Value of Cash Flows	Sketch of Cash Flows (thousands)					
			0	1	2	3	4	5
A. Continue with common carriers:								
500,000 lbs. @ $.26	2.9906	$(388,778)		(130)	(130)	(130)	(130)	(130)
B. Purchase truck:								
Cost of truck	1.0000	(40,000)	(40)					
Cash operating costs*	2.9906	(672,885)		(225)	(225)	(225)	(225)	(225)
Back-haul revenue, 50 trips @ $2,400	2.9906	358,872		120	120	120	120	120
Present value of net cash flows		$(354,013)						
Difference in favor of truck		$ 34,765						

*500,000 lbs. ÷ 10,000 lbs. = 50 trips
 50 trips x 5,000 miles x $.90 per mile = $225,000

2.   The PV of back-haul revenue must fall by $34,765 before the net present value equals zero. Therefore, the total present value of back-haul revenue would be $358,872 less $34,765, or $324,107.

Let X = number of trips
(2.9906) x ($2,400) x (X) = $324,107
$7,177 X = $324,107
X = 45.2 trips

Consequently 45 trips would be slightly insufficient, and 46 trips would have to be guaranteed to yield a non-negative present value.

3. The greatest difficulty is the reliability of the numbers in a world of uncertainty. Although "the numbers" indicate the truck is a favorable alternative, the following other factors could influence the final decision:

    (a) If the back-haul agreement can be canceled by Retro at any time, the truck becomes a more risky investment since the back-haul revenue is needed to make the investment produce a return of 20% or more.

    (b) What is the outlook for other investments over the life of the truck investment? Does purchasing the truck preclude taking advantage of more favorable opportunities during the 5-year life of the truck?

    (c) Does the management have the required expertise to run the truck operation efficiently?

    (d) Will the truck give the company better service than common carriers?

    (e) How certain are the predicted cash flows? Are shipment figures and operating cost predictions considered to be relatively accurate?

11-54 (15 min.)

1. Straight-line depreciation:
   Annual depreciation = $30,000 ÷ 5 = $6,000 per year
   PV of tax savings = $6,000 x .40 x 3.6048 = $8,652

2. MACRS depreciation:

Year	Tax Savings		PV factor	Present Value
1	.2000 x $30,000 x .4 =	$2,400	.8929	$2,143
2	.3200 x 30,000 x .4 =	3,840	.7972	3,061
3	.1920 x 30,000 x .4 =	2,304	.7118	1,640
4	.1152 x 30,000 x .4 =	1,382	.6355	878
5	.1152 x 30,000 x .4 =	1,382	.5674	784
6	.0576 x 30,000 x .4 =	691	.5066	350
Total present value of tax savings				$8,856

You can also use Exhibit 11-7: .7381 x $30,000 x .4 = $8,857 The difference between this and $8,856 is due to rounding error.

3. Immediate write-off:
   $30,000 x .4 = $12,000

4. Mr. Tan would prefer immediate write-off. Note that the total tax savings is $12,000 under all three methods. However, only the immediate write-off provides the entire savings immediately. Straight-line depreciation delays receipt of the tax savings the longest, and therefore it has the lowest present value.

11-55 (30 min.)

1. See Exhibit 11-55 on the next page for the solution to requirement 1.

2. Net present value as in Exhibit 11-55 $ (654)
    Add Year 6 operating cash savings, $5,500 x .5066   2,786
    Add Year 7 operating cash savings, $5,500 x .4523   2,488
    Deduct PV of residual value   (1,560)
    Net present value is positive, so buy. $ 3,060

EXHIBIT 11-55

1. There is a net disadvantage in purchasing because the net present value is slightly negative. However, such a slight quantitative disadvantage could be more than offset by positive factors not quantified here.

	Present Value	Discount Factors, @12%	Total Present Values
Recurring operating cash savings	$10,000		
Income taxes, @ 45%	(4,500)		
After-tax operating cash savings	$ 5,500	3.6048	$ 19,826
Tax savings due to depreciation:			
5-year property @ $33,000			10,960*
Residual value, all subject to tax			
because book value will be zero	$ 5,000		
Less: 45% income tax on disposal gain	(2,250)		
Net cash inflow	$ 2,750	.5674	1,560
Initial required investment			(33,000)
Net present value of all cash flows			$ (654)

*The tax savings due to MACRS depreciation can be calculated as follows:

(1) Year	(2) MACRS Percentage	(3) Income Tax Deduction $33,000x(2)	(4) Present Value Savings, .45x(3)	(5) Total Present Factors, @12%	(6) Values (4)x(5)
1	.2000	$ 6,600	$2,970	.8929	$ 2,652
2	.3200	10,560	4,752	.7972	3,788
3	.1920	6,336	2,851	.7118	2,029
4	.1152	3,802	1,711	.6355	1,087
5	.1152	3,802	1,711	.5674	971
6	.0576	1,901	855	.5066	433
					$10,960

Sketch of Cash Flows at End of Year

0	1	2	3	4	5	6
	2,970					
		4,752				
			2,851			
				1,711		
					1,711	
						855

The tax savings due to MACRS depreciation can also be computed using Exhibit 11-7: .7381 x $33,000 x .45 = $10,961.

11-56 (30 min.)

Investment		$(45,000)
Cash operating savings		
Annual savings	$14,000	
Income taxes @ 40%	5,600	
After-tax effect on cash	$ 8,400	
Present value ($8,400 x 4.5638)		38,336
PV of tax savings from depreciation:		
Investment x PV factor (Exhibit 11-7) x Tax rate =		
$45,000 x .7381 x .40		13,286*
Overhaul required:		
Total cost	$ 5,000	
Less income tax savings @ 40%	2,000	
Total after-tax effect	$ 3,000	
Present value ($3,000 x .6355)		(1,907)
Residual value:		
Cash received	$ 6,000	
Book value	0	
Gain	$ 6,000	
Income tax @ 40%	2,400	
Total after-tax effect	$ 3,600	
Present value ($3,600 x .4523)		1,628
Net present value of all cash flows		$ 6,343

The investment is desirable.

*The PV of the tax savings from depreciation can also be calculated as follows:

Year	Tax Savings	PV factor	Present Value
1	.2000 x $45,000 x .4 = $3,600	.8929	$ 3,214
2	.3200 x 45,000 x .4 = 5,760	.7972	4,592
3	.1920 x 45,000 x .4 = 3,456	.7118	2,460
4	.1152 x 45,000 x .4 = 2,074	.6355	1,318
5	.1152 x 45,000 x .4 = 2,074	.5674	1,177
6	.0576 x 45,000 x .4 = 1,037	.5066	525
Total present value of tax savings			$13,286

11-57 (45-60 min.)

A. Investment: $310,000 + (20 x $12,000) = $550,000

B. PV of cash inflows from operations:
    Monthly rental payments = ($380 x 12) + ($440 x 8) = $8,080
    Repair and maintenance = .15 x $8,080 = $1,212
    Annual before-tax cash inflow = 12 x ($8,080 - $1,212) = $82,416
    Annual after-tax cash inflow = .62 x $82,416 = $51,098
    Present value of inflows @ 10% = $51,098 x 6.1446 = $313,977

C. PV of tax savings:
    Annual depreciation = $550,000 ÷ 27.5 = $20,000
    Annual tax savings = $20,000 x .38 = $7,600
    PV of tax savings for 10 years = $7,600 x 6.1446 = $46,699

D. PV of cash effects of disposal:

Cash received	$950,000
Book value [$550,000 - (10 x $20,000)]	350,000
Gain	$600,000
Income taxes @ 38%	$228,000
Net cash received at disposal ($950,000 - $228,000)	$722,000
Time 0 present value ($722,000 x .3855)	$278,331

E. Net present value at time 0:

A.	Investment	$(550,000)
B.	PV of operating cash inflows	313,977
C.	PV of income tax savings	46,699
D.	PV of cash effect of disposal:	
	PV of net cash received	278,331
	Net present value	$ 89,007

The net present value is positive, so the NPV model indicates that Rabinowitz should purchase the apartment complex.

11-58 (15-20 min.) Amounts are in thousands of Japanese yen.

1. Depreciation expense: (¥380,000 - ¥60,000) ÷ 10 = ¥32,000

2. Net income:

Revenues		¥320,000
Less expense:		
Depreciation	¥ 32,000	
Other	165,000	197,000
Operating income		¥123,000
Less income tax (60%)		73,800
Net income		¥ 49,200

3. Cash flow: ¥49,200 + ¥32,000 = ¥81,200 per year
   or ¥320,000 - ¥165,000 - ¥73,800 = ¥81,200

4. Payback period: ¥380,000 ÷ ¥81,200 = 4.7 years

   You might note that 4.7 years is a reasonably long payback period for United States companies, and many companies would be inclined to reject such a project. However, in Japan managers tend to take a longer-run point of view, and a 4.7-year payback period is often acceptable.

5. Accounting rate of return: ¥49,200 ÷ ¥380,000 = 12.9%
   or, if average investment is used:
     (¥380,000 + ¥60,000) ÷ 2 = ¥220,000 average investment;
     ¥49,200 ÷ ¥220,000 = 22.4%

6. NPV:

Annual cash flows, ¥81,200 x 5.2161 =	¥ 423,547
Salvage value, ¥60,000 x 0.2697 =	16,182
Gross present value	¥ 439,729
Less: Investment	380,000
Net present value	¥ 59,729

11-59 (50-60 min.)

1.

Table of Cash Flows:

End Of Year	Operating Cash Inflow	Operating Cash Outflow	Net After-Tax Operating Cash Flow	Depreciation Tax Shield	Net Cash Flow
2004	$0	$199,500	$(199,500)	$0	$(199,500)
2005	100,000	100,000	0	11,400*	11,400
2006	220,000	180,000	24,000**	11,400	35,400
2007	340,000	260,000	48,000	11,400	59,400
2008	460,000	320,000	84,000	11,400	95,400
2009	470,000	280,000	114,000	11,400	125,400
2010	410,000	200,000	126,000	11,400	137,400
2111	150,000	120,000	18,000	11,400	29,400

* ($199,500 ÷ 7) x .4 = $11,400

** ($220,000 - $180,000) x (1 - .4) = $24,000; etc.

Table of Cumulative Cash Flows:

End Of Year	Cumulative Net Cash Flow	18% PV Factor	PV of Net Cash Flow	Cumulative PV of Net Cash Flow
2004	$(199,500)	1.000	$(199,500)	$(199,500)
2005	(188,100)	.8475	9,662	(189,838)
2006	(152,700)	.7182	25,424	(164,414)
2007	(93,300)	.6086	36,151	(128,263)
2008	2,100	.5158	49,207	(79,056)
2009	127,500	.4371	54,812	(24,244)
2010	264,900	.3704	50,893	26,649
2111	294,300	.3139	9,229	35,878

2. The payback time is just under four years as shown by the Cumulative Net Cash Flow column. Because the maximum allowable payback period is 3 years, AIC would not produce IC-968 if the company uses the payback method.

3. The NPV is $35,878. The project has an NPV greater than zero at a discount rate of 18%. Therefore, the company would produce IC-968 if it uses the NPV method.

4. See Exhibit 11-59 on the following page.

5. The payback model and NPV model lead to different decisions. In general, the NPV method leads to better decisions than the payback model because the payback model doesn't measure profitability. Therefore, AIC should probably accept the project and produce IC-968. A final recommendation would also depend on other factors such as

> Potential for proprietary position – such as an important patent that provides a market advantage,
> Potential for collaborations and outside funding,
> Need to establish competency in a technology,
> Potential for spin-off products, and
> Need to round out a profitable product line.

Students should note the advantage of the graphical approach. Rather than a simple single-point measure for the payback time, in this case about 4 years, the graph shows the project's life-cycle cash flow. This approach overcomes one of the main drawbacks of the payback period method. Some companies combine the payback and NPV models and look at the time it takes for the cumulative present value of net cash flow to reach zero. For this project, this is about 5.5 years, as shown on the graph.

Exhibit 11-59

Graph for of Payback Time and NPV

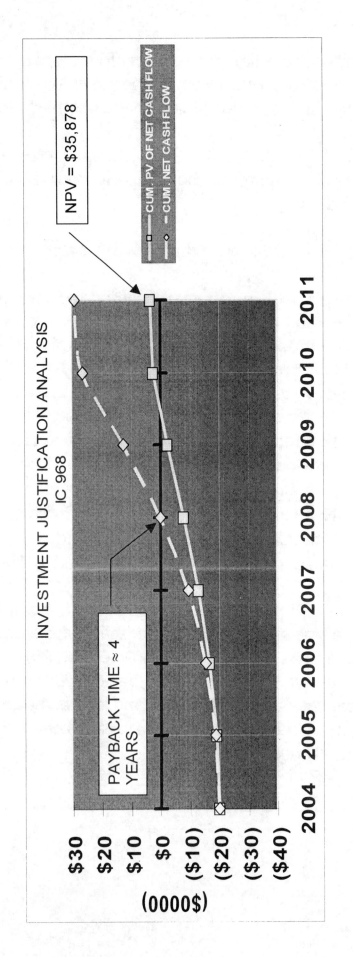

11-60 (20-35 min.)

1. $51,000 x 3.8887 factor = $198,324
    ($22,000 + $16,000) x .4556 factor =   17,313
    Total present value $215,637
    Less initial investment:
      $193,000 + $16,000 =   209,000
    Net present value (NPV) $ 6,637

2. a. Annual depreciation is ($193,000 - $22,000) ÷ 6 = $28,500
        Increase in expected average annual operating income = $51,000 -
          $28,500 = $22,500
        Initial investment is $209,000
        Rate of return is $22,500 ÷ $209,000 = 10.8%

    b. Note the rate of return is not twice the 10.8%. Why? Because the
        investment at the end of six years is not zero:

        Investment at end of 6 years: $22,000 + $16,000 = $ 38,000
        Initial investment   209,000
        Total $247,000

        "Average" investment: $247,000 ÷ 2 = $123,500
        Rate of return is $22,500 ÷ $123,500 = 18.2%

3. The models in requirements 1 and 2 would induce a positive decision.
    However, the 10.8% accounting rate of return based on an initial investment
    might induce a negative decision because it is less than 14%. An
    administrator's reluctance to buy would be understandable if there is no
    reasonable consistency between the decision model and the performance
    evaluation model. If decisions are supposed to be based on DCF models,
    and performance is evaluated on accrual accounting models, the latter tend
    to be persuasive.

11-61 (20 min.)

1. Investment = $2,000,000 + $1,300,000 = $3,300,000
Annual cash inflow = 300 skiers x 40 days x $60/skier-day = $720,000
Annual cash outflow
= (200 days x $500/day)+($10/skier-day x 300 x 40) = $220,000

PV of cash flows @ 14% = ($720,000 - $220,000) x 6.6231 = $3,311,550

NPV = $3,311,550 - $3,300,000 = $11,550

The new lift will create value of $11,550, so it is a profitable investment.

2. After-tax cash flows = $500,000 x .6 = $300,000

PV of after-tax cash flows @ 8% = $300,000 x 9.8181 = $2,945,430

PV of tax savings = $3,300,000 x .4 x .7059 (from Exhibit 11-7) = $931,788

NPV after-tax = $2,945,430 + $931,788 - $3,300,000 = $577,218

The investment in the lift is more profitable on an after-tax basis than on a pretax basis.

3. Subjective factors that might affect this decision include:
   - Profits on sales of food, rental of equipment, and other items purchased by the additional skiers.
   - More satisfied customers because of less crowding on the days that the additional lift does not result in additional skiers being attracted to Deer Valley.
   - Additional skiers may not be as many as estimated if the weather is poor.

<u>11-62</u> (40-50 min.)

1. See Exhibit 11-62 for the solution to requirement 1.

2. The greatest difficulty is the reliability of the numbers in a world of uncertainty. Although "the numbers" indicate the truck is a favorable alternative, the following other factors could influence the final decision:

    (a) If the back-haul agreement can be canceled by Retro at any time, the truck becomes a more risky investment since the back-haul revenue is needed to make the investment produce an after-tax return of 20% or more.

    (b) What is the outlook for other investments over the life of the truck investment? Does purchasing the truck preclude taking advantage of more favorable opportunities during the 5-year life of the truck?

    (c) Does the management have the required expertise to run the truck operation efficiently?

    (d) Will the truck give the company better service than common carriers?

    (e) How certain are the predicted cash flows? Are shipment figures and operating cost predictions considered to be relatively accurate?

EXHIBIT 11-62

After-Tax Cash Flows (in dollars)

Alternative 1: Continue w/ common carrier

500,000 lbs @ 26¢	$130,000
Income tax savings @ 40%	(52,000)
After-tax (Year 0)	$78,000

Adjust $78,000 for 10% inflation
$78,000 x 1.1; x 1.1^2; x 1.1^3; x 1.1^4; x 1.1^5

	Total Present Value	Year 0	Year 1	Year 2	Year 3	Year 4	Year 5	Year 6
Adjust $78,000 for 10% inflation			(85,800)	(94,380)	(103,818)	(114,200)	(125,620)	
Present value factor @ 20%			.8333	.6944	.5787	.4823	.4019	
Present value	$(302,679)		(71,497)	(65,537)	(60,079)	(55,079)	(50,487)	

Alternative 2: Purchase truck

	Total Present Value	Year 0	Year 1	Year 2	Year 3	Year 4	Year 5	Year 6
Initial cash investment		(40,000)						

Depreciation deductions:

Year	%	Deduction	Tax Savings
1	20	$8,000	$3,200
2	32	12,800	5,120
3	19.2	7,680	3,072
4-5	11.52	4,608	1,843
6	5.76	2,304	922

	Total Present Value	Year 0	Year 1	Year 2	Year 3	Year 4	Year 5	Year 6
(Depreciation Tax Savings)			3,200	5,120	3,072	1,843	1,843	922

Back-haul revenue*

50 trips** @ $2,400	$120,000
Income tax @ 40%	(48,000)
After-tax	$72,000

Cash operating costs:

250,000 miles† @ 90¢	$225,000
Income tax savings	(90,000)
	$135,000

	Total Present Value	Year 0	Year 1	Year 2	Year 3	Year 4	Year 5	Year 6
(Back-haul After-tax)			72,000	72,000	72,000	72,000	72,000	

Adjust $135,000 for inflation after Year 1
$135,000 x 1.1; x 1.1^2; x 1.1^3; x 1.1^4

	Total Present Value	Year 0	Year 1	Year 2	Year 3	Year 4	Year 5	Year 6
Adjust $135,000 for inflation after Year 1			(135,000)	(148,500)	(163,350)	(179,685)	(197,654)	
Total cash flow		(40,000)	(59,800)	(71,380)	(88,278)	(105,842)	(123,811)	922
Present value factors @ 20%		1.0000	.8333	.6944	.5787	.4823	.4019	.3349
Present value	(290,982)	(40,000)	(49,831)	(49,566)	(51,086)	(51,048)	(49,760)	309
PV difference in favor of purchasing truck	$ 11,697							

*Not subject to inflation due to 5-year agreement. **500,000 lbs ÷ 10,000 lbs/trip = 50 trips †50 trips @ 5,000 round-trip miles = 250,000 miles

<u>11-63</u> (20-30 min.)

1 & 2. See Exhibit 11-63 for the solution to requirements 1 and 2.

3.   Correct analysis of inflation can affect decisions. Using a required
          rate of return that includes an inflation element but neglecting to
          adjust cash inflows for inflation will understate the present value,
          causing possible rejection of desirable projects.

EXHIBIT 11-63

			Sketch of Relevant Cash Flows (in dollars)					
Description	**14% PV Factor**	**Total Present Value**	**20X0**	**20X1**	**20X2**	**20X3**	**20X4**	**20X5**
1. Per Problem Instructions (But that is an incorrect analysis, which includes an inflation element in the discount rate but does not adjust the predicted cash flows for inflation.)								
Cash operating savings	3.4331	$ 6,866		2,000	2,000	2,000	2,000	2,000
New machine, investment	1.0000	(7,300)	(7,300)					
Net present value		$ (434)						
2. Correct Analysis: (Includes an inflation element in both the discount rate and the predicted cash flows.)								
Cash operating savings:	.8772	$ 1,860		2,120*				
	.7695	1,729			2,247			
	.6750	1,608				2,382		
	.5921	1,495					2,525	
	.5194	1,390						2,676
		$8,082						
New machine, investment	1.0000	(7,300)	(7,300)					
Net present value		$ 782						

*2,000 x 1.06, then 2,000 x $(1.06)^2$, then 2,000 x $(1.06)^3$, etc.

624

<u>11-64</u> (25-30 min.) Amounts are in Swedish Kroner (SKr).

Annual cash savings (SKr 260,000 x 5)	SKr 1,300,000
Additional operating expenses	(900,000)
Net annual savings	SKr 400,000
Investment	SKr 1,500,000

1. NPV = (SKr 400,000 x 4.9676*) - SKr 1,500,000
   = SKr 1,987,040 - SKr 1,500,000
   = SKr 487,040

   *From Table 2, 12% column, 8-year row.

   The system should be purchased because the NPV is positive.

2. Pessimistic:
   Annual savings = SKr 400,000 - SKr 260,000 = SKr 140,000
   Economic life = 5 years
        NPV = (SKr 140,000 x 3.6048) - SKr 1,500,000
             =SKr 504,672 - SKr 1,500,000 = SKr (995,328)

   Optimistic:
   Annual savings = SKr 400,000 + SKr 260,000 = SKr 660,000
   Economic life = 10 years
        NPV = (SKr 660,000 x 5.6502) - SKr 1,500,000
             = SKr 3,729,132 - SKr 1,500,000 = SKr 2,229,132

   Most likely: NPV = SKr 487,040 (from requirement 1)

   This analysis shows that predictions of savings and economic life can greatly affect the decision. Although the expected NPV is SKr 487,040, it is possible that the realized NPV might be as low as (SKr 995,328). It might be worthwhile to gather more information about the savings and economic life before making the decision.

3. Investment in new technology often has many effects that are difficult to quantify. A special report in *Business Week* reported that most companies do not provide a quantitative cost justification for the purchase of computers. However, the article goes on to point out that analyses such as NPV are being increasingly demanded by top management to justify investment in new technology.

The company should be concerned with the amount of investment specified. The system can be purchased for SKr 1,500,000, but might additional costs be incurred in implementing the system?

Will the quality of design be improved by the new system? Or might the system be incapable of meeting current standards?

Maybe most important, the analysis is based on the implementation of CAD only. Is there any chance that the CAM portion will be used? If so, the purchase has more value than shown in the analysis of CAD only.

11-65 (30-40 min.) This case focuses on the appropriate baseline for NPV analysis for an investment in a high technology production system. It highlights the possible loss of competitive position if the company does not undertake the investment. The potential magnitude of errors from omission of some factors in an NPV analysis is shown.

1.   This is a straightforward NPV analysis:

End of Year	Present Value @ 12% from Table 1	Differential Net Cash Flow	Present Value of Differential Cash Flow
2004*	1.0000	$(5,500,000)	$(5,500,000)
2005	.8929	(400,000)	(357,160)
2006	.7972	1,600,000	1,275,520
2007	.7118	1,600,000	1,138,880
2008	.6355	1,600,000	1,016,800
2009	.5674	1,600,000	907,840
2010	.5066	1,600,000	810,560
Total			$ (707,560)

* Or beginning of 2005.

The investment in the CIM has a negative NPV of more than $700,000. It appears that it would be a mistake to invest.

2.   An additional advantage of the CIM must be recognized in this analysis. In the absence of investment in the CIM, some of the existing contribution margin will be lost each year. Investment avoids this loss, so the amount of the contribution margin that would have been lost is in essence a savings from investment in the CIM.

The current market share of 40% and sales of $12 million implies that each 1% of the market is worth sales of $12,000,000 ÷ 40 = $300,000. Current sales are $12,000,000 and variable costs are $4,000,000 + $2,000,000 = $6,000,000, making the contribution margin percentage 50%. Therefore, for each $1 of lost sales, Lexington Auto Parts loses $.50 in contribution margin. The loss of $300,000 in sales results in a loss of $150,000 in contribution margin.

627

Therefore, the potential lost contribution margin each year is:

Year	Lost Market Share	Lost Sales	Lost Contribution Margin
2005	3%	$ 900,000	$ 450,000
2006	6	1,800,000	900,000
2007	9	2,700,000	1,350,000
2008	12	3,600,000	1,800,000
2009	15	4,500,000	2,250,000
2010	18	5,400,000	2,700,000

Combining the savings from variable costs with the savings in contribution margin, the NPV becomes a positive $3,956,069, computed as follows:

Year	Present Value @ 12% from Table 1	Investment and Cost Savings *	Savings in Contribution Margin	Total Differential Cash Flow	Present Value of Differential Cash Flow
2004	1.0000	$(5,500,000)			$(5,500,000)
2005	.8929	(520,000)	$ 450,000	$ (70,000)	(62,503)
2006	.7972	1,360,000	900,000	2,260,000	1,801,672
2007	.7118	1,240,000	1,350,000	2,590,000	1,843,562
2008	.6355	1,120,000	1,800,000	2,920,000	1,855,660
2009	.5674	1,000,000	2,250,000	3,250,000	1,844,050
2010	.5066	880,000	2,700,000	3,580,000	1,813,628
Total					$ 3,956,069

*These cost savings differ from those in part 1 because the variable costs decline with the decrease in sales, thus savings, which are 40% of variable costs, also decline each year. Each year there is $120,000 less savings than the year before because variable costs decrease $300,000 each year.

The picture has changed radically from that in requirement 1. Avoiding the lost contribution margin has made the CIM a very desirable investment.

3. To the Board of Directors:

I recommend that Kentucky Auto Parts invest in the new CIM system. I have made two net present value analyses, the first one showing a negative NPV of more than $700,000 and the second showing a positive NPV of over $3.9 million. Let me explain why the second analysis is better.

The first analysis compares revenues and costs under the CIM to those that would be incurred if operations continue exactly as they did in 2004. However, if we do not invest in CIM, operations will not continue the way they are today. Many of our competitors are investing in technologically sophisticated production systems, and if we do not invest, they will have advantages over us in quality of products, response to design changes desired by our customers, and flexibility of delivery schedules. Investment in the CIM will not only save variable costs of production, it will allow us to maintain our market share.

The second analysis uses the correct baseline for comparisons. It compares the costs and revenues with the CIM to those we expect if we do not invest. It includes consideration of the lost sales, and therefore lost contribution margin, that we would experience if our competitors gain a competitive advantage by investing in CIM while we do not. If we do not upgrade to CIM or some similar system in the next six years, we risk losing nearly half our business. This risk is much greater than that of not achieving all the cost savings projected for the CIM.

In addition to the items included in my analysis, there are other potential benefits to investing in the CIM. First, it encourages our employees to think about the production process and places where we might eliminate or reduce non-value-added activities. It also introduces technologically sophisticated operations so that future expansion of similar activities may be easier.

In summary, cost savings alone do not justify investment in the CIM. But cost savings are not the only advantage of investment. When we add the extra contribution margins from business we will maintain only if we invest in the CIM, plus other qualitative advantages, the investment is certainly desirable.

11-66 (30-40 min.)

This problem includes a complex analysis of relevant costs in addition to its focus on an investment decision. This solution will first identify the relevant costs in four categories:

1. Initial investment
2. Current annual quality control costs
3. Annual quality control costs with new process
4. Forgone profits if quality is not improved

Initial investment:

Worker training	$800,000	
X-ray machine	250,000	
Total investment		$1,050,000

Current annual quality control costs:

Inspection cost	$ 40,000	
Correction of defects (1,500 x $85)	127,500	
Refunds to customers (500 x $210)	105,000	
Total current quality control costs		$ 272,500

Annual quality control costs with new process:

Inspection cost ($40,000 + $50,000)	$ 90,000	
Correction of defects (450 x $50)	22,500	
Refunds to customers (50 x $315)	15,750	
Total new quality control costs		128,250

Net savings in quality control costs		$ 144,250

630

Difference in contribution margin if quality is not improved:

20X2	$ 0	
20X3	350,000	(5,000 x $70)
20X4	700,000	(10,000 x $70)
20X5	1,050,000	(15,000 x $70)

Therefore, the total annual cash flows from the change in the quality control process are:

	Net Savings in Quality Control Costs	Differences in Total Contribution Margin	Net Cash Flow from Operations
20X2	$144,250	$ 0	$ 144,250
20X3	144,250	350,000	494,250
20X4	144,250	700,000	844,250
20X5	144,250	1,050,000	1,194,250

The net present value of the investment in the new quality control is positive, so invest:

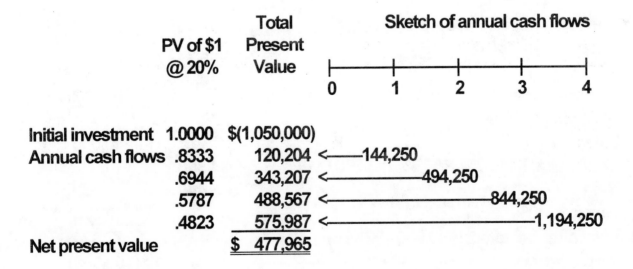

	PV of $1 @ 20%	Total Present Value	
Initial investment	1.0000	$(1,050,000)	
Annual cash flows	.8333	120,204	←—144,250
	.6944	343,207	←————494,250
	.5787	488,567	←—————844,250
	.4823	575,987	←——————1,194,250
Net present value		$ 477,965	

11-67 (50-75 min.)

This is a complex problem because it requires comparing three alternatives. It reviews Chapter 6 as well as covering several of the topics of Chapter 11. The following answer uses the total project approach. The total net future cash outflows are shown for each alternative.

1. Alternative A: Continue to manufacture the parts with the current tools.
Annual cash outlays

Variable cost, $9.20 x 8,000	$(73,600)	
Fixed cost, 1/3 x $4.50 x 8,000 x .6	(7,200)	
Tax savings, .4 x ($73,600 + $7,200)	32,320	
After-tax annual cost	$(48,480)	
Present value, 3.6048 x $48,480		$(174,761)
PV of remaining tax savings on MACRS:		
11.52% x $200,000 x .4 x .8929		8,229
5.76% x $200,000 x .4 x .7972		3,673
Total present value of costs, Alternative A		$(162,859)

Alternative B: Purchase from outside supplier
Annual cash outlays

Purchase cost, $11.00 x 8,000	$(88,000)	
Tax savings, $88,000 x .4	35,200	
After-tax annual cost	$(52,800)	
Present value, $52,800 x 3.6048		$(190,333)
Sale of old equipment:		
Sales price		$40,000
Book value [(11.52% + 5.76%) x $200,000]	34,560	
Gain	$ 5,440	
Taxes @ 40%		(2,176)
Total after-tax effect ($40,000 - $2,176)		37,824
Total present value of costs, Alternative B		$(152,509)

<u>Alternative C:</u> Purchase new equipment

Investment		$(180,000)
Annual cash outlays		
Variable cost, $7.30 x 8,000	$(58,400)	
Fixed cost, (same as A)	(7,200)	
Tax savings, .4 x ($58,400 + $7,200)	26,240	
After-tax annual cost	$(39,360)	
Present value, $39,360 x 3.6048		(141,885)
Tax savings on new equipment*		57,922
Effect of disposal of new equipment		
Sales price	$50,000	
Book value	0	
Gain	$50,000	
Taxes @ 40%	20,000	
Total after-tax effect	$30,000	
Present value, $30,000 x .5674		17,022
Effect of disposal of old equipment (see Alternative B)		37,824
Total present value of costs, Alternative C		$(209,117)

*Using the MACRS schedule for tax depreciation, the depreciation rate for each year of a 3-year asset's life is shown in Exhibit 11-6:

Year	Depreciation Rate	Tax Savings	PV Factor	Present Value
1	33.33%	.3333 x $180,000 x .40 = $23,998	.8929	$21,428
2	44.45%	.4445 x 180,000 x .40 = 32,004	.7972	25,514
3	14.81%	.1481 x 180,000 x .40 = 10,663	.7118	7,590
4	7.41%	.0741 x 180,000 x .40 = 5,335	.6355	3,390
Total present value of tax savings				$57,922

Using Exhibit 11-7, we get .8044 x $180,000 x .4 = $57,917, which differs from $57,922 by a $5 rounding error.

    The alternative with the lowest present value of cost is Alternative B, purchasing from the outside supplier.

2. Among the major factors are (1) the range of expected volume (both large increases and decreases in volume make the purchase of the parts relatively less desirable), (2) the reliability of the outside supplier, (3) possible changes in material, labor, and overhead prices, (4) the possibility that the outside supplier can raise prices before the end of five years, (5) obsolescence of the products and equipment, and (6) alternate uses of available capacity (alternative uses make Alternative B relatively more desirable).

11-68 (20-30 min.) For the solution, see the Prentice Hall Web site, www.prenhall.com/

11-69 (20 min.)

The purpose of this exercise is to see how financial analyses and behavioral and ethical issues interact in decision making. We first present the NPV analysis that should form the basis of Santelli's meeting with Krishnamurthi. Then we discuss other items that are likely to surface in the meeting.

To gain a 16% rate of return, the net present value at 16% must be positive. For Krispie Krinkles, optimistic, expected, and pessimistic present values of predicted cash inflows, assuming cash flows at the end of each year, are (in thousands of dollars):

	(1)	(2)	(3)	(4)	(5)	(6)	(7)
			Optimistic		Expected		Pessimistic
Year	PV of $1 at 16%	Cash Flow	Present Value (1) x (2)	Cash Flow	Present Value (1) x (4)	Cash Flow	Present Value (1) x (6)
1	.8621	800	690	600	517	400	345
2	.7432	1,800	1,338	1,200	892	600	446
3	.6407	2,500	1,602	1,500	961	500	320
4	.5523	4,000	2,209	2,200	1,215	400	221
5	.4761	5,000	2,381	2,600	1,238	200	95
Total			8,220		4,823		1,427

The investment and salvage values do not depend on the optimistic and pessimistic forecasts:

Investment (1.0000 x $6,000,000)	$(6,000,000)
Salvage value of facilities (.4761 x $800,000)	380,880
Salvage value of working capital (.4761 x $500,000)	238,050
Total	$(5,381,070)

Therefore, net present values are:

Optimistic ($8,220,000 - $5,381,070)	$ 2,838,930
Expected ($4,823,000 - $5,381,070)	$ (558,070)
Pessimistic ($1,427,000 - $5,381,070)	$(3,954,070)

If you believe the expected amounts, the product has a negative present value and should not be launched.

Krishnamurthi might raise some of the following issues supporting the project:

- The required rate of return is less than 16%.
- The optimistic scenario is more likely than the pessimistic scenario, making the expected cash flows more than those listed.
- The cash flow predictions for either the optimistic or pessimistic scenarios (or both) are understated.
- The contribution margin is 58% rather than 50%.
- The investment is less than $6 million.

For example, he might maintain that the required rate of return for a project of this risk should be 12% instead of 16%. Then the product's net present value would be $5,434,000 - $6,000,000 + (.5674 x $800,000) + (.5674 x $500,000) = $171,620:

Year	(1) PV of $1 at 12%	(2) Optimistic Cash Flow	(3) Optimistic Present Value (1) x (2)	(4) Expected Cash Flow	(5) Expected Present Value (1) x (4)	(6) Pessimistic Cash Flow	(7) Pessimistic Present Value (1) x (6)
1	.8929	800	714	600	536	400	357
2	.7972	1,800	1,435	1,200	957	600	478
3	.7118	2,500	1,780	1,500	1,068	500	356
4	.6355	4,000	2,542	2,200	1,398	400	254
5	.5674	5,000	2,837	2,600	1,475	200	113
Total			9,308		5,434		1,558

Or he might maintain that each expected cash flow should be $200,000 higher, making the net present value $4,823,000 + ($200,000 x 3.2743) - $5,381,070 = $96,790. Or. if the contribution margin were 58% rather than 50%, the net present value would be [$4,823,000 x (58/50)] - $5,381,070 = $213,610. Finally, if the investment is less than $6,000,000 by at least $558,070, the net present value would be positive.

Krishnamurthi could use some combination of these changes to make the net present value of the product positive.

The ethical issues in this exercise can be revealing. If Santelli believes her information is accurate, it would be unethical to produce biased numbers just to satisfy Krishnamurthi. Among the ethical requirements for management accountants are to "communicate information fairly and objectively," "disclose fully all relevant information," and "prepare concise and clear reports and recommendations after appropriate analyses of relevant and reliable information." These standards would be violated if Santelli were to change her analysis just to satisfy Krishnamurthi.

Therefore, Santelli should report numbers that she believes are accurate. This may upset her supervisor, Krishnamurthi, and that may create problems for Santelli. Nevertheless, using biased information to justify a manager's pet projects can create more serious problems.

<u>11-70</u> (35-50 min.)

NOTE TO INSTRUCTOR. This solution is based on the web site as it was in early 2004. Be sure to examine the current web site before assigning this problem, as the information there may have changed.

1. Carnival Corporation operates 66 cruise ships under the following lines: Carnival Cruise Lines, Princess Cruises, Holland America Line, Windstar Cruises, Seabourn Cruise Line, Costa Cruises, Cunard Line, P&O Cruises, Ocean Village, Swan Hellenic, AIDA, and P&O Cruises Australia. At the time this solution was prepared, Carnival planned to add 11 new cruise ships between 2004 and 2006. This is a substantial investment, reflecting plans for significant growth in business.

2. From Carnival's 2003 annual report, its capacity has increased each of the last five years:

	Passengers Carried	Available Lower Berth Days
1999:	2,365,720	14,336,480
2000:	2,669,153	15,888,404
2001:	3,385,080	20,685,123
2002:	3,549,019	21,435,828
2003:	5,037,553	33,309,785

The passengers carried (capacity used) and available lower berth days (capacity available) both more than doubled from 1999 to 2003-.

3. Carnival continues its expansion plans, with both geographic expansion and expansion of its fleet. Specifically, in 2003 the completed its acquisition of P&O Princess Cruises for approximately $8 billion. In addition it has plans to launch 7 new ships in a 9 month period.

4. In 2003 Carnival invested more than $2,516 million in property and equipment and used about $2,333 million in total for investment activities. This was more than the $1,933 million cash generated by operating activities. Because of its need for cash for capital investments, Carnival had a net increase in long-term debt of $986 million during the year.

CHAPTER 12
COVERAGE OF LEARNING OBJECTIVES

LEARNING OBJECTIVE	FUNDA-MENTAL ASSIGN-MENT MATERIAL	CRITICAL THINKING EXERCISES AND EXERCISES	PROBLEMS	CASES, EXCEL, COLLAB. & INTERNET EXERCISES
LO1: Explain the major reasons for allocating costs.			31,32,33,43	45,46,47,50
LO2: Allocate the variable and fixed costs of service departments to other organizational units.	B1	19,23	37	
LO3: Allocate the central costs of an organization.	A3	20,21,24		
LO4: Use the direct and step-down methods to allocate service department costs to user departments.	A1,A2,B2	25,26	38,39,40	48
LO5: Use activity-based costing to allocate costs in a modern manufacturing environment to products or services.	A2,B3	22	34,35,36, 41,42,43	49
LO6: Use the physical-units and relative-sales-value methods to allocate joint costs to products.	A4,B4	27,28	44	

CHAPTER 12
Cost Allocation

<u>12-A1</u> (30-50 min.)

The numerical answers for requirements 1 and 2 are in Exhibit 12-A1. It seems most logical to use the following cost drivers: cafeteria – number of employees; engineering – engineering hours; and general factory administration – labor hours.

Most students will favor the direct method because the final allocations are not affected significantly.

Special Note: As an example of rounding errors, reconsider footnote (4) in Exhibit 12-A1. If fractions were used instead of percentages, the allocations would become:

36/1,296	x 950,000	=	26,389
120/1,296	x 950,000	=	87,963
300/1,296	x 950,000	=	219,907
720/1,296	x 950,000	=	527,778
120/1,296	x 950,000	=	87,963
Total			950,000

In turn, the computations in footnotes (5) and (6) would also be changed.

EXHIBIT 12-A1

	Total	General Factory Administration	Cafeteria	Engineering	Machining	Assembly	Finishing and Painting
Total labor hours	1,296,000	-	36,000	120,000	300,000	720,000	120,000
Percentage	100.0%	-	2.8%	9.3%	23.1%	55.5%	9.3%
Employees	780	-	-	60	120	540	60
Percentage	100.0%	-	-	7.7%	15.4%	69.2%	7.7%
Engineering hours	80,000	-	-	-	50,000	20,000	10,000
Percentage	100.0%	-	-	-	62.5%	25.0%	12.5%

Cost Drivers

	Total Labor Hours	Employees	Engineering Hours	Machining	Assembly	Finishing and Painting
Method 1, Direct Method						
Total department overhead before allocation	$950,000	$150,000	$2,500,000	-----	Not Given	-----
General factory administration	(950,000)			$ 250,000 [1]	$ 600,000	$100,000
Cafeteria		(150,000)		25,000	112,500 [2]	12,500
Engineering			(2,500,000)	1,562,500 [3]	625,000	312,500
Totals				$1,837,500	$1,337,500	$425,000
Method 2, Step-Down Method						
Total department overhead before allocation	$950,000	$150,000	$2,500,000	-----	Not Given	-----
General factory administration	(950,000)	26,600 [4]	88,350	$219,450	$527,250	$88,350
Cafeteria		(176,600)	13,598 [5]	27,196	122,207	13,598
Engineering			(2,601,948)	1,626,218 [6]	650,487	325,244
Totals				$1,872,864	$1,299,944	$427,192

[1] 300 + 720 + 120 = 1,140;   300/1,140 x 950,000 = 250,000;   720/1,140 x 950,000 = 600,000; etc.

[2] 120 + 540 + 60 = 720;   120/720 x 150,000 = 25,000;   540/720 x 150,000 = 112,500; etc.

[3] 50 + 20 + 10 = 80;   50/80 x 2,500,000 = 1,562,500;   20/80 x 2,500,000 = 625,000; etc.

Rounding in (4), (5), and (6) can cause discrepancies of hundreds of dollars:

[4] 2.8% x 950,000 = 26,600;   9.3% x 950,000 = 88,350; etc.

[5] 7.7% x 176,600 = 13,598;   15.4% x 176,600 = 27,196; etc.

[6] 62.5% x 2,601,948 = 1,626,218;   25.0% x 2,601,948 = 650,487; etc.

12-A2 (30-40 min.)

1. To properly classify an assigned cost, it is necessary to specify the cost object. For example, power cost is a direct cost if the cost object is the power department but an indirect cost if the cost objective is the maintenance department, the assembly department, or the display types.

Type of Cost Assignment per Exhibit 12-1	Example from Exhibit 12-10
1. Directly traced cost to departments	Power cost in power department (power department is the cost object); $90,000 of direct costs of the maintenance department (maintenance department is the cost object); parts and direct labor costs in the assembly department (the cost object is the assembly department).
2. Indirect costs allocated to departments	General costs such as occupancy allocated to the maintenance and the assembly departments.
3. Service department costs allocated to other service departments	Power department costs allocated to the maintenance department.
4. Service department costs allocated to producing departments	Power costs allocated to the assembly departments; maintenance department costs allocated to the assembly department.
5. Producing department costs allocated to other producing departments	Since there is only one producing department, no example exists.
6. Directly traced costs to departments that an organization can also trace directly to products and services	Parts and direct labor costs in the assembly department.
7. Producing department costs that an organization allocates to products or services	All assigned costs of setup and assembly activities, including assembly supervisor salaries, machine depreciation, power, maintenance, and occupancy.

2. The assembly facility uses the step-down method. Power department costs are first allocated to the maintenance service department and the assembly department before the maintenance department costs are allocated to the two major activities in the assembly department.

3.

	Power Department	General Costs	Maintenance Department	Setup Activity	Assembly Activity
Direct costs	$ 60,000*	$ 600,000	$ 90,000		
Allocated general Costs**		$(600,000)	60,000	$120,000	$420,000
Allocated power department costs***	$(60,000)		6,000	6,000	48,000
Allocated maintenance department costs****			$(156,000)	52,000	104,000
Total				$178,000	$572,000

* 10 x $600 + 10 x $600 + 80 x $600

** 10 + 20 + 70 = 100; (10 ÷ 100) x $600,000; etc.

*** 10 + 10 + 80 = 100; (10 ÷ 100) x $60,000; etc.

**** 2,000 + 4,000 = 6,000; (2,000 ÷ 6,000) x $156,000; etc.

4.

	Cost per Driver Unit	Display Type A		Display Type B		Display Type C	
		Driver Units	Cost	Driver Units	Cost	Driver Units	Cost
Parts			$1,053,800		$ 575,000		$239,700
Direct labor			344,000		303,000		123,000
Setup activity	$1,310	20	26,200	60	78,600	120	157,200
Assembly activity	203	1,000	203,000	1,800	365,400	1,200	243,600
Total			$1,627,000		$1,322,000		$763,500
Displays			100,000		50,000		15,000
Cost per display			$ 16.27		$ 26.44		$ 50.90

643

<u>12-A3</u>   (15-20 min.)

1.   Allocations are in millions:

Divisions:	Actual Revenue	Allocated Costs
Northeast	$120	$ 6
Mid-Atlantic	200	10
Southeast	280	14
Total	$600	$30

2.   Northeastern's manager would probably be indifferent, Mid-Atlantic's would be pleased, and Southeast's would be displeased.

The major weakness of using revenue as a basis for cost allocation is that it often fails to portray underlying cause-and-effect relationships. The major point of this problem is to show how strange results occur when the costs being allocated to *a given* segment are dependent on the activity of some *other* segment. The Southeast Division may have done the most to reduce the unit cost of central services, but it is being charged with a heavier dose of common costs. Indeed, Mid-Atlantic may have received more rather than less attention because of its current competitive troubles.

Most of the central costs are discretionary. Pinpointing cause-and-effect relationships is hard. Such costs are usually predetermined by management fiat or by *budgeted* revenue.

Serious consideration should be given to one or more of the following:

a. No allocation, because no convincing allocation base is available.
b. Dividing the services into sub-categories and allocating by the use of several different cost drivers.
c. Using budgeted revenues rather than actual revenues as a cost driver for allocation. Of course, the use of budgeted revenues may induce more "gamesmanship" than is typically encountered during the budgetary process. There is a tendency to "under-budget" whenever a lower cost allocation will result.

3. Allocations are in millions:

	Budgeted Revenue	Allocated Costs
Divisions:		
Northeast	$120	$ 5.625
Mid-Atlantic	240	11.250
Southeast	280	13.125
Total	$640	$30.000

Many managers prefer this method because it portrays causes and effects somewhat better than in requirement (1). That is, at least the overall level of costs tend to be planned rather than just happen after the fact.

In requirement (1), the allocated costs were each 5% of *actual* revenue. However, in requirement (3), the allocation is predetermined, and therefore the percentages of actual revenue vary:

	(1) Actual Revenue	(2) Allocated Costs	(3) Percentage (2) ÷ (1)
Divisions:			
Northeast	$120	$ 5.625	4.7%
Mid-Atlantic	200	11.250	5.6%
Southeast	280	13.125	4.7%
Total	$600	$30.000	

Note that Mid-Atlantic 's budgeted percentage would have been $11.25 ÷ $240 = 4.7%. The resultant deviation of the actual percentage (5.6%) from the budgeted percentage (4.7%) would highlight the effects of Mid-Atlantic 's troubles.

4.   Many accountants and managers oppose allocating any central costs when no convincing causes and effects can be established in any economically feasible way. The opponents of cost allocation feel that the managers of subunits will have better attitudes and will make better decisions if no allocation occurs.

<u>12-A4</u> (20-30 min.)

Note that total joint costs are $10 x 800,000 + $4 x 800,000 = $11,200,000.

1.   Physical units method:

	Pounds	Weighting	Allocation of Joint Costs
A	200,000	(200 ÷ 800) x $11,200,000	$ 2,800,000
B	600,000	(600 ÷ 800) x $11,200,000	8,400,000
	800,000		$11,200,000

2.   Relative sales value method:

	Relative Sales Value at Split-off		Weighting	Allocation of Joint Costs
A	$30.00 x 200,000 =	$ 6,000,000	(6 ÷ 15) x $11,200,000	$ 4,480,000
B	$15.00 x 600,000 =	$ 9,000,000	(9 ÷ 15) x $11,200,000	6,720,000
		$15,000,000		$11,200,000

3.   The sales value of B at the split-off point must be approximated:

Sales value of B   = Final sales value - Separable costs
   = ($21.50 x 600,000) - [$300,000 + ($1 x 600,000)]
   = $12,900,000 - $900,000
   = $12,000,000

	Relative Sales Value at Split-off	Weighting	Allocation of Joint Costs
A	$ 6,000,000	(6 ÷ 18) x $11,200,000	$ 3,733,333
B	12,000,000	(12 ÷ 18) x $11,200,000	7,466,667
	$18,000,000		$11,200,000

12-B1 (10-15 min.)

1.

	Business	Engineering
Fixed costs per month:		
210 ÷ 700, or 30% of $100,000	$30,000	
490 ÷ 700, or 70% of $100,000		$ 70,000
Variable costs @ $200 per hour:		
210 hours	42,000	
390 hours		78,000
Total costs	$72,000	$148,000

2.

	Business	Engineering
Fixed costs per month:		
210/600 x $100,000	$35,000	
390/600 x $100,000		$ 65,000
Variable costs, as before	42,000	78,000
Total costs	$77,000	$143,000

The dean of Business would probably be unhappy. The Business School has operated exactly in accordance with the long-range plan. Nevertheless, Business is bearing an extra $5,000 of fixed costs because of what *another* consumer is using. The dean would prefer the method in Requirement 1 because it insulates Business from short-run fluctuations in costs caused by the actions of other users.

12-B2 (30-40 min.)

1. Direct method:

	Personnel	Administrative	Residential	Commercial
Direct departmental costs before allocation	$ 70,000	$ 90,000	$240,000	$400,000
Personnel	(70,000)		28,000	42,000
Administrative		(90,000)	33,750	56,250
Total costs after allocation			$301,750	$498,250

Calculations:

12 + 18 = 30
(12 ÷ 30) x $70,000 = $28,000
(18 ÷ 30) x $70,000 = $42,000
240,000 + 400,000 = 640,000
(240,000 ÷ 640,000) x $90,000 = $33,750
(400,000 ÷ 640,000) x $90,000 = $56,250

2. Step-down method:

	Personnel	Administrative	Residential	Commercial
Direct departmental cost before allocation	$ 70,000	$ 90,000	$240,000	$400,000
Personnel	(70,000)	10,000	24,000	36,000
Administrative		$(100,000)	37,500	62,500
Total cost after allocation			$301,500	$498,500

Calculations:
5 + 12 + 18 = 35
(5 ÷ 35) x $70,000 = $10,000
(12 ÷ 35) x $70,000 = $24,000
(18 ÷ 35) x $70,000 = $36,000
240,000 + 400,000 = 640,000
(240,000 ÷ 640,000) x $100,000 = $37,500
(400,000 ÷ 640,000) x $100,000 = $62,500

3. (a) Residential: $301,500 ÷ 24,000 hours = $12.56 per direct-labor hr
    (b) Commercial: $498,500 ÷ 9,970,000 sq. ft. = $.05 per square foot

12-B3 (20-30 min.)

		Standard Kiwis	Giant Kiwis
1.	Unit costs:		
	Direct materials	$1.30	$2.20
	Materials receiving and handling	.24	.48
	Production setup (60÷600, 60÷240)	.10	.25
	Cutting, sewing, and assembly	.40	.40
	Total unit cost	$2.04	$3.33
	x Number of units	100	50
	Cost before packing and shipping	$204.00	$166.50
	Packing and shipping	10.00	10.00
	Total cost	$214.00	$176.50

2.   This requirement calls for an understanding of cost drivers. Instead of setup costs being added as an average unit cost, they are added as a total cost for each product in this order. In essence, setup costs are driven by the order because the new requirements call for one setup for each product in each order:

Unit costs:	Standard Kiwis	Giant Kiwis
Direct materials	$1.30	$2.20
Materials receiving and handling	.24	.48
Cutting, sewing, and assembly	.40	.40
Total unit cost	$1.94	$3.08
x Number of units	100	50
Cost before setup and packing and shipping	$194.00	$154.00
Setup	60.00	60.00
Packing and shipping	10.00	10.00
Total cost	$264.00	$224.00

3. The activity-based costing system recognizes the behavior of the costs. Because Maori Novelty has no category for direct labor, it apparently is not a significant cost. Therefore, it is unlikely to have a cause-effect relationship with the other costs. The activity-based costing system allocates costs based on their causes. Therefore, Maori can better assess the costs of individual products. In addition, special situations such as the setups needed in requirement 2 can be costed more easily and accurately.

12-B4 (15 min.)

The joint costs include the purchase cost of $1,000,000 x $.60 = $600,000 and the processing cost before the split-off point of $.30 x 1,000,000 = $300,000, a total of $900,000.

1.

	Pounds	Weighting	Allocation of Joint Costs
Oat flour	800,000	800/1,000 x $900,000	$720,000
Oat bran	200,000	200/1,000 x $900,000	180,000
	1,000,000		$900,000

2.

	Relative Sales Value at Split-off*	Weighting	Allocation of Joint Costs
Oat flour	$1,200,000	1,200/1,600 x $900,000	$675,000
Oat bran	400,000	400/1,600 x $900,000	225,000
	$1,600,000		$900,000

*$1.50 x 800,000 and $2.00 x 200,000

3. Estimated value of oat flour at split-off:

Sales value of oat flakes, $2.90 x 800,000 pounds	$2,320,000
- Processing cost after split-off point, ($.60 x 800,000 pounds) + $240,000	720,000
	$1,600,000

	Relative Sales Value at Split-off	Weighting	Allocation of Joint Costs
Oat flakes	$1,600,000	1,600/2,000 x $900,000	$720,000
Oat bran	400,000	400/2,000 x $900,000	180,000
	$2,000,000		$900,000

<u>12-1</u>   Companies use cost accounting systems to collect and classify costs and assign them to cost objects in order to measure the cost of designing, developing, producing (or purchasing), selling, distributing, and servicing particular products or services.

<u>12-2</u>   No. The costs in a cost pool are not *physically traced* to cost objectives. They are *allocated* to cost objectives using a single cost driver as a base.

<u>12-3</u>   Some possible terms are reallocate, trace, assign, distribute, redistribute, load, apportion, reapportion, attribute, and burden.

<u>12-4</u>   The four purposes of cost allocation are (1) to predict the economic effects of planning and control decisions, (2) to obtain desired motivation, (3) to compute income and asset valuations, and (4) to justify costs or obtain reimbursement.

<u>12-5</u>   The seven types of cost assignments (from Exhibit 12-1) are

(1) directly traced costs to departments,

(2) indirect costs allocated to departments,

(3) service department costs allocated to other service departments,

(4) service department costs allocated to producing departments,

(5) producing department costs allocated to other producing departments,

(6) directly traced costs to departments that can also be directly traced to products and services, and

(7) producing department costs that an organization allocates to products or services.

12-6 The preferred guidelines for allocating service department costs are:

a. Evaluate performance using budgets for each service (staff) department, just as they are used for each production or operating (line) department. When feasible, maintain distinctions between variable-cost pools and fixed-cost pools.

b. Allocate variable- and fixed-cost pools separately. This is sometimes called the dual method of allocation. Note that one service department (such as a computer department) can contain a variable-cost pool and a fixed-cost pool. That is, costs may be pooled within and among departments if desired.

c. Establish part or all of the details regarding cost allocation in advance of rendering the service rather than after the fact.

12-7 The distinction between direct and indirect depends on the cost object. A cost such as the salaries of service department personnel are a direct cost when the cost object is the service department. However, when the cost object is outside the service department, such as a producing department that uses the services of the service department, the salaries of the service department must be allocated to the producing departments and hence are indirect.

12-8 Using budgeted rather than actual cost rates protects the using departments from inefficiencies in the service departments and from intervening price fluctuations.

12-9 The motivation to underestimate long-run usage is a common problem with allocation methods using lump-sums based on long-range plans. To counteract this tendency, management can evaluate predictions of long-run usage and provide rewards for accurate predictions.

12-10 Two methods of allocating service department costs are the *direct method* and the *step-down* method. The direct method ignores other service departments when any given service department's costs are allocated. No costs are allocated from one service department to another. The step-down method recognizes that some service departments provide services to other service departments as well as to producing departments. The costs of the first service department are allocated to all other service departments and the producing departments. Then the second service department's costs are allocated to *the remaining* service departments (i.e., all service departments *except* those whose costs have already been allocated) and the producing departments. Once a service department's costs have been allocated, no subsequent service department's costs are allocated back to it. This procedure continues until all service department costs have been allocated.

12-11 No. Both the direct and step-down methods allocate the same total amount of costs to the producing departments.

12-12 Non-volume-related cost drivers are causes of costs that are not pro-portional to the volume of output. For example, number of hours of engineering design services is a non-volume-related cost driver that can be used to allocate engineering costs. Another non-volume-related cost driver is product complexity - more specifically, possibly number of components in a final product.

12-13 First, managers identify the key activities in the organization, and they collect overhead costs for each activity. Cost drivers are then selected for each activity, and those cost drivers are used to allocate the costs to the cost objects.

12-14 It would be ideal if every cost pool would contain only fixed or only variable costs. This should be the goal. In practice, there are many reasons why this goal may not be achieved. For example, the identification of fixed and variable costs is not perfect; most costs have some fixed and some variable cost characteristics. Perfect separation into fixed and variable cost categories may not be possible. In addition, it may not be economically feasible to have separate cost pools for fixed and variable costs if most (but not all) of the cost fits into one of the categories. For example, if 90% of a cost is variable and 10% is fixed, it may be best to treat the entire cost as variable.

12-15 Some possible activities and cost drivers are:

Activity	Cost driver
Group of machines	Machine hours
Set-up costs	Number of set-ups
Quality inspection	Units passing inspection point
Personnel department	Number of employees

12-16 Joint costs are allocated to products or services for purposes of inventory valuation and income determination. They may also be allocated for cost-reimbursement contracts.

12-17 The *physical units* method allocates joint costs in proportion to some physical property of the products (e.g., weight or volume) at the split-off point. The *relative sales value* method allocates joint costs in proportion to the amounts for which the products can be sold at the split-off point.

12-18 By-products, like joint products, are not separately identifiable before the split-off point. However, by-products have relatively insignificant sales values compared to main products. Only separable costs are applied to by-products; no joint costs are allocated to them. Revenues from by-products, less separable costs, are deducted from the cost of the main product.

12-19 Fixed costs are often allocated separately from variable costs because they are caused by different activities. Fixed costs are affected primarily by long-range decisions about the overall level of service. In contrast, variable costs depend on short-run fluctuations in actual usage.

12-20 Sales dollars are often a poor basis for allocation of costs because they reflect efficiency of sales effort and variations in pricing margins, neither of which is related to costs. Further, changes of sales in one department can affect costs allocated to the other departments.

12-21 One way to allocate national advertising costs to territories is on the basis of *expected* sales in each territory, computed by some formula combining population, income, appeal, competition, and supply capability.

12-22 No. The main reasons that activity-based costing is becoming so popular relate to planning and control, not product costing: (1) decisions about product mix, prices, and other product-related decisions, and (2) control of costs focused on managing activities instead of products. The term activity-based management refers to the use of activity-based costs for planning and control purposes.

12-23 (10-15 min.)

1. Rate = $\dfrac{\$2,500 + (\$.05 \times 100,000)}{100,000} = \$.075$ per copy

    Cost allocated to City Planning in August = $\$.075 \times 42,000 = \$3,150$.

2. Fixed cost pool allocated as a lump sum depending on predicted usage:

    To City Planning: $(36,000 \div 100,000) \times \$2,500 = \$900$ per month

    Variable cost pool allocated on the basis of actual usage:
    $\$.05 \times$ number of copies

    Cost allocated to City Planning in August: $\$900 + (\$.05 \times 42,000) = \$3,000$.

3. The second method, the one that allocated fixed- and variable-cost pools separately, is preferable. It better recognizes the causes of the costs. The fixed cost depends on the size of the photocopy machine, which is based on predicted usage and is independent of actual usage. Variable costs, in contrast are caused by actual usage.

12-24 (10 - 15 min.)

	Sunnyville	Wedgewood	Independence
1. Allocation based on budgeted sales*	$60,000	$100,000	$40,000
2. Allocation based on actual sales**	66,667	77,778	55,555

*$200,000 x (600/2,000); $200,000 x (1,000/2,000); $200,000 x (400/2,000)
** $200,000 x (600/1,800); $200,000 x (700/1,800); $200,000 x (500/1,800)

3.	The major argument against using actual sales as a cost driver for cost allocation is that a department's allocation depends on the success of other departments. Here, Sunnyville is allocated an extra $6,667 because sales in the Wedgewood store are below budget, even though Sunnyville's sales came in right on target. Further, stores with poor sales results probably do not cause reduced central office costs. If anything, a department with poor performance requires more central attention. Also, using budgeted sales reduces surprises; managers know what amount of allocated cost to expect. Often managers are more upset by unexpected changes in allocated amounts than by the size of the allocation itself.

12-25 (25-30 min.)

1.	See Exhibit 12-25. Calculations for the exhibit follow:

	3 + 12 + 18 + 8 = 41
	(3 ÷ 41) x $92,000 = $6,732
	(12 ÷ 41) x $92,000 = $26,927
	(18 ÷ 41) x $92,000 = $40,390
	(8 ÷ 41) x $92,000 = $17,951
	$240,000 + $400,000 = $640,000
	($240,000 ÷ $640,000) x $180,000 = $67,500
	($400,000 ÷ $640,000) x $180,000 = $112,500

2. See Exhibit 12-25. Calculations for the exhibit follow:

$5 + 3 + 12 + 18 + 8 = 46$
$(5 \div 46) \times \$92,000 = \$10,000$
$(3 \div 46) \times \$92,000 = \$6,000$
$(12 \div 46) \times \$92,000 = \$24,000$
$(18 \div 46) \times \$92,000 = \$36,000$
$(8 \div 46) \times \$92,000 = \$16,000$
$\$240,000 + \$400,000 = \$640,000$
$(\$240,000 \div \$640,000) \times \$190,000 = \$71,250$
$(\$400,000 \div \$640,000) \times \$190,000 = \$118,750$

3. The allocation bases used by each division to allocate activity costs to products will be the cost drivers for activities 1 through 5. For example, suppose activity 1 in the residential division is "cleaning windows," and the cost driver is "number of windows." Further assume that service type RA has a total of 3,000 units (customers) with an activity-consumption rate of 6 (an average of 6 windows per RA-type customer) and service type RB has 500 units with an activity-consumption rate of 40. The allocation of activity 1 cost using the step-down method would be:

Activity cost per driver unit =
$\$66,000 \div$ (3,000 RA Customers x 6 windows per customer + 500 RB Customers x 40 windows per customer)
$= \$66,000 \div 38,000$ windows
$= \$1.7368421$ per window.

To service type RA: $\$1.7368 \times 18,000$ windows $= \$31,262.40$

To service type RB: $\$1.7368 \times 20,000$ windows $= \$34,736.00$

Exhibit 12-25

Direct method:

	Personnel	Admin.	Residential Division			Commercial Division			
			Activity 1	Activity 2	Total	Activity 3	Activity 4	Activity 5	Total
Direct costs	$92,000	$180,000	$60,000	$240,000	$300,000	$400,000	$90,000	$110,000	$600,000
Personnel	(92,000)	0*	6,732	26,927	33,659	40,390	0	17,951	58,341
Administrative		(180,000)	0	67,500	67,500	112,500	0	0	112,500
Total costs after allocation			$66,732	$334,427	$401,159	$552,890	$90,000	$127,951	$770,841

*Note that on the process map shown in Exhibit 12-14, the direct method ignores the link and the related allocated costs from the Personnel Department to the Administrative Department.

Step-down method:

	Personnel	Admin.	Residential Division			Commercial Division			
			Activity 1	Activity 2	Total	Activity 3	Activity 4	Activity 5	Total
Direct costs	$92,000	$180,000	$60,000	$240,000	$300,000	$400,000	$90,000	$110,000	$600,000
Personnel	(92,000)	10,000	6,000	24,000	30,000	36,000	0	16,000	52,000
Administrative		(190,000)	0	71,250	71,250	118,750	0	0	118,750
Total costs after allocation			$66,000	$335,250	$401,250	$554,750	$90,000	$126,000	$770,750

12-26 (15-20 min.)

1. Direct method:

	Personnel	Custodial	Machining	Assembly
Direct department costs before allocation	$32,000	$70,000	$600,000	$800,000
Personnel*	(32,000)		14,222	17,778
Custodial**		(70,000)	20,000	50,000
Total cost after allocation	$ 0	$ 0	$634,222	$867,778

* $(200 \div 450)$ x $32,000; $(250 \div 450)$ x $32,000
**$(10 \div 35)$ x $70,000; $(25 \div 35)$ x $70,000

2. Step-down method:

	Personnel	Custodial	Machining	Assembly
Direct department costs before allocation	$32,000	$70,000	$600,000	$800,000
Personnel*	(32,000)	2,000	13,333	16,667
Custodial**		(72,000)	20,571	51,429
Total cost after allocation	$ 0	$ 0	$633,904	$868,096

* $(30 \div 480)$ x $32,000; $(200 \div 480)$ x $32,000; $(250 \div 480)$ x $32,000
**$(10 \div 35)$ x $72,000; $(25 \div 35)$ x $72,000

12-27 (15-20 min.)

1.

	Gallons	Weighting	Allocation of Joint Costs
Solvent A	9,000	9/15 x $300,000	$180,000
Solvent B	6,000	6/15 x $300,000	120,000
	15,000		$300,000

2.

	Relative Sales Value at Split-off*	Weighting	Allocation of Joint Costs
Solvent A	$270,000	27/54 x $300,000	$150,000
Solvent B	270,000	27/54 x $300,000	150,000
	$540,000		$300,000

* $30 x 9,000 and $45 x 6,000

12-28 (10 min.)

1.

	Gallons	Weighting	Allocation of Joint Costs
Solvent A	20,000	20/30 x $400,000	$266,667
Solvent B	10,000	10/30 x $400,000	133,333
	30,000		$400,000

2.

	Relative Sales Value at Split-off*	Weighting	Allocation of Joint Costs
Solvent A	$ 400,000	400/1,000 x $400,000	$160,000
Solvent B	600,000	600/1,000 x $400,000	240,000
	$1,000,000		$400,000

* $20 x 20,000 and $60 x 10,000

12-29 (10-15 min.)

1. *None*. The entire joint cost is allocated to the main product.

2. $35,000. The total inventory cost of the pulp is the separable cost, that is, the cost incurred after the split-off point.

3. Inventory cost of apples:

Direct materials (apples)	$1,000,000
Pressing cost	130,000
Filter, pasteurize, and pack cost	150,000
Total	$1,280,000
Less: Revenue less separable costs of by-product ($50,000 - $35,000)	(15,000)
Net cost of apple juice	$1,265,000

<u>12-30</u> (20 min.)

This problem is based on a description in *Cost Finding and Rate Setting for Hospitals* (Chicago: American Hospital Association), p. 6 and p. 74. It illustrates the idea of using a weighted average, which is really a version of equivalent units (explained in the chapter on process costing). If process costing is covered in this course, the applicability of equivalent units in a hospital context is important to see.

The cost driver would be "weighted number of pounds processed" instead of "number of pounds processed." The new computations are:

Laundry department costs		$180,000
Weighted number of pounds processed:		
Radiology, (7,500 x 5) and (7,500 x 1)	45,000	
Other centers, 600,000 - 15,000	585,000	
Divided by total weighted pounds		630,000
Cost per weighted pound		$ .286
Total costs to radiology:		
Using unweighted base, 15,000 x $.30		$ 4,500
Using weighted base, 45,000 x $.286		$12,870

The practical problems of cost allocation are described in the cost-finding publication:

One basis for the allocation of laundry costs is pounds of soiled laundry. This is a good basis provided it is possible for the hospital to identify the source of soiled linens by department. However, because of the use of linen chutes, or for other reasons, many hospitals cannot identify the source of laundry by department. In smaller hospitals the use of an outside commercial laundry service also is common, and some hospitals do not have weighing facilities.

In every hospital there must be a linen distribution function, and a study of the amount and type of linen distributed to the various departments of the hospital will produce a reliable basis for allocation. As a minimum, the number of pieces, adjusted for weight differentials, should be tallied for a period of perhaps two weeks, two or three times a year. The weight factor, however, needs to be established only once. Reliable weight factors can be developed by simply weighing the various pieces and establishing standard piece weights for each type of laundry. The average of the several two-week tests can be used as the basis for distributing laundry costs for cost-finding purposes.

Another method is to use commercial laundry prices as a weighting factor for the different types of pieces. This method has the advantage of allowing for the relative difficulty of different processing functions, such as pressed versus mangle finishing.

Hospitals can conduct very refined studies if they so desire. It may be appropriate, especially in larger institutions, to give special consideration to refinements. For example, where the laundry processes a large volume of uniforms for student nurses and doctors, and for dietary, housekeeping, and other service personnel, it may be desirable to separate washing and pressing costs and to develop separate allocation bases for each of these functions based on the production statistics. Furthermore, it may be desirable to consider the effect of different processing cycles, such as the special rinse cycles for operating room linens or the special cold wash cycles for woolen blankets. Through discussions with the laundry manager, it is possible to determine whether further analysis is justified. Another example of possible refinements is the personal laundry done for medical interns, residents, student nurses, and others; if the volume is large, it might have to be recognized in the departmental operations.

(15 min.)

1.   What is the purpose of this cost allocation? Primarily, it is to help set a "fair" price. (Note the SP representative's reference to "it is not fair.") Regulatory authorities set prices based on cost allocations in many industries, including utilities, natural gas, and railroads, where free markets are allowed to reign only to a limited degree. The most troublesome problems usually arise when there is a significant amount of common costs.

Obviously, this specific illustration will not lead to any clear-cut answers. Those commissioners who favor "full costing" will be sympathetic to the SP position, while those commissioners who favor "incremental costing" will be sympathetic to the PUC staff.

Those who favor full costing should nevertheless be cautious in applying "system-wide" overhead rates to a small operation. The problem is akin to using plant-wide overhead rates for a particular factory department's operations; sometimes the final results are not affected significantly, but big potential differences lead toward developing departmental rates.

Those who favor incremental costing should be concerned about more costs than just "above-the-rail" costs like fuel, labor, and equipment maintenance. The SP representative cited two examples of "common" costs that would indeed be affected if commuter service were discontinued. In addition, if regulatory commissions allowed only incremental costs to be covered by prices, companies would eventually go out of business. In the long run, all costs must be covered.

2.   This question was raised to demonstrate the dangers of having a cost allocation to one segment be heavily dependent on what is happening in another segment. Commuter passenger traffic is unlikely to be as sensitive to changes in business conditions as is freight traffic. Therefore, a sudden decline in freight traffic would result in passenger traffic's bearing a higher fraction of common costs.

<u>12-32</u> (20-25 min.)

1.   Annual costs for 24,000 miles: Fixed $2,400

                                              Variable ($.10 x 24,000)   <u> 2,400</u>

                                                                       <u>$4,800</u>

Cost per mile = $4,800 ÷ 24,000 miles = $.20 per mile

2.   Two factors caused the April allocation of $.38 per mile to exceed the average of $.20 per mile:

(1) The motor pool's operating inefficiencies are passed on to the user departments. The cost of 50,000 miles in April should have been [($2,400 ÷ 12 months) x 50 autos] + ($.10 x 50,000 miles) = $10,000 + $5,000 = $15,000. Therefore, $4,000 of "unnecessary" cost was assigned to user departments, which is $4,000 ÷ 50,000 miles = $.08 per mile.

(2) April was a month of low general usage. In an average month, 100,000 miles are driven (2,000 miles per auto), and the fixed cost per mile is ($2,400 ÷ 12 months) ÷ 2,000 miles = $200 ÷ 2,000 miles = $.10 per mile. In April the $200 fixed cost of each auto was spread over only 1,000 miles, so fixed cost per mile was $200 ÷ 1,000 = $.20 per mile. This factor accounts for an extra $.10 per mile.

3.   Undesirable behavioral effects include:

(a) The total actual motor pool cost is allocated. The manager is not motivated to control these costs.

(b) Allocated costs are affected by auto usage in other departments. A department is better off if its auto usage happens to fall in a month when other departments have high mileage.

(c) Decisions about whether driving another mile is worth its cost are not appropriately made. The city incurs only $.10 more expense for an additional mile, but departments are charged more.

(d) The cost allocation is affected only by miles driven, not number of autos assigned to a department. A department with two autos each being driven 15,000 miles per year is allocated the same cost as one with one auto driven 30,000 miles per year. But each auto causes the same average fixed costs, so fixed costs should be allocated on the basis of number of autos rather than miles driven. This may be the reason the city planner was continually concerned with her auto costs. Her department's autos were driven an average of 3,000 miles per month, but the city's average was only 2,000 miles. Because both fixed and variable costs are allocated on a per-mile basis, her department's autos are allocated more fixed cost than the average auto in the city. If fixed costs were allocated on the basis of number of autos, each auto would be charged $200 per month. This becomes $.07 per mile for the city planner's autos compared to $.10 for the average auto in the city.

4. Two basic principles should be applied:

(a) Allocate budgeted, not actual, costs. Inefficiencies of the motor pool should not be passed on to user departments.

(b) Separate costs into fixed and variable cost pools. The fixed costs should be allocated on the basis of number of autos assigned to a department or long-run predicted use of autos. Variable costs are appropriately assigned on a per-mile-driven basis.

This cost-allocation method illustrates why the city planner has a legitimate complaint. In April she paid $.08 per mile extra because of motor pool inefficiency, $.10 per mile extra because other departments had light usage in April, and $.03 per mile extra because fixed costs are charged on a per-mile basis rather than a per-auto basis.

12-33 (20-30 min.)

1.

Actual costs	$750,000 + $.75(500,000)	=	$1,125,000
Rate per ton-mile*	$1,125,000 ÷ 500,000	=	$2.25
To North	250,000 x $2.25	=	$562,500
To South	250,000 x $2.25	=	$562,500

*Rate is per thousand net ton-miles

2.

Actual costs	$750,000 + $.75(400,000)	=	$1,050,000
Rate per ton-mile	$1,050,000 ÷ 400,000	=	$2.625
To North	150,000 x $2.625	=	$393,750
To South	250,000 x $2.625	=	$656,250

Note that South's costs increased from $562,500 to $656,250 or 16.7%, solely because North's volume declined.

3.

Rate per ton-mile	$1,250,000 ÷ 500,000	=	$2.50
To North	250,000 x $2.50	=	$625,000
To South	250,000 x $2.50	=	$625,000

Such allocation seems unjustified because the operating departments have to bear another department's cost of inefficiency. Note that the use of a predetermined or budgeted total amount geared to the various levels of activity of the operating departments would eliminate this difficulty. For example, the $2.25 rate of part (1) would be used here despite the excess of actual costs over budgeted costs.

1. Basic maximum capacity:

    360,000 + 240,000 = 600,000 ton miles.

Fixed costs:	North	South
To North, 36/60 x $750,000	$450,000	$ -
To South, 24/60 x $750,000	-	300,000
Variable costs:		
To North, $.75 x 150,000	112,500	-
To South, $.75 x 250,000	-	187,500
Total costs	$562,500	$487,500

Note that North's costs are $562,500 rather than the $393,750 in part (2).

This method has the following advantages:

a. The use of a predetermined unit rate for variable costs prevents the total charges from being affected by the efficiency of price changes of the service department.

b. The use of a predetermined lump-sum for fixed costs prevents the total charges from being affected by the consumption of service or the activity levels of other operating departments or the activity level of the service department.

12-34 (25-30 min.)

There a several ways to organize an analysis that provides product costs. We like to focus first on determining total activity-cost pools and activity cost per driver unit. Then, an analysis similar to the one shown in Exhibit 12-8 on page 538 can be used.

Schedule a   Activity center cost pool

Resources Supporting the Setup/Maintenance Activity Center	Allocation Calculation	Allocated Cost
Assembly supervisors	$92,400 x 2.6%	$ 2,402
Assembly machines	$247,000 x (400 ÷ 1,900)	52,000
Facilities management	$95,000 x (400 ÷ 1,900)	20,000
Power	$54,000 x (10 ÷ 90)	6,000
Total assigned cost		$80,402
Cost per driver unit (setup)	$80,400 ÷ 40	$ 2,010

Resources Supporting the Assembly Activity Center	Allocation Calculation	Allocated Cost
Assembly supervisors	$92,400 x 97.4%	$ 89,998
Assembly machines	$247,000 x (1,500 ÷ 1,900)	195,000
Facilities management	$95,000 x (1,500 ÷ 1,900)	75,000
Power	$54,000 x (80 ÷ 90)	48,000
Total assigned cost		$407,998
Cost per driver unit (machine hour)	$408,000 ÷ 1,500	$ 272

Exhibit 12-34

Contribution to cover other value-chain costs by product

Activity/Resource	Cost per Driver Unit (Schedule a)	Standard		Deluxe		Custom	
		Driver Units	Cost	Driver Units	Cost	Driver Units	Cost
Setup/Maintenance	$2,010	20	$ 40,200	12	$ 24,120	8	$ 16,080
Assembly	$ 272	1,000	272,000	400	108,800	100	27,200
Parts			1,003,800		115,080		15,980
Direct labor			298,000		72,000		68,000
Total			$1,614,000		$320,000		$127,260
Units			100,000		10,000		1,000
Cost per display			$16.14		$32.00		$127.26
Selling price			20.00		50.00		250.00
Unit contribution			$ 3.86		$18.00		$122.74
Total contribution			$ 386,000		$180,000		$122,740

The total contribution of these products is $386,000 + $180,000 + $122,740 = $688,740.

12-35 (25-30 min.) See solution to problem 12-34.

12-36 (10-15 min.)

	Contribution per Unit	Customer Type 1		Customer Type 2	
		Units Sold	Contribution	Units Sold	Contribution
Standard display	$ 3.86	75,000	$289,500	25,000	$ 96,500
Deluxe display	18.00	5,000	90,000	5,000	90,000
Custom display	122.74	0	0	1,000	122,740
Total			$379,500		$309,240

12-37 (20-30 min.)

1. Basic long-run usage:
    75 + 50 = 125 X-rays per month

    Total costs incurred:
    $12,000 + 100 X-rays ($30) = $15,000

	University Hospital	Children's Hospital
Fixed costs:		
75/125 x $12,000	$ 7,200	
50/125 x $12,000		$4,800
Variable costs:		
50 x $30	1,500	
50 x $30		1,500
Total allocated costs	$8,700	$6,300

2. For budgetary control and motivation purposes, it is best not to allocate the $1,500 efficiency variance ($16,500 minus the $15,000 computed above). For cost recovery purposes, if reimbursement is based on actual costs, it should be allocated.

3.

	University Hospital	Children's Hospital
Total costs incurred, $15,000:		
50/100 x $15,000	$7,500	
50/100 x $15,000		$7,500

Children's Hospital bears $1,200 more costs than in part (1) despite the fact that its volume was exactly in accordance with its long-run average usage. In short, Children's Hospital's costs have increased *solely* because of a fellow consumer's actions, not its own actions. University Hospital's failure to reach its predicted usage results in shifting $1,200 more fixed costs to Children's Hospital.

A behavioral effect of this method would be toward more erratic scheduling (to the extent this discretion exists). For instance, if University Hospital had a relatively light month, it would be motivated toward not scheduling procedures during the final week and bunching them in the first week of the second month. In this way, its unit costs of the second month would be lowered.

4. Both University and Children's Hospitals would be induced to underestimate usage. Of course, if both play the same game, the final fraction borne by each would be little changed. One way to counteract these tendencies is to exert higher arbitrary (and unreimbursable) cost allocations to both University and Children's Hospitals if they consistently exceed their predicted usage. Also, first priority on scarce resources can be extended to those consumers who are committed to the higher fractions.

12-38 (20-30 min.)

1.

	Building Services	Materials Receiving and Handling	Mechanical Instruments	Electronic Instruments
Direct department costs before allocation	$150,000	$120,000	$680,000	$548,000
Building services	(150,000)		100,000	50,000
Materials receiving and handling		(120,000)	40,000	80,000
Total costs after allocation			$820,000	$678,000

Calculations:

50,000 + 25,000 = 75,000

(50,000 ÷ 75,000) x $150,000 = $100,000

(25,000 ÷ 75,000) x $150,000 = $50,000

No. of components: 10 x 8,000 = 80,000; 16 x 10,000 = 160,000

80,000 + 160,000 = 240,000

(80,000 ÷ 240,000) x $120,000 = $40,000

(160,000 ÷ 240,000) x $120,000 = $80,000

2. Mechanical instruments:

$820,000 ÷ 30,000 hours = $27.33 per direct-labor hour

Electronic instruments:

$678,000 ÷ 160,000 components = $4.24 per component

3. Total cost = direct materials cost + manufacturing cost:

M1: $74 + ($27.33 x 4) = $74 + $109.32 = $183.32

M2: $86 + ($27.33 x 8) = $86 + 218.64 = $304.64

E1: $63 + ($ 4.24 x 10) = $63 +   42.40 = $105.40

E2: $91 + ($ 4.24 x 15) = $91 +   63.60 = $154.60

12-39 (20-30 min.)

1.

	Building Services	Materials Receiving and Handling	Mechanical Instruments	Electronic Instruments
Direct department costs before allocation	$150,000	$ 120,000	$680,000	$548,000
Building services	(150,000)	9,375	93,750	46,875
Materials receiving and handling		$(129,375)	43,125	86,250
Total costs after allocation			$816,875	$681,125

Calculations:

$5,000 + 50,000 + 25,000 = 80,000$

$(5 \div 80) \times \$150,000 = \$9,375$

$(50 \div 80) \times \$150,000 = \$93,750$

$(25 \div 80) \times \$150,000 = \$46,875$

No. of components: $10 \times 8,000 = 80,000$; $16 \times 10,000 = 160,000$

$80,000 + 160,000 = 240,000$

$(80 \div 240) \times \$129,375 = \$43,125$

$(160 \div 240) \times \$129,375 = \$86,250$

2. Mechanical instruments:

$\$816,875 \div 30,000$ hours = $27.23 per direct-labor hour

Electronic instruments:

$681,125 \div 160,000$ components = $4.26 per component

3. Total cost = direct materials cost + manufacturing cost

M1: $74 + (\$27.23 \times 4) = \$74 + \$108.92 = \$182.92$

M2: $86 + (\$27.23 \times 8) = \$86 + \$217.84 = \$303.84$

E1: $63 + (\$4.26 \times 10) = \$63 + \$42.60 = \$105.60$

E2: $91 + (\$4.26 \times 15) = \$91 + \$63.90 = \$154.90$

12-40 (40 min.)

1 & 2. The solutions to requirements 1 and 2 are in Exhibit 12-40.

3. Single Plantwide Rate: $165,000 ÷ 24,000 = $6.875 per direct-labor hour.

4. Comparison of methods:

Step-down method:

Job K10,	19 x $10 +	2 x $5.83 =	$190 + $ 11.66 =	$201.66
Job K12,	3 x $10 +	18 x $5.83 =	$ 30 + $104.94 =	134.94
Total				$336.60

Direct method:

Job K10, 19 x $9.88 +	2 x $5.87 =	$187.72 + $ 11.74 =	$199.46
Job K12, 3 x $9.88 +	18 x $5.87 =	$ 29.64 + $105.66 =	135.30
Total =			$334.76

Blanket rate:

Job K10,	21 x $6.875 =	$144.38
Job K12,	21 x $6.875 =	144.38
Total		$288.76

EXHIBIT 12-40

1. Step-down Method

	Building & Grounds	Personnel	General Factory Administration	Cafeteria Operating Loss	Storeroom	Machining	Assembly
Direct department costs	$20,000	$1,200	$28,020	$1,430	$2,750	$40,100	$71,500
(1) Building & grounds @ 20¢/sq. ft.	$20,000	400	1,400	800	1,400	6,000	10,000
(2) Personnel @ $8/employee		$1,600	280	80	40	400	800
(3) General factory admin. @$.9167/labor hour			$29,700	1,100	1,100	8,800	18,700
(4) Cafeteria @ $22/employee				1,100	1,100	1,100	2,200
(5) Storeroom @ $1.20/requisition				$3,410	110	3,600	1,800
(6) Total					$5,400	$60,000	$105,000
(7) Divide (6) by direct labor hours						÷6,000	÷18,000
(8) Overhead rate per direct-labor hour						$10.00	$5.83

2. Direct Method

	Building & Grounds	Personnel	General Factory Administration	Cafeteria Operating Loss	Storeroom	Machining	Assembly
Direct department costs	$20,000	$1,200	$28,020	$1,430	$2,750	$40,100	$71,500
(1) Building & grounds:	(20,000)					7,500	12,500
(2) Personnel:		(1,200)				400	800
(3) General factory admin.:			(28,020)			8,966	19,054
(4) Cafeteria:				(1,430)		477	953
(5) Storeroom:					(2,750)	1,833	917
(6) Total						$59,276	$105,724
(7) Divide (6) by direct-labor hours						÷6,000	÷18,000
(8) Overhead rate per direct-labor hour						$9.88	$5.87

(1) Building & grounds: $\frac{20,000}{80,000}$ =25¢

(2) Personnel: 1/3 & 2/3

(3) General factory admin.: $\frac{28,020}{30,000}$ = $0.934

(4) Cafeteria: $\frac{1,430}{150}$ or 1/3 & 2/3

(5) Storeroom: $\frac{2,750}{4,500}$ or 2/3 & 1/3

681

12-41 (15-25 min.)

1. See Exhibit 12-41, Part 1.

2. See Exhibit 12-41, Part 2.

The cost of the model 1 circuit boards decreases from ¥961,600 to ¥891,120, a decrease of ¥70,480. But because the decrease is due to a lower allocation and this is from fixed costs that do not change, the decrease is now allocated to models 2 and 3. The costs of models 2 and 3 increase to absorb the decrease in model 1 cost. So, why would Yamaguchi's management want to implement this process improvement? Because the improved efficiencies will free up processing capacity in resources used for these two activities. The freed up capacity can be deployed to meet other needs such as an increase in demand. The total cost (¥6,120,000) of all three models does not change.

Exhibit 12-41, Part 1

	Model 1	Model 2	Model 3
Direct materials:			
Model 1: ¥4,000 x 80 boards	¥320,000		
Model 2: ¥6,000 x 160 boards		¥960,000	
Model 3: ¥8,000 x 300 boards			¥2,400,000
Material handling activity[1]:			
Model 1: ¥26 x 20 x 80	41,600		
Model 2: ¥26 x 15 x 160		62,400	
Model 3: ¥26 x 10 x 300			78,000
Assembly activity[2]:			
Model 1: ¥67 x 40 x 80	214,400		
Model 2: ¥67 x 30 x 160		321,600	
Model 3: ¥67 x 16 x 300			321,600
Soldering activity[3]:			
Model 1: ¥47 x 60 x 80	225,600		
Model 2: ¥47 x 40 x 160		300,800	
Model 3: ¥47 x 20 x 300			282,000
Quality assurance activity[4]:			
Model 1: ¥400 x 5 x 80	160,000		
Model 2: ¥400 x 3 x 160		192,000	
Model 3: ¥400 x 2 x 300			240,000
Total cost for circuit boards	¥961,600	¥1,836,800	¥3,321,600
Cost per circuit board	¥ 12,020	¥11,480	¥ 11,072

1 ¥182,000 ÷ (80 x 20 + 160 x 15 + 300 x 10) = ¥26 per distinct part
2 ¥857,600 ÷ (80 x 40 + 160 x 30 + 300 x 16) = ¥67 per automatic insertion
3 ¥808,400 ÷ (80 x 60 + 160 x 40 + 300 x 20) = ¥47 per part
4 ¥592,000 ÷ (80 x 5 + 160 x 3 + 300 x 2) = ¥400 per minute

Exhibit 12-41, Part 2

	Model 1	Model 2	Model 3
Direct materials:			
Model 1: ¥4,000 x 80 boards	¥320,000		
Model 2: ¥6,000 x 160 boards		¥960,000	
Model 3: ¥8,000 x 300 boards			¥2,400,000
Material handling activity[1]:			
Model 1: ¥29.35484 x 10 x 80	23,484		
Model 2: ¥29.35484 x 15 x 160		70,452	
Model 3: ¥29.35484 x 10 x 300			88,065
Assembly activity[2]:			
Model 1: ¥67 x 40 x 80	214,400		
Model 2: ¥67 x 30 x 160		321,600	
Model 3: ¥67 x 16 x 300			321,600
Soldering activity[3]:			
Model 1: ¥47 x 60 x 80	225,600		
Model 2: ¥47 x 40 x 160		300,800	
Model 3: ¥47 x 20 x 300			282,000
Quality assurance activity[4]:			
Model 1: ¥448.48485 x 3 x 80	107,636		
Model 2: ¥448.48485 x 3 x 160		215,273	
Model 3: ¥448.48485 x 2 x 300			269,091
Total cost for circuit boards	¥891,120	¥1,868,125	¥3,360,756
Cost per circuit board	¥11,139	¥ 11,676	¥11,203

[1] ¥182,000÷ (80 x 10 + 160 x 15 + 300 x 10) = ¥29.35484 per distinct part
[2] ¥857,600÷ (80 x 40 + 160 x 30 + 300 x 16) = ¥67 per automatic insertion
[3] ¥808,400÷ (60 x 80 + 40 x 160 + 20 x 300) = ¥47 per part
[4] ¥592,000÷ (3 x 80 + 3 x 160 + 2 x 300) = ¥448.48485 per minute

684

12-42 (25 min.)

1. Recording and record-keeping cost: $16.50 x 550 = $ 9,075
   Labor cost: ($23,000 / 460,000) x 80,000 =   4,000
   Inspection cost: $2.75 x 4,000 =   11,000
   Total cost $24,075

2. Recording and record-keeping cost: $16.50 x 330 = $ 5,445
   Labor cost: No savings; fixed cost *   0
   Inspection cost: $2.75 x 1,500 =   4,125
   Total cost $9,570

   * Capacity is made available. If there is a profitable use of that capacity (that is, if the opportunity cost is not zero) a savings would result equal to the benefit from the use of the capacity.

3. Receiving cost per pound: $24,075 ÷ 80,000 = $.30

   Estimated cost saved from 20,000 pounds = $.30 x 20,000 = $6,000

   The company would have underestimated the savings by $9,570 - $6,000 = $3,570, and they may have continued to purchase and stock small-sales-level brands that are actually unprofitable.

12-43 (20 min.)

1.

	Variable Cost	Fixed Cost	Full Cost
Subcomponents	$1,100		$1,100
Receiving	22	$ 22	44
Assembly	144	144	288
Inspection	56		56
Total	$1,322	$166	$1,488

2.   Price = .9 x $1,990 = $1,791

On a full cost basis, the profit would be $1,791 - $1,488 = $303 per computer, or a total of 15 x $303 = $4,545. The contribution margin on the order would be $1,791 - $1,322 = $469 per computer, or a total of 15 x $469 = $7,035. (Of course, some of this "profit" must be used to cover other value-chain costs such as research and development, design, marketing, distribution, and customer service.) If Dell had excess capacity, so that this order did not require additional resources and did not have any affect on the ability to fill other orders, the extra profit from the order is $7,035. However, in a long-term perspective, Dell has to pay for all its resources, both those represented by variable costs and those represented by fixed costs. On this basis, the profit is only $4,545.

3.   Cost is an important factor, but by no means the only factor, to consider in making pricing decisions. In this case, it tells the Dell managers that this is a profitable product at the discounted price. But it does not say whether it is the most profitable product that could be produced with Dell's resources. Cost is important in answering one what-if question: what would profits be if Dell accepts this order at a particular predicted price. Cost data must be combined with a great deal of other data, such as market data and capacity data, to make intelligent pricing decisions.

1. (a) The allocation of joint costs would be in a 1:5 ratio:

	Product A	Product B	Total
Sales value	$1,000	$1,000	$2,000
Joint costs	$200	$1,000	$1,200
Separable costs	350	200	550
Total costs	$550	$1,200	$1,750
Operating profit	$450	$ (200)	$ 250

(b) No. Joint costs are not relevant for this decision because you cannot stop incurring that part allocated to one product and still continue to incur only the other part. If the total process is profitable, you should process any product that shows a positive contribution after the split-off point. Although Product B shows a book loss of $200, it has a contribution after the split-off point of $1,000 - $200, or $800.

2. (a) The relative sales value method deducts separable costs to arrive at an imputed sales value at split-off point:

	A	B	Total
Sales value	$1,000	$1,000	$2,000
Separable costs	350	200	550
Sales value imputed at split-off point	$650	$800	$1,450
Allocation of joint cost, 650/1,450 and 800/1,450, respectively	538	662	1,200
Operating profit	$112	$138	$ 250

(b) No. Product B does have the greater book profit and contribution after the split-off point, but Product A has the greatest contribution per pound, which is the scarce resource in this case. If, for example, the engineer changes the process by 40 pounds, so that we end up with 440 pounds of B and 40 pounds of A, separable costs would become $175 for A and $220 for B, totaling $395 (assuming separable costs are all variable). Sales values would become $500 for A and $1,100 for B, and total of $1,600. Total contribution after the split-off would drop from $1,450 to $1,205 and total profit would drop from $250 to $5.

	A	B	Total
Pounds	40	440	480
Sales value	$500	$1,100	$1,600
Separable costs	175	220	395
Contribution to joint costs	$325	$ 880	$1,205
Joint costs			1,200
Operating profit			$ 5

<u>12-45</u> (25-30 min.)

1. $1,080,000 ÷ 45,000 hours = $24 per direct-labor hour

2. (a) $630,000 ÷ 15,000 hours = $42 per direct-labor hour
    (b) $450,000 ÷ 30,000 hours = $15 per direct-labor hour

3. (a) $630,000 ÷ 105,000 hours = $6 per machine hour
    (b) $450,000 ÷ 30,000 hours = $15 per direct-labor hour

4. (a) $24 x (1.0 + 14.0) = $360.00
       $24 x (1.5 + 3.0) = $108.00
       $24 x (1.3 + 8.0) = $223.20

    (b) ($42 x 1.0) + ($15 x 14.0) = $42.00 + $210.00 = $252.00
        ($42 x 1.5) + ($15 x 3.0) = $63.00 + $ 45.00 = $108.00
        ($42 x 1.3) + ($15 x 8.0) = $54.60 + $120.00 = $174.60

    (c) ($6 x 10.0) + ($15 x 14.0) = $ 60.00 + $210.00 = $270.00
        ($6 x 17.0) + ($15 x 3.0) = $102.00 + $ 45.00 = $147.00
        ($6 x 14.0) + ($15 x 8.0) = $ 84.00 + $120.00 = $204.00

    (d) A major change in costs results from using departmental instead
        of firm-wide rates. Departmental rates that use direct-labor hours
        as the base decrease the cost applied to units of A and C, which
        use relatively more assembly time, and do not affect the cost of B.
        Changing to a base of machine hours in machining causes
        smaller changes in unit costs compared to one firm-wide rate.
        Product B is the only one with an increase in cost in (c) compared
        to (a). Why? Because B's proportion of the machine hours in
        machining exceeds its proportion of direct-labor hours in
        machining. Therefore, it receives more costs with a base of
        machine hours than with a base of direct-labor hours. Both A and
        C have a higher proportion of the direct-labor hours than of the
        machine hours in the machining department.

12-46 (30-45 min.)

1.

Cost pool*	Board L**	Board M	Board N
0. Direct-material cost	£ 660,000	£ 70,400	£ 225,000
1. Direct-labor hours	560,000	201,600	630,000
2. Machine hours	560,000	96,000	280,000
3. Pounds of materials	90,000	9,600	30,000
4. Number of production setups	80,000	40,000	40,000
5. Number of production orders	13,500	9,000	3,150
6. Number of orders shipped	30,000	24,000	60,000
Total budgeted cost	£1,993,500	£450,600	£1,268,150
Number of units	÷ 10,000	÷ 800	÷ 5,000
Unit cost	£ 199.35	£ 563.25	£ 253.63

*Identified by the cost driver used

**Calculations for Product L (Products M and N are similar):

0. 10,000 x £66 = £660,000
1. [(4 x 10,000) ÷ (4 x 10,000 + 18 x 800 + 9 x 5,000)] x £1,391,600 = £560,000
2. [(7 x 10,000) ÷ (7 x 10,000 + 15 x 800 + 7 x 5,000)] x £936,000=£560,000
3. [(3 x 10,000) ÷ (3 x 10,000 + 4 x 800 + 2 x 5,000)] x £129,600 = £90,000
4. [100 ÷ (100 + 50 + 50)] x £160,000 = £80,000
5. [300 ÷ (300 + 200 + 70)] x £25,650 = £13,500
6. [1,000 ÷ (1,000 + 800 + 2,000)] x £114,000 = £30,000

2. Total cost (except direct materials) per direct-labor hour:

£2,756,850 ÷ (4 x 10,000 + 18 x 800 + 9 x 5,000)
= £2,756,850 ÷ 99,400 = £27.735 per direct-labor hour

	Board L	Board M	Board N
Direct material cost per unit	£ 66.00	£ 88.00	£ 45.00
Other manufacturing cost per unit*	110.94	499.23	249.62
Total manufacturing cost per unit	£176.94	£587.23	£294.62
Number of units	x 10,000	x 800	x 5,000
Total budgeted cost**	£1,769,400	£469,784	£1,473,100

* £27.735 x 4; £27.735 x 18; £27.735 x 9
** Total = £1,769,400 + £469,784 + £1,473,100 = £3,712,284, which differs from £3,712,250 due to rounding error in the £27.735 rate.

3. The new system is more complex and more costly. The added expense would be justified if the added value of better decisions made using the new system exceeds the added cost of the system.

12-47 (50-60 min.)

1.

	Systems Department First Quarter Budget	Claims Department Historical Usage	Claims Department First Quarter Budget
Hardware and other capacity-related costs	$150,000	50%	$ 75,000
Software development	141,750	40	56,700
Computer-related operations	189,000	15	28,350
Input/output-related operations	75,600	75	56,700
	$556,350		$216,750

2. Solution is in Exhibit 12-47.

3. a. The new charging system should improve cost control in the Systems Department (if the rates are valid) because inefficiencies can no longer be passed on to the user departments. Thus, the Systems Department would be forced to watch its costs closely.

   b. The recommended system for charging costs to user departments should improve planning and cost control in the user departments. Decisions that affect capacity-related costs will affect the allocation of those costs, while decisions affecting only short-run operating costs will affect the allocation of only the operating costs.

EXHIBIT 12-47

	Total First Quarter Systems Department Costs	Not Allocated	Total	Allocated Department			
				Records	Claims	Finance	Outside
Hardware and other capacity-related costs	$155,000	$5,000	$150,000	$ 37,500 (1)	$ 75,000 (2)	$ 30,000 (3)	$ 7,500 (4)
Software development	130,000	2,500	127,500	13,500 (5)	54,000 (6)	48,000 (7)	12,000 (8)
Computer-related operations	187,000	3,000	184,000	108,000 (9)	38,800 (10)	25,200 (11)	12,000 (12)
Input-output-related operations	78,000	(1,000)	79,000	15,400 (13)	55,400 (14)	4,100 (15)	4,100 (16)
	$550,000	$ 9,500	$540,500	$174,400	$223,200	$107,300	$35,600

(1) $150,000 x .25
(2) $150,000 x .50
(3) $150,000 x .20
(4) $150,000 x .05

(5) $30 x 450
(6) $30 x 1,800
(7) $30 x 1,600
(8) $30 x 400

(9) $200 x 540
(10) $200 x 194
(11) $200 x 126
(12) $200 x 60

(13) $10 x 1,540
(14) $10 x 5,540
(15) $10 x 410
(16) $10 x 410

12-48 (40-35 min.) For the solution, see the Prentice Hall Web site, www.prenhall.com/

12-49 (100 min. or more)

The purposes of this exercise are to conduct library research in the current management accounting literature and to gain a better understanding of activity-based costing and activity-based management. Students must find their own article on ABC or ABM, and this will test their skills with library searches. Using electronic search procedures is likely to be a time-saver, but names of journals are given so that someone could just browse the library holdings of one of the journals to find an appropriate article.

Textbooks are limited in the space they can devote to stories about actual cost-accounting systems. This exercise requires students to deal with real-world issues relating to ABC or ABM. All applications of ABC or ABM are not successful, either because it was not an appropriate techniques where applied or because of mistakes in implementation. Although the literature will be dominated by success stories (companies do not often advertise their failures), by looking at several companies who have implemented ABC or ABM, students should be able to make some of the generalizations called for in requirement 2. By sharing information among group members, students should get a broader perspective on ABC and ABM than they would get from reading a single article.

12-50 (30-40 min.)

NOTE TO INSTRUCTOR. This solution is based on the web site as it was in early 2004. Be sure to examine the current web site before assigning this problem, as the information there may have changed.

1. Three companies are listed under the umbrella of Target Corporation: Target, Marshall Fields, and Mervyn's, in addition to an online store combining all three. The number of these companies listed in an area will be specific to the location of the school.

2. Marshall Field's is in the department store group. The focus of this group is to provide great service, distinctive merchandise, fashion leadership, and a convenient shopping environment. The store strives to meet current trends in both fashion and home items. Marshall Field's has its own Web site for selling and showcasing its products. While Marshall Field's does link from the corporate page of Target, it is unlikely that someone looking for Marshall Field's would look at the Target Web site to find it. So it is unlikely that a good case can be made for allocating part of the cost of the Target Corporation Web site to Marshall Field's. If such an allocation was made, a possible cost driver would be the number of direct links measured in transferring from the Target site to the Marshall Field's site.

3. On the financial review section for 2002, Target provides pre-tax segment profits, number of stores, and total square footage of the stores in each of it's three main segments – Target, Mervyn's and Marshall Field's. The pre-tax segment profits sum to $3,088,000,000 + $238,000,000 + $135,000,000 = $3,461,000,000. The income before taxes on the 2002 income statement is $2,676,000,000. The difference of $785,000,000 is caused by expenses that are incurred by the company that were not allocated to segments.

4. Data are in millions of dollars.

	Pre-tax Income	Percent	Allocation of $785.0
Target	$3,088	89%	$698.7
Mervyn's	238	7%	55.0
Marshall Field's	135	4%	31.4
Total	3,461	100%	$785.1*

	Number of Stores	Percent	Allocation of $785.0
Target	1,147	78%	$612.3
Mervyn's	264	18%	141.3
Marshall Field's	64	4%	31.4
Total	1,475	100%	$785.0

* Difference due to rounding.

CHAPTER 13
COVERAGE OF LEARNING OBJECTIVES

LEARNING OBJECTIVE	FUNDA-MENTAL ASSIGN-MENT MATERIAL	CRITICAL THINKING EXERCISES AND EXERCISES	PROBLEMS	CASES, EXCEL, COLLAB. & INTERNET EXERCISES
LO1: Compute budgeted factory-overhead rates and apply factory overhead to production.	A1,B2	30,31,35,36, 37	47,48,55,58	64,65,69,70
LO2: Determine and use appropriate cost drivers for overhead application.		29,37,38	47,48,55	64,65,70
LO3: Identify the meaning and purpose of normalized overhead rates.		39	58	
LO4: Construct an income statement using the variable-costing approach.	B4	40	50,51,52,53, 54,59,60	66,67
LO5: Construct an income statement using the absorption-costing approach.	A4,B4	40	50,51,52,53, 54,59,60	66,67
LO6: Compute the production-volume variance and show how it should appear in the income statement.		33,43,44,45, 46	55,56,57,62, 63	66,68
LO7: Explain why a company might prefer to use a variable-costing approach.			50,51,56,59	66,67

CHAPTER 13
Accounting For Overhead Costs

13-A1 (15-20 min.)

This is a solid basic problem concerning overhead application.

1. Overhead rate = $\dfrac{\text{Budgeted overhead}}{\text{Appropriate cost driver}}$

    Department A = $\dfrac{\$2,170,000}{350,000}$ = $6.20 per machine hour

    Department B = $\dfrac{\$1,000,000}{125,000}$ = $8.00 per direct-labor hour

2. Department A = $6.20 x 3,500 $21,700
    Department B = $8.00 x 1,250   <u>10,000</u>
    Total applied overhead   <u>$31,700</u>

3.

	Dept. A	Dept. B	Total
Direct material	$12,000	$32,000	$44,000
Direct labor	10,800	10,000	20,800
Applied factory overhead	21,700	10,000	31,700
Totals	$44,500	$52,000	$96,500

Unit cost, $96,500 ÷ 200			$482.50

4.   Students must be on guard to get their definitions clear. "Overapplied" essentially means that "actual" overhead is less than that absorbed by (applied to) the products worked on during the period.

Computations follow:

	Dept. A	Dept. B	Factory as a Whole
Actual	$1,600,000	$1,200,000	$2,800,000
Applied, 300,000 x $6.20 and 120,000 x $8.00	1,860,000	960,000	2,820,000
Underapplied (overapplied)	$ (260,000)	$ 240,000	$ (20,000)

<u>13-A2</u> (15 min.) Note that the direct materials inventory is irrelevant.

1. Underapplied overhead = $224,000 - $216,000 = $8,000

2. Adjusted gross profit = $70,000 - $8,000 = $62,000

3. Proration schedule:

(in thousands)	Unadjusted Balances	Proration of Underapplied Overhead	Adjusted Balances
Work in process	$ 75,000	75/750 x $8,000 = $ 800	$ 75,800
Finished goods	150,000	150/750 x $8,000 = 1,600	151,600
Cost of goods sold	525,000	525/750 x $8,000 = 5,600	530,600
Totals	$750,000	$8,000	$758,000

Adjusted gross profit = $70,000 - 5,600 = $64,400

4. Overapplied overhead = $216,000 - $214,000 = $2,000

Adjusted gross profit = $70,000 + $2,000 = $72,000

13-A3 (15-20 min.) Gross margin and ending direct-materials inventories are irrelevant.

1,2.

	(1) Absorption Costing	(2) Variable Costing
Direct materials used	$ 3,000	$ 3,000
Direct labor	4,500	4,500
Variable manufacturing overhead	2,500	2,500
Fixed manufacturing overhead	4,000	-
Total production costs	$14,000	$10,000
Ending inventories are 1/5 of total production costs	$ 2,800	$ 2,000

3. The $800 difference in ending inventories is accounted for by 1/5 of the $4,000 fixed manufacturing overhead that is lodged in ending inventory under absorption costing. Operating income would be $800 lower under variable costing because all of the fixed manufacturing overhead is released to expense in the current period. (That is why the fixed cost is sometimes called a "period cost" by variable costers; period costs are those that are totally released to expense in the current period rather than being inventoried.)

Note also that the difference in operating income is a function of the *change* in inventory levels, which happened to be zero at the beginning of the year. It is not a function of the ending inventories alone. See the next problem.

13-A4 (20-30 min.)

1.

TRAHN COMPANY
Income Statement
For the Year Ended December 31, 20X5

Sales		$14,080
Deduct cost of goods sold:		
Beginning inventory, 110 @ $9*	$ 990	
Add: Absorption cost of goods manufactured, 1,200 units @ $9	10,800	
Cost of goods available for sale	$11,790	
Ending inventory, 30 @ $9	270	
Cost of goods sold – at standard	$11,520	
Production volume variance (unfavorable)	400**	
Adjusted cost of goods sold		11,920
Gross margin		2,160
Selling and administrative expenses ($600 + 350)		950
Operating income		$ 1,210

*Fixed overhead rate: $2,800 ÷ 1,400 units = $2 per unit. Unit production cost: $7 + $2 = $9

** (1,400 - 1,200) x $2 = $400 underapplied

2. Change in inventory units 110 - 30 = 80 decrease
   Fixed factory overhead rate is $2
   Difference in operating income: 80 x $2 = $160 *less* under absorption costing

13-B1 (10-15 min.) Note that the direct materials inventory is irrelevant.

1. Adjusted cost of goods sold is $250,000 less $20,000 or $230,000.

2.

(in thousands)	Unadjusted Balances	Proration of Overapplied Overhead		Adjusted Balances
Work in process	$100	100/500 x $20 =	4	$ 96
Finished goods	150	150/500 x $20 =	6	144
Cost of goods sold	250	250/500 x $20 =	10	240
Totals	$500		$20	$480

Gross profit would be lower in requirement 2 by $20,000 - $10,000, or $10,000. Adjusted cost of goods sold would be $250,000 - $10,000 = $240,000 in requirement 2 but $250,000 - $20,000 = $230,000 in requirement 1. The higher cost of goods sold in requirement 2 would make gross profit lower.

13-B2 (15-20 min.)

1. Overhead rate = $\dfrac{\text{Budgeted overhead}}{\text{Budgeted cost driver level}}$

    Pharmacy = $\dfrac{\$225,000}{90,000}$ = $2.50 per prescription

    Medical Records = $\dfrac{\$300,000}{60,000}$ = $5.00 per patient visit

2. Pharmacy = $2.50 x 4 $ 10.00
    Medical records = $5.00 x 2   10.00
    Total applied overhead $20.00

3. Students must be on guard to get their definitions clear.
    "Overapplied" essentially means that "actual" overhead is less than
    that absorbed by (applied to) the products worked on during the
    period.

    Computations follow:

	Pharmacy	Medical Records	Total
Actual	$217,000	$325,000	$542,000
Applied, 85,000 x $2.50			
and 63,000 x $5.00	212,500	315,000	527,500
Underapplied	$ 4,500	$ 10,000	$ 14,500

13-B3 (10 min.)

Production costs:	(1) Absorption Costing	(2) Variable Costing
Direct materials used	$3,500	$3,500
Direct labor	4,200	4,200
Variable manufacturing overhead	300	300
Fixed manufacturing overhead	2,200	-
Total	$10,200	$8,000
Ending inventories are 1/4 of total production costs	$2,550	$2,000

13-B4 (30-40 min.)

1.

DESK PC DIVISION
Income Statement (Variable Costing)
For the Year 20X5
(in thousands of dollars)

Sales (15,000 x $500)		$7,500.0
Opening inventory, at variable standard cost of $300	$ 900.0	
Add: Variable cost of goods manufactured	4,650.0	
Available for sale	5,550.0	
Deduct: Ending inventory, at variable standard cost of $300	1,050.0	
Variable cost of goods sold, at standard	$4,500.0	
Net variances for all variable costs, unfavorable	18.0	
Variable cost of goods sold, at actual	4,518.0	
Variable selling expenses, at 5% of dollar sales	375.0	
Total variable costs charged against sales		4,893.0
Contribution margin		2,607.0
Fixed factory overhead	1,560.0*	
Fixed selling and administrative expenses	650.0	
Total fixed expenses		2,210.0
Operating income		$ 397.0

*This can be shown in two lines, $150,000 budget plus $6,000 variance.

DESK PC DIVISION
Income Statement (Absorption Costing)
For the Year 20X5
(in thousands of dollars)

Sales		$7,500.0
Opening inventory, at standard cost of $400	$1,200.0	
Add: Cost of goods manufactured, at standard	6,200.0	
Available for sale	7,400.0	
Deduct: Ending inventory, at standard	1,400.0	
Cost of goods sold, at standard	6,000.0	
Net variances for variable manufacturing costs,		
unfavorable	$18.0	
Fixed factory overhead budget variance, unfavorable	60.0	
Production-volume variance, favorable	(50.0)*	
Total variances	28.0	
Cost of goods sold, at actual		6,028.0
Gross profit, at "actual"		1,472.0
Selling and administrative expenses:		
Variable	375.0	
Fixed	650.0	1,025.0
Operating income		$ 447.0

*Production-volume variance is $100 x (15,000 expected production volume – 15,500 actual production).

2. The $50,000 difference in operating income is attributable to the 500-unit increase in inventory levels. This means that $50,000 of fixed factory overhead (500 units x fixed rate of $100) was held back in inventory under absorption costing, whereas all fixed overhead was released as expense under variable costing.

13-1 The budgeted overhead application rate is the predicted factory overhead for the budget period divided by the predicted machine hours for that period. The amount of factory overhead applied to a job is the budgeted overhead application rate times the actual machine hours used on that job.

13-2 No. In the past, most organizations have used only one cost driver per department. However, the trend is toward using multiple cost drivers. Whether more than one cost driver is used is a cost/benefit issue. If most overhead costs are caused by a single cost driver, using that one cost driver for cost application is logical. If overhead costs are caused by multiple cost drivers, managers must compare the value of more accurate product costs versus the cost of a complex accounting system that uses multiple cost drivers for overhead application.

13-3 Yes. Direct-labor cost may be the best cost driver for overhead allocation even if wage rages vary within a department. For example, higher skilled labor (with higher wage rates) may require more overhead because it may use more costly equipment and have more indirect labor support. Moreover, many factory overhead costs include costly labor fringe benefits such as pensions and payroll taxes, which are higher for more highly paid employees.

13-4 Cost drivers might include direct labor cost, direct labor hours, direct material cost, total direct cost, machine hours, number of batches, number of engineering hours used, number of change orders, etc.

13-5 The comparison of actual overhead costs to budgeted overhead costs is part of the control process. It tells managers when the actual results differ from what was expected.

13-6 Incurred overhead will differ from applied overhead in much the same way as any estimate will differ from actual experience. Specific causes might be: variations in suppliers' prices; inefficiencies in production (excessive down-time, for example); failure of sales to materialize; failure to meet production quotas; and unexpected increases in fixed overhead (increase in insurance rates, for example). They also can arise because of inaccurate overhead cost predictions.

13-7   No. Using "actual" overhead rates, unit costs will be lower as production volume increases and higher with low volume. The variable overhead rate will be approximately constant; the fixed overhead rate will vary inversely with volume. The two rates together form the total overhead rate.

13-8   Normal costing is the product-costing method whereby inventory is carried at actual direct-material costs plus actual direct-labor costs plus applied factory overhead at a budgeted rate.

13-9   The best theoretical method of allocating underapplied or overapplied overhead is to disregard it completely and recompute an actual overhead rate based on actual costs incurred allocated over actual production units. Proration is usually a reasonable approximation to this theoretical ideal.

13-10 The following are examples of costs that are now classified as direct costs in many service industries: secretarial; photocopies; phone calls; power; and costs of computer time.

13-11 No. Variable costing means that all *variable* costs of manufacturing are inventoried. These include direct material, direct labor, and the overhead costs that are incurred in direct proportion to the volume of production, even though these costs may only indirectly affect the production process and thus are categorized as "overhead."

13-12 Fixed manufacturing overhead is considered a noninventoriable or period cost under variable costing but a product cost under absorption costing.

13-13 No. Variable costing is not acceptable for external reporting. However, an increasing number of firms are using variable costing for *internal* reporting. This is especially true for companies that implement multi-stage activity-based costing systems (as described in Chapter 4). These costing systems make heavy use of cost behavior for planning and control purposes.

13-14 The tax authorities and those in charge of the rules for financial reporting do not allow use of variable costing. Why? They believe it violates the matching principle.

13-15 The contribution margin is revenue less variable costs (including both variable manufacturing costs and variable selling and administrative costs). In contrast, gross margin is revenue less manufacturing costs (including both variable manufacturing costs and fixed manufacturing costs).

13-16 Fixed overhead is applied to product via a budgeted unit overhead rate multiplied by an actual cost driver activity level such as machine hours or production units.

13-17 First, the unit product cost in absorption costing includes an allocation of fixed costs, while in variable costing it consists of only variable manufacturing costs. Second, fixed costs appear as a single line in a variable-costing statement, but they are in two places (part of product cost and as a production volume variance) in an absorption-costing statement. Finally, a variable-costing statement separates costs into fixed and variable components, while absorption-costing statements separate them into manufacturing and nonmanufacturing components.

13-18 This statement describes the treatment of fixed costs in an absorption-costing system. Production volume does not affect total fixed costs, but it does affect applied fixed costs, which are proportional to the units of production.

13-19 Variable costing and cost-volume-profit analysis are both based on separate measurements of fixed and variable costs. Both focus on computation of the contribution margin, the difference between revenue and all variable costs.

13-20 Yes. Only when actual production volume exactly equals the expected volume is the applied fixed manufacturing overhead equal to that budgeted. Although the exact equality is rare, most of the time the difference will not be great.

13-21 The production-volume variance depends on the expected volume of production used as the denominator in setting the fixed-overhead rate. The higher the level chosen, the lower the rate. The total amount of the variance is a function of the rate and the deviation of actual volume from the volume used to set the rate.

13-22 Direct labor is a variable cost. The expected amount (i.e., flexible-budget amount) for a variable cost is the same as the amount allocated (or applied) to the product. There is no conflict between the budgeting and control purpose and the product-costing purpose. Therefore, no variance is caused by production volume differing from an expected volume.

13-23 No. Production-volume variances provide no information about the control of fixed manufacturing costs. Such variances arise solely because the actual production volume differs from the expected volume.

13-24 Yes. The unit fixed cost is inversely proportional to the denominator, expected units of production.

13-25 No. When the number of units sold exceeds the number produced, that is, when inventory decreases, variable-costing income exceeds absorption-costing income.

13-26 The manager might produce extra units even if they will not be sold. Each unit produced will increase operating income by the amount of the fixed manufacturing overhead per unit. By producing enough units, the manager can assure that the operating income budget is met and the bonus received.

13-27 Variable- and absorption-costing incomes differ only when the level of inventory changes. Furthermore, the amount of the difference in income is proportional to the change in inventory. When inventories are small, changes in inventory are also generally small. Therefore, companies without much inventory will report nearly the same operating income with variable costing as with absorption costing.

13-28 No. Only the overhead production-volume variance is unique to an absorption-costing system. All other overhead variances occur in both variable- and absorption-costing systems.

13-29 A strong relationship between the factory overhead incurred and the cost driver used for application is the best available indication of a cause-and-effect relationship. That is, the more of the cost driver that is used, the higher the actual overhead incurred. It is important to consider the time period involved. Some overhead costs, equipment for example, have a weak or no relationship to machine hours used in the short run but a strong relationship to providing the capability to operate machines over extended time periods. Such costs are often called capacity costs.

13-30 No. Some service firms trace only direct-labor costs to individual jobs. However, with advances in computer technology and because competition causes a need for better cost information about specific services, jobs, or customers, more service firms are tracing additional costs to jobs. The more costs that are traced to jobs instead of being allocated, the more accurate are the job costs.

13-31 Fixed costs are difficult to deal with because revenue must be enough to cover fixed as well as variable costs before a company makes a profit, but fixed costs do not change with variations in volume of production. Suppose that a company views a product cost as the amount that needs to be received in revenue *in the long-run* to be profitable. Such companies often want to assign fixed costs to the products. Remember that the separation of fixed and variable costs is inherently a short-run phenomenon. In the long run, where capacity can be altered and all commitments can be renegotiated, nearly all costs are variable. Thus, knowing the long-run product cost can be important for strategic decisions. However, the long-run product cost may differ from the accounting cost that includes an allocation of fixed costs, because many fixed costs (for example, depreciation) represent historical costs that may differ significantly from the future cost needed to provide the same services. Thus, it makes sense to include fixed costs in a prediction of long-run product costs, but measuring those fixed costs by allocating fixed historical costs to the products may not provide an accurate measure. Yet, it may be better than the alternatives.

13-32 Most pricing and promotion decisions are short-run decisions. They can be easily reversed if conditions in the marketplace change. Thus, the decisions are unlikely to affect fixed costs unless they increase or decrease demand enough that the volume moves outside the relevant range. The immediate effect on the company's profits is measured by the revenue less the variable cost – that is, the contribution margin. If the pricing or promotion decision has long-term effects as well, for example provides a level of market penetration that will affect future sales levels, then the short-term impact must be compared to the long-term effects. Separating long-term effects from short-term effects is often useful. We can predict short-term effects from current accounting data, while the long-term effects are often poorly measured by data directly from the accounting system. Allocation of fixed costs to products may give some information about long-term effects, but it is usually better to separately estimate these effects.

13-33 A production-volume variance arises when production exceeds or falls short of the volume used to set the fixed overhead rate, often the expected volume. However, unlike the sales-volume variance, the production-volume variance does not directly measure the economic consequences of the production volume. If production falls 10% short of the predicted volume, the production-volume variance merely indicates that 10% of the fixed costs were not applied to the products produced. It does not indicate that the company incurs 10% more fixed costs than planned. A sales-volume variance of $10,000 means that if sales had met the target, the company would have been $10,000 better off. If the production-volume variance was $10,000, it does not mean that production of the additional products would have generated $10,000 of benefit to the company.

13-34 Some companies apply all costs from various stages of the value chain to their products or services. This gives a measure of all of the costs that have to be covered by revenues during the product's life cycle. It is most useful for strategic decisions – decisions relating to long-run commitments to product lines and facilities and establishing product mix and pricing policies. Such allocations are less useful for tactical decisions – those relating to short-term sales and production effects. There is no single measure of cost that is appropriate for all decisions. Rather, cost measures must be tailored to reflect the decisions for which they are being used.

Total budgeted amount of cost driver $= \dfrac{\$248,000}{\$4} = 62,000$ machine hours

Total applied overhead $= \$4 \times 66,000$ machine hours $= \underline{\$264,000}$

Overapplied overhead = applied overhead – actual overhead incurred
$$= \$264,000 - \$256,000$$
$$= \underline{\$8,000}$$

Actual costs must be reported in the income statement. So the $8,000 overapplied overhead must be deducted from cost of goods sold.

13-36 (10-15 min.)

Budgeted overhead application rate:

$$\dfrac{\text{total budgeted factory overhead}}{\text{total budgeted amount of cost driver}} = \dfrac{\$525,000}{75,000 \text{ lab. hours}} = \$7/\text{DLH}$$

Applied overhead = overhead rate x actual number of driver units

Actual number of direct labor hours $= \$560,000 \div \$7 = \underline{80,000}$ direct labor hours.

Actual costs must be reported in the income statement. So the $7,000 underapplied overhead must be added to cost of goods sold.

A major lesson of this exercise is the distinction between budgeted, actual, and applied overhead. Case 2 is more challenging, but it forces the student to learn basic relationships.

1.   c. $750,000 ÷ $500,000 = 150% of direct-labor cost

       f.   1.50 x $570,000 = $855,000

       g. $825,000 - $855,000 = $30,000 overapplied

2.   f. $415,000 - $25,000 = $390,000

       d. $390,000 ÷ 1.20 = $325,000

       b. $420,000 ÷ 1.20 = $350,000

13-38 (10-15 min.)

		(in thousands)	
		Case 1	Case 2

1. Applied overhead: 30 x $9.00 = $270
                         36 x $9.00 = $324

2. Overhead incurred:
     $32 + $22 + $35 + $138 =   227
     $40 + $32 + $47 + $214 =   333

3. Overapplied overhead: $270 - $227 =   43
    Underapplied overhead: $333 - $324 =   9

Note the irrelevant items:
     Sales commissions are selling expenses.
     Depreciation of finished goods warehouse is also a selling
         expense, because the manufacturing processing has been
         completed.
     Cost of goods sold is an overall figure of no use in this problem.
     Direct-labor cost and direct-material cost are not pertinent either.

(10-15 min.)

Overhead is overapplied by $457,000 - $409,000=$48,000.

First Way: Direct Write-off

Unadjusted cost of goods sold	$400,000
Deduct: Overapplied overhead	48,000
Adjusted cost of goods sold	$352,000

Second Way : Proration

	Unadjusted	Proration of Overapplied Overhead	Adjusted
Cost of goods sold	$400,000	400/800 x $48,000 = $24,000	$376,000
Work in process	200,000	200/800 x 48,000 = 12,000	188,000
Finished goods	200,000	200/800 x 48,000 = 12,000	188,000
Totals	$800,000	$48,000	$752,000

Unadjusted cost of goods sold	$400,000
Deduct: Overapplied overhead	24,000
Adjusted cost of goods sold	$376,000

Cost of goods sold would be $376,000 - $352,000 = $24,000 lower (and gross profit higher) under the first way (no proration).

13-40 (20 min.)

This exercise helps students obtain a fundamental look at the essential conceptual differences between the variable and absorption costing methods. Amounts are in thousands of dollars.

Absorption Costing

Balance Sheets					Income Statements	
January 1, 20X4						
Cash	150	Capital Stock	150			
December 31, 20X4					**Year 20X4**	
Cash,150-60	90	Capital stock	150		None	
Inventory,+60	60					
	150					
December 31, 20X5					**Year 20X5**	
Cash,90+42	132	Capital stock	150	Revenue	42	
Inventory,60-30	30	Retained inc.,+12	12	Expense	30	
	162		162	Net income	12	
December 31, 20X6					**Year 20X6**	
Cash,132+42	174	Capital stock	150	Revenue	42	
Inventory,30-30	0	Retained inc.,12+12	24	Expense	30	
	174		174	Net income	12	

Variable (Direct) Costing

Balance Sheets				Income Statements	
January 1, 20X4					
Cash	150	Capital Stock	150		
December 31, 20X4				**Year 20X4**	
Cash,150-60	90	Capital stock	150	Revenue	0
Inventory,+44	44	Retained income,-16	-16	Expense	16
	134		134	Net loss	-16
December 31, 20X5				**Year 20X5**	
Cash,90+42	132	Capital stock	150	Revenue	42
Inventory,44-22	22	Retained inc.,-16+20	4	Expense	22
	154		154	Net income	20
December 31, 20X6				**Year 20X6**	
Cash,132+42	174	Capital stock	150	Revenue	42
Inventory,22-22	0	Retained income,4+20	24	Expense	22
	174		174	Net income	20

Ask the students to ponder how the income statements differ for each year. As inventory levels build (20X4), the fixed overhead is lodged in inventory, so income under variable costing is less. But, as inventory levels decline, that fixed overhead is released so that income under absorption costing is less.

13-41 (15 min.)

1. Variable-costing operating income equals absorption-costing operating income whenever the inventory level is unchanged (beginning inventory equals ending inventory). No change in inventory level implies that units produced equals units sold, as in *20X5.*

2. Absorption-costing operating income exceeds variable-costing operating income when inventory levels *increase,* because (under absorption costing) some fixed costs are applied to the units in the enlarged inventory. Units produced exceed units sold in *20X3 and 20X4.*

3. Repeat the idea in part (1), now considering the four-year total operating income, which is the same ($230,000) under both variable and absorption costing. Thus beginning inventory in 20X3 (0 units) equals ending inventory in 20X6 *(0 units),* or $0.

4. As in part (2), 20X6's absorption-costing operating income exceeds the variable-costing operating income by the amount of fixed costs borne by the increased inventory ($30,000). At $3.00 per unit, units sold exceeds units produced by *10,000 units.*

13-42 (10-15 min.)

1. Variable manufacturing cost per unit
    = $105,000 ÷ 15,000 = $7.00

    Variable nonmanufacturing cost per unit
    = $24,000 ÷ 12,000 = $2.00

    Operating income
    = (12,000 x $17) - (12,000 x $7.00) - (12,000 x $2.00) -$63,000 - $18,000
    = $204,000 - ($84,000 + $24,000 + $81,000)
    = $15,000

2. a. $(15,000 - 12,000) \times (\$7.00 + \dfrac{\$63,000}{18,000})$

    = 3,000 units x $10.50 unit cost
    = $31,500

    b. Total costs incurred
    = $105,000 + $63,000 + $24,000 + $18,000
    = $210,000

    Operating income = Sales - (Total costs - Costs in inventory)
    = $204,000 - ($210,000 - $31,500) = $25,500

    or: $\$15,000 + (\dfrac{\$63,000}{18,000} \times 3,000) = \$25,500$

    Fixed cost in inventory

    From part (1)

720

<u>13-43</u> (5-10 min.)

This exercise requires sorting the relevant information from the irrelevant. Computing the production-volume variance requires knowledge of the fixed-overhead rate:

Fixed-overhead rate = ¥25,620,000 ÷ 6,100 units = ¥4,200 per unit

The actual overhead costs are irrelevant. In addition to the fixed-overhead rate, the only items needed are expected and actual production volume:

$$
\begin{aligned}
\text{Production-volume variance} &= \text{(actual volume - expected volume)} \\
&\quad \text{x fixed-overhead rate} \\
&= (5,800 - 6,100) \times ¥4,200 \\
&= 300 \times ¥4,200 \\
&= ¥1,260,000 \text{ unfavorable}
\end{aligned}
$$

<u>13-44</u> (10-15 min.)

1. (a) $7 x 10,500 = $73,500
    (b) $7 x 1,500 = $10,500 F
    (c) $18,000 – ($7 x 1,000) = $11,000

2. Fixed costs charged by variable costing $73,500
    Fixed costs charged by absorption costing:
        In cost of goods sold, $7 x 11,000 $77,000
        Production-volume variance, favorable   -10,500
        Total fixed cost   66,500
    Difference in fixed cost $ 7,000

Because fixed costs are $7,000 less under absorption costing, operating income is $7,000 greater under absorption costing than under variable costing.

13-45 (15 min.)

Variances in dollars:

Flexible-budget variance	4,000 U	Fixed	1,700 U[1]
		Variable	2,300 U[2]
Production-volume variance	900 U	Fixed	900 U[3]
		Variable	NA
Spending variance	3,600 U	Fixed	1,700 U[4]
		Variable	1,900 U[5]
Efficiency variance	400 U	Fixed	NA
		Variable	400 U[6]

NA = not applicable

1. $14,200 - $12,500
2. $13,300 - $11,000
3. $12,500 - $11,600
4. $14,200 - $12,500
5. $13,300 - $11,400
6. $11,400 - $11,000

13-46 (15-20 min.)

Note that the budget for standard hours allowed for actual output achieved for variable overhead must be $41,000, the same as applied. In contrast, the budget for actual output achieved for fixed overhead must be $70,000, the same as the budget for actual hours of input. Variances are in dollars. The answers follow:

	Total Overhead	Variable	Fixed
1. Spending variance	2,000U	3,500U	1,500F
2. Efficiency variance	4,000U	4,000U	NA
3. Production-volume variance	5,200U	NA	5,200U
4. Flexible-budget variance	6,000U	7,500U	1,500F
5. Underapplied overhead	11,200U	7,500U	3,700U

NA = not applicable

These relationships could be presented in the same way as in Exhibit 13-11:

	Cost Incurred: Actual Inputs x Actual Prices	Flexible Budget Based on Actual Inputs x Expected Prices	Flexible Budget Based on Standard Inputs Allowed for Actual Outputs Achieved x Expected Prices	Product Costing: Applied Overhead
Variable	48,500	45,000	41,000	41,000

Spending, 3,500U	Efficiency, 4,000U	ProdVolume, NA

Flexible-budget variance, 7,500U	NA

Underapplied overhead, 7,500U

	Cost Incurred: Actual Inputs x Actual Prices	Flexible Budget Based on Actual Inputs x Expected Prices	Flexible Budget Based on Standard Inputs Allowed for Actual Outputs Achieved x Expected Prices	Product Costing: Applied Overhead
Fixed	68,500	70,000	70,000	64,800
	Spending, 1,500F	Efficiency, NA	Prod.-volume, 5,200U	
	Flexible-budget variance, 1,500F		Prod.-volume 5,200U.	
	Underapplied overhead, 3,700U			

13-47 (20-35 min.)

1. $10,000,000 ÷ $5,000,000 = 200% of direct labor

2. ($10,000,000 - $3,000,000) ÷ $5,000,000 = 140% of direct labor
    ($10,000,000 - $3,000,000) ÷ ($5,000,000 + $3,000,000) = $7,000,000 ÷
    $8,000,000 = 87.5% of total direct costs

3.

	Engagement	
	Eagledale	First Valley
Direct labor	$15,000	$15,000
Applied overhead @ 200%	30,000	30,000
Total costs	$45,000	$45,000
Total direct costs	$25,000	$21,000
Applied overhead @ 140% of $15,000	21,000	21,000
Total costs	$46,000	$42,000
Total direct costs	$25,000	$21,000
Applied overhead @ 87.5%	21,875	18,375
Total costs	$46,875	$39,375

4.   The billings would differ significantly:

	Engagement	
	Eagledale	First Valley
Method 1:		
Total costs	$45,000	$45,000
Total billings @ 130%	$58,500	$58,500
Method 2:		
Total costs	$46,000	$42,000
Total billings @ 130%	$59,800	$54,600
Method 3:		
Total costs	$46,875	$39,375
Total billings @ 130%	$60,938	$51,188

5.   The first method is inferior to the other two because the latter give more accurate measures of how specific jobs cause increases in costs. In general, the more costs that are directly charged to jobs, the more accurate the picture of where the money is really spent.

As between the other two methods, the answer depends on what causes the indirect costs to rise. If direct labor is the dominant cause, then the 140% rate is better. If the increases in indirect costs are more closely related to increases in all direct costs, then the 87.5% rate is preferable. Additional studies of how indirect costs behave would be necessary to answer this question.

13-48 (15 min.)

1. If other departments are indeed providing services to the water and sewer department, it is certainly appropriate to include the cost of these services in the water and sewer department's budget and to have them paid for by the water and sewer customers. Charging administrative overhead is not a ruse; it is a real cost of providing water and sewer services. However, it is not clear from the case whether the administrative overhead allocation is accurately measured. It appears that there is only one overhead pool and consequently only one cost driver used for allocation. It is likely that the services are quite varied and a single cost driver may not be appropriate.

2. It would be useful to identify the activities involved when other departments provide services to the water and sewer department. If it is not too expensive, it would be worthwhile to measure each type of service and charge the water and sewer department only the cost of those services actually used. In essence, it would be good to directly (physically) trace as many costs to the department as possible, charging directly for the services. At a minimum, using multiple cost pools and cost drivers for allocating diverse costs to the water and sewer departments should be considered.

13-49 (15-25 min.) This problem is intended to highlight the distinction and relation between accounting for control and accounting for product costing.

1. First six months:
    (55,000 x $4.50) - $236,500 = $11,000, overapplied

    Last six months:
    $206,500 - (41,000 x $4.50) = $22,000, underapplied

2. Overhead rate:

Fixed, $325,000 ÷ 100,000 DLH	$3.25 per DLH	
Variable, $125,000 ÷ 100,000 DLH	1.25 per DLH	
Overall rate	$4.50	

    (a) In the first period, direct-labor hours used exceeded half of the year's total budget (50,000) by 5,000. This makes fixed overhead overapplied by 5,000 x $3.25 = $16,250. Actual variable overhead was $236,500 - (50% x $325,000) = $74,000. Variable overhead applied is $55,000 x $1.25 = $68,750, so it is underapplied by $74,000 - $68,750 = $5,250. Therefore, the total overhead is overapplied by $16,250 - $5,250 = $11,000.

    (b) In the last period, direct-labor hours used were less than half the year's total budget by 9,000. Fixed overhead was thus underapplied by 9,000 x $3.25 = $29,250. Actual variable overhead was $206,500 - (50% x $325,000) = $44,000. Variable overhead applied was $1.25 x 41,000 = $51,250, so variable overhead was overapplied by $51,250 - $44,000 = $7,250. Therefore, total overhead is underapplied by $29,250 - $7,250 = $22,000.

Notice that fixed costs were always equal to the budget. Variable overhead was underapplied the first half of the year when total overhead was overapplied. Similarly, variable overhead was overapplied in the second half of the year when total overhead was underapplied. The total over- or under-applied overhead is not a good measure of performance compared to budget because it includes a production-volume variance that is not useful for cost control purposes.

13-50 (35-45 min.) This is an excellent problem for presentation in class. It is less satisfactory as a homework assignment because students tend to make the problem harder than it really is.

1.   One way to present the problem in class is to begin with 9 columns on the board or overhead projector. Each column lists the sales and production quantities. Provide six rows for the variable-costing statement and seven rows for the absorption-costing statement, labeled as in the format provided in the problem, there are 18 "income statements" to be completed. Ask a different student to complete each statement. Patterns soon become clear, and students fill in the statements quickly. If students fail to recognize some patterns, you can prod them with discussion of the patterns as the statements are completed. The completed statements follow:

Variable costing (in thousands of dollars)

	(1)	(2)	(3)	(4)	(5)	(6)	(7)	(8)	(9)
Revenue	300	400	500	400	500	600	500	600	700
Cost of goods sold	(120)	(160)	(200)	(160)	(200)	(240)	(200)	(240)	(280)
Contribution margin	180	240	300	240	300	360	300	360	420
Fixed mfg costs	(150)	(150)	(150)	(150)	(150)	(150)	(150)	(150)	(150)
Fixed selling & admin. exp.	(30)	(30)	(30)	(30)	(30)	(30)	(30)	(30)	(30)
Operating income	0	60	120	60	120	180	120	180	240

Absorption costing (in thousands of dollars)

	(1)	(2)	(3)	(4)	(5)	(6)	(7)	(8)	(9)
Revenue	300	400	500	400	500	600	500	600	700
Cost of goods sold	(210)	(280)	(350)	(280)	(350)	(420)	(350)	(420)	(490)
Gross profit at standard	90	120	150	120	150	180	150	180	210
Favorable (Unfavorable) production-volume var.	(30)	(30)	(30)	0	0	0	30	30	30
Gross profit at "actual"	60	90	120	120	150	180	180	210	240
Selling and admin. exp.	(30)	(30)	(30)	(30)	(30)	(30)	(30)	(30)	(30)
Operating income	30	60	90	90	120	150	150	180	210

The following points are key to rapid completion of the statements·

729

(a) Cost of goods sold under variable costing is *variable* cost ($8) times units *sold*.

(b) Fixed costs are $150,000 and $30,000 on *each* variable-costing statement.

(c) Cost of goods sold under absorption costing is full-absorption cost ($14) times units *sold*.

(d) No separate row for fixed manufacturing cost appears on an absorption-costing statement. Fixed manufacturing cost are included in cost of goods sold and in the production-volume variance.

(e) Production-volume variance is *production* units less expected unit volume times fixed manufacturing cost per unit ($6).

(f) Selling and administrative expenses are not inventoried; even on an absorption-costing statement the $30,000 is charged each period.

Patterns of operating income are discussed in question 2.

If the student did not prepare the problem as a homework assignment, but you use it for class discussion, you might list the following information on the board before proceeding to the statements:

Sales price = $20 per unit
Variable cost = $8 per unit
Fixed manufacturing cost = $150,000 per year
Fixed-overhead rate = $150,000 ÷ 25,000 units = $6 per unit
Full cost = $8 + $6 = $14
Fixed selling and administrative cost = $30,000 per year

2.   (a) Variable-costing income is greater than absorption-costing income when sales exceed production: (3), (6), and (9).

Variable-costing income is lower than absorption-costing income when production exceeds sales: (1), (4), and (7).

Variable-costing income equals absorption-costing income when production equals sales: (2), (5), and (8).

(b) Production-volume variance is unfavorable when expected volume exceeds actual volume: (1), (2), and (3). It is favorable when actual volume exceeds expected volume: (7), (8), and (9).

(c) Each additional unit sold adds $20 - $8 = $12 to profit under variable costing and $20 - $14 = $6 under absorption costing. For example, compare (1) and (2). Production is 20,000 units in each case, but sales are 5,000 units greater in (2). Operating income is $60,000 greater in (2) than in (1) under variable costing and $30,000 greater under absorption costing. $60,000 ÷ 5,000 = $12 per unit for variable costing, and $30,000 ÷ 5,000 = $6 per unit for absorption costing.

(d) Producing an additional unit does not affect operating income under variable costing. Compare, for example, (2) and (4). But under absorption costing, production of one unit increases profit by $6. Again, compare (2) and (4). The only difference is production of 5,000 additional units in (4) and operating income is $30,000 higher: $30,000 ÷ 5,000 = $6 per unit.

(e) Variable costing provides a better measure of performance. Why? Because differences in operating income arise from differences in sales, not production, under variable costing.

731

<u>13-51</u> (25-35 min.)

Please allow ample time for classroom discussion.

1.   <u>Comments on the Following Statements</u>

The accounting for fixed overhead in absorption costing is affected
primarily by what expected production volume is selected as a base
(the denominator) for applying fixed overhead to product. In this case,
is 1,500,000 gallons per year, 3,000,000 gallons, or some other activity
level the most appropriate base? We usually place the above
possibilities on the board and then ask the students to indicate by
vote how many used one version of absorption costing versus
another. Incidentally, discussion tends to move more clearly if
variable-costing statements are discussed first, because there is little
disagreement as to computations under variable costing.

<u>Variable Costing</u> (in thousands of dollars)

	20X4	20X5	Together
Sales (and contribution margin)	900	900	1,800
Fixed costs	800	800	1,600
Net income	100	100	200

Absorption Costing (in thousands of dollars)

	Option One*			Option Two**		
	20X4	20X5	Together	20X4	20X5	Together
Sales	900	900	1,800	900	900	1,800
Less cost of goods sold:						
Beginning inventory	-	300	-	-	600	-
Cost of goods manufactured	600	-	600	1,200	-	1,200
Cost of goods available for sale	600	300	600	1,200	600	1,200
Ending inventory	300	-	-	600	-	-
Cost of goods sold – at normal cost	300	300	600	600	600	1,200
Under applied overhead – loss from idle capacity	-	600	600	-	600	600
Over applied overhead – gain from over-utilization	-	-	-	(600)	-	(600)
Other expenses	200	200	400	200	200	400
Total charges	500	1,100	1,600	200	1,400	1,600
Net income (loss)	400	(200)	200	700	(500)	200

* $600,000 ÷ 3,000,000 gallons as "normal capacity" = $.20 per gallon

** $600,000 ÷ 1,500,000 gallons as "normal capacity" = $.40 per gallon

2. Break-even point $= \dfrac{\text{Fixed expenses}}{\text{Contribution margin per gallon}}$

$= \dfrac{\$800,000}{\$.60} = 1{,}333{,}333$ gallons

If the company would sell 166,667 fewer gallons per year at $.60 each, it would just break even.

Most students will say that the break-even point is 1,333,333 gallons per year under both absorption and variable costing. The logical question to ask a student who answers 1,333,333 units for absorption costing is: "What profit do you show for 20X5 under absorption costing?" If a student answers any negative profit, such as $(200,000), ask: "But you say your break-even point is 1,333,333 gallons. How can you show a loss on 1,500,000 gallons sold during 20X5?"

The answer to the break-even point dilemma is that net income is affected by *both* sales and production under absorption costing. The variable-costing approach dovetails precisely with the cost-volume-profit analysis that the students learned earlier, but absorption costing does not unless some special assumption is made regarding inventory changes. The latter usually entails assuming that all production for a given period is sold—that no inventory changes exist.

3. *Absorption costing:* Either $300,000 or $600,000 at the end of 20X4 and zero at the end of 20X5. *Variable costing:* Zero at all times. This is a major criticism of variable costing and focuses on the issue of the definition of an asset. Supporters of variable costing answer that zero is the correct inventory value because the existence of inventory does not save any future cost.

4.   Comments should include the following:

(a) The central issue is the *timing* of release of fixed factory overhead to expense.

(b) Variable costing dovetails exactly with general break-even analysis, while absorption costing does not.

(c) Variable costing rests on a simple basic assumption that is easy to understand, while results under the same set of facts can differ considerably when absorption costing is applied.

(d) Variable costers would inventory the units at zero cost because they believe no costs should be carried forward to the future if they cannot obviate a future cost incurrence, while the absorption-costing adherents view potential cost *recovery* as the criterion for carrying costs as assets.

13-52 (25-30 min.)

1. Variable Costing (in thousands of dollars)

	20X4	20X5	Together
Sales	900	900	1,800
Variable cost of sales @ $.14 per gallon	210	210	420
Contribution margin	690	690	1,380
Fixed costs	590	590	1,180
Net income (loss)	100	100	200

Absorption Costing (in thousands of dollars)

	Option One*			Option Two**		
	20X4	20X5	Together	20X4	20X5	Together
Sales	900	900	1,800	900	900	1,800
Less cost of goods sold:						
Beginning inventory	-	405	-	-	600	-
Cost of goods manufactured	810	-	810	1,200	-	1,200
Cost of goods available for sale	810	405	810	1,200	600	1,200
Ending inventory	405	-	-	600	-	-
Cost of goods sold	405	405	810	600	600	1,200
Under applied overhead	-	390	390	-	390	390
Over applied overhead	-	-	-	(390)	-	(390)
Other expenses	200	200	400	200	200	400
Total charges	605	995	1,600	410	1,190	1,600
Net income	295	(95)	200	490	(290)	200

*Variable cost per unit, $.14 + Fixed costs per unit, $.13 ($390,000 ÷ 3,000,000 gallons) = $.27

**Variable cost per unit, $.14 + Fixed costs per unit, $.26 ($390,000 ÷ 1,500,000 gallons) = $.40

2.

	Variable Costing	Absorption Costing Option One	Option Two
Inventory:			
December 31, 20X4	$210,000	$405,000	$600,000
December 31, 20X5	-0-	-0-	-0-

13-53 (30-35 min.)

1.

Standard Variable Costing
TRAPANI COMPANY
Income Statement
For the Year Ended December 31, 20X4

(1)	Sales – at standard prices (13,000 x $75)	$975,000
	Opening inventory	-
	Add variable cost of goods manufactured at standard*	660,000
	Variable cost of goods available for sale	660,000
	Deduct ending inventory at standard variable cost:	
	2,000 x $44	88,000
	Variable manufacturing cost of goods sold	572,000
	Variable selling and administrative costs at	
	budget of $9 per unit sold	117,000
(2)	Total variable costs	689,000
(1) - (2)	Contribution margin at standard	286,000
	Fixed factory overhead at budget	98,000
	Fixed selling and administrative costs	80,000
	Total fixed costs	178,000
	Operating income	$108,000

   *15,000 x $44 = $660,000

Standard Absorption Costing
TRAPANI COMPANY
Income Statement
For the Year Ending December 31, 20X4

Sales – at standard prices (13,000 x $75)	$975,000
Opening inventory	-
Add cost of goods manufactured at standard[a]	765,000
Absorption cost of goods available for sale	765,000
Deduct ending inventory at standard absorption cost:	
2,000 x $51[b]	102,000
Absorption cost of goods sold at standard	663,000
Gross profit at standard	312,000
Deduct selling and administrative costs:	
Variable at standard (13,000 x $9)	117,000
Fixed at budget	80,000
Total selling and administrative costs	197,000
Operating income before variances	115,000
Variances: Production-volume variance[c]	7,000F
Operating income	$122,000

[a]15,000 x $51 = $765,000.

[b]Variable cost of $44 + fixed factory overhead of $7 = $51.

[c](15,000 - 14,000 expected volume) x $7 = $7,000F.

2. If inventories increase, operating income will be higher under absorption costing:

Difference in operating income
    = Change in inventory units x Fixed overhead rate
    = (2,000 - 0) x $7
    = $14,000

13-54 (40-45 min.) This problem should not be assigned without also assigning problem 13-54.

1.

Standard Variable Costing
TRAPANI COMPANY
Income Statement
For the Year Ended December 31, 20X5

(1)	Sales – at standard prices (14,000 x $75)	$1,050,000
	Opening inventory, at standard variable cost: 2,000 x $44	88,000
	Add variable cost of goods manufactured at standard*	572,000
	Variable cost of goods available for sale	660,000
	Deduct ending inventory at standard variable cost: 1,000 x $44	44,000
	Variable manufacturing cost of goods sold	616,000
	Variable selling and administrative costs at budget of $9 per unit sold	126,000
(2)	Total variable costs	742,000
(1)-(2)	Contribution margin at standard	308,000
	Fixed factory overhead at budget	98,000
	Fixed selling and administrative costs	80,000
	Total fixed costs	178,000
	Operating income before variances	130,000
	Variances:	
	Selling prices (a)	18,000F
	Variable manufacturing costs (b)	76,800F
	Variable selling & administrative costs (c)	7,600F
	Fixed factory overhead (d)	3,000F
	Total variances	105,400F
	Operating income	$ 235,400

*13,000 x $44 = $572,000.
(a) $1,068,000 - (14,000 x $75)
(b) $285,000 + $174,200 + $36,000 - $572,000
(c) $118,400 - $126,000
(d) $98,000 - $95,000

Standard Absorption Costing
TRAPANI COMPANY
Income Statement
For the Year Ending December 31, 20X5

Sales – at standard prices (14,000 x $75)	$1,050,000
Opening inventory – at standard absorption cost: 2,000 x $51[a]	102,000
Add cost of goods manufactured at standard[b]	663,000
Absorption cost of goods available for sale	765,000
Deduct ending inventory at std. absorption cost: 1,000 x $51[a]	51,000
Absorption cost of goods sold at standard	714,000
Gross profit at standard	336,000
Deduct selling and administrative costs:	
Variable at standard (14,000 x $9)	126,000
Fixed at budget	80,000
Total selling and administrative costs	206,000
Operating income before variances	130,000
Variances:	
Selling prices	18,000F
Variable manufacturing costs	76,800F
Variable selling & administrative costs	7,600F
Fixed factory overhead:	
Budget variance	3,000F
Production-volume variance[c]	7,000U
Total variances	98,400F
Operating income	$ 228,400

[a]Variable cost of $44 + fixed factory overhead of $7 = $51.
[b]13,000 x $51 = $663,000.
[c](14,000 - 13,000) x $7 = $7,000 U.

2.   If inventories decrease, operating income will be lower under absorption costing:

Difference in operating income= Change in inventory units
$$\text{x Fixed overhead rate}$$
$$= (1,000 - 2,000) \times \$7$$
$$= \$\text{-}7,000$$

(30-40 min.) This is a straightforward problem that is quite informative for most students.

1. $60,000 ÷ 7,500 hrs. = $8.00 per hour, or
                          = $16.00 per unit ($8.00 x 2 hours)

2.

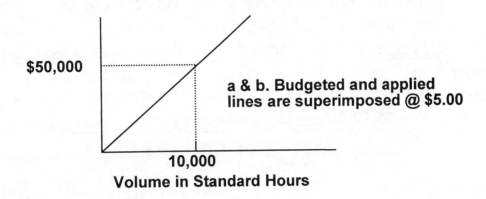

$50,000

a & b. Budgeted and applied
lines are superimposed @ $5.00

10,000
Volume in Standard Hours

3.

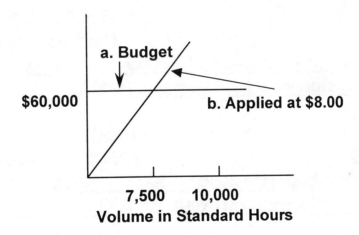

a. Budget

$60,000

b. Applied at $8.00

7,500   10,000
Volume in Standard Hours

We suggest using graphs in class as you explain the subsequent parts.

	(A) Cost Incurred: Actual Inputs x Actual Prices	(B)* Flexible Budget Based on Actual Inputs x Expected Prices	(C) Budget Based on Standard Inputs Allowed for Actual Outputs Achieved x Expected Prices	(D) Product Costing: Applied Overhead
4. Variable Overhead	$31,000		6,000x$5= $30,000	$30,000

Flexible-budget variance, 1,000U │ No variance

Under applied overhead, 1,000U

Fixed Overhead	$62,000		Lump-sum $60,000	6,000x$8= $48,000
				(7,500-6,000)x$8= Prod.-volume var.,

Flexible-budget variance, 2,000U │ 12,000U

Under applied overhead, 14,000U

5. Variable Overhead	$37,700		7,800x$5= $39,000	$39,000

Flexible-budget variance, 1,300F │ No variance

Over applied overhead, 1,300F

Fixed Overhead	$62,000		Lump-sum $60,000	7,800x$8= $62,400
				(7,800-7,500)x$8= Prod.-volume var.,

Flexible-budget variance, 2,000U │ 2,400F

Over applied overhead, 400F

*Not given in this problem.

13-56 (15-20 min.)

1. Variable manufacturing costs per unit, $175,000,000 ÷ 700,000 $250
    Fixed manufacturing costs per unit, 105,000,000 ÷ 700,000   150
    Total manufacturing costs per unit $400

2. Production-volume variance = (700,000 - 750,000) x $150 = $7,500,000 F

3.

Revenue (720,000 x $500)	$360,000,000
Cost of goods sold (720,000 x $400)	288,000,000
Gross margin	72,000,000
Production-volume variance	7,500,000
Profit	$ 79,500,000

4.

Revenue (720,000 x $500)	$360,000,000
Cost of goods sold (720,000 x $250)	180,000,000
Contribution margin	180,000,000
Fixed costs	105,000,000
Profit	$ 75,000,000

5. Neither measure is inherently better. They give different signals about performance. The variable-costing profit is a better measure of the effect of sales on profit. It is not affected by production volumes. The absorption-costing profit is affected by both sales and production volumes. Because production volume exceeded sales volume, the profit is higher under absorption costing.

    From an incentive point of view, the variable-costing profit has the advantage of not being affected by production decisions. Under absorption costing, a manager can increase profits merely by producing more units, even if they are not sold.

(10 min.)

Overhead rates: $720,000 ÷ 60,000 = $12 and $720,000 ÷ 45,000 = $16.

	Cost Incurred: Actual Inputs x Actual Prices	Flexible Budget Based on Actual Inputs x Expected Prices	Budget Based on Standard Inputs Allowed for Actual Outputs Achieved x Expected Prices	Product Costing: Applied Overhead
1. Using Practical Capacity	$747,000		$720,000	54,000x$12 =$648,000
				(54,000-60,000)x $12.00= Prod.-volume var
		Flexible-budget variance, $27,000U		=$72,000U
		Under applied overhead, $99,000U		
2. Using Expected Activity	$747,000		$720,000	54,000x$16= $864,000
				(54,000-45,000) x $16.00= Prod.-volume var.,
		Flexible-budget variance, $27,000U		144,000F
		Over applied overhead, $117,000F		

3.   The flexible-budget variance for fixed overhead is the difference between the amount incurred and the budget figure. The budget figure is the same regardless of the actual level of activity and the rate used in applying fixed overhead. Consequently the flexible-budget variances in parts (1) and (2) would be identical.

The production-volume variance is the difference between fixed overhead applied and the budgeted amount. Fixed overhead applied is the product of standard hours allowed and the standard fixed-overhead rate. The difference arises from the different measures of volume used in computing the standard fixed-overhead rate, the rate being $12 per standard hour in part (1) while being $16 per standard hour in part (2). The difference in variances would be computed by multiplying the difference in rates by standard hours allowed: ($16 - $12) x 54,000 = $216,000.

Note how the production-volume variance will never be favorable when based on practical capacity. Also note how different expected volume assumptions can produce radically different production-volume variances. Both accountants and managers should be aware of these possibilities when analyzing fixed overhead variances.

13-58 (25-30 min.)

1. Total dollars and machine hours are in thousands:

Year	Base a	Base b*	Base c
20X3	$36,400 ÷ 2,450 = $14.86	$36,400 ÷ 2,550 = $14.27	$36,400 ÷ 2,800 = $13.00
20X4	$36,400 ÷ 2,700 = $13.48	$36,400 ÷ 2,550 = $14.27	$36,400 ÷ 2,800 = $13.00
20X5	$36,400 ÷ 2,800 = $13.00	$36,400 ÷ 2,550 = $14.27	$36,400 ÷ 2,800 = $13.00

*Average volume (in thousands): (2,250 + 2,450 + 2,700 + 2,800) ÷ 4 = 2,550.

2. Method a: This is the most popular method. It keeps the fixed-overhead rate constant over a year and generates no <u>expected</u> production-volume variance for the year in total.

Method b: This method keeps the fixed-overhead rate constant over four years, but annual budgets must recognize an expected unfavorable production-volume variance in the first two years and an expected favorable production-volume variance in the last two.

Method c: This method consistently generates unfavorable production-volume variances. The variances show the potential to spread fixed costs over a larger output whenever operations are below capacity.

3. Most students will prefer Method a because the text indicates that it is most popular. However, a case can also be made for either of the other methods. For example, practical capacity has increased in popularity in recent years, principally because the Internal Revenue Service permits its use. For tax purposes, practical capacity permits faster write-off of factory overhead.

13-59 (30 min.)

1. Because Leeds Tool Company uses absorption costing, the net income is influenced by both sales volume and production volume. Sales volume was increased in the November 30, 20X4 forecast, and at standard gross profit rates this would increase gross margin before taxes by £4,800. However, during the same period production volume was below the January 1, 20X4 forecast, causing an unplanned production-volume variance of £6,000. The production-volume variance and the increased selling expenses (due to the 10% increase in sales) overshadowed the added gross margin from sales as shown below:

Increased sales	£15,600
Increased cost of sales at standard	10,800
Increased gross margin at standard	£ 4,800
Less: Increased selling expense	1,120
Expected increase in earnings	£ 3,680
Production-volume variance	6,000 U
Decrease in earnings	£(2,320)

2. The basic cause of the lower forecast of profits is low production. If raw materials can be obtained, and if it is reasonable in light of expected future sales, Leeds Tool Company could schedule heavy production which would reduce the unfavorable production-volume variance.

3. Leeds Tool Company could adopt variable costing. Then fixed manufacturing costs would be treated as period costs and would not be assigned to production. Consequently, earnings would not be affected by production volume but only by sales volume. The following statements are prepared on a variable-costing basis.

LEEDS TOOL COMPANY
Forecasts of Operating Results

	Forecasts as of			
	January 1, 20X4		November 30, 20X4	
Sales		£156,000		£171,600
Variable costs:				
Manufacturing	£78,000		£85,800*	
Selling expenses	11,200**		12,320	
Total variable costs		89,200		98,120
Contribution margin		£ 66,800		£ 73,480
Fixed costs:				
Manufacturing	£30,000		£30,000	
Administration	20,000		20,000	
Total fixed costs		50,000		50,000
Earnings before taxes		£ 16,800		£ 23,480

*(171,600 ÷ 156,000) x £78,000 = £85,800

**Because selling expenses increased by 10% when sales increased by 10%, they are variable costs.

4. Variable costing would not be acceptable for financial reporting purposes because generally accepted accounting principles seem to require the allocation of some fixed manufacturing costs to inventory.

13-60 (30-40 min.)

SCHLOSSER CO.
Variable Costing Income Statement

Sales, 150,000 units at $20.00		$3,000,000
Variable expenses:		
Beginning inventory, 15,000 at $11.00	$ 165,000 (a)	
Production, 145,000 * at $11.00	1,595,000	
Available for sale	$1,760,000	
Ending inventory, 10,000 at $11.00	(110,000)	
Standard variable cost of sales	$1,650,000	
Add variance in variable costs of production	33,000	
Variable manufacturing cost of sales	$1,683,000	
Variable selling and administrative expenses	450,000	(2,133,000)
Contribution margin		(b) $ 867,000
Fixed expenses:		
Manufacturing	$ 165,000	
Selling and administrative	650,000	(815,000)
Operating income		(c) $ 52,000

*Production = sales – decrease in inventory = 150,000 – 5,000 = 145,000 units

SCHLOSSER CO.
Absorption Costing Income Statement

Sales, 150,000 units at $20.00		$3,000,000
Cost of sales:		
Beginning inventory, 15,000 at $12.10*	$ 181,500 (d)	
Production, 145,000 at $12.10	1,754,500	
Available for sale	$1,936,000	
Ending inventory, 10,000 at $12.10	(121,000)	
Standard cost of sales	$1,815,000	
Add unfavorable variances:		
Variable manufacturing costs	33,000	
Prod.-volume variance, 5,000 at $1.10	5,500	(1,853,500)
Gross margin		(e) $1,146,500
Selling and administrative expenses:		
Variable, 150,000 at $3.00	$ 450,000	
Fixed	650,000	(1,100,000)
Operating income		(f) $ 46,500

*$165,000 fixed overhead ÷ 150,000 units = $1.10; $1.10 + $11.00 = $12.10.

13-61 (20-30 min.)

1.

	(in thousands)	
	a.	b.
Revenue, 75,000 x $18	$ 1,350	$ 1,350
Standard cost of goods sold, 75,000 x ($8 + $5 + $4)	(1,275)	(1,275)
Gross margin at standard	$ 75	$ 75
Manufacturing variances	(40)	(30)*
Operating income	$ 35	$ 45

*Total variance = $40,000U. Proration to sales = (75,000 ÷ 100,000) x $40,000 = $30,000

2.   a. Ending inventory, Method (a): 25,000 units x $17 = $425,000
     b. Ending inventory, Method (b): (25,000 units x $17) + (25,000 ÷ 100,000) x $40,000 = $425,000 + $10,000 = $435,000

Note that Method (b) provides $10,000 more operating income and $10,000 higher inventory because $10,000 of the variances was allocated to inventory rather than to expense.

3.   Supporters of Method (a) claim that variances arise from inefficiencies or efficiencies of the period and therefore should affect the current period's income statement. They are not necessary costs of production and therefore should not be inventoried.

Supporters of Method (b) claim that the income statement gives a better picture of *actual costs* using Method (b).

13-62 (35-45 min.)

	Cost Incurred: Actual Inputs x Actual Prices	Flexible Budget Based on Actual Inputs x Expected Prices	Flexible Budget Based on Standard Inputs Allowed for Actual Outputs Achieved x Expected Prices	Product Costing Applied to Product
Direct	12,000 x $12.50	12,000 x $13.00*	10,800 x $13.00*	
Labor:	= $150,000	= $156,000	= $140,400	$140,400

Price variance, 12,000 hrs. x $.50 = $6,000F | Usage variance, 1,200 hrs. x $13 = $15,600U

Flexible-budget variance, $9,600U

		12,000 x $3.00*	10,800 x $3.00*	
Variable Overhead:	$37,000*	= $36,000	= $32,400	$32,400

Spending variance, $1,000U | Efficiency variance, 1,200 hrs. x $3.00 = $3,600U

Flexible-budget variance, $4,600U

Under applied overhead, $4,600U

		Lump-sum	Lump-sum	10,800 x $3.30**
Fixed Overhead:	$38,000*	$39,600	$39,600	= $35,640

Spending variance, $1,600F | No variance | Prod.-Vol. Var., $3,960U

Flexible-budget variance, $1,600F*

Under applied overhead, $2,360U

*Given
**39,600 ÷ (2,000 x 6) = $3.30

13-63 (35-40 min.)

	Cost Incurred: Actual Inputs x Actual Prices	Flexible Budget Based on Actual Inputs x Expected Prices	Flexible Budget Based on Standard Inputs Allowed for Actual Outputs Achieved x Expected Prices	Product Costing Applied to Product
Direct Labor	1,000 x € 42.5 = € 42,500*	1,000 x € 44* = € 44,000	900 x € 44* = € 39,600	€ 39,600

Price variance, 1,000 hrs. x € 1.5 = € 1,500F	Usage variance, 100 hrs. x € 44 = € 4,400U
Flexible-budget variance, € 2,900U	No variance

		Flexible Budget Based on Actual Inputs x Expected Prices	Flexible Budget Based on Standard Inputs Allowed for Actual Outputs Achieved x Expected Prices	Product Costing Applied to Product
Variable Overhead	€ 10,400*	1,000 x € 11 = € 11,000	900 x € 11* = € 9,900	€ 9,900

Spending variance, € 600F	Efficiency variance, 100 hrs. x € 11 = € 1,100U
Flexible-budget variance, € 500U	No variance
Under applied overhead, € 500U	

		Lump-sum	Lump-sum	900 x € 6**
Fixed overhead:	€ 6,300*	€ 6,600	€ 6,600	= € 5,400

Spending variance, € 300F	No variance	Prod.-Vol. Var., € 1,200U
Flexible-budget variance, € 300F*		
Under applied overhead, € 900U		

*Given
**€ 6,600 ÷ (220 x 5) = € 6

753

13-64 (15-20 min.)

1.

	Factory Overhead
Activity	Costs Applied
1.	1 x $ 1.20 = $ 1.20
2.	39 x .07 = 2.73
3.	28 x .20 = 5.60
4.	15 x .40 = 6.00
5.	1 x 3.20 = 3.20
6.	8 x .60 = 4.80
7.	.15 x 80.00 = 12.00
8.	.05 x 90.00 = 4.50
Total	$40.03

Direct materials	$ 55.00
Factory overhead applied	40.03
Total manufacturing product cost	$95.03

2. Direct labor is no longer traced separately via time tickets to individual products. Instead, it becomes part of activity cost pools and is included in each activity's factory overhead application rate. This reduces accounting costs because there is no elaborate tracking of labor.

3. Managers would primarily favor this multiple overhead rate, activity-based costing system because of more accurate product costing. In this way, managers will have more confidence in their decisions regarding pricing and emphasizing or de-emphasizing various products. The older system may be easier to understand but less believable.

13-65 (20-30 min.)

1.

	Machining	Finishing	Plant
Factory overhead	SFr960,000	SFr800,000	SFr1,760,000
Divide by direct labor	SFr300,000	SFr800,000	SFr1,100,000
Application rate	320%	100%	160%
Divide by machine hours	60,000	20,000	80,000
Application rate	SFr16	SFr40	SFr22

2.   a.

	Order	
	K102	K156
Machining:		
Direct materials	SFr 4,000	SFr 4,000
Direct labor	3,000	1,500
Factory overhead applied, 160% of direct labor	4,800	2,400
Finishing:		
Direct labor	1,500	3,000
Factory overhead applied, 160% of direct labor	2,400	4,800
Total cost	SFr15,700	SFr15,700

b.

	Order	
	K102	K156
Machining:		
Direct materials	SFr 4,000	SFr 4,000
Direct labor	3,000	1,500
Factory overhead applied, 1,200 hrs.		
x SFr16 and 100 hrs. x SFr16	19,200	1,600
Finishing:		
Direct labor	1,500	3,000
Factory overhead applied,		
100% of direct labor	1,500	3,000
Total cost	SFr29,200	SFr13,100

3. The answers in 2(b) are preferable to those in 2(a). Why? Because the use of machine hours is probably an important cause of increases in the company's overhead costs. Machine hours are cost drivers. The plantwide rate based on direct labor fails to distinguish between those jobs that make heavy and light use of machinery. In general, the use of departmental overhead rates is preferable to plantwide rates. Why? Because the use of key activities (cost drivers) is pinpointed more accurately. Decisions regarding pricing and product lines should improve.

13-66 (35-50 min.)

1. The income statements are based on absorption costing because the cost of goods sold of $45 per unit includes both variable costs ($14 + $10 + $8) and fixed costs ($13).

2. (a)

Boulder Division
Income Statement Based on
Standard Absorption Costing
For the Year Ended December 31, 20X4

Sales (114,000 x $55)	$6,270,000
Cost of goods sold (114,000 x $45)	5,130,000
Gross margin at standard	$1,140,000
Production-volume variance*	0
Gross margin at actual	1,140,000
Selling and administrative expenses	540,000
Operating income	$ 600,000

*There was no production-volume variance because both actual production volume and expected volume were 120,000 units.

(b) Operating income is short of budget by $660,000 - $600,000 = $60,000. Wolcott could produce extra units; each unit of production will increase operating income by the amount of fixed manufacturing overhead per unit, which is $13 per unit. (The $13 per unit can be calculated as total unit cost less variable unit cost, $45 - $32, or as monthly budgeted fixed overhead divided by monthly budgeted production, $130,000 ÷ 10,000 units = $13 per unit.) Wolcott must produce an extra $60,000 ÷ $13 = 4,616 units to achieve the budgeted profit level. Inventory has already increased by 5,000 units (110,000 production units - 105,000 sales units), and producing an extra 4,616 units in December would increase inventory even more. Of course, it may not be possible to produce a total of 14,616 units in one month, but if it were, Wolcott could meet her operating-income target by producing units for which there is no demand.

3. (a)   **Boulder Division**
              Income Statement Based on Variable Costing
                For the Year Ended December 31, 20X4

Sales		$6,270,000
Variable cost of goods sold (114,000 x $32)		3,648,000
Contribution margin		$2,622,000
Fixed costs:		
Fixed overhead	$1,560,000	
Fixed selling and administrative expenses	540,000	2,100,000
Operating income		$ 522,000

(b) If sales cannot be increased, there is nothing Wolcott can do to achieve the budgeted operating income. Changing the level of production has no effect on variable-costing income.

Notice that the Boulder Division has $78,000 less operating income using variable costing than when using absorption costing. Why? Because production exceeds sales by 6,000 units. For each of these units, $13 of fixed manufacturing overhead was added to inventory with absorption costing but was charged as an expenses with variable costing. This accounts for the 6,000 x $13 = $78,000 extra expense on the variable-costing statement.

4.   The variable-costing system motivates the better decision. Inventory has already been increased 5,000 units above plan by the end of November. An incentive to produce even more units for inventory in December is most likely dysfunctional. Such production will probably result in large unnecessary handling and storage costs.

<u>13-67</u> (40-60 min.) Note that € is the symbol for the Euro.

1. (a)   The division manager would want to build inventory and thereby maximize current income:

	Units
Desired ending inventory, maximum possible	25,000
December sales	6,000
Total needs	31,000
November 30 inventory, 110,000 + 10,000 - 100,000	20,000
Production scheduled	11,000

(b) Sales, 106,000 units at € 400   € 42,400,000

Less cost of goods sold:		
Beginning inventory, 10,000 at € 250	€ 2,500,000	
Manufacturing costs, 121,000 at € 250	30,250,000	
Total standard cost of goods available for sale	€ 32,750,000	
Ending inventory, 25,000 at € 250	6,250,000	
Standard cost of goods sold	€ 26,500,000	
Less over applied fixed manufacturing overhead, 1,000 at € 85, favorable	85,000	26,415,000
Gross margin		15,985,000
Other expenses:		
Variable, 106,000 at € 40	€ 4,240,000	
Fixed	10,200,000	14,440,000
Operating income		€ 1,545,000

(c) If December production were 4,000 units instead of 11,000 units, the under applied overhead would be 6,000 units at € 85, or € 510,000. Net income would be € 1,545,000 less the € 595,000 difference in the applied overhead, or € 950,000. The ending inventory would be 18,000 units (20,000 + 4,000 production - 6,000 sales).

The following tabulation may be helpful:

	Cumulative Manufacturing Costs		
	Incurred	Applied	Variance*
December production, 11,000 units:			
Variable	€ 19,965,000	€ 19,965,000	€ 0
Fixed	10,200,000	10,285,000	85,000F
December production, 4,000 units:			
Variable	€ 18,810,000	€ 18,810,000	€ 0
Fixed	10,200,000	9,690,000	510,000U

*U = under applied, F = over applied.

2. (a)(b)

Sales, 106,000 units at € 400		€ 42,400,000
Variable costs:		
Manufacturing, 106,000 at € 165	€ 17,490,000	
Other, 106,000 at € 40	4,240,000	21,730,000
Contribution margin		€ 20,670,000
Fixed costs:		
Manufacturing	€ 10,200,000	
Other	10,200,000	20,400,000
Operating income		€ 270,000

Operating income is the same under variable costing regardless of December production schedules, because income is influenced by sales alone rather than by sales and production.

2. (c)

	11,000	4,000
December production schedule, units	11,000	4,000
Operating income as shown in requirement (1)	€ 1,545,000	€ 950,000
Inventory increase for the year:		
15,000 units at fixed-overhead rate of € 85	1,275,000	-
8,000 units at € 85	-	680,000
Operating income as shown in requirement (2)	€ 270,000	€ 270,000

3. The division manager should set the minimum production schedule of 4,000 units. This will reduce the inventories by 2,000 units. She may be tempted to ask for permission to reduce production even below 4,000 units, because the outlook is for ending inventories far in excess of reasonable sales demands.

   Note that production scheduling can influence short-run reported operating income under absorption costing, but such scheduling has no effect on operating income under variable costing. Thus, the *accounting technique* used may influence the manager's decision in the former case but not in the latter. It is undesirable to have the accounting technique in itself influence decisions in a direction that may conflict with overall company goals.

4. 4,000 units should be scheduled in December. This will minimize income for the current year and will therefore minimize current income taxes. Additional income taxes will be paid in the future when the rates will be lower.

13-68 (20-30 min.)

1. The fixed overhead variance does not reveal how well fixed overhead costs have been controlled. The standard is not an appropriate basis of comparison. Why? Because the standard accounts for a fixed cost as if it were variable. Note that volume decreased by 10.5%, from 1,520,000 cwt. to 1,360,000 cwt., so the standard fixed overhead decreased by 10.5%, from $2,432,000 to $2,176,000. But *fixed* overhead would not be expected to change. The flexible (control) budget for fixed overhead, based on 20X4 costs, is $2,432,000. From a control perspective, there was a $2,432,000 - $2,412,000 = $20,000F variance.

   The standard used by Jensen is the same as the applied amount in a standard-cost system. The difference between the actual amount and this applied amount can be summarized as follows:

Actual Fixed Overhead	Flexible Budget: Fixed Overhead	Applied Fixed Overhead
$2,412,000	$2,432,000	$2,176,000
	Flexible-budget variance, $20,000F	Production-volume variance, $256,000 U

   The major part of the total variance is the production-volume variance, which serves a product-costing purpose not a control purpose.

2. Setting standards based on last year's costs is not uncommon. Managers must carefully interpret the resulting variances. Such variances do not necessarily measure efficiency, as they do with currently attainable standards. Instead, such variances simply indicate changes in costs. Such information can be useful. However, managers should be alert for any past inefficiency built into the standards. Otherwise, inefficiencies will probably persist over a series of years.

13-69 (20-30 min.) For the solution, see the Prentice Hall Web site, www.prenhall.com/

13-70 (180 min. or more)

The purpose of this exercise is to learn how real companies allocate costs. It involves learning what costs are included in overhead, how they are categorized, whether cost allocations recognize cost-behavior patterns, what cost drivers are used for allocation, and the process by which costs are allocated to final products or services.

The requirement for a diagram makes students put what they learn into a coherent package. It is easy to sit and listen to what seems like a very logical explanation but not understand it fully. The diagram of a cost allocation system cannot be done without a thorough understanding of the system.

A very useful exercise is to have several groups present their findings to the class. In addition to learning about different cost allocation systems, the students making the presentation will hone their communication skills and those listening will learn a great deal about a variety of companies. We find that several short (approximately 5-minute) presentations can be more effective that a couple of longer ones. Students learn to focus quickly on the most important issues.

<u>13-71</u> (30-40 min.)

NOTE TO INSTRUCTOR. This solution is based on the web site as it was in early 2004. Be sure to examine the current web site before assigning this problem, as the information there may have changed. For numbers 2 to 4, students will need to access the 10K report because Dell provides very limited financial information in its annual reports of 2001-2004.

For students to answer questions 2 and 4, they need to be given the following information:

For number 2, specify that "computers" in the last sentence means only notebook computers. Dell's notebook products include the Latitude and Inspiron. Latitude notebooks are sold only to businesses or educational institutions. Inspiron notebooks are essentially the same product sold to individuals. Have students assume that the total revenue reported for notebooks sold in the most recent year is evenly split between Latitude and Inspiron computers.

For number 4, assume that PCs include desktop and notebook computers but not enterprise computers and that the average sales price for PCs is the same as for notebooks.

The answers below are derived from Dell's 2003, 10K report.

1.   Answers will vary depending on the product family and computer chosen. In the home and home office computer family, there are several models of notebook computers. Inspiron notebooks range in price from about $750 to $3,000 (loaded). The same price range holds for the Latitude notebooks sold to individuals – the two products being essentially the same. Information includes the size of the display, memory, computing speed, weight, and other hardware included such as DVD. Features vary which can cause the price to be different from the base price.

2.	From Dell's 10K, FY03 report listed under the SEC Reports, Part II, Item 7, unit shipments increased 21% from 2002 compared to a decrease of 1% in the industry. From footnote 9, segment information, notebook revenue was $9,638,000,000. If the average price is assumed to be about $1,500, then $9,638,000,000 ÷ $1,500 = 6,525,000 notebooks were shipped during the year ending January 31, 2003.

3.	The average price assumed for Latitude computers is $1,500 while the price range is from $750 to more than $3,000. The differences result from the numerous options that are available and discounts given to businesses and educational institutions for volume purchases.

4.	From Dell's 2003, 10K, the cost of goods sold (cost of revenue) was $29,055,000,000. Selling, general and administrative expenses were $3,050,000,000 and research, development, and engineering expenses were $455,000,000. Depreciation and amortization was $211,000,000.

To compute the estimated breakeven point in PCs, estimates of fixed cost, sales price per computer, and variable cost per PC are needed.

Sales price is assumed to be $1,500 per PC. Fixed costs of PCs are estimated to be 80% x $211,000,000 = $168,800,000. Variable costs of PCs are (millions of dollars):

Cost of revenue	$29,055
Selling, general, and administrative, expenses	3,050
Research, development, and engineering expenses	455
Total	$32,560
Less fixed costs	211
Variable costs	$32,349
Variable costs of PCs (x 80%)	$25,879

From footnote 9, segment information, PC revenue was $28,503,000,000. If the average price is assumed to be about $1,500, then $28,503,000,000 ÷ $1,500 = 19,002,000 PCs were shipped during the year ending January 31, 2003. The variable cost per PC is then $25,879,000,000 ÷ 19,002,000 = $1,362.

The number of PCs sold to breakeven is calculated as

$$\text{BEP} = \frac{\text{Fixed Cost}}{\text{Unit Sales Price} - \text{Unit Variable Cost}}$$

$$= \frac{.8 \times \$211,000,000}{\$1,500 = \$1,362} = \frac{\$168,000,000}{\$138} = 1,217,391$$

Does this seem reasonable? Assume that income from PC operations is about 80% of total income from operations. The estimated income from PC operations using our figures would be

Unit CM [Actual PC volume – Breakeven PC volume]

= $138 x [19,002,000 – 1,217,391] = $2,454,276,042.

The estimated total income from operations would be $2,359,265,986 ÷ .8 = $3,067,845,053 or about $3.07 billion which is not far off from the $2.84 billion reported in the annual report and 10K.

CHAPTER 14
COVERAGE OF LEARNING OBJECTIVES

LEARNING OBJECTIVE	FUNDA-MENTAL ASSIGN-MENT MATERIAL	CRITICAL THINKING EXERCISES AND EXERCISES	PROBLEMS	CASES, EXCEL, COLLAB. & INTERNET EXERCISES
LO1: Distinguish between job-order costing and process costing.	A1,B1	16,18		50,51
LO2: Prepare summary journal entries for the typical transactions of a job-costing system.		22,25	41	
LO3: Use an activity-based-costing system in a job-order environment.				
LO4: Show how service organizations use job costing.		17,23	42	
LO5: Explain the basic ideas underlying process costing and how they differ from job costing.		29		51
LO6: Compute output in terms of equivalent units.	A2,B2	30,31,32,36	44,45,46,47	
LO7: Compute costs and prepare journal entries for the principal transactions in a process-costing system.	A2,B2	31,32,33,34, 37,38	43,45,46,47	
LO8: Demonstrate how the presence of beginning inventories affects the computation of unit costs under the weighted-average method.	A3,B3		48	49
LO9: Use backflush costing with a JIT production system.	A4,B4	19		

14-A1 (15-20 min.) Answers are in thousands.

1.

a. Direct materials inventory   450
      Cash   450

b. Work in process inventory   420
      Direct materials inventory   420

c. Work in process inventory   125
      Accrued payroll   125

d. Factory department overhead control   175
      Various accounts   175
        (80 + 55 + 40 = 175)

e. Work in process inventory   225
      Factory department overhead control   225
        (180% x 125)

f. Finished goods inventory   705
      Work in process inventory   705

g. Cost of goods sold   460
      Finished goods inventory   460

2.

Direct Materials Inventory			
a.	450	b.	420
* Bal.	30		

Finished Goods Inventory			
f.	705	g.	460
* Bal.	245		

Work in Process Inventory			
b.	420	f. 705	
c.	125		
e.	225		
	770		
* Bal.	65		

Cost of Goods Sold	
g.	460

Factory Department Overhead Control			
d.	175	e.	225

* 12/31/X4 Balance

14-A2 (10-15 min.)

1.

Flow of Production	(Step 1) Physical Units	(Step 2) Equivalent Units Direct Materials	Conversion Costs
Started and completed	17,000	17,000	17,000
Work in process, ending inventory	2,000		
Direct materials added: 2,000 x 1		2,000	
Conversion costs added: 2,000 x .5			1,000
Total accounted for	19,000		
Total work done		19,000	18,000
Costs:			
Total costs to account for (Step 3):	$147,000	$57,000	$90,000
Divide by equivalent units (Step 4)		19,000	18,000
Unit costs	$ 8.00	$ 3.00	$ 5.00

2.

	Totals	Details
Application of costs (Step 5):		
To units completed and transferred to Testing, 17,000 units ($8.00)	$136,000	
To units not completed and still in process, Feb. 28, 2,000 units:		
Direct materials	$ 6,000	2,000($3.00)
Conversion costs	5,000	1,000($5.00)
Work in process, Feb. 28	$ 11,000	
Total costs accounted for	$147,000	

770

14-A3 (25-30 min.)

Flow of Production	(Step 1) Physical Units	(Step 2) Equivalent Units Direct Materials	Conversion Costs
Work in process, beginning inventory	10,000 (25%)*		
Started	80,000		
To account for	90,000		
Completed and transferred out during current period	70,000	70,000	70,000
Work in process, ending inventory	20,000 (50%)*	20,000	10,000
Units accounted for	90,000		
Work done to date		90,000	80,000

*Degree of completion for conversion costs.

	Costs	Totals	Details Direct Materials	Conversion Costs
	Work in process, beginning inventory	$ 175,500	$138,000	$ 37,500
	Costs added currently	1,494,500	852,000	642,500
(Step 3)	Total costs to account for	$1,670,000	$990,000	$680,000
(Step 4)	Divisor, equivalent units for work done to date		÷ 90,000	÷ 80,000
	Cost per equivalent unit	$ 19.50	$ 11.00	$ 8.50

	Costs	Totals	Details Direct Materials	Details Conversion Costs
(Step 5)	**Application of Costs**			
	Completed and transferred			
	(70,000 units)	$1,365,000	70,000 ($19.50)	
	Work in process, ending			
	inventory (20,000 units):			
	Direct materials	$ 220,000	20,000($11.00)	
	Conversion costs	85,000		10,000($8.50)
	Total work in process	$ 305,000		
	Total costs accounted for	$1,670,000		

14-A4 (15-20 min.)

1.

Materials inventories	46,000	
Accounts payable		46,000
Conversion costs	30,000	
Accrued payroll		11,000
Miscellaneous accounts		19,000
Finished goods inventories (2,000 x $37)	74,000	
Materials inventories (2,000 x $22)		44,000
Conversion costs (2,000 x $15)		30,000
Cost of goods sold (1,980 x $37)	73,260	
Finished goods inventories		73,260

2.

Cost of goods sold	2,000	
Conversion costs		2,000

To recognize actual conversion costs that were
$2,000 greater than the amount applied to the products.

14-B1 (20-25 min.) Entries are in thousands of British pounds (£).

1. a. Direct materials inventory ... 112
        Accounts payable ... 112

    b. Work in process inventory ... 98
        Direct materials inventory ... 98

    c. Work in process inventory ... 105
        Accrued payroll ... 105

    d. Factory department overhead control ... 90
        Various accounts, such as cash or
        accounts payable ... 90

    e. Work in process inventory ... 84
        Factory department overhead control ... 84
        (80% x 105)

    f. Finished goods inventory ... 280
        Work in process inventory ... 280

    g. Cost of goods sold ... 350
        Finished goods inventory ... 350

    h. Accounts receivable ... 600
        Sales ... 600

2. Direct Materials Inventory

12/31/X4 Bal. 18	b.		98
a.	112		
12/31/X5 Bal. 32			

Work in Process Inventory

12/31/X4 Bal. 25	f.		280
b.	98		
c.	105		
e.	84		
	312		
12/31/X5 Bal. 32			

Finished Goods Inventory

12/31/X4 Bal. 100	g.		350
f.	280		
12/31/X5 Bal. 30			

Cost of Goods Sold

g.	350	

Factory Department Overhead Control

d.	90	e.	84

14-B2 (10-15 min.)

1.

Flow of Production	(Step 1) Physical Units	(Step 2) Equivalent Units Direct Materials	Conversion Costs
Started and completed	600,000	600,000	600,000
Work in process, ending inventory	300,000	300,000	150,000*
Units accounted for	900,000		
Units work done to date		900,000	750,000
Total costs to account for (Step 3):	$2,370,000	$1,620,000	$750,000
Divide by equivalent units (Step 4)		900,000	750,000
Unit costs	$ 2.80	$ 1.80	$ 1.00

*300,000 x .5

2. Application of costs (Step 5):	Totals	Details
To units completed and transferred to Finishing, 600,000 units ($2.80)	$1,680,000	
To units not completed and still in process, end, 300,000 units:		
Direct materials	$ 540,000	300,000 ($1.80)
Conversion costs	150,000	150,000($1.00)
Work in process, end	$ 690,000	
Total costs accounted for	$2,370,000	

14-B3 (25-35 min.)

Flow of Production	(Step 1) Physical Units	(Step 2) Equivalent Units Direct Materials	Conversion Costs
Work in process, beginning inventory	550 (40%)*		
Started	7,150		
To account for	7,700		
Completed and transferred out during current period, 550 + 7,150 - 400	7,300	7,300	7,300
Work in process, ending inventory	400 (20%)*	400	80
Units accounted for	7,700		
Work done to date		7,700	7,380

*Degree of completion for conversion costs.

	Costs	Totals	Details Direct Materials	Conversion Costs
	Work in process, beginning inventory	$ 5,104	$ 3,190	$ 1,914
	Costs added currently	100,326	65,340	34,986
(Step 3)	Total costs to account for	$105,430	$68,530	$36,900
(Step 4)	Divisor, equivalent units for work done to date		÷ 7,700	÷ 7,380
	Cost per equivalent unit	$ 13.90	$ 8.90	$ 5.00

(Step 5)	Application of Costs		
	Completed, (7,300 units)	$101,470	7,300 ($13.90)
	Work in process, ending inventory (400 units):		
	Direct materials (400)	$ 3,560	400($8.90)
	Conversion costs (80)	400	80($5.00)
	Total work in process	$ 3,960	
	Total costs accounted for	$105,430	

14-B4 (15 min.)

1. Materials inventories   16,000
      Accounts payable   16,000

    Conversion costs   6,300
      Accrued payroll and miscellaneous accts.   6,300

    Cost of goods sold (1,500 x $14.20)   21,300
      Materials inventories (1,500 x $10.00)   15,000
      Conversion costs (1,500 x $4.20)   6,300

2. Conversion costs   400
      Cost of goods sold   400
    To recognize actual conversion costs that were
    $400 less than the amount applied to the products.

14-1   Three purposes of product costing are to satisfy differing demands for (a) inventory valuation and income determination in accordance with generally accepted accounting principles, (b) income tax reporting, and (c) guiding strategic and operational decision-making.

14-2   The distinction between the job cost and the process cost methods centers largely around how product costing is accomplished. Unlike process costing, which deals with broad averages and great masses of like units, the essential feature of the job-cost method is the attempt to apply costs to specific jobs that may consist of either a single physical unit (a custom sofa) or a few like units (a dozen tables) in a distinct batch or job lot.

14-3   The basic record for the accumulation of job costs is the job-cost sheet or job-cost record. Exhibit 14-1 shows a Job-Cost Sheet, and it also shows the related source documents. A file of current job-cost sheets becomes the supporting details for the Work-in-Process Inventory account.

14-4   Source documents include materials requisitions and labor time tickets (time cards).

14-5   Examples of service industries that use the job-costing approach include repairing, consulting, legal, accounting, painting, dentistry, and income tax preparation.

14-6   No, the amount of value-chain activity not captured in either job-cost or process-cost systems is independent of the type of operating system used.

14-7   Examples of process costing include flour, glass, paint, and beer.

14-8   Examples of process costing include handling of mail, income tax returns, automobile registrations, and drivers license examinations.

14-9   Five key steps in process cost accounting are
        Step 1: Summarize the flow of physical units
        Step 2: Calculate output in terms of equivalent units
        Step 3: Summarize the total costs to account for, which are the
           total debits in Work in Process (that is, the costs applied to Work
           in Process)
        Step 4: Calculate unit costs
        Step 5: Apply costs to units completed and to units in ending work
           in process

14-10   The first two steps concentrate on what is occurring in physical or
engineering terms. The financial impact of the production process is
measured in the final three steps.

14-11 $(1 \times 10,000) + (.5 \times 5,000) = 12,500$ full-time-equivalent students.

14-12   Beginning inventories + Units started = Units transferred out + Ending
inventories.

14-13   Transferred-in costs are accounted for operationally the same as
direct materials added at the beginning of a production process. They differ
from direct material costs because they are a combination of direct material
and conversion costs from a previous department; thus, calling them a
direct-material cost is inappropriate.

14-14   When actual conversion costs exceed the amount applied, the excess
in the conversion cost account is charged directly to cost of goods sold; the
treatment is similar to accounting for underapplied overhead.

14-15   In addition to inventory valuation and income determination,
managers want accurate job costs as guides to pricing and to allocating
effort among particular products, services, or customers. They are also
necessary in contracts that reimburse the cost of a product or service.

14-16 The most important point is that product costing is an averaging process. The unit cost used for inventory purposes is the result of taking some accumulated cost and dividing it by some measure of production. The basic distinction between job order costing and process costing is the breadth of the denominator: in job order costing, it is small (for example, one painting, 100 advertising circulars, or one special packaging machine); but in process costing, it is large (for example, thousands of pounds, gallons, or board feet).

14-17 No. Some service firms trace only direct-labor costs to individual jobs. However, with advances in computer technology and needs for better job-cost information because of competition, more service firms are tracing additional costs to jobs. The more costs that are traced to jobs instead of being allocated, the more accurate are the job costs.

14-18 The central product costing problem in process costing is how each department should compute the cost of goods transferred out and the cost of goods remaining in the department.

14-19 No, but they are especially appropriate for companies with just-in-time systems. Any company with small inventories might find backflush costing appealing.

14-20 (10-15 min.) You may wish to use T-accounts. Amounts are in millions of dollars. You can also use the expression: ending balance (of any account) equals the beginning balance plus additions less subtractions or EB = BB + A - S. In this case "Purchased" is "additions" and "Used" is "subtractions."

1.   8 + 5 - 7 = 6 (BB + A - S = EB)

2.   8 + 9 - 6 = 11 (BB + A - EB = S)

3.   5 + Purchases - 7 = 8.   Purchases = 10

4.   Beginning inventory + 8 - 3 = 7.   Beginning inventory = 2

14-21 (5 min.) Amounts are in millions of dollars.

Beginning inventory + purchases - uses = ending inventory

Beginning inventory + $15 - $12 = $9
Beginning inventory = $9 - $15 + $12
Beginning inventory = $6

14-22 (10-15 min.) Amounts are in thousands of dollars.

1.	Finished goods inventory	128	
	Work in process inventory		128
	Finished goods = 72 + 56 = 128		

2.	Debits: 12 + 50 + 25 + 55 =	142	
	Credits: 72 + 56	128	
	Balance, April 30	14	

3.	Accounts receivable	101	
	Sales		101
	Sale of Job A13		
	Cost of goods sold	72	
	Finished goods inventory		72
	Cost of Job A13 sold		

14-23 (10-15 min.)

			Unit		
Reference	Date	Quantity	Cost	Amount	Summary
Direct Materials:					
Var. medical supplies	Jan. 5			$ 925	
Various chemicals	Jan. 7			780	$ 1,705
Direct Labor:					
Research associates	Jan. 5-12	120 hrs.	$32	$3,840	
Research assistants	Jan. 7-12	180 hrs.	$19	3,420	7,260
Project overhead applied	Jan. 12	$7,260 x .70		$5,082	5,082
Total costs					$14,047

Medical School — Cancer Research Project

14-24 (10 min.)

1. $6,500 + $3,900 = $10,400

2. $8,100

3. $3,200 + $8,800 = $12,000

14-25 (15 min.) Answers are in thousands of dollars.

1.

	a	b	c	a	b	c
Job No.	Construction in Process Sept. 30	Finished Houses, Sept. 30	Cost of Houses Sold Sept.	Construction in Process Oct. 31	Finished Houses, Oct. 31	Cost of Houses Sold Oct.
43			180			
51			170			
52		150				150
53	200					250[1]
61	115				135[2]	
62	180					205[3]
71	118			154[4]		
81	106			154[5]		
	719	150	350	308	135	605

[1]200 + 50   [2]115 + 20   [3]180 + 25   [4]118 + 36   [5]106 + 48

2.

	Sept.		Oct.	
Finished houses inventory	500		590	
Construction in process		500		590

Sept.: 180 + 170 + 150 = 500
Oct.: 250 + 135 + 205 = 590

3.

Cash		345	
Sales			345

To record sale of Job 53

Cost of houses sold		250	
Finished houses inventory			250

To record cost of Job 53 sold

<u>14-26</u> (30 min.)

The answers (in millions) are $15, $5, and $240.

Step-by-step entries are keyed alphabetically. The sequence depends on where the student prefers to start. You may wish to raise the question of whether the underapplied overhead should be prorated among the affected accounts at the end of the year.

Direct Materials				Work in Process				
Bal.	15	(a)	210	Bal.		5	(e) Completed	420
(b)	225			(a) Dir. Materials	210			
	240		210	(c) Dir. Labor	125*			
Bal.	30			(d) Applied overhead	200			
					540			420
				Bal.	120			

Finished Goods				Cost of Goods Sold	
Bal.	240	(f)	500	(f) 500	
(e)	420				
	660		500		
Bal.	160				

* $200 ÷ 160% = $125

14-27 (30 min.)

The answers (in millions) are $25, $22, and $32.

Step-by-step entries are keyed alphabetically. The sequence depends on where the student prefers to start. You may wish to raise the question of whether the underapplied overhead should be prorated among the affected accounts at the end of the year. Note the heavy ending Finished Goods.

Direct Materials			
Bal.	25	(a)	265
(b)	305		
	330		265
Bal.	65		

Work in Process			
Bal.	22	(e) Completed	523
(a) Dir. Materials	265		
(c) Dir. Labor*	100		
(d) Applied overhead	150		
	537		523
Bal.	14		

Finished Goods			
Bal.	32	(f)	350
(e)	523		
	555		350
Bal.	205		

Cost of Goods Sold	
(f)	350

* 150% x Direct labor = $150; therefore, Direct labor = $100.

14-28 (5-10 min.)

  Case A, $\$3,400,000 \div \$2,000,000 = 170\%$ of direct-labor cost
  Case B, $\$5 \times 450,000 = \$2,250,000$
  Case C, $\$1,750,000 \div 250,000 = \$7$ per machine hour

14-29 (5 min.)

  (1) The debit to the work in process account when transferring a subcomponent from Process A to the assembly process is a transferred-in cost.

  (2) The direct materials used in process A and assembly are variable-cost resources.

  (3) Direct labor costs in process A and assembly are directly traced fixed- cost resources.

  (4) An example of an indirect resource cost is the indirect material and indirect labor used for process A and the assembly process.

14-30 (5 min.)

  The direct material is the limestone rock that is delivered to the plant. Because crushing and screening the rock can begin immediately, we assume that direct material is always 100% completed. Thus, the equivalent units of direct material is the entire 400 tons. The 320 tons of rock that have been stocked are 100% complete with respect to both direct labor and overhead.

The 80 tons of rock that are in process at the end of March are 40% complete. This is 32 equivalent tons (80 tons x .40). Thus, the total work done during March is 400 tons of direct material and 352 (that is, 320 + 32) equivalent tons of direct labor and overhead.

14-31 (10-15 min.)

1.

Flow of Production	(Step 1) Physical Units	(Step 2) Equivalent Units Direct Materials	(Step 2) Equivalent Units Conversion Costs
Started and completed	650,000	650,000	650,000
Work in process, ending inventory	220,000	220,000	132,000*
Units accounted for	870,000		
Work done to date		870,000	782,000
Costs:			
Total costs to account for (Step 3)	$4,601,200	$3,741,000	$860,200
Divide by equivalent units (Step 4)		870,000	782,000
Unit costs	$5.40	$4.30	$1.10

*220,000 x .60

2.

Application of costs (Step 5):	Totals	Details
To units completed and transferred,		
650,000 units ($5.40)	$3,510,000	
To units still in process, end,		
220,000 units:		
Direct materials	$ 946,000	220,000($4.30)
Conversion costs	145,200	132,000($1.10)
Work in process, end	$1,091,200	
Total costs accounted for	$4,601,200	

14-32 (15-20 min.)

1.

	(Step 1) Physical Units	(Step 2) Equivalent Units	
Flow of Production		Direct Materials	Conversion Costs
Units started and completed	68,000	68,000	68,000
Work in process, end:	6,000		
Materials added: 6,000 x .90		5,400	
Conversion costs: 6,000 x .70			4,200
Units accounted for	74,000		
Work done to date		73,400	72,200

2.

	Total Costs	Details	
		Direct Materials	Conversion Costs
Costs to account for (Step 3)	$602,620	$205,520	$397,100
Divide by equivalent units (Step 4)		73,400	72,200
Unit costs	$8.30	$2.80	$5.50

Application of costs (Step 5):

To units completed and transferred, 68,000($8.30)	$564,400	
To units still in process, end, 6,000 units:		
Direct materials	$ 15,120	5,400($2.80)
Conversion costs	23,100	4,200($5.50)
Work in process, end	$ 38,220	
Total costs accounted for	$602,620	

14-33 (10-15 min.)

1. Work in process inventory – Assembly 57,000
       Direct materials inventory 57,000
       Materials added to production in February

2. Work in process inventory – Assembly 50,000
       Accrued payroll 50,000
       Direct labor in February

3. Work in process inventory – Assembly 40,000
       Factory overhead control 40,000
       Factory overhead applied in February

4. Work in process inventory – Testing 136,000
       Work in process inventory – Assembly 136,000
       Cost of goods completed and transferred in
       February from Assembly to Testing

The Key T account would show:

Work in Process Inventory – Assembly			
1. Direct materials	57,000	4. Transferred out	
2. Direct labor	50,000	to Testing	136,000
3. Factory overhead	40,000		
Costs to account for	147,000		
Bal. February 28	11,000		

14-34 (10-15 min.)

1. Work in process inventory – Assembly 1,620,000
        Direct materials inventory   1,620,000
    Materials added to production

2. Work in process inventory – Assembly 475,000
        Accrued payroll   475,000
    Direct labor

3. Work in process inventory – Assembly 275,000
        Factory overhead control   275,000
    Factory overhead applied

4. Work in process inventory – Finishing 1,680,000
        Work in process inventory – Assembly   1,680,000
    Cost of goods completed and transferred
    from Assembly to Finishing

The key T account would show:

Work in Process Inventory – Assembly

1.	Direct materials	1,620,000	4.	Transferred out	
2.	Direct labor	475,000		to Finishing	1,680,000
3.	Factory overhead	275,000			
	Costs to account for	2,370,000			
Balance		690,000			

14-35 (5 min.)

$$\text{Let } x = \text{unknown}$$

$$\text{Beginning inventory} + \text{Units started} = \text{Units transferred} + \text{Ending inventory}$$

$$\text{Case A: } 1{,}500 + 6{,}500 = x + 2{,}000$$
$$x = 6{,}000$$
$$\text{Case B: } 4{,}000 + x = 8{,}000 + 3{,}300$$
$$x = 7{,}300$$

14-36 (10-15 min.)

| | | (Step 1) | (Step 2) Equivalent Units | |
| | | Physical | Direct | Conversion |
Flow of Production		Units	Materials	Costs
Work in process, beginning inventory*		20,000		
Started		80,000		
To account for		100,000		
Completed and transferred out				
(100,000-10,000)		90,000	90,000	90,000
Work in process, ending inventory**		10,000	2,000[a]	3,000[a]
Units accounted for		100,000		
Work done to date			92,000	93,000

*Degree of completion: materials, 80%; conversion costs, 40%
**Degree of completion: materials, 20%; conversion costs, 30%
[a] .20 x 10,000 and .30 x 10,000

14-37 (5-10 min.)

1.	Work in process inventory, Department A	65,340	
	Direct-materials inventory		65,340
2.	Work in process inventory, Department A	34,986	
	Various accounts		34,986
3.	Work in process inventory, Department B	101,470	
	Work in process inventory, Department A		101,470

14-38 (5-10 min.)

1.	Work in process inventory, Assembly Dept.	852,000	
	Direct materials inventory		852,000
2.	Work in process inventory, Assembly Dept.	642,500	
	Various accounts		642,500
3.	Work in process inventory, Finishing Dept.	1,365,000	
	Work in process inventory, Assembly Dept.		1,365,000

14-39 (10-15 min.)

Dell would most likely use a job-cost system with each order considered a job. Because each order is assembled from a set of common parts, there is a single cost for each part. Most of the parts are purchased, so the cost is the purchase price. If some parts are made, the production cost would be used as the cost of the part.

Each order would call for several materials, and each would be added to the order's job-cost sheet. Labor would be incurred in assembly, so the direct-labor cost could be allocated to each order based on the number of hours used for assembly. If assembly is highly automated, it is possible that no labor is considered "direct", and labor becomes one more overhead item.

Overhead costs would be allocated based on one or more cost drivers. Possible drivers include direct-labor hours or cost (if direct labor is measured separately), hours in assembly, or number of component parts. For a highly automated process, that latter would be a likely cost driver.

Testing and quality control costs might be part of overhead. Alternately, costs of testing final computers could be charged directly to the order (job). If different types of computers require different amounts of testing, this is a logical allocation method.

14-40 (15-25 min.)

1. Ending inventory = Beginning inventory + Purchases - Usage

    $$75 = 55 + \text{Purchases} - 455$$

    Purchases = 475

2. Total manufacturing costs = Direct + Direct + Factory
    charged to production   materials   labor   overhead

    $$851 = 455 + DL + .8\, DL$$
    $$851 - 455 = 1.8\, DL$$
    $$1.8\, DL = 396$$
    $$DL = 220$$

3. Cost of goods = Cost of goods available - Beginning finished
    manufactured   for sale   goods

    $$= 981 - 90$$
    $$= 891$$

4. Cost of goods = Cost of goods available - Ending finished
    sold   for sale   goods

    $$= 981 - 110$$
    $$= 871$$

14-41 (25-35 min.)

1.   Job 412 ($ 9,000 + $4,000 + $8,000) $21,000
        Job 413 ($12,000 + $5,000 + $10,000)   27,000
        Work-in-process inventory, April 30 $48,000

2.   The job-cost records indicate an overhead application rate of $8,000 ÷
        $4,000 = 200% or $10,000 ÷ $5,000 = 200%.

3.   a.   Work-in-process inventory   15,500
           Direct materials inventory   15,500
        Job 412 of $2,500 + Job 414 of $13,000

     b.   Work-in-process inventory   6,000
           Accrued payroll   6,000
        $1,500 + $2,500 + $2,000

     c.   Work-in-process inventory   12,000
           Factory department overhead control   12,000
        $6,000 x 200%

     d.   Finished goods inventory (Job 412)   28,000
           Work-in-process inventory   28,000
        $21,000 + $2,500 + $1,500 + 200% of $1,500

     e.   Cost of goods sold   33,000
           Finished goods inventory   33,000
        The $33,000 amount is given.

Direct Materials Inventory			
Bal.	19,000	(a)	15,500
Bal.	3,500		

Work-in-Process Inventory			
Bal.	48,000	(d)	28,000
(a)	15,500		
(b)	6,000		
(c)	12,000		
	81,500		
Bal.	53,500		

Accrued Payroll		
	(b)	6,000

Fact. Dept. Overhead Control		
	(c)	12,000

Finished Goods Inventory			
Bal.	18,000	(e)	33,000
(d)	28,000		
Bal.	13,000		

Cost of Goods Sold		
Bal.	450,000	
(e)	33,000	
Bal.	483,000	

4.
Job 413 ($27,000 + $2,500 + 200% of $2,500)	$34,500
Job 414 ($13,000 + $2,000 + 200% of $2,000)	19,000
Work-in-process inventory, May 31	$53,500

<u>14-42</u> (20 min.)

1. Overhead

	Compensation for nonchargeable time, .15 x $3,600,000	$ 540,000
	Other costs	1,449,000
(a)	Total overhead	$1,989,000
(b)	Direct labor, .85 x $3,600,000	$3,060,000
	Overhead application rate, (a) ÷ (b)	65%

2. Hourly rate:
    $60,000 ÷ (48 x 40) = $60,000 ÷ 1,920 $31.25

    Many students will forget that "his work there" includes an overhead application:

Direct labor, 10 x $31.25	$312.50
Applied overhead, $312.50 x .65	203.13
Total costs applied	$515.63

    We point out that direct-labor time on a job is usually compiled for all classes of engineers and then applied at their different compensation rates. Overhead is usually not applied on the piecemeal basis demonstrated here. Instead, it is applied in one step after all the labor costs of the job have been accumulated.

<u>14-43</u> (30-40 min.) See details below.

1. $265 per ton

2. $2,525

3.   This requirement cannot be answered directly from the data using the weighted average process cost method. We must look at the equivalent units of conversion work done in May only:

Work done through the end of May	302 tons
Work done before May (3/4 x 24 tons)	<u>18</u> tons
Work done in May	<u>284</u> tons

Budget for 284 tons:
$16,000 + ($80 x 284) = $38,720

Budget - Actual = $38,720 - $40,670 = $1,950 unfavorable

During May, conversion costs were $1,950 (or 5%) above budget.

	(Step 1)	(Step 2) Equivalent Units	
Flow of Production	Physical Units	Direct Materials	Conversion Costs
Work in process, beg. inv.	24 (3/4)*		
Started	<u>288</u>		
To account for	<u>312</u>		
Completed and transferred out during current period	297	297	297
Work in process, end. inv.	<u>15</u> (1/3)*	<u>15</u>	<u>5</u>
Units accounted for	<u>312</u>		
Work done to date		<u>312</u>	<u>302</u>

*Degree of completion for conversion costs.

| | | Details | |
Costs	Totals	Direct Materials	Conversion Costs
Work in process, beg. inv.	$ 6,000	$ 2,880*	$ 3,120
Costs added currently	75,230	34,560*	40,670
(Step 3) Total costs to account for	$81,230	$37,440	$43,790
(Step 4) Divisor, equivalent units for work done to date		÷ 312	÷ 302
Cost per equivalent unit	$ 265	$ 120	$ 145

(Step 5) **Application of Costs**

Completed and transferred (297 tons)	$78,705	297 ($265)	
Work in process, end. inv. (15 tons):			
Direct materials	$ 1,800	15($120)	
Conversion costs	725		5($145)
Total work in process	$ 2,525		
Total costs accounted for	$81,230		

* $120 x 24 = $2,880; $120 x 288 = $34,560.

14-44 (15-20)

1. Potato chips are a homogeneous product with low unit cost that must be processed through a sequence of continuous steps (sequential processing). Potato chips are produced continuously rather than to order. As a result, a process-cost system is the most logical cost accounting system to use for product-costing purposes.

2. Activity-based accounting systems are most beneficial when products and/or processes are characterized by diversity. Diversity can be in the volume of product produced or the degree of complexity in the production process across product lines. Since neither of these forms of diversity characterize the potato chip industry, it is doubtful that activity-based accounting would pass the cost-benefit test. It may be that some specialty producers of gourmet potato chips (for example, Saratoga Potato Chip Company in New York) may have sufficient diversity to warrant use of an activity-based accounting system.

3. Frito-Lay produces over 6,000 pounds of potato chips each hour, 24 hours a day. This translates into more than 52 million pounds per year. Since at any point in time the work-in-process amounts to no more that one-half an hour (it takes 30 minutes to completely produce the end product), work-in-process accounts for about 3,000/52,000,000 or .006 percent of total annual production. The implication is that work-in-process can be ignored for product-costing purposes due to its immaterial amount.

14-45 (15-20 min.)

1.

	(Step 1) Physical Units	(Step 2) Equivalent Units	
		Materials & Supplies	Conversion Costs
Units started and completed	1,800,000	1,800,000	1,800,000
Work in process, end	1,200,000	1,200,000	900,000*
Units accounted for	3,000,000	-	-
Work done to date		3,000,000	2,700,000

* 1,200,000 x .75

2.

	Total Costs	Details Materials & Supplies	Conversion Costs
Cost to account for (Step 3)	$5,325,000	$ 600,000	$4,725,000
Divide by equivalent unit (Step 4)		3,000,000	2,700,000
Unit costs	$1.95	$.20	$1.75

3. Ending work in process, 1,200,000 units:

Materials and supplies, 1,200,000 x $.20	$ 240,000
Conversion costs, 900,000 x $1.75	1,575,000
Cost of 1,200,000 returns not yet completed	$1,815,000

14-46 (20 min.)

1.

Flow of Production	(Step 1) Physical Units	Plastic	(Step 2) Equivalent Units Softening Compound	Conversion Costs
Work in process, beginning	0			
Started	60,000			
To account for	60,000			
Completed	40,000	40,000	40,000	40,000
Work in process, ending	20,000 (40%)	20,000	0	8,000
Units accounted for	60,000			
Work done to date		60,000	40,000	48,000

Costs	Total Costs	Plastic	Softening Compound	Conversion Costs
Costs to account for (Step 3)	$620,000	$300,000	$80,000	$240,000
Divide by equivalent units (Step 4)		÷ 60,000	÷40,000	÷ 48,000
Cost per equivalent unit	$12.00	$5.00	$2.00	$5.00

2. Application of Costs (Step 5)	Totals	Details	
Units completed (40,000 x $12)	$480,000		
Work in process, ending:			
Material – Plastic	$100,000	20,000($5)	
Conversion costs	40,000		8,000($5)
Total work in process, ending	$140,000		
Total costs accounted for	$620,000		

14-47 (20-30 min.)

1.

	(Step 1)	Step 2 Equivalent Units		
Flow of Production	Physical Flow	Direct Materials	Cartons	Conversion Costs
Units started and completed	145,000	145,000	145,000	145,000
Work in process, end	5,000	—	—	—
Direct materials added:				
5,000 x 1.00	—	5,000	—	—
Cartons added: none				
Conversion costs:				
5,000 x .95	—	—	—	4,750
Units accounted for	150,000	—	—	—
Work done to date		150,000	145,000	149,750

		Details		
	Total Costs	Direct Materials	Cartons	Conversion Costs
Costs accounted for (Step 3)	£3,738,000	£2,250,000	£290,000	£1,198,000
Divide by equivalent units (Step 4)		150,000	145,000	149,750
Unit costs	£25.00	£15.00	£2.00	£8.00

2. Application of costs (Step 5):

To units completed,		
145,000 (£25.00)	3,625,000	
Work in process, end,		
5,000 units:		
Direct materials	75,000	5,000(£15.00)
Conversion costs	38,000	4,750(£8.00)
Work in process, end	113,000	
Total costs accounted for	£3,738,000	

14-48 (15-20 min.)

1.	Materials and parts inventory	287,000	
	Accounts payable or cash		287,000
	Conversion costs	92,000	
	Accrued payroll, accounts payable,		
	accumulated depreciation, etc.		92,000
	Finished goods inventory (11,500 x $32)	368,000	
	Materials and parts inventory (11,500 x $24)		276,000
	Conversion costs (11,500 x $8)		92,000
2.	Cost of goods sold	368,000	
	Finished goods inventory		368,000
	Cost of goods sold	11,000	
	Materials and parts inventory		11,000

Cost of goods sold is $379,000. All costs incurred during April are charged to cost of goods sold in April. This assumes that all altimeters are sold and shipped immediately upon production. Therefore, the balance in Finished Goods Inventory is zero at the end of the month. Also, the balance in the materials and parts inventory should be zero, so the addition of $11,000 to cost of goods sold is necessary.

3. Because the balance in the Conversion Costs account must be zero at the end of the month, and because only $92,000 was transferred out of the Conversion Costs account while $94,600 was added to the account, the remaining $2,600 must be transferred to Cost of Goods Sold:

Cost of goods sold	2,600	
Conversion costs		2,600

14-49   (30-40 min.) For the solution, see the Prentice Hall Web site, www.prenhall.com/

14-50   (45 min. or more)

The purpose of this exercise is to make students think about the characteristics of real production processes and how to account for them. Depending on the assumptions students make about the type of production process used in each of these examples, they may suggest a different type of accounting system than those listed below. These are just suggestions about what the groups might conclude.

a. Process costing, because there are large volumes of identical product.

b. Process costing. Although each application is unique, it is likely that identifying the differences and trying to account for them is not cost-benefit efficient.

c. Probably job costing. It depends on how many identical couches students think that Ethan Allan makes at one time. If each is unique, or if small batches are produced, a job-costing system is most likely used.

d. Job costing. Major construction projects are generally treated as a single job.

e. Process costing. Refining oil into gasoline is a classic process-costing environment, where there is a single continuous process.

f. Job costing. Each order at Kinko's is unique. The only question is whether it is cost-benefit efficient to determine job costs for each order.

g. Job costing. Each ship built is a single job, although there may be parts that are produced in a process that allows process costing.

<u>14-51</u> (30-40 min.)

NOTE TO INSTRUCTOR. This solution is based on the Web sites as they were in early 2004. Be sure to examine the current Web sites before assigning this problem, as the information there may have changed.

1. Land's End is mainly a merchandising firm. The main activity of the firm is selling clothing to individuals, although the firm also engages in some corporate sales. Process-costing systems are used to determine the average cost of like products that are produced. Land's End purchased large quantities of finished products but the costs are readily determinable so averaging is not really necessary.

2. La-Z-Boy is a manufacturing firm. Its main activity is manufacturing furniture. The firm states that it has an extensive line of furniture products – in many types and designs. The decision by La-Z-Boy to use a job-order cost system or a process-costing system (or some hybrid) depends on the nature of the products and production system. If the company produces large enough quantities of a type of furniture using the same processes, a process-cost system might be best. For small quantities of products that are custom manufactured for a specific customer, a job-order costing system might be best.

3. Tasty Baking Company is a manufacturing firm. The firm makes large volumes of snack cakes in a continuous process. The cakes are moving in a continuous flow through the factory. Because each cake is alike, produced in large volumes with small unit costs, a process-costing system would be ideal.

4. In the 2002 annual report, the types of inventories included finished goods, work-in-process, and raw materials. This information was found in the footnotes to the annual report. From the information in the financial statements and footnotes, it is not possible to determine what type of costing system the company uses.

CHAPTER 15
COVERAGE OF LEARNING OBJECTIVES

LEARNING OBJECTIVE	FUNDAMENTAL ASSIGNMENT MATERIAL	ADDITIONAL ASSIGNMENT MATERIAL	EXCEL, COLLAB., & INTERNET EXERCISES
LO1: Read and interpret the basic financial statements.		19, 20, 25, 30 36	43
LO2: Analyze typical business transactions using the balance sheet equation.	A1, A2, B1, B2	22, 23, 26, 27 28, 29, 30, 31 36, 37	41, 42
LO3: Distinguish between the accrual basis of accounting and the cash basis of accounting.	A3, B3	21, 36	
LO4: Relate the measurement of expenses to the expiration of assets.		27	42
LO5: Explain the nature of dividends and retained earnings.		24, 39, 40	
LO6: Select relevant items from a set of data and assemble them into a balance sheet, an income statement, and a statement of retained earnings.	A2, B2	25, 28, 30, 38 39, 40	41
LO7: Distinguish between the reporting of corporate owner's equity and the reporting of owner's equity for partnerships and sole proprietorships.			
LO8: Identify how the measurement conventions of recognition, matching and cost recovery, and stable monetary unit affect financial reporting.			43

CHAPTER 15
Basic Accounting: Concepts, Techniques, and Conventions

15-A1 (20-30 min.)

1. E = 150 - 120 = 30
    D = 40 + 30 = 70
    C = 15 because there were no additional investments by stockholders
    A = 85 - 15 - 40 = 30; or 85 - (15 + 40) = 30
    B = 95 - 15 - 70 = 10; or 95 - (15 + 70) = 10

2. K = 20 + 170 = 190
    J = 50 + 20 - 5 = 65
    H = 10 + 30 = 40
    F = 50 + 10 + 100 = 160
    G = 275 - 65 - 40 = 170

3. P = 300 - 270 = 30
    Q = 100 + 30 - 110 = 20
    N = 85 - 35 = 50
    L = 105 + 50 + 100 = 255
    M = 95 + 85 + 110 = 290

This problem was designed for an equation-type solution, but some students may find a different approach more helpful in understanding the solution and its steps. Such an approach can be easily developed on the board as follows, using Case 1 as an example:

Given:	Beginning	End	Steps:
Liabilities	A	B	1. $A = 85 - (40 + 15) = 30$
Paid-in capital	15	C	2. $E = 150 - 120 = 30$
Retained earnings	40	D	3. $D = 40 + 30 - 0 = 70$
Total (equal to total			
assets)	85	95	4. $C = 15 + 0 = 15$
			5. $B = 95 - (70 + 15) = 10$

Revenues	150
Expenses	120
Net earnings	E

15-A2 (40-55 min.)

1. See Exhibit 15-A2 on the following page.

2.

SRINIVAS COMPANY
Income Statement
For the Month Ended April 30, 20X1

Sales (revenue)		$100,000
Deduct expenses:		
Cost of goods sold	$40,000	
Wages, salaries and commissions	43,000	
Rent, 2,000 + 10,000	12,000	
Depreciation	1,000	
Total expenses		96,000
Net income		$ 4,000

EXHIBIT 15-A2

SRINIVAS COMPANY
Analysis of Transactions for April 20X1
(in thousands of dollars)

Description	Cash +	Accounts Receivable +	Mer-chandise Inventory +	Pre-paid Rent +	Equip-ment and Fixtures	=	Note Payable +	Accounts Payable +	Paid-in Capital +	Retained Earnings
			Assets			=	**Liabilities**		**Stockholders' Equity**	
a. Incorporation	+120					=			+120	
b. Purchased merchandise	-35		+35			=				
c. Purchased merchandise			+25			=		+25		
d1. Sales	+30	+70				=				+100(revenue)
d2. Cost of inventory sold			-40			=				- 40(expense)
e. Collections	+15	-15				=				
f. Disbursements to trade creditors	-18					=		-18		
g. Purchased equipment	-12				+36	=	+24			
h. Prepaid rent	- 6			+6		=				
i. Rent expense	-10					=				- 10(expense)
j. Wages, etc.	-43					=				- 43(expense)
k. Depreciation					- 1	=				- 1(expense)
l. Rent expense				-2		=				- 2(expense)
Balances, April 30, 20X1	+41	+55	+20	+4	+35	=	+24	+7	+120	+ 4

155 = 155

SRINIVAS COMPANY
Balance Sheet
April 30, 20X1

Assets		Liabilities and Stockholders' Equity	
		Liabilities:	
Cash	$ 41,000	Note payable	$ 24,000
Accounts receivable	55,000	Accounts payable	7,000
Merchandise		Total liabilities	$ 31,000
inventory	20,000	**Stockholders' equity:**	
Prepaid rent	4,000	Paid-in capital $120,000	
Equipment and		Retained earnings 4,000	
fixtures	35,000	Total stockholders'	
		equity	124,000
Total assets	$155,000	Total liabilities and	
		stockholders' equity	$155,000

3. Most businesses tend to have net losses during their infant months, so Srinivas's ability to show a net income for April is good. Indeed, the rate of return on beginning investment is $4,000 \div \$120,000 = 3.33\%$ per month, or 40% per year. Many points can be raised, including the problem of maintaining an "optimum" cash balance so that creditors can be paid neither too quickly nor too slowly. See the next solution also.

<u>15-A3</u> (5-10 min.)

Revenue (cash basis):

Cash sales	$30,000
Cash collected from credit customers	15,000
Total revenue	$45,000

The accrual basis provides a more accurate measure of economic performance. As long as the two recognition criteria are met (earned and realized), the $100,000 measure of revenue on the accrual basis is preferred to the $45,000 measure of revenue on the cash basis. The $100,000 is the more accurate measure of accomplishments *for April*.

<u>15-B1</u> (10-15 min.)

This is straightforward. Computations are in millions of dollars.

$$A = 8,363.2 - (4,213.5 + 2,921.3) = 1,228.4$$
$$B = 2,589.0 + 907.0 = 3,496.0$$
$$C = 2,921.3 - 907.0 - 0.0 + 2.2 = 2,016.5$$
$$D = 4,213.5 + 136.6 = 4,350.1$$
$$E = 1,188.8 + 4,350.1 + 2,016.5 = 7,555.4$$

Instructors may wish to comment about the $136.6 million additional investments by stockholders; many companies have stock purchase plans for employees and/or stockholders.

<u>15-B2</u> (30-40 min.)

1.   See Exhibit 15-B2 on the following page.

EXHIBIT 15-B2

PACCAR
Analysis of Transactions for January 2003
(in millions of dollars)

| | Assets | | | | | = | Equities | | |
Transaction	Cash +	Accounts Receivable +	Inven- tories +	Property, Plant, & Equip. +	Prepaid Exp. & Other Assets	=	Liabilities Accounts Payable +	Other Liabilities	Stockholders' Equity Paid-in Capital & Retained Earnings
Balances 1/1/03	+773	+5,064	+311	+1,577	+978	=	+1,275	+4,827	+2,601
a1.	+155	+500				=			+655 (increase revenue)
a2.			-390			=			-390 (increase expense)
b.			+500			=	+500		
c.	+300	-300				=			
d.	-250				+250	=			
e.	-450					=	-450		
f.	-100					=			-100 (increase expense)
g.					- 90	=			- 90 (increase expense)
h.				- 20		=			- 20 (increase expense)
Balances, 1/31/03	+428	+5,264	+421	+1,557	+1,138	=	+1,325	+4,827	+2,656
		+8,808					+8,808		

814

2.

PACCAR
Statement of Earnings
For the Month Ended January 31, 2003
(in millions)

Sales		$655
Deduct expenses:		
Cost of goods sold	$390	
Selling and administrative expenses	100	
Rent and insurance expense	90	
Depreciation	20	
Total expenses		600
Net earnings		$ 55

PACCAR
Balance Sheet
January 31, 2003
(in millions)

Assets		Liabilities and Stockholders' Equity	
Cash	$ 428	Accounts payable	$1,325
Accounts receivable	5,264	Other liabilities	4,827
Inventories	421	Stockholders' equity	2,656
Prepaid expenses & other assets	1,138		
Property, plant, and equipment	1,557		
Total	$8,808	Total	$8,808

<u>15-B3</u> (5-10 min.)

Revenue (cash basis):	
Cash sales	$155,000,000
Collections from credit customers	300,000,000
Total revenue	$455,000,000

The accrual basis provides a more accurate measure of economic performance. As long as both recognition criteria are met (earned and realized), the $655 million measure of revenue on the accrual basis is preferred to the $455 million measure of revenue on the cash basis. The $655 million is the more accurate measure of accomplishments for January.

<u>15-1</u>   The income statement answers questions about financial performance over a span of time. The balance sheet answers questions about financial status at a point in time.

<u>15-2</u>   Assets are economic resources that a company owns and expects to benefit future activities. Liabilities are a company's obligations to nonowners.

<u>15-3</u>   The income statement is the main link between two balance sheets. The income statement explains how operations have changed the balance sheet values over a span of time.

<u>15-4</u>   This statement is fallacious because it does not take into consideration withdrawals (dividends) or increases in ownership investment, both of which affect the ownership capital account but not net income.

<u>15-5</u>   Under the accrual basis, companies recognize revenue as it is earned and realized and expenses in the period when costs expire. In contrast, the cash basis recognizes revenue as cash is collected and most expenses as cash is disbursed.

15-6 Adjusting entries differ from routine entries in that they deal with implicit transactions in contrast with the explicit transactions that trigger nearly all the day-to-day routine entries.

15-7 The manager acquires goods and services (including advertising), not expenses per se. These goods and services become expenses as they are used in obtaining revenue.

15-8 It is preferable to refer to the costs rather than the values of assets such as plants or inventory because the word value has many meanings and is more vague than the word cost. Cost explicitly recognizes that balance sheet amounts are based on the amounts spent on assets, not their current values.

15-9 Yes. Depreciation is simply the allocation of the acquisition cost of assets over the periods that benefit from the asset's use. It is not a measure of the changes in market value of an asset.

15-10 Retained earnings is neither an asset nor a preferred claim against cash or any other asset, but it represents a general claim against total assets. In most instances no "pot of gold" exists, as the cash inflow from operations will be largely reinvested in other assets.

15-11 Although profitable operations are typically a prerequisite to dividends, dividends are actually a distribution of assets that "liquidate" a portion of the ownership claim.

15-12 Congress has delegated the setting of generally accepted accounting principles to the Securities and Exchange Commission (SEC). In turn, the SEC has delegated the task to the Financial Accounting Standards Board (FASB), which is a private-sector body supported by those with interests in preparing, auditing, and using financial statements.

15-13 Accountants create value through the information they supply to decision makers. If users cannot trust the information, it will have little value. Therefore, accountants must be especially careful to adhere to strict ethical guidelines and exhibit the utmost integrity.

15-14 Accountants record revenue when the company has both earned and realized the revenue. This is important because it triggers the recognition not only of the revenue, but also of the related expenses.

15-15 The use of the dollar as the principal accounting measure has been criticized because the changing purchasing power of a monetary unit over time is not taken into account.

15-16 The going-concern concept is a notion that implies that companies will use existing resources to fulfill the general purpose of a continuing concern rather than sell them in tomorrow's real estate or equipment market.

15-17 In the accounting sense, objectivity means freedom from bias or accuracy that can be verified by other independent accountants.

15-18 Economic feasibility sometimes inhibits the adoption of new ways to measure financial performance and position because the apparent benefits may not exceed the obvious costs of gathering and interpreting the information.

15-19 Because land is recorded at its historical cost and is not depreciated, the land purchased in 1910 would still be listed at its purchase price. The market value of that land nearly 100 years later is likely to be substantially more than the amount on the books. The equipment purchased in 1998 would be listed at its purchase price less the depreciation taken on it since 1998. This may be more or less than the current market price of the equipment. Even though the book value of the equipment may differ from its market price, the difference between the book value and the market price of the equipment is likely to be much less than the difference between the book value of the land and its market price.

15-20 A marketing manager generally focuses on changes in assets, not the general level of the assets. Marketing decisions deal with generating revenues and the costs of those revenues. Such items are recorded on the income statement. Although the income statement and balance sheet articulate, that is, the income statement explains changes in the balance sheet, the most direct measures of marketing performance are in the income statement.

15-21 A principle of good performance measures is that they recognize performance as close as possible to the time of the performance. If the goal of the sales staff is to close sales, then such staff should be evaluated on the amount of sales closed. Any delay between the closing of the sale and the recognition of sales staff performance weakens the motivational effects of the performance measure. One potential delay is the time between closing the sale and the time the company receives payment for the goods or services. Accrual accounting does not wait until the receipt of cash before recognizing a sale, whereas cash accounting does. Thus, accrual accounting generally provides a more relevant sales performance measure than does cash-basis accounting.

15-22 We know that stockholders' equity will be $400,000, and the difference between the amount of assets and the amount of liabilities will also be $400,000. But we do not know the exact amount of the assets and the liabilities.

15-23 (10-15 min.)

1.   False. Accounts receivable should be classified as an asset.

2.   False. Retained earnings should be accounted for as a stockholders' equity item.

3.   False. Machinery used in the business should be recorded at original cost less accumulated depreciation.

4.   False. A large retained earnings balance is the best evidence of previous profitable operations.

5.   True

6.   False. From a single balance sheet, you can find stockholders' equity for a specific day.

<u>15-24</u> (15-20 min.)

The theme of this solution is that retained income is not a pot of cash awaiting distribution to stockholders.

1.	Cash	<u>$1,500</u>	Paid-in capital	<u>$1,500</u>
2.	Cash	$ 900	Paid-in capital	<u>$1,500</u>
	Inventory	600		
	Total assets	<u>$1,500</u>		

Note in both Requirements 1 and 2 that the ownership equity is fundamentally a claim against the total assets (in the aggregate). For example, 60% of the shareholders do not have a specific claim on cash, and 40% of the shareholders do not have a specific claim on inventory. Instead, they have an undivided claim against (or interest in) all of the assets.

3.	Cash	<u>$1,750</u>	Paid-in capital	$1,500
			Retained earnings	250
			Total liabilities and	
			stockholders' equity	<u>$1,750</u>

Retained earnings is part of the stockholders' equity. Even though cash and retained earnings have increased by identical amounts, the retained earnings is fundamentally a *general* interest in *total* assets (just as paid-in capital is a general interest in total assets). Retained earnings is the net rise in ownership claim attributable to profitable operations. However, the assets themselves should not be confused with the claims against the assets.

4.	Cash	$ 600	Paid-in capital	$1,500
	($1,750-$400-$750)		Retained earnings	250
	Inventory	400		
	Equipment	750	Total liabilities and	
	Total assets	$1,750	stockholders' equity	$1,750

The same explanation applies here as in Requirement 3. However, Transaction 4 should clarify the lack of a specific link between retained earnings (and paid-in capital) and any particular assets. The ownership claims are general, not specific.

5.	Cash	$ 600	Accounts payable	$ 350
	Inventory		Paid-in capital	1,500
	($400+$350)	750	Retained earnings	250
	Equipment	750	Total liabilities and	
	Total assets	$2,100	stockholders' equity	$2,100

The meaning of retained earnings was explained in answer 3. Purchases on "open account" usually create a general liability; that is, the trade creditors usually hold only general claims against the total assets, not specific claims against particular assets (as created by mortgages on buildings). In sum, both the creditors *and* the owners hold general claims against the assets. Of course, if the corporation is liquidated (all assets converted to cash to be distributed to claimants), the creditors' general claims must be satisfied before the owners get one dollar. Thus, the stockholders are said to have *residual claim* or *residual interest.*

15-25 (10-15 min.)

1. The name of the statement is antiquated. This statement is ordinarily either a statement of profit *or* a statement of loss, not profit *and* loss. It is usually titled *income statement* or *statement of earnings* or sometimes a *statement of operations.*.

2. The line with the date should not be for an *instant* of time but for an indicated span of time.

3. Companies do not usually recognize increases in market values when using historical cost accounting.

4. Dividends are not expenses, and companies do not deduct them when calculating net profit.

5. The appropriate deduction is the cost of goods *sold*, not *purchased.*

6. The bottom line is more often titled *net income* or *net earnings*, although *net profit* is acceptable.

7. Although this is not the major point of the problem, the income statement has apparently omitted some expenses. For example, neither rent nor depreciation is shown; at a minimum, one or the other would ordinarily be included.

8. "Cash received from loan" should not be listed on the income statement.

15-26 (10 min.)

	Sony					United Airlines			
	A		= L +	SE		A	=	L +	SE
		Prepaid						Unearned	
		Travel		Travel				Sales	Sales
	Cash	Expense		Expense		Cash	=	Revenue	Revenue
1. Dec. payment	-70,000	+70,000	=			+70,000	=	+70,000	
2. Feb. travel		-70,000	=	-70,000			=	-70,000	+70,000

15-27 (10-15 min.)

	Winsted Hardware, Tenant					Hutchinson, Landlord			
	A		= L +	SE		A	=	L	+ SE
								Unearned	
		Prepaid		Rent				Rent	Rent
	Cash	Rent		Expense		Cash		Revenue	Revenue
1.	-6,000	+6,000	=			+6,000	=	+6,000	
2.		-2,000	=	-2,000			=	-2,000	+2,000
3.		-2,000	=	-2,000			=	-2,000	+2,000
4.		-2,000	=	-2,000			=	-2,000	+2,000

15-28 (15-20 min.)

$$\text{Assets} - \text{Liabilities} = \text{Stockholders' equity}$$

Dec. 31:	B125,000	- B55,000	= B70,000
Jan. 1:	B100,000	- B40,000	= B60,000
Change:	B 25,000	- B15,000	= B10,000

1. As above, B60,000. This is the easiest computation.

2. Change in stockholders' equity + Cash dividends = Net income
$$B10,000 + B16,000 = B26,000$$

3. Let X = Cost of goods sold
Sales - Cost of goods sold - Operating expenses = Net income
$$B265,000 - X - B50,000 = B26,000$$
$$-X = B26,000 - B265,000 + B50,000$$
$$X = B189,000$$

15-29 (20-30 min.)

				Case			
	1	**2**	**3**	**4**	**5**	**6**	**7**
X	$10,000	$3,000	$9,000	$14,000	$7,500	$ 8,000	$ 4,200
Y		6,000	6,000			2,000	3,600
Z		2,000	2,000			9,000	(200) Loss
A						4,500	4,800
B						16,500	15,200

Computations:

1:     X = $ 9,000 + $ 3,000 - $ 2,000 = $10,000

2:     X = $ 9,000 - $ 6,000 = $ 3,000

:   Y = $11,000 - $ 5,000 = $ 6,000

:   Z = $ 5,000 - $ 3,000 = $ 2,000

3:     X = $ 6,000 + $10,000 - $ 7,000 = $ 9,000

:   Y = $15,000 - $ 9,000 = $ 6,000

:   Z = $ 6,000 - $ 4,000 = $ 2,000

4:     X = $ 8,000 + $12,000 - $ 6,000 = $14,000

5:     X = $ 3,000 + $ 4,500 = $ 7,500

6:     X = $14,000 - $ 6,000 = $ 8,000

:   Y = $ 6,000 - $ 4,000 = $ 2,000

:   Z = $ 8,000 + $ 7,000 - $ 6,000 = $9,000

:   A = $10,000 - $ 2,000 + $ 1,500 - $5,000 = $4,500

:   B = $ 4,500 + $12,000 = $16,500

7:     X = $ 8,200 - $ 4,000 = $ 4,200

:   Y = $ 9,600 - $ 6,000 = $ 3,600

:   Z = $ 3,600 + $ 400 - $ 4,200 = $ (200)

:   A = $ (200) + $ 5,000 = $ 4,800

:   B = $20,000 - $ 4,800 = $15,200

<u>Note:</u> The formula for cost of goods sold is not discussed in the chapter, but it is given in the problem.

The following framework may help on cases 6 and 7:

Stockholders' equity:	Case 6	Case 7
Beginning	$? = 4,500	$8,200 - 4,000 = 4,200
Additional investments	+5,000	0
Net profit	Y = 6,000 - 4,000 = +2,000	? = -200
Dividends	-1,500	-400
End	$10,000	$9,600 - 6,000 = 3,600

$$\text{Then A} = \text{L} + \text{SE}$$
$$= 12,000 + 4,500$$
$$= 16,500$$

In case 6, the $4,500 is the beginning balance, $10,000 - ($5,000 + $2,000 - $1,500) = $4,500. In case 7, the net loss of $200 is $4,200 - ($3,600 + $400) = $200.

15-30 (45-75 min.)

1. See Exhibit 15-30 on the following page.

2. UNIVERSITY WIRELESS
    Statement of Income
    For the Month Ended October 31, 20X1

Sales		$60,000
Cost of goods sold		30,000
Gross profit		$30,000
Operating expenses:		
Rent	$ 500	
Depreciation	50	
Advertising	9,000	
Wages and salaries	11,000	
Miscellaneous	1,510	22,060
Operating income		$ 7,940
Interest expense		40
Net income		$ 7,900

EXHIBIT 15-30

	Assets					=	Equities						
		Accounts		Pre-paid	Fixtures and Equip-	=	Accounts	Notes	Liabilities Accr.	Accr.	Stockholders' Equity Paid-in	Retained
Trans.	Cash +	Receivable +	Inventory +	Rent +	ment	=	Payable +	Payable +	Wages +	Int. +	Capital +	Earnings
a.	+36,000					=					+36,000	
b.	-20,000		+40,000			=	+20,000					
c1.	-1,000			+1,000		=						
c2.*				- 500		=						- 500 (E)
d1.						=	+ 3,000					- 3,000 (E)
d2.	- 6,000					=						- 6,000 (E)
e1.	+10,000	+50,000				=						+60,000 (R)
e2.			-30,000			=						-30,000 (E)
f1.	- 5,000					=						- 5,000 (E)
f2.						=			+6,000			- 6,000 (E)
g.	- 1,510					=						- 1,510 (E)
h.	- 1,000				+6,000	=		+5,000				
i.						=				+40**		- 40 (E)
j.					- 50	=						- 50 (E)
k.	- 6,000					=						-6,000 (D)
Balance						=						
10/30	+5,490	+50,000	+10,000	+ 500	+5,950	=	+23,000	+5,000	+6,000	+40	+36,000	+1,900

*This and other adjustments could be made at the end of this series of entries.

**.096 x $5,000 x 1/12 = $40

828

UNIVERSITY WIRELESS
Balance Sheet
October 31, 20X1

Assets		Equities	
		Liabilities:	
Cash	$ 5,490	Accounts payable	$23,000
Accounts receivable	50,000	Notes payable	5,000
Inventory	10,000	Accrued wages and	
Prepaid rent	500	salaries payable	6,000
Fixtures and equipment	5,950	Accrued interest payable	40
		Total Liabilities	$34,040
		Stockholders' equity:	
		Paid-in capital $36,000	
		Retained earnings 1,900	37,900
Total assets	$71,940	Total equities	$71,940

UNIVERSITY WIRELESS
Statement of Retained Earnings
For the Month Ended October 31, 20X1

Retained earnings, October 1, 20X1	$ 0
Add: Net income for October	7,900
Total	$7,900
Deduct: Cash dividends	6,000
Retained earnings, October 31, 20X1	$1,900

3. The picture in this set of financial statements is not unusual for new businesses. Some of the liabilities are very current: accounts payable, $23,000 and accrued wages, $6,000. Yet there is a small amount of cash. Unless much of the accounts receivable can either be collected or discounted (sold to a bank or other lender) the company may be unable to meet its payroll and pay its bills on time. Moreover, the inventory badly needs replenishment if sales are to continue at their current pace. Payment of a $4,000 dividend may not have been wise.

Many new businesses can show a respectable net income but nevertheless be at the brink of financial disaster because they are "under-capitalized." That is, there is insufficient long-term investment capital to sustain a smooth growth. Too often, creditors and employees need cash far in advance of when customers provide the cash to the business. This may be such a case, unless customers pay promptly.

15-31 (5 min.)

1. Cr.   2. Cr.   3. Cr.   4. Dr.   5. Cr.   6. Cr.   7. Cr.

15-32 (10 min.)

The following statements are true: 4, 5, 8, 9.

Explanations for the false statements follow:
1. The first sentence is correct. However, credit entries always must be on the right.
2. Amounts borrowed are *debited* to Cash and *credited* to Notes Payable.
3. Decreases in assets are shown on the *credit* side, but decreases in liabilities and stockholders' equity are shown on the debit side.
6. *All* credits are on the right.
7. Payments on mortgages are *credited* to cash and *debited* to Mortgage Payable.
10. Purchases of inventory should be *debited* to Inventory and *credited* to Accounts Payable.
11. Decreases in liability accounts should be on the *left* (or decreases in *asset* accounts should be on the right).

15-33 (10-15 min.)

1 and 2.

Cash	
a. 300	
b. 150	
d. 200	

Dues Receivable	
	a. 300

Accounts Receivable	
b. 200	d. 200

Equipment	
c. 120	b. 350

Accounts Payable	
	c. 120

15-34 (20-30 min.) See Exhibit 15-34.

15-35 (20-40 min.) See Exhibit 15-35.

EXHIBIT 15-34   Amounts are in thousands of dollars.

Cash

(a) 120	(b) 35
(d1) 30	(f) 18
(e) 15	(g) 12
	(h) 6
	(i) 10
	(l) 43
Bal. 41	

Accounts Receivable

(d1) 70	(e) 15

Merchandise Inventory

(b) 35	(d2) 40
(c) 25	

Prepaid Rent

(h) 6	(l) 2

Equipment and Fixtures

(g) 36	(k) 1

Note Payable

	(g) 24

Accounts Payable

(f) 18	(c) 25

Paid-in Capital

	(a) 120

Retained Earnings

	Net Inc. 4

Sales

	(d1) 100

Cost of Goods Sold

(d2) 40	

Wages, Sal., & Comm.

(j) 43	

Rent Expense

(i) 10	
(l) 2	

Depreciation Expense

(k) 1	

*Details of the revenue and expense accounts appear in the income statement. Their net income effect appears in Retained Earnings in the balance sheet.

Note: Ending balances should be drawn for each account, but they are not shown here because they can be computed mentally.

832

EXHIBIT 15-35

Cash		
(a)	36,000	(b) 20,000
(e1)	10,000	(c1) 1,000
		(d2) 6,000
		(f1) 5,000
		(g) 1,510
		(h) 1,000
		(k) 6,000
Bal.	5,490	

Accounts Receivable	
(e1)	50,000

Inventory		
(b)	40,000	(e2) 30,000

Prepaid Rent		
(c1)	1,000	(c2) 500

Fixtures and Equipment		
(h)	6,000	(j) 50

Note Payable	
	(h) 5,000

Accounts Payable	
	(b) 20,000
	(d1) 3,000

Accrued Wages & Sal.	
	(f2) 6,000

Accr. Interest Payable	
	(i) 40

Paid-in Capital	
	(a) 36,000

Retained Earnings		
(k) 6,000	Inc.	7,900

Cost of Goods Sold	
(e2)	30,000

Rent Expense	
(c2)	500

Advertising Expense	
(d1)	3,000
(d2)	6,000

Wages & Sal. Expense	
(f1)	5,000
(f2)	6,000

Sales	
	(e1) 60,000

Depreciation Expense	
(j)	50

Interest Expense	
(i)	40

Miscellaneous Expense	
(g)	1,510

Note: Ending balances should be drawn for each account, but they are not shown here because they can be computed mentally.

833

15-36 (30 min.)

1.

DR. VERONICA BRIDGE, DENTIST
Income Statement
For the Year Ended December 31, 20X1

	Cash Basis	Accrual Basis
Fee revenue	$81,000	$99,000[1]
Expenses:		
Rent	$ 7,500	$ 6,000 [2]
Utilities	600	700 [3]
Salaries	16,000	17,000 [4]
Depreciation		12,000 [5]
Total expenses	$24,100	$35,700
Operating income	$56,900	$63,300

[1]$81,000 collected - $2,000 unearned + $20,000 receivable
[2]$7,500 - $1,500 applicable to the first quarter of 20X2
[3]$600 + $100 owed
[4]$16,000 + $1,000 owed
[5]$72,000 ÷ 6 = $12,000

The term "cash basis" is ambiguous. A strict interpretation of cash basis would permit deducting the full $72,000 paid for equipment as an expense in 20X1. Operating income would be $56,900 - $72,000 paid for equipment = a loss of $15,100.

2. The accrual basis provides a better measure of economic performance because it encompasses all assets and liabilities arising from operations rather than their immediate cash effects alone. For example, the $2,000 advance payment has not yet been earned and therefore represents an obligation of Dr. Bridge. However, the $20,000 fees billed have been earned and represent a legitimate economic resource of that magnitude (unless their full collectibility is in doubt).

The government permits the cash basis primarily to ease the cash demands on taxpayers and to ease the record keeping tasks of small businesses. In short, if you extend credit to your customers, the government does not feel it equitable to demand payment for taxes if you have not yet received your cash.

Remember, therefore, that income measurement may *legitimately* differ for different purposes. In this case, the cash basis may be the preferable way to measure income for tax purposes. But to measure her own economic performance as a dentist, Dr. Bridge would probably prefer the accrual basis. This is a major point—there is nothing inherently evil about having "two sets of books."

15-37 (10-15 min.)

1. The bank's assets (cash) and liabilities (deposits) would each increase by $1,000. Personal assets would change, but liabilities and owners' equity would not, assuming that the cash on hand had already been recorded as, say, cash on hand (asset) and personal capital (owners' equity). If the latter recording had been made, the deposit would merely represent the transforming of one asset (cash on hand) into another (cash in bank); no liabilities or owners' equities would be affected.

2. The bank's total assets and liabilities would be unaffected. The only change would be in the form of assets. Cash would decrease by $800,000, and notes receivable would increase by the same amount.

3. Personal cash (asset) would increase, and personal liabilities (note payable) would increase.

15-38 (20 min.)

KELLOGG COMPANY
Balance Sheet
March 29, 2003
(in millions of dollars)

<u>Assets</u>		<u>Liabilities and Stockholders' Equity</u>*	
Cash and equivalents	$ 138.8	Accounts payable	$ 583.3
Receivables	811.1	Accrued liabilities	1,227.9
Inventory	594.2[a]	Long-term liabilities	5,830.5
Property, plant, & equip.	2,776.2	Other liabilities	1,707.3
Other assets	5,937.7	Total liabilities	9,349.0[c]
		Common stock $ 148.4	
		Retained earnings 760.6	
		Total stockholders' equity	909.0[b]
Total assets	$10,258.0	Total liab. and stk. equity	$10,258.0**

 *This is the heading used in most actual annual reports.
**Same amount as total assets.

(a) $10,258.0 - $138.8 - $811.1 - $2,776.2 - $5,937.7 = $594.2.
(b) $148.4 + $760.6 = $ 909.0
(c) $10,258.0 - $909.0 = $9,349.0 or
     $583.3 + $1,227.9 + $5,830.5 + $1,707.3 = $9,349.0

Note that net sales is not a balance sheet account.

15-39 (20-25 min.)

The following statements follow the general format used by Disney. Obviously, various alternatives are possible:

1. (a)   **WALT DISNEY COMPANY**
                              Income Statement
                            For Fiscal Year 2002
                                (in millions)

Revenues	$25,329
Operating Costs and expenses	22,924
Operating income	2,405
Other income, net	137
Net interest expense	(453)
Income before taxes*	2,089
Income taxes*	853
Net income	$ 1,236

*This is the nomenclature used by Disney. Note how the title of this income statement uses "income," whereas the title of the retained income statement uses "retained earnings."

    (b)   **WALT DISNEY COMPANY**
                        Statement of Retained Earnings
                            For Fiscal Year 2002
                          (in thousands of dollars)

Balance at beginning of year	$12,171
Net income for the year	1,236
Dividends paid	(428)*
Balance at end of year	$12,979

    * $12,171 + $1,236 – Dividends = $12,979
       Dividends = $428

2. The cash dividend is $428 ÷ $1,236 = 35% of net income. This is a relatively large dividend for Disney. Generally their cash dividends have been less than 20% of net income because the company financed much of its growth from profits reinvested in the business. Part of the reason for the dividend in recent years being high is that net income was lower than it had been in previous years. To maintain reasonable dividend payouts, Disney had to pay cash dividends that were a high proportion of its net income.

15-40 (15-25 min.)

The following is a reproduction of Procter & Gamble's statements. Students may use other acceptable formats. Accounts payable and cash are irrelevant.

1.
PROCTER & GAMBLE COMPANY
Statement of Earnings
Year Ended June 30, 2002
(in millions)

Net sales and other income		$40,238
Costs and expenses:		
Cost of products sold	20,989	
Marketing, research, and administrative expenses	12,571	
Interest and other expenses	295	
(No label given)		33,855
Earnings before income taxes		6,383
Income taxes		2,031
Net earnings		$ 4,352

2.
PROCTER & GAMBLE COMPANY
Statement of Retained Earnings
Year Ended June 30, 2002
(in millions)

Balance at beginning of year	$10,451
Net earnings	4,352
Dividends to shareholders	(1,971)
Other decreases in retained earnings	(852)
Balance at end of year	$11,980

15-41 (45-60 min.) For the solution, see the Prentice Hall Web site, www.prenhall.com/

15-42 (20 – 30 min.)

The purpose of this game is to help students identify different types of implicit transactions. Usually implicit transactions are harder for students to understand than explicit transactions, and this game makes students identify and classify a large number of implicit transactions. The game has an element of chance because of the roll of the die, and there is competition both within groups and between groups. The game will become more interesting and more challenging when the examples in the text have all been used and students must come up with their own examples. Students with experience in business will have an advantage in the competition, but it is also a good chance for students without such experience to learn from those with it.

15-43 (15-25 min.)

NOTE TO INSTRUCTOR. This solution is based on the web site as it was in early 2004. Be sure to examine the current web site before assigning this problem, as the information there may have changed.

1. McDonalds' largest asset is property and equipment, comprising about 78% of the company's assets. This and other assets such as inventories and prepaid expenses are unexpired costs. Accruals of unrecorded expenses include accrued interest, accrued restructuring and restaurant closing costs, and accrued payroll.

2. One measure of the size of a company is its total assets. McDonalds' total assets grew about 7%, from $22.5 billion to $24.0 billion. This is shown on the balance sheet.

3. McDonalds' sales grew about 3%, from $14.9 billion to $15.4 billion. Meanwhile, net income fell from $1.6 billion to $.9 billion. It is not a good sign that income falls despite an increase in revenues.

4. Each of the basic financial statements includes clues that McDonalds is a corporation. Most obvious is that each statement is labeled "consolidated." The Income Statement shows information about the earnings and dividends per share and the number of shares outstanding. The balance sheet reports Shareholder's Equity. The Statement of Shareholders' Equity shows why the amounts in the various shareholders' investment accounts on the balance sheet changed. Finally, the Statement of Cash Flows reports treasury stock purchases and common stock dividends under the Financing Activities section.

5. Both the "Report of Independent Auditors" and the "Management Report" indicate that McDonalds' financial statements comply with GAAP. The notes to the financial statements also make many references to GAAP standards.

6. McDonalds uses accrual accounting. This is evident from the inclusion of accounts such as prepaid expenses and accrued liabilities on the balance sheet.

CHAPTER 16
COVERAGE OF LEARNING OBJECTIVES

LEARNING OBJECTIVE	FUNDAMENTAL ASSIGNMENT MATERIAL	ADDITIONAL ASSIGNMENT MATERIAL	EXCEL, COLLAB., & INTERNET EXERCISES
LO1: Recognize and define the main types of assets in the balance sheet of a corporation.	A1, B1	36, 37, 41, 42 59, 61, 62, 63	73, 74
LO2: Recognize and define the main types of liabilities in the balance sheet of a corporation.	A1, B1	42, 60, 61, 62	73, 74
LO3: Recognize and define the main elements of the stockholders' equity section of the balance sheet of a corporation.	A1, B1	42, 61, 62	73, 74
LO4: Recognize and define the principal elements in the income statement of a corporation.	A1	36, 37, 38, 42 63	73, 74
LO5: Recognize and define the elements in the statement of retained earnings.		61	
LO6: Identify activities that affect cash, and classify them as operating, investing, or financing activities.	A2, B2	43, 44, 45, 46, 49, 52, 53, 64, 65	
LO7: Assess financing and investing activities using the statement of cash flows.	A2, B2	39, 49, 52, 53	
LO8: Use both the direct method and the indirect method to explain cash flows from operating activities.	A2, A3, A4, B2, B3	43, 44, 45, 46, 47, 48, 49, 50, 52, 53, 65, 66, 67	74
LO9: Explain the role of depreciation in the statement of cash flows.		36, 51	
LO10: Describe and assess the effects of the four main methods of accounting for inventories (Appendix 16A).		54, 55, 56, 57, 58, 68, 69, 70, 71	72, 74

CHAPTER 16
Understanding Corporate Annual Reports: Basic Financial Statements

<u>16-A1</u> (20-25 min.)

WEIKART COMPANY
Balance Sheet
December 31, 20X0

ASSETS:

Current assets:

Cash and equivalents	$ 49,000
Accounts receivable, net	48,000
Inventories	36,000
Prepaid expenses	15,000
Total current assets	148,000

Noncurrent assets:

Property, plant, and equipment, at cost	580,000
Less: Accumulated depreciation	170,000
Property, plant, and equipment, net	410,000
Goodwill, patents, and trademarks	75,000
Other long-term assets	110,000
Total noncurrent assets	595,000
Total assets	$743,000

LIABILITIES AND SHAREHOLDERS' EQUITY:

Current liabilities:

Notes payable	$ 40,000
Accounts payable	48,000
Income taxes payable	37,000
Current portion of long-term debt	16,000
Total current liabilities	141,000

Noncurrent liabilities:

Long-term debt	210,000
Deferred income tax liability	44,000
Total noncurrent liabilities	254,000

Shareholders' equity:

Common stock (50,000 shares @ $.50)	25,000
Additional paid-in capital	121,000*
Retained earnings	202,000
Total shareholders' equity	348,000
Total liabilities and shareholders' equity	$743,000

To determine the amount of additional paid-in capital, you must begin by computing total liabilities and shareholders' equity = total assets = $743,000.

Then:

Total shareholders' equity = $743,000 - current liabilities - noncurrent liabilities

= $743,000 - $141,000 - $254,000

= $348,000

Additional paid-in capital = shareholders' equity - common stock – retained earnings

= $348,000 - $25,000 - $202,000

= $121,000.

WEIKART COMPANY
Income Statement
For the Year Ended December 31, 20X0

Revenues	$800,000
Cost of sales	460,000
Gross profit	$340,000
Selling and administrative expenses	150,000
Income from operations	$190,000
Other income (expense):	
Interest expense	$ (55,000)
Interest income	20,000
Total other income (expense)	$ (35,000)
Income before income taxes	$155,000
Provision for income taxes	60,000
Net income	$ 95,000
Earnings per share ($95,000 ÷ 50,000)	$1.90

16-A2 (15-20 min.) Although the requirements do not call for it, many students will find it useful to prepare a balance sheet equation (without beginning balances, which are not given). Comparing the entries in the Cash column to those in the Retained Earnings column shows why net income differs from cash provided by operations. This understanding is necessary to interpret (or prepare) the schedule that reconciles net income to net cash provided by operating activities (see 16-A3).

ALTOBELLI AUTO PARTS
Statement of Cash Flows
For the Year Ended December 31, 20X1
(in thousands)

Cash flows from operating activities		
Cash collections from customers		$ 1,450
Cash payments:		
To suppliers	$(775)	
To employees	(180)	
For other expenses	(100)	
For interest	(11)	
For income taxes	(30)	
Cash disbursed for operating activities		(1,096)
Net cash provided by operating activities		354
Cash flows from investing activities:		
Purchase of plant and facilities		(335)
Cash flows from financing activities:		
Issued debt	110	
Paid dividends	(39)	
Net cash provided by financing activities		71
Net increase in cash		90
Cash, December 31, 20X0		50
Cash, December 31, 20X1		$ 140

16-A3 (10-15 min.)

ALTOBELLI AUTO PARTS
Supporting Schedule to Statement of Cash Flows
Reconciliation of Net Income to Net Cash Provided by
Operating Activities
For the Year Ended December 31, 20X1
(in thousands)

Net income	$364*	
Adjustments to reconcile net income to net cash		
provided by operating activities:		
Add: Depreciation, which was included in computing		
computing net income but does not affect cash	45	
Deduct: Increase in accounts receivable	(150)	[1,600-1,450]
Deduct: Increase in inventory	(50)	[900-850]
Add: Increase in accounts payable	125	[900-775]
Add: Increase in salaries and wages payable	10	[190-180]
Add: Increase in income taxes payable	10	[40-30]
Net cash provided by operating activities	$354	

* Sales revenues		$1,600
Less expenses:		
Cost of goods sold	$850	
Salaries & wages	190	
Depreciation	45	
Interest expense	11	
Other expenses	100	1,196
Income before income taxes		$404
Income taxes		40
Net income		$364

16-A4 (10 min.)

1.

Sales	$720,000
Nondepreciation expenses [600,000-90,000]	(510,000)
Depreciation	(90,000)
Net income	$120,000
Add back depreciation	90,000
Net cash provided by operating activities	$210,000

2.

Sales	$ 720,000
Nondepreciation expenses [600,000-90,000]	(510,000)
Depreciation	(270,000)
Net income (loss)	$ (60,000)
Add back depreciation	270,000
Net cash provided by operating activities	$ 210,000

Notice that the additional depreciation expense did not affect net cash provided by operating activities. The direct method clearly shows this phenomenon:

Direct method:

Sales for cash	$ 720,000
Operating expenses in cash	(510,000)
Net cash provided by operating activities	$ 210,000

16-B1 (15-20 min.)

INTEL
Balance Sheet
December 28, 2002
(in millions)

ASSETS
Current assets:

Cash and cash equivalents	$ 7,404	
Short-term investments	5,183	
Accounts receivable	2,574	
Inventories	2,276	
Other current assets	1,488	$18,925
Property, plant, and equipment, at cost	$36,912	
Accumulated depreciation	(19,065)	17,847
Long-term investments		1,234
Goodwill		4,330
Other assets		1,888
Total assets		$44,224

LIABILITIES AND SHAREHOLDER'S EQUITY
Current liabilities:

Short-term debt	$ 436	
Accounts payable	1,543*	
Accrued compensation and benefits	1,287	
Deferred income on shipments to distributors	475	
Other accrued liabilities	1,697	
Income taxes payable	1,157	$ 6,595*
Long-term debt		929
Deferred tax liabilities		1,232
Common shareholders' equity:		
Common stock and capital in excess of par value	$ 7,641	
Retained earnings	27,827	35,468
Total liabilities and shareholders' equity		$44,224

*Total Current Liabilities = $44,224 - $35,468 - $1,232 - $929 = $6,595
 Accounts Payable = $6,595 - $436 - $1,287 - $475 - $1,697 - $1,157 = $1,543

16-B2 (25 min.) This is a good exercise in recognizing items that fit in a Statement of Cash Flows and placing them in the proper section of the statement. Three items listed in the problem do not appear in a Statement of Cash Flows: net sales, retained earnings, and total assets.

WALGREEN COMPANY
Statement of Cash Flows
For the Year Ended August 31, 2002
(in millions)

Cash flows from operating activities:	
Net earnings	$ 1,019.2
Adjustments to reconcile net earning to net cash provided by operating activities:	
Depreciation and amortization	307.3
Deferred income taxes	22.9
Other non-cash expenses	48.2
Changes in current assets and liabilities:	
Inventories	(162.8)
Trade accounts payable	289.6
Accrued expenses and other liabilities	75.0
Accounts receivable	(170.6)
Other current assets	30.7
Income taxes payable	14.3
Net cash provided by operating activities	1,473.8
Cash (Used for) Provided by Investing Activities:	
Additions to property and equipment	(934.4)
Disposition of property and equipment	368.1
Proceeds from the surrender of corporate owned life insurance	14.4
Net cash used for investment activities	(551.9)
Cash (Used for) Provided by Financing Activities:	
Cash dividends paid	(147.0)
Repayments of short-term borrowings	(440.7)
Net proceeds from employee stock plans	111.1
Other cash used for financing activities	(12.3)
Net cash used for financing activities	(488.9)
Changes in Cash and Cash Equivalents:	
Net increase in cash and cash equivalents	433.0
Cash and cash equivalents at beginning of year	16.9
Cash and cash equivalents at end of year	$ 449.9

<u>16-B3</u> (10-15 min.)

All of the items listed, except provision for income taxes and interest expense, are additions to (or deductions from) net income that are required in computing net cash flow from operating activities. The main problem is to decide whether each one should be added to or deducted from net income.

TARGET CORPORATION
Supporting Schedule to Statement of Cash Flows
Reconciliation of Net Income to Net Cash Provided by
Operating Activities
For the Year Ended February 1, 2003
(in millions)

Net earnings	$1,654
Add non-cash expenses:	
Depreciation and amortization	1,212
Other non-cash charges	934
Deduct increases in non-cash current assets:	
Receivables	(2,194)
Inventories	(311)
Other assets	(159)
Add increases in operating current liabilities:	
Accounts payable	524
Deduct decreases in operating current liabilities:	
Accrued liabilities	(21)
Income taxes payable	(79)
Other operating cash inflows	30
Net cash provided by operating activities	$1,590

The net cash from operating activities falls short of the net income by $1,654 - $1,590 = $64 million, primarily due to a large increase in receivables. Target could not maintain this relationship in the long run. Successful companies generally have cash flow from operations greater than net earnings unless they are growing very quickly.

16-1   The operating cycle is the time span during which cash is spent to acquire goods and services that are used to produce the organization's output, which in turn is sold to customers, who in turn pay for their purchases in cash. This may be much longer than one year for some firms, such as large construction companies.

16-2   Prepaid expenses belong in current assets because if they were not present more cash would be needed to conduct current operations.

16-3   Current assets usually include cash and cash equivalents, trade receivables, inventories, and prepaid expenses.

16-4   The cost of an asset is allocated to the periods benefiting from use of the asset by charging a portion as depreciation expense. The total amount charged since the acquisition of the asset – the accumulated depreciation – is deducted from the cost to obtain the "net book value" of the asset.

16-5   Accumulated depreciation is not cash; if specific cash is being accumulated for the replacement of assets, such cash will be an asset specifically labeled as a "cash fund for replacement and expansion" or a "fund of marketable securities for replacement and expansion."

16-6   Depreciation is a method of cost *allocation*, not valuation. Therefore, it represents the decrease in book value but not the decrease in market value.

16-7   The useful life of depreciable assets is most heavily influenced by economic obsolescence and technological changes rather than physical wear and tear.

16-8   Yes. Goodwill is simply the excess of the purchase price over the current value of the separable assets acquired, less the liabilities.

16-9   Subordinated debentures are like any long-term debt except that "subordinated" means that such bondholders are junior to other general creditors in exercising claims against assets, and "debenture" means a general claim against all unencumbered assets rather than a specific claim against particular assets.

16-10 Unlike individual proprietors or partners, stockholders' personal assets cannot be confiscated to satisfy the debts of an incorporated entity.

16-11 Stock frequently has a designated *par* or *legal* or *stated* value that is printed on the face of the certificate. For preferred stock (and bonds), par is a basis for computing the amount of dividends (or interest). Par value of common stock has no practical importance. Historically, it was used for establishing the maximum legal liability of the stockholder in case the corporation could not pay its debts. Currently, it is set at a nominal amount (say $1) in relation to the market value of the stock upon issuance (say $20).

16-12 Treasury stock is indeed negative stockholders' equity. It is a contraction of or deduction from outstanding capital stock. It is *not* an asset.

16-13 A multi-step income statement contains subtotals that provide users an easy way to examine the types of performance, such as gross margin or operating income, that may give insights into the company's overall performance.

16-14 No. The statement of cash flows is a required statement with a required format.

16-15 A cash flows statement shows the relationship of net income to changes in cash balances. It aids in predicting future cash flows, evaluating management's generation and use of cash, and determining a company's ability to pay dividends and interest and pay debts when due. It also reveals commitments to assets that may restrict or expand future courses of action.

16-16 Operating activities, investing activities, and financing activities are the three major types of activities summarized in the statement of cash flows.

16-17 Major operating activities include collections from customers, collections of interest or dividends, payments to suppliers, payments to employees, payments for interest, and payments for taxes.

16-18 Major investing activities include sales and purchases of property, plant, and equipment, sales and purchases of securities that are not cash equivalents, and making and collecting loans.

16-19 Major financing activities include borrowing from creditors, issuing equity securities, repaying creditors, repurchasing equity securities, and paying dividends.

16-20 Interest paid or received appears in the operating activities section. Some commentators favor showing interest paid as a financing activity and interest received as an investing activity. However, the FASB decided that, because interest income and interest expense are included in income, they should be included in operating activities.

16-21 Borrowing or repaying cash are not investment activities. They are financing activities because they provide capital to the company.

16-22 The investing section of the statement of cash flows shows the total cash received when a company sells an asset. The book value is irrelevant. Thus, the $8,000 cash received would be cash provided by investing activities.

16-23 Non-cash investing and financing activities generally could have been accomplished identically in substance (though not in form) by cash transactions. For example, issuing debt to purchase an asset could have been accomplished by issuing debt for cash and then using the cash to purchase the asset. Companies should not be able to prevent disclosure of such a transaction to readers of the statement of cash flows simply by using a non-cash form of transaction.

16-24 The direct method and indirect method are the two major ways of computing net cash provided by operating activities. The direct method shows cash inflows and outflows directly. The indirect method begins with net income and adds adjustments to get net cash provided by operating activities.

16-25 The erroneous impression is that depreciation is a source of cash. Depreciation is an allocation of original cost to expense that does not entail a current outlay of cash; that is, depreciation is a non-cash expense. It is added to net income when using the indirect method only to offset its deduction in computing net income.

16-26 Sales revenue is recognized on an accrual basis, not a cash basis. Therefore, cash collections from customers will not ordinarily equal sales revenues during any given period.

16-27 Strictly speaking, net losses, by themselves, do not drain cash. A net loss is an excess of expenses over revenues; it is an income statement item rather than an item on a statement of cash flows. Indeed, equipment may be sold for a net loss. Any cash proceeds resulting from the transaction would be an addition to cash, not a cash drain.

16-28 Cash flow from operations does not recognize the investment necessary to replace the fixed resources used in generating the period's revenues. If a company does not generate enough cash to both carry out its operations and to replace the assets it uses up, it cannot stay in business long. Free cash flow tells us whether the cash generated by operations is enough to support the investment needs of the company.

16-29 Depreciation belongs in a supporting schedule to the body of the statement of cash flows. Depreciation is one of the items that reconciles net income to net cash flow from operating activities. However, it does not appear on a direct-method cash flow statement because it does not directly affect cash.

16-30 The newsletter reinforces the widely held erroneous impression that depreciation provides cash.

16-31 Specific identification recognizes the actual cost paid for the particular physical item sold. First-in, first-out (FIFO) assumes that the items acquired earliest are sold or used up first. Last-in, last-out (LIFO) assumes that the items acquired most recently are sold or used up first. Weighted average assumes that the cost of all items available for sale during the period are divided by the number of items to get an average unit cost.

16-32 FIFO will have the highest net income, because the older (and hence lower cost) items comprise the cost of goods sold, making cost of goods sold lower and net income higher.

16-33 Purchases under LIFO can affect income immediately, because the latest purchases are regarded as cost of goods sold.

16-34 No. It is true that if replacement cost falls and lower ultimate sales prices are expected, the inventory is written down. But once written down, the inventory is *never* written up again. The cost to which inventory is written down becomes the "new cost" and is therefore the ceiling for any future valuation of the inventory.

16-35 No. The opposite is true. Tax expense on reports to shareholders has exceeded the actual tax payments.

16-36 Most accounting measures are based on historical cost, not market values. Companies record fixed assets at the cost paid for them, and they spread this cost as depreciation over the years they expect to use the asset. The book value of the asset is the remainder of the cost that has not yet been charged as depreciation expense; it is not intended to be even an approximation of the market price of the asset. When asset values increase, U.S. GAAP does not allow a revaluation upward of the asset's book value. In come countries, such revaluation is allowed in specific circumstances. If it were allowed, fixed asset book values would be closer to the market values of the assets.

16-37 Companies invest in research and development (R&D) activities because they believe such investments will bring future value. In one sense, investments in R&D are like investments in fixed assets – they are worthwhile only if the value created is greater than the cost of the investment. Thus, recognizing the future value of investments in R&D is important for decision making. This would be more consistent with a policy of capitalizing R&D expenditures than with expensing them immediately. The value created is often very uncertain, but it is certainly not expected to be zero, the amount implicitly assumed by expensing R&D expenditures. It is the subjectivity in estimating the future value of R&D investments and the possibility of manipulation of this number by management that has led to the conservative policy of expensing R&D for financial reporting purposes. But to make informed decisions, managers need to estimate the future value from investment in R&D in order to make intelligent investments.

16-38 The gross margin on an income statement might be an appropriate measure for assessing the success of a sales department. Sales managers are generally responsible for the price charged for goods or services (and therefore the margin received for them) and the volume of sales. Both of these factors are reflected in the gross profit (or gross margin). To separate the effects of volume and profit margin, managers might look at the gross margin percentage as a measure of margin and total sales revenues as a measure of volume.

16-39 The statement of cash flows has three sections. The section on investing activities generally shows how much cash the company needed for expansion and replacement of facilities. The cash flow from operations section shows how much cash was generated by the company's operating activities that might be available for the needed investment. If the cash flow from operations is insufficient to cover the investment needs, then the cash from financing activities section shows the sources of additional capital – generally from issuing either debt or equity. Or, in the case where operating cash flows are more than sufficient for the planned investing activities, the financing activities might reflect distributions of cash to holders of debt or equity interests in the company.

16-40 If the purchasing officer wishes to maximize her performance evaluation by reporting the largest possible gross margin, she will not buy the oil at $30 per barrel if the company uses LIFO. Why? Because the $30 spent for the most recent purchase of oil becomes part of cost of goods sold under LIFO, replacing oil charges at $20 per barrel or less. This would reduce the gross margin. Under FIFO, the purchase decision would not affect current year's gross margin. Therefore, the purchasing officer would not have any special incentive to either purchase or avoid purchasing the oil. With an incentive not to purchase under LIFO and no particular incentive under FIFO, she is more likely to purchase the oil if the company uses FIFO than if it uses LIFO.

16-41 (10-15 min.) The purpose of this problem is to stress the limitations of the use of historical costs, particularly where there are significant amounts of property, plant, and equipment. € stands for the euro, the European measure of currency.

The balance sheet values do not come close to the current market value of the land and building, € 1,800,000 ÷ .60, or € 3,000,000. Consequently, in terms of current values before expansion and modernization, stockholders' equity is understated (in thousands):

Market value of land and building		€ 3,000
Net book value:		
Land	€ 300	
Building	160	460
Excess of market value over net book value		€ 2,540

As conventionally prepared after the expansion and modernization, the balance sheet would be (in thousands):

Cash		€ 400	Liabilities:	
Land		300	Mortgage payable	€ 1,800
Building at cost	€ 2,600		Stockholders' equity	860
Accum. depreciation	640			
Net book value		1,960		
			Total liabilities and	
Total assets		€ 2,660	stockholders' equity	€ 2,660

The balance sheet would be unusually deceiving. The mortgage would appear to be exceedingly high in relation to the book value of the assets. The historical cost and resulting stockholders' equity have lost all meaning.

For more elaborate examples entailing both specific and general price level effects, see Appendix 17.

16-42 (25-30 min.) This problem is similar to 16-A1 but is more difficult because items not shown in exhibits 16-1 and 16-5 are included and terminology is varied slightly.

HOKKAIDO COMPANY
Balance Sheet
May 31, 20X1
(in millions)

ASSETS:	
Current assets:	
Cash and equivalents	¥ 31,000
Receivables	22,000
Inventories	29,000
Other current assets	6,000
Total current assets	88,000
Noncurrent assets:	
Fixed assets, net	217,000
Capital construction fund	28,000
Intangible assets	21,000
Long-term investments	15,000*
Total noncurrent assets	281,000
Total assets	¥369,000

*To compute the amount for long-term investments, recognize that total assets must be ¥369,000 (equal to total liabilities and stockholders' equity). Then:

$$\text{Total noncurrent assets} = \text{Total assets} - \text{Total current assets}$$
$$= ¥369,000 - ¥88,000$$
$$= ¥281,000$$

$$\text{Long-term investments} = \text{Noncurrent assets} - \text{Fixed assets, net} - \text{Capital construction fund} - \text{Intangible assets}$$
$$= ¥281,000 - ¥217,000 - ¥28,000 - ¥21,000$$
$$= ¥15,000$$

LIABILITIES AND STOCKHOLDERS' EQUITY:

Current liabilities:

Accounts payable	¥ 19,000
Accrued expenses payable	16,000
Other current liabilities	9,000
Total current liabilities	44,000

Noncurrent liabilities:

Mortgage bonds	84,000
Debentures	77,000
Deferred income tax liability	12,000
Total noncurrent liabilities	173,000

Stockholders' equity:

Redeemable preferred stock	15,000
Common stock, at par	5,000
Paid-in capital in excess of par	102,000
Retained income, appropriated for self-insurance	16,000
Retained income, unrestricted	27,000
Less: Treasury stock	(13,000)
Total stockholders' equity	152,000
Total liabilities and stockholders' equity	¥369,000

HOKKAIDO COMPANY
Income Statement
For the Year Ended May 31, 20X1
(in millions except net income per share)

Net sales	¥410,000
Cost of goods sold	(190,000)
Gross margin	220,000
Operating expenses:	
Administrative and general expenses	(65,000)
Research and development expenses	(42,000)
Selling and distribution expenses	(41,000)
Total operating expenses	148,000
Operating income	72,000
Other income (expenses), net	(12,000)
Income before income taxes	60,000
Income taxes	(51,000)
Net income	¥ 9,000
Net income per share*	¥180,000

*¥9,000,000,000 ÷ 50,000 = ¥180,000

16-43 (5 min.)

The split between cash and credit sales is irrelevant for purposes of this problem.

Sales	$650,000
Less increase in accounts receivable	(8,000)
Cash received from customers	$642,000

16-44 (5 min.)

Cost of goods sold	$360,000
Add increase in inventory ($120,000-$95,000)	25,000
Deduct increase in accounts payable ($51,000-$24,000)	(27,000)
Cash paid to suppliers	$358,000

16-45 (5-10 min.)

Wage and salary expense	$195,000
Cash paid to employees	165,000
Increase in accrued wages and salaries payable	$ 30,000

Beginning balance, accrued wages, and salaries payable	$ 15,000
Increase in accrued wages and salaries payable	30,000
Ending balance, accrued wages, and salaries payable	$ 45,000

16-46 (5-10 min.)

EKERN AND ASSOCIATES
Statement of Cash Flows from Operating Activities
For the Year Ended December 31, 20X0

Collections from customers (NK480,000 – NK9,000)	NK471,000
Cash expenses (NK280,000 - NK50,000)	230,000
Net cash provided by operating activities	NK241,000

16-47 (5-10 min.)

EKERN AND ASSOCIATES
Reconciliation of Net Income to Net Cash Provided by Operating Activities
For the Year Ended December 31, 20X0.

Net income	NK 200,000
Add depreciation, which was deducted in computing net income but does not affect cash	50,000
Deduct increase in accounts receivable	(9,000)
Net cash provided by operating activities	NK241,000

16-48 (10 min.)

HERNANDEZ COMPANY
Reconciliation of Net Loss to Net Cash Provided by Operating Activities
For the Year Ended December 31, 20X2

Net loss	$(39,000)
Add depreciation	22,000
Add decrease in accounts receivable	4,000
Deduct increase in inventory	(2,000)
Add increase in accounts payable	17,000
Add increase in wages and salaries payable	5,000
Net cash provided by operating activities	$ 7,000

<u>16-49</u> (15-25 min.)

NEW ULM BOTTLERS
Statement of Cash Flows
For the Year Ended December 31, 20X1
(in thousands)

Cash flows from operating activities:		
Cash collections from customers		$2,901
Cash payments:		
To suppliers	$(2,140)	
To employees	(305)	
For other operating expenses	(105)	
For interest	(26)	
For income taxes	(108)	
Cash disbursed for operating activities		(2,684)
Net cash provided by operating activities		217
Cash flows from investing activities:		
Purchase of warehouse	$ (540)	
Proceeds from sale of equipment	37	
Net cash used in investing activities		(503)
Cash flows from financing activities:		
Issued common stock	28	
Retired long-term debt	(25)	
Dividends paid	(89)	
Net cash used in financing activities		(86)
Net decrease in cash		(372)
Cash, January 1, 20X1		380 *
Cash, December 31, 20X1		$ 8

* $372 + $8

16-50 (10-20 min.)

NEW ULM BOTTLERS
Supporting Schedule to Statement of Cash Flows
Reconciliation of Net Income to Net Cash Provided by
Operating Activities
For the Year Ended December 31, 20X1
(in thousands)

Net income		$239
Adjustments to reconcile net income to net cash provided by operating activities		
Add:	Depreciation	151
Deduct:	Increase in accounts receivable (3,003-2,901)	(102)
Deduct:	Increase in inventory	(56)
Add:	Increase in accounts payable (2,096+56-2,140)	12
Deduct:	Decrease in salaries and wages payable	(24)
Deduct:	Decrease in income taxes payable (108-105)	(3)
Net cash provided by operating activities		$217

16-51 (10 min.)

OKANAGON COMPANY
(in millions)

1. Income Statement:

Sales		$215
Nondepreciation expenses ($188 - $17)	$171	
Depreciation	29	200
Net income		$ 15

Reconciliation of net income to net cash
provided by operating activities:

Net income	$ 15
Add non-cash expenses:	
Depreciation	29
Deduct net increase in non-cash operating working capital	(15)
Net cash provided by operating activities	$ 29

2. An increase in depreciation does not affect net cash flow from operating activities. The $12 million increase in depreciation *decreases net income* by $12 million and *increases the addback* by $12 million. The net effect is zero. We add depreciation to net income merely to offset its deduction when computing net income, not because it provides cash.

16-52 (20-30 min.)

1.

JUNEAU COMPANY
Statement of Cash Flows
For the Year Ended December 31, 20X2
(in millions)

Cash flows from operating activities:

Net income		$ 60
Adjustments to reconcile net income to net		
cash provided by operating activities:		
Depreciation		20
Increase in receivables		(35)
Increase in inventories		(50)
Increase in current liabilities		75
Net cash provided by operating activities		$ 70

Cash flows from investing activities:

Purchase of fixed assets		(190)*

Cash flows from financing activities:

Issue of long-term debt	$120*	
Dividends paid	(6)	
Cash provided by financing activities		114
Net decrease in cash		$ (6)
Cash balance, December 31, 20X1		31
Cash balance, December 31, 20X2		$ 25

* This assumes that the debt was issued for cash and the cash used to buy the fixed assets. If the debt were issued directly to the seller of the fixed assets, the cash outflow for purchase of fixed assets would be $70 million, there would be no cash from issuance of long-term debt, and a supporting schedule would have a investment and financing activity of $120 million for acquiring the fixed assets.

2. Dear Ms. Tallman:

Severe shortages of cash commonly accompany rapid corporate growth. Profitable operations usually produce heavy supplies of cash. But the insatiable demand for cash to expand receivables, inventories, and fixed assets may deplete the cash on hand despite profitable operations. This is why so many so-called growth companies usually pay little or no dividends.

Note also that the ratio of current assets to current liabilities is 3.7 to 1 on December 31, 20X1 but only 1.8 to 1 on December 31, 20X2. It appears that the need for cash to support increases in receivables and inventory has come primarily from increases in current liabilities.

16-53 (30-40 min.)

1.

SHANGHAI IMPORTS COMPANY
Statement of Cash Flows
For the Year Ended December 31, 20X1
(in millions)

Cash flows from operating activities:		
Cash collections from customers ($265-$27)		$238
Cash payments:		
To suppliers ($140+$20-$14)	$(146)	
For general expenses ($51+$1)	(52)	
For taxes ($10-$1)	(9)	
Cash disbursed for operating activities		(207)
Net cash provided by operating activities		31
Cash flows from investing activities:		
Acquisition of plant assets	(102)	
Proceeds from sale of plant assets	6	
Net cash used for investing activities		(96)
Cash flows from financing activities:		
Issue long-term debt	50	
Pay cash dividends	(4)	
Net cash provided by financing activities		46
Net decrease in cash		(19)
Cash balance, December 31, 20X0		25
Cash balance, December 31, 20X1		$ 6

2. **Reconciliation of Net Income to Net Cash**
Provided by Operating Activities

Net income	$ 24
Adjustments to reconcile net income to net cash provided by operating activities:	
Depreciation	40
Increase in accounts receivable	(27)
Increase in inventory	(20)
Increase in prepaid general expenses	(1)
Increase in accounts payable for merchandise	14
Increase in accrued taxes payable	1
Net cash provided by operating activities	$ 31

3. Chen's stress may be reduced but not eliminated. The statement of cash flows shows why cash has fallen by $19 million. Operating activities provided $31 million, and financing activities provided an additional $46 million, a total of $77 million. However, $96 million was needed for the net acquisition of plant assets.

Severe crunches on cash commonly accompany quick corporate growth. There may be large net income and working capital provided by operations, but heavy demands for cash to expand receivables, inventories, and plant assets diminish the cash on hand despite profitable operations. Hence, most "growth" companies pay skimpy or no dividends.

16-54 (15 min.)

1.   a. FIFO Method:

        Inventory shows: 600 tons on hand.

Costs:		
	300 tons @ $10.00	$3,000
	250 tons @ $ 9.00	2,250
	50 tons @ $ 8.00	400
July 31 inventory valuation		$5,650

    b. LIFO Method:

        Inventory shows: 600 tons on hand.

Costs:		
	500 tons @ $7.00	$3,500
	100 tons @ $8.00	800
July 31 inventory valuation		$4,300

T accounts (not required) are:

Inventory (FIFO)

Balance	3,500	To cost of goods sold	11,100
Purchases:	8,000		
	2,250		
	3,000		
Available	16,750		
Balance	5,650		

Inventory (LIFO)

Balance	3,500	To cost of goods sold	12,450
Purchases:	8,000		
	2,250		
	3,000		
Available	16,750		
Balance	4,300		

2.

	FIFO	LIFO
Revenue	$16,000	$16,000
Cost of goods sold	11,100	12,450
Gross profit	$ 4,900	$ 3,550

16-55 (5-10 min.)

The inventory would be written down from $100,000 to $75,000 on December 31, 20X0. The new $75,000 valuation is "what's left" of the original $100,000 cost. In other words, the $75,000 is the unexpired cost and may be thought of as the new cost of the inventory for future accounting purposes. Thus, because subsequent replacement values exceed the $75,000 cost, and write-ups above "cost" are not acceptable accounting practice, the valuation remains at $75,000 until it is written down to $70,000 on the following December 31, 20X1.

16-56 (20 min.)

1.

	Units	LIFO	FIFO
Sales	30,000	$360,000	$360,000
Cost of goods sold:			
Inventory, December 31, 20X0	15,000	90,000	90,000
Purchases	52,000	396,000	396,000
Cost of goods available for sale	67,000	486,000	486,000
Inventory, December 31, 20X1	37,000	246,000*	291,000**
Cost of goods sold	30,000	240,000	195,000
Gross margin or gross profit		$120,000	$165,000

$$*15,000 @ \$6 = \$ 90,000$$
$$20,000 @ \$7 = 140,000$$
$$2,000 @ \$8 = \underline{\ \ 16,000}$$
$$\underline{\$246,000}$$

$$**32,000 @ \$8 = \$256,000$$
$$5,000 @ \$7 = \underline{\ \ 35,000}$$
$$\underline{\$291,000}$$

2. Gross margin is higher under FIFO. However, cash will be higher under LIFO by .40($165,000 - $120,000) = .40 x $45,000 = $18,000.

873

16-57 (40-60 min.)

1.

	Do Not Buy[a]	Buy More Units[b]
Sales, 1,000,000 @ $7	$7,000,000	$7,000,000
Cost of goods sold (LIFO basis):		
300,000 units @ $4 = $1,200,000		
700,000 units @ $3 = 2,100,000	3,300,000	
or 600,000 units @ $5 = $3,000,000		
300,000 units @ $4 = 1,200,000		
100,000 units @ $3 = 300,000		4,500,000
Gross profit	$3,700,000	$2,500,000
Other expense	2,400,000	2,400,000
Income before taxes	$1,300,000	$ 100,000
Income taxes	650,000	50,000
Net income	650,000	$ 50,000
Earnings per share	$ .65	$ .05

[a]Ending inventory, 100,000 units @ $3, $ 300,000
[b]Ending inventory, 700,000 units @ $3, $2,100,000

2.

	Do Not Buy[c]	Buy More Units[d]
Sales, 1,000,000 @ $7	$7,000,000	$7,000,000
Cost of goods sold (FIFO basis):		
800,000 units @ $3 = $2,400,000		
200,000 units @ $4 = 800,000	3,200,000	3,200,000
Gross profit	$3,800,000	$3,800,000
Other expense	2,400,000	2,400,000
Income before taxes	$1,400,000	$1,400,000
Income taxes	700,000	700,000
Net income	$ 700,000	$ 700,000
Earnings per share	$ .70	$ .70

[c]Ending inventory, 100,000 units @ $4, $ 400,000
[d]Ending inventory, 600,000 units @ $5, $3,000,000
                        100,000 units @ $4,   400,000
                Total $3,400,000

3. Consider this question from a strict financial management standpoint – ignoring earnings per share. When prices are rising, it may be advantageous – subject to prudent restraint as to maximum and minimum inventory levels – to buy unusually heavy amounts of inventory at year-end, particularly if income tax rates are likely to fall. Under LIFO, the tax savings would be a handsome $600,000. The effects on later years' taxes will depend on inventory levels, prices, and tax rates.

    Tax savings can be generated because LIFO permits management to influence immediate net income by its purchasing decisions. In contrast, this decision would not affect FIFO results.

    However, if management buys the 600,000 units and uses LIFO, the first year earnings per share would be only five cents. Note too that LIFO will show less earnings per share than FIFO ($.65 as compared to $.70), even if the 600,000 units are not bought. Such results may cause management to reject LIFO. Earnings per share (EPS) is a critical number, and many managers are reluctant to adopt accounting policies that hurt EPS.

    The shame of the matter is that the same business events can lead to dramatically different measures of performance, depending on whether LIFO or FIFO is adopted ($.05 versus $.70). Moreover, the *smart decision* would be to adopt LIFO and buy the 600,000 units. Yet this decision produces the worst earnings record!

4a. The income statements for year two are:

	LIFO		FIFO	
In first year	Do Not Buy	Buy	Do Not Buy	Buy
Sales	$7,000,000	$7,000,000	$7,000,000	$7,000,000
Cost of goods sold	5,000,000	5,000,000	4,900,000	4,900,000
Gross profit	2,000,000	2,000,000	2,100,000	2,100,000
Other expenses	1,800,000	1,800,000	1,800,000	1,800,000
Income before taxes	200,000	200,000	300,000	300,000
Income taxes	80,000	80,000	120,000	120,000
Net income	120,000	120,000	180,000	180,000
Earnings per share	$ .12	$ .12	$ .18	$ .18

	(a)	(b)	(c)	(d)
Beginning inventory, see parts (1) and (2)	$ 300,000	$2,100,000	$ 400,000	$3,400,000
Purchases				
1,600,000 units @ $5	8,000,000		8,000,000	
1,000,000 units @ $5		5,000,000		5,000,000
Available for sale	$8,300,000	$7,100,000	$8,400,000	$8,400,000
Ending inventory (100,000 units @ $3 +				
600,000 units @ $5)	3,300,000			
700,000 units @ $3		2,100,000		
700,000 units @ $5			3,500,000	3,500,000
Cost of goods sold	$5,000,000	$5,000,000	$4,900,000	$4,900,000

4b. FIFO shows $100,000 higher income before taxes ($60,000 after taxes) because 100,000 units of old, lower-cost inventory is in cost of goods sold:

LIFO	
1,000,000 units @ $5 =	$5,000,000

FIFO	
900,000 units @ $5 =	$4,500,000
100,000 units @ $4 =	400,000
	$4,900,000

4c. The ending LIFO inventory is $1,200,000 higher in column (a) because the 600,000-unit layer is priced at the second-year acquisition cost of $5. In column (b), the 600,000 units purchased @ $5 near the end of the first year were charged immediately to cost of goods sold, leaving all of the ending inventory at the old unit cost of $3. Under the LIFO assumption, this inventory is regarded as untouched in the second year, so the old $3 unit cost applies to the ending inventory of the second year.

4d.

	Alternatives			
	a	b	c	d
Income tax for the two years	$730,000	$130,000	$820,000	$820,000

Unless the LIFO layers are depleted, the adoption of LIFO will result in permanent postponement of income taxes. However, if the layers are invaded, these low-cost layers will cause higher tax payments in later years than under FIFO.

4e. As far as the financial decision is concerned, the computations in part (4) substantiate the conclusions in part (3). As far as EPS is concerned, note that each EPS declines in the second year, except for the second alternative (a rise from $.05 to $.12). This favorable "trend" may lead some managers to lean toward choosing LIFO and buying 600,000 units in year one.

16-58 (20-30 min.)

1. and 2.

	Requirement 1		Requirement 2	
	(1)	(2)	(3)	(4)
	FIFO	LIFO	FIFO	LIFO
Sales, 28,000 @ $22	$616,000	$616,000	$616,000	$616,000
Deduct cost of goods sold:				
Inventory, December 31, 20X0				
20,000 @ $10	200,000	200,000	200,000	200,000
Purchases: 30,000 @ $12 and				
$8, respectively	360,000	360,000	240,000	240,000
Cost of goods available for sale	560,000	560,000	440,000	440,000
Deduct: Inventory, December				
31, 20X1, 22,000 bags:				
22,000 @ $12	264,000			
or				
20,000 @ $10 + 2,000 @ $12		224,000		
or				
22,000 @ $8			176,000	
or				
20,000 @ $10 + 2,000 @ $8				216,000
Cost of goods sold	296,000	336,000	264,000	224,000
Gross margin	$320,000	$280,000	$352,000	$392,000

3a. LIFO results in more cash by the difference in income tax effects. LIFO results in a lower cash outflow of .40 x ($320,000 - $280,000) = $16,000.

3b. FIFO results in more cash when inventory prices are falling. Why? Because income tax cash outflow would be more under LIFO by .40 x ($392,000 - $352,000) = $16,000.

16-59 (10-15 min.)

1.   (a)   Operating income was lower by the $1,066 million, because R&D must be charged to expense.

        (b)   Operating income would be $1,100 + $1,066 = $2,166 million, almost twice as large.

        (c)   There would be no balance-sheet effect if R&D were expensed. However, if patents were purchased instead of Dow itself conducting the R&D (as in requirement (b)), assets would be higher by $1,066 million, the cost of the patents.

2. $40 million ÷ 4 = $10 million

3.   The balance in pre-opening costs decreased by $2,390,000 - $1,840,000 = $550,000. Because the addition to this account was $2,100,000, the deduction must have been $2,100,000 + $550,000 = $2,650,000. Thus, this $2,650,000 must have been amortized.

    Let x = amortization for 2003. Look at the account Pre-opening costs:

12/31/02 balance	2,390,000
Additions	2,100,000
Subtractions	(x)
12/31/03 balance	1,840,000

$$2,390,000 + 2,100,000 - x = 1,840,000$$
$$x = 2,650,000$$

4. $13 billion - $2 billion = $11 billion of goodwill

    The goodwill would remain on Philip Morris's books until management decided that its value had fallen below the amount initially recorded. At that time, it would be written down (or written off entirely if its value had fallen to zero).

16-60 (15-20 min.)

1. Cash or accounts receivable and sales would increase by $4,000,000.

    Warranty expense and liability for warranties would rise by .032 x $4,000,000 = $128,000.

    Liability for warranties and cash would decrease by $114,000.

2. Cash and the liability account called Deposits on Bottles would be increased by $99,000.

    In turn, both accounts would be decreased by $93,000.

3. Cash and the liability account called Deposits would be increased by $2,000 on April 1. On June 30, Interest Expense and Deposits would be increased by 3/12 x .05 x $2,000 = $25. On July 1, Cash and Deposits would be decreased by $2,000 + $25 = $2,025.

4. (a) Cash and the liability, Unearned Sales Revenue, would be increased by $160,000 on December 31 for the ticket sales.

    (b) On January 31, Unearned Sales Revenue would be decreased by $160,000 ÷ 4 = $40,000. On the income statement, Sales would be increased by $40,000.

<u>16-61</u> (15 min.)

1.	2002 accounts receivable was $219,974,000 - $21,506,000 - $651,000 = $197,817,000.

2.	2002 liabilities for warranties was $102,706,000 - $167,252,000 + $131,687,000 = $67,141,000.

3.	2002 retained earnings were $616,420,000 - $297,718,000 - $11,323,000 = $307,379,000.

<u>16-62</u> (10-15 min.)

The framework of assets = liabilities + stockholders' equity has been changed to assets – liabilities = stockholders' equity. Thus, the bottom line of the balance sheet is assets – liabilities which equals stockholders' equity. Further, the accounts are presented in different orders with different subtotals.   Consider first the assets:
► Fixed assets are listed first, whereas in the U. S., current assets would be first.
► Inventories are called "stocks."
► Accounts receivable and short-term debt are combined and called "debtors," with both those due within a year and those due in more than a year classified as current assets.
► Cash is listed last instead of first among the current assets, and the term cash equivalents is not used.
► Current liabilities are called "creditors."
► Current liabilities are subtracted from current assets to give a subtotal for net current assets, to which the statement adds fixed assets to get a subtotal called total assets, which is really total assets less current liabilities.
► The statement next deducts long-term liabilities to give a subtotal for net assets, which will equal the subtotal for stockholders' equity.
► The main title for stockholders' equity is "capital and reserves," and it includes an account called "reserves."
► Retained earnings is called "profit and loss account."
► Called up capital and share premium account refer to paid-in capital.

Although Johnson Matthey's financial statements contain most of the same basic information that U. S. statements contain, the format is quite different.

16-63 (10-20 min.) A lively discussion usually ensues. This problem can be the basis for a discussion of the strengths and weaknesses of accounting theory.

1. There would be a "gain from insurance on crashed airplane" recognized on the income statement:

Insurance payments received	$6,500,000
Book value of airplane	962,000
Gain from insurance on crashed airplane	$5,538,000

    Total assets would increase by $5,538,000, the amount of the gain. The fleet of airplanes would be the same as before the crash, but a 727 with a book value of $6.5 million has replaced a similar 727 with a book value of only $962,000.

2. Accounting for casualties is very controversial. It gets to the heart of the question of what is income and what is capital. Does the $6.5 million represent a return of capital or a payment of both capital and income?

    The traditional accounting model ignores changes in general purchasing power and intervening changes in specific prices while an asset is held. When an asset is disposed of, the gain or loss is measured in nominal dollars (almost always without regard to the intended use of the proceeds).

    Many theorists and practitioners (as explained much more fully in Appendix 17 on inflation accounting) define the income of a going concern to be a function of whether the proceeds will be reinvested in the same types of assets. These individuals maintain that no gain is realized on the airplane crash, because the $6.5 million is really a return of capital (where capital is thought of in physical terms as airplanes, inventories, etc.). Thus, the "gain" would not be shown in the income statement. Instead, it would appear as a special balance sheet item called Revaluation Equity, or some similar title.

16-64 (5-10 min.)

a.	Operating *	d.	Financing	g.	Financing
b.	Investing	e.	Financing	h.	Financing
c.	Operating *	f.	Investing	i.	Operating *

* Only on a statement of cash flows when using the indirect method.

16-65 (10-15 min.)

1. The only line for interest on the statement of cash flows will be under operating activities:
   Cash payments for interest   ($10,613,000)

2. The *decrease* of $10,613,000 - $8,752,000 = $1,861,000 in interest payable would be *deducted from* net income in computing net cash provided by operating activities. Why? Because the interest *expense* of $8,752,000 was deducted in computing net income, but the cash *payment* of $10,613,000 million, $1,861,000 more, should be deducted in computing cash flow.

16-66 (30 min.)

1. **CONAGRA FOODS**
Statement of Cash Flows From Operating Activities (Indirect Method)
For the Year Ended May 26, 2002
(in millions)

Net income	$783.0
Adjustments to reconcile net income to net	
cash provided by operating activities:	
Depreciation and amortization	623.2
Other noncash expenses	133.2
Decrease in receivables	169.5
Decrease in inventories	658.4
Decrease in accounts payable and accrued liabilities	(17.8)
Net cash provided by operating activities	$2,349.5

2. **CONAGRA FOODS**
Statement of Cash Flows From Operating Activities (Direct Method)
For the Year Ended May 26, 2002
(in millions)

Cash collections from customers (27,629.6 + 169.5)	$27,799.1
Cash payments to suppliers (23,536.5 – 658.4 + 17.8)	(22,895.9)
Cash payment for selling, general, and administrative	
expenses (2,423.4 – 623.2 - $133.2)	(1,667.0)
Cash payments for income taxes	(483.2)
Cash payments for interest and other expenses	(403.5)
Net cash provided by operating activities	$ 2,349.5

16-67 (25-35 min.)

1.

NORDSTROM, INC.
Cash Flows from Operating Activities
For the Year Ended January 31, 2003
(in millions)

Cash collections from customers ($5,975 - $58)		$5,917
Other income, net		74
Total cash receipts		$5,991
Cash payments:		
To suppliers of goods (3,971 + 117 +10)	$4,098	
For selling, general, and administrative expenses		
(1,814 - 234 - 54 - 24 - 17 - 1)	1,484	
For interest (82)	82	
For income taxes (92 - 44)	48	
Cash disbursed for operating activities		5,712
Net cash provided by operating activities		$ 279

16-68 (30-40 min.) Unisys used the terminology given here regarding sales and cost of goods sold. Amounts are in millions.

1.

	FIFO	LIFO	Weighted Average	Specific Identification
Net sales of products (150 @ $8 + 160 @ $8)	$2,480	$2,480	$2,480	$2,480
Deduct cost of sales of products:				
Inventory, December 31, 2002, 100 @ $4	400	400	400	400
Purchases (200 @ $5 + 140 @ $6)	1,840	1,840	1,840	1,840
Cost of goods available for sale	2,240	2,240	2,240	2,240
Deduct: Inventory, June 30, 2003, 130 units:				
130 @ $6	780			
or				
100 @ $4 + 30 @ $5		550		
or				
130 @ ($2,240 ÷ 440) or 130 @ 5.09			662	
or				
80 @ $4 + 50 @ $5				570
Cost of sales of products	1,460	1,690	1,578	1,670
Gross margin	$1,020	$ 790	$ 902	$ 810

2a. Income before income taxes will be lower under LIFO: $1,020 - $790 = $230. The income tax will be lower by .40 x $230 = $92.

2b. Income before income taxes will be lower under LIFO: $902 - $790 = $112. The income tax will be lower by .40 x $112 = $44.80.

<u>16-69</u> (20-30 min.)

This problem explores the effects of LIFO layers.

There would be no effect on gross margin, income taxes, or net income under FIFO. The balance sheet would show a higher inventory by $420. A detailed income statement would show both purchases and ending inventory as higher by $420, so the net effect on cost of goods sold would be zero.

LIFO would show a lower gross margin, $670, as compared with $790, a decrease of $120. Hence, the impact of the late purchase would be a savings of income taxes of 40% of $120 = $48. For details, see the accompanying tabulation.

		Without Late Purchase		With Late Purchase
Net sales of products, as before		$2,480		$2,480
Deduct cost of sales of products:				
Inventory, December 31, 2002, 100 @ $4		$ 400		$ 400
Purchases, 340 units, as before, and 400 units		1,840		2,260*
Available for sale		$2,240		$2,660
Ending inventory:				
First layer ,100 @ $4	$400			
Second layer, 30 @ $5	150	550		
First layer, 100 @ $4			$400	
Second layer, 90 @ $5			450	850
Cost of sales of products		1,690		1,810
Gross margin		$ 790		$ 670
*340 units, as before	$1,840			
60 units @ $7	420			
	$2,260			

887

Although purchases are $420 higher than before, the new LIFO ending inventory is only $850 - $550 = $300 higher. The cost of sales is $1,810 - $1,690 = $120 higher.

To see this another way, compare the ending inventories:

Late purchase added to cost of goods available for sale: 60 @ $7	$420
Deduct 60-unit increase in ending inventory:	
Second layer is 90 - 30 = 60 units higher @ $5	300
Cost of sales is higher by 60 @ ($7 - $5)	$120

16-70 (15 min.)

1. Inventory would have increased by $.3 billion less under LIFO than under FIFO. Therefore, cost of merchandise sold would have been $.3 billion higher, and operating income would have been $.3 billion lower.

   Cost of Merchandise Sold = $40.1 billion + $.3 billion = $40.4 billion
   Operating Income = $5.8 billion - $.3 billion = $5.5 billion, or 5% less

2. At a tax rate of 40%, the $.3 billion reduction in income would result in a tax savings of $.3 x 40% = $.12 billion (or $120 million).

3. Prices were rising during fiscal 2003. The most recent prices must be higher than the beginning prices because the ending inventory under FIFO (which contains the most recent prices) is greater than the ending inventory under LIFO (which contains older layers of inventory). Alternatively, the cost of merchandise sold under LIFO (which contains the most recent prices) is higher than the cost of merchandise sold under FIFO (which includes older prices).

16-71 (20 min.)

The inventory method determines how costs will be divided between ending inventory and cost of goods sold. Under the FIFO method, inventory would have increased by $4 million (that is, $31 million - $27 million) less than it did under LIFO (in millions):

	LIFO	FIFO
2003	$1,082	$1,082 + $27 = $1,109
2002	1,055	1,055 + 31 = 1,086
Increase in inventory	$ 27	$ 23

Therefore, cost of goods sold would have been $4 million higher under the FIFO method. Operating income would have been $4 million lower: $1,925 million - $4 million = $1,921 million.

Total inventory under FIFO would have exceeded that under LIFO by $27 million. Therefore, cumulative operating income would have been $27 million higher under FIFO.

16-72 (30-40 min.) For the solution, see the Prentice Hall Web site, www.prenhall.com/

16-73 (30 min.)

The purpose of this exercise is to learn which accounts belong to the income statement and which to the balance sheet. Doing the exercise in teams of two persons each allows each student to recall income statement and balance sheet accounts himself or herself and also to react to accounts listed by someone else. Discussion of those accounts for which there is disagreement should generate consideration of what criteria make an account an income statement account or a balance sheet account. It also forces consideration of the labels put on accounts and how well they identify the nature of the account.

<u>16-74</u> (15-25 min.)   NOTE TO INSTRUCTOR. This solution is based on the web site as it was in early 2004. Be sure to examine the current web site before assigning this problem, as the information there may have changed.

1.   Safeway Inc. is one of the largest food and drug retailers in North America. The company operates more than 1,700 stores in the Western, Southwestern, Rocky Mountain, and Mid-Atlantic regions of the United States and in western Canada.

2.   Safeway calls its income statement a "Consolidated Statement of Operations." It uses a multiple-step format, with subtotals for gross profit and operating profit. The company had a net loss of $828.1 million in 2002, after a profit of $1,253.9 million in 2001. However, Safeway's 2002 income from continuing operations before an accounting change and before accounting for discontinued operations was a positive $568.5 million.

3.   Safeway's largest current asset is merchandise inventories, and its largest current liability is accounts payable. This is a common case for retail companies. Safeway's goodwill is $2,846.2 million. This must have arisen from the purchase of companies for more than the fair value of the assets less liabilities acquired.

4.   Safeway's $3,904.7 million of treasury stock means that it has repurchased its own shares and is holding them for possible resale – possibly as part of an executive stock option or employee stock purchase plan.

5.   Despite a net loss of more than $800 million, Safeway had a large positive cash flow from operating activities of $1,938.1 million. The cash flow from operating activities was considerably larger than even the $568.5 million income before the accounting change and discontinued operations. This is mainly due to adding depreciation and amortization back to net income and also adding back a charge for impairment of goodwill. In total cash and cash equivalents increased by $8.0 million in fiscal 2002.

6. Safeway's depreciation and amortization of $812.5 million is considerably smaller than the investment in additions to property of $1,370.5 million. This means that Safeway must be growing.

CHAPTER 17
COVERAGE OF LEARNING OBJECTIVES

LEARNING OBJECTIVE	FUNDAMENTAL ASSIGNMENT MATERIAL	ADDITIONAL ASSIGNMENT MATERIAL	EXCEL, COLLAB., & INTERNET EXERCISES
LO1: Contrast accounting for investments using the equity method and the market method.	A1, B1, B3	26, 29, 40, 41 49	54
LO2: Explain the basic ideas and methods used to prepare consolidated financial statements.	A2, A3, B2	25, 30, 32, 34 35, 39, 40, 42 43, 44, 49	54
LO3: Describe how goodwill arises and how to account for it.	A4	31, 32, 33, 45 46	
LO4: Explain and use a variety of popular financial ratios.	A5, B4, B5	27, 36, 47, 48	52, 53, 54
LO5: Identify the major implications that efficient stock markets have for accounting.			
LO6: Explain and illustrate four methods of measuring income: historical cost/nominal dollars, current cost/nominal dollars, historical cost/constant dollars, and current cost/constant dollars (Appendix 17).		28, 37, 38, 50, 51	

CHAPTER 17
Understanding and Analyzing Consolidated Financial Statements

17-A1 (15-20 min.) Answers are in millions of dollars.

1.

	Equity Method			
	Assets	=	Liab. + Stk. Eq.	
	Cash	Invest-ments	Liabil-ities	Stock. Equity
a. Acquisition	-72	+72 =		
b. Net income of Akron		+12 =		+12
c. Dividends from Akron	+8	- 8 =		
Effects for year	-64	+76 =		+12

The journal entries that would accompany this table are:

a. Investment in Akron   72
       Cash   72

b. Investment in Akron   12
       Investment revenue*   12

c. Cash   8
       Investment in Akron   8

*More frequently called Equity in Earnings of Affiliates

Under the equity method, General Motors recognizes income as Akron earns it rather than when GM receives dividends. Cash dividends do not affect net income; they increase cash and decrease the investment balance. In a sense, the dividend is a partial liquidation of the investor's "claim" against the investee. The receipt of a dividend is similar to the collection of an account receivable. The revenue from a sale of merchandise on account is recognized when the receivable is created; to include the collection also as revenue would be double-counting. *Similarly, it would be double-counting to include the $8 million of dividends as income after the $12 million of income is already recognized as it is earned.*

2.

		Market Method		
	Assets	=	Liab. + Stk. Eq.	
	Cash	Invest-ments	Liabil-ities	Stock. Equity
a. Acquisition	-72	+72 =		
b. Dividends from Akron	+8	=		+8 (Revenue)
c. Increase in market value		+4 =		+4 (Valuation acct)
Effects for year	-64	+76 =		+12

The journal entries that would accompany this table are:

a. Investment in Akron	72	
Cash		72

b. Cash	8	
Dividend revenue**		8

c. Investment in Akron	4	
Unrealized gain on available-for-sale securities		4

** Frequently called "dividend income"

17-A2 (25-35 min.) A common mistake is to think that the $50 million is additional money flowing into the Trudeau Company rather than into the pockets of the Trudeau shareholders as individuals. Amounts are in millions.

1.

| | Assets | | =Liab.+ Stockholders' Equity | |
	Investment in Trudeau +	Cash and Other Assets =	Accounts Payable, etc. +	Stockholders' Equity
Vancouver's accounts, Jan. 1:				
Before acquisition		330 =	110 +	220
Acquisition of Trudeau	+50	- 50 =		
Trudeau's accounts, Jan. 1		70 =	20 +	50
Intercompany eliminations	-50	=		- 50
Consolidated, Jan. 1	0 +	350 =	130 +	220

2.

	Vancouver	Trudeau	Consolidated
Sales	$330	$100	$430
Expenses	245	90	335
Operating income	$ 85	$ 10	$ 95
Pro-rata share (100%) of unconsolidated subsidiary net income	10	-	
Net income	$ 95	$ 10	

3. Vancouver's parent-company-only income statement would show its own sales and expenses plus its pro-rata share of Trudeau's net income, as the equity method requires. Reflect on the changes in Vancouver's balance sheet equation (in millions):

	Assets		=	Liab.+Stockholders' Equity		
	Invest- ment in Trudeau +	Cash and Other Assets =		Accounts Payable, etc.	+	Stockholders' Equity
Vancouver's accounts:						
Beginning of the year	50 +	280 =		110	+	220
Operating income		+ 85 =				+ 85
Share of Trudeau's income	+10	=				+ 10
End of year	60 +	365 =		110	+	315
Trudeau's accounts:						
Beginning of the year		70 =		20	+	50
Net income		+ 10 =				+ 10
End of the year		80 =		20	+	60
Intercompany eliminations	-60	=				- 60
Consolidated, end of year	0 +	445 =		130	+	315

Trudeau's balance sheet accounts would have increased by $10 million.

At this point, review to see that consolidated statements are the summation of the individual accounts of two or more separate legal entities. These statements are prepared periodically via worksheets. *A consolidated entity does not have a separate continuous set of books like its legal entities.* Moreover, a consolidated income statement is merely the summation of the revenue and expenses of the separate legal entities being consolidated after the elimination of double-counting.

4. Consolidated accounts would be unaffected. Trudeau's cash and stockholders' equity would decline by $7 million. Vancouver's investment in Trudeau would decline by $7 million, but Vancouver's cash would rise by $7 million.

17-A3 (30-45 min.) A common error is to think that the $40 million is additional money flowing into Trudeau rather than into the pockets of the Trudeau shareholders. Amounts are in millions.

1.

	Assets		=	Liab.+Stockholders' Equity		
	Investment in Trudeau +	Cash and Other Assets =		Accounts Payable, etc. +	Minority Interest +	Stockholders' Equity
Vancouver's accounts, Jan. 1:						
Before acquisition		330	=	110		220
Acquisition of Trudeau	+40	- 40	=			
Trudeau's accounts, Jan. 1		70	=	20		50
Intercompany eliminations	-40		=		+10	- 50
Consolidated, Jan. 1	0 +	360	=	130 +	10 +	220

2. The same basic procedures are followed by Vancouver and Trudeau regardless of whether Trudeau is 100% owned or 80% owned. However, the presence of a minority interest changes the *consolidated* statements slightly. The income statements would include:

	Vancouver	Trudeau	Consolidated
Sales	$330	$100	$430
Expenses	245	90	335
Operating income	$ 85	$ 10	$ 95
Pro-rata share (80%) of unconsolidated subsidiary net income	8	-	
Net income	$ 93	$ 10	
Minority interest (20%) in consolidated subsidiaries' net income			2
Net income to consolidated entity			$ 93

3.

	Assets		=	Liab.+Stockholders' Equity		
	Investment in Trudeau	+ Cash and Other Assets	=	Accounts Payable, etc.	+ Minority Interest	+ Stockholders' Equity
Vancouver's accounts:						
Beginning of year	40	+ 290^a =		110		+ 220
Operating income		+ 85 =				+ 85
Share of Trudeau's income	+ 8	=				+ 8
End of year	48	+ 375 =		110	+	313
Trudeau's accounts:						
Beginning of year		70 =		20		+ 50
Net income		+ 10 =				+ 10
End of year		80 =		20	+	60
Intercompany eliminations	-48	=		+ 12^b		- 60
Consolidated, end of year	0	+ 455 =		130 + 12	+	313

^{a}330 beginning of year - 40 for acquisition = 290
^{b}10 beginning of year + .20(10) = 10 + 2 = 12

4. *Consolidated* accounts would be affected because the minority interest's claim would be partially liquidated in the amount of 20% of $7 million, or $1.4 million. Trudeau's cash would decline by $7 million, Vancouver's investment in Trudeau would decline by .80 x $7 million = $5.6 million, but Vancouver's cash would rise by $5.6 million. See following balance sheet equations:

	Assets		=	Liab.+Stockholders' Equity		
	Invest-ment in Trudeau	Cash and Other +Assets	=	Accounts Payable, etc.	Minority +Interest +	Stockholders' Equity
End of year balances:						
Vancouver's accounts	48.0 +	375.0 =		110	+	313
Effect of Trudeau dividend	- 5.6	+ 5.6 =				
Balance	42.4 +	380.6 =		110	+	313
Trudeau's accounts (from 3):		80.0 =		20	+	60
Effect of Trudeau dividend		- 7.0 =				- 7
Balance		73.0 =		20	+	53
Consolidated accounts	42.4	453.6 =		130	+	366
Intercompany eliminations	-42.4	=			+10.6	- 53
Balance	0	+ 453.6 =		130 +	10.6	313

17-A4 (25-35 min.)

1.

	Investment in Trudeau +	Good- will +	Cash and Other Assets =	=	Accounts Payable, etc.	+	Stockholders' Equity
Vancouver's accounts, Jan. 1:							
Before acquisition			330	=	110	+	220
Acquisition of 100% of Trudeau	+80		- 80	=			
Trudeau's accounts, Jan. 1			70	=	20	+	50
Intercompany eliminations	- 80	+30		=			- 50
Consolidated, Jan. 1	0 +	30* +	320	=	130		220

* The $30 million "goodwill" would appear in the consolidated balance sheet as a separate intangible asset account. It often is shown as the final item in a listing of assets. It remains on the books until its value is impaired.

2. **a.** If the book values of the Trudeau's individual assets are not equal to their fair values, the usual procedures are:

    (1) Trudeau continues as a going concern and keeps its accounts on the same basis as before.

    (2) Vancouver records its investment at its acquisition cost (the agreed purchase price).

    (3) For consolidated reporting purposes, the excess of the acquisition cost over the book values of Trudeau is identified with the individual assets, item by item. (In effect, they are revalued at the current market prices prevailing when Vancouver acquired Trudeau.) Any *remaining excess* that cannot be identified is labeled as purchased goodwill.

The balance sheet accounts immediately after acquisition would be the same as in Requirement 1, except that goodwill would be $18 million instead of $30 million (that is, $27 million - $15 million = $12

899

million less), and other assets would be higher by $12 million. The $12 million would appear in the consolidated balance sheet as an integral part of the "other assets." That is, Trudeau's equipment would be shown at $12 million higher in the consolidated balance sheet than the carrying amount on Trudeau's books. Similarly, the depreciation expense on the consolidated income statement would be higher. For instance, if the equipment had four years of useful life remaining, the straight-line depreciation would be $12 \div 4 = $3 million higher per year. As in the preceding tabulation, the $18 million "goodwill" would appear in the consolidated balance sheet as a separate intangible asset account.

b.   Consolidated income would be lower by the amount of depreciation on the additional individual assets:

Extra annual depreciation, $12,000,000 \div 4 years = $3,000,000

The assigning of a "basket purchase price" to the various assets can have a dramatic effect on income. Every dollar assigned to individual assets rather than goodwill will become an expense sometime, but dollars assigned to goodwill might remain indefinitely on the books if the value of the goodwill is maintained.

17-A5 (10-15 min.)

1.   (a) $400 million x 12% = $48 million

            (b) $48 million ÷ 6% = $800 million

            (c) $800 million ÷ $400 million = 2.0 times; or

                   12% ÷ 6% = 2.0 times

2.   (a)   ¥300 million ÷ 5 = ¥60 million

            (b)   ¥15 million ÷ ¥300 million = 5%

            (c)   ¥15 million ÷ ¥60 million = 25%; or 5% x 5 = 25%

17-B1 (15 min.) The year-end balance in Investment in Jain is $67 million under the equity method, and $43 million under the market method.

1.

	Assets		=Liab.+Stockholders' Equity	
				Stockholders'
	Cash	+Investments	= Liabilities	+ Equity
Equity Method:				
1. Acquisition	-55	+55	=	
2. Net income of Jain		+20	=	+20
3. Dividends from				
Jain	+ 8	- 8	=	___
Effects for year	-47	+67	=	+20
Market Method:				
1. Acquisition	-55	+55	=	
2. Dividends from Jain	+ 8		=	+8 (revenue)
3. Adjustment to market				
value	___	-12	=	-12 (loss)
Effects for year	-47	+43	=	-4

Journal entries (not required):

Equity Method

1. Investment in Jain   55
      Cash   55

2. Investment in Jain   20
      Investment revenue*   20

3. Cash   8
      Investment in Jain   8

* More frequently called Equity in Earnings of Affiliates

Market Method

1. Investment in Jain   55
      Cash   55

2. Cash   8
      Dividend revenue**   8

3. Loss on trading securities 12
      Investment in Jain   12

** Frequently called "dividend income"

Microsoft would be required to use the equity method because its ownership of 33% is between 20% and 50%.

17-B2 (25-40 min.) Amounts are in millions of dollars.

A common mistake is to think that the $400 million is additional money flowing into Bayliner rather than into the pockets of Bayliner shareholders as individuals.

1.

	Assets			=Liab.+Stockholders' Equity		
	Invest- ment in Bayliner +	Cash and Other Assets	=	Accounts Payable, etc.	+	Stockholders' Equity
Brunswick's accounts, Jan. 1:						
Before acquisition		1,400	=	800	+	600
Acquisition of Bayliner	+400	- 400	=			
Bayliner's accounts, Jan. 1:		600	=	200	+	400
Intercompany eliminations	-400		=			-400
Consolidated, Jan. 1	0	+ 1,600	=	1,000	+	600

2.

	Brunswick	Bayliner	Consolidated
Sales	$1,800	$600	$2,400
Expenses	1,300	500	1,800
Operating income	$ 500	$100	$ 600

Pro-rata share (100%) of
  unconsolidated subsidiary
  net income
	100		

Income of parent company	$ 600		

3. Brunswick's parent-company-only income statement would show its own sales and expenses plus its pro-rata share of Bayliner's net income (as the equity method requires). Reflect on the changes in Brunswick's balance sheet equation (in millions of dollars):

	Assets			=Liab.+Stockholders' Equity	
	Investment in Bayliner	+ Cash and Other Assets	=	Accounts Payable, etc.	+ Stockholders' Equity
Brunswick's accounts:					
Beginning of year	400	+ 1,000	=	800	+ 600
Operating income		+500	=		+500 ret. inc.
Share of Bayliner's income	+100		=		+100 ret. inc.
End of year	500	+ 1,500	=	800	+ 1,200
Bayliner's accounts:					
Beginning of year		600	=	200	+ 400
Net income		+100	=		+100
End of year		700	=	200	+ 500
Intercompany eliminations	-500		=		-500
Consolidated, end of year	0	+ 2,200	=	1,000	+ 1,200

4. The important point to see is that the *consolidated* accounts would be unaffected. Bayliner's cash and stockholders' equity would decline by $15 million. Brunswick's investment in Bayliner would decline by $15 million, but Brunswick's cash would rise by $15 million.

<u>17-B3</u> (15-20 min.)

1. Under the equity method Ford will recognize 33% of Mazda's net income: 33% x $67,000,000 = $22,110,000.

2. The balance is increased by Ford's share of Mazda's net income ($22,110,000 from requirement 1) and decreased by the cash dividends received from Mazda (33% x $20,000,000 = $6,600,000): $2,100,000,000 + $22,110,000 - $6,600,000 = $2,115,510,000.

    Using a T account might help:

Investment in Mazda

Beginning bal.	2,100,000,000	Dividends received	
Equity in Mazda's		from Mazda	6,600,000
net income	22,110,000		
Ending balance	2,115,510,000		

3. (a) Of course, the market method is not an acceptable accounting method under these circumstances. If it were, the dividends received from Mazda would be recognized as income by Ford:
        33% x $20,000,000 = $6,600,000

    (b) The account balance would be adjusted to market value, $2.5 billion.

    (c) The $400 million increase would be added to a valuation account in stockholders' equity.

4. Ford is obliged to follow the generally accepted accounting principles for investments:

    (a) Investments that represent more than a 50% ownership interest must be consolidated. A subsidiary is a corporation controlled by another corporation. The usual condition for control is ownership of a majority (more than 50%) of the outstanding voting stock. In parent-company-only statements, the equity method is used.

    (b) The equity method is also generally used for a 20% through 50% interest because such a level of ownership is regarded as a presumption that the owner has the ability to exert significant influence. However, consolidated statements are not reported.

    (c) All other investments in *equity* securities must be accounted for using the market method.

17-B4 (10-20 min.)

1. Total asset turnover: 8.9% ÷ 4% = 2.225 times*
2. Net income: 8.9% x $27.3 billion = $2.4297 billion
3. Total revenues: $2.4297 billion ÷ 4% = $60.7425 billion
    (or 2.225 x $27.3 billion = $60.7425 billion)
4. Average stockholders' equity: $2.4297 billion ÷ 18.9% = $12.8556 billion
5. Gallons sold: $2.4297 billion ÷ 3.6 cents = 67.492 billion gallons
* Alternatively, the total asset turnover can be computed after determining net income and total revenues: $60.7425 billion ÷ $27.3 billion = 2.225 times

<u>17-B5</u> (20 min.)

1. $4{,}268 \div 3{,}448 = 1.24$
2. $10{,}014 \div 5{,}197 = 192.7\%$
3. $10{,}384 \div 35{,}626 = 29.1\%$
4. $485 \div 35{,}626 = 1.4\%$
5. $485 \div [(1/2) \times (5{,}197 + 5{,}915)] = 8.7\%$
6. $(485 - 0) \div 397 = \$1.22$
7. $21 \div 1.22 = 17.2$
8. $0.76 \div 21 = 3.6\%$
9. $0.76 \div 1.22 = 62\%$

<u>17-1</u>   Trading securities are investments that management intends to sell shortly. Available-for-sale securities are investments that management does not intend to sell in the near future.

<u>17-2</u>   Under the equity method, investments are carried in the balance sheet at original cost plus the investor's share of accumulated retained income since acquisition.

<u>17-3</u>   The equity method recognizes income as it is earned by the investee and accounts for dividends as a reduction of the investment. The market method recognizes income or loss from changes in market value and from the receipt of cash dividends from the investee.

<u>17-4</u>   The equity method is usually appropriate for long-term investments where the investor has an ownership interest of 20% or more, because the owner would usually have the ability to exert significant influence over the investee.

<u>17-5</u>   According to law, control cannot exist unless an ownership interest exceeds 50%. Significant influence is presumed if the ownership interest is between 20% and 50%.

<u>17-6</u>   A parent-subsidiary relationship exists when one corporation owns more than 50% of the outstanding voting shares of another corporation.

17-7 The reasons for establishing subsidiaries include limiting the liabilities in a risky venture, saving income taxes, conforming with government regulations with respect to a part of the business, doing business in a foreign country, and expanding in an orderly way.

17-8 No. After adding together the separate statements, intercompany eliminations must be undertaken to avoid double-counting.

17-9 If the parent owns less than 100% of the subsidiary stock, then outsiders to the consolidated group own the remainder. The account Outside Stockholders' Interest in Subsidiaries is a measure of this minority interest. Note that this minority interest is in the subsidiary, *not* in the parent company *or* the consolidated company.

17-10 Goodwill is measured by the excess of purchase price over the fair-value, not the *book* value, of the *net* assets (assets less liabilities) acquired.

17-11 Not necessarily. Rules require that assets in a consolidated statement reflect the fair market value at the time of the acquisition. When leeway exists, recording goodwill avoids the depreciation charges incurred on the individual assets.

17-12 No. Pro forma statements are budgets or predicted amounts. Formal financial statements report historical results.

17-13 Three types of comparisons are: 1) time-series comparisons, 2) comparisons with benchmarks, and 3) cross-sectional comparisons.

17-14 It is difficult to compare financial statements of firms that differ in size. Using component percentages (or common-size statements) allows direct comparison of percentages across companies that differ in size.

17-15 Pre-tax operating rate of return on total assets = operating income percentage on sales x total asset turnover.

<u>17-16</u> Ratios are mechanical because their computation requires following a set rule. They are incomplete because they give only a hint as to their importance or relevance; they must be used in conjunction with further information.

<u>17-17</u> No. An efficient capital market is one in which market prices "fully reflect" all information publicly available at a given time. Therefore, searching for "underpriced" securities using public information is fruitless.

<u>17-18</u> Three sources of information include dividend announcements, industry statistics, and national economic indicators.

<u>17-19</u> The quote assumes that the market applies a fixed price-earnings ratio to income, regardless of the accounting methods used to calculate net income. There is much evidence that this is not so. If software development costs are already disclosed, it is highly unlikely that requiring them to be capitalized will affect IBM's share price.

<u>17-20</u> There is much evidence showing that the stock market is not likely to be "fooled" by manipulating reported income. Only an accounting change that discloses *new* information will affect stock prices.

<u>17-21</u> Return *on* capital is essentially a rental charge for the use of money. It is a return received in addition to getting back the original investment. Return *of* capital is the recoupment of the original investment itself.

<u>17-22</u> The physical concept of capital maintenance is that no income can emerge until provisions are made for replacing the physical assets (for example, inventories and equipment) used to generate revenue. In contrast, the financial concept of capital maintenance is that no income can emerge until the amount of money invested in generating revenue is recovered.

<u>17-23</u> Although the choice is often expressed that way, there are actually four major concepts. The fourth arises because constant-dollar (general-price-level) accounting may be combined with either historical-cost accounting or current-cost accounting.

17-24 The major reason for excluding holding gains from income is that no income can emerge unless a company can replace the physical capital devoted to operations during the current period.

17-25 The amount that P pays above the book value of the net assets of S consists of two parts. The first part is an adjustment of the book values of S to market values of net assets. This amount becomes part of the depreciation of S's assets in the consolidated statements. In addition, P must have paid even more than the market value of the net assets. This additional amount is goodwill. It was initially recorded as an asset. Because some of the goodwill was written off, management must have determined that the future value of the goodwill asset had declined since the purchase.

17-26 A purchase of about 20% of another company is right at the borderline of allowing the market or equity methods. More than 20% and the equity method should be used; less than 20% and Disney should use the market method. Under the equity method, changes in market value are ignored. The book value of the investment will increase only by Disney's share of the company's profits, which is likely to result in only a very small increase in the reported asset value. In contrast, the market method would record the asset at its market value, which Disney expects to increase significantly. Thus, if Disney's expectations are met, the market method would result in much larger asset value recorded in Disney's investment account on its balance sheet.

17-27 If a company reduces its inventories (a component of current assets), its current ratio will decrease. Because holding inventories costs resources, both for the capital invested in them and for costs of handling and storing the inventories, it is often good to reduce inventories. However, many analysts think that a higher current ratio is better. This seems to generate a conflict. In general, analysts will look at the current ratio differently for companies that use a just-in-time inventory system. They will expect such companies to have a lower current ratio and thus will not downgrade their estimate of the liquidity of such companies. An old rule of thumb was that most companies should have a current ratio of about 2.0 to have sufficient liquidity. However, recently that standard has been lowered, especially for companies using just-in-time inventory methods.

17-28 To maintain financial capital, the Treasurer can pay out to investors all of the net income as measured by the traditional historical cost method. That leaves the company an amount equal to the historical cost of the assets consumed during the period to use to replace those resources. The company will have maintained the dollar value of its investments. In contrast, if the Treasurer want to maintain physical capital, he can pay out only the amount of net income measured by the current cost method. This method maintains enough capital to replace assets consumed at their current prices. For example, if a unit of inventory was purchased for $4 but costs $5 to replace today, and if it is sold for $6, financial capital maintenance would allow payment of $2 to investors; the company would still have the $4 financial measure it started with, although it is now $4 of cash and not $4 of inventory. However, since it costs $5 to buy a new unit of inventory, the company cannot maintain its physical capital with that $4 – it now requires $5 to buy the inventory that keeps the company in the same physical position as before the sale of the unit. Thus, only $1 is available to pay to investors and still maintain physical capital.

Which measure an investor might prefer depends on the investor's objectives, especially relating to income versus capital appreciation. An investor who wants current income would probably prefer the financial capital maintenance method even though it might imply a decreasing investment in the firm as the financial resources buy less and less in an inflationary environment. An investor who seeks appreciation wants the company to grow, so a measure that implies a positive income even though the company cannot maintain its physical capital often does not lead to the needed reinvestment in the company for the capital to grow substantially.

17-29 (15 min.) The year-end balance in Investment in Y is $47 million under the equity method, and $50 million under the market method:

	Cash	+Investments=	Liabilities	+	Stockholders' Equity
		Assets		**=Liab.+Stockholders' Equity**	
Equity Method:					
1. Acquisition	-45	+45	=		
2. Net income of Y		+ 5	=		+5
3. Dividends from Y	+ 3	- 3	=		
Effects for year	-42	+47	=		+5
Market Method:					
1. Acquisition	-45	+45	=		
2. Net income of Y			No entry and no effect.		
3. Dividends from Y	+ 3		=		+3
4. Increase in market value of Y		+ 5	=		+5
Effects for year	-42	+50	=		+8

The year-end balance is $47 million under the equity method and $50 million under the market method. If this were a trading security, the $5 million increase in market price would be included in income. If it were an available-for-sale security, the $5 million increase would be added directly to a valuation reserve account in Stockholders' Equity.

913

17-30 (35-50 min.) The formal statements are not presented here because the following tabulations are easier to understand (in thousands of dollars):

1.

	Salt Lake	Provo	Consolidated
Sales (other income reclassified below)	5,300*	1,100	6,400
Expenses	5,100	1,000	6,100
Operating income	200	100	300
Salt Lake's share of Provo's net income	100	-	
Net income	300	100	

*5,400 - 100 = 5,300

	Assets		=	Liab.+Stockholders' Equity		
	Invest-ment in Provo +	Cash and Other Assets	=	Accounts Payable, etc.	+	Stockholders' Equity
Salt Lake's accounts:						
Beginning of year	200 +	600^a	=	450	+	350^b
Operating income		+ 200	=			+200
Share of Provo's income	+100		=			+100
End of year	300 +	800		450	+	650
Provo's accounts:						
End of year		400	=	100	+	300
Intercompany eliminations	-300		=			-300
Consolidated, end of year	0 +	1,200	=	550	+	650

^{a} Working backwards, end-of-year balance 1,000 minus 200 investment minus 200 operating income of Salt Lake = 600

^{b} 550 end-of-year balance - 200 Salt Lake income = 350

2.

	Salt Lake	Provo	Consolidated
Sales (other income reclassified below)	5,300*	1,100	6,400
Expenses	5,100	1,000	6,100
Operating income	200	100	300
Salt Lake's share (60%) of Provo's net income	60	-	
Net income	260	100	
Minority interest (40%) in Provo's net income			40
Net income to consolidated entity			260

*5,360 - 60 = 5,300

The consolidated balance sheet would be as follows:

	Assets		=	Liab.+Stockholders' Equity		
	Investment in Provo	+ Cash and Other Assets =		Accounts Payable, etc.	+ Minority Interest	+ Stockholders' Equity
Salt Lake's accounts:						
Beginning of year	120 +	680[a] =		450 +		350
Operating income		+ 200 =				+200
Share of Provo's income	+60	=				+ 60
End of year	180 +	880		450 +		610
Provo's accounts:						
End of year		400 =		100 +		300
Intercompany eliminations	-180	=			+120[b]	-300
Consolidated, end of year	0 +	1,280 =		550 +	120 +	610

[a] Working backwards, end-of-year balance 1,000 minus 120 investment minus 200 operating income.

[b] 80 at beginning + .4(100) = 80 + 40 = 120

17-31 (10 min.)

The $100,000 "goodwill" would appear as a separate intangible asset account in the consolidated balance sheet. As long as the goodwill is not impaired, the consolidated balance sheet at year-end would continue to show goodwill at $100,000. Consolidated net income would not be affected.

17-32 (20-25 min.) Amounts are in millions of dollars.

1.

	Assets				=	Stockholders' Equity	
	Cash	Inven-tories	Plant Assets, Net	Invest-ment in Tulsa	=	Common Stock, etc.	Retained Income
El Paso's accounts:							
Before acquisition	700 +	350 +	390		=	470 +	970
Acquisition of Tulsa	-290			+290	=		
Tulsa's accounts	80 +	70 +	60		=	120 +	90
Intercompany eliminations			+ 80	-290	=	-120	- 90
Consolidated	490 +	420 +	530* +	0	=	470 +	970

*The $80 million would appear as an integral part of the *plant assets* because they would be carried at $80 million higher in the consolidated balance sheet than the carrying amount on Tulsa's books. Therefore, plant assets would appear on the consolidated balance sheet as ($390 +$60) + $80 = $530.

2.   The Tulsa plant assets would be carried in the consolidated balance sheet at $100 million instead of $140 million, and the $40 million goodwill would appear as a separate intangible asset.

3. Cash would be $50 million less, and a goodwill account of $50 million would be created. The balance in El Paso's Investment in Tulsa's account would be $340 million instead of $290 million. Of the $340 million, $140 million would pertain to plant assets, and $50 million to goodwill in the consolidated statement.

17-33 (10-15 min.)

Many students will fail to see that depreciation must be adjusted. The assumption here is that a 20% rate is appropriate for the year in question. Why? Because Tulsa's depreciation is $12 million; therefore, the rate must be $12 ÷ $60 = 20% of Tulsa's cost basis.

1. The computation (in millions) follows:

	Consolidated
Net income before adjustments, $105 + $35	$140
Adjustments:	
Extra investment, $340 - $210 = $130*	
Depreciation, 20% of $80	(16)
Net income	$124

* Of this $130, $80 is assigned to individual assets and $50 to goodwill.

2. Goodwill write-off is $25 million. Net income would be $124 - $25 = $99 million.

<u>17-34</u> (30 min.)

This problem is based on the actual acquisition of Paramount Pictures by Gulf & Western, although Gulf & Western accounted for the purchase as a pooling, which was then permissible.

1.   The combined company would have the following balance sheet accounts immediately after the acquisition (in millions of dollars):

Cash and receivables	30 + 22 =	52
Inventories	120 + 3 + 70 =	193
Plant assets, net	150 + 95 =	<u>245</u>
Total assets		<u>490</u>
Current liabilities	50 + 20 =	70
Common stock	100 + 170 =	270
Retained income	=	<u>150</u>
Total equities		<u>490</u>

2.
Net income for 20X0	$19 million
Net income for 20X1:	
20 + [21 - (.25 x 70)]	$23.5 million

If the $70 million were assigned to goodwill and no goodwill was written off, net income for 20X1 would be:

   20 + 21 = $41 million

The chairman of MCM may prefer to assign as much as possible to goodwill because MCM could generate net income almost "on demand" by the timing of rentals or sales of its films. This avoids revelation of the cost of the library of films acquired. The immense size of this impact on income is vividly demonstrated by the fact that net income could jump to $41 million in just one year. This could take place because MCM would carry the film library at zero rather than the $70 million actual cost.

The point of this example is to stress that, as a practical matter depending on earnings-per-share objectives, there will be a general pressure by management towards assigning as much of the total purchase price as possible to goodwill rather than to other assets.

17-35 (50-65 min.)

This is a worthwhile problem because it provides an overall view of relationships. It helps to call the attention of the students to the diagram in the chapter, and it helps to place a similar diagram on the board:

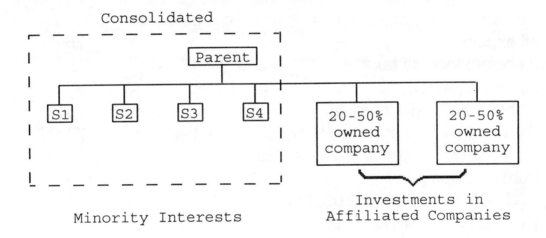

On balance sheets the minority interest typically appears just above the stockholders' equity section; however, some accountants place it as a subpart of the stockholders' equity section. On income statements, the minority interest in net income is deducted as if it were an expense of the consolidated entity.

RAMNATH MEDICAL INSTRUMENTS COMPANY
Consolidated Income Statement
For the Year Ended December 31, 20X1
(in millions)

Net sales and other operating revenue	$900
Cost of goods sold and operating expenses, exclusive of depreciation and amortization	650
Depreciation and amortization	20
Total operating expenses	670
Operating income before share of unconsolidated net income	230
Equity in earnings of affiliated companies	20
Total income before interest expense and income taxes	250
Interest expense	25
Income before income taxes	225
Income tax expense	90
Income before minority interest	135
Minority interest in consolidated subsidiaries' net income	20
Net consolidated income to Ramnath Medical Instruments Company	115*
Preferred dividends ($3.50 x 2,000,000)	7
Net income to Ramnath Medical Instruments Company common stockholders	$108
Earnings per share of common stock:	
On shares outstanding (9,000,000 shares)	$12.00**
Assuming full dilution, reflecting conversion of all convertible securities (11,000,000 shares)	10.45***

* This is the total figure in dollars that the accountant traditionally labels net income. It is reported accordingly in the financial press.

**This is the figure most widely quoted by the investment community.

***$115,000,000 ÷ 11,000,000 = $10.45. Fully diluted earnings per share is not discussed in the chapter. It also shows the potential effect of conversion of the preferred stock to common stock. There is significant potential dilution. Note that $115,000,000 is used rather than $108,000,000, because no preferred dividends would exist. Total common shares would be 9,000,000 + 2,000,000 = 11,000,000.

RAMNATH MEDICAL INSTRUMENTS COMPANY
Consolidated Balance Sheet
As of December 31, 20X1
(in millions of dollars)

Current assets:	
Cash	$ 30
Short-term investments at market value	45
Accounts receivables, net	175
Inventories at average cost	340
Total current assets	590
Investments in affiliated companies	100
Property, plant, and equipment, net	125
Other assets:	
Goodwill	95
Total assets	$910
Current liabilities:	
Accounts payable	$210
Accrued income taxes payable	20
Total current liabilities	230
Long-term liabilities:	
First mortgage bonds, 10% interest, due Dec. 31, 20X9	80
Subordinated debentures, 11% interest, due Dec. 31, 20X7	100
Total long-term liabilities	180
Minority interest in subsidiaries	90
Total liabilities	500
Stockholders' equity:	
Preferred stock, 2,000,000 shares, $50 par*	100
Common stock, 9,000,000 shares, $1 par	9
Paid-in capital in excess of par	103
Retained income	198
Total stockholders' equity	410
Total liabilities and stockholders' equity	$910

* Dividend rate is $3.50 per share; each share is convertible into one share of common stock.

17-36 (40-50 min.) Amounts are in millions of Norwegian kroner.

1.   (a)   Current ratio:

      20X1: $(5 + 70 + 85) \div 55 = 2.9$ to 1
      20X2: $(30 + 85 + 120) \div 70 = 3.4$ to 1

   (b)   Rate of return on sales:
      (Sales: 20X1: 380+620 = 1,000; 20X2: 520+980 = 1,500)

      20X1: $60 \div 1,000 = 6.0\%$
      20X2: $95 \div 1,500 = 6.3\%$

   (c)   Rate of return on stockholders' equity:

      20X1: $60 \div 1/2(205 + 10 + 205 + 55) = 25.3\%$
      20X2: $95 \div 1/2(205 + 55 + 205 + 120) = 32.5\%$

   (d)   Ratio of total debt to stockholders' equity:

      20X1: $(65 + 55) \div (205 + 55) = 46.2\%$
      20X2: $(80 + 70) \div (205 + 120) = 46.2\%$

   (e)   Ratio of current debt to stockholders' equity:

      20X1: $55 \div (205 + 55) = 21.2\%$
      20X2: $70 \div (205 + 120) = 21.5\%$

   (f)   Gross profit rate:

      20X1: $380 \div 1,000 = 38\%$
      20X2: $520 \div 1,500 = 34.7\%$

   (g)   Average collection period for accounts receivable:
      20X1: $[(1/2) \times (40 + 70) \times 365] \div 1,000 = 20.1$ days
      20X2: $[(1/2) \times (70 + 85) \times 365] \div 1,500 = 18.9$ days

(h) Price-earnings ratio (Earnings per share are $60 \div 10 = 6$ for 20X1 and $95 \div 10 = 9.5$ for 20X2):

20X1: $30 \div 6 = 5$
20X2: $40 \div 9.5 = 4.2$

(i) Dividend-payout percentage (Dividends per share are $15 \div 10 = 1.50$ for 20X1 and $30 \div 10 = 3.00$ for 20X2):

20X1: $1.50 \div 6 = 25\%$
20X2: $3.00 \div 9.5 = 31.6\%$

(j) Dividend yield:

20X1: $1.50 \div 30 = 5.0\%$
20X2: $3.00 \div 40 = 7.5\%$

2.
(a)	No, f	(d)	No, g	(g)	Yes, h	(j)	No, j
(b)	No, b	(e)	Yes, i, j	(h)	Yes, b, c	(k)	Yes, g
(c)	Yes, c	(f)	No, d, e	(i)	No, a		

3. The company has grown rapidly and profitably (ratios b and c). Sales have tripled; earnings have nearly quadrupled; dividends have increased 500%; and total assets have increased 64%. Moreover, the large increase in retained income indicates that the expansion has been financed largely by internally generated funds. The expansion has been accompanied by increased liquidity of current assets (ratio a). The stock is priced attractively (h), and the dividend policy seems conservative (i and j).

17-37 (25-30 min.) This problem can prompt a discussion of differing views regarding the meaning of income. (Amounts in thousands of dollars.)

1.

	Historical Cost Nominal Dollars	Current Cost Nominal Dollars	Historical Cost Constant Dollars	Current Cost Constant Dollars
Selling price	460	460	460	460
Cost of goods sold	100	460[a]	315[b]	460[a]
Income from continuing operations	360	-	145	-
Holding gain	-	60[c]	-	40[d]

[a] The problem deliberately omitted comment of whether this going concern would have to pay $460 or something less than $460 to replace the inventory of land. If less than $460, some income from continuing operations would arise.

[b] $(100 \times 3.00) \times 1.05$

[c] The holding gain for 20X1 is the difference between the current cost at the beginning and end of 20X1: $460 - $400 = $60.

[d] Holding gain = $460 - (400 \times 1.05)$

2. The $360,000 operating income is the result of matching historical outlays against historical revenue without adjusting for the fact that the $460,000 and $100,000 are not expressed in common dollars. In contrast, the third column provides these in common dollars; the $145,000 net income excludes the $215,000 of illusory gain of column one and gives a better measure of the gain in *general* purchasing power that resulted from the transaction.

In contrast, the current cost basis has recognized previous increases in the value of the land throughout the holding periods, year by year. These gains would be recognized as "holding gains," with $300,000 of holding gains before December 31, 20X0 and $60,000 during 20X1. Consequently, operating income for 20X1 would be less than under the historical-cost basis. Under current costs with nominal dollars the entire $60,000 increase in value during 20X1 is a holding gain. When constant dollars are used with current costs, only the amount of value increase greater than the price-level increase is a holding gain.

17-38 (40-50 min.) See Exhibit 17-38.

EXHIBIT 17-38

ZAMORA COMPANY
(Amounts are in dollars)

Balance Sheets as of December 31

	NOMINAL DOLLARS Historical Cost 20X0	20X1	NOMINAL DOLLARS Current Cost 20X0	20X1	CONSTANT DOLLARS Historical Cost 20X0	20X1	CONSTANT DOLLARS Current Cost 20X0	20X1
Cash	-	3,900	-	3,900	-	3,900	-	3,900
Inventory, 100 and 40 units respectively	5,000	2,000ᵃ	5,000	2,400ᵇ	5,750ᵈ	2,300ᵈ	5,750ᵈ	2,400ᵇ
Total Assets	5,000	5,900	5,000	6,300	5,750	6,200	5,750	6,300
Paid-in capital	5,000	5,000	5,000	5,000	5,750ᵈ	5,750ᵈ	5,750ᵈ	5,750ᵈ
Retained income	-	900	-	300	-	450	-	300
Revaluation equity (accumulated holding gains)	-	-	-	1,000	-	-	-	250
Total equities	5,000	5,900	5,000	6,300	5,750	6,200	5,750	6,300

Income Statements for 20X1

	NOMINAL DOLLARS Historical Cost 20X1	NOMINAL DOLLARS Current Cost 20X1	CONSTANT DOLLARS Historical Cost 20X1	CONSTANT DOLLARS Current Cost 20X1
Sales, 60 units @ $65	3,900	3,900	3,900	3,900
Cost of goods sold	3,000ᵃ	3,600ᵇ	3,450ᵈ	3,600ᵇ
Income from continuing operations	900	300	450	300
Holding gains:				
On 60 units sold		600ᶜ		150ᵉ
On 40 units unsold		400ᶜ		100ᵉ
Total holding gains (to revaluation equity)		1,000		250

ᵃ 40 x $50
  60 x $50

ᵇ 40 x $60
  60 x $60

ᶜ 60 x ($60 - $50)
  40 x ($60 - $50)

ᵈ 115/100 x 5,000
  115/100 x 2,000
  115/100 x 3,000

ᵉ 3,600 - restated cost of 3,450; or 60 x ($60 - $57.50*)
  2,400 - restated cost of 2,300; or 40 x ($60 - $57.50*)

*115/100 x $50 = $57.50

17-39 (5-10 min.)

1. Generally the last item under long-term liabilities. Sometimes a part of stockholders' equity.
2. Current liability.
3. Investments section of long-term assets.
4. Current asset.
5. Current liability.
6. Deduction from total stockholders' equity.

17-40 (10 min.)

The first two items indicate that there are minority shareholders in the *subsidiaries*, whose individual sales, assets, and other detailed accounts have been added together in the DuPont consolidated statements. The minority interests' share of earnings appears in the income statement; the other account usually appears among "other liabilities" on the balance sheet.

The last two items summarize DuPont's investments in affiliated (or associated) companies. The first appears under long-term assets in the balance sheet, and the second generally appears under "other income" in the income statement.

17-41 (15 min.)

1. ConocoPhillips recognized $337 million of income from the affiliated companies. The amount of dividends paid by the investees is irrelevant to computing ConocoPhillips's income. This was 16% of ConocoPhillips's pretax income.

2. ConocoPhillips invested $3,088 million in equity method investment in 2002. The balance sheet equation and T-account summaries are shown below (in millions of dollars):

Equity Method Investments			Equity Method Investments			
Beg. Bal.	2,788		Beg. Bal.	2,788		
Income	+337		Income	337	Dividends	313
Dividends	-313		Add. Inv.	X		
New Investment	+ X		End. Bal.	5,900		
End. Bal.	5,900					

$$\$2{,}788 + \$337 - \$313 + X = \$5{,}900$$
$$X = \$3{,}088$$

3. The income recognized would remain at $337 million. The amount of dividends paid by investees does not affect the parent's income.

17-42 (5-10 min.)

The parent company could not easily achieve the window-dressing of income under the equity method. For example, if the subsidiary were wholly owned, the parent's share of subsidiary losses would be 100% and would be completely reflected in the parent's accounts. That is why the equity method is often called a "one-line consolidation." However, a possibility for window-dressing is to sell assets (including inventories) to the subsidiary at inflated prices. Until the subsidiary sells or uses the assets, the parent company's income (including its share of the subsidiary's income) will be higher.

<u>17-43</u> (20 min.) Dollar amounts are in millions.

1. ¥47,866 − ¥19,707 = ¥28,159 or ¥27,311 + ¥848 = ¥28,159

2. Let X = subsidiaries' net income
.10 x X = ¥848
X = ¥8,480

3. ¥18,856 - ¥848 = ¥18,008

<u>17-44</u> (15 min.) Amounts are in millions.

1. $1,736 million; the GM income would not change.

2. $1,736 million - $1,870 million = $134 million loss.

3. The consolidated statement allows a comprehensive look at the financial results of the entire entity owned by the shareholders of General Motors. For example, it would combine the amount of goods and services sold to customers of General Motors and GMAC. The unconsolidated statement does not show all of these revenues. Similarly, the unconsolidated statement does not show all the individual expenses because those of GMAC are offset against its revenues when the single line, earnings of nonconsolidated affiliates, is included in the General Motors unconsolidated statement.

   In contrast, the unconsolidated statements avoids combining assets, liabilities, revenues, and expenses for totally different types of operations (e.g., auto production and lending money). Some critics of consolidation maintain that adding the accounts of such unlike operations is like adding apples and oranges – it may make numerical sense but it does not make economic sense.

17-45 (10-15 min.)

1. Goodwill = $5.0 billion – (1.5 billion + .7 billion - .5 billion) = $3.3 billion. This entire amount will stay on P&G's balance sheet until the value of the goodwill has decreased (or been impaired).

2. Goodwill would have been $4.8 billion, which would remain on the books until it is impaired. In contrast, P&G would amortize the $1.5 billion of identifiable intangible assets over 9 years, resulting is amortization of $1.5 billion ÷ 9 = $167 million per year. Thus, income will be less by $167 million.

3. A manager might prefer to have this as goodwill and avoid an amortization charge for each of the next 9 years. This will serve to increase the reported income in these years. Offsetting this is the need to write off the entire $1.5 billion if the goodwill should become impaired.

17-46 (15-20 min.) Amounts are in millions.

1. Goodwill would equal the purchase price less the fair value of the intangible assets less the fair value of the net tangible assets. Since the net tangible assets are a negative $38.4 million, the goodwill becomes:

    Goodwill = $328.6 million – $165.8 million + $38.4 million
    = $201.2 million

2. Consolidated net income is the Medtronic net income plus (minus) the VidaMed net income (loss) less the amortization of the intangible assets, which is $165.8 million ÷ 15 = $11.1 million. Therefore, Consolidated net income = $984.0 million - $9.4 million - $11.1 million = $963.5 million.

3. There would be no depreciation of the intangible assets. Assuming no impairment of goodwill, the consolidated net income would be:

    $984 million - $9.4 million = $974.6 million

17-47 (10-20 min.) Dollar amounts are in millions.

1. Average assets:
    ($1,475,193 + $1,356,601) ÷ 2 = $1,415,897

    Net income percentage of average assets:
    $80,638 ÷ $1,415,897 = 5.695%

2. Total revenues: $80,638 ÷ .04865 = $1,657,513

3. Average stockholders' equity:
    $80,638 ÷ .16719 = $482,314

4. Asset turnover:

    (a) $1,657,513 ÷ $1,415,897 = 1.171

    (b) 5.695% ÷ 4.865% = 1.171

17-48 (15-20 min.) Monetary amounts are in billions of yen.

HONDA MOTOR COMPANY
Income Statement
For the Year Ended March 31, 2003

	Amount	Percentage
Net sales	¥7,971	100.0%
Cost of sales	5,410	67.9
Gross profit	2,561	32.1
Selling and administrative expenses	1,435	18.0
Research and Development	437	5.5
Operating income	689	8.6
Other income (expense):		
Interest income	7	0.1
Interest expense	(11)	(0.1)
Other	(13)	(0.2)
Earnings before income taxes	672	8.4
Income taxes	245	3.1
Net income	¥ 427	5.3%

2.   a.   Current ratio = Current assets ÷ Current liabilities

$$= ¥3,292 ÷ ¥3,122 = 1.1$$

    b.   Total debt to equity = Total liabilities ÷ Stockholders' equity

$$= (¥3,122 + ¥1,929) ÷ ¥2,630$$
$$= 192.1\%$$

    c.   Gross profit rate = Gross profit ÷ Sales

$$= ¥2,561 ÷ ¥7,971 = 32.1\%$$

Note that the gross profit rate is shown in the common-size statement of earnings.

d. Return on stockholders' equity = Net income ÷ Avg. stockholders' equity

$$= ¥427 ÷ 1/2(¥2,630 + ¥2,574)$$
$$= 16.4\%$$

e. Price-earnings ratio = Market price per share ÷ Earnings per share
$$= ¥4,000 ÷ ¥439 = 9.1$$

g. Dividend-payout ratio= Dividends per share ÷ Earnings per share
$$= ¥31 ÷ ¥439 = 7.1\%$$

3. These ratios themselves are difficult to interpret. Comparisons are necessary. It would be helpful to know Honda's ratios for the past few years to aid the identification of trends. It would also be helpful to have average industry ratios for comparison. General benchmarks for Japanese rather than U.S. firms would also be useful.

17-49 (15-20 min.)

1. Because Medusa Electronics accounts for its 19% investment in Rasmussen Transport using the market method, and because the securities are available-for-sale securities, changes in the market value of Rasmussen are entered directly into stockholders' equity. They are not included in the income statement. In contrast, the amount of dividends paid by Rasmussen are part of the income of Medusa Electronics. Thus, regardless of what happens to the market value of Rasmussen, Medusa will include only Rasmussen's dividends in income. By increasing the Rasmussen dividends, Medusa will increase its net income.

This opportunity for Medusa to increase its income by influencing the dividend policy of Rasmussen does not seem desirable. The FASB apparently concluded that ownership interests under 20% do not allow influence over dividend policy, but when that influence is present, manipulation of the income of the investor is definitely possible.

2.   At least two ethical issues arise. First is the investment by Medusa in Rasmussen. If the decision was made by Alex Renalda based only on his friendship with Hans Rasmussen, and if it was not in the best interests of the shareholders of Medusa, Renalda was not appropriately carrying out his duties as an officer of Medusa. Presently this may not be of much concern because the investment appears to have turned out to be profitable to the Medusa shareholders. Nevertheless, if the decision had been based on predicted personal rather than corporate benefits, it was not appropriate.

Second is the influence of Renalda on Rasmussen's dividend policy. Not only does this manipulation of Rasmussen's policy violate the intent of the accounting principles, it may not be in the best interests of Rasmussen's other shareholders (i.e., those shareholders other than Medusa). If Rasmussen pays out $4 million in dividends and then borrows to meet its capital needs, future profitability of Rasmussen may be diminished. The personal obligation of Rasmussen to Renalda should not influence the corporate decisions.

On the other hand, Rasmussen and Medusa may be essentially forming an implicit strategic alliance. When one company needs special help, the other is willing to provide it. Companies in Japan have had such alliances for years, and they have worked well. Often it is hard to judge the ethical implications of actions without being able to assess intent. Still, this situation at least possesses the appearance of possible ethical violations.

<u>17-50</u> (15-20 min.)

	Historical Cost/ Nominal Dollars	Current Cost/ Nominal Dollars	Historical Cost/ Constant Dollars	Current Cost/ Constant Dollars
1. (In millions)				
(a) Beginning inventory	$3,275.0	$3,275.0	$3,602.5	$3,602.5
(b) Ending inventory	3,537.5	3,800.0	3,701.3	3,800.0
(c) Cost of goods sold	1,637.5	1,900.0	1,801.3	1,900.0
(d) Holding gains (losses):				
On units sold	—	262.5	—	98.8
On units unsold	—	262.5	—	98.8
2. Gross margin	362.5	100.0	198.7	100.0

Computations:

1a. (110/100) x $3,275 = $3,602.5

1b. ½ x $3,275 + $1,900 = $3,537.5; 2 x $1,900 = $3,800; ½x (110/100) x
$3,275 + $1,900 = $3,701.25

1c. ½ x $3,275 = $1,637.5; ½x $3,800; (110/100) x $1,637.5 = $1,801.3

1d. ½ x ($3,800 - $3,275) = $262.5; ½ x ($3,800 - $3,602.5) = $98.8

2. $2,000 - $1,637.5 = $362.5; $2,000 - $1,801.3 = $198.7; $2,000 - $1,900 =
$100

<u>17-51</u> (15-20 min.)

The general price level increased, as shown by positive values under "effect of increase in general price level." Therefore, the asset values of all three firms would have to increase to keep pace with inflation, Gannett by $37.5 million, Zayre by $55.5 million, and Goodyear by $252.0 million. The specific prices of Gannett's assets increased by $45.8 million, $8.3 million more than the rate of inflation. Zayre's increased by $24.9 million, but this is less than the inflation rate by $30.6 million. Goodyear's specific asset prices actually fell by $4.7 million, dropping them $256.7 million (in inflation-adjusted dollars) behind their beginning-of-the-year value.

<u>17-52</u> (25-35 min.) For the solution, see the Prentice Hall Web site, www.prenhall.com/

<u>17-53</u> (60 min. or more)

The purpose of this exercise is two-fold. The first is to establish familiarity with four basic ratios. The second is to deduce why these ratios might vary from company to company.

Computing the ratios will cause students to find and read a company's annual financial statements. They will become familiar with some aspects of that particular company as well as learning where in the financial statements to find the needed information.

Students' reasoning skills will be developed when they come together as a group and try to determine reasons for differences in companies' ratios. Some of the conclusions they may draw are:

a.   Earnings per share depend on the number of shares issued compared to the value of the company. If one share costs nearly $70,000, as for Berkshire Hathaway class A shares, earnings per share will be much higher than for a share that costs $10. Earnings per share is also a good measure of the economic success of a company over the last year. If earnings per share decline from one year to the next, it is likely that economic results were not favorable.

b.   The price-earnings ratio depends primarily on the growth prospects for a company's earnings. The greater the expected earnings growth, the greater the P-E ratio.

c & d. Dividend yield is a measure of the amount of dividends a shareholder can expect per dollar invested. Dividend payout ratio is the percentage of income paid out in dividends. These two ratios are highly related. Companies that have excellent internal investment opportunities for cash (often growing companies) will generally pay out a low percentage of their income and have a low dividend yield.

936

<u>17-54</u> (30-40 min.)

NOTE TO INSTRUCTOR. This solution is based on the web site as it was in early 2004 when the 2002 annual report was the latest one available. Be sure to examine the current web site before assigning this problem, as the information there may have changed.

1.   General Electric labels its financial statements "Consolidated Financial Statements." Therefore, the company must consolidate some subsidiaries into its statements. On the income statement there is an account called "Minority interest in net earnings of consolidated affiliates," so there must be some subsidiaries that are not 100% owned.

2.   GE calls its balance sheet a "Statement of Financial Position." GE does not have subtotals for current assets and current liabilities, although the current items are listed first under both assets and liabilities. Its minority interest is $5,473 million. This means that of the equity in the consolidated subsidiaries, GE owns all but $5,473 million. That means that $5,473 of the equity in the subsidiaries is held by outside shareholders.

3.   The income statement shows cash dividends of $.73 per share, out of net income of $1.52 per share, for a payout ratio of $.73 ÷ $1.52 = 48%.

4.   GE's return on stockholders' equity for the last two years is:

2002: $14,118 ÷ (1/2 x ($63,706 + $54,824)) = 23.8%

2001: $13,684 ÷ (1/2 x ($54,824 + $50,492)) = 26.0%

The return fell slightly in 2002 from what it was in 2001, which is not good for investors.

5.   GE has a separate section of its annual report on "Citizenship." It emphasizes education throughout the world and community outreach programs.